FILM HISTORIES

THE UNIVERSITY OF WINCHESTER

FILM HISTORIES

AN INTRODUCTION AND READER

Paul Grainge, Mark Jancovich and
Sharon Monteith

EDINBURGH UNIVERSITY PRESS

© Selection and editorial material Paul Grainge,
Mark Jancovich and Sharon Monteith, 2007

Extracts are reprinted by permission of other publishers

Edinburgh University Press Ltd
22 George Square, Edinburgh

Reprinted 2008, 2009

Typeset in 10/12.5 Sabon
by Servis Filmsetting Ltd, Manchester and
printed and bound in Great Britain by
CPI Antony Rowe, Chippenham, Wiltshire

A CIP record for this book is available from the British Library

ISBN 978 0 7486 1906 1 (hardback)
ISBN 978 0 7486 1907 8 (paperback)

The right of the contributors
to be identified as authors of this work
has been asserted in accordance with
the Copyright, Designs and Patents Act 1988.

CONTENTS

PREFACE

This book emerges out of our teaching and our dissatisfaction with the available books in film history. Kristin Thompson and David Bordwell's now classic volume, *Film History: An Introduction*, best represents the main tendency, and it provides students with an absolutely indispensable narrative history of film that focuses on the aesthetic development of the medium. However, while we recognise that students need to be familiar with this kind of history, if only so that they know the key points of reference in relation to which most existing scholarship is produced, we were also concerned that students should not be given the impression, from early in their studies, that film history is largely about the processes of aesthetic development. However, while Robert Allen and Douglas Gomery's equally classic volume, *Film History: Theory and Practice*, provides the main alternative, and focuses on the wide variety of objects, methods and practices involved in 'doing' film history, it presupposes a great deal of knowledge about the narrative of film history, the very knowledge provided by books such as Bordwell and Thompson's.

In one sense, then, we felt that a book was needed that combined both tendencies: that provided both a narrative history of the medium as it is usually presented, while also introducing students to a wide range of different objects and methods. We also felt that students could best understand what was involved in the practice of historical film research if, rather than simply describe objects and methods in the abstract, we presented them with specific exemplars of those types of research; if they saw examples of the actual practice of film history. As a result, the following book is divided into two parts: the first covers the period from 1895 to 1945 and the second covers the period from 1946 to the present. Each part is then made up of twelve sections, each of which usually covers a period of about five years and is made up of four different elements: a segment of a larger narrative history of film; an introduction to an extract from a classic example of research in film history that deals with roughly the same period as the segment of the narrative history; a set of questions for the student to think about while reading the extract; and the extract from the research itself.

However, we want to make it quite clear that the introductions at the start of each section should not be taken as a definitive history. On the contrary, we want to encourage students to remain aware of another problem with such histories: they are always structured by specific values and so privilege certain aspects over others. For example, given the dominance of Hollywood, most histories (and this volume will be no exception) tend to spend much of the time on American cinema at the expense of other cinemas from around the world, and when not concentrating on Hollywood they tend to focus on art cinema traditions rather than indigenous popular traditions. For example, in Bordwell and Thompson's *Film History*, their discussion of British Cinema in the 1960s spends several pages on the British social realist cinema of directors such as Lindsay Anderson, John Schlesinger and others, despite the fact that most of the films associated with this movement had a small middle-class audience. However, they spend only a sentence or two on the horror films produced by Hammer during the same period, which were extremely successful in commercial terms internationally, and they fail even to mention the 'Carry On' films of the same period, a series of low comedies that were commercially successful inside Britain but were never made with a view to the international market. The reason for this apparent discrepancy is that while the Hammer horror films and 'Carry On' films were popular films with few artistic pretensions, the British social realist films were self-consciously made in relation to the international art cinema of the period and have been critically well-received internationally. In other words, film histories tend to focus on those films that have an international presence rather than ones that may be important to an indigenous community but are rarely consumed elsewhere; and on films that have developed critical reputations rather than those that have been commercially successful. Similarly, many histories associate French cinema with a small number of internationally celebrated art movements, and ignore the vast majority of French film production.

This book also has its absences and omissions. For example, students will find little on animation here, and this reveals another problem. Most film histories are actually the history of the feature film rather than of film more generally but, until very recently in the history of film, the feature film was only one element in a programme of entertainment, of which animated features often formed a significant element. Not only is there little work on the programme as a whole, but the history of animation is therefore a complex one that does not always neatly map onto narratives dominated by the feature film.

In other words, narrative histories are always forced to streamline the complexities of history in order to find a clear and linear narrative of development.

As a result, narratives cannot examine films from too many angles, which is why they cannot give equal weight to the processes of aesthetic development, the economics, politics and creative practices that shape filmmaking, and their marketing, distribution, exhibition and consumption by audiences. However, while this means that one has to face choices in the construction of a narrative history and must decide to privilege one line of analysis over others, no choice is ever neutral and every choice has its consequence. For example, many accounts of film history do not mention Africa until the emergence of directors such as Ousmane Sembene in the 1960s, and the reason for this omission is that they focus on histories of aesthetic production. But, even if we accept that Africa was not a significant producer of films, commercially or aesthetically, until the 1960s, this does not mean that there is no history of film in Africa before this point. On the contrary, there are complex histories of the colonial uses of film, of distribution, exhibition and consumption, and as Chapter 14 demonstrates, we have much to learn from such histories, if only we can escape the assumption that film history is synonymous with the history of aesthetic production.

However, while we encourage students to pay attention to the gaps and absences in the following account, and to that which is privileged or marginalised, we would also stress that this should not imply that one could ever produce a full and accurate account of the history of film. As we have pointed out, narrative inevitably privileges and streamlines history, but this is a strength as much as a weakness. Research is always about finding a focus. The attempt to capture and reproduce the richness and fullness of the historical past is not only impossible but seeks to mirror its object of study, rather than identify a purpose for studying it and studying what is relevant or irrelevant to that purpose. As a result, the intense conflicts over the relevance and irrelevance of specific details, or over what is significant and insignificant, is not simply a conflict over absences or omissions but over the appropriate focus and purpose of historical research.

Finally, we hope not only that the book will equip students with a sense of what others have researched and written about, but also that the variety of objects and methods – the economics, politics and creative practices associated with filmmaking; the processes of aesthetic development; the marketing, distribution, exhibition and consumption of film, and so on – will encourage students to think about the practice of 'doing' film history and encourage them to remember that there is a range of sources available. Certainly, there is a huge amount of material available online but a shift from production-based histories should remind us both that there is a wealth of material in our own neighbourhood, and also that, as Allen and Gomery put it, 'rather than merely sift through the interpretations of others, the local researcher has the opportunity to find and use a great variety of primary materials [and since] so little has been done to document filmgoing at a local level, it is possible to make a contribution to the state of historical film knowledge'.[1] As a result, students do not have to bemoan their lack of access to the papers of major studios and great directors but can begin to think about the ways in which film as a medium has been embedded in everyday life in the local areas in which they live and in which they study. This may include traces of the past that exist in records held in libraries and other organisations; in advertising and other media such as television, magazines, papers, and so on; in the shape of cinema buildings, whether they are currently used to show films, transformed into supermarkets, or even lie derelict; and in the memories of family, friends and others whose stories have much to tell us about the history and meaning of cinema in the past.

NOTE

1. Robert Allen and Douglas Gomery (1985), *Film History: Theory and Practice*, Boston, MA: McGraw-Hill, p. 193.

PART I
FILM HISTORY FROM ITS ORIGINS
TO 1945

I

THE EMERGENCE OF CINEMA

The history of motion-pictures is not easily defined by a single invention or inaugural event. While inventors such as Thomas Edison, and early cinema pioneers such as the Lumière brothers, have become central to legends surrounding the 'birth of cinema', the emergence of cinema was the result of a series of technological and entrepreneurial developments that came together in the 1890s. Seeking to capitalise on new capacities of photographic development, the invention of celluloid, and the refinement of machines that could project images in sequence, a number of individuals saw commercial possibilities in projecting moving images to paying audiences. Cinema did not arise as a fully fledged industry with a set of aesthetic norms and conventions in place, but developed as a novelty entertainment, one of a number of emergent visual forms within popular culture at the end of the nineteenth century.

The invention of moving pictures has complex origins that can be traced back to sixteenth-century experiments with the camera obscura and the use of magic lanterns. While the former was a dark chamber in which an image of outside objects could be thrown upon a screen, the latter was a device that enabled images, painted on glass, to be projected by means of an artificial light source. Magic lanterns were used to present a succession of images for the purpose of telling a story, often illustrating and helping to narrate satirical scenes, theatrical tragedies and miracle plays. While magic lanterns could arrange eight scenes in a long glass slide, phantasmagoria exhibitions would project slides from behind a screen using different lanterns to produce a composite image. Instead of a single operator, several skilled technicians were required, helping to create a complex screen performance that, often shown in theatres and museums, held particular appeal for sophisticated urban audiences. These would become especially popular in France, England and the United States in the late eighteenth and early nineteenth century.

Lantern displays formed a basis upon which technologies and cultural practices of screen projection would develop. This was specifically marked in the nineteenth century. With scientific developments in the study of vision, and industrialisation producing new forms of machine technology (in particular, communication technologies like the telegraph, telephone and phonograph), the nineteenth century created the necessary pre-conditions for the technical development of motion-pictures. At one level, this was linked to particular experiments in the field of vision, growing out of a popular and scientific fascination with moving images. While optical toys such as the Zoetrope, invented in 1833, helped give the illusion of continuous movement by spinning a narrow disc of drawings in a revolving drum, anatomical motion experiments carried out by Eadweard Muybridge in 1878 helped refine not only the study of moving forms, but the technical methods for recording movement photographically. Creating a special lantern to project his famous experiments of galloping horses, Muybridge played a significant part in the long history of what has come to be called 'screen practice'.

The emergence of cinema must be understood in relation to a pre-history of visual experimentation, and to practices of visual representation ranging from magic lantern shows to dioramas and panoramas. Specific technologies were developed in the late nineteenth century, however, that would create the basis for the rapid development of cinema as an artistic and industrial form. The basic apparatus for producing moving images relies on a system where a series of images can be passed in quick succession in front of a light source. This process is reliant on two kinds of device – cameras that can expose an image on a strip of film and projectors that can pass this strip in front of a beam of light at great speed. To create the illusion of continuous movement, a projector has to pass sixteen frames a second in front of a light source, stopping intermittently to expose the frame. While the American inventor George Eastman introduced celluloid roll film in 1889 – a transparent material flexible enough to be used in cameras and projection machines – the technology required to show moving photographs and films was developed concurrently in a number of countries, principally in the United States, France and Britain.

Thomas Edison and a team of technicians working under William Kennedy Laurie Dickson in New Jersey were responsible for the earliest of these, inventing the Kinetograph camera and the Kinetoscope viewing device. The latter was a machine that pulled 35mm film stock in front of an electric lamp and shutter using toothed gears, a device that would mechanically pull the film at a consistent speed. The Kinetograph was based on peephole viewing. Rather than watch images on a screen, individuals would bend and press their eyes to holes in a self-standing machine. While first displayed at the World's Columbian Exhibition in Chicago in 1893, the Kinetograph was designed as a form of popular amusement. Having patented and perfected the use of the new technology, Edison was quick to seek avenues for commercial exploitation. This led in 1894 to the first Kinetoscope parlour, a rented storefront in New York City with room for ten viewing machines.

These reproduced short moving films recorded at Edison's primitive studio in New York, popularly dubbed the 'Black Maria'. Films lasted for no longer than twenty seconds and would often feature vaudeville acts, performances by dancers or acrobats, or appearances by popular sporting figures such as the boxing champion Gentleman Jim Corbett. Because of the individualised nature of the viewing experience, subject material was often voyeuristic and sexually charged, tailored for masculine amusement. Film history has often underestimated the pleasures of the Kinetoscope for women, however. While films that displayed the physique of bodybuilders such as the famous Sandow held their own fascination, particularly the spectacle of the male body, films were increasingly made for mixed-sex audiences, drawing for their subject material upon popular amusements of the day.

At the same time that Edison unveiled the Kinetoscope, Auguste and Louis Lumière were developing a compact camera/projection device known as the Cinématographe. In 1895, the Lumière brothers staged one of the first public moving picture demonstrations. This was held at the Grand Café in Paris. To a crowded room of fashionable society members, the Lumière brothers showed a sequence of short films made using their new system. This included views of Lumière and his wife feeding a baby, a comic scene of a boy stepping on a garden hose, and a train pulling into a station. The last of these, *Arrival of a Train at the Station at Ciôtat* (1895), produced legends of viewers fleeing their seats, but these probably owe more to cinematic myth than anything else. Although the idea persists that early cinema audiences were laughably naïve in their apparent inability to distinguish between image and reality, it has been shown that audiences maintained a complex relationship with the screen. For example, a film such as *The Countryman and the Cinematograph* (1901), made by the British filmmaker Robert William Paul, demonstrates that audiences were encouraged from an early point to see themselves as sophisticated consumers of the viewing experience. With clear reference to Lumière, the film mocks a country bumpkin who dives away from a cinema screen showing a train approaching a station (the film would be remade in the United States as *Uncle Josh at the Moving Picture Show* (1902)). While this may suggest something of the way that urban film audiences sought to compare themselves with ignorant country figures, audiences of all kinds were rarely the dupes they have often been assumed to be, swiftly assimilating the peculiar dimensions of cinematic space and its various forms of spectacle.

The Cinématographe, and the thrall of 'living pictures', was met with widespread fascination. Accordingly, the Lumières moved quickly to capitalise on their invention at home and abroad. The Cinématographe was both portable and adaptable and this enabled the Lumières and their representatives to tour Europe and America, swiftly turning cinema into an international phenomenon. Showing films in rented theatres and cafés, the Lumière Cinématographe represented the earliest known public screening in several countries. This helped establish an early footing for French film production in a growing moving picture market. Not least, it enabled the commercial rise of the Pathé Company (established by Charles Pathé in 1896), the firm's aggressive policy of expansion turning it into the biggest single film company by the mid-1900s, with distribution offices in all corners of the world.

Recognising the waning popularity of the Kinetoscope, and witnessing the success of the Cinématographe, Edison moved quickly into screen projection, acquiring the patents for a projector designed by Thomas Armat and C. Francis Jenkins called the Vitascope. This had its first public première at Koster and Hall's Music Hall in New York in 1896. The commercial possibilities of cinema, especially in the domestic US market, were becoming ever more apparent to those willing to invest in, and exploit, its potential. This led to the swift proliferation of independent exhibitors and projection machines. It also generated intense rivalries between the major film producing companies. This was particularly marked in the United States between the Edison Manufacturing Company and American Mutoscope, a company that made peepshow and projected films on sharper 70mm film.

Changing its name to American Mutoscope and Biograph in 1899, Edison brought a lawsuit against the company for infringement of patents and copyrights. This was a characteristic move by Edison but one that in this instance failed, a landmark case in 1902 deciding that American Mutoscope's camera was sufficiently different from Edison's, using the friction of a roller to guide cinematographic film through a camera, rather than a system that used sprockets, or a toothed cylinder, to drive it through. Legal disputes about the rights to motion-picture equipment defined the American film industry's early history, entangling American Mutoscope and Biograph but also Edison's other major domestic rival, the Vitagraph Company of America. Established in 1898 by James Stuart Blackton and Albert Smith, Vitagraph successfully fed the demand for moving pictures created by the Spanish–American War (1897–8), in particular the appetite for topical war images which Vitagraph satisfied through films staged on its rooftop studio in New York City. Soon establishing itself as a primary American film producer, Vitagraph, like American Mutoscope and Biograph, lived with the risk of copyright lawsuits. This was only briefly calmed in 1902 by the legal ruling against Edison.

If America and France became the most significant film-producing countries in the late 1890s, they were quickly joined by Britain. With Edison failing to patent the Kinetoscope abroad, Robert William Paul was legally able to replicate the viewing machine. When Edison tried to assert control over his technology, cutting off the supply of films, Paul developed his own camera and went into production for himself, demonstrating *Rough Sea At Dover* to the Royal Photographic Institute in 1896. By selling film projectors, rather than renting them, Paul facilitated the rapid spread of film exhibition up and down the country, films being shown mainly in theatres or music halls. He also developed filmmaking activity by opening the first British film studio in 1899. Like that of British filmmaker Cecil Hepworth, Paul based operations out of small premises in London, soon joined by studios on the south coast of Britain operated by George Albert Smith and James Williamson, key figures of the so-called 'Brighton School'. This was renowned for its early experimentation with special effects and editing in films like *The Big Swallow* (1901), a short film where a man reluctant to have his picture taken perceptibly swallows the camera. Including work by Hepworth such as *How it Feels to be Run Over* (1900), a single-shot film creating the illusion of a motorcar colliding with the spectator/camera, English cinema was innovative, internationally popular, and as with R. W. Paul's *The Countryman and the Cinematograph*, frequently imitated.

From its first beginnings, cinema was international in scope and development. The period between 1895 and 1907 was specific in terms of the industrial make-up of the film industry and the style and exhibition of its product. This was a period of ferment and change that would give rise to the frameworks that would later shape motion-picture practice. However, it also revealed a strikingly different understanding of cinema industrially, aesthetically and in terms of exhibition. With regard to film style, this was especially apparent between 1894 and 1902 where the majority of films consisted of one-shot 'actualities'. These were often non-fictional scenes, short travelogues offering views of exotic locales, or films of topical news events that could include parades, world fairs and funerals.

In the fairgrounds and carnivals where film was frequently shown, scenes of local places and crowds became popular subject material, together with sporting occasions such as football matches and horse races. Operators of the Lumière Cinématographe would often make scenics of local interest that would combine with a repertoire of one-shot films. One of the Lumières' first actualities, *Workers Leaving the Lumière Factory* (1895), was a film showing employees spilling out of a factory door, dispersing from either side of the cinematic frame. Indicative here is the fascination that film audiences developed in the simple recording and reproduction of moving images. Cinema opened up new kinds of visual experience, and afforded the chance for people to witness events, people and places never seen before.

Actualities were made with a stationary camera, set far enough back to show the entire length of the human body. Concerned with the individual shot, rather than connections between shots, early cinema was distinguished by a tableau style, replicating perspectives drawn or inspired by visual media of the period, including postcards, stereographs and images from the theatre. Rather than create continuous linear narratives, one-shot actualities based their appeal on visual spectacle. Tom Gunning has called this 'the cinema of attractions', a film style less dependent on cinematic conventions of storytelling, and the creation of temporal and causal relations between shots, than on the sheer novelty of moving pictures.

This does not mean to say that one-shot films were without narrative or experimental elements. Indeed, historians have increasingly shown that one-shot films did not exist in a vacuum, but relied heavily on narrative and visual conventions drawn from other forms of popular entertainment. This included vaudeville, and its particular emphasis on pantomime and melodrama, as well as the performance style of theatre.

The French filmmaker Georges Méliès was an especially significant innovator of staged film theatre. Méliès was a performing magician who, in building a camera based on projection equipment obtained from R. W. Paul, decided to add film to his theatre show, employing a host of camera tricks to create novel fantasy illusions. In his first trick film, *The Vanishing Lady* (1896), Méliès transformed a woman into a skeleton by stopping the camera between shots. Méliès pioneered the use of stop-motion techniques to create early special effects. Examination of early prints also show, however, that Méliès frequently spliced film, cutting and reconnecting it to create a particular sense of filmic reality. In historical debate about the origins of film editing, the early work of Méliès has until recently been overlooked. Indeed, Méliès' stop-motion technique was not simply a case of stopping and restarting the camera at strategic points; it relied on the importance of maintaining unity in the framing and viewpoint of an image. Creating a seamless illusion was a far more complex technique, in this sense, than is often given due. Indeed, while pre-narrative cinema is sometimes thought 'primitive' in its mode of filmmaking, this belies the sophisticated means by which the likes of Méliès combined the magic theatre and new cinematic technology to create visual effects that very skilfully controlled spectators' perceptions.

Méliès' Star Film Company was founded in 1896 and would soon become a leading producer of fiction film, opening distribution offices in London, Barcelona, Berlin and New York. Building a glass-enclosed studio in 1897, Méliès experimented with the cultural and creative potential of the new medium. For example, *The Dreyfus Affair* (1899) was a film made in ten shots. While these shots were released as separate films, which was common practice at the time, they could also be combined to convey the contemporaneous story of a Jewish officer falsely convicted of treason. More popular than staged topicals like *The Dreyfus Affair* were Méliès' fantasy films. The most notable, *A Trip to the Moon* (1902), was a multi-shot film that used editing techniques to emphasise the event of a space capsule landing on the moon. A comic science-fiction film, where a group of scientists meet hostile extraterrestrials, *A Trip to the Moon* used overlapping action and dissolves to link shots together. This was indicative of the move towards more complex narrative filmmaking in the early 1900s, film experimenting with shot-length, point of view and camera tricks to organise cinematic space and time in particular ways. With its multiple tableaux, including, for example, a rocket passing from a cliff on the lunar surface, through space, towards the sea and down to the seabed, *A Trip to the Moon* used the thread of a story to assemble a series of decors and trick effects. While Méliès did not consider himself a storyteller as such, use of multiple shots obliged him to consider the production of spatial coherence in and between scenic episodes.

While cinema would move towards greater levels of narrative integration, the early years of cinema were nevertheless dominated by one-shot actualities, transforming from a brief peepshow amusement to a full-length feature of variety programming. While specific venues for the exhibition of film did not emerge until 1905, film was incorporated into most aspects of American and European entertainment in the late nineteenth century. It was shown in vaudeville theatres, music halls, cafés, in temporary storefronts, at fairs and carnivals, and by travelling showmen who toured with their own projectors and who might give educational lectures to audiences in local churches and opera houses.

Cinema was a vagrant cultural form in many respects, and the experience of film exhibition would likely differ according to place, context and the performance style of the exhibitor. Typically, the presentation of film would be accompanied by music, sometimes by a piano and, in vaudeville theatres, by a house orchestra. Alternatively, exhibitors might synchronise noise with the action on screen, producing sounds to replicate gunfire, hammer blows or other associative links between sound and image. Different still, exhibitors might choose to lecture beside a film, or announce titles to explain the action. While a complete lack of sound accompaniment was a possibility, film was rarely 'silent' in its style of exhibition.

Whatever the venue, exhibitors had considerable control over the organisation of film's presentation and, ultimately, its meaning. The prevalence of one-shot films meant that exhibitors had the choice of buying a series of shots and running them together, or of buying a few shots and combining them with other films or lantern slides. In putting together a projection programme, exhibitors made decisions about the arrangement of scenes and the running order of material. Rather than strive for thematic, generic or narrative continuity between shots, exhibitors often sought diversity and contrast, placing quite different one-shot units next to each other. Within a twelve-shot programme, a scene of Niagara Falls might run beside a film of children playing, which might come before a literary tableau from *Rip Van Winkle*. The exhibitor could play a highly creative role in providing both sound accompaniment to programmed films (voice, music, effects) and in constructing narrative sequences.

Presentational decisions would often take into account the composition of the audience. In general terms, the audience for cinema was socially varied, drawing upon working, middle and élite classes. While vaudeville and opera houses could offer a scale of prices, ranging in the United States from twenty cents to a dollar fifty, storefronts might offer motion-pictures for as little as ten cents. Meanwhile, amusement parks such as Coney Island offered film as one of many cheap distractions, significantly addressed to affluent members of the urban working class. Early film audiences were reasonably heterogeneous. This does not mean to say that élite and working classes watched film presentations together. Exhibitors often took into account the economic status and cultural orientation of particular social groups, emphasising particular kinds of film in their presentations. While commercial amusement often distinguished 'clean entertainment' from (male-oriented) burlesque films more sexual in nature, exhibition that took place under church sponsorship or that appeared in more auspicious cultural venues appealed to distinct social groups through the promise of refined entertainment.

Different kinds of full-length screen entertainment became popular in 1897–8. These were film presentations that could potentially run for an hour and that would focus on a single non-fiction subject. According to Charles Musser in *The Emergence of Cinema: The American Screen to 1907* (1990), these not only demonstrated the potential for the creative role of the exhibitor, but also underscored a 'reassertion of social and cultural differences in the realm of reception or spectatorship'. In America, these evening entertainments were focused around three distinct genres: re-enactments of prize fights, Passion Plays and travel lectures. While the first appealed to those who favoured sensationalist amusements – the apparent barbarism of boxing drawing strong opposition from religious groups and cultural élites – the second appealed to devoted churchgoers, Passion Plays staging single-shot scenes from the life of Jesus. Meanwhile, travel lectures embodied the principles of refined culture, addressing themselves to élitist groups and delivered in rarefied locations such as the Brooklyn Institute. In different ways, these became a means of integrating moving pictures within cultural practice while maintaining established distinctions of social class.

By 1898, hundreds of projectors were in use. Despite the popularity of full-length programmes and other experiments in film exhibition, many films soon appeared staid and familiar. Because producers sold rather than rented their films, motion-pictures began to circulate widely as they were successively *re*sold, generating audience boredom with predictable subject matter. New kinds of film helped revive the film industry at various moments in time. While the Spanish–American War gave the motion-picture industry a new role, investing film with a patriotic and ideological function, the establishment of film as a permanent vaudeville attraction in 1899 gave film companies a significant boost. With vaudeville managers beginning to show films on a permanent basis, new pictures were required each week. This not only helped the major New York-based firms like Edison, it gave support to the companies of William Selig and Sigmund Lubin, active in the emerging film-producing centres of Chicago and Philadelphia.

In the early years of cinema's history, a significant industrial theme was the attempt by film companies to establish stability in the supply of its product and in the search for dependable outlets. While the establishment of film as a permanent vaudeville attraction went some way towards establishing this situation, there remained a significant amount of flux, caused by legal disputes over patents, technological incompatibility, intense competition between companies, and growing audience indifference to film programming. The last of these was not helped by a particular stagnancy in the formulas used to attract early film audiences. One result was an increase in production activity between 1900 and 1903.

This period saw the production company become the principal site for cinematic creativity, assuming control over editing and the construction of multi-shot narratives. While these responsibilities had been previously shared with the exhibitor, commercial crisis at the turn of the century led production companies to search for new cinematic forms. Specifically, it saw an emerging conception of cinema based around storytelling. While this cannot be reduced to the work of any single individual, it was nevertheless influenced by the innovations and commercial success of particular films and filmmakers. Notable among them was Edwin S. Porter.

Porter is often credited with making the first story film in *Life of an American Fireman* (1902). Porter was a film projectionist who was assigned to improve cameras and projectors at the Edison Manufacturing Company. Coinciding with the construction of an enclosed glass rooftop studio in 1900, Porter began to operate a camera and became one of Edison's most important filmmakers. While fictional films were not entirely new at this point, Porter drew upon Méliès' *A Trip to the Moon* and James Williamson's *Fire!* (1901) to make a short rescue story.

Life of an American Fireman begins with a long shot of a sleeping fireman. Conveyed at the top of the screen is a dream or 'vision scene' – that of a woman and child threatened by fire. The film then illustrates the fireman racing to the scene, using a mixture of location and studio filming. The film conveys the rescue twice, using overlapping action. The first time, the rescue is seen from inside the house. The second time, the rescue is conveyed again but this time from a perspective outside the house. For many years, a modernised and re-edited version of the film, held at the Museum of Modern Art, led scholars to vaunt Porter's singular contribution to continuity editing, attempting to match time and space across cuts. The logical ordering of shots in this version would ultimately reveal the difficulty of researching early film, however, in particular what films were being used to make conclusions about early cinematic style. Not only is a good deal of early cinema either lost or incomplete, its traces remain in quite different historical versions. In fact, the original film of *Life of an American Fireman*, held at the Library of Congress, relied heavily on extreme forms of narrative repetition. Indeed, displaying the same event from different viewpoints, such as the rescue scene, was common to the period, a form of 'nonlinear continuity' that differed radically from the linear narrative style that would later distinguish classical Hollywood cinema.

Critics such as Tom Gunning and Charles Musser have argued for the importance of understanding the conventions of early cinema on its own terms. In this context, *Life of an American Fireman* is as significant for its ruptures and repetitions as it is for its similarities with later styles of filmmaking. That said, Porter's early work does suggest a move towards a principle of continuity in its mode of storytelling, illustrated in a different way by *Uncle Tom's Cabin* (1903). Made as a series of one-shot scenes conveying episodes from Harriet Beecher Stowe's novel, the film was one of the first to link scenes using printed intertitles.

Porter's most important film was *The Great Train Robbery* (1903). A significant commercial success, this used eleven shots to tell the story of a train robbery by a gang of bandits. *The Great Train Robbery* is one of the first cinematic Westerns, and incorporates the popular structure of the chase to link together various shots: of the robbery, of a telegraph operator alerting the authorities, and of a posse ambushing the thieves. Significantly, Porter included an emblematic shot of the outlaw leader Barnes firing his gun directly at the camera. According to the Edison catalogue, this shot could come at the beginning *or* the end of the film. In this respect, *The Great Train Robbery* was a story film but one that did not employ the techniques of classical narrative storytelling that would later emerge. Shots are neither 'motivated' in narrative terms (that is, they do not serve a deliberate narrative function) nor are they designed to explain character action.

While not linear in narrative terms, Porter's work was indicative of the rise of fiction filmmaking in the early 1900s, moving away from actuality and documentary subjects towards story-based films. These were still based on pre-existing media for their conventions and storytelling devices, but major changes were beginning to occur within motion-picture practice, transformations in film production and exhibition that would affect both the aesthetic and industrial basis of cinema in its style and organisation. Beginning as a novelty entertainment, itinerant in nature, the film industry began to stabilise in the early 1900s, moving towards a transitional period that would see the development of cinema as a commercial mass medium.

In his seminal essay, 'The Cinema of Attractions: Early Film, its Spectator and the Avant-Garde', Tom Gunning explores the period before the film industry achieved relative stability. Specifically, he examines the pleasures afforded by early cinema, focusing on the modes of film display and exhibition that made cinema a distinctive, and curiously modern visual attraction. Gunning suggests that the cinematic apparatus itself became a source of spectacle, heightened by the means by which performers would self-consciously acknowledge the camera and interact with the audience. Instead of the continuous action of narrative cinema, organised around storytelling, Gunning suggests that 'the cinema of attractions directly solicits spectator attention, inciting visual curiosity, and supplying pleasure through an exciting spectacle – a unique event, whether fictional or documentary, that is of interest in itself.'

In methodological terms, Gunning concentrates on the development of film as an artistic form. Within older schools of aesthetic film history, criticism has often focused on 'classic' works that have been taken to represent key moments in the evolution of film art. While this style of criticism continues, Gunning's work can be situated within a reformulation of aesthetic film history that has largely taken place since the mid-1980s. This puts stress on the study of signifying practices rather than the history of film art as such; it is concerned with the aesthetic norms that govern the style of film in particular periods, and the historically specific relationships that can develop between films and audiences.

In terms of evidence, Gunning makes an argument about exhibition and spectatorship through his reading of the film text. His concern with spectatorship remains abstract, but in considering how film *addressed itself* to an audience, Gunning is able to draw out the historically specific means by which cinema established itself as an attraction. He suggests that the primacy of spectacle and theatricality in early cinema is entwined with the history of the avant-garde. However, the 'cinema of attractions' also provides a significant historical perspective on Hollywood's own aesthetic propensities, particularly its enduring concern with visual and sensory enthralment.

- What kind of evidence does Gunning use to make claims about the appeal of early cinema?
- To what degree can the film text reveal the pleasures of early cinema for audiences, and how else might you examine the status of cinema as a popular attraction?
- Are there ways in which a 'cinema of attractions' may still be said to exist? How would you go about examining this?

THE CINEMA OF ATTRACTIONS: EARLY FILM, ITS SPECTATOR AND THE AVANT-GARDE

Tom Gunning

Writing in 1922, flushed with the excitement of seeing Abel Gance's *La Roue*, Fernand Léger tried to define something of the radical possibilities of the cinema. The potential of the new art did not lie in 'imitating the movements of nature' or in 'the mistaken path' of its resemblance to theatre. Its unique power was a 'matter of *making images seen*'[1] It is precisely this harnessing of visibility, this act of showing and exhibition, which I feel cinema before 1906 displays most intensely. Its inspiration for the avant-garde of the early decades of this century needs to be re-explored.

Tom Gunning, *Wide Angle* 8(3/4), Autumn 1986.

Writings by the early modernists (Futurists, Dadaists and Surrealists) on the cinema follow a pattern similar to Léger: enthusiasm for this new medium and its possibilities; and disappointment at the way it has already developed, its enslavement to traditional art forms, particularly theatre and literature. This fascination with the *potential* of a medium (and the accompanying fantasy of rescuing the cinema from its enslavement to alien and passé forms) can be understood from a number of viewpoints. I want to use it to illuminate a topic I have also approached before, the strangely heterogeneous relation that film before 1906 (or so) bears to the films that follow, and the way a taking account of this heterogeneity signals a new conception of film history and film form. My work in this area has been pursued in collaboration with André Gaudreault.[2]

The history of early cinema, like the history of cinema generally, has been written and theorized under the hegemony of narrative films. Early film-makers like Smith, Méliès and Porter have been studied primarily from the viewpoint of their contribution to film as a storytelling medium, particularly the evolution of narrative editing. Although such approaches are not totally misguided, they are one-sided and potentially distort both the work of these film-makers and the actual forces shaping cinema before 1906. A few observations will indicate the way that early cinema was not dominated by the narrative impulse that later asserted its sway over the medium. First there is the extremely important role that actuality film plays in early film production. Investigation of the films copyrighted in the US shows that actuality films outnumbered fictional films until 1906.[3] The Lumière tradition of 'placing the world within one's reach' through travel films and topicals did not disappear with the exit of the Cinématographe from film production. But even within non-actuality filming – what has sometimes been referred to as the 'Méliès tradition' – the role narrative plays is quite different from in traditional narrative film. Méliès himself declared in discussing his working method:

> As for the scenario, the 'fable,' or 'tale,' I only consider it at the end. I can state that the scenario constructed in this manner has *no importance*, since I use it merely as a pretext for the 'stage effects,' the 'tricks,' or for a nicely arranged tableau.[4]

Whatever differences one might find between Lumière and Méliès, they should not represent the opposition between narrative and non-narrative film-making, at least as it is understood today Rather, one can unite them in a conception that sees cinema less as a way of telling stories than as a way of presenting a series of views to an audience, fascinating because of their illusory power (whether the realistic illusion of motion offered to the first audiences by Lumière, or the magical illusion concocted by Méliès), and exoticism. In other words, I believe that the relation to the spectator set up by the films of both Lumière and Méliès (and many other film-makers before 1906) had a common basis, and one that differs from the primary spectator relations set up by narrative film after 1906. I will call this earlier conception of cinema, 'the cinema of attractions'. I believe that this conception dominates cinema until about 1906–7. Although different from the fascination in storytelling exploited by the cinema from the time of Griffith, it is not necessarily opposed to it. In fact the cinema of attractions does not disappear with the dominance of narrative, but rather goes underground, both into certain avant-garde practices and as a component of narrative films, more evident in some genres (e.g. the musical) than in others.

What precisely is the cinema of attractions? First, it is a cinema that bases itself on the quality that Léger celebrated: its ability to *show* something. Contrasted to the voyeuristic aspect of narrative cinema analysed by Christian Metz,[5] this is an exhibitionist cinema. An aspect of early cinema which I have written about in other articles is emblematic of this different relationship the cinema of attractions constructs with its spectator: the recurring look at the camera by actors. This action, which is later perceived as spoiling the realistic illusion of the cinema, is here undertaken with brio, establishing contact with the audience. From comedians smirking at the camera, to the constant bowing and gesturing of the conjurors in magic films, this is a cinema that displays its visibility, willing to rupture a self-enclosed fictional world for a chance to solicit the attention of the spectator.

Exhibitionism becomes literal in the series of erotic films which play an important role in early film production (the same Pathé catalogue would advertise the Passion Play along with 'scènes grivoises d'un caractère piquant', erotic films often including full nudity), also driven underground in later years. As Noël Burch has shown in his film *Correction Please: How We Got into Pictures* (1979), a film like *The Bride Retires* (France, 1902) reveals a fundamental conflict between this exhibitionistic tendency of early film and the creation of a fictional diegesis. A woman undresses for bed while her new husband peers at her from behind a screen. However, it is to the camera and the audience that the bride addresses her erotic striptease, winking at us as she faces us, smiling in erotic display

As the quote from Méliès points out, the trick film, perhaps the dominant non-actuality film genre before 1906, is itself a series of displays, of magical attractions, rather than a primitive sketch of narrative continuity. Many trick films are, in effect, plotless, a series of transformations strung together with little connection and certainly no characterization. But to approach even the plotted trick films, such as *Voyage dans la lune* (1902), simply as precursors of later narrative structures is to miss the point. The story simply provides a frame upon which to string a demonstration of the magical possibilities of the cinema.

Modes of exhibition in early cinema also reflect this lack of concern with creating a self-sufficient narrative world upon the screen. As Charles Musser has shown,[6] the early showmen exhibitors exerted a great deal of control over the shows they presented, actually re-editing the films they had purchased and supplying a series of offscreen supplements, such as sound effects and spoken commentary. Perhaps most extreme is the Hale's Tours, the largest chain of theatres exclusively showing films before 1906. Not only did the films consist of non-narrative sequences taken from moving vehicles (usually trains), but the theatre itself was arranged as a train car with a conductor who took tickets, and sound effects simulating the click-clack of wheels and hiss of air brakes.[7] Such viewing experiences relate more to the attractions of the fairground than to the traditions of the legitimate theatre. The relation between films and the emergence of the great amusement parks, such as Coney Island, at the turn of the century provides rich ground for rethinking the roots of early cinema.

Nor should we ever forget that in the earliest years of exhibition the cinema itself was an attraction. Early audiences went to exhibitions to see machines demonstrated (the newest technological wonder, following in the wake of such widely exhibited machines and marvels as X-rays or, earlier, the phonograph), rather than to view films. It was the Cinématographe, the Biograph or the Vitascope that were advertised on the variety bills in which they premièred, not *Le Déjeuner de bébé* or *The Black Diamond Express*. After the initial novelty period, this display of the possibilities of cinema continues, and not only in agic films. Many of the close-ups in early film differ from later uses of the technique precisely because they do not use enlargement for narrative punctuation, but as an attraction in its own right. The close-up cut into Porter's *The Gay Shoe Clerk* (1903) may anticipate later continuity techniques, but its principal motive is again pure exhibitionism, as the lady lifts her skirt hem, exposing her ankle for all to see. Biograph films such as *Photographing a Female Crook* (1904) and *Hooligan in Jail* (1903) consist of a single shot in which the camera is brought close to the main character, until they are in mid-shot. The enlargement is not a device expressive of narrative tension; it is in itself an attraction and the point of the film.[8]

To summarise, the cinema of attractions directly solicits spectator attention, inciting visual curiosity, and supplying pleasure through an exciting spectacle – a unique event, whether fictional or documentary, that is of interest in itself. The attraction to be displayed may also be of a cinematic nature, such as the early close-ups just described, or trick films in which a cinematic manipulation (slow motion, reverse motion, substitution, multiple exposure) provides the film's novelty. Fictional situations tend to be restricted to gags, vaudeville numbers or recreations of shocking or curious incidents (executions, current events). It is the direct address of the audience, in which an attraction is offered to the spectator by a cinema showman, that defines this approach to film-making. Theatrical display dominates over narrative absorption, emphasizing the direct stimulation of shock or surprise at the expense of unfolding a story or creating a diegetic universe. The cinema of attractions expends little energy creating characters with psychological motivations or individual personality. Making use of both fictional and non-fictional attractions, its energy moves outward towards an acknowledged spectator rather than inward towards the character-based situations essential to classical narrative.

The term 'attractions' comes, of course, from the young Sergei Mikhailovich Eisenstein and his attempt to find a new model and mode of analysis for the theatre. In his search for the 'unit of impression' of theatrical art, the foundation of an analysis which would undermine realistic representational theatre, Eisenstein hit upon the term 'attraction'.[9] An attraction aggressively subjected the spectator to 'sensual or psychological impact'. According to Eisenstein, theatre should consist of a montage of such attractions, creating a relation to the spectator entirely different from his absorption in 'illusory depictions'.[10] I pick up this term partly to underscore the relation to the spectator that this later avant-garde practice shares with early cinema: that of exhibitionist confrontation rather than diegetic absorption. Of course the 'experimentally regulated and mathematically calculated' montage of attractions demanded by Eisenstein differs enormously from these early films (as any conscious and oppositional mode of practice will from a popular one).[11] However, it is important to realize the context from which Eisenstein selected the term. Then, as now, the 'attraction' was a term of the fairground, and for Eisenstein and his friend Yutkevich it primarily represented their favourite fairground attraction, the roller coaster, or as it was known then in Russia, the American Mountains.[12]

The source is significant. The enthusiasm of the early avant-garde for film was at least partly an enthusiasm for a mass culture that was emerging at the beginning of the century, offering a new sort of stimulus for an audience not acculturated to the traditional arts. It is important to take this enthusiasm for popular art as something more than a simple gesture to *épater les bourgeois*. The enormous development of the entertainment industry since the 1910s and its growing acceptance by middle-class culture (and the accommodation that made this acceptance possible) have made it difficult to understand the liberation popular entertainment offered at the beginning of the century. I believe that it was precisely the exhibitionist quality of turn-of-the-century popular art that made it attractive to the avant-garde – its freedom from the creation of a diegesis, its accent on direct stimulation.

Writing of the variety theatre, Marinetti not only praised its aesthetics of astonishment and stimulation, but particularly its creation of a new spectator who contrasts with the 'static', 'stupid voyeur' of traditional theatre. The spectator at the variety theatre feels directly addressed by the spectacle and joins in, singing along, heckling the comedians.[13] Dealing with early cinema within the context of archive and academy, we risk missing its vital relation to vaudeville, its primary place of exhibition until around 1905. Film appeared as one attraction on the vaudeville programme, surrounded by a mass of unrelated acts in a non-narrative and even nearly illogical succession of performances. Even when presented in the nickelodeons that were emerging at the end of this period, these short films always appeared in a variety format, trick films sandwiched in with farces, actualities, 'illustrated songs', and, quite frequently, cheap vaudeville acts. It was precisely this non-narrative variety that placed this form of entertainment under attack by reform groups in the early 1910s. The Russell Sage Survey of popular entertainments found vaudeville 'depends upon an artificial rather than a natural human and developing interest, these acts having no necessary and as a rule, no actual connection'.[14] In other words, no narrative. A night at the variety theatre was like a ride on a streetcar or an active day in a crowded city, according to this middle-class reform group, stimulating an unhealthy nervousness. It was precisely such artificial stimulus that Marinetti and Eisenstein wished to borrow from the popular arts and inject into the theatre, organizing popular energy for radical purpose.

What happened to the cinema of attractions? The period from 1907 to about 1913 represents the true *narrativization* of the cinema, culminating in the appearance of feature films which radically revised the variety format. Film clearly took the legitimate theatre as its model, producing famous players in famous plays. The transformation of filmic discourse that D. W. Griffith typifies bound cinematic signifiers to the narration of stories and the creation of a self-enclosed diegetic universe. The look at the camera becomes taboo and the devices of cinema are transformed from playful 'tricks' – cinematic attractions (Méliès gesturing at us to watch the lady vanish) – to elements of dramatic expression, entries into the psychology of character and the world of fiction.

However, it would be too easy to see this as a Cain and Abel story, with narrative strangling the nascent possibilities of a young iconoclastic form of entertainment. Just as the variety format in some sense survived in the movie palaces of the 20s (with newsreel, cartoon, sing-along, orchestra performance and sometimes vaudeville acts subordinated to, but still coexisting with, the narrative *feature* of the evening), the system of attraction remains an essential part of popular film-making.

The chase film shows how, towards the end of this period (basically from 1903 to 1906), a synthesis of attractions and narrative was already underway. The chase had been the original truly narrative genre of the cinema, providing a model for causality and linearity as well as a basic editing continuity. A film like Biograph's *Personal* (1904, the model for the chase film in many ways) shows the creation of a narrative linearity, as the French nobleman runs for his life from the fiancées his personal column ad has unleashed. However, at the same time, as the group of young women pursue their prey towards the camera in each shot, they encounter some slight obstacle (a fence, a steep slope, a stream) that slows them down for the spectator, providing a mini-spectacle pause in the unfolding of narrative. The Edison Company seemed particularly aware of this, since they offered their plagiarized version of this Biograph film (*How a French Nobleman Got a Wife Through the New York Herald 'Personal' Columns*) in two forms, as a complete film or as separate shots, so that any one image of the ladies chasing the man could be bought without the inciting incident or narrative closure.[15]

As Laura Mulvey has shown in a very different context, the dialectic between spectacle and narrative has fuelled much of the classical cinema.[16] Donald

Crafton in his study of slapstick comedy, 'The pie and the chase', has shown the way slapstick did a balancing act between the pure spectacle of gag and the development of narrative.[17] Likewise, the traditional spectacle film proved true to its name by highlighting moments of pure visual stimulation along with narrative. The 1924 version of *Ben-Hur* was in fact shown at a Boston theatre with a timetable announcing the moment of its prime attractions:

8.35 *The Star of Bethlehem*
8.40 *Jerusalem Restored*
8.59 *Fall of the House of Hur*
10.29 *The Last Supper*
10.50 *Reunion*[18]

The Hollywood advertising policy of enumerating the features of a film, each emblazoned with the command, 'See!' shows this primal power of the attraction running beneath the armature of narrative regulation.

We seem far from the avant-garde premises with which this discussion of early cinema began. But it is important for the radical heterogeneity which I find in early cinema not to be conceived as a truly oppositional programme, one irreconcilable with the growth of narrative cinema. This view is too sentimental and too ahistorical. A film like *The Great Train Robbery* (1903) does point in both directions, towards a direct assault on the spectator (the spectacularly enlarged outlaw unloading his pistol in our faces), and towards a linear narrative continuity. This is early film's ambiguous heritage. Clearly in some sense recent spectacle cinema has reaffirmed its roots in stimulus and carnival rides, in what might be called the Spielberg-Lucas-Coppola cinema of effects.

But effects are tamed attractions. Marinetti and Eisenstein understood that they were tapping into a source of energy that would need focusing and inten-sification to fulfil its revolutionary possibilities. Both Eisenstein and Marinetti planned to exaggerate the impact on the spectators, Marinetti proposing to literally glue them to their seats (ruined garments paid for after the per-formance) and Eisenstein setting firecrackers off beneath them. Every change in film history implies a change in its address to the spectator, and each period constructs its spectator in a new way. Now in a period of American avant-garde cinema in which the tradition of contemplative subjectivity has perhaps run its (often glorious) course, it is possible that this earlier carnival of the cinema, and the methods of popular entertainment, still provide an unexhausted resource – a Coney Island of the avant-garde, whose never dominant but always sensed current can be traced from Méliès through Keaton, through *Un Chien andalou* (1928), and Jack Smith.

NOTES

First published in *Wide Angle* vol. 8, no. 3/4 (Fall 1986).
1. Fernand Léger, 'A Critical Essay on the Plastic Qualities of Abel Gance's film *The Wheel*', in Edward Fry (ed.), *Functions of Painting*, trans. Alexandra Anderson (New York: Viking Press, 1973), 21.

2. See my articles 'The Non-Continuous Style of Early Film', in Roger Holman (ed.), *Cinema 1900–1906* (Brussels: FIAF, 1982), and 'An Unseen Energy Swallows Space: The Space in Early Film and its Relation to American Avant garde Film', in John L. Fell (ed.), *Film before Griffith* (Berkeley: University of California Press, 1983), 355–66, and our collaborative paper delivered by A. Gaudreault at the conference at Cerisy on Film History (August 1985) 'Le cinéma des premiers temps: un défi à l'histoire du cinéma?', I would also like to note the importance of my discussions with Adam Simon and our hope to investigate further the history and archaeology of the film spectator.

3. Robert C. Allen, *Vaudeville and Film: 1895–1915, A Study in Media Interaction* (New York: Arno Press, 1980), 159, 212–13.

4. Georges Méliès, 'Importance du scénario', in Georges Sadoul, *Georges Méliès* (Paris: Seghers, 1961), 118 (my translation).

5. Christian Metz, *The Imaginary Signifier: Psychoanalysis and the Cinema*, trans. Celia Britton, Annwyl Williams, Ben Brewster and Alfred Guzzetti (Bloomington: Indiana University Press, 1982), particularly 58–80, 91–7.

6. Charles Musser, 'American Vitagraph 1897–1901', *Cinema Journal*, vol. 22, no. 3, Spring 1983: 10.

7. Raymond Fielding, 'Hale's Tours: Ultrarealism in the Pre-1910 Motion-Picture', in Fell, *Film before Griffith*, 116–30.

8. I wish to thank Ben Brewster for his comments after the original delivery of this paper which pointed out the importance of including this aspect of the cinema of attractions here.

9. Sergei Eisenstein, 'How I Became a Film Director', in *Notes of a Film Director* (Moscow: Foreign Language Publishing House, n.d.), 16.

10. 'The Montage of Attractions', in S. M. Eisenstein, *Writings 1922–1934*, ed. Richard Taylor (London: BFI, 1988), 35.

11. Ibid.

12. Yon Barna, *Eisenstein* (Bloomington: Indiana University Press, 1973), 59.

13. 'The Variety Theater 1913', in Umbro Apollonio (ed.), *Futurist Manifestos* (New York: Viking Press, 1973), 127.

14. Michael Davis, *The Exploitation of Pleasure* (New York: Russell Sage Foundation, Dept. of Child Hygiene, Pamphlet, 1911).

15. David Levy, 'Edison Sales Policy and the Continuous Action Film 1904–1906', in Fell, *Film before Griffith*, 207–22.

16. 'Visual Pleasure and Narrative Cinema', in Laura Mulvey, *Visual and Other Pleasures* (London: Macmillan, 1989).

17. Paper delivered at the FIAF Conference on Slapstick, May 1985, New York City.

18. Nicholas Vardac, *From Stage to Screen: Theatrical Method from Garrick to Griffith* (New York: Benjamin Blom, 1968), 232.

2

ORGANISING EARLY FILM AUDIENCES

The enthusiasm that greeted story films in the early 1900s led many studios to shift decisively towards this type of film in meeting popular demand. The five main American production companies – Edison, Biograph, Lubin, Selig and Vitagraph – all moved into fiction filmmaking, as did the major film studios of Europe. From 1905 to 1906, this included the French studios Pathé and Gaumont, the Danish production company Nordisk, as well as the principal film companies of Britain and Italy such as Hepworth and Cines.

If cinema began to flourish in the 1900s, creating a soaring demand for new product, it was linked significantly to the rise of film exchanges. These first emerged in 1903 and had a profound effect on distribution and exhibition practices. Film exchanges enabled film producers to rent rather than sell their films. This had revolutionary implications. On the one hand, film exchanges helped to standardise film and turn it into an interchangeable commodity. On the other hand, they helped decouple the industrial arms of distribution and exhibition. These features would soon become central elements in the organisational structure of the wider film industry. Chicago became the largest centre of film exchanges in the mid-1900s, fifteen of the city's exchanges controlling 80 per cent of the rental business in the United States. These provided new prints to those exhibitors willing to pay a weekly premium. Frustrated at the power of the film exchanges, however, and their propensity to rent 'clap-trap and stale stuff', the initial grip of Chicago exchanges gave rise to a proliferating number of rival exchange and film services, located in both traditional distribution centres like New York and Philadelphia, and in regional cities like St Louis, Pittsburgh and Kansas City.

By purchasing films from manufacturers and renting them to exhibitors, the burgeoning network of film exchanges facilitated the rise of permanent venues. Specifically, they led to the rapid proliferation in the United States of nickelodeons. These were specialised storefront theatres designed for the purpose of showing motion-pictures. Because nickelodeons regularly changed their programme (sometimes up to seven times a week), they could attract repeat customers. These were invariably drawn from working-class neighbourhoods. Clustering in tenement districts, nickelodeons made film cheap and readily available to new kinds of blue-collar audience, transforming cinema into a site of mass entertainment.

Charging a nickel admission fee, storefront theatres swiftly challenged pre-existing forms of exhibition such as vaudeville, amusement parks and penny arcades. Creating new conditions for watching film, and proving immensely profitable for those entering the business, nickelodeons would become the dominant site of film exhibition in America by 1908. While there were approximately 3,000 nickelodeons in 1907, this had risen to 10,000 by 1910, cinema attendance reaching 45 million each week. Appearing first in Midwest cities like Pittsburgh and Chicago, the greatest concentration of nickelodeons could soon be found in New York City.

The nickelodeon boom transformed the industry and the status of film in a number of ways. Not least, it created a new form of spectator: the moviegoer. Providing cheap and regular amusement, nickel theatres encouraged greater frequency of attendance. The sheer ubiquity of nickelodeons, with programmes lasting anywhere between ten minutes and an hour, meant that moviegoing could be incorporated into everyday habits and routines. This was especially marked in the United States for the urban and immigrant poor. With industrialisation concentrating productive energies in the city, urban centres like Chicago and New York became a destination for great tides of immigration in the late nineteenth century. Immigrants came from Europe and the agricultural South, moved to the city and frequently experienced its worst deprivations. Immigrants transformed the social and ethnic mix of city life in the early 1900s. Seeking cheap entertainment, they also formed a core audience for the nickelodeon.

Rather than scaled admissions, nickelodeons charged one price. Instead of separating different social groups, nickel theatres were both cheap and inclusive, unconcerned with preserving class distinctions. In this way, they enabled greater mixing between peoples, bringing together different races, ethnicities, genders and ages in the darkened space of the film theatre. Often, nickel theatres would become the centre of local communities and a popular venue for socialising. Heavily patronised by immigrant communities, they also provided women and children with unprecedented access to popular amusement. While it should not be forgotten that cinema also circulated in rural areas, small towns and medium-sized cities, providing a significant and potentially different regional dimension to cinema's early development, the nickel theatres remained central to the place and experience of moving pictures in urban centres.

In practical terms, nickel theatres were cheap to run and were often established by enterprising blue-collar workers and immigrants who would operate the projection machines, deliver film narrations and collect the nickel fees themselves. As nickelodeons developed, they grew in size. Consisting of wooden seats that could hold as many as 200 people, nickel theatres would invariably provide a singer to perform while the projectionist changed reels, and would accompany film with musical or spoken accompaniment. Nickelodeons retained key elements of show presentation but were much cheaper, and often much shabbier, than previous sites of variety amusement.

Distinguished by dim lighting and poor ventilation, nickelodeons were often seen as deathtraps, with the threat of fires, panics and collapsing balconies becoming a cause for concern for civic reform groups and state officials; but this kind of criticism was often a mask for wider social concerns about the urban working class and their exposure to the perceived physical and moral dangers of cinema. While film had once been dominantly shown in 'respectable' venues such as vaudeville theatres, the rise of nickelodeons created fear among the middle classes, particularly of the effects that cinema might have if opened up to the urban poor.

This created a new impetus to police film content and to scrutinise theatrical venues. This was expressed in a series of regulatory measures. Cast by reformers as recruiting stations of prostitution, robbery and all manner of social ills, nickelodeons became the target for legal censure. Reformers feared that 'immoral films' such as those dealing with crime and adultery would unduly influence susceptible audiences. This led to the regulation of film content in particular cities. In Chicago, for example, a board of police censors was established in 1907 to review films in its jurisdiction and to enforce a code that would excise 'offensive' material. Similarly, a private body of progressive reformers in New York established a board of censorship in 1909 aimed at improving film content. This focused especially on themes of infidelity, violence and lawlessness. In seeking to forestall the creation of national censorship laws, the emerging film industry complied with such bodies in early moves towards self-censorship. Rather than invite federal regulation, the National Board of Censorship (as it became known) took steps to regulate the content of film, the motion-picture industry agreeing to submit films to the Board and not release any film unless approved by it.

Debates about the status of cinema have become an important site of historical investigation, scholars examining the social, political and cultural histories that have powerfully shaped cinema's development in aesthetic and institutional terms. Not simply a question of film content, however, studies have shown that reform efforts also focused on the dark and unsanitary conditions of the nickel theatres themselves. These were seen as environments that not only created fire hazards, but that also encouraged unwholesome possibilities for moral and sexual transgression, especially threatening to the well-being of children. Attempting to improve the plight of the 'other half', reform initiatives in the 1900s often belied middle-class anxiety about threats to the social order. The urban poor were seen both as a social responsibility to be addressed and a social danger to be diffused. In this context, state and local authorities instituted various measures to combat the moral dangers posed by cinema. This included regulations that prohibited activities on the Sabbath, that insisted that children be accompanied by an adult, and that prohibited theatres operating in the vicinity of schools and churches.

These initiatives attacked the box office profits of the nickel theatres and were resisted by the film industry. Within these struggles were competing assumptions about the social influence of cinema and its impact on particular kinds of audience. While certain reformers in the United States produced studies confirming their view that popular cinema had adverse effects on young and impressionable spectators, the film industry provided alternative evidence, casting film as a positive influence offering information and amusing entertainment to those with little opportunity for diversion.

Some reformers maintained that cinema could be used for educational purposes. Progressives like Jane Adams, for example, believed that film could be used to elevate and uplift the poor. As such, Adams showed moving pictures in her Chicago settlement, Hull House, concentrating on films that might 'build character' and that could provide positive models of imitation, especially helpful in 'Americanising' a growing immigrant populace. Despite the industry's best efforts, however, the pressure to reform popular cinema was intense. As a measure of risk, the mayor of New York closed down all of the city's nickelodeons in 1908. While the official reason may have been poor safety conditions, a more pressing motivation was the moral threat caused by 'unsuitable' films consumed by susceptible audiences in darkened rooms.

One response by the film industry to the increasing threat of regulation was to make cinema respectable. By improving exhibition venues and investing in quality film, the motion-picture industry sought to appeal to a broader middle-class audience. Cinema was not only made a 'suitable' place for women and children, attempts were made to legitimise film in cultural terms. This marked the evolution of film not simply in America, but also in countries such as Britain, France and Germany.

In Britain, film shows gradually moved out of music halls, fairground sideshows and 'penny gaffs' in the mid-1900s and into new, permanent exhibition venues. This led to similar debates about safety and social regulation. Notably, the Cinematographic Act was passed in 1909, a law designed to protect audiences from the threat of fire by obliging exhibition sites to apply for licences. This Act served to control cinema in more ways than one. In seeking to give cinema respectability, it denied licences to seedier venues and often enforced the separation of film consumption from that of food and drink. The Act also opened a legal path to forms of film censorship. While public concern about the vulgarity of film went back to the 1890s, the new law enabled authorities to include as a condition of licence a rule that films should not be indecent or immoral. As concern about content could only be enforced after the fact, film censorship remained uneven. However, it prompted the film industry to stem the possibility of more serious state censorship by establishing the British Board of Film Censors (BBFC) in 1912. As in the United States, this was a voluntary organisation and its decisions were advisory rather than mandatory. However, as a self-regulating body, it did set about rejecting films that were perceived to be excessively sexual, gruesome, blasphemous, cruel, or that dealt with 'native customs in foreign lands abhorrent to British ideas'.

In France, the primary location for early film shows had been café-concerts, music halls and fairgrounds. While a catastrophic fire in a temporary cinema in 1897 raised national concern, killing 121 people, a majority of whom were high-society women, public debate did not focus in this case on the dangers of cinema. However, the development of permanent exhibition venues in France was linked to industrial efforts to maintain a bourgeois audience. This led to attempts in the mid-1900s to create more salubrious venues for the consumption of film. Of central importance was Pathé's effort to move beyond its fairground clientele to attract a large urban white-collar audience. This saw the proliferation of Pathé cinemas in the mid-1900s, established in Paris, Lyon, Marseilles and other major urban centres. Unlike the American nickelodeons, there is evidence that working-class audiences still preferred the music hall to the cinema as late as 1910. However, the same effort to instil cinema with respectability was evident in France as it was in Britain and the United States.

Seeking to attain cultural legitimacy, the film industry in America and Europe capitalised on the boom in permanent venues, but quickly sought to refine the atmosphere and appeal of cinema in the interests of future development. Together with commitment to internal censorship and improved exhibition venues, film production began to emulate respectable entertainment. The conception of film as high art was especially developed in France by the Film d'Art Company, established in 1908. With close links to prestigious Paris theatres, productions of literary adaptations became a staple, together with historical films based on nineteenth-century plays and operas. Notable among these was *The Assassination of the Duc de Guise* (1908), a film that used stars from the theatrical stage, and that was respectively written and scored by a famous dramatist and classical composer. While the production of 'high-culture' film was by no means new, quality film production became significant as debates about the deleterious effects of cinema began to spread.

Vitagraph, for example, made a series of films based on Shakespeare classics. This ranged from *As You Like It* and *Macbeth* in 1908, to *King Lear* and *A Midsummer Night's Dream*, a year later. As the largest producer of quality films, Vitagraph also made films based on historical and biblical topics and on literary works such as *Oliver Twist* (1909) and *A Tale of Two Cities* (1911). Likewise, Biograph made a number of literary adaptations, while the Edison Company released films such as *Les Misérables* (1910). It is important not to overstate the importance of these films. They were but one production trend among many. However, in coinciding with the peak of the nickelodeon boom in 1908–9, the emergence of 'quality film' was indicative of the attempt to give cinema cultural, as well as aesthetic, respectability.

The nickelodeon boom had various effects on the industrial and representational structure of film. Nickelodeons created enormous demand for product and this served to energise the film industry. However, it also created new competition between established industry powers and emerging independents. Indeed, the nickelodeon business would provide a crucial footing for businessmen who would later shape the Hollywood studio system. This included the Warner Brothers, Carl Laemmle (who would found Universal), Louis B. Mayer (MGM), Adolph Zukor (Paramount), William Fox (Twentieth Century Fox) and Marcus Loew (Loews). The rise of powerful new figures in the fields of distribution and exhibition created disquiet among established film producers. Fearing their influence might be lost in the very period where film demand was surging, steps were taken to standardise industrial practice and, in the process, reassert market control.

The creation of the Motion Picture Patents Company (MPPC) in 1908 was a key development in this context. This was a tactical move by Edison and Biograph to incorporate the main American and foreign film companies into a single body. In strategic terms, the creation of the MPPC was an attempt to exert oligopolistic control over the film industry through the pooling of patents on film stock, cameras and projectors. Otherwise known as The Trust, the MPPC enabled a small number of companies to block out competition, eliminating other firms by suing them for patent infringement. The MPPC included the American companies Edison, Biograph, Vitagraph, Selig, Essanay, Kleine, Kalem and Lubin, and the French companies Méliès and Pathé. It derived its power through licence agreements that producers, film exchanges and exhibitors had to sign in order to operate. This helped stabilise the film industry in organisational terms, generating assembly-line methods where film was produced according to uniform standards and release schedules. It also mobilised a number of independent producers, however, who continued to supply product to unlicensed exchanges and nickelodeons.

In realising the profits to be made through film, the MPPC tried to freeze out non-affiliated companies and create a stable system for the supply of product. This can be seen alongside regional strategies of dominance undertaken by the likes of Pathé, which sought to create a near monopoly in France by vertically integrating the operations of film production, distribution and exhibition. As the face of the organised film industry in America, the MPPC tried to improve the public image of film. Eileen Bowser (1990) suggests that one of the avowed goals of the MPPC was to improve motion-pictures and its customers at the same time. This became a theme within the industry trade journal, *Moving Picture World* (established in 1909), suggesting that particular subjects be barred from the screen. These included scenes from the inside of prisons and police stations, murders, executions, sensational crime and comedies that relied for their humour on people's defects. Instead, films that were based on cultural masterpieces were vaunted, exemplifying film's capacity for cultural uplift.

While quality film was supported by the MPPC, it was not the only, or most significant type of film made available to cinema audiences during the nickelodeon period. The ascendancy of the story film gave rise to a wide range of genres, displaying ideological diversity in the worldviews they expressed. While high-culture films were a formal expression of the industry's attempt to legitimise itself, focusing around middle-class beliefs and cultural aspirations, story films were more varied in form and address. Together with the classical dramas and sermonising melodramas that distinguished efforts at cultural uplift, cinema was characterised by genre staples ranging from westerns and slapstick comedies to detective films and newsreels.

One of the most popular genres of the period was the western. Selig and Essanay specialised in this form and were the first companies to shoot in the western states. Borrowing from traditional Western elements found in dime novels and the famous shows of Buffalo Bill Cody, films like *The Cattle Rustlers* (1908) used authentic landscapes rather than painted backdrops. While slapstick comedies made up more than 70 per cent of fiction film before 1908, they subsided in the peak nickelodeon period, re-emerging in the mid-teens. Their momentary decline was explained, in part, through reform efforts to suppress the genre, perceived as vulgar, tasteless and loaded with cliché. Comedy remained popular with audiences but dramas took on new significance, often incorporating topical issues of the day. While the Vitagraph film *Daisies* (1910) addressed the suffragette struggle for women's rights, the heroine insisting on her rights to education over the objections of her fiancé, Essanay's *The Long Strike* (1911) dealt with contemporary themes of labour unrest.

While many early story films, particularly those of Vitagraph, explored the dynamism and vitality of urban life, working within a range of established genres such as the fire rescue and the chase film, genre film developed as a consequence of the film industry's attempt to standardise its product. Emphasising speed and quantity, film production was increasingly based on a division of labour that saw the emergence of directors and other specialists such as producers, scriptwriters and property men. Discouraging lengthy rehearsals and shooting times, film companies organised their release schedules around a steady supply of single-reel films. The genre film became a means of organising this supply, larger companies producing between two and five reels a week – releasing, say, a military film, a drama, a Western and a comedy – with smaller companies concentrating on one specific genre.

Standardising the manufacture and distribution of film was central to the newly organised film industry. The genre film enabled audiences to foster expectations of what they might see, and how particular films might deliver and vary narrative formulas. These satisfactions were dependent, however, on audiences being able to make film comprehensible in the first place.

Developments in film genre were predicated on a more fundamental process of standardisation, namely that based on resolving issues of narrative clarity.

With the rise of the nickelodeon boom between 1907 and 1908, narrative clarity was perceived as a particular problem. This was especially linked to the cultural diversity of the expanding nickel theatre audience. Without sharing the same cultural background, audiences no longer held in common, or were familiar with, narrative conventions that had previously made film comprehensible. If early cinema was based on extra-textual knowledge drawn from other cultural fields, particularly Anglo-Saxon literature, theatre and myth, the rise of story films complicated matters. Becoming longer and composed of multiple shots, story films threatened to confuse audiences who invariably lacked a common frame of reference. While nickel theatres often used lecturers to overcome this, explaining narrative development, filmmakers increasingly sought to guide the spectator's attention by using explicit cinematic techniques. In Tom Gunning's terms, this represented a shift in emphasis from the 'cinema of attractions', based on visual pleasure, to the 'cinema of narrative integration', organised around formal cinematic conventions designed to enhance narrative clarity.

These conventions drew upon a range of stylistic elements. Lighting, composition, editing and dialogue intertitles all worked to produce a heightened sense of narrative cause and effect. Editing, in particular, moved towards a principle of continuity, creating temporal and spatial relations between shots. Orienting the viewer through new devices such as intercutting, filmmakers sought to create unbroken connections between scenes. In Pathé's *The Runaway Horse* (1907), for example, scenes of a cart horse eating a bag of oats are intercut with those of a driver making a delivery. In different shots, slightly larger animals are used to give the impression of the cart horse gaining weight, resulting in a chase between the well-fed animal and its driver. Intercutting first emerged in 1906 and was one of a number of formal techniques used to make stories comprehensible.

New editing methods not only enabled the construction of more complex forms of narrative, they helped increase the potential for enlisting the spectator's emotions in film. In films such as Vitagraph's *The Mill Girl* (1907), for instance, editing techniques are used for the purpose of highlighting narrative action. The story of a girl in a textile mill, rescued from the unwanted advances of her employer, the film intercuts scenes to create flowing continuous action. In this, *The Mill Girl* helps emphasise emotions and climactic scenes by having actors move into the centre of the frame, reducing camera distance in key shots to heighten dramatic significance. These techniques were indicative of a new narrative system taking shape, a film style that organised relations between shots and that helped integrate the spectator more deeply into the film experience.

An influential exponent of editing technique was D. W. Griffith. Directing more than 400 films for Biograph between 1908 and 1913, Griffith became known for the bold deployment of intercutting. In his wide range of films, this often served to increase suspense. In *The Lonely Villa* (1909), narrative action is created through fifty shots, intercutting between a man, some thieves and an isolated country house. As the man learns by telephone that his wife and children are endangered, swift parallel editing sequences are used to create tension leading up to the rescue scene. For instance, the telephone call is made up of seventeen alternating shots, including various interruptions and the telephone wire eventually being cut. While telephone calls were often previously shown by dividing the screen, editing gave new opportunities for constructing narrative action and excitement.

Together with its key narrative function, editing also had a significant influence on acting style. With the introduction of the nine-foot line – a convention that from 1909 brought camera positioning closer to the actors, filming them from below the hips rather than from head to foot – new possibilities were created for externalising characters' thoughts and emotions. As a result, character psychology assumed greater significance. Rather than the stock characters of early cinema, invariably drawn from vaudeville and the melodramatic stage, characters became more credible and individualised. This had an effect on performance style. Film acting began to model itself on realist drama rather than exaggerated forms of melodrama. While the previous 'histrionic' style was predicated on a pre-established series of gestures and poses, unanchored to any sense or relation to 'the real', a new style of 'verisimilar' acting tried to mimic everyday behaviour.

If the histrionic style was prone to exaggerate emotions through distinct forms of body language, verisimilar acting was a more intimate style that relied on facial expressions. This developed with the increasing use of point-of-view shots, a technique where the camera cuts between a character, what that character sees, and back to the character again. While extreme close-ups were rarely used, closer views and point-of-view shots were often employed to draw out moments of psychological and dramatic intensity. The restrained acting style was symptomatic of a change in the very perception of cinema. Rather than a form of spectacle, film aspired towards the illusion of reality. As such, it was far less common for actors to acknowledge the presence of the camera. Instead of exaggerated pantomime gestures, acting became more naturalistic, a transition attributable to the very difference between the mediums of stage and film.

As film became longer during the nickelodeon period, running to fifteen minutes, intertitles were also increasingly used. While originally deployed in expository ways, used to summarise the action preceding a scene, intertitles became shorter and dispersed throughout scenes. The introduction of dialogue intertitles in 1910 enabled information to be conveyed from within story action. Initially placed before the shot in which dialogue took place, it became common for intertitles to come just after the character had begun to speak. This further enhanced the development of character subjectivity, the responsibility of narration transferring from the third person of the expository titles to the dialogue titles of individual characters.

These formal techniques were instrumental to the growth of film as a commercial amusement. As a burgeoning screen entertainment, with a developing system of exhibition venues and industrial structures, cinema developed its own aesthetic conventions. In both Europe and America, cinema was marked by acute efforts in the late 1900s to organise its cultural status, its narrative meaning and its market potential. This was linked to the expansion of the moviegoing audience. From the period of 'nickel madness' grew a new understanding of the formal properties of film and of cinema as a cultural practice. No longer a casual or novelty entertainment, 'going to the movies' had come into its own.

The transformation of cinema into a site of mass amusement in the mid-1900s did not occur without conflict. Indeed, it inspired organised crusades against the growth of nickel theatres. Lee Grieveson concentrates on one such campaign in his essay, 'Why the Audience Mattered in Chicago in 1907'. Focusing on the sustained efforts by the *Chicago Tribune* to alert its white, middle-class readers to the inherent dangers posed by the city's nickelodeons, Grieveson examines the social struggles that coalesced around cinemagoing in the first decade of the twentieth century. In particular, he considers the production of knowledge about the cinemagoing audience, focusing on middle-class assumptions that immigrant and working-class audiences were at best wayward and at worst delinquent and potentially criminal. Linking this to wider discussions about governance and citizenship in the period, Grieveson examines the hard-fought debates about the social function of moving pictures, connecting the discourse of cinema in the mid-1900s to particular 'regulatory interventions' that took place, from the introduction of censorship to quite literal forms of policing.

Rather than concentrate on the aesthetic history of film, Grieveson examines cinema as a social phenomenon. In methodological terms, he is less concerned with matters of stylistic innovation in the realm of film art, but focuses instead on debates about the social effects of cinema, especially in this case the perceived impact of moving pictures on children. Individual films are less important to his argument than the specific ways that cinema has been historically discussed, understood and regulated within the social terrain. Grieveson concentrates on a particular sense of moral panic that developed around cinema in the mid-1900s. Portrayed as 'schools for crime' by such as the *Chicago Tribune*, cinema was linked to wider concerns about 'the emergence and proliferation of an ungovernable urban lower-class and immigrant population'. Nickelodeons became a conduit for middle-class anxiety about threats to the social order, generating discussion about the boundaries of what could be seen on cinema screens and of what cinema could be used for.

In his analysis, Grieveson draws upon specific kinds of evidence, concentrating on primary materials that help understand how cinema has been framed in precise historical moments. Using daily and weekly newspapers such as the *Chicago Tribune*, trade periodicals such as *Moving Picture World*, as well as court records and reports from contemporaneous reform organisations, Grieveson is able to build a picture of the social discourses that were circulating at the time, and the kinds of discussion that underpinned initiatives to transform the role and reputation of cinema. In Grieveson's essay, the crusade launched by the *Chicago Tribune* against nickel theatres provides a means of analysing the arguments about cinema that were put forward by those who feared its negative effects, and who sought as a result to redefine through regulation cinema's social function in everyday life.

- Looking at the endnotes, how do you distinguish between the primary and secondary sources that Grieveson draws upon?
- What assumptions can be made about the actual behaviour of audiences from Grieveson's research, and what research might you have to do to examine the practices of early cinema audiences?
- Can you think of other panics about media effects on audiences? What materials might you look at to research this topic?

WHY THE AUDIENCE MATTERED IN CHICAGO IN 1907

Lee Grieveson

In the midst of its 'crusade' against 'nickel theaters' in early 1907, the *Chicago Tribune* carried a front-page report on a fire that had broken out in one of the city's theatres of this kind.[1] The theatre, like 'practically all the others', was without 'adequate protection'. 'Disorder followed', and, in the 'panic' that ensued, one audience member was trampled on.[2] Behind the concern about physical safety, and the call for governmental regulation of building codes, lay concerns about moral danger. In other theatres, the paper noted, 'the fire panic was lacking but the continuous performance panic of cheap songs, tawdry singers, and suggestive pictures reigned'. Typically in early writing on such nickel theatres, an 'intrepid man or woman' would visit a theatre in the poorer region of the city to report back on the sights (and, frequently, on the smells) of these recently developed spaces. This work became a subcategory of what Walter Rauschenbusch termed a 'new literature of exploration', which was visible not only in aesthetic discourse but also in reform efforts to shine light on the moral darkness of the city through vice commissions, police investigations,

Lee Grieveson (ed. Melvyn Stokes and Richard Maltby), *American Movie Audiences: From the Turn of the Century to the Early Sound Era* (London: BFI, 1999).

tenement house commissions and moral crusades against prostitution.[3] In a manner typical of the genre, the *Tribune* began its exploration by claiming: 'Here is what was seen', and describing, first, the series of 'suggestive' pictures shown on the screen. In *Bad Son*, as the *Tribune* journalist describes it, the eponymous son goes to a gambling den, loses money and then enlists in the French navy. He then joins in a mutiny in which an officer is killed, enters a Turkish harem and at last returns home. In *Burglars at the Ball*, burglars steal silver and jewellery from a house where a masked ball is in progress, but are finally caught and clubbed by the police. The *Tribune* noted, however, that boys in the audience felt that 'the burglars could have made their "getaway" if they had been a little smoother'. Another film showed a 'mob' of French waiters on strike, waving such banners as 'Down with the Bosses' and 'The Striker Forever', and fighting with the police.[4]

As the aside about boys watching *Burglars at the Ball* suggests, an account of the audience watching these films was even more important to this narrative of exploration than a description of the films themselves. 'The crowd', the *Tribune* assured its largely white, middle-class readers, 'was watched closely'. They were mainly 'the children of the poor. They were of the families of foreign laborers and formed the early stage of that dangerous second generation which is finding such a place in the criminals of the city'.[5] The disorderly, 'panicky' and potentially criminal 'crowd' in those fetid, dark, smelly nickel theatres emerged at this moment as a critical site for investigation, not only for papers like the *Tribune* but also for a series of reform organisations attempting to gather knowledge about the audience. This knowledge focused almost exclusively on children of an urban immigrant population, and was clearly predicated on the development of the nickel theatres which had opened moving pictures to a working-class and immigrant audience who had not previously frequented theatrical-style entertainments. This chapter will examine the production of knowledge about this audience in Chicago at this precise moment, and will pose the questions: how was this audience made visible?[6] Why did it need to be watched so closely? And how did these discourses about child audiences function?[7]

To pre-figure my argument, I wish briefly to outline the two strands of my account. First, I want to suggest that the regulatory intervention into the new nickel theatres was part of a wider regulatory regime which focused on concerns about immigration, governance and citizenship, enforced in differing ways, by such regulatory agents as settlement workers, citizen groups, probation officers and juvenile courts. These concerns about governance and citizenship were particularly acute in relation to children, who were positioned as citizens-information, as *tabula rasa* for the imprinting of values, behaviours and ideals of what the *Chicago Tribune* called 'good citizenship', and thus frequently cast in a synechdochal relationship to an audience and population that threatened disorder in terms mainly of class and ethnicity.[8] As critical legal theorist Alan Hunt suggests, regulatory interventions are frequently responses to the 'discovery' of some social problem, and this concern about the child audience was part of a complex articulation of discourses on race, ethnicity, urban unrest and youth that gelled into the figure of the 'delinquent' in the late nineteenth and early twentieth century.[9] The audience of the new nickel theatres emerged as a problem of knowledge as part of debates about youthful delinquency that were themselves informed by wider concerns to do with the emergence and proliferation of an ungovernable urban lower-class and immigrant population. The production of knowledge about these potentially wayward audiences can be linked, then, to the more general procedures and apparatuses of government through which, in Michel Foucault's conception, the attributes of modern citizenries have been formed.[10]

The further point I want to develop from this perception of the relationship between debates about audiences and debates about population and governance concerns the shaping of the discourse of cinema. Debates about the social functioning of moving pictures – what moving pictures are for, how they should function in society – had at this time a material effect on the formation of cinema as a social construct. As Alan Hunt observes, the collection of knowledge 'plays a central role in the formulation of regulatory policies and strategies'.[11] The concerns about audiences made cinema liable to intervention; discourses make possible institutions which, in turn, sustain those discourses. In this sense, the emergence of a police censorship board in Chicago in late 1907 figures as the end-point of my account here. The police censorship board prohibited 'immoral or obscene' films and required the police department to issue a permit before any picture was shown. As a prototype for the establishment of state censorship boards in the 1910s, it was a critical aspect of the structure of governance set in place for the emerging cinema.

Schools for Crime

The first nickel theatre opened in Chicago in mid-1905. There were a handful in operation by January 1906, and theatres multiplied quickly thereafter, primarily along the main thoroughfares of immigrant neighbourhoods. In February 1907 it was estimated that there were 158 nickel theatres in the city, visited by 100,000 people a day.[12] By the end of 1906, there were attempts to gather knowledge about this new development in the city. Sherman C. Kingsley, a prominent charity administrator, undertook an investigation of the nickel theatres and penny arcades in the poorer sections of Chicago. His report, published in *Charities and the Commons* in January 1907, pronounced them 'objectionable'.[13] Alongside other Charity Organisation Society workers, Kingsley called for the building of more playgrounds in the city's slum districts to counteract the problematic influence of nickel theatres. Under the proper guidance, Kingsley argued, the child's 'instinct for play' could become a force for 'character building', inculcating the correct 'social virtues' and allowing 'moral growth' to occur.[14] Kingsley's concern to develop supervised playgrounds for the inner-city youth was part of a broader strategy of

Progressive reform linked to new ideas about adolescence and play that were closely connected to anxieties about the urban, immigrant working class.[15] Play-reformers believed that the correct management of the juvenile lifecycle and the proper provision of play facilities would socialise children into the roles, behaviours and values expected of workers and citizens. From Kingsley's objections, it appears that moving pictures were perceived as a factor which might well interfere with this process.

Another report on Chicago's nickel theatres, carried out by the Chicago City Club, was also undertaken in late 1906 and published in April 1907. The City Club was a civic reform organisation aiming to bring together those upper- and middle-class white men 'who sincerely desire to meet the full measure of their responsibility as citizens . . . who are united in the sincerity of their desire to promote public welfare'.[16] The report suggested that the theatres were 'distinctly harmful to the children of the city', because of the immoral environment and the immoral content of many moving pictures, and also because moving pictures had a hypnotic effect on children and could thus induce criminal acts.

The City Club asked the Chicago Juvenile Courts and probation officers about the effect of moving pictures on the criminality of children. They reported that daring hold-ups, shop lifting and murders depicted by moving picture machines were getting the children of the city into trouble'.[17] The report on nickel theatres thus participated in a discourse on delinquency that had a fairly recent provenance and was predicated on concerns about the wayward children of the urban lower classes.[18] The creation of special judicial and correctional institutions for the labelling, processing and management of 'troublesome' youth brought attention to – and in doing so, invented – new categories of youthful misbehaviour around the turn of the century.[19]

The first juvenile court in the United States was founded in Chicago in 1899, in part as an expression of anxieties about the development of a criminal underclass. The superintendent of the Illinois Reform School reasoned that, since it was the aim of the criminal class 'to undermine the confidence of the community and to weaken the strength of the Commonwealth', crime could be reduced by 'stopping production' of criminals and regulating the upbringing of children who had criminal propensities.[20] Such propensities were frequently found, commentators suggested, among lower-class immigrant groups. '[I]t is not at all unlikely', one penologist wrote, 'that juvenile delinquency of the most serious kind in the United States is in some measure to be set down to the boundless hospitality of her shores'.[21] Reformers hoped to convert the mainly recent immigrant juvenile delinquents into law-abiding citizens through the development of a reformatory system.

The City Club's reliance on the juvenile courts and probation officers for information and Kingsley's concern to enact play reform indicate that their reports were closely connected to the developing discourse on delinquency. Nickel theatres emerged as problems of knowledge in relation to debates about youthful delinquency that were quite closely linked to concerns about an ungovernable urban immigrant population. This concern became more explicit when the Juvenile Court Committee themselves undertook investigations of Chicago's nickel theatres in early 1907 and again in 1909. The Juvenile Protective Association also conducted highly critical investigations in 1909 and 1911.[22]

The early reports on nickel theatres and juvenile delinquency posited a model of spectatorship akin to hypnosis. This model was deeply affected by debates over crowd psychology, sociology and the emerging field of social psychology. The pioneering work of Gustave LeBon and Gabriel Tarde in the late nineteenth century attempted to develop a theory of the 'popular mind' in order to control it. In the preface to his *Psychology of the Crowd*, for example, LeBon stated that 'knowledge of the psychology of crowds is today the last resource of the statesman who wishes not to govern them – that is becoming a very difficult matter – but at any rate not to be too much governed by them'.[23] For LeBon and Tarde, individuals were suggestible – capable of being influenced by others – via a process of transference that was heightened in relation to images. Their work greatly influenced Edward A. Ross, whose books *Social Control* (1901) and *Social Psychology* (1908) defined the parameters of the debate in the US.[24] For Ross, suggestibility was 'not a weakness produced by civilization', but was intimately related to factors of age, race, ethnicity and gender, and 'at its maximum in young children'. Ross also maintained that 'hysteria, the mental side of which is exaggerated suggestibility, is much more common in women than in men'.[25] Given the long-standing association between independence and worthy citizenship, suggestible subjects were frequently seen as being beyond the borders of the citizen ideal. Groups identified as being most vulnerable to suggestibility were also likely to go on to imitate what they saw. 'Suggestion and imitation', Ross wrote, 'are merely two aspects of the same thing, the one being the cause, the other effect'.[26] It is this combination of effects that made moving pictures both harmful to these groups and, more importantly, a potential problem for society. LeBon went so far as to suggest that moving pictures should be placed in governmental hands.

The City Club report was published on 13 April 1907, just three days after the *Tribune* had begun its crusade against the nickel theatres. This is unlikely to have been a coincidence. The *Tribune* almost certainly had access to the report prior to publication, and some of its staff may well have been involved in the City Club. The paper's readership was largely white, native born and middle class, and its stance, which developed through the spring of 1907 in a series of editorials, news reports and letters to the editor, mirrored the positions outlined in the City Club report. The nickel theatres, the *Tribune* argued,

> minister to the lowest passions of childhood. They make schools of crime where murders, robberies and holdups are illustrated. The outlaw life they portray in their cheap plays lends to the encouragement of wickedness. They manufacture criminals to the city streets.[27]

These schools of crime, the *Tribune's* argument ran, 'manufactured' not 'good citizens' but criminals. The nickel theatre's potential usurpation of the role of the school as the primary instrument of Americanisation was viewed with considerable unease.[28] The *Tribune's* first contribution to the growing debate about nickel theatres concluded by asserting that the theatres should not be 'tolerated for a day in a community where truth and honor and good citizenship are urged as worthy of the aspirations of childhood'.[29]

Three days later, in an article titled 'Nickel Theaters, Crime Breeders', the paper set in play the stance that would effectively structure its understanding of the effects of moving pictures on young audiences. Moving pictures, the paper argued, affected the audience differently according to gender: young girls could be seduced into sexual immorality, young boys influenced to commit criminal acts.

Two examples from the paper illustrate this. The paper reported that one fourteen-year-old boy 'walked out from these pictures of murder and robbery, which he gazed at for hours, with his eyes popping and his mouth open in wonderment, went home, secured his father's revolver and walked on the street ready to kill'. Accosted by the man he attempted to rob, the boy was taken to juvenile court where 'His mother wept for him and promised to teach him better'. His sentence was suspended 'on the promise that he would never again venture into a 5 cent theater'.[30] In a report the day after the 'Nickel Theaters, Crime Breeders' piece, the paper asserted that 'There were a number of little girls who should have been playing with dolls who were ruined through going to the nickel theatre'. This was illustrated with an example of a girl who had run away from home with a man named Sorenson, the manager of a 'tawdry' nickel theatre on Halstead Street:

> The young girl was 15 years old and from all the evidence in the case was of pure and unsophisticated mind until she began looking at the scenes of love and passion supplied by Sorenson's tawdry place. Day by day she frequented the place. . . . The man saw her pretty cheeks and fresh young face and laid his nets. Finally there came a day when she did not go home and when the police found her she was living in a room in a West Madison street hotel with Sorenson.

The conclusion of the story would perhaps be salutary to other girls and parents: 'She wept when she saw her mother', the paper noted, 'but it was too late. She was sent to the Erring Women's Refuge'.[31]

Although, according to the *Tribune*, moving pictures affected male and female members of the audience differently, it suggested that there was a consistency of effect in matters of class and ethnicity. The *Tribune* staff were concerned that moving pictures and nickel theatres would, in their words, sow 'the seeds of class hatred', a concern that was no doubt exacerbated by the urban unrest that had plagued the city for some years.[32] George Kibbe Turner, writing about Chicago in April 1907, termed this a 'wave of crime'.[33] There had been a series of disturbances in the city, which could perhaps be traced back at least to 1903, when a streetcar strike had led to violence and when there had been a series of highly publicised confrontations between police and a gang of working-class bandits. The city witnessed a series of major strikes between 1904 and 1906.[34] The *Tribune* suggested that audiences at the city's nickel theatres were mostly children 'of the families of foreign labourers . . . [who] formed the early stage of that dangerous second generation which is finding such a place in the criminals of the city'. These movie-goers were part of a population that seemed to many middle-class Americans at this time visibly out of control. Moving pictures and nickel theatres were identified as problems of governance, in close connection with the wider fears about 'mobs', 'crowds' and rioting addressed by Tarde, Le Bon and Ross. They became what Steve Redhead terms a 'site of intervention' in the disciplining and policing of working-class culture'.[35] Reform groups articulated a set of 'regulatory strategies' for cinema, transforming the knowledge gained about audiences into the form of procedures, ordinances and statutes.[36] The following two parts of this essay address the debates over this.

Uplift Theatres, Big Lizards from Java and Films with Hustle

On 2 May 1907, less than three weeks after the publication of the Chicago City Club's report on Chicago's nickel theatres, a special meeting of the club was convened to debate its findings and to work out a policy for regulating the nickel theatres. At the meeting, Judge Julian Mack, a juvenile-court judge, argued for the complete exclusion of children under thirteen from these theatres, a stance already adopted by the *Tribune*, based on comments by juvenile-court Judge McKenzie Cleland and on the research of the Juvenile Protective League. Arguing against this, Jane Addams, founder of the Hull House settlement, suggested that moving pictures and nickel theatres could be productive of social virtue and moral growth if more closely supervised by the police and by citizen groups.[37] Addams placed the cinema in a category reserved by others for playgrounds, as a potentially positive force in the reshaping of subjectivity and of the urban environment. The debate in the City Club effectively established two distinct and opposing positions on the nickel theatre business: on the one hand, a coercive approach aimed, if not at the total eradication of nickel theatres, at least at prohibiting children from visiting them; on the other hand, an attempt to shape the institution in such a way as to help mould a population of cultivated, moral and socially responsible city dwellers.

The debate about the City Club report had visible and productive effects in relation to the nickel theatre business: Addams set up a nickel theatre within the confines of Hull House, attempting to reorient the business away from commercialised pleasure towards some form of municipal or reform-generated control. The *Chicago Tribune*, reporting positively on this, noted that moving pictures would now be 'operated in connection with settlement work'.[38] Such work was closely associated with the assimilation of immigrants into American society and culture. The settlement house movement itself emphasised the role of environmental factors in shaping the lives of the immigrant masses, and attempted to create a physical environment that would help mould responsible citizens. Education was seen as central to the assimilation of immigrants and to the creation of a new American 'type'. In her autobiography, *Twenty Years at Hull House*, Addams wrote generally of the aims of Hull House in this respect. 'It seemed to me', she observed, 'that Hull House ought to be able to devise some educational enterprise which should build a bridge between European and American experience in such ways as to give them both more meaning and a sense of relation'.[39] For a short period of time, moving pictures were seen as one element of this strategy of acculturation and education, linked mainly to the education of boys and the shaping of their 'moral codes' in line with those of the 'more fortunate boys' who read the 'chivalric tales' of Homer and Stevenson.[40]

The *Moving Picture World* termed this 'the uplift theater' when it opened on 16 June 1907. It was located on Halstead Street, like Sorenson's tawdry nickel theatre, the two perhaps existing for a few months side by side as diametrically opposed understandings of the social functioning of cinema. The uplift nickel theatre showed mainly 'actualities' and travel pictures, interspersed with lectures. The educational value of moving pictures had been discussed from the moment they were first exhibited, but what emerged here was a strong sense of how this educational role could be moved to centre stage in the cinematic institution as a whole, with the nickel theatre in effect becoming like a school. Many defenders of moving pictures argued that it could become an important educational tool. Thomas Edison, for example, claimed that 'I look for the time, and it's not far distant, when every college and school in the world will boast of its projecting machine and library of educational films'. Travelling exhibitor Lyman Howe asserted that 'The day is not far distant when every schoolroom will have its moving picture machine . . . I have the same forecast from more than 500 teachers who now realise the educational possibilities of the animated camera'.[41] Far from being schools of crime, the argument ran, moving pictures and nickel theatres were in reality valuable adjuncts to the school.

The uplift theatre closed after just three months. Gertrude Britton, the manager of the theatre, blamed the closure on the inability to obtain suitable films: 'Funny pictures of the kind desired by Hull House theater were difficult to find. Those of the "slap stick" and vulgar variety were numerous but not wanted'.[42] This is one example of how industrial strategies influenced a stance on the social functioning of cinema, effectively marginalising a conception of it as linked to education and acculturation. Addams, too, acknowledged this, arguing in 1909 that the aims of Hull House in regard to nickel theatres were better served by assisting the Juvenile Protection Association in their campaign to gain knowledge about nickel theatres and thus to improve them.[43] It is worth noting also that Addams's work had a general and long-term influence on the beginning of large-scale mass communications research.[44] The Payne Fund Studies on moving pictures and youth, which developed out of the research agenda of the department of sociology at the University of Chicago in the late 20s, deliberately harked back to Addams's 1909 book *The Spirit of Youth and the City Streets* in their projected volume titled *Boys, Movies and City Streets*.[45] A published volume of that series, entitled *Movies, Delinquency and Crime*, paid close attention to the question of the immigrant spectator in an analysis of the connection between cinema and delinquency.

There may have been a more prosaic reason for the demise of the uplift theatre. It was seemingly unable to attract a large enough audience. The *Moving Picture World* had a report in June on the theatre which, significantly, quoted children disaffected with the show:

> 'Bet your life its pretty, all right, and its lasts good and long and dat *Cinderella* show was swell, but its slow to make a go of it on dis street', he said. 'Things has got ter have some hustle. I dont say its right, but people like to see fights 'n' fellows getting hurt, 'n' love makin', 'n' robbers, and all that stuff. This show here ain't even funny, unless those big lizards from Java was funny.'[46]

Audiences, even supposedly malleable children, voted with their feet. The uplift theatre itself was seemingly not immune to the industry's commercial aesthetic and, in any case, it was located next door to Sorenson's tawdry nickel theatre.

Policing the Cinema

On 23 April 1907, in the midst of this intensified surveillance of moving pictures and nickel theatres, Police Commissioner Theodore Bingham announced an investigation of New York City's penny arcades and nickel theatres.[47] By July, Bingham had recommended that the Mayor revoke the licences held by scores of penny arcades, nickel theatres and cheap vaudeville houses because they admitted children unaccompanied by parents, showed obscene pictures or violated building and fire regulations.[48] Linked to a discourse of efficiency, scientific investigation and expertise, police interest in the cinema was also explicitly concerned with questions of morality. Policing in the US was in any case often linked to moral issues. Raymond Fosdick, an authority on European and American policing, suggested in 1920 that 'Nowhere in the world is there so great an anxiety to place the moral regulation of social affairs in the hands of the police [as in the United States]'.[49] The concern to regulate morality was part of the profound influence of what Robert Fogelson calls 'the catchall tradition of American policing', linked to a broader regulation of the urban environment through such activities as suppressing vice, curbing juvenile delinquency and looking for missing persons.[50] The transformation of the police during the early twentieth century into a semi-military force was linked to larger changes in the structure of urban governance. Most police work, Sidney Harring has suggested, 'consisted of patrolling the city for deviations from middle-class standards of public order'.[51] Nickel theatres and moving pictures would emerge as significant police issues in relation to morality and urban governance.

In Chicago in November 1907, a momentous city ordinance was passed which made it unlawful to show moving pictures without first securing a permit from the chief of police.[52] All moving pictures were to be submitted to a ten-man police censorship board and would be banned from Chicago if the police found them to be 'immoral or obscene'.[53] This ordinance set in place the legal parameters for municipal and state censorship and, thus, had an enormous impact on the system of state censorship that emerged in the US through the 1910s. It introduced a shift away from the literal policing of the space of nickel theatres, visible in Bingham's investigation in New York City and also in many cases where the police actually stopped the exhibition of certain moving pictures, towards the policing of the films that could be exhibited.[54] This was an important innovation in the development of a governance of cinema.

The constitutionality of the board was challenged by an exhibitor, Jake Block, who had been denied a permit for two films, *The James Boys in Missouri* and *Night Riders*, in late 1908. Block argued that the law deprived him of rights under the Constitution and that the films he had shown in his theatre were 'moral and in no way obscene'.[55] His case was denied and the constitutionality of the police censorship board was upheld in 1909 by the Illinois Supreme Court. It was the purpose of the law, Chief Justice James H. Cartwright argued, 'to secure decency and morality in the moving picture business, and that purpose falls within the police power'.

In upholding the constitutionality of the board, Justice Cartwright explicitly invoked the need to protect youthful audiences. 'On account of the low price of admissions', he noted, nickel theatres

> are frequented and patronized by a large number of children, as well as by those of limited means who do not attend the productions of plays and dramas given in the regular theaters. The audiences include those classes whose age, education and situation in life especially entitle them to protection against the evil influence of obscene and immoral repre-sentations.

He concluded that exhibition of the pictures 'would necessarily be attended with evil effects upon youthful spectators'.[56] The concern about the effect of moving pictures and nickel theatres on children, and indeed on those of 'limited means', that emerged so forcefully in early 1907, contributed both to the creation of a police censorship board and to the defence of its constitutionality in the state Supreme Court.

In 1909, reformers in Chicago lobbied for and won the right to institute an eleven-person censorship board to sit alongside the police censorship board. This dual board gave way in 1914 to a single board made up entirely of reformers. The new board introduced the 'pink permit' system whereby children could be entirely barred from movies that received an 'adults only' rating, one of the first age-rating systems in the country.[57] This brings the narrative I have outlined here full circle: the reform-generated concern about nickel theatres contributed directly to the creation of a police censorship board, which in turn gave way to private forms of governance carried on through reform boards. The withdrawal of direct state action was further facilitated by an internal 'reformation' of cinema signalled by the formation of the National Board of Censorship in 1909. Shifts in signifying practices, particularly the emergence of formations of narrative capable of (in part at least) directing the moral and emotional response of movie-goers, can be linked to the intensified reform concern shown from early 1907. These shifts have been connected by Miriam Hansen to an 'invention of spectatorship' as a standardisation of the diverse and sometimes unpredictable acts of reception that threatened various forms of disorder.[58] This invention, underpinned by the regulatory intervention I have described in this chapter, was critical to the emergence of what we call Hollywood.

NOTES

1. The *Chicago Tribune*, 3 May 1907, p. 2.
2. The *Chicago Tribune*, 15 April 1907, p. 1.
3. Walter Rauschenbusch, *Christianity and the Social Crisis*, 1907, quoted in Paul Boyer, *Urban Masses and Moral Order in America, 1820–1920* (Cambridge: Harvard University Press, 1978), p, 127. For more on this linkage of social and aesthetic discourse on the 'underworld' of the city, see my 'Mapping the City: Early Moving Pictures of the "Underworld" of New York City', *OverHere: A European Journal of American Culture*, vol. 17, no. 1 (Summer 1997).
4. The *Chicago Tribune*, 15 April 1907, p. 1.
5. *Ibid.*
6. It is important to note that Chicago served as a port of entry for immigrants and had a broader mixture of classes than other American cities. Some of the concern about lower-class and immigrant audiences was specific to Chicago and New York City. It cannot be taken as representative of wider patterns. It is, however, true that the system of regulation of moving pictures and nickel theatres set in place in both Chicago and New York City came to have wider applicability and greater ramifications for the film industry in the US.
7. Let me make clear at the outset that I will not be discussing audiences themselves, or how they responded to either films or these projects to gather knowledge about them and to speculate on the effects of moving pictures on them. That is a separate project. My concern here is to trace out the emergence and proliferation of discourses about audiences, a concern that is consistent with Michel Foucault's general work on the relations between knowledge and power within specific discursive formations.
8. The *Chicago Tribune*, 10 April 1907, p. 10.
9. Alan Hunt, *Explorations in Law and Society: Toward a Constitutive Theory of Law* (London: Routledge, 1993). See, in particular, 'Law as a Constitutive Mode of Regulation'; pp. 301–33.
10. Graham Burchell, Colin Gordon and Peter Miller (eds), *The Foucault Effect: Studies in Governmentality* (London: Harvester Wheatsheaf, 1991).
11. Hunt, *Explorations in Law and Society*, p. 317.
12. For details, see Kathleen D. McCarthy, 'Nickel Vice and Virtue: Movie Censorship in Chicago, 1907–1915; *Journal of Popular Film*, 5, no. 1 (1976), p. 39; the *Moving Picture World*, 29 June 1907, p. 263; and Charles Musser, *The Emergence of*

Cinema: The American Screen to 1907 (Berkeley: University of California Press, 1990), pp. 422–4, 428.

13. Sherman C. Kingsley, 'The Penny Arcade and the Cheap Theater', *Charities and the Commons*, XVIII (January 1907), quoted in Kenneth L. Kusmer, 'The Functions of Organized Charity in the Progressive Era: Chicago as a Case Study', *The Journal of American History*, vol. LX, no. 3 (December 1973), p. 663.

14. Kingsley, in Kusmer, 'The Functions of Organized Charity', p. 663.

15. Roy Rosenzweig, *Eight Hours For What We Will: Workers and Leisure in an Industrial City, 1870–1920* (Cambridge: Cambridge University Press, 1983), pp. 143–4. See also the discussion in Boyer, *Urban Masses and Moral Order*, pp. 240–5. The first annual convention of the Playground Association of America took place in Chicago in 1907.

16. City Club of Chicago Statement of Purpose, quoted in Maureen A. Flanagan, 'Gender and Urban Political Reform: The City Club and the Woman's City Club of Chicago in the Progressive Era', *American Historical Review*, vol. 95, no. 4 (October 1990), p. 1032. Flanagan also provides details of the membership of the City Club.

17. The *Moving Picture World*, 29 June 1907, p. 263.

18. Anthony M. Platt, *The Child Savers*; Ian Hacking, 'The Making and Molding of Child Abuse', *Critical Inquiry*, vol. 17 (Winter 1991), pp. 265–6.

19. See Platt, *The Child Savers*, and on juvenile courts more generally, see Schlossman, *Love and the American Delinquent: The Theory and Practice of 'Progressive' Juvenile Justice, 1825–1920* (Chicago: The University of Chicago Press, 1977), pp. 55–78.

20. J. D. Scouller, quoted in Platt, *The Child Savers*, p. 32.

21. William Douglas Morrison, quoted in Platt, *The Child Savers*, p. 37.

22. For brief details on these reports see McCarthy, 'Nickel Vice and Virtue', p. 53; Alan Havig, 'The Commercial Amusement Audience in Early 20th-Century American Cities', *Journal of American Culture* (Spring 1982), pp. 2–4; and David Nasaw, 'Children and Commercial Culture: Moving Pictures in the Early Twentieth Century', in Elliot West and Paula Petrik, *Small Worlds: Children and Adolescents in America, 1850–1950* (Kansas: University Press of Kansas, 1992), pp. 19–22.

23. Gustave LeBon, *The Crowd*, 1895 (New York: Viking, 1960), p. xxi. For a discussion of this work, see Robert Nye, *The Origins of Crowd Psychology: Gustave LeBon and the Crisis of Mass Democracy in the Third Republic* (London: Sage Publications, 1975).

24. Edward Ross, *Social Psychology: An Outline and Source Book* (New York: Macmillan, 1908); Edward Ross, *Social Control: A Survey of the Foundation of Order*, 1901 (Cleveland: Case Western Reserve University Press, 1969). For an insightful discussion of this work, see Dorothy Ross, *The Origins of American Social Science* (Cambridge: Cambridge University Press, 1991).

25. Ross, *Social Psychology*, pp. 13–16. On how a notion of 'civilisation' was entwined with a discourse of race, see Gail Bederman, *Manliness and Civilization: A Cultural History of Gender and Race in the United States, 1880–1917* (Chicago: The University of Chicago Press, 1995).

26. Ross, *Social Psychology*, p. 13.

27. The *Chicago Tribune*, 10 April 1907, p. 10.

28. For more on discourses about moving pictures and schools see William Uricchio and Roberta E. Pearson, *Reframing Culture: The Case of the Vitagraph Quality Films* (Princeton: Princeton University Press, 1993). The *Chicago Tribune* commented favourably in summer 1907 on vacation schools using 'dramatic recitals' to 'offset the allurements of the 5 cent theaters'. The *Chicago Tribune*, 13 June 1907, p. 3.

29. The *Chicago Tribune*, 10 April 1907, p. 10.

30. The *Chicago Tribune*, 13 April 1907, p. 3.

31. The *Chicago Tribune*, 14 April 1907, Section I, p. 5.
32. The *Chicago Tribune*, 15 April 1907, p. 4.
33. George Kibbe Turner, 'The City of Chicago: A Study of the Great Immoralities', *McClure's* (April 1907), in Arthur and Lila Weinberg (eds), *The Muckrakers* (New York: Capricorn Books, 1964), p. 389.
34. See Sidney L. Harring, *Policing a Class Society: The Experience of American Cities, 1865–1915* (New Brunswick: Rutgers University Press, 1983), pp. 228–33. See also Turner, 'The City of Chicago', pp. 404–5.
35. Steve Redhead, *Unpopular Cultures: The Birth of Law and Popular Culture* (Manchester: Manchester University Press, 1995), p. 43.
36. Alan Hunt writes: 'Not only is knowledge "produced" but it must also be transformed into a form that is capable of being expressed as a regulatory policy or strategy, which in turn is capable of being incorporated into legislative form'. Hunt, *Explorations in Law and Society*, p. 319.
37. See the account in the *Moving Picture World*, 11 May 1907, p. 147.
38. The *Chicago Tribune*, 16 June 1907, p. 3.
39. Jane Addams, *Twenty Years at Hull House* (New York: Signet, 1960), p. 172.
40. Jane Addams, *The Spirit of Youth and the City Streets* (New York: Macmillan, 1909), pp. 80–1.
41. Thomas Edison, quoted in *The Nickelodeon*, 1 August 1910, p. 64; Lyman Howe, quoted in Charles Musser and Carol Nelson, *High-Class Moving Pictures: Lyman H. Howe and the Forgotten Era of Traveling Exhibition, 1880–1920* (Princeton: Princeton University Press, 1991), p. 174.
42. Gertrude Britton, quoted in the *Moving Picture World*, 29 June 1907, p. 262.
43. Addams, *Twenty Years at Hull House*, p. 267.
44. Dorothy Ross has suggested that the empirical stance of the department of sociology at the University of Chicago in the late 20s was indebted to the work of Hull House prior to that. 'The inspiration . . . came largely from Hull House and the urban charity movement. Hull House widened the sympathies of its academic visitors and the writings of Jane Addams were regularly consulted . . . More specifically, *Hull House Maps and Papers* (1895) began the urban studies and use of maps for which Chicago sociology later became famous.' Ross, *The Origins of American Social Science*, pp. 226–7.
45. Lea Jacobs suggests this in her 'Reformers and Spectators: The Film Education Movement in the Thirties', *Camera Obscura*, no. 22 (January 1990), p. 34.
46. The *Moving Picture World*, 29 June 1907, p. 262.
47. This investigation followed on from a conference between the Department of Health and Fire. The aim, the *Moving Picture World* prophesied, was 'to subject these places to a more rigorous supervision'. The *Moving Picture World*, 4 May 1907, p. 137.
48. The *Moving Picture World*, 20 July 1907, p. 312.
49. Raymond Fosdick, *American Police Systems*, 1920, quoted in Robert M. Fogelson, *Big-City Police* (Cambridge: Harvard University Press, 1977), p. 108.
50. Fogelson, *Big-City Police*, p. 88.
51. Harring, *Policing a Class Society*, p. 29.
52. For details on this ordinance, see 'Police Supervision in Chicago', *The Nickelodeon*, January 1909, p. 11. It was passed on 4 November and came into effect on 15 November 1907.
53. The category of the immoral was, as Edward De Grazia and Roger Newman show, 'a legal net big and durable enough to condemn almost any picture'. The suppression of 'immoral' movies would continue for more than fifty years. Edward De Grazia and Roger K. Newman, *Banned Films: Movies, Censors and The First Amendment* (New York: R. R. Bowker Company, 1982), p. 10.
54. For example, exhibition of the controversial *The Unwritten Law: A Thrilling Drama Based on the Thaw–White Case* (Lubin, 1907), was stopped by police in early 1907 in Worcester, Houston and Superior, Wisconsin. See details in

Rosenzweig, *Eight Hours for What We Will*, p. 205; The *Moving Picture World*, 20 April 1907, p. 93; and the *Moving Picture World*, 27 April 1907, p. 119.

55. Quoted in De Grazia and Newman, *Banned Films*, p. 177. For further discussion of the implications of this case see my 'The Birth of Fiction, 1907–1915', in Leonardo Quaresino, ed., *The Birth of Film Genres* (forthcoming).

56. Justice James H. Cartwright, quoted in De Grazia and Newman, *Banned Films*, p. 178.

57. De Grazia and Newman, *Banned Films*, p. 9; McCarthy, 'Nickel Vice and Virtue', p. 45.

58. Miriam Hansen, *Babel and Babylon: Spectatorship in American Silent Film* (Cambridge: Harvard University Press, 1991), pp. 15–16.

3

NATIONALISM, TRADE AND MARKET DOMINATION

While the United States had the greatest number of film theatres during the nickelodeon period, the films they played very often came from Europe. Indeed, by the start of the First World War in 1914, France and Italy were the two leading film-producing countries in the world. Although the history of popular film is often associated with Hollywood and the development of the American film industry, this ignores the international scope and status of early cinema, and the particular significance of European production companies.

The prominence of the French film industry was based on the activity of Pathé-Frères. Not only did Pathé films make up to half of those shown in American nickelodeon programmes, the company dominated world markets, exporting its product in areas such as Western and Eastern Europe, Russia, India, Singapore and Japan. Pathé-Frères was a vertically integrated company, one of the first to control simultaneously the different sectors of production, distribution and exhibition. As well as manufacturing its own cameras, projectors and film stock, Pathé produced and distributed film, and in Europe owned the theatres in which they played. By 1909, Pathé had a circuit of 200 cinemas in France and Belgium. This combined with a network of agencies across the globe to administer the sale and rental of its films. By 1907, Pathé-Frères was the largest film company in the world, using mass-production methods to release as many as six film titles a week.

With production overseen by Ferdinand Zecca, Pathé released films across a broad swathe of genres. This included actualities, historical films, trick films, drama, vaudeville acts and chases. As in the United States, however, this gave way in the late 1900s to a more integrated narrative cinema. Of particular note were the popular serials that Pathé released from 1907. These were organised around a central character or single actor and would often star well-known comics. For example, the 'Boireau' series was named after a character played by André Deed. Meanwhile, the 'Rigadin' series featured the music-hall star Charles Prince.

The most successful series featured Max Linder, a comic artist whose performance style would later influence Charlie Chaplin. Adopting the character of a handsome bourgeois dandy, distinguished by a neat moustache and silk hat, the Linder series would find Max continually extricating himself from socially embarrassing situations. Whether thwarted in love or carried through the streets in a bathtub, the character of Max would find ingenious methods to overcome humiliating situations. This distinguished films ranging from *The Little Nag* (1911) to *Max the Pedicure* (1914). Linder's subtlety of expression and comic elegance proved hugely popular, and his films became a regular feature of theatrical programmes in France and around the world.

Pathé's major French rival was Gaumont, a company that also experienced rapid expansion from the mid-1900s. Established by Léon Gaumont, the company was also vertically integrated, constructing its own circuit of palace cinemas and producing a wide repertoire of films under the supervision of Alice Guy and Louis Feuillade. In particular, Feuillade was associated with the 'Fantômas' crime serial that began in 1913, a popular series of films based on a master criminal who eludes a detective through mastery of disguise. Capitalising on the demand for French film exports, a number of smaller companies also emerged in the late 1900s. These specialised in particular genres, such as the Film d'Art Company that focused output on literary adaptations, and Éclair that became associated with the male adventure series, inspired by the international success of *Nick Carter, King of the Detectives* (1908). With an established production infrastructure, and a solid base for distributing and exhibiting its films, the French film industry was both prosperous and influential in cinema's early period of development.

The same was also true of Italy. Although film production developed later there than many other European countries, Italy became a major force in world cinema before the outbreak of the First World War. From 1905, the Italian film industry experienced a period of brisk expansion. This focused on a number of key production companies, including Cines, based in Rome (established in 1905), and Ambrosio (1905) and Itala (1906), located in Turin. Instead of temporary venues, cinematic exhibition in Italy was based from the outset on a network of permanent theatres. This gave cinema a more immediate sense of legitimacy and status, and gave rise to longer, more expensive, three-reel films.

Italian film in the late 1900s had several strands. While the Italian market was dominated by French film, the newly formed studios developed strategies to adapt and customise popular genres, specifically historical films, documentaries and comedies. Of these, comedies and historical epics were especially popular. Hiring André Deed from Pathé in 1909, Itala made comic serials based around characters such as Cretinetti ('the little cretin'). These relied for their humour on visual tricks, clownery and the vibrancy of the comedians' fashioned personalities, Ferdinand Guillaume adding to the genre with his comic creation, Tontolini.

Equally popular were historical epics, frequently drawing upon Ancient Greece, Rome and the Renaissance for their inspiration. The genre was typified by *The Fall of Troy* (1911), a three-reel film directed by Giovanni Pastrone and Romano L. Borgnetto. Aspiring to the status of high art, historical epics were central to the reputation of the Italian film industry between 1911 and 1914. Such films were especially reliant on visual spectacle. Enrico Guazzoni's *Quo Vadis?* (1913), for example, recreated Ancient Rome using lavish sets and a cast of hundreds, and employing extras in their thousands. Made on nine reels, and lasting two hours in length, *Quo Vadis?* was not made for the nickelodeon. While nickel theatres relied on short varied programmes that would ensure rapid audience turnover, multi-reel films ran in legitimate theatres and opera houses, enabling exhibitors to charge higher ticket prices. Historical spectacles were a form of prestige entertainment that, in spectacle and length, helped usher in the era of the feature film.

Within American cinema, the rise of the feature film is often associated with multi-reel films such as Vitagraph's *The Life of Moses* (1910). A biblical spectacle depicting the life of the Hebrew leader, the film was made in five reels. These could be shown separately but also within a single programme. The organisation of the nickel theatres under the MPPC militated against multi-reel films, however, depending as they did on a regular supply of shorter one-reel titles. While the rise of the 'superspecial', describing films of deliberate cost and scale, is typically associated with D. W. Griffith's *The Birth of a Nation* (1915), it was really the success of foreign imports that set in place a transition to 'feature' programming within upmarket theatres and movie palaces. Indeed, it was *Quo Vadis?* that influenced Griffith's first long (four-reel) feature, *Judith of Bethulia* (1913). Far from an American development, the rise of the spectacular feature film in the early teens was closely aligned with the popular success, and evident profitability, of Italian historical epics.

Giovanni Pastrone's *Cabiria* (1914) was emblematic of this trend. If *Quo Vadis?* used chariots and real lions for the purposes of historical recreation, *Cabiria* staged spectacular scenes based on the Punic Wars fought between Rome and Carthage. This included the eruption of volcanoes, the destruction of the Roman fleet, and Hannibal's crossing of the Alps. A twelve-reel epic, again using lavish sets, *Cabiria* pioneered the use of long tracking shots. Filming scenes using a sophisticated system of tracks, camera movements could be used in far more complex ways, creating a greater sense of depth and movement across the enormous sets used by Pastrone. Tracking shots would become increasingly common after 1910 as narrative film continued to experiment with expressive formal techniques. *Cabiria* was in many ways the apotheosis of the Italian historical spectacle, majestic in scale and basing its appeal on large-scale battle scenes, extravagant sets and huge numbers of actors.

Furthermore, the success of *Cabiria* foreshadowed a tradition of 'strongman' films such as *Maciste* (1915) and *Maciste Alpino* (1916), indicating a rising star system within Italian cinema. Inspired by the character of the slave Maciste in *Cabiria* (played by Bartolomeo Pagano), strongman films were a variant of the adventure film and were based on the athletic prowess and emotional simplicity of the leading protagonist. If Pagano became the emblematic strongman of Italian cinema, Lyda Borelli became its most famous 'diva'. Based on a charismatic and beautiful 'goddess' figure, diva films such as *Love Everlasting* (1913) were often set in opulent bourgeois surroundings, the diva representing a sensual and tortured figure, enmeshed in plots of intrigue and love. Strongman and diva films developed into distinctive national genres, becoming staples of Italian filmmaking in the 1920s.

Through production of a range of popular genres, including the comic series and the historical spectacle, France and Italy became major exporters of film. Also significant in the 1900s were the prosperous film industries of Britain and Denmark. Like France, the history of British film production had origins that went back to the very emergence of cinema. In particular, the production company of Cecil Hepworth was responsible for many of the cheap spoofs, serials and parodies that became popular within Britain's home market. And yet, despite the contribution of British filmmakers to early editing and shooting practices, and the commercial success of Hepworth's *Rescued by Rover* (1905), Britain was not as responsive to changes in film style as certain of its European neighbours. This gave it presence, but not prevalence, in world markets. By the early teens, Britain had become influential more as a distribution centre than as a vital hub of film production.

On these terms, Britain was outpaced by Denmark. Focusing around a production company called Nordisk (established in 1906 by the exhibitor Ole Olsen), the Danish film industry established a reputation for superb acting and production values. While Nordisk's most lucrative foreign market was Germany, it swiftly established distribution offices in New York, where its films were released under the brand name of Great Northern. Nordisk specialised in thrillers and melodramas, notably those based on the circus – in large part the result of Olsen installing a permanent circus set in one of the company's glass-walled studios. However, Nordisk was also influential in the development of 'sensational' film. These included 'white-slave', or prostitution, stories set in the worlds of crime and vice and distinguished by the frank treatment of sexual themes.

By 1910, Nordisk was the world's second largest production company after Pathé, buying up or driving out of business many smaller companies. While Danish filmmakers were less concerned with developing narrative technique, they were influential in the realm of lighting, camera-positioning and set design. This was a consequence of sensational dramas that relied for their power on atmospheric intensity. For example, the use of shadows and silhouettes were distinctive in the films of Benjamin Christensen, whose melodramatic spy story *The Mysterious X* (1913) was defined by its bold visual compositions.

Half-lit images also heightened the sexual atmosphere of *The Abyss* (1910), a film directed by Urban Gad that famously saw Asta Nielson tie up her lover with a whip before performing an erotic dance before him. Like Max Linder, Nielson was one of the first international stars of cinema. Trained in the theatre, she was made famous by her performance in *The Abyss*. Nielson's depiction of a respectable girl led astray made her an international sensation. She would develop a reputation for playing unconventional women, entangled by conventions of class and sex, in a series of roles that would draw upon her intelligence and dark-eyed beauty. In her acting style, Nielson was able to express inner conflict through subtle expressions perfectly suited to the cinematic screen. For aesthetic effect, these combined with experimental tricks in *The Abyss*, including mirror angles that showed characters who remained out of the camera's field of vision. Through use of expressionist camera technique and a nascent star system, Danish cinema helped further shape international developments in stylistic form and performance.

Like Italian film production, Nordisk moved towards longer, multi-reel, films in the early teens. The company's principal director, August Blom, made *Atlantis* in 1913, inspired by the *Titanic* disaster the year before. Based on the spectacular sinking of an ocean liner, this ran to eight reels and was tremendously successful in international markets. Indeed, the income generated through export allowed the film's high budget. These same export possibilities were not available to filmmakers in all countries, however. Sweden was a case a point. While highly influenced by the Danish film industry, and the rise of Nordisk, Swedish film drew heavily upon local customs and literatures. As Swedish film was not widely exported, it served to foster a deeper interest in national traits. These were often conveyed in distinctive films by three directors, Georg af Klecker, Mauritz Stiller and Victor Sjöström. These all worked for a small Swedish firm established in 1907 called Svenska Biografteatern. Making comedies and dramas, each director contributed to an intricate and sometimes austere film style that would grow in influence, especially helped by Sweden's neutrality in the First World War.

Before the start of the war, European countries dominated international film production and distribution, controlling trade patterns and the flow of motion-pictures across borders. This did not come without attempts by the leading American producers to arrest and contain this influence. Indeed, the MPPC tried to limit competition within the United States by restricting imports. A year after the creation of the MPPC in 1908, imports constituted less than half of all films released. Numerous European companies were simply shut out of the MPPC, including Nordisk and all Italian firms. With the domestic film industry controlled by a small number of powerful companies (as outlined in Chapter 2), it became much harder for foreign companies to gain access to the American market.

This gave American film companies a lasting advantage within international film commerce. The United States was by far the largest film market in the world and by securing exclusive access for American producers, domestic film companies could recoup all of their costs at home before maximising the profit potential of their films abroad. This continued to provide a basis for American industrial power. By controlling the domestic market, American producers were able to invest in, or capitalise on, their films at higher levels than foreign competitors. This allowed for better production values, a regular supply of product, and the capacity for American film to be sold at affordable rates to foreign exhibitors. In short, control of the lucrative domestic market enabled American film companies to outperform their foreign rivals in terms of the size, scale and overall profitability of their operations.

And yet American film companies did not move into the business of film export until relatively late, absorbed as they were in the competition for the domestic market. While Vitagraph opened a distribution office in London in 1906, American companies only started to expand internationally in the late 1900s. Selling foreign rights to export agents, London became a dominant centre for the circulation of American films. With a large domestic exhibition market, and an established colonial and commonwealth trade network, Britain became the heart of international film export in the early 1910s. This strengthened distribution agents, who re-exported American movies around the world, but also weakened investment in British film production. Indicative of growing American pre-eminence, it is estimated that 70 per cent of films imported to Britain in 1911 came from the United States.

Of course, American film would eventually dominate world markets. However, this should not be taken for granted, as it was by no means inevitable before the war. Indeed, the international flow of film in the pre-war period stemmed mainly from Europe, a fact that is sometimes overlooked. Because of small domestic demand, the business of the major European producers was predicated on international export. Penetrating foreign markets was essential in this respect. The major companies of France, Italy, Denmark and Britain distributed their product in countries such as Germany, Austria, Hungary, Russia and the Netherlands, as well as in wider import markets such as Latin America, Asia, Africa and Australia. None of these regions had the trade protection of the United States, and were therefore easier to penetrate. Neither, though, did they have the rich commercial possibilities of the American market.

Despite organised resistance, European producers continued to attack the American market. For companies affiliated with the MPPC, such as Pathé, this meant investing in film that would deflect growing resistance to foreign, and especially French, imports by the American film industry and its trade press. To offset ranging complaints that imports were inferior in quality, and were dangerously 'alien' or 'un-American' in moral content, Pathé moved towards literary adaptations and historical epics. Excluded from the MPPC entirely, companies like Nordisk (Great Northern) adopted a different strategy, supplying the growing number of unlicensed film exchanges and nickelodeons. While European film producers were a vital force in supplying the US market in the nickelodeon and pre-war period, they had to negotiate domestic efforts to protect and nationalise American cinema. These attempts would lay the foundation for America's strength as a film-producing nation, especially as it began to enlarge its field of vision.

Strategic expansion into film export would strengthen the position of American movies within world film markets. Its pre-eminent global position was fully realised, however, by the seismic transformations brought about by the First World War. Beginning in 1914, following the assassination of Archduke Ferdinand of Austria, the Great War would alter the balance of political, economic and cultural power in ways that would shape the entire history of the twentieth century. Ravaging the dominant European powers in material and human cost, the war also disrupted the trade patterns that had given France, Italy and Britain a superior position within international film commerce. Film production in many countries came to an abrupt halt when the war began. Mobilisation would drain studios of their staff, production facilities would be transformed for wartime usage, and new problems would present themselves in acquiring and transporting film stock, the flammable nature of celluloid nitrate being carefully controlled.

In the major film-producing countries of Europe, output declined. This was not entirely explained by the war. Indeed, the French film industry had already begun to lose its influence. In 1913, Pathé cut back on production and moved towards distribution and exhibition. While profitable, concentration in these areas would eventually marginalise Pathé as an industry leader. Withdrawing its membership from the MPPC in 1913, Pathé established its own distribution company, releasing a number of popular serials, including *The Perils of Pauline* (1914) starring Pearl White. Popular serials were co-productions by newspapers and film companies, in this case between the Hearst newspaper empire and Pathé's American branch, the Eclectic Film Company. Designed as packaged sensationalism, popular serials were released in tandem with print versions that appeared in newspapers and magazines. While commercial tie-ins are often thought to be a contemporary development, cross media alignments have their origins in early cinema. Serialised in film and print form, the publicity for serials such as *The Perils of Pauline* reached millions. Like other Pathé serials such as *The Exploits of Elaine* (1915), serial heroines tapped into revised models of femininity associated with the 'New Woman', moving away from Victorian models of domesticity towards heroines that assumed traditionally 'masculine' attributes such as bravery, toughness and intelligence. Serials were geared to the mass market but were never simplistic in their appeal, striving to attract men and women with varying class tastes and competences.

Despite Pathé's influence in foreign and domestic markets, the company's focus on distribution would ultimately create new opportunities for American film, notably in the French market itself. American comedies and Westerns were met with great enthusiasm by French audiences, and would effect changes in popular taste that would underpin continued US penetration of markets.

It would be a simplification to suggest that American power in world film markets owed itself entirely to the First World War. However, trade relations would never be the same again. Certain countries that remained neutral during the war, such as Denmark and Sweden, were able to maintain and increase their production levels. For France, Italy and Britain, the experience was of a stark dismantling of their dominant pre-war strength. War severely damaged the major European film industries but, at the same time, it helped transform the status of film, generating a tacit consensus about cinema's national importance. While American cinema was cast as a morale booster in Allied nations such as Britain and France, war would also generate distinct national identities in the cinemas of Germany and Russia.

In countries that found themselves politically isolated and cut off from imports, efforts to supply the domestic market encouraged the development of new and singular filmmaking styles. Until the war, Germany had only a modest film industry. Rapid growth of permanent exhibition sites in the early teens led to cultural debates about the status of film, similar to those witnessed in America. Cinema was attacked by reformers for its potentially malign influence, leading to various initiatives to shape film into an educational and artistically worthy medium. While reformers pressed the German industry to make *Kulturfilme*, educational films focusing on topics such as geography, folklore and hygiene, literary intellectuals encouraged moves towards an artistic cinema based upon literary adaptations. This was akin to the output of the Film d'Art company in France. German efforts were vested in the *Autorenfilm* (or author's film), emerging briefly in 1913 with theatrical adaptations such as Max Reinhardt's *A Venetian Night* (1913) and *Island of the Blessed* (1913).

Although Germany had a fledgling industry before the war, film production was energised by conflict. Consolidating its domestic market and expanding its influence in occupied countries, German film became a more determined cultural and economic force. This was significantly helped by government and industrial capital, and the realisation of film's potential to serve a propaganda function. By 1916, the German government had taken steps to ban foreign films, concerned with their anti-German content. This encouraged a surge in domestic production and in 1917 the purchase and reorganisation of existing German and European companies (including Nordisk) into Universum Film Aktien Gesellschaft (UFA). This established the industrial basis of what would become a highly creative cinema emanating from Germany in the 1920s (see Chapter 6).

In the same way, Russian cinema would be stimulated by the onset of war. In the pre-war period, the Russian film industry was dominated by imports, particularly those of Pathé and Gaumont, both of which established distribution offices in Moscow in 1908–9. With imports making up to 90 per cent of the market at this time, the production of Russian film was small in scale. With film gaining respectability in the early teens, however, a number of companies such as Khanzhonkov (established in 1908) began to satisfy demand for the tragic form of cinema beloved by Russian audiences.

Influenced by German, Danish and Italian films, the work of Yevgeny Bauer was especially notable, a director who was prolific in output and whose films were marked by a distinctive melancholia. With the war affecting imports, domestic production surged, directors such as Bauer and Yakov Protazanov developing the deliberate and internalised acting styles that would define the sober mood of their many films. As with other cinemas of the period, film was shaped less by the international cross-pollination of form and technique, witnessing instead the development, or hardening, of particular national filmmaking styles.

In the 1910s, American filmmaking developed as one such style. While Europe dominated world film markets in the first decade of the twentieth century, this situation would begin to change as the business organisation of the American film industry was streamlined, and the Hollywood studio system developed. This gave rise to industrial struggles of a particular kind. If, on the one hand, attempts were made to nationalise American cinema in the late 1900s, protecting the domestic market from insipient foreign influence, these industrial manoeuvres were matched with trade battles fought inside the domestic market.

In the emerging history of Hollywood, the established powers of the MPPC positioned themselves against a growing lobby of independent producers, distributors and exhibitors in a fight for market control. It was from this struggle that the industrial and aesthetic dominance of the American studio system would emerge and come to assert itself in national and international terms. To understand the dominance that American film would assume in world markets, one must understand in more detail the industrial and aesthetic transitions that took place between 1909 and 1914. This period saw the early development of classical Hollywood cinema, a film style and mode of film production that would dominate markets for generations to come.

In his article, 'The Perils of Pathé, or the Americanization of Early American Cinema', Richard Abel concentrates on a period before the concerted expansion of Hollywood into world markets, but one that is no less significant in establishing the foundations upon which a nationalised American cinema would develop. Analysing the attempt to 'make cinema American' during the nickelodeon period, Abel examines the means by which cinema became a contested site of Americanisation. It is amidst historical debates about the capacity of cinema to inscribe American values that Abel draws out implications for trade and market domination in the film industry.

Abel's essay considers the social and ideological function of cinema, including questions in the mid-1900s concerning the effect of moving pictures on working-class and immigrant populations. In this respect, Abel operates in a similar critical sphere to that of Lee Grieveson in the previous chapter. Where Grieveson is concerned with efforts to regulate cinema, Abel concentrates on a discourse of cinema that is driven by the imperatives of business and the desire to achieve trade supremacy. As a form of historical research, Abel foregrounds the rivalries that have long distinguished the film industry, including the struggles that take place between companies to control national and international markets. He complicates the picture that early cinema was about the dominance of American film companies. He examines instead the means by which the United States was, itself, a hugely profitable market for foreign film companies during cinema's early development. Ultimately, this inspired attempts to protect and nationalise American cinema, a strategy that would later be developed by other film industries, albeit less successfully, in response to the pressing dominance of Hollywood abroad.

Abel's focus on trade situates the film industry within systems of capitalist enterprise that are international in scope, and that are frequently overlaid with debates about nationalism, imperialism and cultural identity. His essay demonstrates the emerging process of American cinema's nationalisation in the 1900s. To this end, he draws evidence from a formidable array of sources that provide insight into the way that French films were dealt with and discussed by the American film industry and its trade press. Outlining changes in the control and organisation of the film industry through journals such as *Show World*, *Moving Picture World* and *Billboard*, as well as documents relating to the activities of the MPPC, Abel conducts a wide-ranging analysis of Pathé's reception in publications including *Variety*, *Harper's Weekly* and a host of regional newspapers. This accumulation of source material builds a textured picture of the way that 'Red Rooster' films changed status in the late 1900s, dictated by the needs, and ambition, of competing film industries.

- To what degree is Abel's research method based on the range and variety of his source material?
- Does Abel's research suggest that the fate of Pathé in America can be applied to other regions and markets of the world? What might be gained in a comparative analysis and how might you go about researching this?
- Can you think of other examples where arguments have been made for or against 'foreign' film as a vehicle of cultural influence? How might examining these arguments help you think about questions of national identity in particular periods or places?

THE PERILS OF PATHÉ, OR THE AMERICANIZATION OF EARLY AMERICAN CINEMA[1]

Richard Abel

[. . .]

Fencing the Rooster In

Pathé's role in stimulating and then exploiting the nickelodeon boom of 1906–1907 sharply defined the issue of who would exercise control over the

Richard Abel (ed. Leo Charney and Vanessa R. Schwartz), *Cinema and the Invention of Modern Life* (Berkeley: University of California Press, 1995).

cinema business in the United States, and how. Once one frames that struggle for control in terms of 'American interests' versus 'foreign interests,' as such were perceived at the time, especially during the period from 1907 to 1909, the 'foreign body' of 'red rooster' films looms large indeed. There is perhaps no better evidence of Pathé's economic threat than a letter from George Eastman, head of Eastman Kodak, which at the time supplied 90 percent of the negative film stock used throughout the world.[1] According to Eastman's figures, the French company was selling on the American market between thirty and forty million feet of positive film stock per year by the fall of 1907, nearly twice as much as all the American companies combined.

As early as 1906, Pathé had drawn up plans to build factories for printing positive film stock in those countries where it was distributing the highest volume of films.[2] Such factories would reduce the high costs that the company already was paying for transportation and import duties, especially in the United States. In the spring of 1907, Pathé was preparing to construct such a facility in Bound Brook, New Jersey, based not only on its ever-expanding business but also on its understanding that a March 1907 court decision upholding the Edison camera patent (against Biograph) did not apply to perforated film.[3] Alarmed by the French company's move to embed itself more firmly in the American market, Edison set up negotiations with Pathé in April, threatening the company with litigation but also sweetening that threat with a 'generous' proposition.[4] To counter the Bound Brook factory plans, Edison made what at first seemed a lucrative proposal, offering to print Pathé's positive film stock (from the shipped negative) at its own facilities and to serve as the principal sales agent of that film stock in the United States. Tempted by the offer, the French company responded favorably, assuming that Edison would print the sum total of its weekly negative output and that, in turn, it might gain exclusive rights to sell Edison films in Europe. However, it was more than a month before the Edison company finally replied, refusing to take Pathé's entire list of weekly subjects and demanding the right to select which French films would be released on the American market.[5] After that, the deal quickly collapsed, and Pathé accused Edison of costing it a good deal of lost revenues.[6]

The result of Edison's delaying tactic was to stall the French company at a critical point in its expansion. Construction could not begin on the Bound Brook factory until early that summer, and Charles Pathé himself hurried across the ocean to join Berst for the factory's groundbreaking as well as for Pathé Cinematograph's incorporation as an American company.[7] Despite the company's record-setting business that fall, Berst remained uneasy because of the persistent 'unsettled conditions' created by the proliferating nickelodeons and rental exchanges. The practice of duping film prints continued to the extent, for instance, that Kalem's Francis Marion warned that it could drive manufacturers like Pathé into the rental business.[8] And Pathé's recent decision to stop selling films in France and to establish its own rental system and exhibition circuit there raised fears that it was about to do the same in the United States.[9]

Another practice that worried Berst as well as others was the subrenting of films without proper authorization. In order to curb these practices, in October Berst sent out new contracts to the exchanges and exhibitors which set forth tighter restrictions on reselling, duping, and 'bicycling' prints (that is, sharing them 'illegally' with other exhibitors) and encouraged customers to take all of the company's weekly releases *en bloc* rather than select several titles from among them.[10] As reported by *Show World*, *Moving Picture World*, and *Billboard*, representatives of the leading rental exchanges convened in Pittsburgh in November and, one month later, in Chicago, to remedy these and other problems.[11] Their solution was the United Film Service Protection Association (UFSPA), which promised to combine all sectors of the industry into a single national 'regulatory' organization.

Behind the scenes, however, Edison was maneuvering to gain control of the new association. Emboldened by a Chicago court decision in October which upheld one of its patent suits against Selig and by the evidence accumulating in its case against Vitagraph – both of which strengthened its legal position – Edison set out to negotiate a licensing agreement with the other manufacturers that would let them, for an annual fee, exploit its patents.[12] Its purpose, besides the obvious one of self-interest, was to shift the industry's profits away from the renters and exhibitors and increasingly towards the manufacturers. Again Edison set up negotiations with Pathé, assuming that once the world's leading film producer fell in line, along with Vitagraph, the others would as well. Although its threat of litigation still loomed large, Edison now focused on assuring the French company that its licensing agreement would disallow or discourage 'foreign imports' other than those from Pathé itself. It was this assurance, Berst later testified, which persuaded Pathé to accept Edison's plan, as well as its insistence on paying only half the fee percentage the other manufacturers did.[13] The Edison licensing group then began securing contracts with members of the UFSPA, transforming it into the Film Service Association (FSA) and, in the process, excluding from its ranks the man who had brokered the original organization, George Kleine, the only other major dealer in 'foreign imports.'[14] In that it 'shut out the importation of foreign stuff . . . not suitable or good enough for the American market,'[15] the FSA seemed to secure Pathé's position not only as the largest film supplier for that market but also as the only significant foreign producer, a position which could only have supported the French company's own strategies of dominance within Europe.[16] Moreover, as Martin Norden has pointed out, the Edison agreement permitted Pathé to begin manufacturing its cameras and projectors at the Bound Brook facility when it finally opened in late 1907 and began processing the fifty million feet of negative it had ordered from Eastman Kodak.[17]

However, not long after Biograph, together with Kleine, set up its own rival licensing group in February 1908 to serve the foreign companies and importers excluded from the FSA, Pathé began to sense that its operations were being blocked, its 'red rooster' films fenced in.[18] First of all, Biograph promised to offer 'a regular weekly supply of from 12 to 20 reels of splendid new subjects' and soon had commitments from a sufficient number of rental exchanges and exhibitors' associations, especially in Chicago, to sustain what was being dubbed the 'Independent Movement.'[19] Then, not only did Biograph refer to the FSA as the 'Edison-Pathé combination' but Kleine, often called the leader of the new 'Independents,' also pointedly blamed Pathé more than Edison for the FSA's exclusionary strategy and for the ensuing 'film war.'[20] As if that were not enough, according to Georges Sadoul, with the revenue from the FSA licensees (which, at its peak, included one hundred and fifty rental exchanges as well as the eight manufacturers), Edison's gross profits equaled and then exceeded those of Pathé for the first time in years.[21] Even as it continued to amass high revenues on the American market, the French company found itself being outflanked by rivals both within and without the FSA. Early in the summer of 1908, as a means of regaining some measure of control, Berst floated an idea that Pathé had used successfully before: If the FSA producers were to cut prices on their positive film stock, the 'Independents' would be unable to compete with them for long.[22] When that failed to win approval, the French company considered something more drastic. Now Charles Pathé himself came to the United States once again to explore the viability of establishing a circuit of film rental exchanges modeled on the system he had recently put in place in France, a system that, in its exploratory stages, may well have included Vitagraph along with the 'Independents.'[23]

That Pathé finally decided against making this move, or felt unable to do so, is revealing. The recession and monetary crisis threatening the United States economy at the time may have played a role in the decision, but the company's revenues, according to its own internal reports, seem not to have been much affected by that threat.[24] More to the point, Berst later admitted that Pathé found itself overextended in its investment and could not afford to set up the kind of rental exchange system that such a huge country as the United States would require.[25] Perhaps most crucially, the French company's internal records reveal that Charles Pathé and his directors were all too aware that, despite the best efforts of Berst in New York and Ivor Montague in Chicago, 'they continued to be considered . . . foreigners.'[26] Pathé was no more able to exert a leadership role in the American cinema industry now than either it or *Views and Films Index* had been two years earlier at the start of the nickelodeon boom.[27] In late September 1908, the *New York Dramatic Mirror* made a cryptic reference to one of the first signs of the French company's retreat. Whereas Vitagraph and Edison were increasing their output, respectively, to three and two reels per week, Pathé's output 'of new subjects' was being cut 'to four reels per week as against the five reels' released previously that year.[28]

Throughout the spring and summer of 1908, the rivalry between the two licensing groups led to much less stability in the industry than either Edison or Biograph had imagined. The FSA set up a regularized schedule of weekly releases in order to encourage stability, but soon there were complaints that it was too inflexible and that rental prices were too high, which increased the operating costs especially for nickelodeon owners.[29] Then, in July, the FSA pegged its pricing system to a film's release date, making those shown on the very first day of their release, as Eileen Bowser has written, the only 'truly "fresh" and valuable' commodities.[30] Among the trade press weeklies, only *Views and Films Index* strongly endorsed the FSA, earning it the reputation of being a mouthpiece for 'Edison and its allied interests.'[31] *Show World*, *Billboard*, and the *New York Clipper*, by contrast, all actively supported the 'Independents,' and *Moving Picture World* was hard-pressed to maintain the neutrality of its professed 'independence.'[32] Finally, as Charles Musser has documented, for the first time exhibitors were complaining, at least in New York, about a dearth of subjects.[33] By July, consequently, Edison was negotiating with both Biograph and Kleine to merge the rival groups into a single patent association – and Pathé's absence from those discussions clearly signaled its waning influence.[34] By September the Motion picture Patents Company (MPPC) was all but in place, and now it was Eastman and Pathé, after a brief flurry of publicity over its proposed rental exchanges, who delayed the MPPC's official institution until December.[35] That the MPPC provisions limited foreign imports even more than before surely addressed one of Pathé's demands, but the provisions also restricted each licensed producer to a maximum of four thousand feet (or four reels) of new positive film stock per week.[36] That restriction contractually bound the company to the concession it already had made in September, and the weekly maximum of four thousand feet was considerably less than its full production capacity.

In the struggle to ensure that 'American interests' rather than 'foreign interests' controlled the American cinema industry, the formation of the FSA and then the MPPC played a significant role by curbing Pathé's considerable, if far from invulnerable, economic power at a crucial stage in that industry's development.

Clipping the Rooster's Wings

Yet the struggle for control of the American cinema industry was hardly confined to the production and circulation of films as 'fresh' and valuable commodities. It also encompassed their venues of exhibition and, especially, their reception and the efforts to mediate that reception. Evidence of this struggle is unmistakable in the trade journals, newspapers, and magazines. It is expressed perhaps most openly in an October 1908 article on the nickelodeon in *World Today*, in which the writer notes that 'competition has lately become very keen between French and American manufacturers' but frames that competition in terms of taste and morality – associating the French with 'bad taste' and immorality.[37] This kind of moral discourse appears repeatedly throughout the previous year and is often invoked to describe Pathé films in circulation. The reviews in *Variety*, which primarily addressed the vaudeville circuit, are especially striking: *The Female Spy* (December 1907) is 'chaotic' and 'disagreeable'; *Avenged by the Sea* (March 1908) is so 'gruesome and morbid' that it 'should not be on the market'; *A Christmas Eve Tragedy* (April 1908) is 'as well conceived for children as an interior view of a slaughter house would be' and reprehensible enough to justify censorship.[38] This attitude toward Pathé films can be found even earlier, however, in the spring of 1907, specifically in the correspondence conveying Edison's refusal to negotiate further with the French company, a refusal couched self-servingly in terms of moral objections to Pathé's subjects.[39] Furthermore, it is important enough that, when he visited the United States in May 1908 in order to assess the FSA's operations, Charles Pathé himself responded implicitly to such criticism by insisting that he would personally select the films his company released in the American market.[40] Indeed, as late as June 1909, the American correspondent for the British trade journal *Bioscope* went so far as to unmask this moralistic attitude toward Pathé films as symptomatic of something else entirely: 'The quality of the Pathé picture is far and away ahead of that of its competition . . . The public like Pathé pictures . . . From this state of affairs there has arisen a condition of mind which one can only call Pathé-mentia.'[41]

All this controversy suggests that, in the United States, Pathé was situated near the center of a debate over early cinema's status as a modern form of mass culture and, more importantly, over its ideological function as 'a new social force' within an increasingly contested public sphere.[42] In one sense, the conflicted discourse about Pathé reveals how the company and its products served a double role in 'legitimating' the cinema in the United States.[43] Initially, that role was to align certain positively perceived attributes of French culture with the 'American' cinema. This can be seen in Pathé's own appeal, in its early advertisements, to the acknowledged high quality of French technology, demonstrated elsewhere by the photography industry (where the Lumière name was held in high regard) and the new automobile industry but also emblematised by such engineering marvels as the Eiffel Tower and the Gallery of Machines at the 1889 Paris Exposition.[44] Exhibitors, journalists, and others, however, also consistently celebrated the cinema by invoking the marvels of Pathé's 'high quality' – from its unique stencil-color process to the 'flickerless images' produced by the superbly crafted apparatuses of its laboratories.[45] That technology continued to be praised as late as 1909 and 1910, when a new version of the Pathé projector came on the market and was soon being installed not only in nickelodeons and the best new New York cinemas but also on ships of the United States Navy.[46] Pathé subjects also allowed vaudeville and nickelodeon exhibitors to treat their programs like a new, but inexpensive and continually renewed, version of the European theatrical tour, a significant form of French (as well as British) cultural influence in the late nineteenth century.[47] And one of the more famous of those tours just happened to coincide with Pathé's rise to power in the American market – the 'Farewell America Tour' of Sarah Bernhardt from 1905 to 1906.[48] Finally, Pathé's 'red rooster' films may well have benefited from the turn-of-the century belief 'that the magical link to everything Parisian was a near guarantee' of sales, especially for department stores, through the mass market introduction of 'Paris' fashion shows in stores like Wanamakers in Philadelphia.[49]

Just as often, however, and more frequently from 1907 on, writers in the trade press as well as exhibitors eschewed such 'legitimating' appeals to play on another conception of French culture as risqué, deviant, and decidedly different from American culture – especially in its display of sexuality, sensational violence, and distasteful comic business. Here, the French *grand guignol* melodramas offer a telling instance of that shift.[50] During the nickelodeon boom, Pathé versions of such melodramas seem to have been not only accepted but also quite popular.[51] This was clearly the case in Des Moines, where a dramatic critic in March 1907 cited 'the tense one-act drama[–]short character plays, vivid pathetic flashes from human life, a whirl of comedy[–]which claims prominent attention on the French stage' (a reference to the Grand Guignol theater in Paris) as a model for vaudeville programs in the city.[52] One month later, when the Colonial Theatre opened there with an entire program of Pathé titles, it ran *The Female Spy* (which *Variety* would later condemn) as a prominent feature.[53] The same film ran two weeks later at the Nickeldom, whose programs the *Des Moines Register and Leader* was then praising for their well-chosen variety, which included 'scenes from foreign countries, unique adventures on land and water, and skillfully posed grotesque pictures.'[54] That summer, according to the manager of the Theatre Film Service, the demand for sensational melodramas began to wane throughout the country, or, rather, he and other renters began to participate in their denigration, probably in response to recent attacks on Chicago nickelodeons.[55] In articles and interviews, the French tradition of grand guignol melodrama now was presented as sharply different from the American tradition of 'ethical melodrama' and its 'bright, happy denouements,'[56] or what William Leach, paraphrasing the department store magnate John Wanamaker, describes as the American 'quest for pleasure, security, comfort, and material well-being.'[57] Perhaps Carl Laemmle put it most succinctly: 'Let's cater more to the happy side of life. There's enough of the seamy side without exposing it to further view.'[58]

This illicit or 'low-other' conception of French culture grew increasingly persistent over the next year or so. And it ranged across the spectrum of French films, encompassing much more than the sensational and the grotesque. One summer day in 1907, for example, a New York nickelodeon advertised its program as 'FRESH FROM PARIS, *Very Naughty*.'[59] In a similar vein, *Variety* repeatedly vilified Pathé's films well into 1909 – as in its disgust at an early Max Linder comedy, *The Servant's Good Joke*, which exploited the effects of a salad deliberately dressed with castor oil.[60] Ironically, the language of approbation which the FSA (including Pathé) invoked to exclude that unwanted 'foreign stuff' from the American market shifted to target and tar the French company itself.[61] The process accelerated as demands grew, especially among Progressive moralists, for a greater measure of control over this new arena of the 'cheap' and the 'low' – whether or not they agreed with economist Simon Patten's view of the nickelodeon as a source of regeneration for the masses – and for the construction of cinemas that would be as spacious and elegant as 'legitimate' theaters and, therefore, would be more suitable for the 'better classes.'[62] In other words, as the nickelodeon boom increasingly came to be inscribed within the rhetoric of moral reform and uplift (with its 'imperialist' notions of responsibility for 'others less fortunate') and described as a 'detour . . . through the lower regions of the entertainment market,'[63] Pathé found itself more and more circumscribed in public discourse as representative of much that was 'low' and 'illegitimate' about the cinema.

As the demands for social control of the cinema converged with those for economic control, the need to deal with 'Pathé-mentia,' otherwise translated into Pathé 'illegitimacy,' took on greater urgency. This is perhaps no more evident than in the actions of the National Board of Censorship, at least for the first year or so after its formation in March 1909.[64] According to documents housed at the Edison National Historical Site, throughout 1909 and 1910, Pathé films were either rejected or returned for alteration much more frequently than were the films of American producers. In May 1909, for instance, the board 'condemned' two Pathé titles it had asked to be altered (*Le Parapluie d'Anatole* and *Le Boucher de Meudon*), but accepted Biograph's *Two Memories* after changes were made.[65] One month later, no less than six of thirteen Pathé titles were rejected or recommended for alteration.[66] As late as February 1910, the board found Alfred Machin's *Moulin maudit* so offensive that, in order to eliminate its adultery, murder, and suicide, it ordered Pathé simply to lop off the second half of the film.[67] An October 1910 article in *World Today* unequivocally supports this evidence: 'In the early days of the censors about one in every ten French pictures had to be condemned.'[68] So does H. N. Marvin's testimony in the antitrust court case against the MPPC, in which he specifically referred to the great number of 'indecent and obscene . . . pictures imported from foreign countries' as a principal reason for the board's formation.[69] In effect, the board's early work neatly complemented that of the FSA and the MPPC, not only in curbing Pathé's economic power but also in curtailing what was seen as an undesirable, immoral, 'foreign' influence.

[. . .]

NOTES

1. Eastman's letter is reprinted in Georges Sadoul, *Histoire générale du cinéma*, vol. 2, *Les Pionniers du cinéma*, 1897–1909 (Paris: Denoël, 1948), pp. 465–6. Although undated, it refers to his recent negotiations with Edison and Pathé representatives in the summer of 1907. Sadoul's account of the FSA and MPPC's formation in that volume, on pages 461–78, is still one of the best available.
2. 'Compagnie générale de phonographes, cinématographes et appareils de précision,' *Les Assemblés générales* (25 June 1906), pp. 656, 658, Carton 1, Pathé Télévision Archive (PTA), Saint-Ouen.

3. 'Trade Notes,' *Views and Films Index*, 16 March 1907, p. 6. For a more detailed analysis of the negotiations between Edison and Pathé, see Kristin Thompson, 'Regaining the American Market, 1907–1913', in Thompson, *Exporting Entertainment: America in the World Film Market, 1907–1934* (London: British Institute, 1985), pp. 4–10. See also Martin Sopocy, 'The Edison-Biograph Patent Litigation of 1901–1907,' *Film History* 3 (1989): 19–22.

4. See G. Croydon-Marks to W. E. Gilmore, 15 March 1907; Gilmore to Croydon-Marks, 10 April 1907; and Dyer to Gilmore, 13 April 1907, 1907 motion-picture folder, Pathé file, Edison National Historical Site (ENHS), West Orange, New Jersey.

5. See Marks to Pathé, 21 May 1907, and Gilmore to William Pelzer and Gilmore to Thomas Edison himself, 28 May 1907, 1907 motion-picture folder, Pathé file, ENHS.

6. See the translation of the 22 May 1907 letter from Pathé to Marks, 1907 motion-picture folder, Pathé file, ENHS.

7. 'Trade Notes,' *Views and Films Index*, 8 June 1907, p. 4; and 'Trade Notes,' *Moving Picture World*, 22 June 1907, p. 249. The 'incorporators' of the new company were William H. Corbin, Collins & Corbin, Ernest A. Ivatts, and Charles Pathé.

8. ' "Duping" of Fine Film Pictures Condemned,' *Show World*, 19 November 1907, p. 16.

9. See, for instance, 'What Will Pathé Do?' *Show World*, 19 October 1907, p. 18; and 'Editorial: What Does It Mean?' *Moving Picture World*, 26 October 1907, pp. 535–6. See also Abel, *The Ciné Goes to Town*, pp. 33–4.

10. 'A New Move: The Pathé Contract,' *Views and Films Index*, 26 October 1907, p. 3; 'Editorial: What Does It Mean?' *Moving Picture World*, 26 October 1907, pp. 535–6.

11. See 'American Moving Picture Captains Meet in Pittsburgh,' *Show World*, 23 November 1907, p. 21; Warren Patrick, 'Chicago Welcomes Captains of Moving Picture Industry,' ibid., 30 November 1907, p. 18; 'The United Film Service Protective Association,' *Moving Picture World*, 30 November 1907. p. 627; 'Film Men's Association Needed, Says Swanson,' *Show World*, 7 December 1907, p. 14; 'Moving Picture Men Organize,' ibid., 21 December 1907, p. 88; 'The U.F.S.P.A.,' *Moving Picture World*, 21 December 1907, p. 682; 'United Film Service Protective Association Meets,' *Billboard*, 21 December 1907, p. 20; and 'Film Convention and Moving Picture News,' *Billboard*, 28 December 1907, p. 9. *Views and Films Index* was unusually reticent about these meetings, having only one story devoted to them – see 'United Film Service Protective Ass'n,' *Views and Films Index*, 21 December 1907, pp. 4–5.

12. Charles Musser, *Before the Nickelodeon: Edwin S. Porter and the Edison Manufacturing Company* (Berkeley, Los Angeles, London: University of California Press, 1991), p. 375.

13. J. A. Berst, Direct Examination, 'USA vs. MPPC and Others, Case No. 889, Eastern Pennsylvania District Court, September 1912–April 1914', (Washington, D.C.: U.S. Government Printing office), vol. 3, pp. 1,768–1,770. See also Musser, *Before the Nickelodeon*, p. 377.

14. The initial listing of the UFSPA included rental exchanges only ('The U.F.S.P.A.,' *Moving Picture World*, 21 December 1907, p. 682). By February the FSA was contractually bound to the following licensed manufacturers: Edison, Essanay, Kalem, Lubin, Méliès, Pathé, Selig, and Vitagraph ('Statement by the Licensed Manufacturers,' *Views and Films Index*, 29 February 1908, pp. 3–4). For the details of Kleine's ill-rewarded diplomacy in the UFSPA's formation, see Eileen Bowser, *History of the American Cinema*, vol. 2, *The Transformation of Cinema, 1908–1915* (New York: Scribners, 1991), pp. 26–7.

15. 'Interview with FSA Members and Others,' *Moving Picture World*, 28 March 1908, p. 260. Among those foreign companies excluded from the FSA agreement were Gaumont, Urban-Eclipse, Cinès, and Nordisk, all of which had begun to carve out a niche in the American market.

16. See, for instance, J. A. Berst to George Eastman, 11 February 1908, MPPC box no. 5, ENHS. Pathé also was allowed to hold an 'inventory sale' of its 'large stock of films on hand' – see the Pathé ad in *Views and Films Index*, 25 January 1908, p. 2.

17. Martin Norden, 'The Pathé-Frères Company During the Trust Era,' *Journal of the University Film Association* 33 (Summer 1981): 16–17. The Bound Brook factory was producing thirteen thousand meters of positive film stock per day by the summer of 1908, with expectations of twenty thousand meters by the end of the year. See the 'Rapport du Conseil d'Administration,' Assemblée Générale Ordinaire, Pathé-Frères (2 June 1908), carton 2, PTA.

18. The Biograph licensing group was announced in an ad in *Moving Picture World*, 22 February 1908, p. 130; and then in similar ads in *Show World*, 29 February 1908, p. 28, and in *New York Clipper*, 29 February 1908, p. 52. Kleine had to sell the stocks he controlled in Kalem in order to avoid a conflict of interest.

19. 'Moving Picture Men Indorse Independent Movement in Chicago,' *Show World*, 14 March 1908, p. 8. See also Musser, *Before the Nickelodeon*, p. 380.

20. See, for instance, 'The Position of the American Mutoscope and Biograph Company,' *Moving Picture World*, 15 February 1908, p. 112; 'Trade Notes: The Film War,' ibid., 29 February 1908, pp. 160–1; and 'Moving Picture Men Indorse Independent Movement in Chicago,' *Show World*, 14 March 1908, p. 8.

21. Sadoul, *Histoire*, p. 467.

22. 'Pathé's Position,' *Views and Films Index*, 13 June 1908, p. 4.

23. See 'Rumors Regarding Pathé-Frères,' *New York Dramatic Mirror*, 12 September 1908, p. 9; 'Pathé Will Not Invade Rental Field,' *Moving Picture World*, 12 September 1908, p. 192; 'Pathé Frères Not to Rent,' *Views and Films Index*, 19 September 1908, p. 4; and Bowser, op. cit., pp. 28–9.

24. 'Rapport du Conseil d'Administration,' Pathé-Frères (2 June 1908), PTA.

25. J. A. Berst, Direct Examination, 'USA vs. MPPC and Others,' vol. 3, p. 1,778.

26. 'Rapport du Conseil d'Administration,' Pathé-Frères (2 June 1908), PTA.

27. By November 1905, Pathé was so entrenched on the American market that, along with Kleine Optical, Vitagraph, Biograph and Méliès (but, significantly, not Edison), it had participated in the first attempt to organise 'the leading manufacturers of films,' the Moving Picture Protective League of America; see 'Moving Picture Makers Organize,' *New York Clipper*, 23 December 1905, p. 1,118. *Views and Films Index* often had encouraged the formation of some kind of protective association for the new industry, beginning in the late summer of 1906; see, for instance, 'Editorial: Association for Protection Against Dishonest Customers in the Moving Picture Trade,' *Views and Films Index*, 18 August 1906, p. 3; 'Problems of the Trade and Their Solution,' *Views and Films Index*, 25 August 1906, p. 3; and 'The Plan to Organize the Protective Association,' *Views and Films Index*, 27 October 1906, pp. 3–4.

28. 'Increasing American Output,' *New York Dramatic Mirror*, 26 September 1908, p. 9.

29. See, for instance, 'Release Dates,' *Views and Films Index*, 11 April 1908, p. 3; 'Now Is the Time,' ibid., 30 May 1908, p. 3; and 'Association Renters Discuss Schedule,' ibid., 6 June 1908, p. 4.

30. Musser, *Before the Nickelodeon*, p. 378; and Bowser, *History*, p. 28.

31. See, for instance, the front covers of *Views and Films Index*, 22 February and 25 April 1908; and 'The Moving Picture Field,' *New York Dramatic Mirror*, 30 May 1908, p. 7.

32 See, for instance, 'Words From the Knocker and Howler,' *Moving Picture World*, 1 February 1908, p. 72; 'The Film Service Association and Ourselves.' ibid., 22 February 1908, p. 131; and 'About Ourselves,' ibid., 21 March 1908, p. 227.

33. Musser, *Before the Nickelodeon*, pp. 380–1.

34. It was Frank Dyer, for Edison, and Harry Marvin and Jeremiah J. Kennedy, for Biograph, who headed these negotiations. For further information on the MPPC's formation, see Thompson, *Exporting Entertainment*, pp. 10–19; Musser, *Before the Nickelodeon*, pp. 433–8; and Bowser, *History*, pp. 27–33.

35. The MPPC was even incorporated that September in New Jersey (Musser, *Before the Nickelodeon*, pp. 435–7). For further information on the delay caused by Eastman and Pathé, see Bowser, *History*, p. 31. Another reason that Pathé briefly considered opening its own rental exchange was to amortise the unsold film prints which were accumulating because of the FSA regulations, but it was able to sell off many of those between September and December, when the MPPC officially replaced the FSA.

36. See the testimony of H. N. Marvin and Frank Dyer, *USA vs. MPPC* (1914), pp. 26 and 1,519.

37. Lucy France Pierce, 'The Nickelodeon,' *World Today*, October 1908; reprinted in Gerald Mast (ed.), *The Movies in Our Midst: Documents in a Cultural History of Film in America* (Chicago: University of Chicago Press, 1982), p. 56.

38. These reviews are reprinted in *Variety Film Reviews, 1907–1920* (New York: Garland, 1983). *The Female Spy* ended with a young Cossack woman being killed and then dragged by a horse, while *A Christmas Eve Tragedy* climaxed with a Breton fisherman throwing his wife's lover, along with the man's horse and cart, over a cliff. This discourse of moral approbation contrasted, however, with the grudging respect that John Collier used to describe New York nickelodeon films in April 1908 (Collier, 'Cheap Amusements,' *Charities and the Commons*, 11 April 1908, p. 74).

39. See W. E. Gilmore to T. Edison, 28 May 1907, 1907 motion-picture folder, EHNS.

40. 'Chas. Pathé Makes a Statement,' *Views and Films Index*, 16 May 1908, p. 4.

41. T. B., 'News from America,' *Bioscope*, 24 June 1909, p. 25. See, also, the letter from a Boston nickelodeon manager who argued that only one American company, Biograph, 'had attained the standard of quality set by Pathé films' ('Correspondence,' *Moving Picture World*, 29 May 1909, p. 716).

42. The phrase 'a new social force' was first used by John Collier in 'Cheap Amusements.' Contrast this with Robert Sklar's statement that Pathé's success in the American market had notably little effect (*Movie-Made America: A Cultural History of American Movies* [New York: Random House, 1975], p. 29).

43. Roberta Pearson and William Uricchio examine a similar contradiction in the appeals made to Italian culture in American discourse on early cinema – see 'English, Italian, and American Shakespearean Cinema in the United States: Differences in Signifying Practices and Reception,' in *Images Across Borders*, ed. Roland Cosandey (Paris: Editions Payot, 1995).

44. Perhaps the earliest evidence of this appeal comes in the Pathé ad in the *New York Clipper*, 28 October 1905, p. 930. Between 1903 and 1905, Lumière's technical advances frequently were highlighted in the prestigious American monthly, *Photo-Era Magazine*. In 1903 France exported 51 million francs worth of automobiles and parts, in 1906, 140 million (Eugen Weber, *France, Fin-de-Siècle* [Cambridge: Harvard University Press, 1986], p. 207). See also Roger Magraw, *France, 1815–1914: The Bourgeois Century* (London: Fontana, 1983), pp. 232–3; and Paul Greenhalgh, *Ephemeral Vistas: The Expositions Universelles, Great Exhibitions, and World's Fairs, 1851–1939* (Manchester: Manchester University Press, 1988), pp. 154–5.

45. See, for instance, 'Trade Notes,' *Moving Picture World*, 11 May 1907, pp. 152–3.

46. See, for instance, the full-page ad for the new Pathé projector in *Moving Picture World*, 3 April 1909, p. 390; 'French Machine Hits Iowa City,' *Views and Films Index*, 5 June 1909, p. 4; 'Pathé Professional Outfit,' *New York Dramatic Mirror*; 31 July 1909, p. 15; 'Pleased with Pathé Machines,' ibid., 30 October 1909, p. 17; 'Quantitative Competition,' *Moving Picture World*, 5 February 1910, p. 158; 'N.I.M.P.A. Meeting,' ibid., 12 February 1910, p. 214; and 'Pathé Machines on United States Warships,' ibid., 28 May 1910, p. 885.

47. Sarah Bernhardt made one of the earliest and most influential of such tours in 1880, then returned for another in 1900; Gabrielle Réjane made her first in 1895 and then

a second in 1904; see, for instance, Hamilton Mason, *French Theatre in New York* (New York: AMS Press, 1940), pp. 6, 28–9, 31.

48. See, for instance, Arthur Gold and Robert Fizdale, *The Divine Sarah: A Life of Sarah Bernhardt* (New York: Knopf, 1991), pp. 294–8.

49. William Leach, *Land of Desire: Merchants, Power, and the Rise of a New American Culture* (New York: Pantheon, 1993), pp. 99–102. A similar point is made by Kathy Peiss in 'Making Faces: The Cosmetics Industry and the Cultural Construction of Gender, 1890–1930,' *Genders* 7 (Spring 1990): 157–8.

50. For a good introduction to French grand guignol, see Mel Gordon, *The Grand Guignol: Theatre of Fear and Terror* (New York: Amok Press, 1988).

51. Vitagraph also briefly stressed the 'sensationalism' of its films during this period; see its ad for *The Automobile Thieves* in *Views and Films Index*, 10 November 1906, p. 11.

52. 'Vaudeville's Higher Aim,' *Des Moines Register and Leader*, 24 March 1907.

53. See the Colonial Theatre ad in ibid., 30 April 1907, p. 5.

54. See the Nickeldom ad in ibid., 13 May 1907, p. 5; and 'This Week's Bills,' ibid., 26 May 1907.

55. F. C. McCarahan, 'Chicago's Great Film Industry,' *Billboard*, 24 August 1907, p. 6.

56. See, for instance, 'The Melodrama,' *New York Dramatic Mirror*, 1 June 1907, p. 14; and 'Public Taste in Pictures as Viewed by M. E. Fleckles,' *Show World*, 7 September 1907, p. 9.

57. John Wanamaker's advertising editorial in *North American*, 5 April 1906, as cited in Leach, *Land of Desire*, p. 3.

58. 'Moving Picture Industry Great,' *Show World*, 29 June 1907, p. 29.

59. 'The Nickel Madness,' *Harper's Weekly*, 24 August 1907, reprinted in Mast, *Movies in Our Midst*, pp. 49–50.

60. See the 2 October 1909 review of *The Servant's Good Joke* reprinted in *Variety Film Reviews, 1907–1920* (New York: Garland, 1983).

61. In 1907 George Kleine had defended French films (especially Pathé's) against press attacks on Chicago's nickelodeons; one year later, allied with the 'Independents' against the FSA, he was maligning French films as 'racy, risqué, and sensational' ('Interview with George Kleine,' *New York Dramatic Mirror*, 27 June 1908, p. 7).

62. See, for instance, 'Moving Picture Industry Shows Marked Improvement, Activity and Development,' *Show World*, 19 October 1907, p. 22; 'Editorial,' *Views and Films Index*, 11 April 1908, p. 4; W. Stephen Bush, 'Who Goes to the Moving Pictures,' *Moving Picture World*, 3 October 1908, p. 378; 'Editorial,' *Views and Films Index*, 7 November 1908, p. 3; 'The Real Problem to be Solved,' ibid., 29 May 1909, p. 3; and Lewis E. Palmer, 'The World in Motion,' *Survey*, 5 June 1909, p. 357. For an analysis of Simon Patten's influential books *The New Basis of Civilization* (1907) and *Product and Climax* (1909), see Daniel Horowitz, *The Morality of Spending: Attitudes toward the Consumer Society in America, 1875–1940* (Baltimore: Johns Hopkins University Press, 1985), pp. 31–7.

63. The descriptive phrase is from Miriam Hansen, *Babel and Babylon: Spectatorship in American Silent Cinema* (Cambridge: Harvard University Press, 1991), p. 69, but the outlines of this redefinition of the nickelodeon period already were in place in H. F. Hoffman, 'What People Want: Some Observations,' *Moving Picture World*, 9 July 1910, p. 77.

64. See, especially, Nancy Rosenbloom, 'Progressive Reform, Censorship, and the Motion picture Industry, 1909–1917,' in *Popular Culture and Political Change in Modern America*, ed. Ronald Edsforth and Larry Bennett (Buffalo: SUNY Press, 1991), pp. 41–59. It should be noted that in April 1909 the board took unusual measures to approve a large number of Pathé's films, but this changed shortly thereafter – see Bowser, *History*, p. 50; and Palmer, 'The World in Motion,' p. 363.

65. See John Collier to Frank Dyer, 10 May 1909, motion-picture folder, censorship file no. 1, ENHS. Ironically, Collier had detected not 'one immoral or indecent picture'

in his investigation of New York nickelodeons just one year earlier (Collier, 'Cheap Amusements,' p. 74).

66. See Collier to Dyer, 18 June 1909, motion-picture folder, censorship file no. 1, ENHS.

67. See Collier to Dyer, 1 February and 9 February 1910, motion-picture folder, censorship file no. 1, ENHS.

68. Charles V. Trevis, 'Censoring the Five-Cent Drama,' *World Today*, October 1910; reprinted in Mast, *Movies in Our Midst*, p. 69. Michael Davis also praises the work of the board in substantially decreasing the number of 'morally objectionable' films; see *The Exploitation of Pleasure: A Study of Commercial Recreation in New York City* (New York: Russell Sage Foundation, 1911), p. 34.

69. H. N. Marvin, Direct Examination, 'USA vs. MPPC and Others' vol. 3, p. 1,282. See also the 15 January 1910 letter from Charles Sprague Smith, the board's first director, to Frank Dyer, arguing that Pathé should not be allowed to advertise its films as approved by the Board for fear that that would 'tend to discredit the censorship,' moving picture folder, censorship file, ENHS.

4

ESTABLISHING CLASSICAL NORMS

The formation of the major Hollywood studios developed from market struggles between the Motion Picture Patents Company (MPPC) and a group of independents spearheaded by Carl Laemmle. Running the largest American distribution firm, Laemmle was unwilling to pay licence fees to the MPPC. This meant he was restricted from purchasing films to supply his customers, unable to buy titles from Biograph, Vitagraph, Edison, Pathé, or any of the other major affiliated companies. As a result, Laemmle began his own firm, founding the Independent Moving Picture Company (or IMP as it became known) in 1909. This company produced its own films, releasing two reels a week together with reels supplied by Italian companies such as Ambrosio and Itala. This marked a surge of activity in the independent sector, unlicensed producers, distributors and exhibitors allying themselves in ways that would unravel the power of the MPPC.

Together with IMP, a number of independent producers emerged in 1910. This included the Centaur Film Manufacturing Company, the Nestor Company, the Thanhouser Company, and the New York Motion Picture Company. In the same year, the independent producers established a co-operative distribution arm called the Motion Picture Distribution and Sales Company. This would help organise the independent field by regulating release dates and film prices and mirrored the function of the General Film Company, established by the Trust in 1910. Both were attempts to monopolise distribution in the domestic market and set in place a power struggle to control the US film industry.

For the MPPC, the struggle against the independents was primarily waged through legal means. It tried to assert its authority by bringing lawsuits against independent producers for patent infringement. This especially applied to the use of film cameras. However, this legal front was forestalled by a court decision in 1912 that judged that IMP cameras, based on a patent called the Latham-loop, did not constitute any kind of infringement. This undermined the MPPC for it meant that independents could use cameras without fear of litigation.

This situation significantly weakened the position of the Trust and its hold over the industry. It was already clear in 1911 that many exhibitors were simply ignoring the rules set down by the MPPC, often combining licensed and unlicensed films on their programmes. Mismanagement and anti-trust initiatives were also hastening the demise of the Trust. Most significantly, the federal government filed a suit against the MPPC in 1912 under the Sherman Antitrust Act. The government case was brought on the grounds that the MPPC had tried to monopolise the business of rental exchanges in the United States, unfairly constraining trade. The lawsuit continued for several years and in 1915 a final decision ordered that the MPPC be dissolved.

This ruling was a symptom of the more general realignment of the American film industry in the 1910s. Specifically, the period from 1909 to 1913 saw the emergence of a new oligopoly based around the independents. This was linked to contiguous developments in the form and development of film itself. In particular, the 1910s saw the rise of both the feature film and the star system. While these were not exclusively associated with the independents, they distinguished film production as the independent sector rose to power, becoming standard features of a nascent, but not yet fully realised, studio system.

Stars began to be central to the publicity mechanisms of this system, outlined more fully in the following chapter. During the nickelodeon boom, the motion-picture industry advertised and distributed its product by way of the company brand. With films conceived as a uniform commodity, the brand name of the production company – Biograph, Vitagraph, Pathé, Lubin – took precedence. Before 1908, there was little impetus to name particular filmmakers or actors. Despite an established star system in the theatre, neither directors nor actors received any kind of screen credit, and were not generally used to publicise film.

There were several industrial factors that delayed the creation of a cinematic star system until the 1920s. Most significantly, the acting profession itself was a highly transient one. Few actors worked consistently in the film industry or with any particular film company. Indeed, many film actors were in the lower ranks of the theatrical profession and were hired by the day. In practical terms, the very distance of the camera also made it difficult for early film audiences to recognise particular actors. As such, fan investments were not readily cultivated. This situation began to change after 1908 when production companies started to employ actors on longer contracts, camera close-ups were increasingly used, and the film industry became a more legitimate professional choice for those trained in theatre. It was at this point that the majority of film companies began to experiment with star publicity, responding to a voracious public interest in lead performers. For example, the licensed company, Kalem, was one of the first to offer photographs of their stock company for display in theatrical lobbies.

The transition to feature film undoubtedly shaped the cinematic star system. Not only did features enable closer and more prolonged identification with performers, they encouraged studios to compete with each other, signing popular actors to long-term contracts in the hope of matching them with star vehicles. Features would become a staple of film production in the early 1910s, stars providing an efficient means of differentiating and giving status to individual film events.

Increasingly consumed as a special attraction, feature films described the multi-reel films that began to emerge, and become popular, from 1909. Initially, these were 1,000 feet long and ran for approximately fifteen minutes. They became longer in the next five years, however, marked by the success of multi-reel foreign imports shown outside of the established distribution system. These included historical epics such as *Dante's Inferno* (1911), *Queen Elisabeth* (1912) and *Quo Vadis?* (1913). These could run for as long as two hours, would play for two weeks at a time, and might charge a dollar admission price. In significant ways, feature films represented a challenge to the standard practices of the organised film industry. While multi-reel films encountered initial resistance, features would become the norm by the mid-1910s, redefining the industry in the process.

Rather than play nickelodeons, features were 'roadshown', meaning that they toured cities and regions across the country, exhibited as a special event in town halls, opera houses and in legitimate theatres. Features were a significant facet of the film industry's attempt to give cinema cultural respectability. Heralding the newfound legitimacy of film, the rise of feature production was duly accompanied by transitions in film exhibition. In both Europe and America, this was symbolised by the arrival of the movie palace, first emerging in 1910 although more fully developed in the later part of the decade. Movie palaces did not entirely replace nickelodeons, which continued to exist in poor urban districts until the mid-1910s. However, they did represent a new phase in the conditions of moviegoing, looking for their inspiration to the refinements of theatre design, using lavish architectural themes and including amenities such as toilets, carpeting, dazzling lights and ornate foyers.

The rise of multi-reel features, shown in elaborate movie palaces, meant that power continued to transfer from exhibitors to film producers. Longer films meant that showmen could not intervene, or organise programmes, as they had done before. While audiences entered a programme at whatever time they wished, film was consumed in a different way, more than one reel at a time and often as a special occasion.

This precipitated the decline of the nickelodeon, unable to afford the costs of feature films. This did not mean to say that the film industry abandoned their needs entirely. Indeed, the rise of the serial in the early teens was an interim means of supplying product to those unwilling or unable to transfer to five- or six-reel features. Serials were generally released in one or two reels and constructed a story through instalments. They were frequently sensational in nature and featured continuous characters whose lives were defined by fights, escapes, explosions and chases. If the film industry was anxious to broaden its appeal to middle-class audiences through quality film, it sought to hold onto its profitable blue-collar audience through serial melodramas.

In effect, serials were a means of negotiating changes in the style, length and status of film. Often, they focused on plucky heroines in serials such as Edison's *What's Happened to Mary* (1912), Selig's *The Adventures of Kathlyn* (1914), Kalem's *The Hazards of Helen* (1914–17) and Pathé's *The Perils of Pauline* (1914). As described in the previous chapter, these featured 'serial queens' who, while frequently adopting the trope of the imperilled woman, also put forward assertive models of femininity. Formulaic in style and with low production values, film serials were popular in numerous film markets, representing adjustments in various countries to the industrial and cultural emergence of multi-reel features, and the need to find a transitional bridge from one kind of film product to another.

Indeed, feature films were a departure from early forms of cinema. Although features initially resembled one-reel films in terms of narrative structure and editing patterns – basically following a single incident towards a climax – multi-reel films gradually developed formal elements of their own. Negotiating the complexities of narrative, producers invariably turned to theatre and novels for inspiration. Features began to include more characters and incidents, with several climactic scenes leading up to a final denouement. In American cinema, intelligible plots were built around characters, focusing on particular traits or motivations that would drive the narrative. Certain long-established principles of storytelling were codified in the feature film. Relieved of requirements that previously governed the length and structure of film, however, new formal and aesthetic strategies also developed.

Editing techniques, in particular, were able to slow down significantly, there being less need to compress stories with rapid cuts. Rather than films being made in one shot from one camera position, a process of scene dissection used editing to combine different shots of the same scene. This helped give variety and depth both to narrative action and character psychology. Meanwhile, emphasis was placed on the value of spectacle, principally as a means of holding audience attention over a longer period of time.

The career of D. W. Griffith is indicative of these transitions. Frustrated at Biograph's reluctance to make feature films, Griffith left the company in 1913. Although his last film for Biograph had been the four-reel historical epic *Judith of Bethulia* (1913), he moved to an independent distribution firm called Mutual where he began work on a number of multi-reel films, including *The Birth of a Nation* (1915). This film became a landmark feature, bringing narrative complexity and visual spectacle, not to say racial controversy, to an historical epic set around the American Civil War. Often described as the defining film of

Griffith's career, *The Birth of a Nation* helped initiate a widespread transition to feature production in the United States.

Griffith's move to Mutual is suggestive of the weakened power of the MPPC and its affiliate companies in the early 1910s. After the 1912 verdict against the Trust, independent production and distribution firms established themselves in ways that would herald the formation of the major studios and inspire the move to Hollywood. Initially, this included the creation of the Universal Film Manufacturing Company by Carl Laemmle (1912), Famous Players by Alfred Zukor (1912) and the Jesse L. Lasky Feature Play Company, established by the eponymous vaudeville producer (1914). It also included a national distributor called Paramount, founded by W. W. Hodkinson in 1914, which agreed to distribute film for 35 per cent of the proceeds. In addition, Paramount agreed to provide cash advances for production and a guaranteed minimum return to the production company, anticipating industry arrangements to come. While a large number of other companies were established at this time, eager to capitalise on the boom in features, not all would survive. The most influential would become those of Warner Bros. (1913), the Fox Film Corporation (1913), Metro (1914) and Goldwyn and Mayer (1917), the last two merging to become MGM in 1924.

Unlike the MPPC, the independents invested heavily in feature production, all the time expanding their reach into distribution and exhibition. As significant as any single film made by the industrial regrouping and expansion of the independents was the production system they put in place. Essentially, the independents developed an efficient system for manufacturing film on a large scale, concentrating specifically on the ninety-minute feature. These might cost anywhere between $100,000 and $500,000 and would be differentiated through publicity and mass advertising. This would draw centrally upon the star system. Companies would sometimes capture stars or 'famous players' from legitimate theatre, such as Sarah Bernhardt who starred in *Queen Elisabeth* (1912). Just as often, however, film companies would nurture their own stars, Alfred Zukor turning Mary Pickford into the highest-paid film star of her day.

In organisational terms, the major film companies, moving towards a studio system, would increasingly emulate the workings of modern capitalist enterprise. Specifically, they instituted a clear division of labour to maximise efficiency in the production process. While the film industry had made early efforts to standardise the production of single-reel films, leading to the emergence of the director and other expert practitioners, division of labour became essential with the growing size and narrative complexity of multi-reel films. A system developed geared towards even greater efficiency, and was especially refined by the producer Thomas Ince. It would be wrong to suggest that Ince gave birth to the studio system. He was instrumental, however, in developing a framework for the working procedures that would eventually take hold.

This focused centrally on a studio boss, a director and a continuity script. The last of these was a means of carefully planning and costing a film. As a means of reducing expense, scripts were increasingly shot out of sequence. This relied on a shooting script that broke the action down into a series of numbered shots and that could be reassembled by an editor after the filming was complete. Shooting scripts were carefully planned, not simply to establish continuity in the story but, just as significantly, to enable the producer to make calculations about the required footage of each scene, and to estimate the given cost of a film.

Shooting scripts enabled greater co-ordination and cost effectiveness within the filmmaking process. Typically, before a movie could be made, shooting scripts would be submitted to a studio boss for approval. Outlining the genre, characters, storyline and sequence of scenes, studio heads would consider the film and approve or reject it on the basis of a planned programme of movies, a roster of films that the studio would undertake over the course of a year. This would establish the basis for a 'factory' system of film production, systematically planned for and geared towards regular and consistent streams of profit.

Once a movie had been approved, a producer such as Ince could oversee the various practical elements of production. These would involve assigning buildings and commissioning writers to devise storylines, dialogue and intertitles, and would also require the work of set designers, scenic artists and fashion designers, responsible for staging, backdrops and costumes. While casting directors would find the actors, make-up artists would provide them with requisite glamour for the screen. Helped by cinematographers and other technical experts, the shooting process would be the overall responsibility of the director who would bring the various creative elements together.

This would see the rise of a number of powerful directors who would exercise an unusual degree of control over their productions and included figures such as D. W. Griffith and Cecil B. DeMille. Invited by Jesse Lasky to direct a film for his new production company, DeMille took charge of *The Squaw Man* (1914), one of the first feature-length movies to be filmed in Hollywood. Like Griffith, DeMille had an eye for innovation, able to experiment with new narrative techniques within the framework of a controlled production system.

The filming process itself was carried out either in purpose-built studios, or outdoors. Early studios had glass roofs and cloth-lined walls to permit the use of artificial light. However, this created problems in the production centres of New York and Chicago. Short hours of daylight in the winter, and severe weather conditions outside, threatened to disrupt the non-stop production of film. As the worldwide popularity of American movies grew in the 1910s, and demand increased, it was vital that operations were not hampered in any way.

As a result, film producers began to look for places with greater shooting potential in terms of both sunshine and variety of landscape. While Jacksonville in Florida became a destination for Selig and the Kalem Company in the late 1900s – trumpeting itself as the 'World's Winter Film Capital' – Southern California was more suited to the general needs of the industry. Year-round sunshine made studio filmmaking less prone to disruption but the close proximity of oceans, beaches, mountains, forests and deserts also supplied natural backdrops for outdoor shooting, especially useful for the popular western genre.

Film companies began to send production units to Southern California from 1908 to 1909. Los Angeles, in particular, became a centre of activity. Selig created a makeshift studio there in 1909 and Biograph set up temporary quarters in 1910. By 1911, Los Angeles had become the location home to Essanay, Lubin, Kalem, Nestor and the New York Motion Picture Company. At this time, Los Angeles was relatively small, with a population of 319,000. This would change as it became home to more and more film companies. With its hospitable climate and limitless possibilities for location shooting, production companies began to migrate to the Los Angeles area, buying property in the small suburb of Hollywood. While companies still had their headquarters in New York, studio facilities would develop in and around the vicinity west of Los Angeles. Although the American film business was not yet synonymous with the name of Hollywood, the move to Southern California set in place a key industry transition, providing a physical and symbolic home for what would become the studio system.

With Hollywood-based production delivering a continuous and reliable output of films, certain genres became renowned within national and inter-national markets. These would become integral to the programme of films scheduled by the major American production companies. Notable among these were slapstick comedies and Westerns.

American screen comedy was especially associated with the Keystone Comedy Studio, established in 1912 under Mack Sennett. This was the comedy division of the New York Motion Picture Company, and included a stock company of comic performers including Charlie Chaplin, Ben Turpin, Mabel Normand and Roscoe 'Fatty' Arbuckle. Sennett was familiar with French comedy and influenced by the innovative film techniques of D. W. Griffith. In shaping a distinctive comedy style, the Keystone Studio brought fast editing and breathless action to the screen. Keystone comedy played upon traditions of vaudeville and the circus, setting characters within everyday scenes drawn from life in modern America.

As production moved towards feature films, comedies functioned as one-reel shorts on theatrical programmes. Keystone pictures were frequently anarchic, captured in the destruction of material goods, the ridiculing of authority, and the breakneck chase sequences featuring the hopeless Keystone Kops. These films often made stars of their comic performers. Most significant was Charlie Chaplin who signed a one-year contract with Keystone in 1914 and immediately became a household name. Chaplin starred in a series of one-reel films at Keystone. He also starred in the first feature length comedy, *Tillie's Punctured Room* (1914). Featuring Chaplin as a con artist who talks Marie Dressler into stealing her father's savings and running off with him to the city, the film combined familiar depictions of dusty streets, clapboard houses, bedrooms and buggies with the trademark style of Chaplin's mime performance, both dexterous and impressively subtle. While making Chaplin into a star, his time at Keystone was short-lived; he soon turned away from fast-paced one- and two-reel films and moved towards feature films that bore the imprint of his self-styled creative independence.

Another significant genre to emerge in the 1910s was the epic western. This was associated with producer Thomas Ince and a studio called 101 Bison, another division of the New York Motion Picture Company. This genre was especially helped by the relocation of film production to Southern California. The magnificent landscapes of California gave the western a ready source of visual spectacle. Re-imagining the American West became a particular occupation of the veteran stage actor William S. Hart whose films set down many of the compositional traits of the classic western. This ranged from the long shot of the wagon train to the slow panning that would give due scale to the rugged scenery. With pretensions towards historical authenticity, Hart would help shape the cinematic western and the established formulas that would continue to instruct national mythology about America's frontier past, replete with its population of cowboys, outlaws and Indians.

Like slapstick comedy, the western would distinguish the output of the major Hollywood studios as they began to form. While an established studio system did not coalesce until later in the decade, the early 1910s were significant in refining the specific film style that would exist at its core. In aesthetic terms, this has become associated with the development of 'classical' norms. It has been argued by David Bordwell, Janet Staiger and Kristin Thompson, for example, that a system for efficiently mass-producing film gave rise in the 1910s to a 'group style' that became central to the aesthetic identity of Hollywood's product. The word 'classical' in this context describes certain rules of composition and aesthetic organisation that produce unity, balance and order within Hollywood film. In *The Classical Hollywood Cinema: Film Style and Mode of Production to 1960* (1985), Bordwell, Staiger and Thompson suggest that 'the principles which Hollywood claims as its own rely on notions of decorum, proportion, formal harmony, respect for tradition, mimesis, self-efffacing craftsmanship, and cool control of the perceiver's response – canons which critics in any medium usually call "classical."'

Put simply, classical norms put emphasis on narrative continuity and the coherent ordering of space. This linked filmmaking technique to a unified mode of storytelling. For example, directors and cinematographers were expected to match the position of actors across cuts so that shifts in framing would not be noticeable. Indeed, the continuity system included various editing techniques for joining shots in ways that developed narrative action while maintaining unbroken connections across time and space. While intercutting cut back and forth between different shots to create relations between characters and events, analytical editing created a frame within a single shot (such as a close-up) to establish narrative emphasis. Meanwhile, contiguity editing kept the direction of movement constant across contiguous shots. This introduced the 180-degree system, a principle whereby the camera stayed within a semicircle on one side of the action to ensure that screen direction was consistent. In all of these ways, complex relationships were established between shots to create an effect of seamlessness. These combined with other editing techniques that further developed characterisation. They included point-of-view shots that would reveal the object of a character's gaze with a specific cut known as an eyeline match, and shot/reverse-shots where the camera would cut between characters, creating, for example, the effect of conversation.

Classical norms were not fixed rules or structures, but set particular boundaries within which innovation could take place. In essence, classical film style rejected formal techniques that were purposely disruptive or jarring to the audience. While it is sometimes implied that classical norms emerged simultaneously with the studio system, it is important to note that the aesthetic principles of classical Hollywood cinema preceded the studio system. The development of film style in this sense (classical norms) did not emerge in the very same historical instant as the mode of production that gave it institutional shape (the studio system). Instead, the relation between the two would develop a gradual symbiosis, such that classical norms would become synonymous with the studio system as it emerged more fully after the First World War.

It is the overall structure of production organisation that concerns Janet Staiger in her essay, 'Mass-produced Photoplays: Economic and Signifying Practices in the First Years of Hollywood'. Addressing the question of 'how economic practices in the first years of Hollywood might be related to the development of representational systems', Staiger examines how production practices in the early 1910s influenced the way that films were developed and made. From the function of the continuity script to the cost factors that led to specific techniques of style, she examines the complex relationship between economic and aesthetic practices in the first years of Hollywood.

In methodological terms, Staiger's essay provides a bridge between economic and aesthetic film analysis, collapsing the boundaries that often set these positions apart. If economic film history situates the movie business within wider industrial frameworks, and aesthetic film history is concerned with the development of film as an artistic form, Staiger marries the two perspectives, showing how economic and representational systems emerge in light of each other. In seeking to describe how movies work, she concentrates on the organisational history of Hollywood's production practices. Staiger is concerned with how production tasks are divided, how technology is employed, how responsibility is delegated, and how estimations are made about what films should be made, and how they should look and sound.

Staiger's argument depends on a wide range of evidence. In establishing the economic practices of the early film industry, she draws upon business records and documents that outline the various means by which the major film companies began to organise themselves in industrial terms. This ranges from systems of accountancy in the film business, evident in reports issued by Price, Waterhouse & Company, to lists of brand names and stock issues detailed by trade publications such as *Photoplay* and *Reel Life*. These help connect the film industry to general economic histories of the period. In allying this kind of evidence to specific kinds of aesthetic practice, however, Staiger also turns to film catalogues, manuals and technical handbooks that set out procedures and conventions for writing photoplays. Bringing these different kinds of evidence together enables Staiger to analyse Hollywood's 'mode of production' in ways that relate, rather than separate, economic and signifying practices in its first years. Staiger's work also represents a mode of historical analysis that draws upon a random selection of films, rather than 'great works', to illustrate the basis of classical film style.

- What primary material does Staiger choose to emphasise in building her argument about standardisation and differentiation in the film industry?
- To what extent can Staiger's research help us understand whether or not consumer attention was drawn to the originality of the feature product in individual cases? How might you research this topic?
- In industrial terms, what significance do the following people have in the filmmaking process, past and present: (1) cinematographers; (2) costume designers; (3) sound technicians? What source material would you hope to find as a means of examining their function and working practices?

MASS-PRODUCED PHOTOPLAYS: ECONOMIC AND SIGNIFYING PRACTICES IN THE FIRST YEARS OF HOLLYWOOD

Janet Staiger

In a 1917 handbook for freelance writers of movies, Marguerite Bertsch writes, 'By the subjective we mean all that takes place within the mind or soul of a character, either in thought or feeling, influencing his future behavior.' She then describes two techniques: the double exposure in which both the character and the subjective thoughts are represented simultaneously in the image, and editing with dissolves in which the subjective material is presented sequentially in shots bracketed by the cues of dissolves. She continues: 'All subjective matter, such as a retrospection into the past, a looking forward into the future, or the hallucinations of a troubled mind, is possible to either, and so these two devices may be used one in place of the other.' Of course, Bertsch is disseminating and

Janet Staiger, *Wide Angle* 4(3), Summer 1981.

formalizing conventions we recognize, as did she, as part of the standard techniques of the Hollywood film of 1917.[1]

As an analyst of films, one area of research is how we explain historically particular representational systems. An apparent explanation of films at least is that the narrative moving pictures the United States film industry produced took theirs initially from representational systems already available in fiction, theater, pantomime, vaudeville, opera, from systems in painting, engraving, still photography, lantern and stereoptican shows, illustrated comic strips and so on. In other words, the industry took representational systems available from other extant products in the culture and innovated them where necessary to suit the moving pictures. The production of these objects constitutes a culture's signifying practices which include its ideologies of representation, its conventions, its aesthetics. We are familiar with the characterization of the representational system which Hollywood produced: a linear, 'closed' sequence of events with emphasis on individual character psychology as motivation for narrative action; the dominance of causal action over spatial and temporal continuity justifying the breaking down, the analyzing of space and time – but a continuity reconstituted through certain rules of linkage such as matches-on-action, frame cuts, establishing and re-establishing shots, systems of screen direction (the 180 degree rule, shot-reverse shot, eyeline and point-of-view constructions). We are familiar with its photographic aesthetics: valuing a 'three-dimensional,' 'stereoscopic' depth; clear, steady images in which the narrative event 'stands out' within the site of its occurrence; human bodies made up and lit for cultural representations of beauty, realism and typage as well as for narrative legibility. At any point of choice for this representational system other possibilities exist, and within the mode there are historical changes as well.[2]

Economic practices, the other part of this process, are also products of and producers of cultures and social institutions. These practices are the economic modes of production – the forces and relations of production. Clearly, signifying and economic practices are not separate. On the one hand, the creation of a product that signifies involves some mode of economic production, even if it is a single individual positioned in relation to a single object. On the other hand, any product of an industry (including the tools and technology produced to create the product) potentially has some signification which may be as basic as an expression of the function of the object. This object is for drinking. That one is for measuring the amount of reflected light. The difference between the two practices, really, is what part of the process one is emphasizing at the moment.

In order to make this more concrete, I want to consider how economic practices in the first years of Hollywood might be related to the development of its representational systems such as, for instance, Bertsch's statement of the equivalence of two methods to signify subjectivity. I shall concentrate on what became the dominant practices, not the options which might have been.

To study this, I am going to construct, first of all, a general description of the economic practices in the society contemporaneous with the initiation of the US film industry. In this description I am going to identify a tension in the economic practices between standardization and differentiation. Second, I am going to describe some of the economic practices of the film industry between 1907 and 1917 which repeat this general tension. Third, I will suggest how and where these economic practices had an effect on the representational systems.

The Contemporary Economic Practices

Economic practices in the United States shifted significantly during the nineteenth century. The introduction of a machine tool industry in the 1810s and 1820s permitted an industrial revolution which emphasized mass production through standardization and interchangeable parts.[3] These machines centralized the location and formalized the labor process into a factory mode of production. Companies formed to capitalize on inventions such as the telegraph and telephone, and massive capital investment in transportation systems, rapidly promoted national and international markets. Aided by state institutions in the form of laws and court decisions, a corporate business structure developed. An unanticipated effect of the fourteenth amendment was the court's decision to define business corporations as 'persons,' giving them due process of law.[4]

When the Standard Oil Trust was broken up in 1892, it re-incorporated as a holding company in New Jersey, a state which had in 1889 foreseen the advantages of creating a liberal incorporation law. The New Jersey law permitted corporations, like persons, to buy and hold stock in other companies, allowing combinations to develop and to capitalize 'without regard to the actual cost of existing plant[s].'[5] From 1896 to 1904, consolidation of firms occurred at an incredible rate, the high point of which was the incorporation of US Steel for over $1,000,000,000, while Moody's listed 318 other industrial combinations with more than 5300 plants and a combined capital of over $7,000,000,000. A thousand railroad lines were consolidated into six systems controlling over $10,000,000,000 in capital.[6] Supreme Court decisions made the Sherman Anti-Trust Act of 1890 almost irrelevant, except when applied to striking unions.[7] Big business produced increasing capital and goods with the United States rivalling Europe as an industrial giant.

With this came the business concept of efficiency as the means to economic success. Efficiency justified the division of labor into smaller and smaller units and the motions of the worker into more and more predetermined sequences of actions. General interest in labor conditions developed after 1900 in the United States due to attacks by labor organizations and muckrakers and by comparisons to the Europeans who adopted Taylorism before US businesses did. 'Scientific management' caught on in the early 1910s.[8]

Efficiency through economies of scale justified the creation of trusts and then holding companies and other legal business structures.[9] John D. Rockefeller sought an end to ' "idiotic, senseless destruction," "the wasteful conditions" of competition.'[10] Discussing in 1902 the reorganization and recapitalization of the railroads, M. G. Cunniff said that Huntington's and Morgan's idea of a 'community of interest' had brought the lines to 'the best condition they have ever known, with the cheapest freight rates, the best equipment, the fastest service, and the largest dividends in the world.'[11]

Efficiency justified the standardization of products. Trade associations which dated from the Civil War provided a means of sharing information, developing standard cost accounting systems and pooling patents.[12] 'Efficiency' spilled over into political and legal decisions. In 1901 Theodore Roosevelt considered 'handling the tariff problem through "scientific management," '[13] and court decisions on wage rates and working conditions for women were made on the basis of business efficiency.

If efficiency justified standardization, another process was simultaneously at work – differentiation of products by advertising. Although advertising is ancient as an economic practice, in the early 1800s in the United States most goods were sold generically. By the mid-1800s companies began advertising goods by name brands, and by the 1870s retailers spent money on local and national printed materials to the consumer and began outdoor display advertising. In 1870, 121 trademarks were registered with the US Patent Office, in 1906 more than 10,000 and by 1926 over 70,000. An early advertising agent set up business in 1841 in Philadelphia, soon expanding to Boston and New York. In 1899 Ayer's became a full-service ad agency, did national campaigns, conducted market surveys and created trade names. Advertising expenditures in 1904 were over $800 million and at 3.4 per cent of the gross national product, the same percentage level current today. In the 1890s as the corporations consolidated, they moved into vertically integrated structures, directly controlling their own retailing and associated advertising to consumers. By the late 1920s only one-third of US goods went through independent wholesalers; the other two-thirds were marketed directly or through corporation-owned outlets.

Thus, the film industry begins in a general industrial structure of a well-developed corporate capitalism which is positioned between the economic practice of standardization for efficient mass production and the economic practice of product differentiation.

The Economic Practices of the Film Industry

The people who entered the film industry had these contemporary examples as their standards for successful economic competition. The formation of a moving pictures patent pool at the end of 1908 followed the general pattern of consolidation of communities-of-interest to end 'vexatious and expensive litigations.'[14] In a brief prepared by the Patents Company for the 1912 investigation by the Department of Justice into their trust, the lawyers argued that without a combination of patents no business could be conducted. A series of lawsuits had determined three patents essential to the industry which were split between three different concerns and their licensees.

The only solution for the industry to continue was cross-licensing. Lawyers cited patent pool precedents in the farm machinery industry as justification for the formation of the company.[15] At the point of organization, all significant manufacturing and importing firms were included in the company.[16] The organising of the Patents Company seemed to indicate a stable business climate, and the individual firms, assured of regular unrestricted national and international sale of their products through the Patents Company, began to run off up to one hundred copies of each negative rather than the ten to twelve previously struck. The increased income provided capital for expanding their operations.

Unfortunately for the company, however, while patents seek a monopoly of control over an invention, publication of patent information upon application also provides knowledge for other inventors.[17] Even if the Patents Company had legal rights, the cameras and projectors were easily manufactured by others. Furthermore, the growth of the exhibition sector of the industry seemed to suggest high profits – warranting a calculated risk of being caught for patent infringement. With low barriers to entry and high profits to tempt new competitors, it is not surprising that in the next twelve months Powers Picture Plays, the Independent Motion Picture Company, the New York Motion Picture Company, Thanhouser, Rex and other films incorporated.[18]

Meanwhile, the manufacturing firms of the Patents Company followed general economic practices of vertically integrating into distributing and retailing by establishing the General Film Company in April 1910. The independents followed suit and consolidated at the distribution level.[19] In 1912 Livingston and Co., members of the New York Stock Exchange, organised the public financing of the distributing firm of Mutual Film, and $1,700,000 common stock and $800,000 cumulative preferred at 7 per cent were authorised for sale. Price, Waterhouse in 1916 issued a fifty-four-page manual on how standard accounting for the film industry should be done.[20]

The mode of production was similarly sophisticated by 1916. Once the industry seemed potentially capable of regular supply of films with a widespread demand in the exhibition sector, mass production began. Multiple shooting units for each company were created to increase the number of releases per company, thus increasing profit potentials. The 'logic' of this economic practice was described in 1911:

> When an industry has reached such a magnitude that many people are employed in its work . . . some employees will develop greater ability in some lines than in others, and the lines of activity become so divergent that they are best cared for separately. As in any manufacturing industry,

the manufacture of motion-picture films for exhibition in a modern factory has its division of labor, and a film picture is the joint product of the various departments and specialists who in turn take it and perfect it with their skills.[21]

This divided labor split into a 'line-and-staff' structure with administrators in New York or Chicago handling general operations and distributing and advertising the films, producers and studio managers administering the nationally distributed studio and on-location production units, departments handling set construction, costuming, properties, special effects, casting, developing negatives and editing, and units headed by directors doing the shooting. In late 1916, an 'efficiency system' in one studio had a four-page manual given to new employees which listed rules, regulations and the duties of every job position. Given a number within the system, the employee entered into a production schedule already organized.[22]

The pattern for the product was the scenario produced by the director and writers.[23] By 1913, detailed continuity scripts were regularly produced by scenario departments. These departments were split into two major functional operations: the writing of original screenplays for the firm and the transference of original plots from freelancers and increasingly from plays, novels and short stories. Trade papers announced as early as 1909 that manufacturers were accepting freelance contributions of stories. In a 1909 article entitled 'Motion-picture play writing as an art' (three months after the new copyright law went into effect and following the court ruling that Kalem's film *Ben-Hur* infringed on copyright protection), the Edison company announced the filming of Mark Twain's 'The prince and the pauper' and the hiring of famous writers to produce scenarios. By 1911 trade papers were regularly publishing articles such as 'Outline of how to write a photoplay,' and books contained sample scenarios.[24]

Producing standard scripts had at least two functions: (1) saving costs and (2) controlling quality. It is easy to see how preplanning the scenes saves costs. Since labor was paid by time not unit of production, all employees needed to be used efficiently. Furthermore, detailed scripts permitted initial estimates of the cost of the film and allowed prior trimming if the film was likely to go over budget.

The second function, quality control, relates to two events simultaneous with the development of this mode of production. Between 1910 and 1915, multiple-reel films increased in number. At the same time, Frank Woods of the *New York Dramatic Mirror* and other writers began reviewing films and responding to patrons' questions and reactions in the general and trade papers. This formalised network of interaction began a dissemination of rules and categories of conspicuous skill and quality in the photoplay.

A study of some of these conceptions of quality and skill should suggest how certain representational systems held in esteem influenced economic practices. (Again, this is a two-sided process.) As examples, two reviews of Woods in

March 1911 should indicate an ideological reason for the development of the continuity script:

> *His Daughter* (Biograph, February 23) . . . the old father's fall was not convincing, and the girl's intention to leave the town was told only by the subtitle, as she ran out bareheaded and with no traveling equipment. There was also a technical error in the management of the scenes, exits from the interiors are to the right, but the immediate entrances to the exteriors are also from the right.[25]

> Attention has been called frequently in *Mirror* film reviews to apparent errors of direction or management as to exits and entrances in motion-picture productions . . . A player will be seen leaving a room or locality in a certain direction, and in the very next connecting scene, a sixteenth of a second later, he will enter in exactly the opposite direction. Now it may be argued quite logically that this need not necessarily be inartistic because the spectator himself may be assumed to [have] changed his point of view, but . . . the spectator will not look at it that way. Any one who has watched pictures knows how often his sense of reality has been shocked by this very thing.[26]

What the continuity script provides is a precheck of the quality of spatial, temporal and causal continuity and *vraisemblance*. This became more problematic as the length of the films developed and as the aesthetics refined to include frame cuts, matches-on-action, inserts, cut-backs, flashes, mixing of interior and exterior sets and narrative 'punch.'

That the industry paid attention to reviews and critics was evident in Woods's column of 22 March 1911 in which he rather gleefully recounts an incident of a film company arguing for half an hour, citing Woods as an authority, whether or not the son in a photoplay should turn toward the camera as he said farewell to his mother.[27] The solution was that the turn was deemed realistic because of spatial positions, but that the son should avoid playing to the camera, an acting practice Woods and others considered unnatural.

The dispersal of these standards of quality and of format was supplemented by the appearance of trade associations in the film industry. In July 1908 a craft union of projectionists formed, in 1911 New York motion-picture exhibitors incorporated, in 1913 cinematographers in New York formed the Cinema Camera Club, in 1914 the Photoplay Authors' League was established and in 1916 the Society of Motion Picture Engineers formed with the 'avowed purpose "the advancement in the theory and practice of motion-picture engineering and the allied arts and sciences, the standardization of the mechanism and practices employed therein and the dissemination of scientific knowledge by publication." '[28]

Furthermore, and this is something I want to stress, the quality control function was placed legally by the courts in the hands of the company. Two law suits in 1917 are typical of this. Charlie Chaplin sued Essanay for stretching a two-reeler of his into a four-reeler after he left. His suit was denied because, among other considerations, the photoplay was declared Essanay's property. In a second case, the director Herbert Brenon unsuccessfully contested Fox's re-editing of *A Daughter of the Gods*.[29]

If these practices provided efficient, standardized mass production of photoplays, simultaneous with them came the need to differentiate the product – to appeal to the exhibitors to order one firm's films rather than another's. It should be pointed out that direct, nationwide, organised advertising to the consumer by the producing and distributing companies did not begin until 1915.[30] At first, exhibitors chose their own films from the distributors who advertised to them, and the exhibitors created their own advertising to attract customers; newspapers, billboards and lobby displays. With the formation of the Patents Company, some aids were offered to the exhibitors. In November 1909 the ABC Company of Cleveland was delegated as official supplier of posters: 'These posters are not "fakes," made up from dead stock previously printed for some melodramatic production, but *real pictorial posters made from actual photographs of scenes in the pictures they advertise*.'[31] At the same time in Edison's catalog, 'stars' (its term) and stock players were being introduced to the exhibitors.[32] (These stars were established theatrical stars; the film companies began to develop their own about a year later.[33]) From this period on, the companies supplied cuts for newspapers and information about the actors and actresses to exhibitors so that they, in turn, could 'boom' the films.

The rise of multiple-reel films coincides with this shift in attack to more controlled advertising of individual films. What was special about each film was specified to the consumer. The concept of a *feature* film goes back at least to this 1904 advice to exhibitors by Kleine Optical Company:

> The exhibitor who purchases a small quantity of films, say from 300 to 500 feet, is necessarily compelled to confine himself to short subjects. But if the purchase is 1000 feet, we advise one feature film of 400 to 500 feet, the balance from 50 to 100 feet each; if 2000 feet, there should be at least one long feature film, such as *The Great Train Robbery*, 740 feet, or *Christopher Columbus*, 850 feet. These long films admit of special advertising, that is to say, special emphasis on one subject, which is more effective than equal emphasis on a number of shorter films. The public has been educated to appreciate these long films which tell an interesting story, and need few words of explanation.[34]

In October 1909 Pathé released *The Drink* in two parts over two days. Quickly exhibitors shifted from sequential days to running the multiple reels on one day and advertising something 'extra and of more importance than the ordinary single reels.'[35] Since business was thriving, more money could be expended on these 'de luxe' films, which went together with better advertising and timing release dates to take advantage of the advertising, which permitted higher admission prices and which could pay the costs of theatrical stars and production values. As a result, the film had a longer exhibition life, providing more income to cover the geometrical increases in cost.[36] In April 1914, a year before the release of *The Birth of a Nation*, one-fifth of New York City's theaters were running multiple-reel features, and people were paying $1.00 on Broadway to see a film that cost $50,0000 to produce.[37] In 1915 Paramount, seeking higher rental rates for a feature film, decided to assist directly the exhibitors in their promotion, reasoning that to get the higher rentals they would need to increase receipts. Advised by an advertising agency to direct ads to the patrons, Paramount's New Department of Exploitation began their initial national advertising with primary demand ads – ones that emphasized the institution of movie-theater-going.[38]

In *Painting and Experience in Fifteenth Century Italy*, Michael Baxandall talks about the difficulties of determing what a patron of the arts might see in an individual work. To locate the 'period eye,' as he calls it, he examines written contracts between painters and patrons and notes that during the first part of the 1400s the quality of the materials to be used was carefully specified. By the second half of the century, what parts of the work the master artist was to paint became important. This leads Baxandall to the conclusion that cultivated people expected to be able to perceive the *conspicuous skill* of the artist.[39] These perceptible skills, of course, were formally taught by rules and categories of discussion within the culture.

What Baxandall is suggesting, I think, is generalizable to the US film industry. An historian can construct where *value* in the product lies as a means, in part, of determining the relationships between economic and signifying practices. In this mode of production, advertising is an economic practice directing consumers to the apparent areas of exchange-value in the product. In the culture in this time, novelty, originality and uniqueness are areas of heavy advertising stress.[40] Additional ones are conspicuous display of certain 'unique' personalities, specific popular genres, 'realism' and expensive means of production (for instance, spectacles in which massive sets and hundreds of people are involved).

These are parts of the catalog and review descriptions of three early films:

> *Life of an American Fireman* (Edison, 1903, Edwin S. Porter): It will be difficult for the exhibitor to conceive the amount of work involved and the number of rehearsals necessary to turn out a film of this kind. We were compelled to enlist the services of the fire departments of four different cities . . . and about 300 firemen appear in the various scenes of this film.[41]

> *The Great Train Robbery* (Edison, 1903, Edwin S. Porter): It has been posed and acted in faithful duplication of the genuine 'Hold Ups' made famous by various outlaw bands in the far West, and only recently the East has been shocked by several crimes of the frontier order, which fact will increase the popular interest in this great *Headline Attraction*.[42]

Il Trovatore (Pathé, 1911): Pathé has an 'innovation': The novelty lies in the special music that goes with the picture. The score of the opera has been carefully arranged by a competent musician so that it times exactly with the dramatic action of the film.[43]

We have, then, in the first years of Hollywood, economic practices with a tension: simplify, standardize and consolidate for efficiency and mass production but differentiate, direct the consumers attention to the originality and production values of the feature product.

Economic Practices and Filmic Representational Systems

In the US film industry, co-extensive with its history of economic practices is a complex history of signifying practices – ideologies, aesthetics, conventions. What might be economically cheap might simultaneously 'violate' an aesthetic of beauty or composition or a convention of *vraisemblance* or continuity or counter ideologies of value and representation. I have suggested a tension between the economic practices of standardization and differentiation. Likewise, I theorise, in general, two other tensions within the processes. First, that of economic practices versus signifying practices: the tension of low-cost – an economic goal for profit maximization – versus high-cost-ideologies of value in originality, spectacles, displays of labor and conspicuous skills such as technological tours de force. The other major tension is within the signifying practices themselves: a tension between codes of *vraisemblance*, what seems 'ordinary life,' and codes of novelty, variation, 'art,' beauty, the non-ordinary. One can begin to postulate the possibilities had the economic or signifying practices been different, had, for instance, on the broader scale, *repetition* rather than originality been valued.

This prevents a simplistic assertion that such and such economic practice determined such and such signifying practice and makes the historical representation more complex, mediated and non-linear. Locating single causes also becomes impossible. This means that in an individual instance, specific historical inquiry will be necessary to understand the impact of the particular practices operating at that time and place on the formation of specific films or groups of films. But this model likewise permits that precision without lapsing into a reflectionism.

In this concluding section, I am merely going to suggest areas in which economic practices of the period pressured the construction of certain signifying practices. I have already indicated how the mode of production, the trade media and trade associations worked toward standardizing the representational systems and how advertising and reviews promoted perception of specifiable values in the product. Now I will suggest some further sites of influence.

Cost factors promoted the reuse of sets and costumes, thus stimulating serials, genres and series. Serials like the multiple-reel films were usually shot at one time so that locations and sets were used only once even though the episodes might extend for weeks in release.[44] Price, Waterhouse, in their 1916 memorandum, advise accountants to charge all scenery and costume costs to the original film since reuse was unpredictable but would thereafter be free any time such reuse could be managed.[45] Companies often called for scenarios that would use established sets. Sometimes an extensive initial investment channeled subsequent films. William Selig's zoo, purchased in 1908 for an African safari film, was used for a series of animal films. Bison's hiring of the Miller Brothers 101 Ranch Wild West Show resulted in several years of westerns and the Civil War films using large casts.[46] Connected to this, a 1913 manual advises freelance writers:

> Unity of place is also of economic importance for the production and will permit the use of the same settings for many scenes. In this way the producer feels justified in spending more money upon the settings themselves. He is more or less limited by the owner of the motion-picture company as to the outlay for each picture – and the result is more elaborate and artistic stage effects.[47]

The writer also advises creating few characters for the plot:

> At the same time more attention could be given by the director to the production; more time taken, because less wasted on supernumeraries, and more money to spend on settings and costumes and additional film, because of the reduced cost of salaries.[48]

Cost factors promoted a limited number of retakes. Price, Waterhouse suggest that there were several ways to distribute overhead costs, but the preferred method was to divide them by the number of exposed feet of negative film on the assumption that 'managers who take many feet of discarded negative are careless, wasteful, and expensive . . .'[49] Rehearsals of actors were considered cheap compared to the costs of all laborers, electricity and film stock involved in actual shooting time. Such an economic practice might also weigh against long takes which are more susceptible to error as the length of the take or its complexity increases.[50]

A more tenuous connection, but one that occasionally surfaces, is that cost factors related to techniques of style. A handbook author writes that dissolves are usually used instead of double exposures to indicate a character's thoughts because the former are cheaper, less complicated and less time consuming. The practice of having the characters 'discovered' in the scene rather than using entrances is cited as saving thirty to forty feet of film. The technique of cutbacks (the period term for cross cutting) can be used to abbreviate the length of the action and save film footage by cutting away to parallel action and then cutting back with the former action completed.[51] Obviously, there are other reasons for the cut-back: it is a means to avoid censorable material, an explicit aesthetics of variation of shots is functioning in the period and it provides a simpler, cheaper technique than a split screen or an unusual set for representing parallel action – not to mention the narrative effects of suspense and complexity which constitute a process for the subject.

Expenditures of funds on spectacles and trick work are often balanced against the effect they produce. Writers of advice to freelancers continually caution against writing photoplays that require wrecking trains, burning mansions and building extravagant sets. John Emerson and Anita Loos go so far as to advise that although night scenes can be done with 'sunlight arcs, mercury lights and spotlights,' the cost of each is $2500, and they are hard to transport. 'It is well,' they write, 'to keep your characters indoors by night.'[52]

On the other hand, the expenditures might be justified. In describing the production technology, one writer in 1913 points out that the camera is heavy and mounted on a 'massive tripod.' Despite this, it is shifted to difficult set ups:

> The body of the camera, without the tripod, may be placed upon the overhead beams in a studio in order to get some novel scenic effect below; or a special platform may be built for the camera and operator, when the producer is determined to get a scene on the side of a cliff.[53]

The reason? '. . . [A]n unusually strong story that justifies the special effort . . .' Innovation of such effects seems motivated by this ideology of value in originality supported by the economic and signifying practices. It explains the occurrence *within the system itself of optional signifying practices* without resorting to a model of these options deconstructing the system.[54] For example, Fred Balshofer describes the decision to use a complicated camera movement rather than analytical editing in a 1915 film:

> Besides being an outstanding picture, *The Second in Command* contained a technical innovation . . . While going over the script for our first picture, it seemed to us that we would have to come up with something new in production to match the class of our new star, [Francis X.] Bushman. We decided to plan the action of some scenes to make it possible to follow the actors, especially Bushman, and to move to a close-up without making a cut. We certainly weren't thinking of anything as elaborate as we wound up with. We drew a rough sketch of a platform large enough to set the tripod on with the camera and cameraman that could be moved on four wheels. When it was constructed, we found we would have to enlarge it to accommodate a second person. As the platform was pushed forward, it became difficult for Adler to crank the camera, watch the actors to judge distance as the platform moved, and to follow the focus all at the same time. And so it went. We were continually taking the rolling platform in to our small carpenter shop and having it altered to meet our needs as they became more and more complex . . .
>
> Making a film this way took more time but after looking at the rushes, we thought it worthwhile. Besides, it added that something extra to the production of the picture.[55]

Of course this sort of 'first-itis' was useful to the individual companies in promoting a studio style and identity for brand-name advertising. The reviewers and trade papers contributed to a perpetuation of searching for novelties and innovations. One reviewer in 1912 writes:

> Biograph's influence on picture production has been important. It was the first company – at least in America – to introduce heroic figures in its pictures. It was the first in America to present acting of the restrained artistic type, and the first to produce quiet drama and pure comedy. It was the first to attempt fading light effects. It was the first to employ alternating flashes of simultaneous action in working up suspense.[56]

Triangle initiated the use of art titles as an 'experiment' in 1916 which 'served to distinguish still further the highly individual character of the Ince plays,'[57] and in an article entitled 'Very latest thing in photoplay subtitles,' Triangle explain that their Photographic and Art Department head had 'set to work to develop the subtitle to a maximum of efficiency.'[58]

Something successful was widely and rapidly imitated by the industry. Classical Hollywood films are not only typified by genres and series but by cycles. This was made possible by short-term production plans, often made less than a year in advance even in the 1930s and 1940s for program features. This was partially due to the standardization which made rapid production possible. In 1913, critics were complaining that the 'time is ripe for another shift,' that everything is a 'repetition' of what had come before.[59] The search for originality leads to some amusing results. Emerson and Loos say that 'the very latest thing' in 1920 is the 'pictorial pun. For example, in "A virtuous vamp," a leading character says to the flirtatious heroine: "Woman, you make me see red." The scene is instantly tinted red.'[60] Emerson and Loos think this 'novelty' will last a couple months. Or the case cited in 1913:

> Death is seldom dramatic. It is even capable of being turned to farce if overdone. One of the funniest stories that was ever screened ended with the suicide of the sole remaining member of the cast. All the others had been murdered. It was meant by producer and author alike to be tremendously sensational, but there is but a short step from the ultrasensational to the travesty of sensation.[61]

Economic practices affected the signifying practices in another way. To some writers they even became part of the aesthetic rationales for the signifying practices. Victor Freeburg in the 1923 book *Pictorial Beauty on the Screen* incorporates efficiency into his theory of aesthetics: 'The pictorial beauty discussed in this book is really a kind of pictorial efficiency, and therefore must have practical economic value.' 'A practical proof is dramatic utility. The motions of a photoplay are in the service of the story. They should perform that work well without waste of time and energy.' 'One might say that the artistic efficiency of a motion-picture may be partly tested in the same way as the practical value of a machine. In either case motions are no good unless they help to perform some work.'[62]

In my initial example, Bertsch's equation of the two procedures for representing subjectivity may have been a bit naive. Technically and economically, a double exposure provided more production complexity than editing with dissolves. By 1917 the perceptible value of the *novelty* of either device may have made them equivalent in signifying subjectivity with the double exposure used for production value and editing with dissolves used when the subjective sequence was extensive or not worth the additional cost. (There are also different implications about the representation of space and subject.) In either case, however, they are incorporated into a general representational mode, the classical Hollywood film. To determine the value and function of any individual practice requires an extensive construction of the history of *both* economic and signifying practices within the culture in order to provide satisfactory production of knowledge about signification by subjects.

NOTES

1. Marguerite Bertsch, *How to Write for Moving Pictures: A Manual of Instruction and Information* (New York: George H. Doran Company, 1917), pp. 97 and 99.
2. In using the term signifying practices, I want to emphasise that the representational systems produced have meaning in the act of the subject's constitution of the signifying object. Assumed, then, are issues of subjectivity.
3. This section relies heavily on three general economic histories: Harry N. Scheiber, Harold G. Vatter and Harold Underwood Faulkner, *American Economic History*, 9th edn (New York: Harper & Row, 1976); Alex Groner, *The American Heritage History of American Business and Industry* (New York: American Heritage, 1972); John Chamberlain, *The Enterprising Americans: A Business History of the United States*, rev. edn (New York: Harper & Row, 1974).
4. On the shift from the formation of corporations for public interests to those for private profit, see Groner, *The American Heritage History*, pp. 60 and 91.
5. Chamberlain, *The Enterprising Americans*, p. 174, and see US Industrial Commission, *Preliminary Report on Trusts and Industrial Combinations . . .* 56th Cong., 1st Sess., House Document no. 476, Part 1 (Washington, DC: Government Printing Office, 1900), pp. 9–13, 16–20, 32–4 rpt. in *American Economic Development since 1860*, ed. William Greenleaf (New York: Harper & Row, 1968), pp. 216–33.
6. The government's investigation in 1900 produced a detailed description and explanation of these mergers; see US Industrial Commission, *Preliminary Report*, pp. 216–33.
7. Groner, *American Heritage History*, pp. 198–9; *Great Issues in American History*, ed. Richard Hofstadter (New York: Alfred A. Knopf and Random House, 1958), pp. 121–2, 125.
8. On the history of scientific management in the US see Don D. Lescohier, 'Working conditions,' in *History of Labor in the United States*, ed. John R. Commons, vol. III (1935; rpt. edn New York: Augustus M. Kelley, 1966), pp. 304–15.
9. Magnus W. Alexander, *The Economic Evolution of the United States: Its Background and Significance* (New York: National Industrial Conference Board, 1929), p. 35.
10. John D. Rockefeller cited in Chamberlain, *The Enterprising Americans*, p. 150.
11. 'Increasing railroad consolidation,' *World's Work*, 3 (February 1902), 1775–1780, rpt. in *American Economic Development since 1860*, pp. 106–15. Not everyone

agreed with this assessment of holding companies; see Richard Hofstadter, *The Age of Reform* (New York: Vintage Books, 1955), p. 232, and William J. Ghent, *Our Benevolent Feudalism* (New York: Macmillan, 1902).

12. Alexander, *The Economic Evolution of the United States*, pp. 34–8; Monte Calvert, *The Mechanical Engineer in America, 1830–1910* (Baltimore: The Johns Hopkins University Press, 1967), p. 172; Thomas C. Cochran and William Miller, *The Age of Enterprise*, rev. edn (New York: Harper & Bros, 1961), p. 243; Ray M. Hudson, 'Organized effort in simplification,' *The Annals* (of the American Academy of Political and Social Science), 87 (May 1928), pp. 1–8; and Frank L. Eidmann, *Economic Control of Engineering and Manufacturing* (New York: McGraw-Hill, 1931), pp. 261–8.

13. William Appleton Williams, *The Contours of American History* (1961; rpt. edn, New York: Franklin Watts, 1973), pp. 405–6.

14. M. B. Phillipp and Francis T. Homer for the Motion Picture Patents Co., 'Memorandum for the Motion Picture Patents Company and the General Film Company concerning the investigation of their business by the Department of Justice,' TS, 18 May 1912 (Museum of Modern Art), p. 17.

15. Phillipp and Homer, 'Memorandum,' pp. 1–17.

16. Ralph Cassady Jr., 'Monopoly in motion picture production and distribution: 1908–1915,' *Southern California Law Review*, vol. 32, no. 4 (Summer 1959), pp. 328–9, 335, 346.

17. Jeanne Thomas Allen [untitled paper], The cinematic apparatus: technology as historical and ideological form, Conference at the Centre for Twentieth Century Studies, University of Wisconsin-Milwaukee, 22–24 February 1978. In the main argument of the essay Allen points out how the general business practice of stand-ardisation of technology relates to the history of the invention of the motion picture machines.

18. Robert C. Allen, 'Motion picture exhibitions in Manhattan 1906–1912: beyond the nickelodeon,' *Cinema Journal*, vol. 18, no. 2 (Spring 1979), p. 11.

19. Phillipp and Homer, 'Memorandum,' pp. 42–6; H. E. Aitken, *Reel Life*, vol. 3, no. 26 (14 April 1914), pp. 17–18; 'C. J. Hire's career,' *Reel Life*, vol. 3, no. 16 (3 January 1914), p. 3; 'Spectator,' ' "Spectator's" Comments,' *New York Dramatic Mirror* [hereafter *NYDM*], vol. 65, no. 1691 (17 May 1911), p. 28; for a list of 1911 manufacturers, brand names and distribution groups, see David Sherrill Hulfish, *Cyclopedia of Motion-Picture Work*, vol. I (Chicago: American School of Correspondence, 1911), pp. 277–82.

20. 'Financing the motion picture Wall Street's latest move,' *Reel Life*, vol. 3, no. 22 (14 February 1914), p. 34. Other firms were organised as stock companies but without public sale; for details of early stock issues see Paul H. Davis, 'Investing in the movies [part 7],' *Photoplay*, vol. 9, no. 3 (February 1916), pp. 71–3. His series of eleven articles runs from August 1915 through August 1916. Price, Waterhouse & Company, *Memorandum on Moving Picture Accounts* (New York: Price, Waterhouse & Company, 1916).

21. Hulfish, *Cyclopedia*, vol. II, p. 76.

22. 'The higher efficiency,' *Cinema News*, vol. 1, no. 1 (15 December 1916), p. 6.

23. For a description of the development in one company of the mode of production using the producer as quality controller and the continuity script as the pattern, see Janet Staiger, 'Dividing labor for production control: Thomas Ince and the rise of the studio system,' *Cinema Journal*, vol. 18, no. 2 (Spring 1979), pp. 16–25. The standard script format is detailed there.

24. 'Motion picture play writing as an art,' *The Edison Kinetogram*, vol. 1, no. 3 (1 September 1909), p. 12; Archer McMackin, 'How moving picture plays are written,' *The Nickelodeon*, vol. 2, no. 6 (December 1909), pp. 171–3; Everett McNeil, 'Outline of how to write a photoplay,' *Moving Picture World*, vol. 9, no. 1 (15 July 1911), p. 27; Hulfish, *Cyclopedia*, vol. II, pp. 78–90.

25. 'Reviews of licensed films,' *NYDM*, vol. 65, no. 1680 (1 March 1911), p. 31.
26. 'Spectator,' "Spectator's" comments,' *NYDM* vol. 65, no. 1681 (8 March 1911), p. 29.
27. 'Spectator,' "Spectator's" comments,' *NYDM*, vol. 65, no. 1683 (22 March 1911), p. 28. Also see 'Significant praise for "Mirror,"' *NYDM*, vol. 65, no. 1674 (18 January 1911), p. 34. Woods is undoubtedly 'biased,' but Epes Winthrop Sargent of *Moving Picture World*, William Lord Wright of *Motion Picture News* and other contemporaries continually acknowledge his (as well as their own) influence on the 'art' of the photoplay.
28. Phil Whitman, 'Western correspondent,' *Motion Picture News*, vol. 5, no. 3 (20 January 1912), p. 35; 'Exhibitors incorporate, *NYDM*, vol. 66, no. 1718 (22 November 1911) p. 25; Lewis W. Physioc, 'The history of the Cinema Camera Club,' *Cinema News*, vol. 1, no. 5 (15 February 1917), pp. 5–6; 'Woods Heads Authors' League,' *NYDM*, vol. 70, no. 1840 (25 March 1914), p. 31; Society of Motion Picture Engineers, *The Society of Motion Picture Engineers* (New York: Society of Motion Picture Engineers, 1930), p. iii.
29. Louis D. Frohlich and Charles Schwartz, *The Law of Motion Pictures including the Law of the Theatre* (New York: Baker, Voorhis, & Co., 1918), pp. 169–71; Anthony Slide, *Early American Cinema* (New York: A. S. Barnes & Co., 1970), pp. 92–5.
30. For a general history see John Francis Barry and Epes W. Sargent, *Building Theatre Patronage: Management and Merchandising* (New York: Chalmers, 1927), pp. 15–27.
31. 'Advertising the pictures,' *The Edison Kinetogram*, vol. 1, no. 7 (1 November 1909), p. 14. (Their italics.)
32. 'The Edison Stock Company,' *The Edison Kinetogram*, vol. 1, no. 4 (15 September 1909), p. 13; 'Our stock company,' *The Edison Kinetogram*, vol. 1, no. 5 (1 October 1909), p. 13; 'Our lobby display frames,' *The Edison Kinetogram*, vol. 1, no. 9 (1 June 1910), p. 2.
33. Anthony Slide, 'The evolution of the film star,' *Films in Review*, no. 25 (December 1974), pp. 591–4.
34. 'About moving picture films,' *Complete Illustrated Catalog* (October 1904) pp. 30–1. rpt. in George C. Pratt, *Spellbound in Darkness: A History of the Silent Film*, rev. edn (Greenwich: New York Graphic Society, 1973), pp. 36–7.
35. 'Spectator,' "Spectator's" comments,' *NYDM*, vol. 65, no. 1676 (1 February 1911), p. 29.
36. 'This list does not mean to suggest any causality or priority of factors. It notes only a conjunction that worked together to promote multiple-reel films.
37. Most of these films were two- and three-reelers, but a shift in exhibition practices was occurring, 'The listener chatters,' *Reel Life*, vol. 4, no. 3 (4 April 1924), p. 6.
38. Barry and Sargent, *Building Theatre Patronage*, pp. 19–21; Howard Thompson Lewis, *Cases on the Motion Picture Industry* (New York: McGraw-Hill, 1930), pp. 435–4.
39. Michael Baxandall, *Painting and Experience in Fifteenth Century Italy: A Printer in the Social History of Pictorial Style* (Oxford: Clarendon Press, 1972), pp. 14–39.
40. Leonard B. Meyer in *Music, The Arts, and Ideas: Patterns and Predictions in Twentieth-Century Culture* (Chicago: University of Chicago Press, 1967) also suggests that novelty as a value is a cultural ideological system for the West from about 1500 to now (pp. 89–133). He does not, however, tie this into the economic supports which perpetuate an appearance of novelty, assuming instead that a shift in our conception of authorship will dilute the force of 'novelty' as a value.
41. *Edison Films*, supplement no. 168 (Orange, New Jersey: Edison Manufacturing Company, February 1903), pp. 2–3, rpt. in Pratt, *Spellbound in Darkness*, pp. 29–30.
42. *Edison Films*, supplement no. 200 (January 1904), pp. 5–7, rpt. in Pratt, *Spellbound in Darkness*, pp. 34–6.

43. 'Spectator, "Spectator's" comments,' *NYDM*, vol. 65, no. 1672 (4 January 1911), p. 8.
44. Epes Winthrop Sargent, *The Technique of the Photoplay*, 2nd edn (New York: Moving Picture World, 1913), p. 123.
45. Price, Waterhouse, *Memorandum*, pp. 11–12.
46. Slide, *Early American Cinema*, p. 23; 'Bison gets 101 ranch,' *NYDM*, vol. 66, no. 1720 (6 December 1911), p. 29; 'Bison Company gets 101 ranch,' *Moving Picture World*, vol. 10, no. 10 (9 December 1911), p. 810; William Lord Wright, *Photoplay Writing* (New York: Falk, 1922), pp. 105–8.
47. Eustace Hale Ball, *The Art of the Photoplay* (New York: Veritas, 1913), p. 50.
48. Ball, *The Art of the Photoplay*, p. 43; also see for example James Irving, *The Irving System* (Auburn, New York: Authors' Press, 1919), p. 159.
49. Price, Waterhouse, *Memorandum*, p. 12–15.
50. See for instance Balshofer's description below of the choice of a long take rather than analytical editing in *The Second in Command*. Another reason may be the inability of the studio to have as many final cut options available with a long take style.
51. The problem of footage length was more serious when exhibition practices limited the narrative to one, two, or three reels. Catherine Carr, *The Art of Photoplay Writing* (New York: Hannis Jordan, 1914), pp. 41–3; Ball, *The Art of the Photoplay*, pp. 52–3; Epes Winthrop Sargent, 'The photoplaywright,' *Moving Picture World*, vol. 23, no. 12 (20 March 1915), p. 1757; Irving, *The Irving System*, p. 179.
52. Sargent, *The Technique of the Photoplay*, p. 117; J. Berg Esenwein and Arthur Leeds, *Writing the Photoplay* (Springfield: Home Correspondence School, 1913), pp. 222–4; Louella O. Parsons, *How to Write for the Movies*, rev. edn (Chicago: A. C. McClurg, 1917), p. 46; John Emerson and Anita Loos, *How to Write Photoplays* (1920 rpt., Philadelphia: George W. Jacobs, 1923), p. 55.
53. Esenwein and Leeds, *Writing the Photoplay*, p. 206.
54. After all, for example, a long take rather than editing does not in itself challenge the general Hollywood classical mode. See its classical function in Balshofer's description. Nor does analytical editing always subordinate itself to a causal chain. Without continuity links, it may function in other ways; see the obvious examples of Eisenstein and Godard.
55. Fred F. Balshofer and Arthur C. Miller, *One Reel a Week* (Berkeley: University of California Press, 1967), pp. 117–18.
56. 'A blot in the "Scutcheon-Biograph,"' *NYDM*, vol. 67, no. 1728 (31 January 1912), p. 56.
57. 'The wonderful year in three corners of Triangle film,' *The Triangle*, vol. 3, no. 3 (4 November 1916), p. 5.
58. 'Very latest thing in photoplay subtitles,' *The Triangle*, vol. 3, no. 7 (9 December 1916), p. 1.
59. 'William Lord Wright's page,' *Motion Picture News*, vol. 7, no. 16 (19 April 1913), pp. 13–14.
60. Emerson and Loos, *How to Write a Photoplay*, p. 104.
61. Sargent, *The Technique of the Photoplay*, p. 104.
62. Victor Oscar Freeburg, *Pictorial Beauty on the Screen* (1923, rpt., New York: Arno Press and *The New York Times*, 1970), pp. 10, 96 and 97.

5

THE AGE OF THE DREAM PALACE AND THE RISE OF THE STAR SYSTEM

By the end of the First World War, the cinema was an established cultural fact in an era of rapid social change. In America, theatres or dream palaces were crucial to the structuring of the film industry. They were the places where cinema came to the masses and the studios successfully exploited such venues as they did the movie stars under contract to them. The first movie palaces were built in 1913. The story of Loew's Corporation in New York is representative. Building on his success and to secure his own suppliers of movies, Marcus Loew bought Metro Pictures in 1919 and went on to buy Goldwyn Pictures, creating Metro-Goldwyn-Meyer (or MGM) – what would become the most powerful studio of the 1930s. The vertical integration of aspects of the industry ensured a corporation like Loew's could control the manufacturing of films, their retailing and their exhibition.

In this period, audience concentration spans would stretch from short one-reel films to features of around seventy-five minutes in direct correlation with their worshipping of stars such as matinée idol John Barrymore, swashbuckler Douglas 'the Great Lover' Fairbanks, Rudolph Valentino and a host of beauties including Mary Pickford, Mae Murray, Gloria Swanson, Pola Negri and Greta Garbo. Cinema had begun by borrowing known quality from the theatre. In Germany Max Reinhardt, an acclaimed theatrical producer, had begun working in the cinema around 1910 and demonstrated a phenomenal ability to spot talent that would work in the studio as well as on the stage. Ernst Lubitsch, the first German director to be head-hunted by Hollywood, began as a stage comedian under Reinhardt and when encouraged to turn to direction found instant success with *One Arabian Night* (1920) and headed for America. Like

Reinhardt and Lubitsch, a number of the most renowned American directors of the silent era began their professional careers in the theatre – D. W. Griffith and Sidney Olcott, amongst others – just like the actors. Sarah Bernhardt and John Barrymore, for example, having enjoyed successful careers in the theatre, began to branch out into the cinema. They were first of all decried for deserting the 'legitimate' theatre for the 'low art' of the movies. Films themselves remained theatrical presentations for some time during the silent era. D. W. Griffith's *The Birth of a Nation* (1915), for instance, was first distributed in theatrical format divided into two 'acts' with an intermission. However, cinematic techniques began to draw away from stagecraft as cinema distinguished itself as a new medium.

The release of *The Birth of a Nation* signalled the beginning of the era of great 'American' pictures that could command huge sales for exhibitors. The year 1915 alone saw epic and melodramatic hits such as Cecil B. DeMille's *The Cheat*, in which a bourgeois American wife and a villainous Japanese businessman are mutually attracted by money and sado-masochistic desire; Raoul Walsh's mob tale *Regeneration*; Theda Bara as the 'vamp' in *A Fool There Was*; 'America's Sweetheart' Mary Pickford as Cho Cho San in *Madame Butterfly*; and Anthony Hope's swashbuckler *The Prisoner of Zenda*, as well as numerous Roscoe 'Fatty' Arbuckle vehicles. Tickets for *The Birth of a Nation* sold for unprecedentedly high prices and each première was a gala, often with Griffith introducing the film flanked by ushers in period costume and an orchestra or marching band. Griffith's was the first film to be released with an accompanying score and it attracted middle-class audiences into the theatres and often ran for months. It also became the first film screened in the White House, in February 1915, with President Woodrow Wilson famously describing it as 'writing history with lightning'. However, its pro-slavery racist overtones and celebration of a plantation aristocracy led to the campaign by the National Association for the Advancement of Colored People (NAACP) to ban its exhibition, and *The Nation* described it as an attempt to humiliate African Americans that could foment race hatred. *The Birth of a Nation* was banned in France and one of the reasons for this was fear that the film would offend African troops fighting for the Allies, but its status as an aesthetic masterpiece was unaffected and the controversy was even a boost to ticket sales. Movies are salient in disseminating ideology, such as anxieties over America's role as an ethnic 'melting pot' or the South's maintenance of racial segregation and the new nativism which proclaimed 'American' identity to be white Anglo-Saxon. *The Birth of a Nation* had presidential approval and the NAACP failed to make inroads into censoring it. One of the reasons for this was probably that society so far had no way of measuring the ideological impact of film on the public. Nevertheless, evidence shows that membership of the Ku Klux Klan soared on its revival in 1915 with Griffith's film used as an aid to recruitment.

The Birth of a Nation's status derived in large part from D. W. Griffith's innovative artistic development of the film medium itself, ensuring its enshrining as a cinematic masterpiece. Griffith spent a phenomenal $110,000 promoting the film as an American epic and he found innovative ways in which to produce spectacular camerawork that would make his films seem distinctively new. For instance, he placed a camera in the back of a car to produce a tracking shot of a chase scene and in *Intolerance* (1916) he mounted a camera in a tall tower that would act as a dolly from where it could survey the entirety of Griffith's gigantic sets. Most significantly, *The Birth of a Nation* was renowned for its parallel editing in the cutting between the American families, the Southern Camerons and the Northern Stonemans; and in scenes on the battlefield that cut quickly between different characters and locations. It was seen as a paragon of American cinema – its coming of age.

Intolerance was a classic example of early cinema's burgeoning visual power with its monumental sets, especially in the Babylonian sequence. It was also generally understood to be Griffith's response to protests over his racism in *The Birth of a Nation* and, consequently, was designed as a history of the bigotry of the world in four epic sequences. Controversy surrounded that film too when the Anti-Defamation League discovered that Griffith intended to represent Jews in what they believed would be an anti-Semitic way, and it was noted that no black people were represented as suffering bigotry, even in the 'America' sequence. Black independent filmmaker Oscar Micheaux can now be understood as a foil to Griffith. It was really only in the 1990s that a lost or neglected history of African American filmmaking in the pre-Second World War period was uncovered and Micheaux was central to that history. He made some forty films, beginning in 1918, an average of three films a year in the silent era. These include *Within Our Gates* (1919), restored in 1993 after a print was discovered in Spain, which does much to challenge the traditional lynching plot Griffith deployed in *The Birth of a Nation* whereby Gus, a black army officer, is lynched to 'protect' not just Flora, the white girl to whom he proposes, but supposedly the whole white American family, North and South. Micheaux's *oeuvre* provides a sharp critique of America's disenfranchisement of African Americans.

Despite the innovations in filmmaking, the setting for the exhibition of films remained very theatrical after the First World War, especially since the first successful picture palaces were former theatres and few were dedicated only to film exhibition. By the coming of sound in the late 1920s, some 20,000 theatres were operating as cinemas in the US. The expanding industry gave rise to myriad business opportunities. Film companies were in their ascendancy, struggling against one another to carve a niche in a fast-growing industry, each investing in a cast of stars to ensure a control of the market. But there was more than one way to forge a monopoly. Paramount Pictures Corporation, founded in 1914, had set up a national distribution network, controlling the distribution of more than a hundred films in their first year and cornering the market. This prompted film producers to find allies to try to ensure that their pictures would be screened by, for example, instigating a 'block booking' system where potential movie triumphs would only be distributed to theatres as part of a larger package of films. Adolph Zukor combined forces with Jesse Lasky in this regard to form the Famous Players-Lasky which went on to produce John Ford's epic western *The Covered Wagon* in 1923. Cinema owners began to combine forces to counter Paramount's stranglehold on exhibition. In 1917 they formed the FNEC (First National Exhibitors' Circuit) in order to establish a hold on distribution and exhibition and began to produce films themselves by 1921.

By 1915 multi-reel films were known as 'features'. The new features demanded larger film theatres with the kind of audience attractions that would make people comfortable to stay for two hours or more. Nickelodeons were becoming more competitive, with cloakrooms in which to leave one's coat and even crèches so that parents, and especially mothers, would not be stopped from seeing the latest releases. 'Women's stories' began to dominate as the nickelodeons metamorphosed from working men's domains, sometimes with peep shows, into legitimate picture palaces where affluent Americans could safely enjoy entertainment for the whole family. Renovation and building work began. The retail of films was the surest way to make money because the American public had begun to regard movies as a necessity rather than a luxury, even if they preferred the surroundings in which they viewed them to be luxurious.

As the cinema industry grew certain of itself in the early 1920s, nickelodeon habits were considered passé: vaudeville acts and popular singers entertaining audiences while a reel was changed gave way to orchestras and Wurlitzer organs. Sound effect machines such as the Kinematophone became popular before up-market theatres began to expect specially prepared scores to accompany each film, like the one that had first accompanied *The Birth of a Nation*. As the visual quality of cinematic productions improved, theatres charged higher admission prices and ploughed profits back into the buildings, making them more opulent and palatial. Those theatre chains that formed part of a vertically integrated company in the 1920s also secured revenue from the association because the picture palace was the public face of the industry and a new picture would be premièred in major cities, in New York on Broadway, for instance. 'Deluxe' picture palaces allocated the first runs of films showed Hollywood's products to best effect, and set the scene for second-run theatres. Further down the chain, the 'fleapits', often converted stores, paid the lowest rental charges for films after a movie's 'run' was over.

Ushers in uniform welcomed patrons and the best picture palaces had grand lobbies that were hugely ornamental with marble and glass, and magnificent staircases. They exuded opulence as the places to see and to be seen like the most successful hotels – such as the Alexandria Hotel in downtown Los Angeles where movie hopefuls tried to mingle with stars, directors and producers – as described in Siegfried Kracauer's classic essay of the 1920s, 'The Hotel Lobby', which emphasises the space as indubitably modern. The picture palaces often favoured themed décor, as in the 'Oriental' fashion popular in the 1920s which is best seen in Grauman's Chinese Theater in Hollywood. Theatre fronts and lobbies also changed like film sets according to the picture they were promoting. In first-run theatres, lobby displays and magnetic billboards kept pace with new releases and new theatres looked like Hollywood sets with rococo and baroque designs.

Correlations have also been made between the picture palaces and department stores, which in their first incarnations were similarly luxurious. Mass entertainment and the incredible growth of motion-pictures did evolve hand in hand with the rise of consumer culture. Theodor Adorno and Max Horkheimer would write their thesis on the 'Culture Industry' in 1940s Los Angeles and, while they aligned the production of films and their star commodities with the production of automobiles, they also recognised film's hegemonic power, bemoaning that 'real life' was becoming difficult to distinguish from the movies. Also looking back from the perspective of the 1940s, Siegfried Kracauer (1995b) took up the idea of a mass-mediated reality when he wrote of 'the cult of distraction' epitomised by movie theatres as an inevitable fact of modernity. Selling luxurious living, picture palaces increased audience consumption of the movies: seating capacity increased because managers were well aware that the operating costs were similar whether the theatre's capacity was 1,000 seats or 6,000. Premier locations, usually downtown or in a wealthy residential area, ensured that industry investors were willing to build and sponsor new theatres. Air conditioning, pioneered by the Balaban and Katz chain in 1917, as Douglas Gomery has shown in *Shared Pleasures*, ensured that cinemas would maintain high audience numbers even in the middle of summer. In fact, the cost that investors were willing to devote to cool-air systems reaped rewards as patrons often increased in hot weather, finding in the cool and airy theatres comfort that was impossible to find at home. During the 1920s, theatre audiences doubled and by the coming of sound cinema were estimated at an amazing 80 million moviegoers a week.

The decade was characterised by the Jazz Age – by sex and pleasure, and guilt and excess following Prohibition. As well as picture palaces and dream factories, tango palaces became an American fashion. Dance had become one of the leading entertainments, with the Charleston the leading dance craze. The ways in which the 'New Woman' behaved had become a subject of social debate and dance provided modern women with an outlet for expressing not just freedom of movement but also female desire. Paramount's Louise Brooks began as a dancer in the Ziegfeld Follies and in her films personified the decadent and feminist flapper, wearing shorter dresses, smoking in public and usually getting her man. Feminist detractors warned that feminine restlessness would have an adverse and destabilising effect on traditional patriarchal institutions such as the family, as in F. W. Murnau's representation of 'The City Girl' in *Sunrise* (1927) who seduces the farmer away from his wife for a while. If women

97

seemed unhappy with the roles of wife and mother, the flapper seemed to represent an alternative lifestyle sold by Hollywood in the 'Roaring Twenties' via the 'It' girl Clara Bow. 'It' was an idea popularised by romantic fiction writer Elinor Glyn to signify sex appeal and she even scripted *It* (1927) as a star vehicle for Bow, the sexiest flapper of them all.

Women were considered the key targets in the sharp upward curve of consumerist success. Advertisers focused on what Thorstein Veblen in his book *The Theory of the Leisure Class* had called 'conspicuous consumption' and 'conspicuous waste', an idea that would later be satirised to effect in George Cukor's film *What Price Hollywood?* (1932). The Hollywood stars audiences paid money to watch were marketed as having an aura of extraordinariness and excess, epitomised by their grand Hollywood mansions, swimming pools and celebrity parties. These were the conspicuous trappings of their success, as in Pickfair, the mansion that Douglas Fairbanks gave Mary Pickford for a wedding present. Stars were also a democratic ideal: Charlie Chaplin, Pickford and Fairbanks had used their star status to promote the war effort by selling Liberty Bonds to Americans around the country. They were world celebrities, the first generation of stars, and they were the nouveau riche, successful in movies regardless of class or background. In this way, stars were salient in the making and reinvigorating of a number of American myths including 'The American Dream' of success, and Mary Pickford and Gloria Swanson were the first women millionaires in Hollywood. The English small-time music hall performer Chaplin became revered like no one else at the time, so that poet Hart Crane coined the term 'Chaplinesque' to express great fame. Chaplin's fame survived the coming of sound and decades of changes – he made his last film at 77 – but the most enduring image is from the silent era, of the 'Little Tramp' skipping into the distance as *The Tramp* (1915) fades out.

Clara Bow, whose spark of fame burned out much more quickly, is a more representative example of Hollywood's fame game. In 1922 Bow, aged 14, entered a competition in a fan magazine and won a bit part in a movie and by 1927 she was starring in *Wings*, the first movie to win the Best Picture Oscar. On the continent, female star power had been best represented by Asta Nielsen (see Chapter 3) who was truly international in her appeal, with a host of tie-in products such as Asta skincare and cigarettes. Greta Garbo and Nielsen, two of the greatest divas, starred in *The Joyless Street* (1925) directed by Pabst, one of German Expressionist cinema's major exponents. It deployed an intriguing gimmick, recently reworked in *Heat* (1995) with Robert de Niro and Al Pacino, by ensuring that Garbo and Nielsen never appeared together on screen. Garbo was always marketed as aloof and mysterious and the statement 'I want to be alone' became axiomatic of the Hollywood star's otherworldliness.

It has been said that stars were discovered not made, but film history tells many tales of Svengali-like creators: Mauritz Stiller, who had already decided on the name Garbo for the unattainable beauty he would make into a legend before he even met her; and Cecil B. DeMille, who 'made' Gloria Swanson.

In 1915 Fox released the studio's first film, *A Fool There Was* and its star, Theda Bara, became known as the 'vamp', a new word coined to capture her sultry appeal. Bara was created by the studio, her fictitious name an anagram of Arab Death, and the Studio invented an exotic past for her: she was 'born in the shadow of the Sphinx' rather than in Cincinatti. D. W. Griffith's star 'discoveries' included Lillian Gish. Gish had already played leading roles but it was Griffith's camera caressing her face in *The Birth of a Nation* and *Broken Blossoms* (1919), and his casting of her as the nation's motherly protector, rocking the cradle of history in *Intolerance*, that ensured she found her star niche in his movies. Gish remains memorable for iconic scenes such as that in *Hearts of the World* (1919) where she wanders helplessly across a First World War blood-soaked battlefield to find the boy she is engaged to marry, a scene that prefigures Vivien Leigh as Scarlett O'Hara walking through the carnal devastation wrought by the Civil War in *Gone with the Wind* (1939). Gish remained a spiritual presence in American cinema; she was never a vamp even though it is reputed that Irving Thalberg in 1928 suggested spicing up her image with a whiff of contrived scandal. Gish refused. Her face remains the cinematic shorthand for the archetypal 'Little Mother', which she played to the full so many years later in Charles Laughton's *The Night of the Hunter* (1955).

While women enjoyed a variety of roles, cinematic representations of children in the silent era were much more various than the saccharine stories that came to dominate later with child actors Shirley Temple, Elizabeth Taylor and Mickey Rooney. Mary Pickford was renowned for feisty roles and such boisterousness was extended in the series of films known as 'Our Gang' or 'The Little Rascals' produced by Hal Roach in the 1920s, which continued into the 1930s and made stars of the children who featured, black and white. Movie stars became a very important aspect of producers' and distributors' marketing strategies in the silent era. The first movie stars had been anonymous: they were known by the brand name of the production company for which they worked. Biograph's Florence Lawrence was perhaps the first American star although she was known only as 'the Biograph Girl' and then the 'Imp Girl', when Independent Motion Pictures producer Carl Laemmle hired her away from Biograph. Laemmle was a showman who in the 1920s would charge the public to sit in the gallery to watch films being made at Universal and he used publicity stunts to secure continued interest in the stars. Florence Lawrence is a case in point. Laemmle promoted a rumour as a sensationalist stunt, ensuring newspapers gave out that Lawrence was believed dead after a streetcar accident. Then he planted editorials as advertising features denying the death ('We Nail A Lie') and reassuring the public that Lawrence would be seen shortly in her new Imp movies.

In America the system of star-making was perfected during the 'Jazz Age', the era that F. Scott Fitzgerald had declared 'open' in 1919. The studios made the stars a phenomenon peculiar to the movies; they were industrial tools and their pictures in theatre lobbies ensured box office success. In an age of excess and heightened consumerism, stars were marketed as having a dual identity, a cinematic 'personality' projected on the screen and a scandalous 'private' life, often created as much by the popular press as by their own antics. Rudolph Valentino is a classic example. Reputed great lover and known as the 'Prince of the Desert' after his role in *The Sheik* (1921), he had women fainting in the movie theatres and is supposed to have inspired the popular song, 'The Sheik of Araby'. In New York, where he died in 1926, thousands lined the streets and his tomb in Hollywood is a shrine. Stars were supremely profitable and their images were reinforced and circulated by extra-textual means including agents and publicity shots, fan magazines, interviews, planted articles and reviews in the movie press. The discourse of stardom was established by 1920 and publicity agents began courting controversy on their behalf, resulting in the appetite for Hollywood scandals that Kenneth Anger popularised in his memoir *Hollywood Babylon*. Hedda Hopper and Louella Parsons would become famous gossip columnists who fed the public's appetite for scandal while ostensibly policing the Hollywood community and acting as its moral conscience.

Moral panics revolved around Hollywood and its stars. Athletic actor Wallace Reid was the first star to die from drug addiction when he became addicted to morphine following an accident. He died in 1922 and his decline was good copy for producer Thomas H. Ince, who filmed it the following year as *Human Wreckage* (1923) starring Reid's widow. Two actresses were believed to have been involved with the murder of a director, William Desmond Taylor. The best known was Mabel Normand, the only comedienne almost as popular as Chaplin or Harold Lloyd, the last to see Taylor alive and a favourite of Hollywood gossips. Such scandals sometimes stalled the release of a film but little else – except in the case of the infamous prosecution of silent comedian Fatty Arbuckle who was believed to have murdered Virginia Rappe in 1921 after a party he threw in San Francisco on Labor Day weekend. Arbuckle was acquitted but the publicity was so great that even President Harding followed the story. Arbuckle's career was over. Scandals in general led to studios inserting 'morality clauses' into their contracts in the 1920s so that a star playing a dramatic role would sign to assure the studio that their behaviour off-screen would have no adverse affects on the marketing of the film. The Motion Picture Producers and Distributors of America (MPPDA) was formed in 1922 with Will Hays (former US Postmaster General under President Harding) at its head to censor material he considered offensive to the public and to create a new clean image for Hollywood. The long-term result would be the infamous Hays Production Code of 1934 (see Chapter 9).

An odd anomaly in the star system was MGM's Irving Thalberg, immortalised in F. Scott Fitzgerald's final and unfinished novel *The Last Tycoon*, who would die young in 1936. Thalberg married actress Norma Shearer and was himself a starmaker in very different ways from Carl Laemmle or Thomas Ince. He promoted Lon Chaney's career, for example, who was one of the very few star actors to fall outside the conventionally handsome model expected of male stars. This was, in fact, the source of Chaney's stardom and he played Quasimodo in *The Hunchback of Notre Dame* (1923) and the Phantom in *The Phantom of the Opera* (1925). Thalberg was the stars' star whose decisions could make or break a career and he stood firmly behind Chaney. MGM, the biggest and most financially powerful of the studios, was also considered the most 'American' of the studios and its marketing slogan, 'More stars than there are in heaven', served to underline the idea.

One way of wresting back some control over their star status was for the stars themselves to command larger salaries, but the biggest stars such as Mary Pickford were soon worth much more than studios were willing to pay. Pickford was an astute businesswoman who had starred in around forty films before she was 20 and formed her own company, Mary Pickford Motion Pictures, to capitalise on the name the studios had exploited to great financial success. With husband Douglas Fairbanks she established United Artists in 1919 as a means by which key protagonists in early cinema – Pickford and Fairbanks, with Charlie Chaplin and D. W. Griffith and William S. Hart – could control the films they made. They issued a 'Declaration of Independence' and made good their star status, distributing their own films. The Declaration, published in the magazine *Moving Picture World* on 1 February 1919, stated specifically that exhibitors would not have to block book pictures but each would be sold individually by United Artists, 'to protect the great motion-picture public from threatening combinations and trusts that would force upon them mediocre productions and machine-made entertainment'. The stars were fighting the studios' oligopoly and the picture palaces would be the bene-ficiaries. United Artists could not follow through on its ideals, however, and its profits began declining quite quickly. Nevertheless, in the 1920s United Artists remained consistent in its attention to quality and became renowned for prestige films including Chaplin's *The Gold Rush* (1925), Valentino's *The Son of the Sheik* (1926) and Buster Keaton's *The General* (1927). United Artists also made it through the Depression of the 1930s.

The picture palaces are the stuff of film heritage today. Sid Grauman's Chinese Theater on Hollywood Boulevard was the most famous theatre of the era, its grand opening in May 1927 attended by stars including Mary Pickford and directors including D. W. Griffith. Grauman had capitalised on the success of his Egyptian Theatre, which premièred Douglas Fairbanks' *Robin Hood* in 1922, but the entrepreneur lost ground in the 1930s. His Egyptian Theatre declined into a porn cinema after its glory years but was restored in 1998 to great public acclaim. The power struggles that characterised the era are encapsulated in the grand old buildings, a fascinating feature of film history. Douglas Gomery's *Shared Pleasures* traces American cinematic presentation from its origins through the rise of the 'dream palaces' down the decades to include the domestic viewing of home videos and the rise of the multiplex.

Gomery's focus in the extract that follows is the most resourceful movie chain of the late 1910s and the 1920s, Balaban and Katz, who would by 1925 merge with Hollywood's Famous Players-Lasky to form the powerful movie company, Paramount Pictures. In this way, Balaban and Katz sought to attract audiences by commodifying their movie pleasures in a business package that would sell. Exhibition practice is an aspect of film history that was very much neglected until the last twenty years or so. It helps film historians to think about some of the different levels on which cinema functions as a business and Gomery digs deep into the internal workings of the business culture that underpinned the rise of the integrated studio system. Examination of a successful regional chain like Loew's, and of precisely how Balaban and Katz succeeded in building their regional chain in Chicago into a national empire, reveals how the cinema industry began to make the successful shift towards globalising mass entertainment in the decade that followed the First World War. It also reveals how film exhibition became one of America's biggest businesses precisely by appealing to a cross-section of the America public.

Rather than focus on film texts or film as text, Gomery's is an institutional study that speaks to the significance of filmgoing as a social practice. Gomery shows film consumption as taking place in very precise circumstances for audiences. These are national and regional; they involve recognising the broader trends of film history and the specifics of local communities, to the extent that Balban and Katz themselves argued that 'we must build in the minds of our audience the feeling that we represent an institution taking a vital part in the formation of the character of the community'. The extract explores the circumstances in which early cinema was distributed and then experienced in a Balaban and Katz venue, from the patrons' entrance into the movie palace to their exit after the show, and in so doing Gomery demonstrates that the movies themselves were never the only reason that audiences frequented the picture palaces.

At the end of the extract, Douglas Gomery has provided a new postscript that indicates some of the new factors that influence his re-assessment of his 1992 study. You might consider what this Afterword tells us not only about the extract you have read but also what it reveals in general terms about the film historian's ever-changing role.

- Enumerate the social factors that contributed to the amazing economic success of the picture palaces after the First World War.
- Distinguish between the types of primary and secondary sources Gomery deploys in order to trace the history of Balaban and Katz and in order to examine how entrepreneurs in other areas of business contributed to their success.
- What sources might you use to pursue a study of the most successful theatre chains in your city or region? And what sources might you use to discover which stars were local favourites between 1915 and 1925?

THE RISE OF NATIONAL THEATRE CHAINS

Douglas Gomery

[. . .]

The successes of Loew's in New York and the achievements of the Stanley Company in Philadelphia tell us much about the development of *regional* theatre chains. Neither, however, established the standard for running a *national* theatre chain. A strategy for a national chain had its origins in the second largest city in the United States, Chicago, Illinois, with the extraordinary accomplishments of Balaban & Katz. By 1924 this one company was making more money than any other theatre chain in the United States and was being copied from coast to coast.

In retrospect this must be considered somewhat surprising. Balaban & Katz entered the exhibition game late. While other regional chains had established their presence by 1920, Balaban & Katz was just beginning its rise. Indeed, as late as 1919 Balaban & Katz owned just six theatres, of which only two were large, formidable movie palaces. What makes the growth of this company so remarkable is that its ascent took place over the course of a mere five years. Balaban & Katz went beyond simply combining vaudeville and movies and forming a company such as MGM, beyond skillful real estate dealings, and beyond careful use of economies of scale. To understand Balaban & Katz is to learn how the movie show captured its place as the dominant mass entertainment form in the United States.

Balaban & Katz started with a single nickelodeon. The Balaban side came first. Oldest brother Barney and second in line Abraham Joseph (simply known as A. J.) and their parents set up a nickelodeon theatre in Chicago's west-side ghetto in 1908. The Balabans did better than many and opened their second theatre in 1909 and a third in 1914. They moved into local film distribution, peddling cheaply made features and shorts to fellow theatre owners. For a time the brothers even operated a restaurant, the Movie Inn, located downtown in the heart of film-sellers row. The Movie Inn served as a meeting place for exhibitors, distributors, and visiting movie folk, and although the restaurant never made much money, it did serve a vital function for their owners. It was there that the Balaban brothers met the dynamic Samuel Katz.[1]

Samuel Katz, 'Sam' to one and all, followed a more traditional route toward success, graduating from high school and even attending college. He supported his education with a series of part-time jobs, one of which found him playing piano for a nickelodeon located in Chicago's south side. There Katz

---

Douglas Gomery, *Shared Pleasures: A History of Movie Presentation in the United States* (Madison: University of Wisconsin Press, 1992).

fell in love with the movies, and he set his sights on becoming an industry leader. In 1912 Katz acquired the Wallace theatre, next door to his father's barbershop; by 1915 he owned three theatres and was in the movie business full time.

In 1916 Sam Katz and the Balaban brothers teamed up and decided to follow the model of Samuel Rothapfel's New York City Rivoli and Rialto theatres. They would open a large theatre, one that could take advantage of the continually growing interest in moviegoing they saw in Chicago. They sought to become giants like Loew's in New York or the Mastbaums in Philadelphia. For their first major theatre they chose the North Lawndale neighborhood of Chicago.[2]

Sam Katz went to work. He approached Julius Rosenwald, president of Sears-Roebuck, the neighborhood's largest employer. Rosenwald put Katz in touch with S. W. Straus, a Chicago mortgage company. On 16 August 1916 Straus granted the Central Park Building Corporation a $125,000 mortgage. Sam Katz and the Balabans put up their theatres as collateral.

Balaban & Katz's Central Park Theatre opened on schedule on Saturday, 27 October 1917. This mighty picture palace was an immediate success and Sam Katz, as corporate planner and president, began to draw up plans for a second picture palace in the fashionable Uptown district of Chicago's far north side. Katz thought big. He proposed and built a three-thousand-seat picture palace, the Riveria.[3]

At this point Sam Katz assembled a syndicate of backers who all were doing so well in their own Chicago-based businesses that they had some extra cash to invest.

Julius Rosenwald had seen Sears-Roebuck grow into America's most important mail-order retailer. During the 1920s Sears would move to the top position in retail sales in the United States, with stores often found just across the street from movie palaces.

William Wrigley, Jr.'s sales were expanding at a furious rate as a nation acquired the chewing-gum habit. In the 1930s his confectionery treat would become a staple in concession stands in movie houses.

John Hertz had become Chicago's taxi king. His yellow cabs made his fortune: the rental car business would come later. And many a taxi took passengers to a night at the movies. Rosenwald, Wrigley, and Hertz added to their fortunes through their backing of Balaban & Katz.[4]

Balaban & Katz opened the Riveria on 2 October 1918 and again had a major success. Katz knew what his next steps must be: open a picture palace on Chicago's south side and then in the downtown Loop area. He moved quickly, although strikes and shortages that remained after the end of the First World War limited rapid expansion. The south side's Tivoli opened 16 February 1921; the Chicago Theatre in downtown's north Loop area opened 26 October 1921. Now Balaban & Katz could offer their brand of movie entertainment to Chicago's west-, north-, and south-siders as well as crowds in the central city. All were hugely profitable from the start.[5]

At the same time Sam Katz began to solidify Balaban & Katz's place in the Chicago moviegoing marketplace. He furiously began to buy theatres, simply with the excess monies produced by his four movie palaces. Balaban & Katz's four remarkable Chicago picture palaces were so successful that excess profits permitted future expansion from internal cash flow. The five-thousand-seat Uptown Theatre, the three-thousand-seat Norshore, and the four-thousand-seat Oriental opened in the mid-1920s and provided Balaban & Katz with total domination of the cinema in Chicago.[6]

From this base of power in Chicago Katz began to seek theatres in the surrounding states. In May 1924 Balaban & Katz acquired Midwest Theatres, a chain in Illinois and Wisconsin. By 1925 Hollywood came to Sam Katz. Skillfully Katz played one studio off another, but in the end he chose to affiliate with the largest Hollywood movie company, Famous Players-Lasky. This alliance guaranteed Balaban & Katz access to Hollywood's top films and secured for Famous Players-Lasky a top manager for its own expanding theatre chain. Thus, in October 1925, Sam Katz moved to New York to run what would be known as the Publix theatre chain.[7]

Balaban & Katz's rise to power symbolized the rise of the theatre chain in the American movie business. Twenty years earlier, in 1905, the field of film exhibition had been one of entrepreneurs who could enter the motion-picture exhibition business with a few hundred dollars. In 1925, with the Balaban & Katz/Famous Players-Lasky alliance, the field of movie exhibition became a part of the pantheon of American big business. By examining why Balaban & Katz was able to expand so rapidly and successfully, we can understand why the movie exhibition business moved from a marginal leisure-time industry to center stage in the business of entertainment.

Remarkably, one of the variables that did *not* count in Balaban & Katz's rise to power and control was the movies themselves. Indeed, the company grew and prospered despite having little access to Hollywood's top films. Balaban & Katz's competitors may have been able to book the films that proved most popular elsewhere, but it did not pose a significant obstacle to Balaban & Katz's rise. Indeed, Balaban & Katz took the films others did not want. Only after 1925, with the alliance with Famous Players-Lasky, did Balaban & Katz gain access to the top Hollywood feature films. By then Balaban & Katz used this extra advantage to wipe out the competition.

Indeed Balaban & Katz knew it could never depend too much on films to form the foundation of its theatrical empire. Barney Balaban and Sam Katz argued: 'We cannot afford to build up a patronage depending entirely upon the drawing power of our feature films as we display them. We must build in the minds of our audience the feeling that we represent an institution taking a vital part in the formation of the character of the community.'[8] Balaban & Katz carefully formed this institution by taking advantage of certain factors where it did hold advantage over the competition. By differentiating its corporate product through five important factors – location, the theatre building, service, stage shows, and air conditioning – Balaban & Katz was able to transform itself, and the film industry as a whole, from a small-time operation into a part of the growing chain store revolution.

Location

Possibly the most important factor in differentiating theatres was one recognised by Loew and the Mastbaums, and even more thoroughly by Balaban & Katz, that is, location. Previously, owners of motion-picture houses had followed the prevailing tendencies of entertainment districts and sought the ideal location downtown. Balaban & Katz established the locus of their power by going to new audiences who lived in what were then the suburbs of America's biggest cities, with easy access to mass transit. Balaban & Katz demonstrated that it was not enough simply to seek the middle class by happenstance; one had to take the movie show to their neighborhoods.

What gave Balaban & Katz their opening was Chicago's construction of a mass transit trolley and elevated lines. As in other cities, rapid mass transit enabled the middle class and rich to move to the edge of the city to the first true suburbs (although many were actually within city boundaries). Thus, as late as the year 1900, Chicago was a compact city, with most citizens living three miles from the Loop; two decades later that distance had doubled. Balaban & Katz took advantage of this revolution in mass transit. The firm built its first three theatres, the Central Park, the Riveria, and the Tivoli, in the heart of *outlying* business and recreational centers of Chicago. Only then did it construct a theatre, the Chicago, downtown in the north Loop area.[9]

The Central Park Theatre came first and was located in an area of Chicago the Balabans and Katzes knew well, North Lawndale. On what was then the far west side of the city, North Lawndale was where immigrant Jewish families like the Balabans and Katzes moved to in order to prove they had 'made it.' The elevated line had reached North Lawndale in 1902, and within two decades this lightly populated outpost had grown into a teeming neighborhood of Jews who had left Maxwell Street. Indeed, the 1920 census determined that three-quarters of the population of this particular neighborhood were Russian Jews who had come to America in the 1880s and 1890s, settled in the neighborhood around Hull House (Maxwell Street), and then resettled in North Lawndale.[10]

Louis Wirth's classic sociological study *The Ghetto* documented this transformation. Wirth found that the children pushed their parents to move to North Lawndale to achieve higher status in life. In turn, these children had acquired a strong desire for upward mobility from education in public school, from reformers such as Jane Addams, and from newly acquired gentile friends and co-workers. This new generation ate non-Kosher food, attended synagogue less frequently, shopped outside the neighborhood, and spoke Yiddish only at home. And as part of this cultural assimilation they also embraced the movie show. The Central Park made its fortune catering to the very people Louis Wirth had studied.[11]

For Balaban & Katz's second picture palace the firms' leaders chose a site in the thriving outlying center of the prosperous north-side neighborhood of Uptown. The 'bright-light' center of this streetcar transfer point was already filling up with dance halls, cabarets, and arcades. In the early 1920s Uptown stood as the largest outlying center in Chicago, with more than 100,000 prosperous residents living in apartment buildings only a walk from the neighborhood center. Since Balaban & Katz came late to this center, the Riveria was initially several blocks from the 'el' station. But because the crowds became so big with the opening of Balaban & Katz's Uptown Theatre in 1924, across the street from the Riveria, the city of Chicago opened up a new station. Uptown became the 'hottest' of the hot spots in Chicago in the Roaring Twenties.[12]

The Central Park and the Riveria, because of their location near the terminus of the 'el' lines, were able to attract patrons from all parts of the west and north sides of Chicago – all the new middle-class patrons who had moved to the periphery of the city. The Tivoli performed the same function for the south side. Again, it was located near the center of an outlying business and recreational center at Sixty-Third and Cottage Grove avenues. The 'el' was nearby, as were thousands who worked or attended the University of Chicago. Indeed 'Sixty-Third and Cottage' was the south side's equivalent of Uptown.[13]

The matrix of theatres appealing to all sectors of the city was complete. The Chicago Theatre downtown in the Loop was almost an afterthought, built with the profits made from the suburban theatres. The Chicago Theatre stood as a symbol of the success of the outlying theatres, not the central movie house that had vaulted the company to the top of the exhibition business. After the outlying theatres were established, it only made sense to construct a theatre for the thousands who journeyed downtown to shop and have fun.

Once these four theatres – the Central Park, the Riveria, the Tivoli, and the Chicago – were in place, Balaban & Katz could advertise that no one need travel more than a half-hour to reach one of its wonder theatres. Acquiring more theatres, as the company did with the millions pouring in, simply reduced the maximum required travel time to fifteen minutes. Sam Katz had leveraged four theatres into an empire, and so by 1924 all power in the theatrical market for movie exhibition in Chicago flowed through his office atop the Chicago Theatre on North State Street.[14]

Balaban & Katz proved that the movie entertainment business was not one of simple *mass* market appeal. Middle-class patrons who had recently settled on the edges of the city went to the movies far more often and were willing to pay more than other citizens of Chicago, New York, Philadelphia, or any other major metropolis. It is crucial to recognise that in the 1920s young, middle-class, upwardly mobile apartment dwellers living in the better parts of the city did not find it in their best interest to acknowledge this love for the movie show. Nonetheless they did go to the movies, as the lines in front of Balaban & Katz's Tivoli, Central Park, or Riveria theatres indicated. (The queues began in earnest at ten in the morning.)

Depending on the shape of the city, theatre owners built most of their movie palaces outside the center city. Chicago is typical of what urban geographers call a fan-shaped city. Built on a body of water, the city spread in the 1920s, with increasing mass transit, in the shape of a fan away from downtown. In other cities there was similar pressure to build theatres on the edges of the fan. The theatre owners in Detroit (John Kunsky), St. Louis (the Skouras brothers), and Milwaukee (the Saxe brothers), to name only three examples of large fan-shaped cities, copied the Balaban & Katz example, and we can still see the three-thousand-seat St. Louis theatre (now Powell Hall) in St. Louis and the two-thousand seat Modjeska in Milwaukee, both miles from their city's central business and recreation areas.

The fan-shaped city saw the greatest development of the outlying theatre. Square-shaped cities had less development per capita. Growth in these square (or circular) urban areas exploded in the 1920s in all directions, not constrained by mountains and/or large bodies of water. Indianapolis had outlying picture palaces in the north, west, south, and eastern parts of the city. Outlying theatres also were more likely in cities where growth was limited by mountains and/or bodies of water spread. Thus the expansion of Madison, Wisconsin, was defined by its lakes.

Or, consider the long, narrow island of Manhattan. Certainly there were more than a dozen movie places in Times Square, all easy to travel to by a variety of mass transit. But if one looked closely at the only section of Manhattan Island that saw population growth in the 1920s, that area north of 145th Street, it can be seen that entrepreneurs built movie palaces far exceeding any section of the island outside Times Square. The area north of 145th Street had one-twentieth of the population but one-fifth of the movie palaces. This area was the only part of the island that in the 1920s offered a high-quality life-style at affordable prices.

In northern Manhattan the newly admitted middle-class and upper middle-class Americans flocked to just-built apartment buildings. Second- and third-generation Americans, educated far in excess of the norm and holding well-paying jobs, had the time and money to spend on the new movie entertainment. But they stayed home, so when Loew's, Inc. decided to expand in 1930 it opened the Loew's 175th Street, a Hindu-Indochinese temple, to this group of movie fans.[15]

The Theatre Building

It was not enough to select the optimal crossroads to locate a theatre. A motion-picture exhibition company had to offer an attractive building. The entertainment commenced with the building, which was a palace for the motion-pictures. Balaban & Katz surpassed the splendor of the vaudeville and legitimate theatre by making their buildings attractions unto themselves. With the pride associated with the opening of a world's fair or new skyscraper, Chicagoans of the 1920s proclaimed and heralded their movie palaces as the finest in the world.

Consider the evocative memory composed by novelist Meyer Levin writing in *The Old Bunch*. He has his characters go to the Chicago theatre in the 1920s:

> As [they] turned into State Street, the Chicago sign blazed at them. Boy, was that a sign! It made daylight of the whole block. Eight stories high. Three thousand bulbs spelled CHICAGO!
>
> After a wait of forty-five minutes they got inside the lobby. Everything white and gold and mirrored.
>
> Up on the promenade was a grand piano, all in white . . .
>
> And overhead, a magnificent chandelier! The largest in the world! Six tons![16]

All Balaban & Katz theatres spelled opulence to the average Chicago moviegoer. It was a special treat to go to these theatres.[17]

The architects for the Balaban & Katz empire came from the Chicago architectural firm headed by the brothers George and C. W. Rapp. The Rapps began with the Central Park Theatre and from that day until 1932 their drawing boards had underway at least one major project for first Balaban & Katz and then Sam Katz's Publix theatres. Katz was their patron for a set of theatres that stretched from New York's Paramount to the Ambassador in St. Louis to the Paramount in Portland, Oregon. Since others, like the Skourases in St. Louis with their Rapp & Rapp Ambassador Theatre, sought to do in their community what Balaban & Katz had done in Chicago. The Rapps became rich men designing movie theatres from one coast to the other.[18]

The Rapps were among the leading architects of the movie palace, establishing a style and look fundamental to the industry. Their opulent designs dazzled patrons with images from Spain, Italy, or France and into the 1930s with art deco renderings. Throughout the 1920s fans marveled at the triumphal arches overhead as they entered the theatre, the monumental staircase (inspired by the Paris Opera House) found in the typical lobby, and the ornate designs filling the sidewall of the auditorium.[19]

The expense of outfitting a theatre was considerable. Consider the Uptown Theatre, opened in 1924. For this five-thousand-seat monument to movie entertainment, Balaban & Katz spent nearly twenty-five thousand dollars on furniture and double that on drapes and carpets. The restrooms, hidden in the basement or in the balcony foyers, were more splendid than many private houses. They were spacious, clean, and decorated with their own sets of drapes, furniture, paintings, and mirrors. The patron could only wonder if the well-to-do had such facilities in their country clubs or boardrooms.

But these overpowering spaces were also highly functional. Everyone had a perfect view of the screen. In vaudeville theatres often there were posts in the way or the angle for viewing the stage was awkward. Acoustical planning for Balaban & Katz movie palaces ensured the orchestral accompaniment to the silent films could be heard even in the furthest reaches of the balcony. Lighting played a key role throughout the performances. Auditoriums were lamped with thousands of bulbs, often in three primary colors. Thus a silent film with live music could also be accompanied by changing light motifs through the show. In general the lights were kept low and patrons kept their seats throughout the show. Too much light invited patrons to move about, and that would have become chaotic with full houses of four thousand or more. This was a dignified setting and patrons responded accordingly.[20]

Since there always seemed to be a line to get into a theatre, keeping the waiting customers happy was as important as entertaining those already in the auditorium. Indeed the rule of thumb was that a Rapp and Rapp lobby ought comfortably to hold ticket holders equal to the number of seats in the auditorium. Indeed one of the main functions of the building was to make sure thousands could enter and exit quickly and safely so the maximum number of shows could be tendered each day. Massive enclosed passageways speeded exit and entry.

Service

Balaban & Katz had a stated policy of treating the movie patron as a king or queen. Theatres offered free child care, attendant smoking rooms, foyers and lobbies lined with paintings and sculpture, and organ music for those waiting in line. Ushers were at the center of this strategy, and they maintained a quiet decorum in the theatre that went along with, and even underlined, the upper-class atmosphere so sought after by suburbanite patrons.

In the basement of each movie palace was a complete playground that included slides, sandboxes, and other objects of fun. For no extra cost children were left in the care of nurses and attendants while families attended the show upstairs. There were afternoon tea shows for women who went shopping with small children and infants. Balaban & Katz advertised that one could come to their movie palace, drop off the children, and enjoy the show. A nurse with complete medical equipment was nearby.

The centerpiece of the special Balaban & Katz service was the corps of ushers. They guided patrons through the maze of halls and foyers, assisted the elderly and small children, and handled any emergencies that might arise in a crowd of four thousand in the auditorium and four thousand waiting for the next show. A picture palace had twenty to forty ushers and doorkeepers in attendance for all shows. Indeed, there was a regular changing of the guard throughout the day.

Balaban & Katz recruited its corps from male college students, dressed them in red uniforms with white gloves and yellow epaulets, and demanded they be obediently polite even to the rudest of patrons. The ushers responded to patrons with 'yes, sir,' or 'no, ma'am' and all requests had to end with a 'thank you.' Even the rowdy were led away with propriety and sensitivity to emphasise that if they opted to be well behaved they were welcome to return. Balaban & Katz emphasised that it was an honor to be selected for the special job of usher.

Ushers worked hard. They used 'spill-cards' to record how full each section of the theatre was at any one moment so patrons could be ushered in to empty areas and not run into each other. Phones and early calculating machines also helped in filling every possible seat. (These data were collected and forwarded to the main office and used to plan future programs.) Ushers received a free week's 'vacation': a special camp during the summer that offered more training and created a special esprit de corps. Any usher who accepted a tip was immediately fired. The special treatment ushers provided was 'free,' a part of the price of admission.[21]

But there were more than nurses, baby-sitters, and ushers who worked in a movie palace. Aside from the manager and direct assistants, there were cashiers, projectionists, maintenance staff, electricians, and others backstage. Musicians and stagehands helped mount the live stage show. Balaban & Katz demanded strict standards to qualify for employment. Ushers had to be white males, seventeen to twenty-one years of age, five feet seven inches tall, 125 to 145 pounds, and enrolled in a local college. In contrast, messenger boys had to be 'the smaller type of negro boy, not over five feet four, of slight, or slender build, well formed and in good proportion, not markedly of negro type with heavy features.'[22] Balaban & Katz regulated its labor to effect a special image and to keep costs to a minimum. Acceptable white males out front in uniform guaranteed an image that most patrons associated with a fine hotel, country club, or bank.

And labor costs were not high. Hollywood may have paid its stars thousands of dollars a week, but the minimum wage of the day was accepted for the privilege to work in a Balaban & Katz theatre. Indeed, most employees, from maintenance and cleaning staff to ushers and even managers, were either young, female, and/or black. None save the musicians, stagehands, and projectionists belonged to a union. All were given specific routine tasks so the management of the chain could regulate their actions like an assembly line. Janitors filled out charts to tell how long it took to clean a certain area of floor. Ushers were of a given size so uniforms could be passed down. These operations were run with an efficiency Henry Ford surely admired.[23]

Stage Shows

The purpose of the location, theatre building, and service was to lead to the entertainment inside the auditorium. In the beginning Balaban & Katz could not offer its patrons at the Riveria, Central Park, Tivoli, and Chicago theatres anything close to the best films coming out of Hollywood. Rival circuits had exclusive booking contracts with the major studios. Balaban & Katz took what was left over. Since they could not offer superior movie entertainment, Balaban & Katz filled the well-located, architecturally splendid, and well-serviced movie houses by producing live stage shows.

[. . .]

[M]ixtures of vaudeville and movies were not new. Samuel Rothapfel and Sid Grauman made big names for themselves in New York City and Los Angeles, respectively, with their stage shows. Grauman's prologues were known from coast to coast; Roxy's 'Rockettes' were hits long before Radio City Music Hall opened in 1932. Balaban & Katz can hardly be credited for the invention or even innovation of the stage show.[24]

But Balaban & Katz carefully exploited the stage show, melding live presentations into a 'product mix' that generated fabulous profits. The company nurtured and developed local talent into stars who would play Chicago exclusively. Balaban & Katz knew that if it could mount popular but tasteful shows, it could solidify its appeal to a middle-class audience so long wedded to vaudeville theatrical entertainment. Moreover, local stars guaranteed that Balaban & Katz would not suffer swings in revenues. The strategy worked. In time Balaban & Katz became more famous for its impressive stage attractions, orchestras, and organists than for any movies it presented.[25]

Consistently Balaban & Katz divided their 150-minute shows between movies and live stage shows. (Often feature films would be shortened to fit the required formula.) The stage show was an elaborate minimusical, with spectacular settings and intricate lighting effects. Much like the stage shows at Radio City Music Hall in recent years, the stage show stood as a separate package of entertainment, emphasizing its theme rather than individual stars. There were shows to celebrate holidays, fads of the day, and heroic adventures, including all the highlights of the Roaring Twenties from the Charleston dance craze to Lucky Lindbergh's solo flight across the Atlantic to the new electronic phenomenon radio. In the entertainment trade, this strategy was known as the 'pure presentation,' as opposed to Sid Grauman's prologues linked dramatically and thematically to the movie that followed or to the Loew's chain strategy for its theatres of putting on a typical vaudeville show with big-name stars.

Typical was 'Jazz and Opera' week. In an era when jazz was looked down upon in the same way rock-and-roll was during the 1950s, the theatre would play one off against the other. It was a 'battle of the sounds,' and jazz always won. By 1925 jazz shows or evenings of syncopation were staged regularly throughout the year. Classical music was reserved exclusively for free Sunday morning concerts by the star organists and orchestras, in order to appease the reformers and city fathers and mothers. It is hard to over-estimate how popular these shows were. One night the Chicago Theatre's curtain would not rise, and although the movie could still be presented, the stage show could not. More than half the audience walked out and demanded their money back.[26]

Brother A. J. Balaban was in charge of these stage attractions. He, his assistant Frank Cambria (who had trained under David Belasco), and their staff put together a new show each week. The talent was initially drawn from bookers at the Western Vaudeville Association. Later Balaban & Katz signed up a stable of talented performers and stage designers of their own. Some would go on to international fame. Noted Hollywood director Vincente Minnelli, the man behind the camera for many of the best Hollywood musicals (*Meet Me in St. Louis and The Band Wagon*), began as a set designer in the Balaban & Katz shop.[27]

Such shows were quite expensive. An average presentation cost between three and five thousand dollars to mount and run for a week. A special show around a holiday might cost more than ten thousand dollars to mount. Consequently Balaban & Katz had the shows play the circuit in true vaudeville fashion. They began downtown at the Chicago Theatre and were reviewed at this venue. Then they played a week at the Riveria, then the Tivoli, and ended at the Central Park. Expenses to create the show thus could be spread over four (and later more) theatres. This repetition did not seem to hurt grosses of outlying theatres and effectively spread the audiences around to all theatres. Again it was a device to wed neighborhood theatregoers to the movie palace entertainment in their community.[28]

For its orchestras and organists who provided music for the silent films and occasional concerts, Balaban & Katz depended on the star system. The company tried any number of musicians until it hit upon two stars. The organist Jesse Crawford became an organist as well known as any Chicagoan of the 1920s. Balaban & Katz had hired him away from Sid Grauman in 1921 to open the Tivoli Theatre and then to open the Chicago eight months later. A year later he commenced his free Sunday morning concerts, with equal parts classical and popular music. By 1923 Crawford's wedding to fellow organist Helen Anderson was the talk of Chicago's tabloids. The couple began to perform together and by 1925 were a Chicago institution, complete with a radio show and a recording contract. When Sam Katz took the pair to New York when he moved to head the complete Paramount theatre circuit, the newspapers mourned the loss in the same way as for a star who had left the Bears, Cubs, or White Sox.[29]

The other music star was a red-haired, flamboyant band leader brought in from the West Coast. Paul Ash may be a footnote in the history of popular music of the 1920s, but in Chicago he was a star unmatched by any band leader of his era. He ran into the audience and conducted singalongs, and his hokum-filled vaudeville act, leading what most conceded was an ordinary jazz band (dressed in a new set of costumes each week), was a smash. During the mid-1920s the lines stretched around the corner to see Ash and his 'Merry, Mad Musical Gang' first at the McVickers and then the new Oriental, which some said was designed with Ash in mind. Sam Katz, again paying him the highest possible compliment, took Ash with him to New York to Paramount's theatre on Times Square.[30]

Air Conditioning

Balaban & Katz's Central Park Theatre, opened in 1917, was the first mechanically air cooled theatre in the world. Other theatre entrepreneurs had tried crude experiments with blowing air across blocks of ice to cool auditoria, but these never functioned without severe breakdown. Prior to the Central Park, most movie houses in the Midwest, South, and far West simply closed during the summer or opened to small crowds. Great progress toward safe

mechanical cooling was made during the first two decades of the twentieth century. Technological change centered in Chicago, because firms in that city still slaughtered and processed most of the meat in the United States. The Kroeschell Bros. Ice Machine Company of Chicago developed a carbon dioxide system that efficiently cooled large spaces but required an investment of thousands of dollars as well as a room full of equipment. Thus Kroeschell Bros. sold it only to industries with a cash flow to justify the expense. Customers remained mainly meat packers, although a carbon dioxide system was installed to cool the banquet hall of Chicago's Congress Hotel.[31]

Before Barney Balaban entered the movie business he worked in the office of the Western Cold Storage Company. He knew firsthand of the advances in the art of air cooling. Consequently as Balaban & Katz planned the Central Park Theatre, they convinced Kroeschell Bros. chief engineer and inventor to work up a system specifically designed to cool movie patrons. Wittenmeyer adapted a carbon dioxide system first for the Central Park and then an improved system for the Riveria a year later. Both only *cooled* the air, by forcing it through vents in the floor. The air then exhausted through ducts in the ceiling. Chicago movie fans became, for the first time, patrons of the movies year round.

But these early systems had two distinct disadvantages. First, the cool air on the floor bothered patrons, especially women with long skirts. Second, the air remained too dry or too moist. So a method of dehumidification to perfect true air conditioning was needed. Wittenmeyer worked on both problems and the improved system for the Tivoli and Chicago theatres solved them. The air entered from the side and was dehumidified.[32]

These air conditioners were no window units. The apparatus took up a vast basement room. For the Chicago Theatre the equipment included more than fifteen thousand feet of heavy duty pipe, a 240-horsepower electric motor, and two all-steel, seven-foot flywheels, each weighing seven thousand pounds. An engineer was always on duty to watch over the equipment and effect necessary repairs.[33]

Once in place, these air cooled fantasy worlds became famous as summertime escapes from the brutal Chicago summers. Balaban & Katz's publicity constantly reminded Chicagoans of the rare treat in store inside. Icicles were hung from all newspaper advertisements. Announcements were made, in an almost public service fashion, that the Balaban & Katz theatre was a marvel of modern-day engineering and comfort. Others helped. The Public Health Commissioner of the city of Chicago proclaimed that Balaban & Katz theatres had purer air than Pike's Peak and that anyone with a lung disease or women in the final trimester of pregnancy ought to regularly spend time 'at the movies.' In their advertisements the Chicago Chamber of Commerce heralded Chicago as a wonderland of summer fun, in part because of the pleasures inside a Balaban & Katz movie palace.[34]

The results of Balaban & Katz's pioneering efforts in building a movie theatre chain were nothing short of phenomenal. Movie trade papers noted the consistently high grosses during the summer months and could find no better explanation than the comfort inside. Indeed, box-office receipts in the summer regularly exceeded those during the normally peak months during the winter. The location, architecture, service, stage shows, and indeed the movies themselves simply did not matter. Movie palaces provided relief from the heat that no other institution in the city could provide from May through September. No wonder millions embraced Balaban & Katz's unique brand of movie show in the years just after the First World War.[35]

Balaban & Katz's Influence

With its five-point strategy of mass entertainment, Balaban & Katz changed the movie business by keeping houses full and costs low. Workers were not paid much, since many wanted to work in the movies and there were no unions, except for the projectionists and certain musicians. The buildings were expensive, but they were filled from morning to night, nearly every day of the week. Prices were higher than the usual five and ten cents and sometimes reached a dollar for the best seats on the best nights of the week for the top attractions.

The Balaban & Katz experience proved, despite the oft-asserted claims, that the profits from the movie exhibition business were not found in the 'common man and woman' but in those striving for the riches offered in twentieth-century urban America. Smaller neighborhood theatres, without a stage show, with limited service, and in less-than-optimal surroundings, were cheaper and thus the province of the working family.[36]

By following the Balaban & Katz strategy, exhibitors around the United States created carefully crafted packages of pleasure that consistently generated high profits. Movies per se were never the sole driving force to attract audiences to ante up their quarters, fifty-cent pieces, and, at times, dollar bills. Instead Balaban & Katz's strategy depended first on finding the location that could appeal to most riders of mass transit. Then the building was made so spectacular that it served as an attraction on its own. There was nothing like the lobby of the Uptown or the exterior of the Chicago Theatre. Once inside you were waited on, led to your seat, and made to feel comfortable – and in the summer cool.

Only then can we properly focus on the Balaban & Katz entertainment show. Its music and stage shows were reviewed, followed, and debated in the 1920s. Many patrons, at times, did not care what was actually playing on the screen. But the movies were there, and they fueled a special brand of entertainment in this well-located, entertainment paradise. Balaban & Katz's multi-media package of pleasure kept audiences enthralled and they looked forward to queuing up for the next show.

It is no wonder the major Hollywood companies scrambled to ally themselves with Balaban & Katz, and few were surprised when in 1925 Famous Players-Lasky, the largest movie company in the world, formally merged with the Chicago exhibitor. Sam Katz moved to New York, and during the late 1920s he successfully transferred the Balaban & Katz system to Paramount's theatres.

Soon the newly christened Publix chain was the world's largest, most profitable, and most imitated. Immediately Katz set in motion on a national scale the five-part strategy that had worked so well in Chicago. The centralisation of the movie business would become the standard that Hollywood would employ in the next twenty years.[37]

The successes of the Loew's, the Stanley Company of America, and the Balaban & Katz chain operations were soon copied around the country. Indeed these three became the bases of three of the largest Hollywood movies companies – Loew's and MGM, Stanley and Warner Bros., and Balaban & Katz and Paramount. By the late 1920s, as sound was apparently transforming the movie business, major regional chains in every city made sure that little was disrupted. They had control, and when Hollywood came to bid and buy, the founders of these great operations sold out. Based on this foundation, the coming of sound would lead to profits unprecedented in the history of Hollywood. From New York and Hollywood offices the chief operating officers and presidents of the five major studios – with their powerful theatre chains – ruled the mainstream movie industry and set up the conditions for filmgoing in what is now labeled the golden age of the movies.

NOTES

1. *Motography*, June 1912, p. 247; *Exhibitor's Film Exchange*, 1 July 1915, p. 28; 21 August 1915, p. 4; 2 October 1915, p. 5; *Exhibitor's Herald*, 26 February 1916, p. 7; *Motion Picture News*, 15 July 1916, p. 315; *Motography*, 7 April 1917, p. 704.
2. *Motography*, March, 1912, p. 105 and 17 April 1915, p. 620; *Exhibitor's Film Exchange*, 9 October 1915, p. 23; *Motography*, 2 December 1916, p. 1220; Joseph P. Kennedy, ed., *The Story of Films* (Chicago: A. W. Shaw, 1927), pp. 349–50; *United States of America v. Motion Picture Patents Co. et al.*, 225 F. 800 (1915), record, vol. V, p. 2737.
3. *Exhibitor's Herald*, 24 November 1917, p. 23 and 15 December 1917, p. 217; *Motion Picture News*, 22 December 1917, p. 4426 and 1 June 1918, pp. 3327–8; F. Cyril James, *The Growth of Chicago Banks* (New York: Harper Bros., 1938), p. 1304; Melchoir Palyi, *The Chicago Credit Market* (Chicago: University of Chicago Press, 1937), p. 71; John Sherman Porter, ed., *Moody's Manual of Industrials* (New York: Moody's Investor Service, 1920), p. 1514.
4. *Who's Who in Chicago and Illinois* (Chicago: A. N. Marquis, 1917), pp. 75, 584; *Who's Who in Chicago and Illinois* (Chicago: A. N. Marquis, 1926), pp. 107, 625; Paul M. Angle, *Philip K. Wrigley* (Chicago: Rand McNally, 1975), pp. 11–41; M. R. Werner, *Julius Rosenwald* (New York: Harper, 1938), pp. 20–2; 'Paramount Pictures,' *Fortune* vol. 15 (March 1937): 87–96; Tedlow, *New and Improved*, pp. 261–300.
5. *Moving Picture World*, 19 October 1918, p. 366; *Exhibitor's Herald*, 7 June 1919, p. 35; *Motion Picture News*, 5 April 1919, p. 4; *Exhibitor's Herald and Motography*, 31 April 1919, p. 37; *Motion Picture News*, 31 May 1919, p. 3574; *Exhibitor's Herald and Motography*, 6 September 1919, p. 46; *Motion Picture News*, 6 December 1919, p. 4065; *Exhibitor's Herald and Motography*, 4 October 1919, p. 47; *Motion Picture News*, 24 January 1920, p. 1038; 26 February 1912, p. 1615; 6 August 1921, p. 759.
6. *Variety*, 26 May 1922, p. 39; *Motion Picture News*, 24 June 1922, p. 3321; *Variety*, 23 June 1922, p. 38 and 7 July 1922, p. 61; *Motion Picture News*, 8 July 1922, p. 178; 15 December 1923, p. 2771; 8 September 1923, p. 1170; *Variety*, 12

July 1923, p. 20; 9 April 1924, p. 16; 23 July 1924, p. 24; *Motion Picture News*, 15 November 1924, p. 2482.

7. *Motion Picture News*, 10 May 1924, p. 2085; *Variety*, 14 January 1925, p. 21; *Motion Picture News*, 14 February 1925, p. 708 and 14 March 1925, p. 1150; *Variety*, 2 September 1925, p. 33; 15 July 1925, p. 23; 4 November 1925, p. 29; 16 December 1925, p. 29; 7 April 1926, pp. 24, 28; Kennedy, *The Story of Films*, p. 75.

8. Barney Balaban and Sam Katz, *The Fundamental Principles of Balaban and Katz Theatre Management* (Chicago: Balaban & Katz, 1926), p. 54.

9. James L. Davis, *The Elevated System and the Growth of Chicago* (Evanston.: Northwestern University, Department of Geography, 1965), pp. 11–49; Homer Hoyt, *One Hundred Years of Land Values in Chicago* (Chicago: University of Chicago Press. 1933), pp. 1–53.

10. Irving Cutler, 'The Jews of Chicago: From Shtetl to Suburb,' in *Ethnic Chicago* eds. Melvin G. Holli and Peter d'A. Jones (Grand Rapids: William B. Eerdman's Publishing, 1984), pp. 46–69.

11. Chicago Plan Commission, *Forty-Four Cities in the City of Chicago* (Chicago: Chicago Plan Commission, 1942), pp. 27–8; Louis Wirth. *The Ghetto* (Chicago: University of Chicago Press, 1928), pp. 241–52. To capture a flavor of what it was like read Meyer Levin, *The Old Bunch* (New York: The Citadel Press, 1937). Levin based his novel on friends and experiences in this Chicago neighborhood.

12. T. V. Smith and Leonard D. White, eds., *Chicago: An Experiment in Social Science Research* (Chicago: University of Chicago Press, 1929), pp. 113–18; Malcolm J. Proudfoot. 'The Major Outlying Business Centers of Chicago,' unpublished Ph.D. dissertation, University of Chicago, 1936, pp. 16–50, 100–224; Hoyt, *One Hundred Years*, pp. 227–31; Balaban and Katz, *The Fundamental Principles*, p. 87.

13. Chicago Plan Commission, *Forty-Four Cities*, pp. 118–19.

14. Michael Conant, *Antitrust in the Motion Picture Industry*, (Berkeley: University of California Press, 1960), pp. 154–5; Chicago Recreation Commission, *The Chicago Recreation Survey*, 1937, vol. II, 'Commercial Recreation' (Chicago, 1938), pp. 36–7; Hoyt, *One Hundred Years*, p. 262.

15. Federal Writers Project, *New York City Guide* (New York: Random House, 1939), pp. 226–52; New York Herald, *The New York Market* (New York: New York Herald, 1922), pp. 60, 63; Allan Nevins and John A. Krout, eds., *The Greater City* (New York: Columbia University Press, 1948), pp. 148–72; Walter Laidlow, *Population of the City of New York, 1890–1932* (New York: Cities Census Committee, 1932), pp. 51–8; Harold T. Lewis, *Transit and Transportation*, Regional Survey, vol. IV (New York: Regional Plan of New York. 1928), pp. 19–69.

16. Levin, *The Old Bunch*, p. 58.

17. But not everyone shared this unabashed enthusiasm. H. L. Mencken wrote in 1928: 'I advocate hanging architects whose work is intolerably bad. Most of them specialise in the design of movie and gasoline cathedrals.' Quoted in 'Editorial Comment,' *Architecture*, vol. 57, no. 6 (June 1928): 319.

18. For an analysis of Rapp & Rapp see Robert A. M. Stern, Gregory Gilmartin, and Thomas Mellins, *Architecture and Urbanism Between the Two World Wars* (New York: Rizzoli, 1987), p. 256.

19. Ben M. Hall, *The Best Remaining Seats* (New York: Bramhall House, 1961), pp. 136–42.

20. 'Uptown Theatre,' *Marquee*, vol. 9, no. 2 (Second Quarter, 1977): 1–27; Theatre Historical Society, *Chicago Theatre* (Notre Dame, Ind.: Theatre Historical Society, 1975), pp. 1–20; 'Special Issue on the Balaban & Katz Tivoli Theatre,' *Marquee*, vol. 17. no. 4 (Fourth Quarter 1985): 1–36; George L. Rapp, 'History of Cinema Theater Architecture,' in *Living Architecture*, ed. Arthur Woltersdorf (Chicago: A. Kroch, 1930), pp. 55–64. John W. Landon, *Jesse Crawford* (Vestal: Vestal Press, 1974), pp. 19–44.

21. Arthur Mayer. *Merely Colossal* (New York: Simon and Schuster, 1953), p. 71; Ira Berkow, *Maxwell Street* (Garden City: Doubleday, 1977), p. 201.
22. Balaban and Katz, *The Fundamental Principles*, pp. 14–15, 54–5.
23. Kennedy, *The Story of Films*, pp. 269–273; *Exhibitor's Herald and Motography*, 21 December 1918, p. 25; Balaban and Katz, *The Fundamental Principles*, pp. 20–33.
24. For more on the history of the stage show see Hall, *The Best Remaining Seats*, pp. 200–6 and Charles Beardsley, *Hollywood's Master Showman: The Legendary Sid Grauman* (New York: Cornwall Books, 1983), pp. 42–7, 57–8, 76–7.
25. Compare this with the success of Sid Grauman, who centered his publicity campaigns around Hollywood-sponsored premieres. Grauman may be credited with the development of the prologue, but his success was due to access to movie stars. Balaban & Katz in distant Chicago (days away by train) had no such means of publicity. See David Karnes, 'The Glamorous Crowd: Hollywood Movie Premièrs Between the Wars,' *American Quarterly*, vol. 38, no. 4 (Fall 1986): 557–60.
26. *Variety*, 22 September 1922, p. 1; Hall, *The Best Remaining Seats*, p. 208; *Variety*, 25 October 1923, p. 18; 14 June 1923, p. 21; 11 March 1925, pp. 39–40; Carrie Balaban, *Continuous Performance* (New York: A. J. Balaban Foundation, 1941), pp. 46–60.
27. Vincente Minnelli, *I Remember It Well* (Garden City: Doubleday, 1974), pp. 52–6; *Variety*, 12 April 1923, p. 30; 12 July 1923, p 27; 1 November 1923, p. 26; 8 November 1923, p. 21.
28. *Variety*, 8 December 1922, p. 37; 29 March 1923, p. 30; 23 September 1925, p. 32; 18 March 1925, p. 27; 31 January 1924, p. 21.
29. Landon. *Jesse Crawford*, pp. 30–42. See David L. Junchen, *Encyclopedia of the American Theatre Organ*, vol. I (Pasadena: Showcase Publications, 1985), pp. 16–22 for a technical history of the remarkable organs manufactured for theatres. The author estimates about seven thousand were made and placed, principally between 1923 and 1929.
30. *Variety*, 22 July 1925, p. 27; 5 August 1925, p. 27; 19 August 1925, pp. 32, 35; 28 October 1925, p. 30; 26 May 1926, p. 23; Hall, *The Best Remaining Seats*, pp. 187–8.
31. Fred Wittenmeyer, 'Cooling of Theatres and Public Buildings,' *Ice and Refrigeration*, July 1922, pp. 13–14; Fred Wittenmeyer, 'Development of Carbon Dioxide Refrigerating Machines,' *Ice and Refrigeration*, November 1916, p. 165, R. E. Cherne, 'Developments in Refrigeration as Applied to Air Conditioning,' *Ice and Refrigeration*, January 1941, pp. 29–30; Walter L. Feisher, 'How Air Conditioning Has Developed in Fifty Years,' *Heating, Piping and Air Conditioning*, January 1950, pp. 120–2.
32. Barney Balaban, 'My Biggest Mistake,' *Forbes*, vol. 50 (1 February 1946) 16; Ruth Ingels, *Willis Haviland Carrier: Father of Air Conditioning* (New York: Doubleday, 1952), p. 143.
33. 'Air Conditioning System in Motion Picture House,' *Ice and Refrigeration*, November 1925, pp. 251–2; 'Heating, Ventilating and Cooling Plant of the Tivoli Theatre,' *Power Plant Engineering*, 1 March 1922, pp. 249–55.
34. 'Air Conditioning,' *Ice and Refrigeration*, November 1925, p. 251.
35. *Variety*, 10 June 1925, p. 31 and 9 September 1925, p. 30; Ingels, *Willis Haviland Carrier*, pp. 65–8; Oscar E. Anderson *Refrigeration in America* (Princeton: Princeton University Press, 1953), pp. 309–11.
36. Lizabeth Cohen, *Making a New Deal: Industrial Workers in Chicago, 1919–1939* (New York: Cambridge University Press, 1990), pp. 121–5 and Lizabeth Cohen, 'Encountering Mass Culture at the Grassroots: The Experience of Chicago Workers in the 1920s,' *American Quarterly*, vol. 41, no. 1 (March 1989); 1–16.
37. *Variety*, 28 October 1925, p. 27; Mason Miller, 'Famous Players in Transition Period,' *The Magazine of Wall Street*, 23 April 1927, p. 1178; *Variety*, 26 June

1929, p. 5; 'Review of Operations – Paramount Famous Lasky,' *Commercial and Financial Chronicle*, 21 April 1928, p. 2490.

An Afterword by Douglas Gomery

What you have just read is a small part of a book I wrote fifteen years ago. In Chapter 3 of 14, I analyse the rise of national chains of cinemas in the USA, with examples of attempts at fashioning a business model, and then the ultimate formula perfected by Chicago's Balaban & Katz. This part of one chapter comes within the Business History section of my book, and is not intended to cover the technical, social or cultural implications of what Balaban & Katz wrought. Yet, as business history, I think it stands the test of time. However, one point has been ignored in literature since I wrote the section: the highly innovative technological change wrought by air conditioning. The Carrier Corporation has now opened an archive and encouraged scholars to accept the myth that Willis Carrier was the most important person in bringing air conditioning to the USA. He certainly should be credited for making air conditioning affordable to US home owners, but Balaban & Katz and the Kroeschell Bros. Ice Company were the true pioneers. These brothers, lost in history, taught Chicagoans and other owners of theatre chains the importance of air conditioning. But there is no archive of this corporation, and no publicity machine celebrating a hero, only data from the trade press of the day. Historians ought to learn an important the lesson from Carrier and Kroeschell Bros. – that just because a corporation has an archive that is easy to use does not mean that the corporation was important. We can see this with the United Artists Corporation, the smallest of the major corporations in the studio system. We have more business records for this company than any other, but that does not make UA the leading Hollywood studio. Also, if extended – and part of a longer history – my segment would include analysis of the ethnicity of the brothers Balaban and their in-law Sam Katz as members of the Jewish migration to Chicago and their success in reading the desires of the Chicago melting pot audiences of the 1920s. It would also include more on the significance of the architectural and service elements. At the time, for example, the leading architectural critics mocked the Rapp & Rapp styling; now we applaud them as true US innovations. In addition, I did not do enough on the combination of live vaudeville shows and the movies. I knew this at the time, but wanted to finish the book before I died.

Balaban & Katz also kept the stage show alive and well into the 1950s when vaudeville became 'vaudeo' and was transferred to television – first by Ed Sullivan and then Milton Berle. This is the weakest section of the unit in that I relied on *Variety*. *Billboard* and other trade papers should be examined, as well as vaudeville sources from collections such as those found at the University of Iowa. Far more research needs to be done and I encourage readers to take up the question: How were silent film narratives presented, with live orchestra music, and live stage shows?

6

COMPETING WITH HOLLYWOOD:
NATIONAL FILM INDUSTRIES OUTSIDE
HOLLYWOOD

A glance around the world in the 1920s reveals a heterogeneous film history but one replete with anxieties about American cultural imperialism and the homogenising tendencies of mass culture. The German film industry competed most successfully with America in that its domestic productions outweighed foreign imports in the 1920s and Britain put up a very good fight at the box office, with 1927 its *annus mirabilis*. However, protectionist measures would characterise a decade in which national cinemas sought to hold their own against Hollywood's incursions into other national cinemas. Audiences in Australia, Canada and India, for example, received a diet of mainly American fare. The American challenge to European and other cinemas was also underwritten by the federal support that the American film industry received from the US Government's Commerce Department, designed to support a developing industry. Nevertheless, the national cinema that produced the highest number of films in the 1920s was Japan's. Japanese cinema was a domestic product, and rarely exported, yet its major studios were highly organised and vertically integrated and directors tended to enjoy more artistic freedom within the evolving studio system. The significance of Japanese cinema may have been 'discovered' in the West by Noël Burch in the 1970s but we see the beginnings of Yasuijuro Ozu's career as an *auteur* in the Japanese cinema of the 1920s.

Japanese cinema was not insular despite its emphasis on the national. One of the earliest successes, *Souls on the Road* (1921), was a loose adaptation of the *The Lower Depths* by the Russian writer Maxim Gorky. Similarly, directors such as Teinosuke Kinugasa drew on German Expressionist cinema, as in

A Page of Madness (1926) which was loosely based on *The Cabinet of Dr Caligari* (1919). Yasujiro Ozu, who would go on to direct *Tokyo Story* in 1953, began his career with *Days of Youth* in 1929 which was heavily influenced by American slapstick comedy, telling the story of a man whose skis run away from him. As these examples indicate, it would be a mistake to assume that national cinemas will be characterised by distinctive and discrete artistic qualities that do not correspond with those of other national cinemas. A detailed study of the cinema of the 1920s reveals intertextual and technical influences at work. Where a thematic approach to film technique and content reveals connections and continuities between types of cinema, reading cinema according to a nation's culture and society will emphasise ways in which local conditions inform film style, but we should be cautious. For example, classical Hollywood continuity editing is generally accepted as comprising techniques of cross-cutting, eyeline matching shots and analytical editing in order to sustain the narrative as it cuts between plot and sub-plot. Griffith's techniques of cross-cutting and flashbacks in *Intolerance* (1916) with its weaving together of four different historical moments is considered exemplary of this style. But, as David Bordwell shows in *The History of Film Style* (1997), there has been a tendency to divide philosophies and techniques of filmmaking into two distinct traditions, with editing often considered 'American' and *mise-en-scène* and visual depth typically 'European'. To polarise cinematic tendencies according to geographical locations or, indeed, by film genres, can be unhelpful, especially when Hollywood cinema was so influenced by European émigrés. Erich von Stroheim's *Greed* (1924) made important use of depth of focus and Abel Gance's *The Wheel* (1923) deploys rapid editing as a form of Impressionist experimentation. Many other examples would also complicate such an approach to the history of film style. One thing is clear: while the emphasis had been on action and movement in the medium's early years, across different national cinemas filmmakers began to explore the emotional and expressive potential of cinematic art.

The First World War had changed the history of cinema: from sharing discoveries and trends, some national cinemas were balkanised (Germany and Russia closed their doors to film imports) and the American industry profited from the economic devastation in Europe that made film production slacken (see Chapter 3). By the late 1920s, the US could boast that it supplied around 80 per cent of pictures for most foreign markets, and 90 per cent in Australia and New Zealand. American success abroad, consolidated by the First World War's effect on European film industries, was reinforced by the very limited exhibition of foreign pictures in American theatres, despite national cinemas sending their products to the US. In fact, the importing of European films stimulated domestic production and Hollywood's push into foreign markets. The domination of European markets by US film exhibition was not achieved overnight in the 1920s, though. It was a cumulative effect in that even before the war it is estimated that between 60 to 70 per cent of films shown in British cinemas, for example, were American in origin. This had led British producers to campaign for a quota system that would guarantee exhibition for their own productions. Their plea went unheard, however, until the Cinematograph Films Act of 1927 finally led to the instigation of a quota system in 1928.

Across Europe, state-supported cinemas called for co-operation to control distribution. To begin with, co-operation led to co-production, as with Michael Balcon's studio Gainsborough and UFA (Universum Film Aktien Gesellschaft) in the case of Hitchcock's *The Pleasure Garden* (1925). Then Film Europe developed to organise quotas across the region, slowly blocking American saturation. The sound era would put paid to co-operation of this kind since foreign languages and accents were a barrier to international communication. European national cinemas could not compete with the sheer volume of movies being released in the US, sometimes 700 a year by the end of the 1920s; or the level of financial investment in each production; or the salaries paid to Hollywood stars. Hollywood films were popular: the classical Hollywood style of telling stories on screen, largely realist in its reliance on continuity editing, would ultimately win out against the competition, especially when that competition came in the form of 'art cinema'. Even the most popular of Hollywood's competitors favoured modernist film styles over more conventional narrative pleasures and by the end of the 1920s Hollywood had an oligopolistic relationship to world cinema. Nevertheless, the European initiative known as 'Film Europe' that ran between 1924 and 1928 endeavoured to ensure a reciprocal distribution of film sales that might rival the US. It enjoyed a certain success in combining small national cinemas but ran out of steam when Germany's UFA, its biggest producer, ran out of money. The final nail in Film Europe's coffin was the introduction of sound film at the end of the decade.

Individual nations had very different histories, of course. Before the First World War, Denmark had been a very successful exporter of films through Nordisk. Later, Danish cinema was dominated by the talents of director Carl Dreyer whose sensitive close-ups of actors' faces conveyed an intensity seemingly rivalled only by D. W. Griffith. For example, his *The Passion of Joan of Arc* (1928) was critically acclaimed for its experimental close-ups though it failed at the box office, despite – or because of – its chilling psychological intensity and scenes of excruciating physical torture. Although best known for *Days of Wrath* (1943), Dreyer forged his film style in the silent era with Nordisk up to 1925. When Germany and Russia closed their doors to imports, Nordisk felt the effects and the loss of key figures in filmmaking and acting to Sweden, Germany and Hollywood – such as star Asta Nielsen and pioneering director Benjamin Christensen – exacerbated Danish cinema's decline.

Italian cinema had also begun well, concentrating on spectacular epics such as *Quo Vadis?* (1912) which influenced D. W. Griffith's first long (that is, four-reel) feature *Judith of Bethulia* (1913) (see Chapter 4). But, once Italy entered the war in 1916, the nation's cinema suffered a sharp decline and even the success of its divas would not ensure that its reduced output could compete with

America's success. Italy did not regain its foothold in the industry at the end of the war. In 1923 the Italians remade that national favourite *Quo Vadis?* but its failure signalled that the cinema could not recover. It would take the coming of sound to reinvigorate the nation's industry. Sweden had perhaps the most self-sufficient national cinema in the period preceding American domination. Concentrating on the domestic market, Swedish films were inspired by the country's landscapes and villages, which featured as distinctive backdrops. In fact, Swedish cinema was so incredibly successful that it emerged as a real challenge to Hollywood's hegemony after the war, its 'Golden Age' dominated by Victor Sjöström, Mauritz Stiller and Georg af Klerker, polymaths, all of whom had been acting and writing screenplays as well as directing since the 1910s. Klerker remains the least well known; at ease with comedy or melodrama, his films were only rediscovered as recently as the 1980s, but Sjöström and Stiller were hugely famous and both moved to Hollywood in the mid-1920s.

In Sweden in the 1920s Sjöström and Stiller were prolific, making films for Svenska, the national company that had modelled itself on Denmark's Nordisk and adapting bestselling Swedish author Selma Lagerlöf's novels to great acclaim. Stiller, actually born in Finland, was best known for comedies of manners which influenced Ernst Lubitsch and others, and for setting Greta Garbo on the path to fame, starring her in *The Atonement of Gösta Berling* (1924) before accompanying her to Hollywood the following year at the behest of Louis B. Mayer of MGM. Unhappy in Hollywood and dogged by ill-health, he returned to Sweden in 1927 and died a year later. Sjöström also returned home, in 1930, but he was by far the more successful at making the transition to the American film factories, as evidenced in his adaptation of Nathaniel Hawthorne's novel *The Scarlet Letter* (1926), *The Tower of Lies* (1925) with Lon Chaney, and *The Wind* (1928), perhaps his own and even Lillian Gish's finest cinematic achievement. That Sweden's phenomenal success in silent film was based on the work of so few directors led to its decline after their departure. Charles Magnusson, head of Svenska, secured the sole distribution rights for MGM releases in Sweden as part payment for losing Sjöström, but as American imports started to dominate so Sweden began to lose its national distinctiveness, to find it again only with Ingmar Bergman and his use of Swedish myths in the art cinema of the 1950s.

The most successful film production company outside Hollywood in the silent era was Germany's UFA, founded by Paul Davidsohn in 1911 but financially underwritten by the German government during the First World War to contribute to the war effort by supplying propaganda films for the troops at the front and Germans at home. In the wake of Germany's defeat, UFA was denationalised and as a result of its considerable success the industry was able to buy out all government interest in 1918. Nevertheless, UFA remained bound to an explicit national aim: to promote German ideas and customs at home and abroad. The industry got off to fine start since between

1916 and 1921 the nation banned the importation of any foreign films. Of a number of small film companies, UFA's strongest competitor was producer Erich Pommer's Decla-Bioscope, which had made *The Cabinet of Dr Caligari* and employed the director Fritz Lang. But in 1921 the two companies merged into UFA and their consolidation led to what is known as German cinema's 'Golden Age' of the 1920s. Even though both Britain and America had banned German imports following the war, they were seduced by reviews of Expressionist films and the ban was lifted. In fact, Alfred Hitchcock leased UFA's studio space to film *The Pleasure Garden* and harnessed aspects of a German Expressionist visual style in *The Lodger* (1927), his first real success, and in *Blackmail* (1929).

The Cabinet of Dr Caligari exhibits the potent combination of horror and fantasy for which German cinema became renowned. Caligari (Werner Krauss) and the zombie Cesare (Conrad Veidt) spawned a clutch of arch villains and criminals including Fritz Lang's criminal Dr Mabuse, as well as the mad scientist Rotwang in *Metropolis (1927)*, and F. W. Murnau's vampire Nosferatu. Such strong characterisation and distinctive Expressionist style, achieved solely in the studio, lent the Weimar cinema an aesthetic sophistication that other national cinemas could only begin to emulate by luring filmmakers away, to Hollywood, for example. German Expressionism was an art movement that began before the First World War but which took hold of Weimar cinema in the 1920s. It is broadly anti-naturalistic, characterised by psychological symbolism and an intense feeling of social alienation. The set designers on *The Cabinet of Dr Caligari* were Expressionist painters and the disorienting sets they created were examples of what Lotte Eisner in her book on Weimar cinema (1969) would call the 'haunted screen'. The film is generally credited with inaugurating Expressionism as a cinema movement. At its most successful Expressionism combines with a strain of German Romanticism and it is certainly the case that *The Golem* (1920), *Nosferatu* (Murnau's 1922 adaptation of Bram Stoker's *Dracula*) and similar successes recall the sinister fairytales of the Brothers Grimm and E. T. A. Hoffman. This Gothic element distinguished German cinema of the period from all other national movements. It involved a highly stylised architecture of death and desire, as in shots of Nosferatu in his necrophilic yearning, gazing at Ellen through windows shaped like coffins. The importance of chiaroscuro lighting in such films cannot be overstated and it would inform the style of American cinema in later years, especially the horror films of the 1930s and *film noir* of the 1940s.

European cinema was becoming synonymous with style and sophistication and it follows that Hollywood would begin to poach Europe's most internationally renowned directors. The creative talent that guaranteed UFA's success would later reinforce Hollywood's own stable. UFA's directors included names that would become prominent in Hollywood filmmaking as the rise of Hitler led them to leave Germany: Robert Siodmak, Michael Curtiz (still known as Mihály Kertész while in Germany), Alexander Korda, Ernst Lubitsch and Fritz Lang. Nevertheless, the 1920s in Germany saw a consistent creative output from *The Golem* through to *The Last Laugh* (1924) and Fritz Lang's *Metropolis* (1927). Also on UFA's creative staff was Karl Freund whose camerawork on *The Last Laugh* was to influence film style around the world. Complementing director Murnau's modernist vision of his character's subjectivity, Freund strapped the camera to a cameraman, barrelling around the drunken porter to create a visual sense of his dizziness, and he stood the camera on a turntable, letting it spin. In the sometimes elliptical relationship between the frames, a feeling of space emerges and Freund exploits ideas of freedom and movement in Murnau's ongoing critique of a cruel and decadent society. In the opening scene, for example, a travelling shot moves down a lift shaft and into a hotel lobby, passing through a glass door, and moving outside to the old porter (Emil Jannings) hailing taxis for patrons. The use of cranes and dollies had begun to free the camera. Fox invited Murnau to Hollywood when *The Last Laugh* became a hit on its American release. UFA had amassed a valuable cache of actors, such as Jannings and the Polish actress Pola Negri, and of technicians at each stage of the production process, such as Freund and Rudolph Maté. UFA enjoyed the talent and expertise of the tried and tested and among the studio's writers, Thea von Harbou and Carl Mayer were the most prolific.

Fritz Lang's *Metropolis* was UFA and Germany's most expensive and ambitious film project of the decade and it established its director as the leading light in the nation's cinema and on the international stage. It was a financial failure for UFA, however, largely due to the hundreds of extras and the spectacular sets influenced by Max Reinhardt's theatrical style. The screenplay by Lang and Thea von Harbou from her novel was a shocking dystopian vision of the year 2000. It tells the story of a classic battle between good and evil but is nevertheless sufficiently complex for it to have been lauded by both ends of the political spectrum during the rise of Nazism. *Metropolis* has been seen to echo Lang's left-leaning politics, the same politics that saw him set sail for America in 1935 – though he had been courted since the film's release in 1927 – once he saw Nazism becoming entrenched. In stark contrast, his wife Thea von Harbou's right-wing politics saw her remain in Germany to become one of the Third Reich's most successful writers. This apparent contradiction is perhaps most accurately expressed in the ideological tension between Expressionism's belief in a basic humanism and Futurism's elevation of new technologies over humanity and human endeavour. In the film, such ideas are also revealed in the gap in the narrative's apparent resolution. While Freder and Maria come together in love, despite their class differences – in a symbolic scene of Capital and Labour hand-in-hand before the Cathedral – the fate of the workers who have revolted is left unclear.

Metropolis would also seem to signal the lavish beginning of the end of German Expressionist cinema primarily because UFA's anxiety over its slipping finances led the company to make a deal with Paramount and MGM.

The 'Parufamet' Agreement (an amalgamation of Paramount, UFA and Metro) secured UFA an American loan in 1926 and thereby the Americans' distribution rights in Germany, saturating the German market and quickly organising their own distributors while buying up theatre chains. In this way German competition with America was weakened and by the end of the decade many of Germany's major talents – from F. W. Murnau to up-and-coming successes like Erich von Stroheim and Marlene Dietrich – were in the US. UFA's Carl Mayer scripted Murnau's *Sunrise* (1927), the film that assured the German director's success on both sides of the Atlantic and secured actress Janet Gaynor one of the first Academy awards for her portrayal of 'The Wife'. It has become a commonplace to describe *Sunrise* as 'German' or at least European in style (the production team comprised predominantly German émigrés, notably Erich Pommer) but it was shot in America with American actors. This has accounted for the critical acclaim it received and for its lack of popular success on release. With the passing of the decades and with the heightened sense of the Expressionist qualities of *film noir*, *Sunrise* has been reconsidered a classically 'American' masterpiece, a shift that is indicative of Hollywood persuading German directors towards distinctively 'American' themes.

A director whose success followed on the heels of the UFA directors was G. W. Pabst whose socially realist cinema was both acclaimed and a cause of controversy, with some countries – England, Italy and France – banning *The Joyless Street* (1925) or cutting it. Austrian-born Pabst made economic deprivation explicit in the scenes in which Greta Garbo (in her first German-produced film) and Asta Nielsen become prostitutes in order to support their families, a theme he would return to in *Pandora's Box* (1929). Pabst was a true exponent of world cinema insofar as his primary influences were Soviet rather than national. While his context was the collapse of the Austrian bourgeoisie in postwar Vienna, his style emphasised Eisenstein's theories of montage and eschewed the German tendency towards *mise-en-scène*. In films such as *The Joyless Street* and *The Love of Jeanne Ney* (1927), he developed his own more fluid montage, designed to privilege the viewer's gaze so that an action begun in one shot would be completed in a single fluid movement in the next. In this way, he found an individual style even within UFA's studio-led productions.

While slapstick comedy became the province of director and producer Mack Sennet and actor and director Charlie Chaplin in the 1920s, it had its film origins in France and Italy, especially in the form of Feuillade's comedies (see Chapter 3). Feuillade had also produced the serial *Les Vampires* (1915–16) which successfully deployed the war-torn streets of Paris as the backdrop before turning to *Judex* (1916) in which the eponymous avenging hero, whose stories were serialised in French newspapers, came to cinematic life in twelve mysterious episodes. Feuillade's serials were popular but were not appreciated as art until the Surrealist movement of the 1920s acknowledged their fantasy elements. The importance of 'art' to national cinema was reflected in Impressionism, a movement which began around 1919 and continued to influence until the end of the 1920s. Impressionism was conceived as distinctively 'French' and was seen as a means to combat American competition but it did not enjoy the success of German Expressionism, largely because its experimentalism did not always attract audiences and American films continued to flood the French market until a quota system was finally launched in the 1930s.

Impressionist filmmakers such as Germaine Dulac, Jean Epstein, Abel Gance and critic Louis Delluc emphasised the importance of conveying feeling; narrative was often auxiliary – Gance's *The Folly of Dr Tube* (1915), filled with distorted images of madness, was so experimental that it was denied release. While Delluc and Epstein refined the theory of Impressionist filmmaking, in general, Impressionists discovered that in order to fund experimental cinema they had to work in the mainstream too – or generate typically Impressionist scenes within conventional narrative films. In *The Wheel* Gance combined aesthetic experimentation with a tragic love story. In the rapid editing of a train's wheels hurtling down the tracks, a synecdoche for the driver's anguish, Gance captures the visual rhythm that Impressionists believed was central to the emotional impressions they wanted to convey while binding that rhythm seamlessly into a story of the 'wheel of fate'. As the decade wore on Impressionist films were harder to market and the coming of sound with its increased production costs made it almost impossible for avant-garde projects to compete on the same terms.

The French Avant-Garde movement of the 1920s had diverged into the Surrealist movement towards the end of the decade and it may be that the flow of different artistic styles was a contributory factor in French cinema failing to find a foothold on the international scene. Germaine Dulac who had directed a number of Impressionist films including *The Smiling Madame Beudet* (1922) formed her own production company, Delia Films, and made *The Seashell and the Clergyman* which, though banned following release in 1927, was later acknowledged as a classic of the Surrealist movement. René Clair, who achieved fame with his comedies of manners such as *The Italian Straw Hat* (1928), began experimenting with fantasy from his very first film, *Sleeping Paris* (1924), and the story of a ray gun that paralyses the city prefigures the Surrealists later in the decade. At the same time, French experimentation with 'Dada' films and Cubist cinema found expression in Luis Buñuel and the painter Salvador Dali's classic *Un Chien Andalou* (1928) which was designed to shock French élite cinemagoers with bizarre sexual and animal images (a man squeezes a woman's breasts and dead donkeys lie putrefying on top of grand pianos). When audiences were fascinated as well as shocked, Buñuel denied the film's 'art' and played up its notoriety. In 1930 his *L'Age d'Or* would be banned mainly due to a scene with a Christ-like figure at an orgy. The nightmare world of the Surrealists, with insanity their avowed inspiration, later found a popular niche when Hitchcock famously deployed Dali's art in the dream sequence in *Spellbound* (1945), his most effective 'pop' at psychologists.

Outside Europe the success of national cinemas was sporadic. In Africa the rise of cinema was inevitably stalled by the deleterious effects of colonialism on indigenous populations. There were many films *about* Africa, such as the anthropological 'explorer' films of Martin Johnson (*Simba* [1928] and *Congorilla* [1932]), filmed on the continent but never distributed there and, of course, the Tarzan serials based on Edgar Rice Burroughs' novels. *Tarzan of the Apes* directed by Scott Sidney in 1918 was a huge hit outside Africa and in the 1930s such films as *Sanders of the River* (1935) would even find success in Africa. African nations did begin to experiment with cinema, as in the Tunisian director Albert Shemama Chikly's *The Gazelle's Eye* (1924) and the films of Egyptian director Widād Urfi who worked for the Italo-Egyptian film company and co-directed *Lailā* in 1927. However, African cinema remained saturated by colonialist representations for many more decades.

One of the most notable of national cinemas, especially in terms of its contribution to film theory and film culture, was Russian cinema which really began to take off in the 1910s. From 1914 when Russia entered the First World War, foreign distributors closed their offices and foreign saturation of the domestic scene ceased. Evgeni Bauer had made some eighty films in just four years, beginning work in the Tsarist era and later exploring the cataclysmic changes in Russian society after the February Revolution of 1917. Bauer died before the October Revolution was under way and early Soviet cinema was superseded by the post-revolutionary aesthetics of montage (see Chapter 8). Dziga Vertov captured the moment with wry emphasis when he stated in 1926, 'Actors who had once played Tsarist officials now play workers, actresses who once played court ladies, now pull faces in the approved Soviet style.' After the fall of the Tsars, the Bolshevik government centralised cinema under a state monopoly believing film to be an important component in the revolutionary struggle. Bauer's contemporary Yakov Protazanov was a rare example of a director who adapted successfully when Russian cinema changed so radically with the change of regime. He had begun directing in 1912, a series of morbid melodramas typical of the day, but after a spell in Paris returned as a successful director after the revolution. It was after 1917 that the Russians made more action films largely as a result of the influence of American cinematic productions and, in this sense, cinema in the USSR seemed to fall into distinct eras and types by the 1920s. While the tendency is always to see the breaks in film history as heralding new forms, there were elements of international continuity. For example, the Yermoliev film company moved to Paris in 1920 to avoid the nationalisation of the industry and re-oriented their style to produce Impressionist films with Jean Epstein and others.

Only after 1925, when a decision was taken to reverse state intervention, would Russian cinema begin to catch up with developments in other national cinemas. By the end of the 1920s, Soviet national cinema had come to international prominence, with such leading lights as Eisenstein, Vertov, Pudovkin and Dovzhenko and including neglected figures such as documentary filmmaker Esther Shub who worked first as a film editor and went on to direct later in the decade. Eisenstein stood at the head of Soviet Montage filmmaking and by the end of the decade Russian cinema's radical techniques were evident in all genres including documentary, as in Vertov's *Man with a Movie Camera* (1929).

Thomas Elsaesser's essay is a revised and updated version of 'Social Mobility and the Fantastic: German Silent Cinema', originally published in the film journal *Wide Angle* in 1982. It is a revisionist study that pays tribute to two classic film studies of the era – Siegfried Kracauer's sociological *From Caligari to Hitler* (1947) and Lotte Eisner's aesthetic study *The Haunted Screen* (1969). Elsaesser critiques what had become their 'consensus' view of the cinema of the period. He launches an inquiry into the 'fantastic' and its possible relation to the social reality of the Weimar republic, especially as mediated through nineteenth-century Romantic tropes by Eisner, and fantastic motifs as reworked in the early twentieth century in artistic and industrial contexts. In linking aesthetics with film technology, Elsaesser turns a critical eye on film's relationship to national culture in the moment prior to the rise of the Nazi movement in Germany. He also explores the extent to which German cinema itself determined the representation of Romantic and fantastic motifs.

This essay is the first example in *Film Histories* of textual analysis that combines literary and art history with cultural studies. It examines a particular national cinema through classic film texts in a particular historical moment, but it also acts as a critique of what that focus implies. Elsaesser seeks to re-orient what he sees as overemphasised connections between national cinema and the idea of a national 'psyche', or character, that homology between cinema and history on which many hermeneutic studies rest. In so doing, he challenges the equation that sees cinema as consciously or unconsciously reflecting a nation and a political agenda. He also reminds us that German Expressionism was an alternative or 'counter' cinema, a national product conceived to counter the saturation of German cinemas by French films prior to the First World War, American cinema and its global tentacles, as well as a more 'mainstream' German product. This is something that can be forgotten when the focus is those film 'texts' that have endured in film studies over the decades and when national cinema is not studied in an international context.

Elsaesser 'reads' German fantastic cinema, most notably through two films, *The Student of Prague* (1913) and *The Cabinet of Dr Caligari* (1919), that could be seen as solidly representative. In nuanced ways, he reads them through a double-voiced discourse, that of the artist-intellectual and the producer as they engage via cinema with a contemporary audience whose consumption of such films is bound up in a complex system of social and aesthetic exchange. His essay has become a classic film study, establishing as it does the idea of the 'social imaginary' in Weimar cinema, a concept that has influenced subsequent studies of national cinemas.

- Summarise the reasons why Elsaesser both values and critiques Kracauer and Eisner's different approaches to film history. How would you describe Elsaesser's methodological approach to a study of national cinemas?
- Evaluate what the film historian gains (or loses) by drawing textual analysis of individual films and aesthetic practices into a discussion of a particular period.
- What other approaches might you apply to a case study of film production in a specific national context?

SOCIAL MOBILITY AND THE FANTASTIC: GERMAN SILENT CINEMA

Thomas Elsaesser

I

Almost all attempts to define the German cinema of the silent era start with the observation that it is a cinema of the 'fantastic', having given rise to such notable figures as Dr Caligari, The Student of Prague, Nosferatu the Vampire, the Golem, or Maria, the female robot in *Metropolis*. The dark, daemonic, haunted and somehow profoundly irrational nature of this tradition has been argued in two well-known books, Siegfried Kracauer's *From Caligari to Hitler* and Lotte Eisner's *The Haunted Screen*.[1] Kracauer's study is a bold extended speculation about the social and political meaning that can be attached to such a pronounced preference for humanoids, vampires, automata, doubles, as well as other creatures hovering between man and beast and man and machine and living in the twilight zone of power and madness. Written in 1947 in New York, where Kracauer spent his enforced exile as a refugee from Nazi Germany, *From Caligari to Hitler* (as the title indicates) unequivocally declares the 'fantastic' tendencies of Weimar cinema to be a prelude or premonition of Nazism. He connects it sociologically to mass-unemployment and the pauperisation of the middle class as a consequence of World War I and the subsequent period of hyperinflation, while psychologically, he detects unresolved (male) conflicts with authority figures. As a methodology, Kracauer's thesis has ever since become the model for correlating the narratives of popular film with other forces in society and political life.[2] Eisner's *The Haunted Screen* is less sociological, and more art-historical in method and inspiration.[3] It connects the cinema of the 1920s not to political horrors to come but to the long tradition of fantastic figures in German literature and art since the Romantics and even further back, to medieval folk traditions.[4]

In looking once more at the fantastic and its possible roots in social life and national traits, I shall begin by taking my cue not from Kracauer, but from Lotte

This essay was first published as 'Social Mobility and the Fantastic: German Silent Cinema', in *Wide Angle* 5 (2), 1982, pp. 14–25. It appears here in a revised version.

Eisner's assertion that '[i]t is reasonable to argue that the German cinema is a development of German Romanticism, and that modern technique [i.e. cinematography] merely lends a visible form to Romantic fancies.[5] This assertion begs two questions: what precisely is the historical reality or indeed is there a precise historical reality to which Romantic figurations and motifs answer, and if so, why should the motifs return with such force in an apparently quite different historical context? And secondly, can we actually assume that a different technology does not affect the meaning and function of themes that the new medium appropriates in the form of an extended quotation?

My hypothesis is that there is indeed a pattern in the recurrence of Romantic motifs in German history, and that the cinema seems to have altered the meaning of this connection. If one studies the relation between the emergence of the Gothic novel and early twentieth-century history, between stories of Romantic agony, tales of horror, the supernatural and the industrial revolution, urbanisation or new forms of social control such as the cinema, then it seems that motifs of the fantastic both represent political conflicts and help disguise them. In particular, the fantastic raises the question of agency and at the same time obscures causal links, by attributing effective power to supernatural forces. The urgency and relevance of certain contemporary social issues is hidden, by translating itself, in the mode of the fantastic, into the urgency and violence of the irruption of these supernatural forces or agents in the fabric of the everyday. Their sudden appearance is, however, more often than not, set in another, more distant age. Medieval courts, Renaissance principalities, or the struggles of the Reformation and counter-Reformation provide the scenery: for depicting class relations, sexuality and its destructive power, and for giving vent to hostile feelings towards the clergy or other father/authority figures.

The Gothic novel at the beginning and at its revival at the end of the nineteenth century, as indeed much else in the Romantic arsenal, is a Europe-wide phenomenon. Gothic horror has variously been attributed to a reaction against Enlightenment rationality and a more explicitly political response to the French Revolution (in Britain) and the Napoleonic Wars (in Germany). At the same time, there is little question that rapid industrialisation provoked its own forms of dislocation, in which the contrast between city and country became profoundly refigured,[6] often with the result of making nature itself seem uncanny, haunting, poised to avenge itself on those despoiling the earth in search of mineral wealth, taking over rivers, lakes and waterfalls as cheap sources of mechanical energy, or clearing the woods for fuel and land.

It is therefore perfectly possible to find parallels between the 1830s and 1840s in Europe (the high tide of Romanticism), and the Germany of the 1910s and early 1920s. For while the unification of the German Reich under Bismarck had finally done away with the small feudal courts and petty aristocratic principalities which had blocked Germany's industrial development and its emergence as a bourgeois nation-state, it had left intact a powerful caste society, and a culture as well as an educational system which were deeply saturated and at the same time made contradictory by its élitist, feudal heritage. The survival in Germany (even after the bourgeois victory of the 1870s) of an imperial court, and of a bureaucratic-military administration (even after the defeat in 1918 and the emergence of strongly politicised working class) gave the struggle for power on the part of various sections of the bourgeoisie quite distinctive traits. The recurrence of Romantic and fantastic motifs might thus be explained as a reflection of this uneven development among social agents, and of the time-lag that separated Germany from its European neighbours, especially Britain and France, in respect of entering modernity.[7]

But while we can find explanations for the popularity and persistence of certain medieval and Romantic themes in German culture of later periods, this does not answer my second set of questions. Why and how do these themes appear specifically in the cinema and to what extent does the cinema itself determine the form in which they appear? Are there properties of cinema technology which make it a particularly suitable vehicle for figurations of the fantastic (which is what Eisner seems to imply)? Or might the issue not centre rather on the place that cinema came to occupy in cultural and social life during the Weimar period? One of the features typical of the German cinema in the early 1920s was the development of film technologies (with respect to lighting, camera movement, special effects) in the directorial mise-en-scène, which enabled it to accommodate an iconography of the fantastic, drawing upon figurations derived from Romanticism. But it did so for the benefit of a particular audience which, in its class composition and its expectations of what the modern world had to offer, was very different from any audience conceivable to the Romantics whose works were thus pillaged for tropes, topics and themes.

Kracauer, unlike Eisner, offers some sort of answer to this question, but it is an answer flawed by the fact that the cinema on which he concentrates in order to validate his historical thesis was not in fact a typical one. The German (Expressionist) silent cinema, however influential it has been on certain aspects of Hollywood filmmaking (the *film noir*, for instance, and the horror film), nonetheless constitutes a body of films whose textual construction did not impose itself on the commercial cinema. It was and has remained an 'alternative cinema', different from the German (commercial) mainstream. So different, in fact, that it has almost become incomprehensible, in much the same way as certain Romantic narrative genres became obsolete once the realist novel had appropriated the codes of representation and conflict in which a society recognised its moral or psychological reality. In other words, the whole body of techniques or hermeneutic traditions, whereby critics talk about the ways a work of literature 'reflects' its society, and by extension, the way films reflect social forces and trends, appears misapplied. And nowhere more spectacularly than in Kracauer's reading of the German cinema.

What seems to me most glaringly obvious, if we are to understand the manner in which history has entered into these films, is the double reduction that Kracauer operates on his material. In order to establish the homology between German cinema and German history on which his thesis rests, he first of all has to construct a very particular 'narrative' for German cinema. By this I do not primarily mean the inevitability he posits, where all events are seen to lead up to Hitler and fascism. What is problematic is the process and selection of the forces and determinants he deems as pertinent to our understanding of history. That he has to narrativise, even personalise, these forces is evident if we look at the protagonist he creates: the German 'soul', the national character, who becomes the plaything of instinct, sex, fate, destiny, tyrants and demons. The history he thus constructs is itself an Expressionist drama, and while he makes it clear that the categories he employs are those that the films themselves suggest, the tautological nature of the reasoning seems inescapable: the films reflect German history, because this history has been narrated in terms and categories derived from the films.

Even more problematic, however, is the way in which Kracauer narrativises the films themselves in his plot/content analyses. For it is only with considerable violence that the visual and narrative organisation of the films he discusses can be made to submit to his reading. The paradox is that his interpretation applies an altogether different textual form than that of Expressionist cinema: Kracauer treats these films as if they conformed to the norms of classical narrative film as it established itself in the late 1920s and early 1930s, under the increasing dominance of Hollywood. This means that the specific stylistic features of the Expressionist films, which alone can give us a clue about their mode of historical inscription, are ignored, in favour of ransacking the films for their most obvious motifs – which then turn out to be those elements borrowed and quoted from Romantic literature and painting.

II

How can one break this hermeneutic circle, which seems to vitiate both Eisner's and Kracauer's construction of the aesthetic or historical specificity of the fantastic, or 'Expressionist' idiom in the German cinema? I think ultimately only by looking at concrete examples. My starting point is a specific motif, a social one: *economic success and social mobility*. What interests me is *how* especially social mobility gets encoded in fantastic forms, and *why* – given that it is a theme not only common to many quite dissimilar films in Germany but one that the cinema of other countries has made use of, especially in America, yet more often in a combination of realistic setting and romance plots (for example in the films of Preston Sturges or Frank Capra). In general terms, the possibility of improving one's fortunes is a subject that appeals to a wide spectrum of possible audiences: from working-class to petty-bourgeois, from intellectuals to white-collar workers, and excludes only those who (at least in Germany) tend not to go to the cinema anyway: the rich, the super-rich and aristocrats. Wherever it appears, it is couched in wish-fulfilling fantasies, but the fantasies tend to stand in some relation to what forms and degrees of mobility are actually possible and feasible in a given society. In the case of the

American cinema, one could say that the more the 'rags-to-riches' theme is treated realistically, the more one may assume that the society or period in question does allow its members a degree of social mobility. In the European cinema, by contrast, the motif comprises two elements, which stand in a certain tension to each other, if not in an outright contradiction. On the one hand, in the German cinema, it seems to be associated with the supernatural, generally reminiscent of a pact with the Devil. On the other hand, in France and Italy, when someone is chosen by fate and chance for social success it is regarded with fewer guilt feelings and more as a personal triumph. But both versions can be seen as distorted versions of the class struggle, insofar as a personal, individual solution is offered by the film, while blocking off and suppressing the question of the whole class or group to which the individual belongs. Social rise in European cinema is thus often a version of class struggle that denies the existence of this struggle.

In popular literature as well as in American films depicting social mobility, one occasionally finds elements of the fantastic, too. But there the theme of social rise crops up most consistently as a fairytale motif, rather than combining with elements from the horror genre. It usually is a version of the Cinderella story, or a tale that involves an orphan and a Prince Charming. In this guise, it has a predominantly female protagonist. But already in Charles Dickens we find a slightly different constellation. Oliver Twist, forced to participate in a robbery, and consumed by a desire to escape into a better world, copes with his fear and anxiety by falling unconscious. He wakes up, and the setting he wakes up into is indeed the cosy world of the middle class, the world of his wish-fulfilling fantasy.

This moment of falling unconscious, under the conflicting pressure of anxiety and desire, becomes, I want to argue, constitutive also for the German silent cinema, and lies behind the use of the fantastic-Gothic, as opposed to the fantastic-fairytale mode. We find the motif, for instance, in Friedrich Murnau's *Phantom* (1922). A poor clerk, his mind full of fantasies and daydreams, is knocked unconscious by a white horse-and-carriage, as he crosses the street with an armful of books. A young lady, also in white, steps out of the carriage, bends over him to make sure he is unharmed, and then rides on. But for the young man, the incident sparks off a vision, and a passion, which pursues him all his life: it becomes the phantom of the title. Turned away by the girl's parents he becomes a criminal, even attempts murder, only so as not to be refused again.

What in *Phantom* is, emblematically, the combination of becoming unconscious, the white horse and the woman in white, at the margins of which are criminality and violent death, is, in *The Student of Prague* (1913, dir: Stellen Rye) the lady on horseback, whom Baldwin, the student of the title, rescues from the lake, after her horse has bolted. From there on, his goal is to possess this woman, which, as it turns out, necessitates eliminating the lady's cousin and fiancé. The film ends with the hero committing suicide.

But on the surface of the film, the question of social rise is altogether a peripheral issue, for, as is well-known, *The Student of Prague* is actually about Baldwin selling his shadow to the mysterious Scapinelli, who in turn promises him riches and happiness. The social rise, to which Baldwin accedes with ease once he has money, belongs altogether to the realm of magic and the fantastic, as if the dream of happiness has to be tabooed and repressed so completely that only a fantastic guise can be made to represent it. The film generously borrows from the Faust legend as well as from E. T. A. Hoffmann and E. A. Poe's 'William Wilson' (1839): what is different is precisely the sociological emphasis. The protagonist who is effectively barred from attaining social status, and who has to pay for his ambitions with his death, is the petit-bourgeois intellectual – the *student*. In Germany throughout the nineteenth century student-intellectuals were made to feel socially inferior to the nobility, while educationally and intellectually having every right to feel superior to the members of an impoverished and decaying aristocracy. The subject was treated in a brutally realistic manner by a dramatist of Goethe's generation. In Reinhold Lenz's *The Tutor* (1774) just such a student-intellectual literally goes mad and castrates himself.

Thus, in *The Student of Prague* the choice of setting and character already contains a covert social dimension, which alludes to German history and its vicissitudes. But also present is another subtext, which the film both points to and then disavows. One of the most popular genres of the German commercial cinema from its earliest days right up to the 1950s were comedies and musicals, set in the carefree milieu of wining and dining, wenching and duelling students, in short, what everyone associates with Heidelberg and *The Student Prince*. A film like *The Student of Prague* sets up expectations of this kind, but does not fulfil them. It works with popular assumptions, but reshapes them in an apparently completely different genre. As Bertolt Brecht noted, the form of humour that sees in student life nothing but carousing and caressing is already the expression of a massive displacement of social reality. German students, especially since the opening up of higher education early in the twentieth century, were particularly abject creatures, acquiring hard-earned knowledge difficult to sell, from professors who vampirised their students' best energies and ideas. Cast out into an uncertain society, they became the very prototype of the anal-aggressive male, depicted in the novels of Heinrich Mann, and analysed as the proto-fascist of *The Authoritarian Personality*.[8]

It is precisely this knowledge of what students' life was really like that *The Student of Prague* makes its starting point: Baldwin is sick of the student scene, which is going on in the background of the opening shot. With a dismissive gesture he sits down at a table apart from the others. He is broke, worried about his future, and in such a morose and depressed state that even his girlfriend cannot cheer him up. But instead of investigating the causes, or what brought him to this state, the film blocks and breaks off the subject at this point to introduce Scapinelli, the mysterious figure in hat and black overcoat. The visual composition with which it does so is significant: throughout this scene, Baldwin sits with his back to his girlfriend dancing lasciviously on the tables behind to attract his eye. He looks straight into the camera, so that he is doubly separated from what goes on; spatially, and in terms of his field of vision. By contrast, we, the spectators are made to identify with two distinct points of view: we participate as spectator-voyeurs in the girl's self-display (and are thus part of the 'student-scene') but we also identify with Baldwin's refusal to participate. As spectators we are already split well before Baldwin's Double appears. While a classically realist film would develop its narrative out of the need to reconcile and mediate between these two levels, after having set up such a division or contradiction, *The Student of Prague* does indeed introduce a mediator, in the figure of Scapinelli, who enters not from the direction of Baldwin's gaze, but sideways, from off-screen, and his black carriage completely blocks out the background of the girlfriend surrounded by Baldwin's fellow-students. If Scapinelli provides the means whereby the contradiction is resolved, he does so in an excessive, monstrous, tabooed way: he enters the frame of the fiction in much the same way as Nosferatu's ghost-ship enters the Bremen harbour to bring the plague in Murnau's 1922 film of that title. The basic strategy of *The Student of Prague* is thus to allude to a 'real' problem with which the audience can identify, interrupt its development, disguise its direct investigation and reinforce it on another level by introducing a magic and demonic chain of causality, via mystery-figures and chance-encounters. These are internalised; they force a split upon the protagonist, and so act as repressive and inhibitive agents rather than simply as fairytale donors or helpers in the sense of Vladimir Propp's analyses.[9]

Thus, what is being repressed is the initial situation, in its social and historical dimension. The fact that it is repressed, rather than simply elided or passed over, is what makes the film belong to the genre of the fantastic, as opposed to, say, social comedy in the style of Chaplin or Capra. The repressed dimension returns to the hero in a horribly altered (disfigured) form, as the nightmare of the split self, as a crisis of identity or a compulsion towards self-destruction and self-annihilation. In Hoffmann, Poe or Dostoevski's *The Double* (1846), the uncanny is the result of trying to defend against a ubiquitous pressure and violence upon the self, but the hero is able to do so successfully only by personalising this violence and at the same time turning it against himself. It is the structure and dynamics of repression itself, more than what is being repressed or what materialises in its stead, which produces the effect of the fantastic. For if one looks at the literary antecedents, one finds that the motif of the Double is quite closely allied in German and English Romantic literature especially with a detection plot, whose solution, as in Poe's 'William Wilson', is the establishment of an identity between criminal and investigator. In other words, an explicitly Oedipal plot is being enacted, which cannot but end in suicide or self-mutilation. In *The Student of Prague* this 'original' story line is complicated by all manner of other motifs (as I indicated, mostly of a sociological nature) until it resurfaces at the end when Baldwin aims at his Double but the shot actually kills Baldwin himself. What seems to happen is that, between hero and world, an alien power interposes itself, and the films of Expressionist cinema thus operate a decisive break between cause and effect, by letting a substitute motivation and a seemingly irrational causality fill the gap – a process which the opening scene of *The Student of Prague* visualises in quite literal terms.

With this, the fantastic film embodies the central characteristics of German silent cinema, namely the virtual absence of narratives based on action or suspense, the preference of composition within the frame over montage, the frequent time ellipses and the generally static impression, which many of the films convey. This is true even of works without a supernatural or fantastic element, such as *The Last Laugh* (1924) or Carl Mayer's other *Kammerspiel* films (*Sylvester* [1924], *Shattered*, *Backstairs* [both 1921]). The manifest lack of, or ambiguous, causal links between sequences (seemingly contravening the rules of continuity editing) become the very hallmark of the German Expressionist cinema, which may be why it invites symbolic interpretations of the kind Kracauer gives. But ironically, it is only by eliminating this characteristic hesitation, the hovering effect of the narratives, and by smoothing out, levelling off, filling in the gaps, breaks, fissures and ellipses of the films he discusses that Kracauer is able to bend their narratives into the shape that his thesis requires, and thereby submit them to the causality and inevitability that their actual textual construction so consistently eschews and renders opaque.

III

If one wants to avoid making such analyses as Kracauer's seem tautological, or turning them into self-fulfilling prophecies, any reasoning about the social or political meaning of Expressionist films has to respect both the autonomy of the textual level, and seek structures not where they overlap or mirror each other, but at their points of contact or even conflict. In other words, focus on those moments, where the text has seized, worked over, displaced or objectified elements of the historical or the social sphere, in order to bring them to representation within the text's own formal or generic constraints. The model I am sketching here is therefore not aimed at discovering homologies of social and narrative structure (as they prevail in Kracauer) or analogies of motifs and *topoi* (typical for Eisner's correlation of art, literature and cinema), but to valorise imbalances, excesses, intensities: that is to say, to focus on the very figures of the fantastic discourse. Hence my focus so far on one *social* moment (mobility between classes) and its transformations/representations in the filmic discourse of Weimar cinema. In a second step, I now want to reverse this procedure, and start with a recurrent *stylistic-textual* feature, to see what it might tell us about its social or material basis.

One of the most typical figures of the fantastic in German cinema is that of the sorcerer's apprentice, that is the creation and use of magic forces which outstrip their creator and over whom he loses control. This familiar Romantic – Faustian,

Promethean, Frankensteinian – motif returns with particular vehemence in settings featuring the so-called first industrial machine age, whether in *The Golem* (1920), or in *Metropolis* (1927), or in the earlier, very popular *Homunculus* serial (1916). The fact that it is a figure very often connected with technology should not, however, lead us to interpret it wholly in such a context. In *The Golem*, for instance, the 'robot' figure is associated with forces of quite a different kind, where Rabbi Loew creates the Golem, a clay figure turned live creature of supernatural strength, in order to defend himself against the arbitrary and (financially as well as sexually) predatory rule of an absolutist aristocracy. In this respect, *The Golem* is an anti-feudal parable, typical for the bourgeoisie in its revolutionary militant phase. At the same time, it could be read as an anti-technological parable (in line with the 'tampering with nature' theme), just as the story makes sense in terms of a minority defending itself, however 'excessively' (when seen from the point of view of the majority) against oppression. Thus, it would be a simplification if one saw the Golem story, no less than the Frankenstein myth, principally as a 'reaction' to industrialisation. At a more formal level, what is at issue (as so often in tales of the fantastic) is a lack, an absence, an imbalance of forces, which is being compensated for by means that turn out to be excessive, irrepressible, destructive. As such, it is an attempt, via narrative, to find a system of equivalence or substitution (which fails – failure of mediation being the mark of the fantastic and the uncanny).[10] Within the context of the nineteenth century, this failure, furthermore, has a definite political character: we find the motif of such imbalance in both conservative and liberal writers when discussing conditions which are recognised as in need of change, but where the cure is suspected to be worse than the ill. It thus becomes the favourite metaphor of the radical turned conservative – a stance as topical for the German Romantics of the 1820s as for German Expressionists disappointed with the socialist revolution of 1919. The model in both cases is that of the 'excesses' of the French Revolution (for instance, as depicted in Thomas Carlyle's popular and influential *History of the French Revolution* [1837]).

However, looked at from a slightly oblique angle, the same motif might yield a quite different historical perspective. If we see the Double, for instance, not as a duplication of the self or a mirror, but as an indication that a part of the self, or a partial drive, has emancipated itself and formed a new monstrous entity, then the motif of the Double is, indeed, structurally quite close to the motif of the creature, emancipating itself from the creator and turning against him. This is important in view of the much-repeated interpretation of the Double and of shadows in Weimar cinema as the expression of the 'soul', as the symbolic representation of internal irrational forces of the self. For it is equally possible – if we take several motifs of the 'fantastic' together – to view them as objectifications and representations of parts or aspects of self, formed under pressure from external events. As I argued with respect to *The Student of Prague*, internalising and psychologising these forces is a consequence, not an origin of the problem, and thus can be seen as a displacement, an abstraction and reification of social and political moments. This displacement, however, has left its own trace: being an unequal substitution, a 'failed' transformation, it manifests itself in the intensity, the uncanniness, with which the displaced and repressed elements irrupt into idyllic worlds and seemingly harmonious relationships.

One way of recovering the historical dimension of the uncanny motif, therefore, is to point not so much to the emergence of the machine, but to the changing relations of production during the Romantic period, especially as they affect the artists and intellectuals, increasingly thrown upon the market with their products, and finding there that they no longer control the modes of (re)production and distribution of their works. To some of Hoffmann's tales, notably 'The Sandman' or 'Mlle de Scuderi', and to Balzac's early stories such as 'Peau de Chagrin' or 'Le Chef d'oeuvre inconnu', applies what Marx (as early as 1830) wrote about alienation and reification, namely that in the capitalist production process, the product confronts the producer as something alien, and his own person comes to seem to him uncanny.

It is this process that we find represented in so many of the films and their typical motifs – the Double, the Faustian overreacher, the creator half-possessed by his creature, and so on. And it reappears as a *dominant* configuration at precisely the point in history when the conditions of production for artists and intellectuals undergo a further significant change. This is especially true for literature and the fine arts with the emergence of cinema. By the early 1920s, the cinema was very much perceived as a dangerously powerful rival to theatre and serious fiction. The role of the writer as the representative of his time, as someone in whom the times reflect themselves and find their ideal (artistic) expression was declining, and another power – that of technological reproduction, the emergent mass-media – interposes itself, as both a lure and a threat. To construct, as I am here suggesting, these films of the German Expressionist cinema as objectifications of the concrete historical situation of their makers (the scriptwriters and directors) would itself be problematic, were it not for the fact already mentioned, namely that we are dealing with a counter-cinema, that is, one conceived in conscious opposition not only to Hollywood films (or more accurately, the flooding of the European market prior to World War I with French films), but also in opposition to the burgeoning mainstream commercial film production in Germany itself. Paul Wegener, Hans Heinz Ewers, Robert Wiene, F. W. Murnau and Fritz Lang saw themselves very much as part of an offensive to make the cinema respectable for bourgeois audiences, and to give it the status of 'art'. We therefore are right to talk of the German Expressionist cinema as an art-cinema, and it is here that the forms of the fantastic are developed, in the context of a self-conscious attempt to make 'art' in the cinema, and to appeal to a self-selected and initially camera-shy part of the general audience.

The latter point applies with especial force to a film like *The Cabinet of Dr Caligari* (1919), conceived and marketed very deliberately as a high-brow product, and by no stretch of credulity can the film be regarded as an unself-conscious bodying forth of the German 'soul' brooding about Fate and Destiny. Thus, a few words about *The Cabinet of Dr Caligari*, once again inverting my perspective, by talking about it as an objectification, as a fantasmatic representation of another kind of alienation: that of the spectators, rather than the producer. This is supported by the fact that the Dr Caligari of *The Cabinet of Dr Caligari* has often been read as an allegory of the film director, making Francis, Jane and Allan, the protagonists, into spectators.

In *The Cabinet of Dr Caligari*, too, the initial situation contains a social aspect involving class/status differences. Caligari, asking deferentially for a permit to put up his tent-show, is treated by the town clerk and his subordinates in a brusque, humiliating and insulting manner. There can be little doubt that this scene transmits to the spectator an identifiable, realistic experience of the arbitrary and haughty behaviour that a militarist bureaucracy (which is what the civil service was, even during the Weimar Republic) displayed towards civilians. What we all at some stage of our lives may have murmured under our breath 'I could have killed him,' Caligari acts out. He takes revenge on the hated town clerk by way of his medium, Cesare, thus setting off the chain of events which make-up the narrative. Yet here, too, any analysis of the origins and causes of such an all-powerful but at the same time petty bureaucracy is blocked and displaced.

Instead, we find a commensurate magic omnipotence, one which in effect overcompensates in Caligari's medium Cesare. As in *The Golem*, a force is set free that at least in part escapes its creator's control. Cesare is Caligari's Double and the embodiment or condensation of rebellious, anti-authoritarian impulses which stand in direct contradiction to Caligari's own authoritarianism. What makes the film significant is not only its striking decor as such, but the degree to which the decor permits a particularly complex and contradictory narrative to articulate itself within the space of a single fiction. There has been much debate about the meaning of the framing device, but it seems to me that it is only one (albeit an important one) of the many strategies in the film for sustaining a multi-perspectival narrative.

Perhaps the easiest way to locate these strategies is to ask some simple questions, such as, why does Francis, the narrator in the frame and Caligari's chief antagonist in the story, 'go mad'? Or: what is the relationship between the murder of the town clerk and the murder of Allan, Francis' friend? These rather naïve questions, which doubtless would be asked by every spectator, if the film were a 'realistic' film, somehow seem irrelevant. And this is so, I think, because questions of motivation and causality have, in the process of editing the film into such a static self-contained series of tableaux, become almost illegible. It would take me too far to enter into the full history of the tableaux-scene as a form of 'negative' dramaturgy of unresolved conflict – one finds its theory in Denis Diderot – but as part of a rhetoric of muteness and self-repression, it is the most direct link between bourgeois drama/melodrama of the stage, and the silent

German cinema. This illegibility of both temporal and causal sequence in the film, the opaqueness of the emotional relationship between, say, Francis, Jane, Allan, and the breaking off or fading out of several scenes, so to speak, in mid-gesture, on a note of suspension, is in fact evidence of the dynamic interplay of forces between fictional world and filmic form, the work of resistances without which there would be no narrative and no narrator. The act of narration *per se* establishes itself in *The Cabinet of Dr Caligari*, and subsequently in countless films of the classic German cinema (with their frame-tales, their narrator-figures, their nested narratives) as a field of force, as a struggle for control over the intensities (and thus comprehensibility) of discourse itself.

The static quality of this as of other films in the German canon, therefore, should not be mistaken for clumsiness of the mise-en-scène, or the 'primitive' state of film-form, but rather as the containment of an agitation, which, banished from articulating itself in a linear fashion, such as we are used to from classical narrative, creates a different kind of economy of filmic discourse. *The Cabinet of Dr Caligari* displaces not only its social themes, by making them into enigmas whose resolutions lead elsewhere (thereby creating the conditions for narration, for there being 'texts' that need deciphering); it also displaces an already constituted cinematic genre to which the film (also) belongs: the (half-hidden) subtext in *The Cabinet of Dr Caligari* is the detective serial, extremely popular in Germany (as in France) in the late 1910s and early 1920s.

The particular, and perhaps unique, textual economy of *The Cabinet of Dr Caligari* shows itself, if one tries to answer what motivates the characters. Putting it in slightly different terms, questions of agency and motivation become questions of narration: who tells the story, whose story is it, and to whom is it told? If one follows accounts like Kracauer's, it is the story of Caligari, the mad doctor, the premonitory materialisation of a long line of tyrants, the faithful image of German military dictatorship and its demonic, mesmerising hold over others. But what if we construct for Caligari's behaviour a certain motivational logic, a certain coherence *within* the story, before we follow Kracauer's allegorical move? The doctor, researching in his archives, finds the secret of somnambulism and brings a patient under his control. Disguising himself as a fairground operator, he uses his power to avenge himself on his enemies (the town clerk) and subsequently, to lure a young woman into his tent. He beckons Jane inside, showing her the upright box, flings it open with a leer to reveal the rigid figure of Cesare, who, as she gets closer, opens his eyes, whereupon she stands transfixed in fascination, until she breaks away with a terrified, distraught expression on her face. The sexual connotations of the scene are unmistakable, and here Caligari's Mesmeric powers compensate a more directly sexual form of impotence, for his behaviour towards Jane is the very epitome of the 'dirty old man' exposing himself. Showing Cesare to Jane is literally an 'exhibition' which is also a (self-) exposure. Cesare's abduction of Jane strengthens this particular interpretation: the medium becomes, as it were, the detachable part of Caligari, not so much his Double as his tool. Caligari's story would be centred on a disturbing relationship to sexuality and political power, in which impotence is being overcompensated by exhibition ('I'll show you'), but where showing involves an alternation of hiding and revealing, that is, flashing and blinking. It is interesting that Cesare, unlike the Golem and other 'creatures', does not turn against his master. Instead, when pursued by Francis, he drops Jane, he weakens, withers or fades away, becoming detumescent, or as the intertitle puts it, dying of exhaustion. In this respect, he is rather similar to Nosferatu, fading with daylight (like over-exposed film-stock). When Cesare does return to his creator, the very sight of him and the necessity to recognise him as part of himself, drives Caligari mad.

IV

But is it possible to see the film centred on Caligari? The story is initiated by Francis, and in this sense it is his story, too: about how he came to be at the place from which he tells it (the asylum), as the recollection of a series of events whose memory is activated by the sight of a figure in white passing by, who subsequently turns out to be Jane. What, then, is Francis' story and why does he go mad? It is, essentially, the tale of a suitor who is ignored or turned down. The narrative comes full circle when Francis pleads with Jane to marry him, and she replies that 'we queens may never choose where our hearts dictate.' In the story itself, the choice is between Francis and Allan. After the visit to the fairground, where Allan is told by Cesare that he has only until dawn to live, the friends part with the remark: 'We must let her choose. But whatever her choice, we shall always remain friends.' In this situation of rivalry, the main beneficiary of Allan's death seems to be Francis, a benefit which his horrified reaction both suppresses and expresses.

This moment of recognition (in the script it appears as 'a look of comprehension') is itself turned into an enigma (that is, disavowed). 'I shall not rest until I get to the bottom of these events,' Francis says, and he thereby opens up the detection-narrative, with its false trails–false suspects strategy, in which substitution plays a major part. In this respect, Cesare becomes Francis' double: he kills the rival and abducts the bride, thus acting out Francis' secret desires. The fact that throughout the rape/abduction scene both Francis and Caligari sit stupidly in front of Cesare's dummy not only accentuates the gesture of disavowal, it also establishes a parallelism of desire between Francis and Caligari, underlined later by the repetition of an identical composition and shot: first Caligari is put into a strait-jacket and locked into a cell, and then Francis is shown in the same position. The investigation of the series of crimes thus culminates in the visual statement that the criminal is the alter ego of the detective, once more the story of Oedipus, in other words, but held in suspense by the reversibility that the framing of the tale imposes on any attempt at determinate decipherment.

Yet it is equally possible to read *The Cabinet of Dr Caligari* as Jane's story, in which case, her doctor-father and Dr Caligari feature as Doubles of each other, with Cesare as the disavowed phallus-fetish of a curiosity which the scene in Caligari's tent marks as explicitly sexual. One recalls that she is motivated to visit Caligari by 'her father's long absence', and that in the face of Francis' protestations that it could not have been Cesare who abducted her, Jane insists vehemently on being right, as if to defend her version against the rival claims of Francis.

What implications can one draw from this? It would appear that in *The Cabinet of Dr Caligari* a visual form and a mode of narration has been found where several different 'versions' or narrative perspectives converge or superimpose themselves on the same fictional space – a procedure we usually associate with much later films such as *Rashomon* (1950), or *Last Year in Marienbad* (1961). Its economy is that of condensation, itself the outcome of a series of displacements which decentre the narrative, while at the same time creating entry-points for a number of distinct and different spectator-fantasies, centred on male and female Oedipal scenarios. Technically, this is accomplished by a disarticulation of action-time in favour of narrated time, and – supported by the decor, but by no means confined to it – the projection of a purely interior space organised to bring to the fore in visual terms the repetitions and parallels which the narrative elides and mutes. What we have is a lacunary, elliptical text, in which the figures of the fantastic can be seen as a particular textual economy of narrative perspectivism and spectator-projection. Paradoxically, this economy (which has the force of repression) here works both towards opening up the text and at the same time condensing its elements into a tight Oedipal logic. *The Cabinet of Dr Caligari* thus posits a very strong internal system of relations between the different characters, where they act as substitutes for each other, either as Doubles or (fetishised) part-objects. The narrative effects these forms of containment by a repression of (male and female) desire, so that in the language of such an (Oedipalised) fantasy a specifically bourgeois renunciation of desire legitimates itself. The 'political' nature of the psychic repression is named, shown, hinted at, only to become in turn the object of further repression. It is as if the social motifs are being substituted by sexual motifs, but these are themselves distorted by the force of narration itself, so that the film offers 'solutions' which leave everything open, or rather, which produce radically equivocal textual ensembles. It would therefore be inaccurate to say that in the German silent cinema all social conflicts become internalised, 'psychologised': unless one added that this interiorisation is of such a virulent kind that it tends to threaten and disturb the very process of psychological containment or resolution, leading to a new form of externalisation, which is in some sense more 'Cubist' than 'Expressionist'.

The problem of 'containment' can also be argued by reference to another film, Murnau's *Nosferatu*. The hero's initial situation has, once again, economic overtones: Jonathan Harper undertakes his journey to Transylvania in order to make money and improve his prospects for advancement in his firm. This entails ignoring the entreaties of his bride, from whose domesticity (flowers, cats) he seems positively anxious to escape. The journey thereby has the signs of a detour: if the economic motif splits the couple, Nosferatu unites them, in the characteristic structure of a lack, an absence, being overcompensated by the insertion of another force, and of a different degree of intensity. Again, as in *The Cabinet of Dr Caligari*, all the characters are closely interwoven: Renfield, the estate agent, manipulates Jonathan, but is himself the tool of Nosferatu, who in turn comes under the power and influence of Nina, who thereby closes the gap of not being able to exert influence on Jonathan. The protagonists are important to the narrative only insofar as they can enter into such substitute relationships, but more explicitly than in any other film of the German fantastic, *Nosferatu* is the enactment of a deal, a bargain, an exchange, where there is blatant incommensurability of the entities being exchanged, and thus once more signs of a 'significant failure', which prompts the fantastic. A crucial scene makes this explicit: as the Count is about to sign the papers, Jonathan accidentally (?) displays/exhibits the medallion, which bears the image of Nina. Nosferatu grasps it, and it is this image which is being exchanged between the men: it substitutes itself for money that would otherwise seal the deal. In a business based on real estate (not unlike the film industry), Nosferatu acquires a view (of Nina: the house serves him as nothing but an observation post) and Jonathan gains social status (for having a Count as his client). If Nosferatu is Jonathan's Double, insofar as Nina acquires the lover that Jonathan seems so reluctant to be, the 'undeadness' of desire is shown to have social consequences. Nosferatu brings with him the plague, itself seen as the reverse-side of trade (Nosferatu is both captain and cargo, producer and product).

V

The films of the German fantastic cinema thus seem to encode in their encounter with the social reality of the Weimar Republic not the street battles, inflation, unemployment, but something else, though no less historical. A double perspective opens the texts of the fantastic towards society: on one hand, that of the artist-intellectual whose changing relations to the modes of cultural production, such as the cinema, are condensed into the neo-Romantic motifs of the sorcerer's apprentice and that of the producer confronting the product of his labour/desire as an alienated self-image. To return to the quotation from Lotte Eisner: one can now argue that the Romantic project – the transformation of history into inwardness, and inwardness into a phenomenological and sensuous immediacy of contemplation – has been accomplished by the cinema, but with a vengeance. For it shows this transformation to have been an act of repression, and the history, which is repressed but also preserved in Eisner's 'Romantic fancies' returns in the form of the uncanny and fantastic. Romanticism wedded to technology has produced a wholly fetishised, reified form of immediacy.

On the other hand, the films open up a perspective towards a class of spectators whose precarious *social* position as 'students', clerks, young men with frustrated ambitions and vague resentments make them members of the petit-bourgeoisie, whose engagement with the class-struggle takes the form of avoiding class-struggle, by imagining themselves above it and outside. Which is to say, a class who compensates for its fear of proletarianisation by dreaming of the by-pass or detour around social conflict in the shape of personal fantasies of erotic conquest and social rise. The logic of the films consists in accommodating this situation and this desire, but translating it into transactions of unequal exchange, which the narrative 'integrates' by its heavily metaphoric economy. Telling is selling, and the cinema offers the spectator a narrative position in exchange for a desire: we arrive at what Roland Barthes has called 'contract-narratives', which is to say, narratives where the strategies of narration (framing, nesting, and so on) are 'determined not by a desire to narrate, but by a desire to exchange: (narrative is a medium of exchange, an agent, a currency, a gold standard)'.[11]

The cinema, in other words, enters the social arena not by a mimesis of class-conflicts or the movements of a collective unconscious, but as that form of social relation which the consumption of narratives and images changes. And it does so in order to block or displace the 'real contradictions' of history and society not into 'imaginary resolutions' (Levi-Strauss), but into effects of disavowal and substitution. Films are not versions of (bourgeois) historiography; rather, they act upon another history: that of commodity-relations and their modes of production and consumption. It is this physical reality, which the cinema, in Kracauer's phrase, attempts to redeem, by inserting itself as a quasi-magical power, a fetish-object, into the reified and abstracted relationships which characterise our 'society of the spectacle'.

NOTES

1. Siegfried Kracauer, *From Caligari to Hitler* (Princeton: Princeton University Press, 1947); Lotte Eisner, *The Haunted Screen*, trans. Roger Graeves (Berkeley: University of California Press, 1969).
2. See, for instance, George Huaco, *Towards A Sociology of Cinema* (New York: Basic Books, 1965); Andrew Tudor, *Image and Influence: Studies in the Sociology of Film* (London: Allen and Unwin, 1974); Paul Monaco, *Cinema and Society: France and Germany in the 1920s* (New York: Greenwood Press, 1981).
3. Eisner's *The Haunted Screen* and Siegfried Kracauer's *From Caligari to Hitler* appeared almost simultaneously, but independently from each other, shortly after World War II. Significantly, the books were published, respectively, in France and the United States, rather than in Germany, where their publishing history is a chapter all by itself (see, for instance, Karsten Witte's preface to *Von Caligari zu Hitler* [1974]). Each book is the work of a Jewish exile, who in the 1920s wrote as a professional film critic or journalist, and each in its distinct way is a profoundly personal attempt to grasp through the cinema something of the tragedy that had befallen the country and the culture they had loved and perhaps even over-identified with: hence the vehemence of their ambivalence about this cinema, reflected in the rather lurid titles they chose for their books.
4. Lotte Eisner concentrates on the stylistic continuities and transformations, what she calls the 'influences' from the other arts, especially the intertextuality between film, theatre and painting. She shows strong echoes of nineteenth- and early

twentieth-century painting in set design, decor, and the use of lighting. That paintings by Caspar David Friedrich are quite evidently the inspiration for certain compositions in Fritz Lang's *Destiny*, just as Arnold Böcklin and Ludwig Thoma's paintings figure in other well-known films (notably *The Nibelungen* and *Nosferatu*), are among the insights which make-up in range what Eisner's argument may lack in rigour.

5. *The Haunted Screen*, p. 113.
6. See Raymond Williams' classic study, *The Country and the City* (London: Chatto and Windus, 1973).
7. More recently, in the light of the 'New German Cinema'and its revival of Romantic motifs by directors as different as Werner Herzog, Werner Schroeter and Hans Jürgen Syberberg, another explanation suggests itself. The revival of Romantic art and fantastic literature in Germany is due to an eminently political fact: aborted social change. After every revolution that has failed – notably in 1798, in 1848, in 1918, and in 1968, one finds an irruption of animist thought and passionate irrationalism. The prevalence of fantasy would then be the reaction, usually by a cultural and/or geographic minority, to their exclusion from a sweep of historical events. As such, it is the expression of a frustrated desire for change, rather than a resistance to change. In this manner, a cyclical movement unites Goethe's Faust/Prometheus figures, E. T. A. Hoffmann's Doubles and artist-magicians, the Golems of the Prague School with the Aguirre of Werner Herzog, and the Hitler figure of Hans Jürgen Syberberg.
8. T. W. Adorno et al., *The Authoritarian Personality* (New York: Harper & Brothers, 1950).
9. Vladimir Propp, *Morphology of the Folk Tale* (Austin: University of Texas Press, 1968).
10. For a more detailed (and classical) analysis of the genre, see Tsvetan Todorov, *The Fantastic: A Structural Approach to a Literary Genre* (Cornell: Cornell University Press, 1975).
11. Roland Barthes, *S/Z*, trans. Richard Miller (New York: Hill and Wang, 1974), p. 90.

7

THE RISE OF THE STUDIOS AND THE COMING OF SOUND

American cinema's domination of world markets coincided with the rise of the Hollywood studios. The Hollywood Studio System would properly take hold by 1930 once five companies – Metro-Goldwyn-Mayer, RKO, Fox (later Twentieth-Century Fox), Warner Bros. and Paramount – had emerged victorious from increasing competition and a scrimmage of mergers and takeovers of production and distribution companies. By 1930 it is estimated that there were around 24,000 cinemas in the US with the five major studios controlling at least 50 per cent of the total industry output. By 1931, D. W. Griffith had made his last film and the film industry was primed to establish the classical Hollywood era with the new technology of sound. In fact, the era from the coming of the sound film to the end of the 1940s is often called Hollywood's 'Golden Age'. During those years the Hollywood film factory fitted a Fordist model of capitalist mass production. In order to understand the success of the American film industry, it is important to examine the 1920s: the decade in which the studios employing thousands of people changed the face of Los Angeles and in which Thomas Ince's idea of the 'factory system' of production took hold.

In 1923 the first Hollywood sign was erected high in the Hollywood hills – at this time it actually said 'Hollywoodland' to signify a housing development. Although the sign was left to deteriorate, until the Chamber of Commerce took responsibility for it from the late 1940s, it signalled the beginning of the Hollywood brand and has remained the patented symbol of the world's most renowned cinema city. Hollywood even rallied quickly after the financial crisis that was the Great Crash hit in 1929, and its escapist fare and documentary realism enabled it to rise above the Depression for most of the decade that followed (see Chapter 9). Calvin Coolidge reassured Congress in December 1928 that the future revealed a pleasing prospect for American society and that prosperity was stable; share prices were still rising on the stock exchange. He was responding to the fact that since the beginning of the decade industrial production had doubled, consumer goods – cars, radios, kitchen white goods and, of course, movies – were generally available, with movies the fifth highest grossing business in the US. While for many historians the decade closed with the Wall Street Crash of October 1929, the cinema decade really closes with the coming of sound. Silent cinema was a casualty of the medium's success, perhaps the first 'art' to die away so soon – and to be celebrated again so soon after its demise in films such as John Ford's *The Informer* (1935) set in Ireland in the 1920s. By the end of the decade, film societies and new arts theatres were already screening the 'classics' of silent cinema and by the 1930s the archiving of those classics would begin.

Finance was always the driving force in cinema's early years forcing smaller companies in and out of each other's orbit, as with Stoll Pictures and Ideal Films in Britain. In France, cinema was traditionally produced by small companies – only Pathé and Gaumont were sizeable – but there too by the end of the decade even the larger companies merged to form production firms such as Pathé-Nathan. Britain tried to establish a studio system on a small scale on the outskirts of London. The first Ealing studio had been built in 1910, serving popular melodramas alongside educational Pathé films. Ealing hoped an eclectic mix of styles and genres would promote the studio's reputation for quality and it built on early success across the 1920s up to its heyday in the post-Second World War years when Rank helped finance production under studio head Michael Balcon. Balcon founded the Gainsborough studio in Islington in 1924 where Alfred Hitchcock had his beginnings in British cinema, including success with *The Lodger* (1927). While Hitchcock was the most successful of Balcon's directors, Gainsborough's eclecticism also gave rise to popular box office hits like those of Ivor Novello, Britain's matinée idol, and others based on the English music hall – as with George Robey's rendition of Ali Baba in *Chu-Chin-Chow* (1934), also starring Anna May Wong. Balcon's Gainsborough years have been read as an apprenticeship for when he took over Ealing Studios in 1937 but they were much more than that. In the late 1920s distributor John Maxwell founded the Associated British Picture Company and went on to merge with British International Pictures at Elstree thereby building Balcon's competition. Elstree was sometimes referred to as Britain's Hollywood and it was here that Britain's first talkies would be made.

In the US the biggest studio, MGM (Metro-Goldwyn-Mayer), had come into existence in 1924. Marcus Loew had originally owned a clutch of movie theatres and his treasurer was Adolph Zukor. Loew disliked Zukor and they became rivals. When Zukor's Famous Players-Lasky was so successful, he made it very difficult for theatres owned by Loew to show any of the company's pictures. As a result, Loew turned to production himself. In 1920 he had bought Metro Pictures which had been sinking but which rose again with the Rudolph Valentino hit *The Four Horsemen of the Apocalypse* (1924). In 1924 Loew also bought up Goldwyn Pictures, one of the oldest of the studios, which had been set up in 1916 by the Selwyn brothers and Samuel Goldwyn. Finally Loew bought Louis B. Mayer Pictures and the conglomerate was in place, with Mayer having negotiated a percentage of profits, rather than selling his holdings, and bringing with him Irving Thalberg, the ace producer. Much of MGM's success was due to Thalberg who had cut his producer's teeth at Universal until 1923. He became MGM's vice-president in charge of production and his ability to manipulate the filmmaking process ensured the studio consolidated its success.

While the seeds of the studio system were planted in the 1910s (Chapter 4), and the division of labour that would characterise studio production was established then, the industrial strategy of having super-producers such as Thomas Ince and Irving Thalberg oversee all facets, their eyes on the budget, became a key feature of the 1920s. Ince's canny business practices, first with the Triangle Film Corporation alongside Griffith and Mack Sennett, enabled him to conceive of the studio as an efficiently run Fordist production line and his vision included building Culver City studios which would later become the home of MGM. It is impossible to know what more he might have achieved had he not died early, in 1924. However, it was also the very success of the factory model and the inevitable diminution of their overall control that made Hollywood studio life difficult for émigré directors such as Mauritz Stiller, France's Maurice Tourneur and later Erich von Stroheim, leading them to return to Europe.

As early as 1916, Adolph Zukor and Jesse Lasky had merged into Famous Players-Lasky Corporation. In 1926, building on the company's success, they expanded premises, taking over a huge $1 million studio, expanding as a result of a new merger a year later to become Paramount, with stars such as Douglas Fairbanks and Mary Pickford and star directors, such as Cecil B. DeMille. As the studios amalgamated and grew, larger production budgets allowed for prestige pictures that were really early blockbusters such as Cecil B. DeMille's *The Ten Commandments* (1923), Fred Niblo's *Ben-Hur* (1925) which was MGM's biggest box office hit, and DeMille's *King of Kings* (1927) for Paramount. *Ben-Hur* was a challenge for Irving Thalberg and Louis B. Mayer in MGM's earliest years. They had apparently inherited the film from Goldwyn when the studio was formed and it had been in production for many years. Their ability to save it was testimony to what MGM became known for: ruthlessly streamlined and clear-eyed film production. DeMille became renowned for historical epics with casts of thousands making blockbusting smashes at the box office, as well as his 'society' films with Gloria Swanson.

If the first studios in Hollywood had been converted stores like Nestor Film Company, the biggest studios expanded their lots in the 1920s buying up real estate to create the huge Hollywood complex. Warner Bros. bought up

Vitagraph's Santa Monica lot in 1925, for example, and Fox, following Zukor and Lasky, constructed a huge new complex off Santa Monica Boulevard in 1927. The film factories' expansion coincided with the smooth technical know-how in lighting and editing that was the polished classical Hollywood style of continuity editing. Each of the big studios had lighting stages where blackouts enabled them to light scenes using artificial lights and to control the effect through what was known as the three-point lighting system (key light, fill light and back light). Techniques in continuity editing had also settled into the kind of consistency that made narrative cinema seem natural to audiences. By the end of the decade cinema had industrialised, the business of Hollywood successfully harnessing technology and creativity to the marketplace. The coming of sound was significant in this regard and it also began to bring the skills of the theatre back to Hollywood, as studios sought dramatic actors to naturalise sound in the 'talkies'.

The arrival of the sound era both reflected the evolution of motion-pictures and demanded a form of cinematic regression that initially forced movie makers back towards stagecraft. The first examples were liminal films that moved in and out of sound. *The Jazz Singer*, directed by Alan Crosland, that premièred on 6 October 1927 in New York was the film that convinced producers and exhibitors alike that the sound film was here to stay and that the industry had to adapt. *The Jazz Singer* was not an 'all-talking picture', characterised as it was by sporadic insertions of sound, but the publicity fomented around its release exceeded any furore created by *Don Juan* a year earlier with its music accompaniment on disc.

There is a surfeit of tales that the coming of sound was a cataclysmic shock, reinforced in Hollywood folklore by movies such as *Singin' in the Rain* (1952), but this is misleading. Certainly sound broke the decade in two and *The Jazz Singer* brought not only sound but huge financial success to Warner Bros. who had banked their business on the success of the sound cinema revolution. It also brought acclaim to Al Jolson, its star. The film's success allowed Warner Bros. to move from a minor Hollywood player to the largest of the movie companies by 1930. But it was not the first time the cinema had produced a 'sound' film: orchestral scores had accompanied pictures in even the smallest of theatres, including the nickelodeons. Thomas Edison had been working on sound for years and he produced the Kinetophone in 1913, although synchronisation of sound to picture remained a problem. AT&T and RCA had conducted experiments in sound, harnessing the resources of discoveries in radio, and in 1928 would form RKO (Radio-Keith-Orpheum). Fox had been producing Movietone newsreels which successfully deployed sound technology, such as the newsreel showing Charles Lindbergh taking off on his trans-Atlantic flight in May of 1927. Jack and Harry Warner had been negotiating for Western Electric's sound technology since 1925, making good use of the new sound-on-disc process to include non-diegetic music and a speech by Will Hays. When the companies merged as Vitaphone, the result was *Don Juan* (1926), Warners' vehicle for new star John Barrymore, actually released before *The Jazz Singer*, although with music rather than dialogue.

In short, experiments in sound were as old as the cinema itself and for audiences the cinema had never actually been silent. Presenters were employed to read intertitles and in Japan the *benshi* commentated on the narrative on screen for theatre audiences; orchestras and singers proliferated in theatres; and musical scores for movies were an art in themselves. D. W. Griffith released each picture with a score; Gottfried Hupperlz's score for Lang's *Metropolis* (1927) had been a modernist revelation; and well-known composers such as Dimitri Shostakovich also worked on films, such as *New Babylon* (1929).

The Warner Bros. studio was simply most effective in launching sound and publicising what it could do. 'You ain't heard nothin' yet' was the catchphrase in one of the brief segments in which Jolson spoke. Other studios were forced to follow Warners' lead. The industry turned itself inside out in order to accommodate sound and by the end of the decade there were few successful silent films on release. French director Abel Gance's *Napoléon* (1927), planned as a six-part biopic, is a representative example of a technically innovative film that failed due to the public's interest in sound. Gance's Impressionist camerawork and innovations in point-of-view shots, attaching the camera to a galloping horse and suspending it over the sea in a storm, were hugely successful. He also created a split screen in nine separate sections, splicing the film expertly by hand without the benefit of an editing suite, and a triptych of shots to create a wide panoramic shot of Napoleon's troops. However, with the coming of sound, the silent *Napoléon* might have remained a cinematic folly had it not been for its rediscovery and restoration by British film historian and film-maker Kevin Brownlow in 1979.

There were two versions of sound cinema to begin with: sound-on-disc, as used in *The Jazz Singer*, and sound-on-film. The first was synchronised and for the second sound was taped onto the film itself. In America, sound-on-film, the most obvious method and in many ways the easiest, would be quickly and widely adapted as the most effective system with Western Electric pioneering the system for a lion's share of the domestic and export market. Considerable resistance was put up in Europe, however, by European radio companies, such as the Torbis-Klangfilm syndicate. The transition to sound was neither entirely welcome nor an unmitigated success. The spectacular scale of *Intolerance* (1916) or Gance's *Napoléon* would begin to be translated down into more intimate stories in which speech drove the narrative. The monumental scale achieved in silent cinema would not be restored until the 1950s in an effort to persuade audiences away from their television sets back into the theatres (see Chapter 15).

In the preceding two years, AT&T had approached all the major producers to introduce new sound equipment but they were loath to tamper with a thriving business and very aware that while they might change the design of studios dedicated to the production of silent pictures, the picture palaces were all equipped for silent films. Such a change would involve the loss of millions of dollars and the investment of still more millions for new sound technology. Subsequently, studios borrowed huge sums from Wall Street in order to harness the new technology and successfully re-equip studios. The economic scramble and the short time between the coming of sound and the end of the decade was dominated by mergers and acquisitions which resulted in the five major and three minor studios – Universal, United Artists and Columbia – emerging triumphant in 1930. One by-product for the film industry was the control financiers placed on standardising the product and on ensuring production efficiency. This was made most apparent during the Depression of the 1930s when financiers would tighten the purse strings.

The coming of sound also made very different demands on actors for whom exaggerated mime and dramatic close-ups had become the staples of silent screen-acting. The voices of some of those who had become its greatest stars – John Gilbert, Norma Talmadge, Pola Negri – did not make a successful transition to 'talkies'. One American star who was immortalised in Europe, Louise Brooks, did not make the transition and she epitomises the adage 'We didn't need dialogue; we had faces', spoken with conviction by Gloria Swanson (as former silent diva Norma Desmond) in *Sunset Boulevard* (1950). Brooks' films are rarely shown now but her face is iconic and her sleek black hairstyle was copied by women around the world. The gutsy femme fatale of the silent age, Lulu, in G. W. Pabst's *Pandora's Box* (1929) became her trademark and she became 'Lulu' to the public, as evidenced in her memoir *Lulu in Hollywood* (1982), but she would remain locked in the silent era. Greta Garbo's first talking picture, *Anna Christie*, was not released until 1930 because MGM were wary of their megastar's ability to transfer successfully to sound cinema. Yet she succeeded, as witnessed in the legendary aloof statement, 'I want to be alone' in *Grand Hotel* (1932) which entered popular culture and only underlined her iconic status.

In Britain Anny Ondra, Hitchcock's first ice-cool blonde and star of *Blackmail* (1929), was a benign casualty. *Blackmail* was a silent film when Hitchcock began work on it but with the coming of sound he added sound segments. Ondra's voice was dubbed, her German accent considered too marked for English-speaking audiences. She returned to Germany and retired. Hitchcock was also significant for his Expressionist use of non-realist sound. In *Blackmail*, the grating of the word 'Knife' that punctuates a breakfast conversation for an agonised Alice (Ondra) brings into sharp relief the murder she committed in self-defence the night before. Most directors were slow in getting to grips with sound technology but Hitchcock, René Clair and King Vidor were among the most innovative in the early years.

A representative genre through which to examine the coming of sound is comedy. Through silent comedy culturally specific social mores could be exposed and satirised but the genre was also transnational and translocal in its appeal. The slapstick tradition perfected in the late 1910s and the 1920s travelled very well and it was variously argued, by self- and Hollywood publicists as different as Charlie Chaplin, D. W. Griffith, and Carl Laemmle, that silent cinema had created a new universal language. Comedy was often salient in advancing such claims, with Chaplin believing that comedy was itself a universal language. From the fumbling of the chaotic Keystone Kops to Buster Keaton's antics in a hot-air balloon or a small boat, silent comedy seemed to transcend cultural differences although there were, of course, odd exceptions: French comedian Max Linder's snappy dressing 'Max' was a significant influence on Chaplin but he was never appreciated in America as in Europe. In any case, the comedian was always locked in silence on the screen, even as audiences brought the house down with their laughter. The silent intensely visual style was epitomised by the 'comedy greats': Charlie Chaplin, whose first silent feature *The Kid* (1921) successfully combined comedy with senti-mentality; Buster Keaton, with his lithe body and expressive face who perfected a hugely physical comedy style in the Civil War film *The General* (1927); Harold Lloyd remembered for scaling skyscrapers as a human fly in *Safety Last* (1923); and Harry Langdon whose comedic talents were nurtured by Frank Capra in his directorial début *The Strong Man* (1926). The image of the comic clown or the sensitive outsider whose failure to 'fit' gave rise to a comedy of errors was augmented by the figures of new immigrant 'outsiders' who found a place in silent cinema.

Vaudeville had relied on ethnic stereotypes for much of its humour and Lon Chaney's cast of grotesque 'alien' misfits, stigmatised as 'freaks' in cinema hits such as *Shadows* (1922) and *Mr Wu* (1927), were an extension of that. Al Jolson came out of vaudeville and his use of blackface in *The Jazz Singer* and *The Singing Fool* (1928) recalled that tradition as well as reflecting the popularity of radio shows such as *Amos 'n' Andy*. By successfully harnessing the tropes of minstrelsy to nativist pressure to understand citizenship as a dialectical relationship between 'black' and 'white', Jolson became the first Jewish person to be an 'American' idol for the masses. Similarly, *The Immigrant* (1917), the most significant of Charlie Chaplin's two-reel films as a director, is more sympathetic social comment than slapstick. Nevertheless, it is a rare thing when compared to the popularity of the characters Chu-Chin Chow or Dr Fu Manchu in the 1920s. The studios' dominant popular representation was of racial fantasies of white heroines under threat from a black or Asian rapist as in *The Yellow Menace* (1916) and *The Perils of Pauline* (1919). Conversely – or even perversely – an ethnic stereotype that held great sway for cinema audiences in this period of fear over mass immigration was the romantic, often sadomasochistic, and at times villainous, aesthete epitomised by Rudolph Valentino and Ramón Novarro – and, to an extent, Sessue Hayakawa in *The Cheat* (1915). Valentino in particular co-opted this stereotype to enormous popular effect and successfully overturned many of its most deleterious aspects.

Comedy is also the genre that changed most with the coming of sound. The visual 'gag', slapstick and farce that made silent cinema so beloved of audiences would give way to a literate genre in which repartee, as that between Laurel and Hardy, would win the day. Comic characters created in the silent era would fade or adapt. Keaton's career was terminated by the coming of sound. Although he continued to appear in films, few were noteworthy, until his cameo comeback in Chaplin's *Limelight* in 1952. Chaplin's 'Little Tramp' persisted into the beginning of the sound era. The Tramp's progress through Chaplin's early films had often been accompanied by sound effects but he never spoke, not even in *City Lights* (1931) or *Modern Times* (1936) in which Chaplin's legendary character retired from the limelight. The wisecracks of Mae West and the banter of Laurel and Hardy would change the comedy genre forever and in 1929 the Marx Brothers would release their film début *The Cocoanuts* (1929).

The coming of sound also restricted the camera which was enclosed and static in order to prevent additional noise; humming lights had to be superseded by silent incandescent lights and lanier microphones hidden in actors' clothing or in stage sets were less than adequate to the task of producing realistic sound accompaniment, a problem made much of in the satirical scenes of non-synchronised sound in *Singin' in the Rain*. When Don Lockwood (Gene Kelly) and Lina Lamont (Jean Hagen) attempt their first sound picture, *The Duelling Cavalier*, her shrill nasal tones ruin the effect so she is secretly dubbed. It is very possible that the scene alludes to Norma Talmadge whose accent was out of place in the costume drama *Du Barry, Woman of Passion* (1930) or maybe Marion Davies, William Randolph Hearst's mistress, parodied so mercilessly in Welles' *Citizen Kane* (1941). Dubbing actors' voices only became really established in the early 1930s. The coming of sound had entrenched fears of American cultural imperialism and an immediate reaction was the banning of American talkies in some countries including Italy and Spain. One way around this was to make the same film in different language versions, using different actors in each case, as in the case of E. A. Dupont's *Atlantic* (1929), until the technique of dubbing became popular.

In fact, the season of 1927–8 was characterised by other technological developments too: panochromatic film stocks were replaced by orthochromatic stock and colour technology created unrest. It was thought that colour would compromise film art, that is to say that colour would distract and confuse, diluting the purity of monochrome cinematography. *The Black Pirate* (1926) with Douglas Fairbanks was subject to mixed reviews in this regard and it was posited that while some genres could exploit colour successfully (animation), others should not (documentary). In 1930, Technicolor was forced to advertise its colour process as naturalistic ('What if a rainbow had always been black and white . . .?') in order to try to control the audience response to colour. Sound was by far the most sweeping change, though, and with *The Jazz Singer* and *Broadway Melody*, the leading box office success of 1929, the American film musical which would exploit sound and colour to great effect began to take hold as the archetypal genre of 'show business' in the 1930s. In *Singin' in the Rain*, a short scene in a long musical number captures the visual and aural iconography of the musical styles – burlesque, vaudeville and revue – that combine in their influence on the 1920s film musical. But the coming of sound proved as distinctive in enhancing other genres too. The authority of newsreels was heightened by commanding voiceovers and D. W. Griffith's first sound film was a historical drama, *Abraham Lincoln* (1930), which won him Best Director.

The cinema has always been self-referential; making movies about making movies has been popular since Victor Sjöström starred in Stiller's *Thomas Graal's Best Film* (1917) and Anthony Asquith made *Shooting Stars* (1928). *Singin' in the Rain* and *Sunset Boulevard* are classic examples. The latter is subtitled 'A Hollywood Story' and star of the silent screen Gloria Swanson became identified with Norma Desmond, the former star aiming to make a comeback (Swanson made at least three comebacks herself). In a clever pun on cinema history, Swanson and budding scriptwriter-turned-gigolo Joe Gilles (William Holden) watch one of Desmond's old movies. The film in which Desmond is supposed to have starred is actually *Queen Kelly* (1928) in which Swanson appeared and which she also produced. She was directed by Erich von Stroheim who as Max der Mayerling runs the projection of the film in *Sunset Boulevard*. *Queen Kelly* was never released in full, a casualty of Stroheim's excesses and the coming of sound. That Stroheim acts, and that Cecil B. DeMille, Hedda Hopper and Buster Keaton appear as themselves in *Sunset Boulevard*, testifies to the composite picture of the era as driven by the studios. Important directors, actors, even stars, could become the most vulnerable parties in the studio configuration. Much more recent examples include Woody Allen's *Bullets over Broadway* (1994) which opens with the strains of *The Jazz Singer* and the box office smash *Forrest Gump* (1994). Gump's name is visually 'explained' in the eponymous 1994 box office smash with recourse to a simulated scene from Griffith's *The Birth of a Nation*; he is a descendant of the 'great Civil War hero' Nathan Bedford Forrest who also founded the revitalised Ku Klux Klan in 1915.

Mark Jancovich and Lucy Faire, with Sarah Stubbings, begin their study of social film history, 'Translating the Talkies: Diffusion, Reception and Live Performance', by reminding the reader of the importance of the context in which the first sound films were consumed. Cinemagoing is a social activity that takes place within a specific cultural geography. Their study of spectatorship and film consumption in a single British city, Nottingham, at the moment in which the talkies came to Nottingham's Elite cinema in June 1929, is significant in its interrelation of the local with a global phenomenon – the coming of sound.

This extract helps to contextualise the coming of sound in terms of wider fears of 'Americanisation' and, conversely, comparative global contexts in which an emphasis on the local reveals telling evidence of cinema as a social phenomenon. For example, *The Jazz Singer*, usually regarded as the first talkie for cinema audiences, was not the first sound film exhibited to Nottingham audiences and when sound came to Nottingham, it was part of a touring exhibition. Nottingham audiences also returned to viewing silent movies before the city's cinemas finally converted to sound technology in 1930. Even then, as research reveals, silent films continued to be shown and enjoyed for a while. Similarly, if one extends the local comparison to another city, Calcutta in India, for example, the first talkie to be exhibited there was a little-remembered film *Melody of Love* (1928) in 1929. It was Universal's first talking picture and was reputedly made by borrowing Fox's equipment after the Fox studios had shut down for the night. Modes of consumption, it soon becomes apparent, are dependent on the specificities of distribution to and exhibition in particular places and on local historical circumstances.

Jancovich and Faire, with Stubbings, perform the kind of film history here that focuses on the city and the sites of exhibition and distribution within that city space. Their study reveals the ways in which a specific city responded to sound cinema, neither homogeneously nor with unqualified appreciation of the new technology that made it possible. Although the coming of sound is often presented as a fait accompli, their research reveals that for cinema audiences in the late 1920s it may not have necessarily seemed like the beginning of the end of the silent cinema.

- How does a consideration of exhibition sites increase our understanding of the significance of film and filmgoing as a cultural phenomenon?
- Why is reception of sound films difficult to assess and what are the potential gains and pitfalls in looking to journalism to provide a picture of audience activity in this particular context?
- Choose a film (a 'first' if possible in your local area) and amass as many newspaper reports as possible that relate to its exhibition and consumption. You might use online newspaper archives or the local library. What conclusions can you draw about the effectiveness of such resources in your study of local film history?

TRANSLATING THE TALKIES: DIFFUSION, RECEPTION AND LIVE PERFORMANCE

Mark Jancovich and Lucy Faire

As Allen and Gomery have argued, one of the problems with histories of the talkies is the focus on one event and one location. As they put it, 'we are skeptical about the ability of one film, *The Jazz Singer*, to alter the course of

Mark Jancovich, Lucy Faire with Sarah Stubbings, *The Place of the Audience: Cultural Geographies of Film Consumption* (London: BFI, 2003).

history'[1] and 'New York City is not the entire country.[2] To this we would also add that it is not the entire world either. Their argument is that the process through which sound was introduced to the cinemagoing public was much longer and more complex than is suggested by those histories that concentrate on the supposed overnight success of *The Jazz Singer*. Instead, they offer both an industrial history of the processes through which technologies were developed, tested and disseminated[3] and a local study. As they argue, most 'historians of technological change in the cinema emphasise the origins of change' and it is rarely asked: 'How does the diffusion of technological change occur at the local level?'[4] It is not simply that the talkies arrived in cities outside New York at different times, but that the processes through which sound technologies were diffused were affected by the specific local conditions within which that diffusion took place.

First, the introduction of the talkies into Nottingham did not occur at the same time as the so-called overnight success of *The Jazz Singer* in New York. Although *The Jazz Singer* was released in New York in 1927, the talkies did not reach Nottingham until June 1929 when they were exhibited at the Elite. Moreover, the first show was not Jolson's performance in *The Jazz Singer*, but the film *Lucky Boy*, which was shown for two weeks. As the NEN observed, the film featured 'George Jessel, the original Jazz Singer, and a magnetic baritone, [who] wrote the story, and his attractive personality dominates the screen production'.[5] The first sound film to be shown in Nottingham that featured Jolson was *The Singing Fool*, shown at the Hippodrome in July 1929, two weeks after the screening of *Lucky Boy*.

As a result, by the time that the talkies reached Nottingham, they had already been preceded by numerous reports about them, and the adverts for these first showings exploited this fact. The first talkie was not a surprise sensation, but rather the final, long awaited arrival of a much-talked-about phenomenon. It was 'Hot from America' and 'the first presentation in the country, apart from the Regal, London',[6] and all references to *The Jazz Singer* assumed that everyone was already aware of the film. Consequently, the talkies were presented as something to which only the cultural centres of London and New York had previously been privy but which had now reached Nottingham and, in the process, it was suggested that Nottingham had some special relationship to these cultural centres. The adverts claimed that the films had come straight to Nottingham after New York and London, and so presented Nottingham as close to the top of the cultural hierarchy of cities.

However, a review article on the event also made reference to other talking films that had been shown in England before this screening:

> The talking sequences came out well, the synchronisation being good, and the accents of the characters not too aggressively American, which has been the great drawback to some of the talking pictures sent over from the States.[7]

Thus, as Allen and Gomery have shown, The *Jazz Singer* did not mark the arrival of the talkies, and there had been numerous experiments that had been exhibited to the public prior to its release. However, these experiments were not always well received and it took some time to overcome various technical difficulties such as synchronisation and sound quality. Like the viewers of the first moving pictures, then, audiences for the 'new' talkies were not unsophisticated ones that simply marvelled at the talking images. On the contrary, the introduction of sound was the product of a lengthy process of trials and readjustments, in which the film companies sought to develop a product that audiences would find acceptable.

Furthermore, this first film showing did not herald the 'arrival' of the talkies. It was projected using a mechanism called 'Portable Talking Pictures' and the Elite promptly stopped showing sound films after its two-week engagement. The Elite had not been converted to sound but was simply staging a touring exhibition, and it did not show another sound film until February 1930.[8]

The Hippodrome was the first Nottingham cinema to show talkies on a full-time basis. It had been recently converted from a music hall in 1927 when it was taken over by Provincial Cinematograph Theatres Ltd and, in the process, the wooden benches were removed from the gods and an organ was installed. The newly converted cinema had 2,000 seats, and its size meant that it became Provincial Cinematograph Theatres' (PCT) premier cinema in Nottingham, displacing the Long Row Picture House from this position and closing it down. Like the Elite, the Hippodrome also reverted to silent films after a couple of weeks of showing sound films but it soon showed talkies again on the improved Western Electric apparatus. By June 1929, sixty-five cinemas in Britain had installed this equipment, and although the equipment did not reach Nottingham until 13 August of that year, the Hippodrome was still one of a small group of cinemas outside London to have acquired the technology. Other Nottingham cinemas also followed the Hippodrome's lead and, six months after the arrival of sound, the papers were advertising five cinemas that had been converted to sound.

However, while Nottingham was keen to present itself as the cultural centre of the region at this time, the picture is more complex. In April, the Victory cinema in Loughborough advertised that it was showing talkies, although the papers give no details as to what these films might have been. However, the claim that the films were British rather than American makes it unlikely that they would have been feature films. The first British sound feature, Hitchcock's *Blackmail*, was not shown until June 1929. Leicester, on the other hand, seems to have had its first sound feature at around the same time as Nottingham: on 20 June, the Palace Variety House gave a presentation of *The Singing Fool*.[9] However, it was a little ahead of Nottingham when it came to the matter of equipment and, on 24 June 1929, the Western Electric Sound was installed at the Picture House[10] This cinema was owned by PCT, which also owned Nottingham's Hippodrome. In contrast, sound came to Lincoln sometime later.

The first sound on disc film (*The Donovan Affair*) was shown on 12 August 1929, and the first sound on film was shown on 23 September 1929: the Grand showed *Showboat* while, at the same time, the Central was showing another sound film.[11]

The Reception of Sound Technology

The reception of sound films is difficult to assess. Reviews of the first talking picture in Nottingham claimed that 'the film and the novelty of its sound effects obviously delighted the crowded audience'[12] and there were also reports of record audiences for the talking pictures shown at the Hippodrome in July.[13] However, journalistic reports are not always a reliable gauge of audience reactions. For example, the *Nottingham Journal* claimed that the audience at the Hippodrome was critical of the synchronisation and the music, but it also claimed that 'there is no denying the wonderful combination of movement and speech' and that the audience 'were startled into silence' when Al Jolson started to sing.[14] Also, as we will see later, many press accounts of the new talking pictures objected to the American accents present in these films but these objections were not shared by many sections of the audience, nor was this situation unique. Journalists often sought to establish a dear and appreciable distinction between their own responses and what they saw as the responses of the 'ordinary' cinemagoer, and one reason for this was that, as Klinger has argued, reviews:

> signify cultural hierarchies of aesthetic value reigning at particular times. As a primary public tastemaker, the critic operates to make, in Pierre Bourdieu's parlance, 'distinctions'. Among other things, the critic distinguishes legitimate from illegitimate art and proper from improper modes of aesthetic appreciation.[15]

It was precisely by distancing themselves from what they saw as the responses of 'ordinary' cinemagoers that journalists asserted and established their own legitimacy.

However, so long as we remain aware of these dangers, and test journalistic accounts against other evidence whenever possible, press coverage has much to tell us about the reception of the talkies.[16] For example, comments in the reviews also suggest that it took some time for audiences to get used to the new sound films:

> The Western Electric Apparatus resulted in a rich and mellow sound from the four 'receivers' (or loud speakers) behind the special screen and it was satisfactory reproduction. The voices (especially the male) were at times a little overwhelming, but little fault could be found with the music which accompanied the silent period.[17]

In this instance the audience found the best parts to be the 'silent' sections. The managing director of the Elite also talked to one reporter about his 'shock' at seeing the talkies in America and at the lack of 'silent relief'.[18] A second article echoed this sentiment:

> But the fact remains unchanged that the talking film is a quite different form of entertainment from the silent. It makes greater demands on the attention of the audience, which had to key up two senses instead of one [and] while that increases one's capacity for enjoyment it makes the 'talkie' much more physically tiring than the silent film.[19]

Indeed, contrary to Horkheimer and Adorno's claim that the sound film simply increased the illusory realism of film and created greater passivity on the part of the audience,[20] the evidence from Nottingham suggests that audiences did not find the sound film easy to consume. The consumption of the sound film required considerable adjustment and could even be an uncomfortable experience.

Of course, at one level, cinemas almost always had some form of music to go along with the silent films, and the problems were partly due to the types of sound technology that were available. Another reviewer, for example, commented that the viewer had to adapt to appreciate the talkies because the 'voice reproductions are a bit artificial'.[21] This opinion might also explain why, although talkies proved popular, they did not simply replace the silent films in the public's interest.

At any rate, the transition to sound could not have taken place overnight, despite audience interest: cinemas needed to be converted and studios needed to switch over to sound production. However, the silent film did not become an inferior object overnight. Both the Elite and the Victoria Picture House not only continued to show silent films, but actively and unembarrassingly identified themselves as 'The Silent House' in their adverts and listings in the papers. Furthermore, on 29 October 1929, one silent film shown at the Elite was described as being a 'sensation in London even at the height of the "talkie" boom'.[22] It should also be remembered that until the opening of the Ritz in 1933, the Elite remained Nottingham's most prestigious movie palace, and even in cinemas that had been converted to sound, silent films continued to be shown, although in many cases they were used to support the talking pictures.

Where the reviewers did register problems with the new talking pictures was, as we will see later, with the American accents of the actors. They also objected to the plots of many of the early films. The NEN, for example, comments on the unvaried subject matter of the talkies: 'The Melody of Broadway does not depart from the talking film habit of being about chorus girls and the night life of Broadway' while Broadway Babies, showing at the Hippodrome in January 1930, was described as having the 'inevitable Broadway as its background'.[23] By the end of October, however, the NEN felt that the audience was beginning to become more critical: 'The talkies having lost their novelty, the public naturally are paying more attention to quality of acting, singing and humour'.[24] Another reviewer was happy with The Great Gabba not only because the stage screens were 'magnificent, but at last chorus girls have not been allowed to entirely dominate the plot'.[25] Furthermore, when *Blackmail* was shown at the Hippodrome, the reviewer in the NEN was delighted, and considered it to be 'genuine drama' and the best talkie production yet seen in Nottingham.[26] It is, however, unclear quite how much this praise was due to the film's status as the first British talkie, given the general disdain for American products in the press.

Music, Variety and Live Performance

There were also other worries about the impact of talking pictures. Music had always been an important part of silent films, especially in the big central cinemas such as the Elite and the Hippodrome that had large orchestras. However, even the smaller local cinemas generally featured some form of musical accompaniment, usually a pianist but sometimes a small band on special occasions. Given that many of the working classes could not afford gramophones or radios before the 1930s, cinemas and dance halls were often the only places where they could hear professional performances.[27] In a reminiscence of early theatregoing in the local press, Kathleen Oakland therefore spoke for many of her generation who considered the music to be an important part of an evening at the theatre:

> Each week I used to book for a Friday evening performance second house for my young man and myself. I always asked for front seats as I enjoyed watching and listening to the orchestra as much as the stage performances. There was a special cello player who always gave us a smile as we went to our seats.[28]

In another account published in the local press, N. Hall even claimed that the music was his primary motivation for going to the cinema. As he explained, he had spent many 'contented hours' at the Picture House because the orchestra there was particularly good. His preference for the music over the films themselves is also demonstrated by his choice of an end seat in the balcony, a seat that no one else wanted due to the poor view of the screen but from which he could see right into the orchestra pit. In addition, he remembers that the conductor was a Belgian who liked French music, and that he would buy the 'piano conductor's' copy of the score as a souvenir of the show.[29]

In his study of Lexington cinemas, Waller observes that there was a great deal of concern about the possible effects that the talkies might have on the nature of the music in cinemas,[30] and similar anxieties were also present in Nottingham:

> Since the advent of the talking film in Nottingham, many picture-goers have had plenty of cause for nursing a grievance because the orchestra at the cinema concerned, which to many was the centre of attraction, had been dispensed with. The 'canned' music that has been associated with the 'talkies' yet shown in the city has not been the slightest compensation

for the loss of a fine orchestra, for without exception it has borne a very striking resemblance in the harsh, strident, unmusical noises which issued from the now obsolete phonograph and the very first gramophones.[31]

In this situation, one reason for the continued appreciation of silent films was that these film showings were still associated with the presence of live music. As one review commented:

> It seems that although the talkie has become very popular in this city, the silent film is still attractive when presented under such ideal conditions. The Elite orchestra is very fine. There is something about the human player that sometimes seems an indispensable part of the showing of a film, and certainly a very large number of people think so, judging by the audiences.[32]

However, this reviewer also went on to explain that the sound film being shown that week was the first example in which the music was 'pleasing to the ear', and he concluded that, if the music in the talking picture continued to improve, 'the cloud which hangs over the "talkie" in the eyes of the music-loving section of the films' goers will be lifted'.[33]

However, it was not only the presence of live music that was threatened by the talking pictures, but the variety format, too. *Movietone Follies of 1929* was almost just a film version of a music hall revue but had 'the additional advantage of going through without the intervals of waiting inseparable from the stage show'.[34] It was also the case that, as Murphy argues, sound had the advantage of providing a cheap alternative to live performances, not only for those cinemas that already had live acts, but also for those cinemas that depended on gramophones.[35] The coming of sound therefore hastened the demise of the music hall and the variety show, and cinemas became less dependent on live entertainment. However, the decline of the music hall had already started before the arrival of sound, as the conversion of the Hippodrome to a cinema in 1927 indicates. None the less, Priestley blamed the lack of live acts in Leicester on the presence of films and, although there was not such a striking absence of live entertainment in Nottingham, his comments are indicative of the impact of sound films on live shows:

> In the whole of Leicester that night there was only one performance being given by living players, in a touring musical comedy. In a town with nearly a quarter of million people, not without intelligence or money, this is not good enough. Soon we shall be as badly off as America, where I find myself in large cities that had not a single living actor performing in them, nothing but films, films, films. There a whole generation has grown up that associates entertainment with moving pictures and nothing else; and I am not sure that as much could not be said of this country.[36]

Although Priestley does go on to say that he liked films, he felt that they did not provide any inside knowledge of a town.[37] These concerns therefore pick up on a more general fear of Americanisation in the period, and the loss of national and local identity that it supposedly caused.[38] However, although there were certainly local acts and performers associated with the variety show, many were also touring players, often from abroad, and it is difficult to see why they, any more than the recordings of American performers and performances, would provide an inside knowledge of a town in which they appeared.[39]

Of course, the arrival of the talkies did not completely shut down the presence of live acts either within the cinema or within culture more generally. The Empire remained open as a music hall until the late 1950s; the Playhouse was opened in an old cinema in 1942; and the Theatre Royal continued to function as a prominent and respected institution. Even in the cinemas, as we shall see, live performers continued to be a major draw with figures such as Jack Helyer, the organist at the Ritz, often being a more important draw than the films shown.

NOTES

1. Robert C. Allen and Douglas Gomery, *Film History: Theory and Practice* (New York: McGraw-Hill, 1985), p. 116.
2. Ibid., p. 196.
3. See Donald Crafton, *The Talkies: American Cinema's Transition to Sound, 1926–1931* (Berkeley, CA: University of California Press, 1997); Douglas Gomery, *Shared Pleasures: A History of Movie Exhibition in America* (London: BFI, 1992); Barbara Stones, *America Goes to the Movies: 100 years of Motion Picture Exhibition* (North Hollywood: National Association of Theater Owners, 1993).
   NEN = *Nottingham Evening News*
   NJ= *Nottingham Journal*
   NDG= *Nottingham Daily Guardian*
   NEP= *Nottingham Evening Post*
4. Allen and Gomery, 1985, p. 194.
5. *Nottingham Evening News* (NEN), 25 June 1929.
6. *Nottingham Journal* (NJ), 24 June 1929.
7. *Nottingham Daily Guardian* (NDG), 25 June 1929.
8. The first sound films were shown in February 1930, but on 1 January, a screen voice did wish the patrons of the cinema a happy new year.
9. David R. Williams, *Cinema in Leicester, 1896–1931* (Loughborough: Heart of Albion Press, 1993), p. 200.
10. Ibid., pp. 200–1.
11. George Clarke, *The Cinemas of Lincoln* (Wakefield: Mercia Cinema Society, 1991), pp. 12, 15.
12. NJ, 25 June 1929.
13. NEN, 9 July 1929.
14. Ibid.
15. Barbara Klinger, *Melodrama and Meaning: History, Culture, and the Films of Douglas Sirk* (Bloomington, IN: Indiana University Press, 1994), p. 70.
16. For a more detailed discussion of the dangers and uses of journalist reviews, see Mark Jancovich, 'Genre and the Audience: Genre Classification and Cultural Distinctions in the Mediation of *Silence of the Lambs*' in Melvyn Stokes and Richard Maltby eds. *Hollywood Spectatorship* (London: BFI, 2000), pp. 33–44.
17. NEN, 13 August 1929.
18. NJ, 25 June 1929.

19. NDG, 4 February 1930.
20. Max Horkheimer and Theodor Adorno, *Dialectic of Enlightenment* (London: New Left Books, 1979).
21. NJ, 25 June 1929.
22. *Nottingham Evening Post* (NEP), 29 October 1929.
23. NEN, 22 October 1929; NEN, 4 January 1930.
24. NEN, 29 October 1929.
25. NEN, 3 December 1929.
26. NEN, 5 November 1929.
27. Some may have had instruments of their own, and even been members of formal or informal bands.
28. *Bygones*, 3 July 1999.
29. NEP, 7 April 1970.
30. Gregory A. Waller, *Main Street Amusements: Movies and Commercial Entertainment in a Southern City, 1896–1930* (Washington DC: Smithsonian Institution Press, 1995).
31. See article 'A Serious Crisis has Arisen in German Musical Circles Owing to the Arrival of the Talking Film (Says Berlin Wire From the Exchange)': NEN, Tuesday 18 June 1929.
32. NEN, 15 October 1929.
33. NJ, 23 September 1929.
34. Ibid.
35. Robert Murphy, 'Coming of Sound to the Cinema in Britain' *Historical Journal of Film, Radio, and Television* 4: 2 (1984), p. 45. According to Murphy, from 1926, 'Kine-Variety' was a popular form of entertainment, and it involved live acts supporting the main film programme. However, the smaller cinemas, which could not afford expensive variety acts, 'were helped by the fortuitous arrival of the electric gramophone'. British Brunswick, for example, claimed that, by 1928, it had installed over 1,000 gramophones in cinemas 'Sound films were envisaged as fulfilling a similar function to the gramophone in providing a cheap alternative to live performers.' Gomery also makes a similar point in his study of movie exhibition in the United States; see Gomery, 1992.
36. J. B. Priestley, *English Journey* (London: Mandarin, 1994), p. 121.
37. Ibid.
38. For work on Americanisation debates, see Dick Hebdige, *Hiding in the Light: On Images and Things* (London: Comedia, 1988); David Morley and Kevin Robins, *Spaces of Identity: Global Media, Electronic Landscapes and Cultural Boundaries* (London: Routledge, 1995); Duncan Webster, *Looka Yonda! The Imaginary American of Populist Culture* (London: Comedia/Routledge, 1988); Andrew Higson, *Waving the Flag: Constructing a National Cinema in Britain* (Oxford: Clarendon Press, 1995).
39. According to Crump, unlike the North East and Lancashire, the success of early music hall in Nottingham and Birmingham 'needs to be located in the context of early integration into a national circuit based in London rather than a regional tradition'. As a result, music halls in the Midlands never really were a reflection of local identity. See Jeremy Crump, 'Provincial Music Hall: Promoters and Public in Leicester, 1863–1929' in Peter Bailey ed. *Music Hall: The Business of Pleasure* (Milton Keynes: Open University Press, 1986).

8

REALISM, NATIONALISM AND 'FILM CULTURE'

The coming of sound was an important phase in the bid for naturalism in the cinema and by the end of the 1920s many filmmakers across different national cinemas were in pursuit of forms of cinematic realism that would convey 'modernity'. The cinema was one of a number of cultural, technological and political developments, or transformations, that coalesced in the larger formation of modernity. The 1920s would also see the beginnings of an intellectual tradition that read cinema as a self-reflexive medium and a distinctively public phenomenon that might translate, or at the very least comment on, modernity for a mass audience. A burgeoning film culture began to involve critics and reviewers as taste-makers, categorising and theorising about films as art, and film journals and magazines as the forum in which the patrons of film clubs and societies could begin to find the films they enjoyed contextualised.

New documentary styles emerged although the term 'new' may seem misleading when it is remembered that Lumière's first frames were actually of workers leaving his factory after their day's work and that early cinema from most national vantage points sought to exploit new technology to find the 'truth value' in everyday realities from its beginnings. The cinema was beginning to experiment with realism and its alternatives and by the late 1920s, the term 'documentary' was in popular usage and in Hollywood too directors aimed at capturing a level of verisimilitude that would amaze audiences. For example, *Wings*, directed to acclaim by William A. Wellman in 1927, had a strong plot and Clara Bow as the love interest, features that secured its Academy Award for Best Picture. It was also carefully naturalistic in detail. Wellman had flown with the French Air Corps and in order to capture

165

realistically the dogfights and bombings, he placed cameras on the planes and actually bombed trees and dug trenches in the Texas scrubland to recreate a bomb-blasted landscape.

With *Nanook of the North* (1922) Robert Flaherty had gained a mainstream Hollywood audience for his anthropological foray into the lives of Eskimos. Flaherty's second feature fared less well and he left Hollywood, but his later film, *Man of Aran* (1934) made in Britain, established him as the leading figure in factual filmmaking, influencing Scottish film producer John Grierson. Grierson, who would go on to head the Canadian Film Board, himself directed only one (silent) film, *Drifters*, in 1929. Its style largely influenced by Eisenstein, it is detailed evocation of herring fishermen, but its larger effect was as a spur to the creation of the British documentary film movement of the 1930s. Henry Bruce Woolfe, head of British Instructional Films, had made reconstructions of wartime battles and, in advance of Grierson, he also pioneered naturalist documentaries with the *Secrets of Nature* series. Flaherty extended still further to collaborate with F. W. Murnau on one quasi-documentary feature called *Tabu* (1930). Murnau's *Sunrise* (1927) had made much of the significance of environment in its agrarian allegory in which the morally corrupt city is set in opposition to rural life under threat from the encroachment of industrialisation. For *Tabu* the co-directors headed for Polynesia and heated debates ensued about their authorial intervention into the quotidian life of the indigenous population they represented in *Tabu*. Like *Sunrise*, the film as finally released is a partly a love story and one feels that Murnau must have won out in debating the importance of narrative. By the time it opened Murnau had died in a car crash and there is no way of knowing whether he might have produced other stylised docudramas.

Flaherty and Grierson shared an educationally driven expressive realism, poetic in the camera's attention to landscape. This feature of documentary realism had already received sustained treatment in Scandinavian cinema. In Denmark, Nordisk retained its trademark of a polar bear sitting on top of the world and wildlife documentaries had cemented the company's early success. In more general terms feature films such as Victor Sjöström's poetic and socially incisive *Give Us This Day* (1913), which prompted improved legislation for the poor in Sweden, had relied heavily on location filming for their impact and exhibited a certain pantheism in their depiction of nature. In Sjöström's *The Wind* (1928), the Texas dustbowl seems to be a character in its own right. French Impressionists saw their film work as an extension of the art of Picasso and Braque and the poetry of Apollinaire but they also looked to the Swedish cinema of Sjöström and Stiller for the artistic ways in which they conveyed landscapes. Gance's *The Wheel* (1923) includes footage of the Alps, for example, and, as one might expect, Canada's first forays into national cinema had included features like David M. Hartford's *Back to God's Country* (1919) which celebrated the distinctive Canadian wilderness. Varick Frissell's *The Viking* (1931) set in Newfoundland and focusing on a seal hunt was funded by the American studio Paramount. It is indicative of Canadian cinema existing in the shadow of Hollywood but is also a striking example of location shooting.

The representation of the cityscape was an important realist and modernist project in films as different as Stroheim's epic *Greed* (1924) and King Vidor's *The Crowd* (1928). In broad trends, it has been argued that American cinema favoured motivational realism over the psychological and metaphorical realism of European cinema but, at the end of the decade, a clutch of German directors, later to find success as proponents of *film noir*, collaborated on a realist project, *People on Sunday* (1929), in which the significance of the city as *noir* subject can be detected. The modernist city became a key trope in the camera's pursuit of truth in urban alienation, from the most well-known art films such as Walter Ruttman's *Berlin: Symphony of a Great City* (1927) to Alberto Cavalcanti's *Nothing But the Hours* (1926) and Marcel Carné's story of Parisians enjoying the Seine at the weekend, *Eldorado du Dimanche* (1929).

Film movements also go to exemplify the key artistic traits of realist-modernist projects as in Germany's 'New Objectivity', for example, for which the city was an important trope. In the mid-1920s *Neue Sachlichkeit* (translated as 'New Objectivity' or 'New Realism') was coined to reflect a feeling of disillusionment with German society. It is a feeling that can be detected in Expressionist features like *The Last Laugh* (1924) but the movement also signalled the decline of the Expressionist movement. It was influenced by painting as stylised as that of the Expressionists but focused on the element of social critique in paintings like those of Otto Dix of the First World War, or the savagery of George Grosz's caricatures. The political aspects of New Objectivity may be usefully read in conjunction with playwright Bertolt Brecht's idea of the 'alienation effect' (*Verfremdungseffekt*) which was intended to provoke a politicised reaction in audiences and became popular in Germany in the 1920s and 1930s. The cold and savage beauty of New Objectivity is best displayed in *Berlin: Symphony of a Great City*. Ruttman had originally studied as a painter and experimented with photographing paintings in sequence. In his film, shots of Berlin's citizens are intercut with shots of tailors' dummies in shop windows, uncannily reminiscent of Lang's automatons in *Metropolis* (1927). People watch seemingly unmoved as a young girl commits suicide by drowning. For the New Realists society was appallingly indifferent to such suffering and audiences were expected to feel the shock of self-realisation. Some social commentators would later make correlations between such sterile scenes and the rise of Nazism in the early 1930s. E. A. Dupont, who directed *Vaudeville* (1925), and G. W. Pabst became exponents of New Objectivity before its decline later in the decade. Pabst's socially committed features, *The Joyless Street* (1925) and *Pandora's Box* (1929), captured the postwar slums in Vienna and London respectively (see Chapter 6).

In Russia, Lenin had famously declared that film was the most important of the arts in Russia. Certainly, in its success as a socialist, educational and propaganda tool, he was proved right in the 1920s. Soviet montage aesthetics would dominate by 1925. Lenin had nationalised the industry in 1919 and a State Film school was formed the same year with Lev Kuleshov a prominent member. Despite the fact that the country's film stocks were low in a period of economic depression and they often had to use the same film stock many times over, Kuleshov and other members of the school (Pudovkin and Vertov) began to experiment with what would become known as the Kuleshov Effect. Individual frames were edited together to provoke associations. An actor's expression would not change but the juxtaposition of his face with variously a grave site, a bowl of soup, or a baby would create the effect of an emotional response to the object (sorrow, hunger or happiness). The actor in the shots was usually Ivan Mozhukin who would later become an important actor in France. Kuleshov's Effect went to prove the salience of montage to any intellectual and political understanding of the uses to which medium could be put. Kuleshov had also trained with filmmaker Evgeni Bauer in the Tsarist era and his overall contribution to cinema was considerable. In 1929 he published *The Art of Cinema*. He also experimented in depth of field and long takes, techniques that flash forward to those celebrated when Orson Welles and William Wyler explored their effects in detail in the early 1940s. Kuleshov influenced Pudovkin's style considerably and *Mother* (1926) is one of the most strongly plotted of the examples of montage cinema: a mother is influenced by her son's political activism around the failed revolution of 1905. *Mother* exhibits a 'montage of attractions' rather than the alienating and discontinuous editing that Eisenstein would pioneer.

Kuleshov, along with Eisenstein and Vertov, was a key theorist of cinema and from the mid-1920s to the end of the decade the most experimental phase of Russian silent cinema involved the theory and praxis of montage. Eisenstein, who had begun his career as an engineer building bridges, described his theory of montage as 'half-industrial and half-music-hall'. He used the machine as a metaphor for assembling his films in a Constructivist conception of montage as collision of images, rather than a way of linking images as in Kuleshov's experiment, both being supremely manipulative. Constructivism was based on the idea of the filmmaker as a technical facilitator whose social vision would echo that of intellectuals and workers alike. In essays such as 'A Dialectical Approach to Film Form' (1929) and 'Methods of Montage' (1929) which with other short works would be gathered in the collections *Film Form* and *The Film Sense* in the 1930s and 1940s, Eisenstein proposed a theory of montage as the organising principle for representing abstract concepts and emotions as well as the visible world. Montage draws on Marx's ideas to formulate a dialectical approach to cinema in which strongly antithetical elements would clash to produce a 'synesthesia' that would provoke political and social awareness in filmgoers. That is to say, film culture itself would be a revolution. Film would be located in a materialist context. *Battleship Potemkin* (1925), for example, commemorated the failed revolution of 1905 and *October* (1927) celebrated the anniversary of the successful October Revolution of 1917. The filmmaker

was a technical innovator whose social vision might echo that of party intellectuals and workers alike.

In the 1920s, a pioneering figure in Soviet documentary filmmaking was
Dziga Vertov, whose philosophy of Kino-Eye upheld the beauty of the everyday
as the cinematic aesthetic with the camera more noticing than the human eye.
He pursued his thesis in the newsreel series of films (Kino-Pravda – or Ciné
Truth) and documented the reaction to Lenin's death in 1924. His idea of film
'truth' was to survey the environment rather than organise a cinematic response
to it. He is best known internationally for *Man with a Movie Camera* (1929),
a day-in-the-life of the city of Moscow. Vertov was radical in his decrying of
film drama as 'the opium of the people' and he would become a significant
influence on the Cinéma-Vérité movement of the 1960s. In Russian cinema
theory and praxis came together to influence ideas of film culture around the
world but Russian cinema was also hugely nationalistic in content and context.
The social context of revolution was as important as a film's location within a
developing film culture. This is made clear in the case of Esther Shub who in
the 1920s reconstructed Russian history in documentaries designed to resonate
with emotion, deploying newsreel footage and archives, as in *The Great Road*
(1927) and *The Fall of the Romanov Dynasty* (1927).

In the context of their national cinema, those filmmakers working outside the
documentary form developed a theory of film directing that was based on
staging, *mise-en-scène* and editing. 'Typage' was also an important element. It
involved the use of non-actors who were chosen because they were deemed to
'look like' a soldier or a doctor. This idea would influence movements including
Italian neo-realism in the 1940s but for Eisenstein the actor was simply an
aspect of *mise-en-scène* and no more meaningful than any other aspect. The
masses, or proletariat were often taken to be the protagonist of his films. In
Strike (1924), the first film of the Montage movement, Eisenstein's theories are
used to effect: he intercuts shots of an abattoir with shots of the striking
workers being massacred. Even more visually startling are the frames of
Eisenstein's famous Odessa Steps sequence in *Battleship Potemkin* in which
'real time' slows and a shot-by-shot analysis reveals physical and emotional
reactions to the storming of the Tsarist militia. Long shots of people fleeing in
terror are cut with close-ups of eyes wide with fear; a bunch of flowers is
crushed underfoot; a mother loses control of a baby in a pram and it bounces
down the Odessa Steps; and the whole is intercut with shots of the boots of the
soldiers who march relentlessly forward.

During this period the importance of theories of editing was a guiding
principle in establishing film technique across widely divergent filmmakers and
genres from Murnau (there are some 540 shots in *Nosferatu* [1922]) and
Eisenstein to D. W. Griffith and Alfred Hitchcock. Despite the nationalism of
the developing Soviet cinema, there were also significant cross-cultural
influences on filmmaking and intertextual connections that influenced wider
film culture. Piotrovsky, for example, believed Griffith to be formative in terms

of the influence that melodrama had on Soviet cinema; and in Hitchcock's *Blackmail* (1929) the intercutting of the heroine Alice's legs with the dead man's lifeless arm, as she walks home after having killed him in self defence, recalls aspects of Soviet montage. Film Europe, in the spirit of international co-operation, staged a 1928 exhibition in The Hague which popularised the Soviet montage aesthetic for European participants and, in the same year, the Communist Party organised its first party conference on film questions and instated a five-year plan that would go on to affect socialist-realist filmmaking in the 1930s. Before 1928 *Battleship Potemkin* had never been screened in Europe. Banned as Soviet film was in most countries, it was not screened by the London Film Society until November of 1929. The growth of film societies campaigning to see new cinema was very important in opening up film culture in an international context and ciné clubs in nations around the world were regularly screening non-fiction and avant-garde films by the end of the 1920s.

The theory and praxis of film culture came together in interesting ways in France. Louis Delluc was a prominent film reviewer and editor of *Le Film* and *Cinéa*, in which he called for a national cinema with the legend 'The French cinema must be cinema and the French cinema must be French!' Although he died very young in 1923, he made his mark on French film culture and his editorials were collected in books with titles such as *Photogénie*, a term he coined to capture the Impressionist project, that artistic 'essence' that distinguished film from the reality it photographed. Even when he and other Impressionist filmmakers filmed on location, the images distilled were believed to be psychologically enriched by point-of-view shots, dream sequences and optical effects that would convey a character's subjectivity. Delluc also coined the term *cinéaste* in which the aesthetic is understood as part and parcel of the filmmaking, however straightforwardly realist a film might seem. Germaine Dulac, another Impressionist filmmaker, extended the Impressionist aesthetic into what became known as *cinéma pur* or 'pure cinema'. Pure cinema was epitomised in the late 1920s in *Ballet Mécanique* (1924) and Dulac's Surrealist *The Seashell and the Clergymen* (1928), non-narrative, essentially abstract works that were purposely non-commercial. Such short works were exhibited in specialist cinemas and their experimentalism, aligned with the work of the Dadaist and Surrealist schools of thought, is discussed in Jean Vigo's book *Vers Un Cinéma Sociale* (1930) and Salvador Dali's 'Abstract of a Critical History of the Cinema' (1932).

Film culture was forged in the late 1920s. The term is notoriously difficult to define but it encompasses the circulation of cinema in a variety of cultural spheres. For example, the cinema's trade press emphasised ways to attract educated audiences into the theatres and how to differentiate clearly an up-market theatre from a downbeat fleapit. It began by stressing cinema as the 'seventh art', as in the early film theorist Ricciotto Canudo's *The Birth of the Seventh Art* (1911), and went on to emphasise the technical artistry of silent movies and the importance of establishing masterworks – *The Birth of a Nation*

(1915), *Battleship Potemkin, The Gold Rush* (1925) – that served to exemplify film as a unique art form. Film history began to be written according to its winners. D. W. Griffith was a very effective self-publicist whose statements that he had invented a clutch of cinema techniques became not only a popular perception but also a feature of film history by the late 1920s. Film historians, critics of film style and reviewers established a canon as well as a sense of national cinemas derived specifically from painterly developments in art: German Expressionism as derived from Romantic painting; Soviet formalism and Constructivism; French *film d'art* and Parisian Cubism and Surrealism. Throughout the 1920s, German cinema was agreed by critics to sit at the apex of cinema art with films such as the psychologically and artistically complex *The Cabinet of Dr Caligari* (1919) positioned as the cinema's definitive break with realism. Such films were screened as avant-garde 'classics' in art-house cinemas by the end of the 1920s. In this way, film culture derived from intellectual movements that worked outside, or pitted themselves against, the norm of Hollywood classical cinema, as in film critic Bela Belazs' devotion to film aesthetics in his essays of the 1920s.

Throughout the 1920s, film critics celebrated silent cinema aesthetics. Few books by film historians that were published in the period remain classics of film history but Paul Rotha's *The Film Till Now* (1930) has become a classic text largely because it is organised according to the major protagonists of film art – the directors. But other studies such as Gilbert Seldes' *The Seven Lively Arts* (1924) were also important at the time. His book was a defence of the popular and a celebration of silent movies. With the coming of sound on the horizon, Seldes was sceptical that directors would exploit its creative possibilities as expertly as they had explored the medium's visual pleasures. Other film studies included Terry Ramsaye's *A Million and One Nights* (1926), in which Griffith is lauded as the creator of modern cinema, and Lewis Jacobs' *The Rise of American Film* (1939). Silent film theory went virtually unchallenged until the 1940s when revisionist film historian André Bazin proposed an alternative version of film history that valued sound cinema's artistic importance and challenged the idea that sound heralded a loss of visual grace and expressivity in such classic essays as 'The Evolution of the Language of Cinema'. Bazin would also develop the idea of Hollywood cinema as a 'classical art' in a critical formulation that would maintain currency in film culture for many decades. The idea of a classical Hollywood cinema would not really generate opposition in the form of a thoroughgoing critique until the 1970s after which time it was sometimes argued that Hollywood cinema had been as nationalist as any other. Hollywood had secured hegemonic control not only through its business practices and distribution (see chapter 6), but also through its success in harnessing the experience of modernity and modernisation and creating out of them mass-mediated stories that produced tears and laughter, highly commercial cultural exports, or what Walter Benjamin would call, 'The Work of Art in the Age of Mechanical Reproduction'.

Benjamin argued that 'Mechanical reproduction of art changes the reaction of the masses toward art' so that with regard to the cinema, 'the critical and the receptive attitudes of the public coincide'.

Hollywood spawned a series of publications that underlined the stories and fantasies that it produced. Fan magazines had begun to be published around 1911, notably *Photoplay* and *Motion Picture Magazine*, as discussed in the extract by Janet Staiger in Chapter 4. In turn, they spawned an industry of publicists, columnists and feature writers dedicated to Hollywood. Trade periodicals also expanded with *Exhibitors Herald* and *Moving Picture World* as leaders in the field. Trade journals and periodicals reinforced aesthetic considerations; while the former concentrated on personalities, the latter reinforced film as art in film culture's early years. Films could demonstrate essential properties and characteristics that distinguished the medium from other modern art forms. This was a defence of the cinema that was returned to at different points in the evolution of film culture over the twentieth century but at the beginning it was based on the medium's artistic and technical potential. An intellectual film culture first developed with journals consistently reviewing silent cinema as an art form. In America, for example, *Cinema Art* (1923) and *Movie Makers* (1928) were closely followed by more specialist magazines such as *Experimental Cinema* (1930). One of the most prestigious film journals was *Close-Up* (1927–33) edited by Kenneth MacPherson and his wife Bryer (who also published the first English language study of Soviet cinema), Americans based in Switzerland. A regular contributor was modernist poet H. D. (Hilda Dolittle) who starred alongside Paul Robeson in *Borderline* (1927), a film produced by the journal that would demonstrate something of its distinctive philosophy of film.

For avant-garde intellectuals, watching films became a major pastime in the 1920s. The establishing of film societies led to the inauguration of arts theatres which would screen seasons of classics. In France there was the French Ciné Club movement with contributors such as critic and filmmaker Germaine Dulac; in London, the Film Society was inaugurated in 1925; and in New York, The Film Arts Guild opened its doors in 1925. Each became linked to specialist film theatres showing silent film classics as well as new releases. France was at the forefront of the arts theatre movement with Delluc and, after his death, Jean Tedesco establishing outlets for the dissemination of the arts such as Théâtre du Vieux-Colombier, an arts cinema which even branched out into production of small avant-garde films whose makers were unable to find funding or commercial distribution. Maurice Bardèche and Robert Braslach's *Histoire du Cinéma* (1935 and translated into English in 1939) notes this tendency. Even Hollywood opened an art-house theatre screening foreign films in 1928.

In 1929 the first Academy Awards were instituted by the Academy of Motion Picture Arts and Sciences with the ceremony taking place at the Roosevelt Hotel in Hollywood. To begin with, the names of the chosen recipients were released to the press and to trade journals prior to the event. Suspense as engineered by the sealed envelope only began in 1941. At the end of the 1920s, the awards began by celebrating the artistic and technical achievements of some of those films most revered by film societies and critics: the cinematography of Murnau's *Sunrise* which was declared a 'unique and artistic picture'; the epic sweep of Wellman's *Wings* which was awarded 'Outstanding Picture'; and the acting of Emil Jannings and the writing of Ben Hecht. Notably in this first year of what would come to be called The Oscars, *The Jazz Singer* received a special award as the pioneering picture that had revolutionised the industry, as did Charlie Chaplin for being 'in a class by himself', acting, writing, directing and producing. The Academy of Motion Picture Arts and Sciences had originally acted as a combination of watchdog (policing the stars whose unions were demanding recognition) and co-operative (encouraging the exchanging of cinema skills). The new awards were designed as a public relations exercise and they succeeded in sanctifying the aura of commercial success with a heightened sense of artistry.

Film critics and cinéphiles who reviewed movies in mainstream newspapers in the 1920s contributed significantly to the establishment of a film intelligentsia. They were at the forefront of the formation of film studies as a discipline. The British modernist writer Dorothy Richardson, for example, wrote about cinema and C. A. Lejeune, the first woman film journalist who worked on the *Manchester Guardian* in the 1920s, produced arch and ironic film criticism which gained her many readers, even if it did not always promote the cinema as comparable with the other arts. In Germany E. A. Dupont began as a film critic before directing *Vaudeville* (1925) and in America Mordaunt Hall of the *New York Times* and novelist and social wit Anita Loos were significant voices. Iris Barry, one of the founders of the London Film Society, had a key role in establishing cinema audiences for different national cinemas and major directors in the 1920s and she would go on to head the Museum of Modern Art's film archive in New York the 1930s.

Haidee Wasson's essay on British-born Barry, 'Writing the Cinema into Daily Life,' focuses on her film journalism of the 1920s. Wasson extrapolates from Barry's two weekly columns for the populist daily newspaper *The Daily Mail* and the more highbrow and specialist weekly, *The Spectator*, to assess her role in opening up film criticism to a massive readership. The *Mail* had the highest circulation in the 1920s and while addressing its readers, Barry also elaborated on cinema in a different register for those intellectual readers of *The Spectator* vexed by what they regarded as the dilution of 'high' culture by film, a 'low' or popular form, that was coming to dominate. Barry combined her advocacy of film as a literate phenomenon with a keen sense of its populist appeal for the masses.

This case study also elucidates the ways in which the early film critic had to negotiate her promotion of American cinema in a decade when anti-American feeling was an inevitable by-product of anxieties about cultural imperialism.

Wasson addresses the various local and global cultural flows that illustrate the nuances of British film culture in the 1920s, including the film critic's own prejudices and preferences as revealed in her film journalism, as well as her critical assessment of the state of the British film industry. In short, Wasson contextualises Barry's contribution to the establishment of 'infrastructures and discourses that have significantly influenced the way films are produced, distributed, exhibited and thought about, and that we now take for granted as basic elements of film culture'. She is read as representative of a wider and more eclectic film culture than that evidenced in specialist film journals such as *Close Up*, for example.

Wasson reveals film criticism to be a historically situated process that is firmly anchored in the social world. Iris Barry can be read as representative of the desire from film culture's inception to frame films as cultural practice within vital debates about modernity, aesthetics, mass culture and consumption, and the culture industry.

- What does this film historian's methodology reveal about a wider film 'culture'?
- The primary sources Wasson deploys derive largely from Iris Barry's journalism as published for two very different readerships. What are the potential limitations with deploying these kinds of sources?
- Do such appellations as 'high' and 'low' culture still pertain in film criticism or film journalism? Select and examine different publications to investigate the different ways in which film critics assess a single film on its release.

Writing the Cinema into Daily Life: Iris Barry and the Emergence of British Film Criticism in the 1920s

Haidee Wasson

Iris Barry is perhaps best known as the influential first curator of the Film Library at the Museum of Modern Art, New York (MoMA), a post she held from 1935 to 1951. During this period, she also helped to found the International Federation of Film Archives, was involved early on with the film programme of the United Nations, and was the first American representative at the fledgling Cannes Film Festival in 1947. She authored several books, among them *Let's go to the Pictures* and *D. W. Griffith: American Film Master.*[1] During a time in which the phrase *film study* struck many as odd if not oxymoronic, Barry effectively advocated the creation of archives, educational programmes, and non-commercial exhibition circuits – spaces in which the significance of cinema as a modern medium would be explored and secured.

Haidee Wasson (ed. Andrew Higson), *Young and Innocent: British Silent Cinema* (Exeter: Exeter University Press, 2001).

Born in 1895, Barry was in fact British, and in the 1920s served as a prominent film critic for the *Spectator* (1923–7) and the *Daily Mail* (1925–30); she was also a founding member of the Film Society (1925). As Rachael Low points out, this was the period in which 'people started treating film seriously in Britain'.[2] One manifestation of this 'seriousness' was the appearance of film writing in daily and weekly, local and national, specialist and mass circulation publications; another was the formation of film societies, clubs and libraries. As an important participant in these shifts, Barry helped establish infra-structures and discourses that have significantly influenced the way films are produced, distributed, exhibited and thought about, and that we now take for granted as basic elements of film culture.

In Britain, some of these institutions, such as the Film Society, reacted against the power exercised by state censorship and the film industry; others accommodated popular and middlebrow interests. Some did both. While Barry's participation in the Film Society has long identified her with 'minority' film culture, her criticism invites assessment of her place in mainstream film culture. Indeed, Barry's writing stands less as a precious outpost of bourgeois and specialized film activity and more as one example of a remarkable pro-liferation of discourses about cinema in 1920s Britain.

Barry's criticism is important for our understanding of this period for two reasons. First, hers was the most widely distributed film writing of its day. *The Daily Mail* was the highest circulating British newspaper in 1925, twice exceeding that of its closest competitor, the *Daily Mirror*.[3] At the same time, she also wrote for the more highbrow and limited circulation weekly magazine, the *Spectator*, ensuring that her prose reached not only the widest but the most diversified readership of its day. Second, Barry's writing raises historiographical questions about how to write about film's social, political and cultural sig-nificance. Until recently, histories of this period have emphasized three things. Some focus on the impoverished state of indigenous film production and the policy debates that ensued to redress this. Others focus on select *auteurs* such as Hitchcock. Still others focus on the development of 'minority' film cultures that emerged as critiques of mainstream film culture the Film Society, Workers' Leagues and the modernist journal *Close Up*.[4] While such work has provided crucial insights into British film history it has also obscured the varied ways in which films – British or otherwise – were taken up in everyday life and in popular critical practices.

One example of the ways conventional histories have contributed to this elision is through the persistent use of the standard dichotomies familiar in so much film scholarship: high/low, art/commerce, American/international. Barry's writing, on the other hand, resonates with contemporaneous theoretical work on the cinema as well as with ordinary concerns about getting along with other moviegoers: 'No hats please!'[5] She discussed popular American cinema within the context of an unfolding international aesthetic project. Her tastes were eclectic, ranging from popular melodramas to science films and time-motion studies. In other words, her writing readily complicates the binaries often employed to understand the period.

To read Barry's writing, then, is to gain access to a somewhat different view of film's cultural status in the 1920s; it is to witness a prominent critic's efforts to articulate both the quotidian and the complex challenges posed by cinema. In what follows, I will explore how Barry balances critical modes with popular practices, and utopian ideas about film with the key debates that characterized film culture of the period. Three themes will be identified: first, the kind of medium film was conceived to be; second, the American presence in British film culture; and third, the recommended British response to that presence.

It is also worth noting in passing that two of the most prominent film critics of the period were women – Barry, and the better known C. A. Lejeune, who wrote for the *Observer*. The *Daily Mail* actively sought out female readers and was one of the first national papers to feature cinema regularly in its pages. Barry herself suggested in the pages of her book, *Let's Go to the Pictures*, that cinema's future resided predominantly with women who would serve as producers and as discriminating consumers. Interestingly, the early feminist meditations present in her book do not surface in her weekly writing.[6]

Taking Film Seriously

Barry was enthralled with the formal and functional possibilities of the cinema; its distinct and protean aesthetic was as exciting as its promise of eliminating national boundaries and transporting new kinds of visual knowledge everywhere. Its promise of global citizens, its mass popularity, as well as its contribution to the 'respectable' arts, were each seen as complementary and constitutive elements of cinema's larger whole. For Barry, cinema's hybridity – art, industry, information, daily experience, national form – was foundational and inescapable, something she embraced, not rejected.

As with any such writing, Barry's was informed by its cultural and institutional context. Unlike the comparatively unrestrained and polemical writing that appeared in now acclaimed journals such as *Close Up*, or the specialised notes that accompanied Film Society screenings, Barry's criticism was shaped by concerns that informed newspaper and periodical content: editorial influence, readership interest, advertising revenue, the tension between urban, regional and national concerns, publishing and distribution schedules and so on.

Writing weekly for two quite different publications, the sprawling nature of Barry's commentary is unsurprising. Rather than reasoned and methodical critique of film form, content or function, it ranges from ruminations on the phantasmagoria of Hollywood's artifice to sober considerations of the problems facing British films. If there is a theme common to her work for both the *Spectator* and the *Daily Mail* it is the redemption of film as an expressive form and as a modern technological system. A key problem, she contended, was that the cinema suffered for too long under the weight of its benighted status as a mechanical art and as a popular entertainment – both attributes Barry refused to consider faults and preferred to see as merits. Summary judgements and prejudiced disposals based on the medium's accessibility and popularity were unacceptable to her. How then was she able to introduce her often populist concerns to the highbrow readers of the *Spectator*?

Writing for the Spectator: What Kind of Medium is Film?

When John Strachey hired Barry in 1923 to 'do something about the cinema', film became part of the *Spectator*'s editorial mission: 'to be a truthful and attractive record of all social movements, and of all that was accomplished in art, science, or literature.'[7] Significantly, Barry inherited a readership predisposed to discussions of poetry, literature, theatre and politics befitting a well-educated, socially respectable and highly literate cohort. The *Spectator*'s early acknowledgement of film as a noteworthy contemporary phenomenon supports observations made by Low and others that attending as well as discussing the cinema was slowly being accepted by a small group of reputable citizens.[8] This acceptance, however, was neither simple nor complete. Barry's writing also coincided with the increasing association of film, by a number of intellectuals, with an attack on traditional cultural values, which they saw as indicative of a broader social breakdown. Such associations emanated from the left and the right, casting film either as an affront to working-class literacy or as a challenge to the necessary and desirable cultural domination of the élite.[9] British censors also registered their mark. 'Taking film seriously' did not always produce the happy environment in which the cinema as a medium was vindicated as art or leisure; it also marked the wider contestation of cinema as a mass medium capable of moulding minds deemed weak and therefore vulnerable.

Barry herself was likely very familiar with the many forms of judgement against film then circulating, from high modernist to culturally reformist. From her earliest days in London, through introductions made by Ezra Pound, Barry was a regular of the Bloomsbury scene. Compounding her involvement with such moderns was her relationship with Wyndham Lewis, lasting several tumultuous years and yielding two children. Against the tide of her daily life, Barry's earliest writing for the *Spectator* addressed the pervasive tendency of the literary and cultural élite to further particular aesthetic and ideological positions against cinema without actually considering cinema at all. She argued persistently that the cinema embodied aesthetic achievement and possessed civic utility and was thus worthy of detailed analysis and discussion.

In the effort to prove that cinema was capable of aesthetic achievement, Barry elaborated the basic components of film art, tending towards characteristically highbrow concepts of formal distinctiveness and individual genius. To a contemporary reader, her strategies will seem familiar. Camera movement and the use of editing to manipulate space, evoke rhythm or create dramatic suspense were often celebrated. She argued that film was essentially a medium for telling stories through moving pictures,[10] as exemplified by her review of Ernst

Lubitsch's *The Marriage Circle* (1924): 'Everything is visualized, all the comedy is in what the characters are seen or imagined to be thinking or feeling, in the interplay, never expressed in words, of wills and personalities.'[11] Also now familiar but at the time unconventional, was her celebration of 'genius' directors emerging from national art cinemas, situating cinematic accomplishment in singular animating personalities rather than more diffuse collaborative processes: Fritz Lang, Ernst Lubitsch, Karl Grüne, Robert Wiene, Victor Seastrom, Charlie Chaplin and D. W. Griffith.[12]

Importantly, Barry's writing extended beyond these now familiar tropes of intellectual film history. She also explored cinema's technological and democratic particularities, paying frequent homage to its informational capacities as well as its ability to offer the spectator new experiences of space and time. A telling example resides in Barry's efforts to free cinema from the constraints of the theatre. For her, the cinema possessed a scope that not only rivalled but far surpassed that of the theatre. She maintained that cinema 'alone can handle natural history, anthropology and travel' as well as more fully develop 'parable, fairystory, pageant, romance and character-study':

> It has infinite variety of scene, endless angles of vision and focus, it can use for its own ends all the resources of landscape and architecture, and, very important indeed, it brings out an enormous significance in natural objects. Chairs and tables, collar-studs, kitchenware and flowers take on a function which they have lost, except for young children, since animism was abandoned in the accumulating sophistications of 'progress'.[13]

Barry wrote of animated objects and of the 'infinite variety' of vision offered by the cinema, which she argued lent a clear expressive edge over the theatre. While the use of these qualities for developing fictional narratives was important, it was not their only significance. Natural history and travel films would benefit as much as parable and romance films. The fascination of visual information – animating the previously lifeless – worked in tandem with cinematic narratives. Each enhanced the value of the medium. Theatre did not stand a chance.

Barry's interest in what film made visible is further evident in her commentary on travel, nature and science films. The camera's slow-motion capacities held particular fascination for her:

> The Film Society recently showed one of these marvels of patience, *The Life of a Plant*, in which a nasturtium germinated, grew up, flowered, was cross-fertilized, languished, shot its seeds off and died in five minutes. Gigantic on the screen, this plant ceased to have any vegetable attributes and became the most temperamental of creatures, dashing itself about, waving its 'arms' like a prima donna in a rage.[14]

Like many others, including members of the surrealist and constructivist movement, Barry became enamoured with the protean, fantastical ability of the cinema to reconfigure the visual world by depicting otherwise abstract or invisible phenomena. Any object could take on renewed symbolic presence, greeting a malleability of form that went hand in hand with a new kind of knowledge made visible by moving photo-realistic images.

As well as slowing time and expanding space, the cinema could also accelerate time and minimize space, endowing the medium with the courage and cause of an explorer. According to Barry, the camera transported its audience, democratising ocular discovery. Thus the travel film *The Epic of Everest*:

> has magnificently that rare quality of communication through the visual sense which is one of the peculiar qualities of the cinema: it communicates an experience which almost none of us can ever have in fact. And it is good for human beings to see, as they do in their hundreds of thousands daily, the appearance of the remoter places, whether they be untouched African forests, the island homes of Papua, or the ghastly face of the Black Country.[15]

For Barry, the cinema provided a privileged form of knowledge, which she rhetorically construed as transcendent of not only geographic space but also historical time and national psychology. Of the 'reasonably intelligent spectator', she remarked:

> He can see more clearly than if he were an actual spectator of race meetings, volcanic eruptions, eminent persons, and landscapes from California to Jerusalem. He can even see the past, whether it be the deeply moving past of reality as films like *Ypres* recreate it, or the romantic past of an historical piece like *Helen of Troy*. And if he be of a reflective mind he can learn as much of German, French, and American mentality as any other who has travelled widely.[16]

This ability to take spectators out of themselves and immerse them in faraway, unfamiliar places was for Barry the 'purest' and most 'plainly socially valuable' quality of the cinema: simplicity of form and clarity of thought combined with a myth of exploration and education. She ascribed these qualities not only to travel pictures and documentaries but also to farces (especially those of Chaplin and Keaton). These film forms, she suggested, sat at opposite ends of the film spectrum but shared this quality of simple beauty, clarity and therefore social value.[17]

Barry's celebration of American popular films deserves mention. Her unapologetic embrace of Chaplin, Fairbanks, Griffith, early animation, cowboy serials and slapstick, while reasonably familiar to the internationalist canon of film writing, must have appeared unusual to her readership. To assuage anxieties about such films, Barry couched her discussions in terms her readers might find more familiar. For instance, in championing Douglas Fairbanks, she likened his swashbuckling to the 'grace of ballet'. In favouring animation and slapstick, she dubbed Felix the Cat and Charlie Chaplin distinctly 'highbrow'. She loved Western serials, celebrating their 'great open spaces', proclaiming such 'horse operas' to be the best of American product.[18] Somewhat more polemical and agitating against the dominance of the established arts was her bold assertion that Chaplin's *Gold Rush* (1925), Fairbanks's *Don Q* (1925), and Griffith's *Sally of the Sawdust* (1925) represented more vitality 'than anything that the other arts are at the moment offering humanity.[19] Barry's strategy was sometimes to familiarize but sometimes to confront.

For Barry, cinema was a polymorphous form with the promise of multiplying utility, presenting new configurations of aesthetics and knowledge. The implied audience was not irretrievably seduced by cinematic pleasure or duped by national ideologies, but was liberated and enlightened by the cinema. This utopian strand in Barry's writing demonstrates her euphoric fascination with film, and is as such typical of an important genre in the history of writing on film.

Writing for the Daily Mail

While the *Spectator*'s mandate granted Barry latitude to ruminate on the particularities of the cinematic image, the *Daily Mail* presented different working conditions. Founded in 1896, the *Daily Mail* was conceived as an inexpensive, accessible and national daily. It was designed to appeal to women as well as to working men by including articles on fashion, marriage, recipes and housekeeping. The strategy was extremely successful, attracting a wide range of readers. The largest portion of these readers were, however, solidly middle-class.[20] In accepting the *Daily Mail* post, Barry thus acquired an audience for her writing unprecedented in size and scope. Now she would have to balance the needs of a large, diverse and diffuse audience with her own sensibilities about film.

As well as inheriting a new readership, Barry was bequeathed a particular set of debates about British film. In the mid-1920s, domestic film production was in decline, despite a concurrent increase in distribution and exhibition circuits. The number of British films on British screens fell steadily, reaching 5 per cent in 1925, while the percentage of American films increased to approximately 85–90 per cent.[21] American practices of block-booking, underselling and high production and marketing budgets combined with the popularity of American films to expedite this imbalance. Film attendance was relatively healthy in Britain; film production was not.[22]

When Barry began writing for the *Daily Mail* in 1925, it was widely acknowledged that the low status of the British film was a serious problem in need of a quick remedy. But there was little agreement as to how to rectify such a complex set of cultural, commercial and political problems. Many constituencies staked out a place in the murky terrain. Importantly, the *Daily Mail*'s editorial pages represented one of the more extreme and persistent of these constituencies, often reducing the role of British exhibitors, distributors, producers and audiences to the victims of an overt act of domination orchestrated by the

American film industry and government. Indeed, during the 1920s, the paper's wide readership supplied Lord Rothermere, figurehead of the *Daily Mail*, with an audience for his increasingly anti-American, protectionist beliefs. The paper's editorials invoked inflammatory nationalist rhetoric in order to support a 'free trade' platform aimed at opening up markets within the British Empire but squeezing out (usually American) competitors. Film fell comfortably within this purview. It was argued that British films should be sent aggressively throughout the colonies and that the dominance of British screens by American films was as undesirable as American dominance by other means. The editorial stance of the *Daily Mail* resonated with the assertion, also evident in policy debates, that American cinema was a powerful and persuasive force, contaminating consumer habits as well as national ideologies. The problem of establishing a native film industry was clearly linked to general concerns about the economic autonomy of the nation as much as its cultural or spiritual well-being. While fostering native film production was a legitimate concern of policymakers and necessarily, in part, of British businessmen, it is important to note that such ideas about the nation and film often depended on concepts of British audiences that infantilized or completely disregarded them. The editorials either penned or sanctioned by Rothermere provide no exception.[23]

In both the *Spectator* and the *Daily Mail*, Barry addressed the state of the British film industry, as well as the place of American cinema within this. Surprisingly, her writing on this issue did not differ greatly between publications, suggesting that she and Rothermere must have more than occasionally disagreed. How she negotiated his nationalism must, unfortunately, be relegated to speculation. In extreme moments however, some of her opinions did seem to resonate with his. For instance, she once declared that American films are on the whole 'deplorable, vulgar, sensational and even dismally stupid'.[24] Nevertheless, even as the great debate escalated, she also boldly claimed that 'we owe the present vitality of the cinema as a whole to the Americans their best films are the best in the world'.[25]

Barry acknowledged the importance of a healthy British production base. Nevertheless, she was unafraid to polemicize against the rising tide of anti-American sentiment, claiming that as a pleasure-loving member of the public she could not be dragged by 'wild horses to a British picture if an American picture could be seen instead.'[26] Concurrently, she also neatly rejected Hollywood's aggressive business practices as well as the bulk of formulaic and sometimes gaudy pictures that flooded British screens. She nevertheless eschewed extreme protectionist measures: 'Take away American films and you close the cinemas.'[27] She dismissed those who confused 'a few bad American films' with the output of an entire nation, let alone an entire medium. English literature, she pointed out, continued to garner respect despite the success of *penny horribles*.[28] Thus at times she rejected and at others she embraced nationalist rhetoric, yet she was steadfastly averse to the more conservative, anti-film and anti-populist elements of this rhetoric.

Perhaps more than any other aspect of the debate about British films, the public's pleasure was clearly, for Barry, a cause in need of an advocate. She argued against the fear-mongering inherent in contamination debates, acknowledging that audiences can actually think, disagree and dislike films for some reasons but like them for others: 'Yes, American films paint an idealized view of America but does it really affect us that much, since bad films also give us reason to reject or dislike America?'[29] In short, Barry saw America's domination of British screens as a highly problematic yet often pleasurable pre-occupation; she liked some American films, but deplored others; she yearned for a superior British film but remained fascinated by America and Hollywood as cinematic spaces unto themselves.

Barry's anti-Americanism is best evidenced by her discussions of Cecil B. De Mille. At its worst, American cinema embodied opulent wealth, moral indulgences, stars but no actors, and spectacle without cleverness or reason. Thus she imagined De Mille directing *Ben-Hur* (1925), standing behind camera, exclaiming through his megaphone: More money!! More money!![30] In a later article, titling him the 'Prince of Hollywood', she continued:

> He it is who chiefly specialises in the making of easily thrilling, inconsistent and expensive films which reveal a world where riches always spell vice and vulgarity, and which always appeal to the 'gallery' with their second-rate ideas about Socialism, or religion, or reincarnation or any other big theme which it happens to occur to Mr. DeMille to cheapen . . . All the DeMille pictures are brilliantly photographed. Technically they are far above the average. Spiritually they reek of the producer's subterranean – and, one fancies, over-heated and over-scented – boudoir.[31]

Even in her scathing criticism of De Mille's excesses, it is clear that Barry enjoyed her distaste too much to utterly dismiss the objects of it.

Barry travelled to Hollywood in October 1927. Exploring her ambivalence toward American film as well as her responsibilities to the readers of the *Daily Mail*, Barry wrote about the film capital from her experience of studio tours, evening parties and flaneurial wanderings. This yielded a series of articles with topics ranging from America's luxury picture palaces to Hollywood's 'English film colony'.[32] Barry expressed a muted fascination with Hollywood, pleasing fans hungry for news of the American film centre but filtering it through ambivalent, sometimes melancholy, prose. In one article, she wrote:

> There are tens of thousands of men and women registered as extra players: there are on an average two thousand of them employed every day. For the rest – managing ways and means, hope, starvation. Hollywood is all heartbreaks: but somehow in the smiling, haunted eyes of the men whom the tide of the Great War swept out here there is something other than heartbreak. There is a sermon for humanity, if they would read it.[33]

Barry observed former European military officers colliding with young starlet hopefuls. She did not interpret such scenes as depictions of exploited labour or suffering diasporas. Instead, she saw both a 'sermon' eulogizing the atrocities of war and the possibility of redemption, evident in the chaotic mix of nations that the cinema turned to relative harmony through the use of crowds choreographed as moving backdrops.

For Barry, Hollywood was not America, nor was it cinema. It was an uncanny, self-enclosed world of infinitely regressive likenesses where everything she encountered it seemed she had seen 'somewhere sometime' before, referring wistfully to films of which she had only vague recollections.[34] The celebrities and other industry members Barry observed were as self-absorbed as the film capital itself: 'Perhaps it is this which is the cause of the lack of proportion, even of common sense, in so many Hollywood films. They do not mirror life, but Hollywood's film world only.'[35] Considered in the context of her editor's policies, Barry's Hollywood seemed compelling, uncanny and most importantly, unthreatening.

The British Film?

Barry's thoughts about American films should be situated within a generalized internationalism, manifest also in her Film Society activities. She made casual and frequent mention of film production in France and Germany, aware both of policy debates and of the aesthetic ferment underway. Importantly, she often used such examples to provide suggestions for addressing the problem facing British films, noting, for instance, that English artists had been much slower to give film its due than artists of neighbouring countries and that this, in part, contributed to the lack of British innovation.[36] (She often used the term 'English' interchangeably with the term 'British'.) Barry did not see the success of other national cinemas primarily as threatening. Rather, she considered such cinemas to provide the raw material necessary for expanding the appeal of British films. She identified the anti-American elements of the British industry as the most responsible for perpetuating British mediocrity and advocated drawing freely on all available cinematic traditions.[37] Such lessons were to be drawn both from the failures as well as the successes of these cinemas. For instance, she suggested that from German films 'we see how wise it is to use stories created specially for the screen and by contrast to avoid persistent morbidity and excessive length'. From America, we learn to avoid plots 'false to human experience', to eschew 'vulgar moralizing', and to resist substituting stars for actors.[38]

While Barry recognised that the domination of American films was a serious challenge to establishing a British industry and a 'properly' British film, she did not hesitate to identify domestic complicity in this. She blamed British distributors and exhibitors – happy with the comfortable profits they made exhibiting American films – as often as she identified an 'abysmal' lack of production talent.[39] On the whole, however, Barry should be read as an optimist. She constantly made recommendations for the kinds of films that might be made, and for the processes required to support those films, and was confident that British audiences would pull their weight by becoming more discriminating. She happily advocated what she believed to be the two primary qualities of popular cinema: 'One, which is narrative, answers the old demand: "Tell me a story." The other, melodrama, replies to the age-old query: "And what happened next?" '[40] She embraced the role of cinema as popular entertainment, arguing that in order to be successful films must appeal to the emotions:

> For the kinema exists primarily to entertain. It does so best not when it clumsily attempts to uplift, but when deep emotions and stirring events of past or present take life on the screen, typified in the deeds of men and women from whom heroes and history alike are made. It is a nation's soul, which flowered so finely in men like Drake, Nelson, and Scott that can most finely inspire films. The dry bones can be left to the museums and libraries where they belong.[41]

She did not believe that British films should compete directly with Hollywood but that they should strive for a specificity that captured British as well as cinematic essence:

> Our new films must be patently English [sic], introducing to the world the spirit as well as the appearance of life here, and showing for the first time normal existence, heightened by drama or comedy, and discovering to audiences for the first time railways, towns, factories, playing fields, schools, shops, horse-shows, and seaside resorts in England.[42]

Despite persistent complaint about British films, she wrote with hope about a select number of promising directors, favouring George Pearson, Maurice Elvey, Adrian Brunel and Alfred Hitchcock, while tolerating Graham Cutts, Walter Sumners and Manning Haynes.[43]

Conclusion

For Barry, the future of British cinema rested in somehow combining the grandeur of American and international cinematic innovation with the specificity of British life. She knew this was a complicated task and required not only support from industry and government but also a shift in consciousness regarding what the cinema could and should become. Achieving a properly British cinema would involve an ongoing dialogue whose resolution required industrial, state and public bodies to admit first of all the many ways in which cinema mattered; detailed discussion of why and how it mattered would need to follow. Her criticism stands as one example of these seemingly simple but then-novel assertions.

The cinema, Barry maintained, was a peculiar phenomenon: a machine art born of the industrial age, made great by the distinctly modern combination of technology, aesthetics, spectacle, industrialism and mass popularity. For this reason, it remained as much potential as it was a reality. Barry's criticism thus provides an interesting example of wishful cinematic thinking, partly grounded in the present and partly in the promise of what might be. Crucially, to take her critical writing seriously is to open up wider consideration of the discourses that set the terms by which film cultures have historically taken shape. Such widely distributed film writing should not be treated necessarily as a lesser discursive site than any other. Such writing not only helps us to characterise film culture of any given period but provides a constitutive site for the very terms by which filmgoers (as well as scholars) understand and shape film culture itself. In Barry's case, such consideration indicates a body of writing that combines an intellectual's cinephilia with a firm commitment to cinema's populist appeal, a rhetoric of technological utopianism with a steady dedication to the quotidian task of building institutions, and a clear desire to forge a British cinema while openly embracing the contradictions of loving and hating American cinema.

NOTES

1. *Let's Go to the Pictures* (London: Chatto and Windus, 1926); *D. W. Griffith: American Film Master* (New York: Museum of Modern Art, 1940).
2. Rachael Low, *The History of the British Film, 1918–1929* (London: George Allen and Unwin, 1970), p. 15.
3. Circulation figures for the *Daily Mail* were 1,743,000 per day, for the *Mirror* 964,000 per day. See Tom Jeffrey and Keith McClelland, 'A World Fit to Live in: *The Daily Mail* and the Middleclasses,' in James Curran, Anthony Smith and Pauline Wingate, eds, *Impacts and Influences: Essays on Media Power in the 20th Century* (London: Methuen, 1987), pp. 27–52.
4. See e.g. Julian Petley, 'Cinema and State,' in Charles Barr, ed., *All Our Yesterdays: 90 Years of British Cinema* (London: British Film Institute, 1986), pp. 31–46; James Donald, Anne Friedberg and Laura Marcus, eds, *Close Up, 1927–1933: Cinema and Modernism* (Princeton: Princeton University Press, 1998); Don Macpherson, ed., *Traditions of Independence: British Cinema in the Thirties* (London: British Film Institute, 1980); Margaret Dickinson and Sarah Street, *Cinema and State: The Film Industry and the Government 1927–84* (London: British Film Institute, 1985).
5. 'Kinema Manners,' *Daily Mail*, 23 February 1926, p. 8.
6. See Barry, *Let's Go to the Pictures*, pp. 60–6; 147–9; 176.
7. Quoted in William Beach Thomas, *The Story of the Spectator, 1828–1928* (Freeport: Books for Libraries Press, 1928; rpt 1971), p. 5.
8. Low, *The History of the British Film*, p. 17.
9. See Peter Miles and Malcolm Smith, ' "The Embattled Minority": Theorists of the Elite,' in *Cinema, Literature and Society: Elite and Mass Culture in Interwar Britain* (London: Croom Helm, 1987), pp. 81–101.
10. Cf. David Bordwell, *On the History of Film Style* (Cambridge: Harvard University Press, 1997), pp. 12–45.
11. Barry, 'The Cinema: Hope Fulfilled,' *Spectator*, 17 May 1924, p. 788.
12. Ibid.
13. Barry, 'The Cinema: A Comparison of Arts,' *Spectator*, 3 May 1924, p. 707.
14. Barry, 'The Cinema: Lesser Glories,' *Spectator*, 6 March 1926, p. 415.
15. Barry, 'The Cinema: "The Epic of Everest" at the Scala,' *Spectator*, 20 December 1924, p. 982.
16. Barry, 'The Lure of the Films,' *Daily Mail*, 9 October 1925, p. 8.

17. Barry, 'The Cinema: "The Epic of Everest" at the Scala,' p. 982. See also 'The Cinema: Back to Simplicity,' *Spectator*, 17 July 1926, p. 88, and 'The Lure of the Films,' p. 8.
18. Barry, 'The Cinema: Laughter Makers,' *Spectator*, 19 September 1925, p. 444. See also 'Cowboy Films for "Highbrows",' *Daily Mail*, 10 August 1927, p. 8, and 'Lesser Glories,' *Spectator*, 6 March 1926, p. 415.
19. Barry, 'The Laughter Makers,' p. 445.
20. See Jeffrey and McClelland, 'A World Fit to Live in,' pp. 27–52.
21. Dickinson and Street, *Cinema and State*, p. 5.
22. Ibid., pp. 5–33.
23. See for instance 'The Foreign Film and the English Soul: An Insidious Form of Attack,' *Daily Mail*, 16 April 1926, p. 8; 'Why We Must Have British Films,' *Daily Mail*, 16 December 1925, p. 8; 'The Film Dictators,' *Daily Mail*, 9 April 1925, p. 8; and 'The Cosmopolitan Film: Made in Germany for Britain,' *Daily Mail*, 2 April 1925, p. 8. For a general history of the paper and Rothermere's influence, see J. S. Taylor, *The Great Outsiders: Northcliffe, Rothermere and The Daily Mail* (London: Phoenix Giant, 1996).
24. Barry, 'The Cinema: Of British Films,' *Spectator*, 14 November 1925, p. 870.
25. Barry, 'The Cinema: American Prestige and British Films,' *Spectator*, 11 July 1925, p. 52.
26. Ibid., p. 52.
27. Ibid., p. 51.
28. Ibid., p. 51.
29. Ibid., p. 52.
30. Barry, 'The Cinema: Ben Hur at the Tivoli,' *Spectator*, 20 November 1926, p. 898.
31. Barry, 'The Prince of Hollywood,' *Daily Mail*, 23 March 1927, p. 10.
32. See Barry, 'American's Giant Cinema,' *Daily Mail*, 21 November 1927, p. 10; and 'Hollywood's English Colony,' *Daily Mail*, 18 November 1927, p. 10.
33. Barry, 'Pity the Extras of Hollywood,' *Daily Mail*, 1 November 1927, p. 10.
34. See especially 'An Outpost of Hollywood,' *Daily Mail*, 14 December 1927, p. 10.
35. Barry, 'Actors Who Dream of Films,' *Daily Mail*, 24 November 1927, p. 10.
36. Barry, 'The New Art,' *Daily Mail*, 15 April 1926, p. 8.
37. Barry, 'New Blood for British Films,' *Daily Mail*, 17 December 1925, p. 7.
38. Barry, 'Films the Public Want,' *Daily Mail*, 21 November 1925, p. 8.
39. See Barry, 'Films We Do Not Want,' *Daily Mail*, 21 September 1926, p. 8; 'The Curse of the Films,' *Daily Mail*, 14 November 1925, p. 8; 'What We Owe to the Kinema,' *Daily Mail*, 18 May 1926, p. 6.
40. Barry, 'Films the Public Want,' p. 8.
41. Barry, 'Nelson and Three Bad Men,' *Daily Mail*, 4 October 1926, p. 8.
42. Barry, 'Films We Do Not Want,' p. 8.
43. Barry, 'Do-Everything Film Makers,' *Daily Mail*, 22 February 1927, p. 17.

9

ADJUSTMENT, DEPRESSION AND REGULATION

During the early 1930s, Hollywood faced a series of problems. First, the industry was still adjusting to the introduction of sound and the period saw a series of technical developments in sound recording. Second, the Great Depression followed the Wall Street Crash of 1929, and this seriously affected the industry: as unemployment grew, audiences declined. Finally, opposition to the industry intensified both at home and abroad, and this led to the introduction of the notorious Hays Code in 1934 and the creation of organisations such as the British Film Institute, which were designed to counter the influence of Hollywood overseas.

Although sound created technical problems for filmmakers, its introduction did not significantly change the structure of the industry, which was dominated by eight companies. The 'Majors', or Big Five, were Paramount (which had previously been known as Famous Players-Lasky), Loew's (which was better known as Metro-Goldwyn-Mayer or MGM), Fox, Warner Bros. and Radio-Keith-Orpheum (RKO), a new company that had been created in order to capitalise on RCA's sound system. Added to the Majors were three 'Minors': Universal, Columbia and United Artists. However, their size did not necessarily imply that these were low-budget enterprises, and United Artists in particular was known for its prestige productions. Much the same is also true of some of the small independent companies, such as those run by Samuel Goldwyn and David O. Selznick, which produced lavish prestige features for the major studios. Even Universal was in no sense a 'poverty row' company, such as Monogram or Republic, whose budgets were considerably smaller and who specialised in 'B' pictures.

In addition to the development of unidirectional microphones and booms (see Chapter 7), the introduction of sound led to the development of multi-track recording in 1932, which enabled sound technicians to record a number of different sounds on different tracks and then alter the relative volume of these sounds for emphasis. It also enabled sound effects or music to be recorded at another time and then added to the soundtrack. This had profound implications for the development of films. For example, it led to the development of non-diegetic musical scores, or the addition of music that was not supposed to represent sounds actually heard within the world of the film but rather acts as an interpretation of the action, implying menace, action or tragedy. As a result, the industry was able to develop impressive symphonic scores and the early 1930s saw the emergence of major film composers such as Max Steiner and Miklos Rózsa.

It also led to the development of the musical. Musical performances were one of the key ways of demonstrating the appeal of sound and, with the development of multi-track recordings, complex musical pieces could be pre-recorded so that equally complex dance sequences could be filmed and later edited together to synchronise with the music. It is hardly surprising, therefore, that the musical emerged as a key genre within the 1930s. Busby Berkeley became famous for films such as *42nd Street* (1933) and *Gold Diggers of 1933* (1933), which featured elaborate musical set pieces in which large numbers of dancers would perform complex, co-ordinated routines on elaborate sets. Also, by the mid-1930s, RKO was producing rather different musicals starring Fred Astaire and Ginger Rogers such as *Top Hat* (1935). These sometimes involved the kind of routines for which Berkeley became famous, but they are better known for the sequences in which the two leads would dance for, or with, one another as expressions of their romantic relationship.

These musical sequences also made use of new techniques for moving cameras, particularly dollies and cranes. The dolly was a piece of equipment onto which the camera was mounted and which enabled the operator to turn the camera to one side or the other (pan), tilt the camera up or down (tilt) or move the whole camera forward or backwards smoothly without it shaking (tracking). The crane, on the other hand, is fairly self-explanatory and was usually a long arm onto which the camera was placed at one end. The crane therefore enabled the camera to soar above the action or sweep in from a great height. These developments allowed the camera to become far more mobile and could be used to create powerful dramatic impact.

Special effects also developed within the period and are probably most notably present in the horror films that followed Universal's film versions of *Dracula* (1931) and *Frankenstein* (1931). Not only were these films famous for their make-up effects, particularly for Boris Karloff's monster, they also used a series of other effects, most notably in the construction of Frankenstein's laboratory. *King Kong* (1933) also used stop-motion animation for its monster. Other special-effects techniques were less obvious. For example, techniques of back projection were developed during the period, which enabled actors to perform on a sound stage while a piece of previously recorded film was projected behind them so that they appeared to be elsewhere: the African jungle, the Houses of Parliament, or the Deep South. Developments in photographic film also enabled filmmakers to create a highly glamorous look through the use of low-contrast lighting. Indeed, the soft, romantic look became so pervasive that, a decade later, high-contrast camerawork was used by thrillers to create a sense of menace and danger. These techniques of lighting and cinematography were employed to great effect by Josef von Sternberg in collaborations with Marlene Dietrich such as *Blonde Venus* (1932).

Despite these developments, the industry was hit hard by the Great Depression. By 1933, there were as many as 14 million unemployed and many believed that American capitalism had failed and that revolution was inevitable. Change did come that year, but in a much more moderate form, when Franklin Delano Roosevelt was elected president. Roosevelt's policies were a major reversal of the laissez-faire economics of earlier administrations, and his New Deal was based on state intervention in the economy. Through government spending on the economic infrastructure (roads, electrification programmes and so on), the New Deal not only put people back to work but also hoped to stimulate the consumer spending necessary to re-energise the economy. Recovery was slow and the first half of the 1930s saw little improvement from these measures.

The Depression meant, of course, that many people had less to spend on leisure, and cinema audiences in America declined dramatically. In many rural areas, cinemas closed and those cinemas that did stay open changed their practices. The large movie palaces could no longer afford the levels of service that they had previously offered and many cinema managers turned to concession stands as a means of generating extra income. For example, cinemas had previously shunned popcorn in a bid for respectability in which they sought to associate themselves with legitimate culture and disassociate themselves from popular amusements such as the funfair. But, with the introduction of concession stands, cinema became virtually synonymous with popcorn.

While cinemas sought to find new sources of income, the introduction of sound had helped remove one form of expenditure. Theatres no longer relied on live entertainers and, in many theatres, the whole programme came to be made up of filmed entertainment. As a result, the film companies received more income and exhibitors did not have to maintain orchestras or other live performers. This situation also meant unemployment for those who had previously performed as part of the cinema programme.

The Depression created a vogue for social problem films, or films that presented themselves as tackling a pressing social issue. *I was a Fugitive from a Chain Gang* (1932) concerns the plight of a First World War veteran driven to a life of crime by harsh social conditions. Indeed, the social problem film and the crime film were often indistinguishable and films that have now become known as gangster movies were often, as the films themselves stressed, 'torn from today's headlines'. *Little Caesar* (1931), *Public Enemy* (1931) and *Scarface* (1932) all centred on the rise to power of a criminal figure but also sought to comment on current social conditions. On the one hand, they added to the growing pressure to repeal the laws that prohibited the sale of alcohol by suggesting that these laws led to the creation of large criminal organisations and, on the other, they suggested that unemployment and poverty also created the conditions for lawlessness and criminality.

Although these films presented themselves as more than mere entertainment, and as addressing serious social problems, they were the target of campaigners who argued that they irresponsibly glamorised their criminal protagonists. These attacks on gangster films were only part of a more general condemnation of Hollywood by reformers, a condemnation that resulted in the introduction of the Hays Code. Will Hays was head of the Motion Picture Producers and Distributors Association (MPPDA) which had been set up in 1922 to combat the attacks on Hollywood that followed the scandals in the late 1910s and early 1920s. With the start of the Great Depression, pressures to reform Hollywood started to mount yet again. Cultural intellectuals and clergymen had long been concerned about the influence of Hollywood but, in the early 1930s, many blamed the start of the Great Depression on the loose morals of 1920s America. Added to these voices were also the findings of the Payne Fund studies, which investigated the influence of films on the general public and particularly children.

Hollywood was therefore attacked for its handling of sex, violence and other issues and, in 1934, the industry publicly backed Will Hays' code for the self-regulation of the industry. The code is usually ridiculed as a list of ludicrously puritan restrictions and Hays himself presented as a stern, humourless censor. However, as Richard Maltby has pointed out, in 'The Production Code and the Hays Office' (1993), the role of the Hays Office was not to prevent films from being made or released, but rather to enable films to achieve the office's seal of approval. In other words, the Hays Code was designed to ward off the threat of censorship, and the office worked hard with filmmakers to find ways to ensure that their films would not violate the code and could be given the industry's official endorsement. Furthermore, the introduction of the code did not result in the sudden and brutal repression of popular entertainment traditions often represented by the Marx Brothers and Mae West, as is often claimed. The Marx Brothers were known for their dizzying and anarchic verbal wit, which irreverently ridiculed social conventions, and Mae West was known for her lewd and suggestive behaviour. However, as Maltby has shown, the code had actually been in operation since the early 1930s and the significance of 1934 was that it was the year in which an arrangement was reached that required Hollywood to acknowledge publicly previous wrongdoing, in return for which the Catholic hierarchy withdrew its call for federal censorship of films.

Furthermore, the code was not sacrosanct and both the studios and the Hays Office were constantly searching for ways to work around it or test its limits.

Indeed, it has been argued that, in certain ways, the code worked productively and made audiences sensitive to connotation and ambiguity. For example, films frequently worked through ellipses in the narrative, where materials were implied but not represented. In these moments, the audience was left to supply the missing information but the result might be more powerful than the actual representation would have been. When a vampire moves in toward a young virgin's throat, and she screams as the screen goes black, the fact that it is left to the imagination to guess at the details may make the sequence far more powerful than an overt depiction would have been.

In addition, the code often required films to work through connotation. For example, homosexuality could not be openly discussed and therefore it was implied. Classical Hollywood films were never as clear and direct as is often suggested. Sometimes the ellipses and connotations made for films that were far more ambiguous or perverse than was ever intended. In *Frankenstein*, for example, the death of a young girl was thought to be too disturbing and was cut, but the cut left the actual cause of her death ambiguous and even suggested the disturbing possibility of child molestation.

Hollywood was also under attack overseas. During the late 1920s in Britain, a cinema-building boom started that continued into the late 1930s. This boom was largely the result of the massive suburban building projects of the period. The nineteenth-century city had come to be seen as a dangerous place producing physical sickness and social unrest. As a result, many cities were redeveloped during the inter-war years and large sections of the population moved to new suburban estates. While the traditional place of working-class amusement and communal interaction had been the public house, temperance organisations usually opposed planning permission for public houses on the new estates. Cinemas, however, did not share the same fate and the vast majority of cinemas built during the building boom were located within the new suburbs where they were often the only amusements and places of communal interaction. As a result, while audiences in the United States declined during the first half of the 1930s, in Britain, audiences reached record levels.

While film audiences were flourishing, there were significant critics of these developments. In 1932, for example, the Commission on Educational and Cultural Films published its report, *The Film in National Life*. For these critics, audiences may have been flourishing but they were watching the wrong films. American films were considered dangerous and the commission wanted to encourage the development of a British cinema that would be distinct from Hollywood and educate and reform the working classes. These attitudes led to the establishment of the Film Society movement, which had a very contradictory attitude to censorship. On the one hand, it was concerned with the influence of Hollywood films upon the population but it was also critical of censorship, which was claimed to prevent films from dealing with serious and adult issues.

The state was also instrumental in fostering this alternative film culture. First, there was the establishment of the British Film Institute in 1933, which had the remit of resisting Hollywood through the development of an indigenous British film culture that was both educational and artistic in its ambitions. Second, there was the emergence of the British 'Documentary' movement led by John Grierson. Rather than simply entertain, these filmmakers were concerned to inform and educate the viewer through films that were supposed to 'document' reality rather than offer the fantasy and escapism associated with Hollywood. They also believed that, in so doing, film could reform society and produce a sense of national collectivity.

Ironically, Grierson had been educated in the US and he championed a cinema that was deliberately non-commercial. This is not to imply that he was in any sense economically independent but rather that he favoured an approach to funding taken by Robert Flaherty for *Nanook of the North* (1922), which was not made with the hope of recouping costs from a paying audience but was funded by a fur company. In much the same way, Grierson did not make films for commercial audiences, but worked with the Empire Marketing Board, where he established a permanent film unit in 1930. However, despite this context, Grierson was influenced by left-wing filmmaking, particularly Soviet montage, and his unit remained concerned to tell the stories of working people. In 1933, the Empire Marketing Board was dismantled and Grierson's unit moved to the General Post Office (GPO), where Harry Watt made *Night Mail* (1935), a film about the postal service that included poetry by W. H. Auden and music by Sir Benjamin Britten. The film depicted the complex routines by which the nightly express took the mail from the south of England up to Edinburgh in the north and, in the process, it suggested that communications were vital to the production of the nation and that they bound its members together by routines and practices. As the narrator comments at the end, 'Soon they will wake and listen for the postman's knock – for who can bear to feel himself forgot?' The same year also saw the publication of *Grierson on Documentary*, which gave a name to this genre of non-fictional filmmaking, and the release of Basil Wright's *Song of Ceylon* (1934), which lyrically contrasted the supposedly timeless 'native' cultures of Ceylon with the modern tea trade.

If Grierson's unit was therefore involved in the production of images of nation and empire, the empire itself was also producing its own images. Indian cinema was certainly the biggest success in these terms and, by the 1920s, India was producing about 100 films per year, more than England, France or the Soviet Union. The country was divided by huge cultural and linguistic differences, which not only resulted in differences in ethnic and regional production but also meant that, even after the introduction of sound, visual imagery remained central to Indian cinema. In the 1930s, three major studios emerged: Prabhat, which was founded in 1929 in Bombay; New Theatres, which was founded in 1930 in Calcutta; and Bombay Talkies, which was founded in 1934. Unlike the Hollywood studios, these firms were not vertically integrated and did not own theatre chains. As a result, they were devastated by competition from the independents.

After the introduction of sound, musical set pieces also became central to most Indian film production but, despite the use of music, there were still several different types of filmmaking. For example, many films were based on established religious or mythological narratives, while others involved the types of swashbuckling adventure for which Douglas Fairbanks and Errol Flynn were famous in Hollywood. Another key genre was the 'social' film, such as *Devdas* (1935), in which two lovers are torn apart by an arranged marriage.

The following extract on *King Kong's* promotional campaign focuses on an aspect of film reception, the marketing of the film. One of the problems with exploring films historically is that our current understanding of a film may be different from the ways in which it was understood in other periods. Analysis of marketing is one way that we can examine how a specific film (or group of films) was presented to the public in different periods. Marketing seeks to inform potential audiences about both the existence of a film and its attractions. In this process, marketing sets up intertexts for the film – different texts that it can be linked to or associated with – and tries to establish terms of reference within which the film might become meaningful to, or provide pleasure for, audiences. As Cynthia Erb makes clear, marketing rarely establishes one set of intertexts. In the search for the broadest audience, marketing seeks to suggest attractions that appeal to different sections of the public. For example, as Rhona Berenstein has demonstrated in *Attack of the Leading Ladies* (1995), exhibitors frequently advertised horror films in the 1930s through poster campaigns, one of which emphasised the 'horror' angle and another of which concentrated on 'romance', and they did so on the assumption that the former would have more appeal for men and the latter would have more appeal for women.

The usefulness of this kind of historical research is demonstrated by Cynthia Erb in 'From Novelty to Romance: *King Kong's* Promotional Campaign' which shows that, although *King Kong* is most commonly seen as a horror film today, its promotional campaign sought to place it in relation to a cycle of films that is now virtually forgotten: jungle adventure films. Thus while most readings today tend to associate Kong with other monsters of the period, Erb is able to explore different historical associations at the time of the film's release that can only be understood by replacing it within a series of industrial and cultural concerns with the jungle as an exotic location.

This is, of course, not to suggest that the analysis of marketing establishes the only way in which the film was understood; even at the time of its release *King Kong* was associated with horror films. But this association with horror was only one of a range of different associations used to attract different audiences with different tastes. It is also important that one does not privilege the meanings of the film in its contemporary period as the 'real' or 'true' meanings of the film. On the contrary, the value of such research is that it demonstrates that the ways in which the film is understood today involves only one particular set of meanings, and ones that are determined by our contemporary historical context.

- Erb examines a range of primary sources in her discussion of *King Kong*. Try to group these into a small number of different types.
- How does Erb use certain materials to compensate for the limitations of other materials?
- The analysis of marketing might tell us how the industry presented films to audiences, but what problems might there be with using these sources to provide an account of how audiences actually made sense of films?

FROM NOVELTY TO ROMANCE: *King Kong*'s PROMOTIONAL CAMPAIGN

Cynthia Erb

[. . .]

I wish instead to consider how *King Kong's* pastichelike qualities gave it the status of a 'showman's dream' – a text highly amenable to proven promotional and exhibition strategies of the early 1930s.[1] Looking at the film's historical reception this way means conceiving of the initial release context, not so much as a fixed locus in which a singular original reading of the film materialized, but rather as a shifting reception dynamic, in which multiple viewing frames became possible, according to both regional and temporal variables present during the release.

In the classical Hollywood period, viewing positions were shaped (but not entirely determined) by various industrial texts and practices, which included materials from three basic groups. The first group consisted of promotional texts created directly by the studio – for example, posters, advertisements, press books, and lobby cards. The second group was comprised of mass media texts, such as newspaper reviews, fanzine features, and interviews with stars and other production personnel. Although media texts such as these might seem to develop in a fashion relatively independent of the film industry, many reception critics agree that the media were probably heavily influenced by the terms of the promotional campaign devised by the studio. Indeed, one of the basic purposes of the press book was to instruct newspaper reviewers on how to summarize and evaluate a film's features – a tactic achieved by providing plot summaries, short features, and even sample reviews. Although William Troy's review of *King Kong* for *The Nation* [for example] was remarkably free of press book influence, it was actually quite exceptional in this respect.

The third and final group was comprised of exhibitors' practices, which were much more varied and elaborate during the classical period than they are today.

Cynthia Erb, *Tracking King Kong: A Hollywood Icon in World Culture* (Detroit: Wayne State University Press, 1998).

Exhibitors' practices included marquee and lobby displays, promotional contests, live prologue shows, and various strategies summed up in the word 'ballyhoo.' Ballyhoo describes the carnivalesque stunts used in the circus, vaudeville, and other popular entertainment forms that were inherited by classical Hollywood. Ballyhoo practices survived in the film industry well into the 1950s, but were gradually replaced by more standardized forms of mass media promotion and advertising.[2] In the 1930s, mass media promotion coexisted with ballyhoo practices, a situation that led to differences, and occasionally even tensions, between the terms of the centralized campaign devised by the studio, and exhibitors' own campaigns and practices waged at the local level. *King Kong*'s release campaign was quite a lavish one, deploying many standardised promotional media strategies, such as a novelization, a magazine serial, a radio serial, radio and newspaper advertisements, a cartoon serial for newspapers, and 'teaser' trailers. Exhibitors, however, sometimes departed from the terms of RKO's official campaign, apparently believing they understood the needs of their local markets better than the studio. As we shall see, one outcome of this was that sensational elements that had been largely censored out of *King Kong* during script preparation and film production were sometimes restored to the film in release settings, as theater owners, wishing to define the film as 'sexy' and exotic, drew upon the formulaic repertoire of the 1930s jungle craze to promote the film.

As I have suggested, one of the reasons for regional and temporal shifts in *King Kong*'s campaign is that, although quite successful in box office terms, the film apparently failed to meet the studio's inflated expectations for it. Historians sometimes depict *King Kong* as the film that saved RKO from bankruptcy, but this is probably reductive. After all, RKO's *Little Women*, released in December 1933, was more successful than *King Kong*, setting a one-day attendance record at the Radio City Music Hall and rapidly shooting into the list of top twenty box office hits up to that time – a feat *King Kong* did not manage.[3] As we have seen, *King Kong* was an unusually expensive film to produce and market. In its first release, the film faced a series of setbacks, not the least of which was the flurry of bank closings which began in Michigan and spread to the national level by Saturday, March 4, two days after *King Kong*'s première in New York City. Although the trade journals offer varying accounts of the damage done by the bank closings, a contraction of the market took place, with *Variety* predicting an overall reduction of approximately 10 per cent in the New York theatrical market.[4] *King Kong*'s ability to garner $90,000 in its first week at the Radio City Music Hall was considered 'good,' in light of 'the tightened money situation,' but the film did not perform much better in its opening week than *Our Betters*, the Constance Bennett vehicle that had played the Music Hall the previous week.[5]

King Kong also opened against unusually heavy box office competition, the major studios having saved their best releases as 'tie-ins' with the presidential inauguration of Franklin Delano Roosevelt in the first week of March. New

Deal rhetoric saturated the film trade press at this time, with writers dedicating optimistic editorials to the presidential incumbent whom they commended for handling his image and campaign like a resourceful, talented showman.[6] Like the famous *42nd Street Special* campaign, in which a train loaded with Warner Bros. stars traveled cross-country, arriving in New York during inauguration week, *King Kong*'s New York campaign also included some attempts to capitalise on the inaugural ceremonies, as when RKO publicity personnel posted bills along major highway and railway routes between New York and Washington, in an effort to attract the attention of those traveling to and from the inauguration.[7] Ultimately, *King Kong* proved unable to compete against some of the biggest hits released at this time, including *42nd Street*, *She Done Him Wrong*, and *Cavalcade*, the Academy Award-winning adaptation of a Noel Coward play. Never quite living up to RKO's inflated expectations, *King Kong* failed to accomplish all the things a film like *42nd Street* did – setting house records, meriting holdovers, and entering the top box office list, not just for 1933, but for all time.

In its first release, then, *King Kong*'s box office performance was good, but uneven. The film opened brilliantly in a few eastern markets, such as Baltimore and Washington, but it proved a disappointment in parts of Los Angeles, particularly at Grauman's Chinese Theater, where an especially lavish première had been designed for it.[8] At a time when a three-week run was standard for an 'A' picture, a pattern developed in which *King Kong* would open strong, but then sales would sag in the second and third weeks. The film's limited success in the initial release, however, actually renders it more interesting from a reception standpoint, since its reception dynamic was a comparatively mobile, shifting one, in which distributors and exhibitors kept recalculating the terms of the campaign in an effort to re-present the film's features in their best (most profitable) light. The temporal shifts evident during the campaign assumed three basic promotional forms or strategies: novelty appeals, genre-based appeals, and romance-based appeals. Within each of the three temporal phases of release, one can also detect regional variations, according to the terms of particular exhibition settings.

Novelty appeals capitalized on immediate sensational images, and were especially amenable to the spectacle- and image-based media that made up the pre-release campaign: posters, advertisements, 'teaser' trailers, and ballyhoo stunts. The studio materials generated for *King Kong*'s main campaign were dominated by novelty strategies highlighting the film's trick effects, and its overall status as spectacle. (Indeed, the trade press tended to identify the film as a melodramatic spectacle, or an animal spectacle.) Novelty appeals, which dominated the New York première, generally appeared early, when potential viewers possessed little information about a film, and were presumed to be susceptible to pure sensational images and sounds. This phase of the release included coverage of the film's technical effects and its famous sound track – sound still constituting something of a special effect in 1933.[9] Other novelty appeals included various forms of ballyhoo exploiting the Orientalist 'ring' of the film's title, and stunts featuring the 'gorilla/girl' image. This last figure was of course prominent throughout the release, but in the novelty phase it received little narrativization, circulating in ways that seem abstracted from the film for purposes of sheer spectacle.

Newspaper coverage of *King Kong*'s technical effects adhered closely to the press book and need not be recapitulated here. Examples of novelty appeals organised around the film's title and the 'gorilla/girl' image offer useful examples of ballyhoo techniques deployed early in the campaign. Historically, *King Kong*'s exotic title has been one of its strongest selling points, so that now it seems surprising that Cooper had trouble selling the title to his superiors. In his journal entry for January 12, 1932, Wallace wrote: 'Apparently they are not going to accept *King Kong* as a title; they think it has a Chinese sound and that it is too much like *Chang*, and I can see their points of view.'[10] Selznick urged Cooper to change the title to *The Jungle Beast*, but Cooper objected that this title lacked romance and suggested to the viewer 'an animal travel picture instead of a mystery, adventure, novelty, which the picture really is.'[11] The Orientalist fantasy suggested in the name *King Kong* was much more amenable to promotion, so that various stunts were devised simply to play upon its exotic ring. In Pittsburgh, for example, an exhibitor rigged a giant amplifier atop his theater so that every two minutes beating drums would sound out, followed by a voice calling, '*King Kong* is coming!' The sound reportedly carried for miles, inspiring both awe and complaints from local residents.[12]

The novelty tactic of highlighting sensational appearances of King Kong and 'the girl' was exemplified in a mini-prologue act a Boston theater owner devised as a 'build up' for a *King Kong* teaser trailer shown during the pre-release campaign. As the theater went dark, giant tinseled letters that spelled out the film's title exploded, and a man in a gorilla costume carrying a 'girl' appeared behind a scrim onstage: Green lights illuminate the gorilla . . . the girl is screaming . . . shots are fired from the wings. As the gorilla almost reaches the footlights, the trailer is thrown on the scrim. During the exhibition of the trailer, which tells what King Kong is about and also gives quotes from the New York critics' reviews, the gorilla is still faintly visible through the scrim . . . the girl is heard screaming . . . and the general commotion continues.[13]

As the campaign wore on, the 'gorilla/girl' image became increasingly narrativized. In the prologue show at Grauman's Chinese Theater, for example, a female trapeze artist appeared onstage as a 'white captive' who escaped from a fake gorilla in a cage (probably another man in an ape suit), climbing into a tree top where her rigging was, and then swinging into her act.[14]

Novelty appeals tended to be of an ephemeral nature, so that in the long run, distributors and exhibitors believed promoting *King Kong* as little more than a 'trick' film would set severe limits on its box office staying power. As the effectiveness of novelty appeals waned, these were gradually supplanted by other techniques featuring a stronger narrative basis. In the case of *King Kong*'s campaign, genre- and romance-oriented appeals were tried out, with varying degrees of success. As mentioned above, the makers of *King Kong* did take the then current popularity of horror films into account as they worked: Wallace watched *Dracula* while working on the screenplay; Cooper looked at *Murders in the Rue Morgue* (1932) to study the 'trick' effects used.[15] Wallace hoped that *King Kong* would attain the popularity of the then current horror cycle issuing from Universal Pictures: 'The pictures which are going best are the horror pictures. *Frankenstein, Dracula.* and *Jekyll and Hyde* are the three money-makers – *Frankenstein* the biggest of all. I am hoping still to get a good horror picture without corpses, and I am certain that *Kong* is going to be a wow.'[16]

During the release, however, the jungle-adventure genre prevailed as the genre frame repeatedly assigned to *King Kong*. This generic definition developed from a combination of factors, including matters of authorship, genre cycles, and exhibition practices. The first two of these will receive more detailed analysis in the next chapter, and will be treated only briefly here. Although I have thus far stressed the prominence of Wallace's name in the *King Kong* campaign, to a lesser extent Cooper and Schoedsack received credit as the film's creators, so that reviewers sometimes discussed their careers as makers of exotic animal and travel films, notably *Grass* (1925), *Chang* (1927), *The Four Feathers* (1929), and *Rango* (directed by Schoedsack alone, 1931). The most famous of these at the time of *King Kong*'s release was *Chang*, an early documentary that featured local persons as amateur performers in a scripted 'nature drama,' shot on location in northern Siam (now Thailand). *Chang* depicts the story of a Lao family struggling to eke out an agrarian existence on the edge of a jungle, facing wild animals and other hazards on a daily basis. It became one of the most profitable and critically acclaimed of the 1920s travel films, earning an Academy Award nomination for 'Artistic Quality of Production,' which it lost to *Sunrise* (1929).[17] Since *King Kong*'s fictional travel filmmaker Carl Denham seems such a huckster today, *Chang*'s artistic success may seem surprising, but a review in *Close Up* is rather typical of the 'raves' the film received: 'See it a dozen times. *Chang* is the film of the year, of the age.'[18] Cooper and Schoedsack were especially celebrated for their photographic skills, achieved under hazardous conditions:

> some of the photographs were astounding, and when one realizes the hours or days or weeks of waiting that must have gone to secure some of the close-ups of jungle beasts, and thinks of the thousands of feet of film that must have been sacrificed for the sake of perhaps no more than ten feet, one begins to get a perspective of the wonderful achievement these two intrepid travellers have made.[19]

As mentioned, Cooper's promotion to production chief at RKO gave him a certain media visibility around the time of *King Kong*'s release, with reporters often characterizing him as a kind of restless, visionary individual, slightly eccentric, and happier out-of-doors than in a studio office.[20] A *Hollywood*

Reporter piece described Cooper thus: 'There's an adventurer who walks up and down his office in Hollywood with restless feet . . . He is a camera explorer at heart . . . Today he is chained by contract to the management of a huge studio. And are his feet fidgety?'[21] Reviewers of *King Kong* often described the fictional Carl Denham as a Frank Buck- or Martin Johnson-type, referring to other men who made wild animal films in the 1920s and 1930s. Some reviewers also marveled that Cooper and Schoedsack, known for 'authentic' travel productions, had chosen a sheer fantasy project like *King Kong*:

> Merian C. Cooper and Ernest B. Schoedsack . . . used to be earnest scientists whose *Chang* and *Grass* were successes of estime which made little money.
>
> Presumably in *King Kong* they deliberately conceived a picture so ridiculous . . . and so exaggerated in its faked views of wild life that other producers of spurious jungle pictures would give up the fight and leave Cooper and Schoedsack free to do reputable work.[22]

King Kong's links to the jungle tradition thus resulted in part from the established reputations of the filmmakers, but this genre frame also developed from a coincidence between *King Kong*'s release date and a cycle of jungle films that grew up in the wake of two MGM jungle hits, both directed by W. S. Van Dyke: *Trader Horn* (1931), and *Tarzan, the Ape Man* (1932). Creelman's scripts for *King Kong* occasionally allude to popular jungle films of the day. In the June draft, Denham enlightens Englehorn and Driscoll about Kong's existence by exclaiming: 'They [the natives] worship this trick animal like a God. Boy, when we shoot that, they'll boil down *Ingagi* and *Trader Horn* for the celluloid.'[23] Around the time of *King Kong*'s release, the *Motion Picture Herald* listed the film as part of a cycle of 'animal pictures' that were either in release or production, others including Universal's *The Big Cage* (Kurt Neumann, 1933), Paramount's *King of the Jungle* (H. Bruce Humberstone and Max Marcin, 1933), MGM's *Tarzan and His Mate* (Cedric Gibbons and Jack Conway, 1934), Warners' *Untamed Africa*, and Monogram's *Jungle Bride*.[24]

In contrast to contemporary viewers' inclination to interpret *King Kong* according to codes of the horror genre, audiences of the 1930s were probably more sensitive to images and themes culled from the classic jungle film tradition. *Trader Horn*, for example, offered a number of visual elements that evidently influenced the makers of *King Kong*: Nina's (Edwina Booth) scanty animal skin clothing, her pale white skin, and long blonde wavy hair apparently established the precedent for Fay Wray's jungle 'look' in *King Kong*. *Trader Horn*'s trio of white characters – the experienced older trader Aloysius Horn (Harry Carey), the young romantic lead (Duncan Renaldo), and the 'wild' white woman (Booth) worshipped by African natives as a fetish – set the terms for the similar trio of lead characters in *King Kong*.

King of the Jungle, a Tarzan-type film starring 1932 Olympic swimming champion Buster Crabbe (billed as 'the most perfectly formed man in the world'), was released at the same time as *King Kong*, the former jungle film exhibiting stock characters and conventions strikingly similar to textual features found in *King Kong*. *King of the Jungle* features a villainous circus entertainer named Forbes who captures the innocent lion man named Kaspa (raised by lions in the wild) and brings him back to 'civilization' with the purpose of making a fortune exhibiting the wild man in his animal act. When Forbes sees Kaspa playing with some lions in a cage, the showman's carny-style speech resembles Carl Denham's, as he exclaims: 'What an act!'[25] Forbes's scheme is foiled when Kaspa escapes and takes shelter in the apartment of a woman (Frances Dee) who has a taming effect on him. An advertisement for the Crabbe vehicle renders salient the two-world structure typical of the jungle film tradition, as well as the importance of a woman's love in taming 'savage,' animal-like behavior: 'the Lion-Man – embattled Man-King of Beasts – brought to civilization in a cage only to discover himself a man – in the arms of a woman he learned to love. A picture that swings its action across two continents.'[26] Although *King of the Jungle* performed poorly at the box office, this example nevertheless indicates that the two-world structure found in *King Kong* was by no means unique, but was rather a stock formula of the jungle-adventure tradition.

The third and final set of contextual factors responsible for *King Kong*'s early definition as a jungle film is comprised of exhibitors' practices. The jungle film tradition was quite amenable to ballyhoo techniques and the live entertainment programs featured as prologues to major film releases in the classical period. Even exhibitors in small regional markets could afford to rent a caged lion for lobby display, or could possibly erect a cut-out version of a white female captive on an altar of ritual sacrifice. Exhibitors in major urban markets devised more elaborate campaigns around the jungle theme, such as the one organised by Sid Grauman for *King Kong*'s première at the Chinese Theater in Los Angeles.

King Kong's New York première at the Radio City Music Hall and the RKO Roxy tapped the visual and sound elements of the jungle genre for portions of the variety-style prologue shows featured at both theaters. The Music Hall's three-part show culminated in a jungle production number in which a male dancer, 'stripped but for a loin cloth,' performed a dance on a drum.[27] The number concluded with a giant cut-out ape rising in the background, its fake arm reaching down to pick up a female dancer, just as the lights dimmed for a fade into *King Kong*'s title sheet. For the most part, however, the New York première foregrounded modern urban and art deco-style elements for *King Kong*'s campaign, and advertisements rather predictably stressed images of Kong's New York rampage. After all, the film furnished an easy opportunity to foreground locations familiar to New York audiences – tapping into their 'stomping grounds,' so to speak. One of the more imaginative advertisements for the New York campaign depicted an enraged Kong chasing panic-stricken crowds down an imaginary avenue separating the two giant RKO theaters where *King Kong* was playing.[28]

Jungle exotica and Orientalist elements played a far more prominent role in the Los Angeles première of *King Kong* than had been the case in New York. Sid Grauman, owner of the Chinese Theater, made his reputation creating elaborate prologue shows devised from a single theme extrapolated from the film – a practice that contrasted with the variety-style prologues used in many other theaters, such as the Radio City Music Hall.[29] In direct contrast to the Manhattan campaign's emphasis on *King Kong*'s urban features, the Los Angeles première heavily foregrounded the film's Orientalist, Africanist features – evidently for 'sexy,' 'racy' purposes. Instead of the art deco lettering used for most of *King Kong*'s advertising campaigns, Grauman's ads used a tropical 'grassy'-style lettering to spell out the film's title. In a fashion that had been used for previous jungle films such as *Trader Horn*, which had also premièred at the Chinese Theater, ads for *King Kong*'s Los Angeles première gave the seventeen-part prologue, entitled 'A Scene in the Jungle,' equal billing with the film itself. In contrast to the Music Hall's use of the white Roxyettes (later Rockettes), the Grauman's prologue heavily stressed black performers: four white principals – a comedian, a juggler, a trapeze artist, and a dancer – were backed up by 'a chorus of dusky maidens' and 'African choral ensembles' (possibly African-American performers, or non-black performers in 'blackface' makeup). Musical numbers, given exotic, Africanist titles, included 'The Voo Doo Dancer,' 'Dance to the Sacred Ape,' 'The Black Ballet,' and 'Goodbye Africa.'[30]

In a certain sense, the prologue shows seemed to offer a sort of 'return of the repressed' as sensational racial and sexual elements, largely censored during the script revision process, returned in some exhibition settings. In these cases, activating the film's Orientalist and primitivist features furnished a means of bypassing censorship strictures enforced in this period. When the serial version of *King Kong* ran in *Mystery* magazine, images of the film's jungle spectacle dominated the layout, as if to promote a sensation-based eroticism not as prominent in the film itself. One of these images was a production illustration of Kong tearing away part of Ann's clothing, exposing her breast. More sexually explicit than the rather chaste scene in the film, this image received a sensational caption: 'A look of surprise came over the great beast's face. Anne [*sic*], paralyzed with fear, could feel his hot breath scorch her body as he curiously inspected her.'[31] One Grauman ad picked up this same image of the stripping scene; another featured an illustration of the ritual sacrifice scene, emphasising the wild movements of the black natives and giving Kong vaguely Asian-looking facial features (hybridising black exotic and Orientalist elements). As Mary Beth Haralovich has shown, in the early 1930s exhibitors sometimes discarded the studio's advertisements, provided in the press book, and made up ads of their own.[32] They did this to bypass the censorship strictures of the 1930 Advertising Code, drawn up with the intention of making motion-picture ads conform to principles of 'good taste.' The images chosen for the Grauman campaign shaped *King Kong*'s features in a fashion that promised 'sexy,' 'racy' spectacle.

As Mary Carbine has shown, however, the film prologue tradition may have been a complex reception moment, for prologue shows often gave a central place to black performers that contrasted markedly with the 'backgrounding' treatment black entertainers notoriously received in the films themselves.[33] At this time, coverage of the jungle film cycle in the pages of the *Chicago Defender*, one of the most prominent of the African-American papers, was generally limited to brief, neutral notes, such as a short notice that MGM's *Tarzan and His Mate* was in production and would need black actors to perform as natives.[34] Although other features in this newspaper often deplored stereo-typical depictions of black people, these brief entertainment notices tended to treat the jungle genre as a place of employment – a dire concern in what was the bleakest stretch of the Depression. The prologue shows, however, received more extended attention from the *Defender*. Significantly, these shows afforded opportunities for discussing various matters of employment and labor disputes in the early 1930s. During a salary dispute at a Warner's theater in downtown Los Angeles, for example, white entertainers were locked out by the theater owner, who then hired black musicians calling themselves 'The Fourteen Gentlemen of Harlem' and comedian Eddie Anderson to create a live show to accompany *42nd Street*.[35] The *Defender's* entertainment columnist Harry Levette commended Earl Dancer, who had assembled the show under pressure: 'Earl deserves much credit for his boldness and confidence in offering to step in where only whites had been featured before . . . 'The Fourteen Gentlemen of Harlem' have proven that Negro musicians can hold the downtown houses and no doubt have opened the way for others.'[36] Another *Defender* piece covered a dispute that arose between a New York theater manager and black chorines performing in a prologue show devised for MGM's *Rasputin and the Empress*. Knowing he had no money for salaries, the (presumably white) manager concealed this from the women, and let them perform as usual. Later, with the film in progress, the chorines dressed for the street and went to pick up their pay, only to discover there were no funds with which to compensate them. The sympathetic reporter noted that 'chiseling' theater managers often refused to pay their performers, sometimes forcing workers to go for weeks without pay.[37] The infuriated dancers then went out into the auditorium and told the audience to leave, whereupon the women proceeded to wreck the place, slashing seats, destroying scenery, and ripping down the curtains. The police arrived but refused to make any arrests, saying: 'The poor kids had to have the money – they did the work.'[38]

Although *King Kong* did not receive extended discussion in the pages of *The Chicago Defender*, the film managed to motivate a brief, but noteworthy mention: a black composer named Harvey Brooks, who with his partner, lyricist Bennie Ellison, had created the music for the Grauman's prologue, received his 'big break' on account of this show. Brooks was subsequently put under contract by Paramount, and assigned to write the songs sung by Mae West in *I'm No Angel* (Wesley Ruggles), one of the biggest box office hits of

1933.[39] Rather than concentrating on the prologue's 'racy' (and racist) images, then, the *Defender* columnist chose to celebrate the black authorship of the show's music. Black reception of such shows may thus have been mixed or ambivalent, as these shows traded in racist spectacle, yet also provided occasions for working through pressing labor-related issues during a bleak moment of economic downturn.

Although the jungle genre was quite prominent in *King Kong*'s promotional campaign, this genre frame ultimately posed a problem, because the flurry of 'animal pictures' released in the early months of 1933 generally performed very poorly at the box office. Noting the disappointing returns of such films as *King of the Jungle*, *The Big Cage*, and Columbia's *Jungle Killer* (1932), a *Variety* reporter commented: 'Last week definitely proved that animal shows are about washed up . . . Tarzan stole the cream of the jungle stuff, and milk that's left is pretty skim.'[40] The poor track records of the jungle films led to certain contradictory tendencies in *King Kong*'s release campaign: on the one hand, some exhibitors continued to favor the exotic appeal potential to jungle-style ballyhoo techniques; on the other, RKO distributors began to warn their exhibitors to find ways to set *King Kong* apart from the then current cycle of mediocre 'animal pictures.' To accomplish this, some exhibitors turned to the most standard of all Hollywood narrative appeals – promotion of the film as a romance. Although *King Kong*'s romance line seems obvious today, such was not the case in 1933. Romance strategies were generally constructed by way of the star system, but *King Kong* had only Fay Wray's name to trade on – the name of a then minor star at that. Despite this problem, some exhibitors set about constructing a 'romance angle' as the centerpiece for their campaigns. An Indianapolis theater owner attracted local press attention by erecting a thirty-six foot cut-out of King Kong atop his theater marquee, then hiring two women to work alternating shifts sitting in the giant ape's hand.[41] This exhibitor then made romance central to both his marquee announcements (' "King Kong" – a Love Story that spans the Ages') and his newspaper advertisements. One ad featured an image of Fay Wray swooning in the arms of Robert Armstrong, underscored by the caption: 'Their Hearts Stood Still . . . for There Stood Kong! A Love Story of Today That Spans the Ages!'[42] The fact that Armstrong (who played Denham) and Wray are not in fact the film's couple did not deter this exhibitor, who selected the publicity still that both suited his romance theme, and featured the better known players. (Bruce Cabot, who played Jack Driscoll, was a complete unknown at this time.) An RKO distributor commended this campaign and a similar one in St. Louis, and he urged other exhibitors to play up the romance theme: 'There truly is a love story in the picture, and unless this is brought to the attention of the public, a number will stay away from the theater because they believe it to be just another animal picture.'[43]

Romance thus became yet another 'angle' for understanding *King Kong* – one created by highlighting selected textual features, and even shuffling these in ways not necessarily 'true' to the film itself. Promoting the film as a romance promised to secure the female audience, who were believed to shy away from films such as *King Kong*.[44] At the same time, romance offered a convenient 'tie-in' for the women's magazines, and the lucrative markets for women's products that supported these publications. One advertisement Fay Wray appeared in for Lux soap is telling in this respect. In the ad, Wray wears the Beauty costume Ann Darrow dons for the screen-test scene (a scene that has received more critical commentary than any other in *King Kong* with the possible exception of the closing sequence). In the context of the film, Wray (as Darrow) wears an expression of abject terror during this scene, and this is the first time we hear her legendary scream. In the Lux ad, however, Wray stands in a placid pose, offering her beauty calmly to the prospective consumer: 'A thousand thrills . . . and hers the thrill of *Supreme Beauty*. Here's one you *must* see – Beauty and the Beast in modern dress. Such a Beast – and such a Beauty! Even the chills and thrills of King Kong pale before the Thrill Supreme . . . Fay Wray's matchless blond loveliness!'[45] In contrast to the promotional ephemera that traded so heavily in sexually loaded images and exotica, the Lux advertisement hails female readers by linking the female star's 'blond loveliness' to the whiteness and light (Lux) of its soap product. The advertisement thus rearranges elements of *King Kong*'s screen-test scene to create a racially loaded constellation of signifiers – light, cleanliness, whiteness, femininity, and idealized beauty. The ad renders a kind of wrenching of the film's intrinsic features, creating a distortion effect that manages the film's discourses of race and gender 'differently,' with the result that these discourses are rechanneled in a certain 'hailing' of the presumably white female readers solicited by newspapers and magazines that ran this ad. In the face of this overcoded (and racist) image of an idealized white feminine beauty, the ad seems to suggest, even King Kong himself can only grow 'pale.'[46]

This single advertisement for soap was only a small part of a large promotional campaign, the effects of which remain difficult to track with precision. In charting aspects of the campaign at some length, I have sought to problematise existing scholarly readings of *King Kong* that glean social significance from textual features, as well as a fairly schematic sense of 1930s social history. In a recent essay on Sessue Hayakawa's performance in *The Cheat* (Cecil B. DeMille, 1915), Donald Kirihara argues that stereotypes (in this case, an Orientalist stereotype) should be assessed in historical terms, according to local and contextual forms of knowledge possessed by spectators within a given period, which may have since become lost to us.[47] Kirihara's point is fundamental but essential, in that he argues for the importance of contextualizing ideological effects by reconstructing forms of information available to viewers within specific reception moments. Against a certain critical tradition that has gauged *King Kong*'s ideological effects primarily on the basis of its textual properties, I have sought to complicate the picture by examining the layers of promotional discourses, which batted up against one another for a series of reasons pertaining to censorship, marketing strategies, exhibitors' showmanship, tie-in campaigns, and so forth. In so doing, I have demonstrated that even during the first release, *King Kong*'s ideological effects were shifting and potential, subject to complex contextual factors. In looking at a particular discursive strain, such as the key issue of racial difference, the reception critic might describe *King Kong* as a virtual 'performance' of racial ideologies which, depending on contextual factors at work, variously 'hailed' different audience and consumer groups, such as the largely white audiences at Grauman's, readers of black newspapers, or readers of women's magazines.

This analysis of *King Kong*'s original release has also been the launching point for a diachronic assessment of *King Kong*'s place in American culture. In this chapter, I have shown how *King Kong* evolved as a pastiche work and complicated, multigeneric text which was, from the start, shifting in its capacity to suit an unusually diverse set of marketing and viewing frames. The case of genre is particularly illuminating: since the 1950s, *King Kong* has largely been regarded as a classic horror film, and yet horror references were far less available to 1930s spectators than jungle and travel film references. In this case, more than one genre framework existed; moreover, the issue of genre developed not only from current film cycles, but also from exhibitors' needs, such as development of the live prologue show. On the basis of this case, one might argue for a need to pose genres as historical reconstructions, composed not only of the elements characteristic of particular film groups, but also of industrial, media, and social discourses and practices.

NOTES

1. The phrase 'showman's dream' appears on the cover page of the 1933 press book for *King Kong*: 'King Kong comes like a gift from a showman's heaven . . . A genius showman's dream comes to reality!' For a copy of the press book, see *King Kong* file, Margaret Herrick Library.
2. For an excellent discussion of the historical transition from ballyhoo practices into modern forms of film advertising, see Jane Gaines, 'From Elephants to Lux Soap: The Programming and "Flow" of Early Motion Picture Exploitation,' *The Velvet Light Trap* 25 (spring 1990): 29–43.
3. *Film Daily Yearbook of Motion Pictures* (New York: Film Daily, 1934), 35; and *Motion Picture Almanac for 1934* (New York: Quigley Publications, 1934), 17.
4. *Variety*, 7 March 1933, 9.
5. Ibid. *King Kong* earned about $38,000 in its first week at the RKO Roxy. *Variety* commented that this was 'not so great,' but worth holding the film over a second week.
6. A *Film Daily* editorial noted: 'Franklin Delano Roosevelt would have shaped up as a gorgeous showman . . . he loves mobs . . . he understands their psychology . . . and like every good showman . . . he never overdoes it . . . Hail to our New Chief . . . a showman at heart' (4 March 1933, 12).
7. *Motion Picture Herald*, 11 March 1933, 53.
8. *Variety*, 21 March 1933, 3: and *Variety*, 28 March 1933, 3.
9. Examples include an article on Willis O'Brien's animation work in *The Washington Post*, 17 March 1933, 12; and a piece on Murray Spivack's sound work in *The Indianapolis News*, 22 April 1933, 3.
10. Wallace, *My Hollywood Diary*, 183. Wallace refers to *Chang*, the critically

acclaimed Cooper/Schoedsack travel film, released in 1927.

11. Merian Cooper to David O. Selznick, memorandum, 23 January 1932, Cooper Collection.
12. *Variety*, 11 April 1933, 21.
13. *Radio Flash*, 18 March 1933, 2.
14. *Variety*, 28 March 1933, 14.
15. Merian Cooper to David Selznick, memorandum, 1 March 1932, Cooper Collection.
16. Wallace, *My Hollywood Diary*, 201–2.
17. J. Hoberman, 'Trouble in Paradise,' *Premiere*, May 1991, 37.
18. Review of *Chang, Close Up* 1, no. 4 (October 1927): 82.
19. Ibid., 83. Scrapbooks devoted to *Chang* in the Cooper Collection indicate that reviewers regarded the film as the best of its type, even better than *Nanook of the North*. Many critics included *Chang* on their lists of the ten best films of 1927, and Cooper and Schoedsack were ranked as the artistic equals of Fritz Lang, whose *Metropolis* was released at the same time as *Chang*. In the 1920s, then, Cooper and Schoedsack were heralded as directors who were artistically uncompromising, refusing to abide by the rules of Hollywood – quite the opposite of Carl Denham. This critical reputation shifted after *King Kong's* release, when they became better known as directors of mainstream entertainment films.
20. Reginald Taviner, 'A Pipe Is His Scepter,' *Photoplay*, July 1933, 42, 113.
21. W. E. Oliver, 'Legend of Beauty and Beast Is Given Astounding Turn,' *Hollywood Reporter*, 15 February 1933, 1.
22. Review of *King Kong*, *Newsweek*, 11 March 1933, 27.
23. Wallace and Cooper, 'Kong' ('The Eighth Wonder'), dialogue and adaptation by Creelman, 16 June 1932, Theater Arts Library, UCLA.
24. 'Animal Pictures a Current Cycle,' *Motion Picture Herald*, 4 March 1933, 57.
25. Mordaunt Hall, review of *King of the Jungle*, *New York Times*, 25 February 1933, 20.
26. Advertisement for *King of the Jungle*, *Mystery*, March 1933, 17.
27. *Variety*, 7 March 1933, 15.
28. Advertisement for *King Kong*, *New York Times*, 28 February 1933, 15.
29. Douglas Gomery, 'The Picture Palace: Economic Sense or Hollywood Nonsense?' *Quarterly Review of Film Studies* 3 (1978): 25.
30. Souvenir program for *King Kong* premiere at Grauman's Chinese Theater, 1933, *King Kong* production file, Margaret Herrick Library.
31. *Mystery*, February 1933, 24–5.
32. Mary Beth Haralovich, 'Mandates of Good Taste: The Self-Regulation of Film Advertising in the Thirties,' *Wide Angle* 6, no. 2 (1984): 50–7.
33. Carbine, ' "The Finest Outside the Loop." '
34. *Chicago Defender*, 22 April 1933, 5.
35. Ibid.
36. Ibid.
37. Ibid., 8 April 1933, 2.
38. Ibid.
39. Ibid., 3 June 1933, 5.
40. *Variety*, 28 March 1933, 3.
41. *Radio Flash*, 29 April 1933, 4–5.
42. Advertisement for *King Kong*, *Indianapolis Star*, 21 April 1933, 10.
43. *Radio Flash*, 22 April 1933, 4–5.
44. One reviewer commented, 'The picture has plenty of shocker stuff . . . While the wiser fans will accept the fantastic affair as grand hokum, some women and children may find it strong.' Review of *King Kong*, *Film Daily*, 25 February 1933, 4.
45. Advertisement, *Los Angeles Examiner*, 27 March 1933.
46. Lux advertisements featuring Hollywood's female stars ran for decades. For other

discussions of this campaign, see Gaines, 'From Elephants to Lux Soap,' 40–1; and Jackie Stacey, *Star Gazing: Hollywood Cinema and Female Spectatorship* (London: Routledge, 1994), 3–5.

47. Donald Kirihara, 'The Accepted Idea Displaced: Stereotype and Sessue Hayakawa,' in *The Birth of Whiteness: Race and the Emergence of U.S. Cinema*, ed. Daniel Bernardi (New Brunswick, N.J.: Rutgers University Press, 1996), 81–99. Kirihara maintains that because original audiences of *The Cheat* were probably familiar with the many films in which Hayakawa played heroic roles, they may have perceived his character as more complex than the villainous stereotype he seems to us today.

10

TOTALITARIANISM, DICTATORSHIP AND PROPAGANDA

If Hollywood managed to avoid regulation by state institutions through the use of the Hays Office, and the British documentary movement relied on state institutions, it is often suggested that in the totalitarian states of the 1930s – the Soviet Union, Nazi Germany, fascist Italy and the Japanese Empire – the cinema was no more than a crude form of state propaganda. Certainly these were not liberal states and overt opposition was not tolerated, but it would be equally wrong to see the films that were produced in these countries as simply propagandist.

Admittedly Soviet cinema had been state controlled since the revolution but in the 1930s there was a push to increase the number of films produced in the Soviet Union. The man placed in charge of this process was Boris Shumyatsky, who was anything but the stern propagandist. On the contrary, he was a champion of entertainment and opposed Soviet montage on the grounds that it was too difficult and intellectual. He therefore favoured a cinema that spoke more directly to popular competences and dispositions.

This did not mean that Soviet cinema was not subject to censorship and, from 1934, socialist realism was the approved style of filmmaking. However, this style of filmmaking is often caricatured by critics who want to present it as simple propagandist affirmation of Soviet society. It was supposed to present Soviet communism as representing historical progress, and as leading the world towards a socialist Utopia, but it was also associated with the rejection of the objective 'documentation' of reality. For example, while it was based around 'typical' characters, and hence tended to favour films that depicted ordinary working people, the word typical had a quite precise meaning that is often misrepresented. Typical characters were supposed to represent historical forces but not necessarily in a one-dimensional way. On the contrary, if typical characters represented specific social types, they were supposed to be viewed dialectically as embodying contradictory historical forces.

It is for this reason that socialist realism was able to justify films that celebrated both ordinary working people and great historical figures. For socialist realism, individuals do not become pivotal historical figures as a result of their unique individuality but due to their position within processes of historical development. Hence, an ordinary person could represent the vanguard of history as much as a great leader. As a result, during this period, the Soviet state made heroes of a whole series of individual working men who were praised for breaking productivity records and so contributing to Soviet industrial development. In this way, there was a fit between the worship of these 'Stakhanovite' record breakers and the developing 'cult of personality' in which Stalin himself was presented as the embodiment of the historical vanguard and was associated with other great leaders of the Russian past. Historical dramas, therefore, became a key feature of Soviet production, with one of the first key examples being a civil war drama, *Chapayev* (1934). In this film, the central character is a typical working-class figure but later films also featured great historical figures whose greatness is attributed to their ties to the people. For example, in the Gorky Trilogy (*My Childhood*, 1938; *My Apprenticeship*, 1939, and *My Universities*, 1940), Gorky's lack of formal education is contrasted with the education that is provided through his encounters with the common people.

In other narratives, historical figures are validated through their historical function. For example, *Ivan the Terrible Part I* (1945) is directly associated with Stalin and portrayed as a ruler who represented the vanguard of history and dragged his country out of feudalism and on the path towards its historical destiny. Similarly, *Alexander Nevsky* (1938) concerns a medieval hero who defeats an invasion by the Germanic Teutonic knights in a brilliantly staged battle on a frozen lake. In the process, he is directly associated with the Soviet opposition to Nazi aggression and his success is attributed to his close relationship to the rank and file of his army.

Historical dramas were not the only films produced by the Soviet film factory and some of the most popular films of the period were musical comedies. Stalin's own favourite is supposed to have been *Volga-Volga* (1938). There was also a series of 'tractor musicals' that celebrated life on the new collective farms. In *Tractor Drivers* (1939), two record-breaking tractor drivers fall in love and, along the way, the workers sing of their lives. Ironically, although it told stories of heroic workers who exceeded their quotas, and although it produced a rich and energetic body of films, Soviet cinema in the 1930s never attained the levels of productivity set for it by the party and Shumyatsky himself was a victim of the Stalinist purges and was executed in 1939.

In Germany, on the other hand, the early 1930s saw a continuation of the Weimar cinema including Fritz Lang's sympathetic portrait of a child murder in

M, which starred Peter Lorre. In 1933, the political democracy that had been created after the First World War was ended by the electoral victory of the Nazi Party. Although democratically elected into power, Hitler became a dictator who suspended the democratic process and began to prepare for war. Nazism was also based on an ideology of racial superiority in which the Germans not only had a right to rule the world but were also threatened with corruption by inferior races such as the Jews, who, along with other 'degenerates' such as socialists and homosexuals, were segregated from the rest of the population in concentration camps where the Nazis sought systematically to exterminate them.

Despite the atrocities of this regime, its film policy was complex. The Nazis did not take control of the film industry, which was left in private hands, at least initially. On the one hand, this meant leaving ownership in the hands of right-wing businessmen such as Alfred Hugenberg and, on the other, it meant the industry was dependent on overseas markets. Converting German cinema into state propaganda would have proved financially disastrous. Even within Germany, the Ministry of Propaganda realised that overt celebrations of fascism were rarely, if ever, popular with audiences, and this situation set up a political contradiction for the ministry. While Goebbels clearly hoped to develop a cinema that expressed Nazism as vividly as Soviet montage expressed communism, he also wanted German cinema to end its reliance on foreign imports and this meant creating a popular German cinema that dominated the domestic market. As a result, he was forced to concentrate on entertainment and fantasy, rather than straightforward propaganda.

Nor was it even the case that feature films needed to be propagandist, given that this function could be given to other parts of the film programme. If entertaining features could be used to attract audiences, they could be fed propaganda via the documentary short or *Kulturfilm* that preceded the main feature. Eventually, the Nazis did take control of the industry, but only late in the day and only after a decline in foreign sales, and a rise in costs, made nation-alisation essential to the survival of the industry. As a result, it is important to recognise that while discussions of German cinema have often concentrated on the films of Leni Riefenstahl and anti-Semitic films such as *Jud Süss* (1940), these films were not typical of Nazi cinema more generally. Nevertheless, Riefenstahl has often been taken as defining the aesthetic of Nazi cinema with her highly stylised images of Aryan perfection. In *Olympia* (1938), for example, she recorded the 1936 Olympic games but concentrated on the perfection of Aryan athletes, rather than non-Aryan medal winners such as the outstanding black runner, Jesse Owens. Similarly much has been written about *Jud Süss* in which an evil Jewish money lender uses his wiles to seize political power.

Out of the 1,094 feature films made in the period, 941 were genre films of which 295 were melodramas and biopics; 123 were detective stories or adventures; and nearly half (523) were musicals and comedies. It was fantasy, though, that was perhaps the most distinctively German genre. Although small in number, these films maintained a clear sense of continuity with UFA's heyday and were therefore used to sell UFA and German cinema more generally. For example, for the twenty-fifth anniversary of UFA, the German film industry invested heavily in *Munchhausen* (1943). An established figure of European fiction, Munchhausen is a German baron who recounts the outrageous and implausible stories of his exploits, such as a trip to the moon, and so provided the perfect subject matter for a fabulous fantasy film that emphasised German powers of imagination and displayed its film industry's amazing special effects. It was an unparalleled showcase for the strengths of German cinema and culture.

If the Nazis eventually chose to nationalise the German film industry, Mussolini's fascists chose to maintain an independent Italian film industry through government subsidy and support. They were even quite disdainful of the Nazis' handling of cinema. In 1934, the Undersecretariat of State for Press and Propaganda created a division to oversee the cinema and appointed Luigi Freddi as its head, a man who would become an outspoken critic of the Nazis' management of the film industry. He believed that the cinema should not be used as a form of propaganda but as a medium of entertainment. For Freddi, an amused and distracted public would be pliant and passive. As a result, while the state maintained oversight of the industry, it hardly ever banned a film.

Italian cinema was therefore a largely commercial affair, but the Depression hit the film industry hard and the government introduced a series of measures to bolster production. In addition to subsidies for Italian films, the fascists set quotas for exhibitors, who were required to show a certain percentage of Italian films. Foreign films were subject to tax and a series of prizes was established to encourage quality film production. The still prominent Venice Film Festival was also a product of this period and its purpose was both to present Italian cinema to the international community and to foster a vital film culture within Italy. Furthermore, after the old Cines studios were destroyed by fire in the mid-1930s, the government built the magnificent Cinecittà studios, which laid the foundations for the postwar Italian film industry and have also been used to film a number of major Hollywood productions from *Ben-Hur* (1959) to *Gladiator* (2002).

One reason that the fascists exerted so little ideological control over the film industry was that Italian fascism was far less developed ideologically than either communism or Nazism, but its rampant nationalism did find expression in historical epics such as *Scipione l'Africano* (1937), which was reputedly written by Mussolini and was the story of the Roman soldier who conquered Northern Africa in 202 BC. As a result, its military adventures had clear parallels with Mussolini's invasion of Ethiopia in 1935. By no means were all historical films nationalistic in this way. For example, Mussolini did not agree with Alessandro Blasetti's interpretation of Garibaldi in his epic masterpiece *1860* (1934) or his pacifist sentiments in *The Iron Crown* (1941).

Epics were, however, by no means the sole or even main tendency within Italian cinema and among the most popular genres were the 'white-telephone' films, idealised stories of the leisured élite. Furthermore, as their association with 'white-telephones' suggests, one of the key features of these films was the emphasis on set design as a means of signifying affluence and modernity. Comedy was also an important genre of the period, and was to prove highly influential on postwar neo-realism. Not only did Vittorio De Sica, a key figure in postwar neo-realism, achieve early success in comedy, but the coming of sound enabled the development of dialect comedy. In Italy, dialect was a key marker of social and regional identity and it was strongly associated with the culture of the common people and everyday life, key concerns of the neo-realists. Indeed, the Italian Marxist Antonio Gramsci developed his theory of hegemony from linguistic studies that concerned the struggles between different dialects within Italy.

While Luigi Freddi's handling of the cinema boosted both audiences and production, fascism was becoming increasingly unpopular among younger intellectuals, and, by the 1940s, critics called for films that dealt more directly with the concerns of ordinary working people. The films that emerged in response often stressed their regional specificity through the use of dialect, location and the use of non-professional actors, and many of these films were made by directors who would become key figures in the postwar period. For example, Rossellini used documentary techniques in his naval drama *La Nave Bianca* (1941), while Luchino Visconti made *Ossessione* (1943), a film version of James M. Cain's *The Postman Always Rings Twice* that was set in the impoverished Po Valley and proved particularly bleak and uncompromising in its realism.

The third member of the Axis powers was Japan, which was ruled by the Emperor Hirohito. Japan had a fully developed studio system that was dominated by three major companies, Nikkatsu, Shochiku and, after 1934, Toho and, despite the repression of socialism after 1937, and the stress on nationalism after the attack on Pearl Harbor in 1941, there was no real attempt to turn the cinema into an organ of political propaganda. On the contrary, the regime's major impact on the industry was that its imperial wars created the conditions for the Japanese film industry's dominance of the Asian film market, a dominance that continued well into the postwar period.

This dominance is probably best seen in the case of China, which had a flourishing film industry during the 1920s and, due to the high levels of illiteracy among the peasantry, was given a further boost with the introduction of sound. Politically, the country was divided by a conflict between Chiang Kai Shek's Kuomintang and Mao Tse Tung's communists, but when Japan invaded Manchuria in 1931, Chiang Kai Shek continued to focus his attention on fighting the communists rather than the Japanese. It is therefore the communists' contribution to Chinese cinema that is best remembered from this period and, in 1932, the Film Group was formed to provide support for communists and others on the political left who were working within the film industry. The head of the Film Group was also head of scripting at the Mingxing Film Corporation, one of the two major Chinese studios, while the left also dominated one of the three production units of the other major studio, the Lianhua Film Company.

During this time, Mingxing made *Spring Silkworms* (1933), which used documentary techniques to tell the story of a peasant family. The film follows them through the year-long cycle of silk production, at the end of which they are devastated by a drop in the market price of silk. Meanwhile, Lianhua made *The Goddess* (1934), which details the life and death of a prostitute, and *The Highway* (1934), which concerns a group of working men as they build a road that will be used to repel the Japanese invasion. Despite the struggles between the left and right, the Chinese industry was virtually destroyed when the Japanese captured Shanghai in 1937. This not only incapacitated one of Japanese cinema's key competitors but also established China as a market for Japanese films.

During this period, Japan was largely a genre cinema and one of its major genres was the Jidai-geki which were historical adventures often featuring samurai warriors. Although some have argued that these were little more than a form of military propaganda, others have stressed the psychological realism of the genre in the 1930s, which made many of its films fairly complex meditations on the nature of combat. Another key genre was the Kindai-geki, which involved realist depictions of the modern Japanese middle class and had subgenres such as 'mother' films and 'salaryman' films. Finally, the Shomin-geki were depictions of the lower middle class.

In addition, the studios tended to associate specific directors with specific genres, and the two directors of the period that have received most critical attention were Mizoguchi and Ozu. Both directors built their reputation while working in a number of different genres but Mizoguchi became best known for his thrillers and for his handling of women characters. Stylistically, his films were distinguished by his use of the extended take. This usually meant that he used long shots rather than close-ups, and relied on the movement of the camera to tell the story. Ozu, by contrast, was known for his depictions of middle-class family life and was stylistically quite different. He used short takes, static cameras, close-ups and editing to tell the story. Together, but in different ways, they represent the accomplishment of Japanese cinema in the period.

One of the problems with seeing films as solely the vehicles of totalitarian propaganda is that, even in totalitarian societies, the state is never a unitary and fixed entity but is always composed of a series of political forces that compete with one another for power. Even particular individuals such as Goebbels may have powerfully conflicting interests: Goebbels was clearly divided by his desire to use cinema to legitimate Nazi power and his interest in film aesthetics. A political history of cinema does not necessarily simply involve an analysis of how individual films or groups of films reflected political ideas but should also examine the relationships between the organisation of cinematic production and political institutions.

As a result, Richard Taylor's examination of the Soviet film industry in 'Ideology as Mass Entertainment: Boris Shumyatsky and Soviet Cinema in the 1930s' demonstrates that, while Soviet cinema is usually seen as an organ of the

Soviet state, it was actually organised as a commercial activity that was 'expected to stand on its own two feet financially'. In other words, while it was required to fulfil certain political requirements, it was actually organised as a relatively autonomous institution that was driven by commercial criteria. In his account, Taylor seeks to provide an alternative to the concentration on state propaganda on the one hand, and great directors and aesthetic movements on the other, and he concentrates on 'those who actually ran the industry at the highest level, those who took the major policy decisions who held the ultimate responsibility'. He therefore concentrates on the figure of Boris Shumyatsky, 'a party activist and administrator', who 'dominated' Soviet cinema from 1930 until 1937.

The extract concentrates on the specific organisation and policies of the Soviet Film Factory during the period and it attempts to do so through an analysis of a variety of materials. In the absence of a trade press comparable to *Variety* in the US, Taylor examines a range of political publications in which issues of policy were proposed, debated and negotiated. Some of these were organs of political organisations and others were specialist organisations associated with film. In the process, he shows not only how the organisation of the film factory was the product of fierce political conflicts over policy, but also how these were linked to specific aesthetic agendas. Although creative workers often present those who manage them as tasteless bureaucrats with no under-standing of the film medium, Taylor demonstrates that even executives have aesthetic agendas, agendas that may not be disinterested but frequently attempt to resolve complex problems.

- Can you distinguish between the primary and the secondary sources that Taylor uses in his study?
- What questions is he trying to answer when he examines these sources?
- If Soviet cinema was more commercially driven than many accounts suggest, Hollywood has always had close ties to the state. Can you think of examples and how might you study them?

IDEOLOGY AS MASS ENTERTAINMENT: BORIS SHUMYATSKY AND SOVIET CINEMA IN THE 1930S

Richard Taylor

A film and its success are directly linked to the degree of entertainment in the plot . . . that is why we are obliged to require our masters to produce works that have strong plots and are organised around a story-line.

Boris Shumyatsky, 1933[1]

Richard Taylor (ed. Richard Taylor and Ian Christie), *Inside the Film Factory: New Approaches to Russian and Soviet Cinema* (New York and London: Routledge, 1991).

The conventional approach to Soviet cinema looks at the films produced almost exclusively in terms of the men who directed them: Eisenstein, Pudovkin, Vertov head a long, and lengthening, list of what film critics and historians would, borrowing from their French counterparts, nowadays call *auteurs*. Yet our approach to Hollywood, which is both more familiar to us, and more influential over us, is rather different: the *auteur* theory persists in the discussion of such important individual directors as Alfred Hitchcock or John Ford but we are much more prepared to concede that a film is the result of a variety of influences, perhaps even of a collective effort – at best a collective work of art, at worst a mere industrial commodity destined for mass consumption. In the Hollywood context, therefore, we talk of a studio style or of the influence of a producer like David O. Selznick. We group American films according to their scriptwriter (Jules Furthman or Clifford Odets), their genre (the western, the musical, the war film) or their star (Marlene Dietrich, Marilyn Monroe, James Dean). But we never apply these criteria to Soviet cinema.

There are, of course, good historical (and ideological) reasons for this: one of the principal reasons is quite simply lack of adequate information. But, if we do not ask different questions, we shall never get different answers or, indeed, much new information at all. In concentrating exclusively on directors, our approach to Soviet cinema lacks an important dimension. We ignore the different styles that emanate from different studios and we ignore the role of a man like Adrian Piotrovsky, head of the script department of the Leningrad studios in the early 1930s, in creating a studio style. We ignore the threads of continuity in the work of a scriptwriter like Mikhail Bleiman, whose first script was filmed in 1924 and who was still active in the 1970s, or Nina Agadzhanova-Shutko, who scripted films for both Eisenstein (*The Battleship Potemkin*, 1926) and Pudovkin (*The Deserter*, 1933). We ignore the importance of Soviet actors like the comedian Igor Ilyinsky or the more serious Nikolai Cherkasov or massively popular stars like Lyubov Orlova or Tamara Makarova. And we ignore the significance in Soviet cinema of genres like musical comedy (*The Happy Guys* [Veselye rebyata. 1934], *The Circus* [1936], *Volga-Volga* [1938] or *The Tractor Drivers* [Traktoristy, 1939]), Civil War films (*Chapayev* [1934], *We from Kronstadt* [1936], *Shchors* [1939]), or 'historical-revolutionary' films (the Maxim trilogy [1934–8], *A Great Citizen* [Velikii grazhdanin, 1937–9], *Lenin in October*, 1937] etc.). As a result our view of Soviet cinema has been both distorted and impoverished.

But perhaps the most surprising omission of all is our constant underestimation of the importance of those who actually ran the film industry at the highest political level, those who took the major policy decisions and who held the ultimate responsibility. This underestimation is a limitation we share with Soviet cinema historians, although the ideological origin of their blind spot is rather different from that of ours. In this chapter I want to look at the role of the man who dominated Soviet cinema for seven years from 1930 until the end of 1937: he was neither a film director nor a scriptwriter, neither an actor nor a cameraman, but a Party activist and an administrator and his influence on Soviet cinema can still be felt today. His name was Boris Shumyatsky.

Boris Zakharovich Shumyatsky was born on 4 November 1886 (old style) to an artisan family near Lake Baikal, joined the Party in 1903, played a leading part in the disturbances in Krasnoyarsk and Vladivostok in 1905–7 and, after 1917, held a number of important position in the Soviet governmental and Party apparatus in Siberia. From 1923 to 1925 he was Soviet plenipotentiary in Iran and on his return he became rector of the Communist University of Workers of the East and a member of the Central Asian Bureau of the Party Central Committee. This might seem an unlikely background for his next appointment, which is the one that concerns us here: in December 1930 he was made the chairman of the new centralised Soviet film organisation, Soyuzkino. But it was precisely this background as Old Bolshevik, Party activist and administrator that did qualify him, in the authorities' eyes, for the task in hand.[2]

There had been two previous attempts to organise Soviet cinema along centralised lines since the film industry had been nationalised in August 1919. In December 1922 Goskino had been established to put Soviet cinema on a secure footing: it had failed, partly because it was underfunded and partly because it had to compete with numerous other organisations, some of which were privately funded. Learning from these mistakes, Narkompros established Sovkino in December 1924 to perform a fundamentally similar task. But even Sovkino did not have the resources to compete adequately with the private sector and Soviet cinema audiences still flocked to see either imported films like *Broken Blossoms* [USA, 1919], *The Mark of Zorro* [USA, 1920], *Robin Hood* [USA, 1922] or Soviet films that imitated imported models. An excellent example of this last category is the film *The Bear's Wedding* [1926],[3] made by Konstantin Eggert in 1925 for Mezhrabpom-Rus, the joint-stock company in which he had a large shareholding, from a story by Prosper Mérimée adapted for the screen by Anatoli Lunacharsky, the People's Commissar for Enlightenment, with Lunacharsky's wife, Nataliya Rozenel, playing the female lead. The story is set in the forests of Lithuania and contains the stock horror-film elements of murky castles, human beasts, hereditary insanity, storms and dungeons. It was unashamedly a commercial film aimed at attracting audiences through entertainment and diversion rather than through edification, agitation or propaganda. Showing in Moscow at the same time as the state film organisation's *The Battleship Potemkin*, it attracted more than twice as large an audience and was advertised as 'the first hit of 1926'.[4] Later in the year 'public demand' led to *Potemkin* being replaced by Douglas Fairbanks in *Robin Hood*.[5]

Since Soviet cinema was expected to stand on its own two feet financially, Sovkino had to make films that were commercially rather than ideologically orientated. What surplus, if any, was left from the production and distribution of *kassovye* (cash) films was to be used to finance *klassovye* (class) films. Sovkino was bitterly attacked from all sides for its heavy-handed attitudes and for its failure to make any real attempt to combine ideological rectitude with box-office success

[. . .]

Our conventional approach to Soviet cinema has tended to obscure that argument by overlooking the wider political context.

We have largely ignored the implications of Lunacharsky's observation that in the Soviet Union too 'cinema is an industry and, what is more, a profitable industry'[6] and his subsequent conclusion that:

> Many of our people do not understand that our film production must whet the public appetite, that, if the public is not interested in a picture that we produce, it will become boring agitation and we shall become boring agitators. But it is well known that boring agitation is counter-agitation. We must choose and find a line that ensures that *the film is both artistic and ideologically consistent and contains romantic experience of an intimate and psychological character.*[7]

The lessons of Lunacharsky's remarks may have been lost on 'many of our people' but they were not lost on Boris Shumyatsky.

Shumyatsky was appointed head of Soyuzkino when the 'proletarian hegemony' was at its height. Many leading directors had turned to making films on contemporary themes drawn from the everyday experience of the Soviet worker or peasant. Ermler was making *Counterplan* [Vstrechnyi, 1932], Ekk *The Path to Life* [1931] and Yutkevich *The Golden Mountains* [1931], while the Kozintsev and Trauberg film *Alone* [1931] was greeted warmly by Sutyrin, the editor of the monthly journal *Proletraskoe Kino*, in a review significantly entitled 'From Intelligentsia Illusions to Actual Reality'[8] (Despite its name, *Proletarskoe kino* was not quite the forcing ground for proletarianisation that it might have seemed, or wanted to seem, to be: its editorial board, in addition to Sutyrin, included the directors Pudovkin and Ermler while Petrov-Bytov became editor of the mass-circulation Leningrad film magazine, *Kadr.*) Shumyatsky himself paid little more than lip service to the campaign, preferring to concentrate on the broader problems of Soviet cinema, which were enormous, and as much industrial as political.

In the year 1927/8 box office receipts from Soviet films had exceeded those from imports for the first time,[9] but this did not mean that Soviet films were intrinsically more popular. It meant that a shortage of foreign currency had led to a severe reduction in the number of films imported while the Soviet films that filled the gap were on the whole imitative of Western models. The rapid expansion of the cinema network during the first Five Year Plan period accentuated the problem and the spread of cinemas to the countryside created a new audience for Soviet films.

While we cannot talk in conventional Western terms of supply and demand, we can say that those responsible for Soviet cinema, from Lunacharsky and

Shumyatsky downwards, realised that the industry was not producing enough films, or enough of the right films to meet the demand that they perceived. Hence the emphases on attracting established authors into writing scripts, on adapting the established classics and on tackling themes and developing genres that were immediately relevant to the ever-widening audience. The shortage of foreign currency meant that Soviet cinema also had to try to achieve self-sufficiency in the production of film stock, projectors and other equipment and to achieve this as quickly as possible.

Lastly, the Soviet Union had, like other countries, to come to terms with the advent of sound film. This meant 'the agitation, the anxieties and the alarm' that the scriptwriter Yevgeni Gabrilovich detected among 'script-writers, directors, actors, cameramen and editors when the screen suddenly, surprisingly and quite unexpectedly began producing sounds'.[10] It also meant a further massive investment in re-equipment and yet another headache for Shumyatsky.

[. . .]

Shumyatsky's ideas were developed in two books published in 1934 and 1935.[11] By then he had the time and the experience to consider the longer-term aims and achievements of Soviet cinema: he was no longer dealing with a period of acute crisis. Like others before him, he asked where Soviet cinema had gone wrong. For him the answer lay not with a predominance of non-proletarian strata (although he made the by now standard reference to sabotage by class enemies and their exposure by OGPU)[12] but with the primacy of montage in Soviet film theory in the 1930s:

> The overvaluation of montage represents the primacy of form over content, the isolation of aesthetics from politics.[13]

The prime object of Shumyatsky's critique was not, as is usually supposed, Eisenstein but Lev Kuleshov whose early concentration on montage he denounced as 'typically bourgeois' because Kuleshov had emphasised form and ignored content. He was therefore a Formalist, one who had no sense of the coherence of life, one for whom 'life is a collection of individual phenomena, incidents and anecdotes'. Kuleshov's early films, such as *The Extraordinary Adventures of Mr West in the Land of the Bolsheviks* [1924], could, in Shumyatsky's view, have been produced in the West: there was nothing specifically Soviet about them, while his most recent film, *The Happy Canary* [Veselaya kanareika, 1929], was 'objectively hostile to Soviet art'.[14]

Kuleshov attracted Shumyatsky's venom because it was he who had first developed the theory of montage as the essence of cinema specificity. Early film theorists had sought to justify cinema as an independent art form and they had in particular to delineate its independence from theatre. In 1917 Kuleshov was the first to argue that the distinctive feature of cinema was montage:

> The essence of cinema art in the work of both director and art director is
> based entirely on composition. In order to make a film the director must

compose the separate, unordered and unconnected film shots into a single whole and juxtapose separate moments into a more meaningful, coherent and rhythmical sequence just as a child creates a whole word or phrase from different scattered letter blocks.[15]

In March 1918 he went further:

> Montage is to cinema what the composition of colours is to painting or a harmonic sequence of sounds is to music.[16]

In a series of film experiments he demonstrated what is now known as the 'Kuleshov effect'. He took a still shot of the actor Ivan Mosjoukine staring expressionless straight ahead of him and cut that shot into three different sequences: the context in which the shot was placed turned Mosjoukine's expressionlessness into expression – into sadness, laughter, anger, hunger.[17] It is from these experiments that the whole notion of the fundamental importance of montage develops. Vsevolod Pudovkin and other members of Kuleshov's Workshop later remarked: 'We make films but Kuleshov made cinema.'[18]

For a newer and younger generation of artists, inspired by the ideals of the October Revolution and dedicated to the construction of a new society and a new way of life, cinema was seen as *the* art form with which to shape the new man. One critic remarked: 'Theatre is a game: cinema is life',[19] another defined it as 'the new philosophy',[20] while a third argued:

> There can be no doubt that cinema, this new art form, is the rightful heir for our time, for its melodiousness, its rhythm, refinement and its machine culture, and it therefore represents the central art form of the current epoch.[21]

Even Lenin stated, 'Of all the arts, for us cinema is the most important.'[22] It therefore mattered uniquely if Soviet cinema was not playing, or was thought not to be playing, a central role in the transformation of Soviet society and this 'backwardness' became a particularly acute embarrassment at the time of the 'cultural revolution' that was to accompany the first Five Year Plan. But, as we have seen, this was not a new problem, rather a more acute manifestation of an old problem.

Shumyatsky argued that the inaccessibility or unintelligibility ascribed to some of the major triumphs of Soviet silent film (Eisenstein's *The Strike* or *October*, the Kozintsev and Trauberg *New Babylon* or almost any of Vertov's documentaries) resulted from an emphasis on the primacy of montage at the expense of other elements such as the script or the acting. This emphasis on montage paralleled a similar emphasis on the director at the expense of the scriptwriter or the actor. People behaved 'as if the director was empowered to do with a film whatever he *and he alone* wanted'.[23] The underestimation of the role of the scriptwriter had, in Shumyatsky's view, made it very difficult to attract good writers to the screen and this had resulted in recurring 'script crises', acute shortages of material that was suitable for filming, and Soviet cinema had suffered from an almost continuous series of such 'crises' since its inception. Although there were some notable exceptions (Mayakovsky and

Shklovsky are obvious examples) the majority of writers regarded scriptwriting as a somewhat inferior and even unworthy activity; this was a view they shared with their colleagues in other countries. Repeated efforts to encourage writers to play a more active part in cinema culminated in a Central Committee decree in the spring of 1933 designed to stimulate such participation on a more regular and organised basis. Gorky was quoted as regarding film scripts not just as a worthwhile activity in themselves but as 'the most complex dramaturgical work'.[24] For Shumyatsky the principal task facing Soviet cinema in the mid-1930s was 'the battle for high-quality scripts'.[25]

Montage had, as I have indicated, played a central part in attempts to distinguish theoretically between silent cinema and theatre: it was prominent in the writings of Soviet film-makers of different schools, from 'fiction' film-makers like Eisenstein, Kuleshov and Pudovkin to documentarists like Shub and Vertov. In silent cinema the absence of sound gave the visual image an inevitable primacy over the word. This had certain political advantages: it could simplify a film's narrative structure, thus broadening its appeal. But it also had certain political disadvantages: it could encourage an experimental search for non-narrative structures of exposition, emphasising visual continuity or discontinuity through montage leading in some instances to an abandonment of conventional plot and story-line altogether. Eisenstein's 'montage of attractions' in which each attraction 'collides' with another is one example that confused worker audiences and Dziga Vertov's Cine-Eye 'factory of facts' and 'life caught unawares' is another. Both represented attempts to replace what were perceived as bourgeois narrative forms imitative of Hollywood with new forms of exposition deemed more appropriate to a revolutionary art form.

But the abandonment of conventional narrative structures and the notion that a film might in some way be 'plotless' were a particular *bête noire* for Shumyatsky:

> The plot of a work represents the constructive expression of its idea. A plotless form for a work of art is powerless to express an idea of any significance. That is why we require of our films a plot as the basic condition for the expression of ideas, of their direction, as the condition for their mass character, i.e. of the audience's interest in them. Certainly, among our masters you will find people who say: 'I am working on the plotless, storyless level.'
> People who maintain that position are profoundly deluded.[26]

Accusing them of 'creative atavism', Shumyatsky maintained that 'they have not yet got used to the discipline of the concrete tasks that our mass audience is setting them'.[27] Without a plot, no film could be entertaining:

> A film and its success are directly linked to the degree of entertainment in the plot, in the appropriately constructed and realistic artistic motivations for its development.

That is why we are obliged to require our masters to produce works that have strong plots and are organised around a story-line. Otherwise they [the works] cannot be entertaining, they can have no mass character, otherwise the Soviet screen will not need them.[28]

In Shumyatsky's view then it was the hegemony of montage and the primacy accorded by montage to the director that represented the root cause of the dalliance with 'plotlessness' that he deplored. Montage lay in complete antithesis to the entertainment film that he considered so important. Montage represented 'creative atavism': plot represented 'the discipline of the concrete tasks that our mass audience is setting'. Plot necessitated script and an effective script had to be worked out carefully, in detail and in advance: 'At the basis of every feature film lies a work of drama, a play for cinema, a script.'[29] The notion that a script was 'a play for cinema' represented a complete reversal of the general desire that we have seen among film-makers to distinguish cinema from theatre. It represented in particular a realisation of the worst fears expressed by Eisenstein, Alexandrov and Pudovkin in their seminal 'Statement on Sound', published in August 1928:

Contemporary cinema, operating through visual images, has a powerful effect on the individual and rightfully occupies one of the leading positions in the ranks of the arts.

It is well known that the principal (and sole) method which has led cinema to a position of such great influence is *montage*. The confirmation of montage as the principal means of influence has become the indisputable axiom upon which world cinema culture rests.

The success of Soviet pictures on world markets is to a significant extent the result of a number of those concepts of montage which they first revealed and asserted.

And so for the further development of cinema the significant features appear to be those that strengthen and broaden the montage methods of influencing the audience.[30]

Those significant features included the development of colour and stereoscopic film but the most important feature of all was the advent of sound:

Sound is a double-edged invention and its most probable application will be along the line of least resistance, i.e. in the field of the *satisfaction of simple curiosity* . . .

The first period of sensations will not harm the development of the new art; the danger comes with the second period, accompanied by the loss of innocence and purity of the initial concept of cinema's new textural possibilities, which can only intensify its unimaginative use for 'dramas of high culture' and other photographed representations of a theatrical order.[31]

It is significant that the shortage of suitable scripts led Shumyatsky to encourage film-makers to turn their attention to adaptations of the classics[32] thus producing precisely those 'dramas of high culture' that the 1928 'Statement' was denouncing. It is also significant that the advent of the doctrine of Socialist Realism and the proclaimed need to produce films that were 'intelligible to the millions' led to an increase in 'photographed representations of a theatrical order', and a reinstatement of more familiar conventional narrative structures so that Eisenstein could write in the spring of 1938, a few months after Shumyatsky's fall from grace, that:

> There was a period in our cinema when montage was declared 'everything'. Now we are coming to the end of a period when montage is thought of as 'nothing'.[33]

But for the time being the primacy of montage and the hegemony of the director were blamed by Shumyatsky for the shortage of suitable scripts.

Similarly the downgrading of the actor's role had in his view led to a deterioration in the standard of film acting. This had even been formalised by some directors. Eisenstein had renounced professional actors for his first four films (*The Strike, The Battleship Potemkin, October* and *The Old and the New* [Staroe i novoe, 1929, a.k.a. *The General Line*]) and resorted to 'typage', where non-actors were selected who simply looked right for the part, who were in some way 'typical' of the mass: this process culminated in the use of worker Nikandrov as Lenin in *October*.[34] Kuleshov had also renounced a conventional theatrical style of acting and deployed the quasi-Meyerholdian *naturshchik* or model, a specialised cinema actor highly trained in specific external movements and gestures that would replicate his internal state of mind. As two recent Soviet critics have observed:

> What was required above all else from the *naturshchik* was the appropriate external trappings – speed of reaction, accuracy and precision of movement – that is, external qualities more reminiscent of the requirements of sport than of the criteria of art.[35]

In Shumyatsky's view the use of both the *naturshchik* and typage had led to a breakdown in communication with the audience who had no one in the film real enough for them to identify with. The cardboard effigies on the screen were not the psychologically real 'living men' that RAPP and ARRK had demanded: they were not convincing.

To some extent of course this lack of realism and exaggerated dependence on mimetic gesture was an inherent attribute of silent film: in the absence, or virtual absence, of words there was no alternative means of communication. But the dependence on the external trappings of mimetic gesture vitiated against a psychologically convincing development of characters and led to an underestimation of the actor's full potential. The film actor's role was a two-dimensional one: small wonder then that, just as creative writers had proved reluctant to furnish scripts, so theatre actors had also proved reluctant to act on film. This, Shumyatsky agreed, was also partly because of the loss of live contact with the audience but mainly because cinema did not use the actor efficiently. He cited the particular instance of the actor Naum Rogozhin who, in the period January–September 1935, worked for only six full days.[36] Rationalisation of acting commitments was another problem to be dealt with by the annual thematic plan, for the actor's role was in fact quite central:

> The Soviet actor creates the popularity of our art. The creative success of cinema is to a significant extent based on the success of our acting resources.[37]

The role of the actor is yet another aspect of Soviet cinema that we in the West have tended to overlook.

If, as Shumyatsky thought, the problem of Soviet cinema lay with the pre-dominance of the director at the particular expense of the scriptwriter and the actor, the obvious question then arose as to how the imbalance could be rectified. Shumyatsky's answer lay in a collective approach in which the plot outline, then the script and then the rushes would be discussed by all concerned to eliminate errors and infelicities at the earliest possible stage; significantly that collective approach was to include the management of the film industry and by clear implication and known practice also direct representatives of the Party – for each film there was to be in effect *a thematic plan in microcosm*. Shumyatsky's argument ran like this:

> The creation of a film is a *collective process* because a film unites the creative potential of many of its participants, from the scriptwriter and the director to the actor, the composer, the designer, the cameraman – and beginning and ending with the management . . . The time has come at last to speak unequivocally of the *direct creative* participation of the management in a film because it is the management that accepts the script and the general plan (and often even the plot outline), the management that criticises and makes suggestions and corrections, views the filmed material and asks for changes if those changes are necessary, it is the management that accepts films and so on and, it must be admitted, it is the management that often authors (without copyright!) both the plan and the details of a work.[38]

It was the management that would direct film-makers, as indeed Shumyatsky directed Eisenstein. In 1934 he praised him for his return to the notions of plot and acting and for his renewed theatrical activity.[39] But in March 1937 he ordered him to stop work on *Bezhin Meadow* [Bezhin lug] because he had wasted 2 million roubles, indulged in 'harmful Formalistic exercises' and produced work that was 'anti-artistic and politically quite unsound'.[40] Shumyatsky admitted 'that I bear the responsibility for all this as head of GUK [Gosudarstvennoe upravlenie kinematografii, State Cinema Enterprise][41] and reiterated that, 'It was inadmissible to allow a film to go into production without establishing beforehand a definite script and dialogues'.[42] The ban on

Bezhin Meadow was not an isolated incident and certainly not the result solely of any antipathy between Shumyatsky and Eisenstein. The tone of the argument in this instance was characterised as much by sorrow for a master gone astray as by anger. In the spring of 1934 there had been a much greater public furore over Abram Room's failure to shoot more than 5 per cent of the footage for his projected film comedy *Once One Summer* [Odnazhdy letom] after spending more than half a million roubles. On that occasion both Pudovkin and Dovzhenko had joined the chorus of denunciation.[43] None the less, by stopping the production of *Bezhin Meadow*, Shumyatsky claimed, 'the Party has shown once again the Bolshevik way of resolving the problems of art'.[44]

This 'Bolshevik way of resolving the problems of art', this enhanced role for management, was in fact of course a way of resolving the political problems of art. When the Central Committee had turned its attention to the strengthening of film cadres in January 1929[45] its concern had been to improve the political rather than the artistic performance of Soviet cinema. Similarly, Shumyatsky's emphasis on a prepared and detailed script facilitated the elimination at an early stage of undesirable elements from the completed film, whose undesirability derived from ideological as well as aesthetic considerations. Nevertheless he claimed:

> This organisation frees creativity and promotes the creative independence of each participant in the film.[46]

We have seen the main thrust of Shumyatsky's critique of Soviet cinema: primacy of montage and the hegemony of the director had led to a series of 'script crises' and to the production of films that were all too often 'unintelligible to the millions'. But we need to consider also the kind of films that Shumyatsky wanted to put in their place. The negative critique was balanced by the positive exhortation. How then was this 'creative independence' to be used?

The Conference of Film-Makers held in the wake of the August 1934 Writers' Congress in Moscow in January 1935 under the slogan 'For a Great Cinema Art'[47] revealed, as Shumyatsky himself admitted, that:

> We have no common view on such fundamental and decisive problems of our art as the inter-relationship between form and content, as plot, as the pace and rhythm of a film, the role of the script, the techniques of cinema and so on.[48]

The first tasks therefore were: (1) to create a common language of cinema, in which sound was to play a vital role and (2) to train suitable masters to use that language.[49]

[. . .]

Shumyatsky was particularly concerned to provide Soviet cinema audiences with a greater degree of variety in their staple diet:

> We need genres that are infused with optimism, with the mobilising emotions, with cheerfulness, joie-de-vivre and laughter. Genres that provide us with the maximum opportunity to demonstrate the best Bolshevik traditions: an implacable attitude to opportunism, with tenacity, initiative, skill and a Bolshevik scale of work.[50]

He urged a concentration on three genres: drama, comedy and, perhaps somewhat surprisingly, fairy tales. He was especially interested in developing these last two. Of comedy he wrote, in a chapter entitled 'The Battle for New Genres':

> In a country where socialism is being constructed, where there is no private property and exploitation, where the classes hostile to the proletariat have been liquidated, where the workers are united by their conscious participation in the construction of a socialist society and where the great task of liquidating the remnants of the capitalist past is being successfully accomplished by the Party even in the consciousness of the people – in this country comedy, apart from its task of exposure, has another, more important and responsible task: the creation of a good, joyful spectacle.[51]

In this instance he argued for the satisfaction of audience demand:

> The victorious class wants to laugh with joy. That is its right and Soviet cinema must provide its audiences with this joyful Soviet laughter.[52]

The two films that Shumyatsky held up as examples were Alexander Medvedkin's satire *Happiness* [1935] and Grigori Alexandrov's jazz musical comedy *The Happy Guys* [1934] which he described as 'a good *start to a new genre*, the Soviet film comedy'.[53] Shumyatsky was particularly incensed by the criticisms levelled at *The Happy Guys* at the Writers' Congress in August 1934: he compared its detractors to preachers from the Salvation Army and retorted:

> Neither the Revolution nor the defence of the socialist fatherland is a tragedy for the proletariat. We have always gone and in future we shall still go into battle singing and laughing.[54]

In Shumyatsky's view, a variety of genres was the spice of socialist cinema art.[55] Shumyatsky used a similar defence for the fairy-tale film:

> There is a new genre that we are now trying to introduce into our plan: it is the fairy-tale film that treats the raw material of scientific fantasy. Here too any notion that there is a limit to what is permissible is dangerous. Here everything is permissible, provided only that it is imbued with definite progressive ideas.[56]

But, lest anyone should imagine that Shumyatsky's blueprint should mean that Soviet cinema concentrate entirely on comic and fairy-tale escapism, he emphasised that Soviet science fiction should be based on reality rather than utopia. Whereas for the scientist, he argued, unfinished experiments

> are merely a job half done, it is another matter for the artist. For him the world of as yet unfinished scientific experiments is a Klondike of creative ideas and story-lines.[57]

Perhaps the best example of the kind of film that Shumyatsky had in mind is Yuri Zhelyabuzhsky's *Cosmic Flight* [Kosmicheskii reis], a Soviet parallel to *Things to Come* [Great Britain, 1936], released in 1935,[58] although the film can hardly be said to contain a 'Klondike of creative ideas'!

Soviet films were to be firmly tied to reality, or at least to the socialist realist perception of it, by their subject-matter which was to be relevant, topical and realistic. Shumyatsky designated five principal themes for film-makers to pursue. The most important of these was the process of the collectivisation of agriculture. The reasons for this are obvious: it was a policy that had encountered more widespread opposition than any other and a greater propaganda effort had therefore to be directed towards making it more palatable, if not to the expanding audiences for cinema in the countryside, who were after all those most closely affected, then at least to audiences in the towns and cities. A large number of films can be counted in this category, from Medvedkin's already mentioned *Happiness* and other, earlier efforts such as Ermler's *Peasants* [Krest'yane, 1934] through Eisenstein's abortive *Bezhin Meadow* to the series of what are best described as 'kolkhoz musicals', such as Savchenko and Schneider's *The Accordion* [Garmon, 1934] and Pyriev's extraordinary *The Tractor Drivers* [1939].

Of almost equal importance are films depicting the socialist construction of industry such as Macheret's *Men and Jobs* [1932], Dovzhenko's *Ivan* [1932] or Ermler's *Counterplan* [1932]. This theme was closely related to another: the depiction of the Revolution through the portrayal of its effect on an individual who, while being a fully developed character in his own right (unlike Eisenstein's 'types' or Kuleshov's *naturshchiki*), also represented the mass. The Kozintsev and Trauberg Maxim trilogy is perhaps the best example of this, although their *Alone*, Ekk's *The Path to Life*, Yutkevich's *The Golden Mountains*, Pudovkin's *The Deserter* or Raizman's *The Pilots* [Letchiki, 1935] would also suffice. This theme was again intertwined with what Shumyatsky termed 'the everyday life of the new man'.[59] One of the most intriguing films in this field, Abram Room's *A Severe Young Man*, from a script by Yuri Olesha, was in fact banned because it confronted in a politically unacceptable way the question of inequalities in Soviet life and both director and scriptwriter were disgraced. It is worth noting, however, that, despite the thorough discussion of the film at all stages of its production, it was actually completed[60] – unlike *Bezhin Meadow*, and unlike Room's earlier project, *Once One Summer*. Quite how it was completed, given the controversial nature of its subject-matter, is one of the many questions that still await an answer.

The last theme that Shumyatsky urged upon Soviet film-makers was that of defence. Again it is difficult to consign particular films to any one thematic division but, if we are to include the defence of the Revolution, then the list is almost endless: Soviet cinema has from its inception produced a steady flow of 'historical revolutionary' films. We could again include the Maxim trilogy, *The Deserter* and, for different reasons, *The Pilots* and *The Tractor Drivers* but we should also recall Barnet's *Outskirts* [1933], Dovzhenko's *Aerograd* [1935], Dzigan's *We from Kronstadt*, the Zarkhi and Heifits *The Baltic Deputy* [Deputat Baltiki, 1936] and, of course, Eisenstein's one completed 1930s film, *Alexander Nevsky* [1938]. Lastly, we might also include films about the rise of anti-Semitism and fascism in the West: Pyriev's *The Conveyor-Belt of Death* (Konveier smerti, 1933], Kuleshov's *Gorizont* [1932], Roshal's *The Oppenheim Family* [Sem'ya Oppengeim, 1938] or the Minkin and Rappaport film *Professor Mamlock* [1938].

But one of the most important themes for Soviet film-makers in the 1930s was the Civil War of 1918–21. Its role for Soviet cinema was comparable to that of the western for Hollywood and it had many of the same ingredients: action and excitement, clearly defined 'goodies' and 'baddies' (Reds and Whites instead of cowboys and Indians), and the security of a known '*kheppi-end*' that established and then confirmed a myth and in this instance helped to legitimise the Revolution and the sacrifices in the eyes of the cinemagoing public.

The great model for the Civil War film was of course *Chapayev*, made by the Vasiliev 'brothers' in 1934, which, perhaps not surprisingly, won the Grand Prix at the 1st Moscow International Film Festival in 1935. No other Soviet film, not even *The Battleship Potemkin*, has ever been accorded such widespread official sanction so quickly and so repeatedly. Shumyatsky wrote:

> In 1934 the best film produced by Soviet cinema in the whole period of its existence was released: it was *Chapayev*, a film that represents the genuine summit of Soviet film art.[61]

The strength of *Chapayev* lay in its action rather than its 'psychologising' and in its simultaneous portrayal of the positive and negative sides of the Red Army in the Civil War period. The hero of the film was portrayed realistically, warts and all, while the Whites were depicted as a powerful enemy that could only be defeated by a considerable effort, an enemy worth defeating:

> In *Chapayev* the heroism of the movement of the masses is depicted alongside the fate of individual heroes and it is in and through them that the mass is graphically and colourfully revealed . . . The film *Chapayev* has proved that in a dramatic work it is the *characters*, the intensity of the tempo, the ideological breadth that are decisive.[62]

The relative subtlety of the characterisation, the clouding of the absolute distinctions between black and white (at least in comparison with films like

The Battleship Potemkin or *October)*, involved the audience more closely in the film and its developing story-line:

> Chapayev's development does not take place *on the actual screen (as in many of our films) but in the audience's own eyes*. Chapayev is not finished and ready made, as all too often happens: he becomes a type through the plot, through dramatic changes. There is no head-on confrontation here, no exaggerated tendentiousness: the tendentiousness derives from the very essence of the action, from the deeds of the characters themselves.[63]

Chapayev then was *the model film*. In his message of congratulation to Soviet film-makers on the fifteenth anniversary of Soviet cinema in January 1935, Stalin said:

> Soviet power expects from you new successes, new films that, like *Chapayev*, portray the greatness of the historic cause of the struggle for power of the workers and peasants of the Soviet Union, that mobilise us to perform new tasks and remind us both of the achievements and of the difficulties of socialist construction.[64]

It was also Stalin who personally suggested to Dovzhenko that he should make 'a Ukrainian *Chapayev*', a project realised in 1939 in the film *Shchors*.[65]

Shumyatsky angrily rejected the view, expressed by the writer and former RAPP activist Vladimir Kirshon among others, that Soviet art was developing in an irregular pattern and that the emergence of *Chapayev* was in some way accidental.[66] Soviet cinema was, he claimed, 'the most organised of all the arts in our country'[67] but it should be raised to the level of the best:

> The *whole* Soviet cinema can work better. The *whole* of Soviet cinema, by aligning itself with the best films, can and must achieve better results.[68]

In order to do this, Soviet cinema had to undergo a radical reorganisation and overcome its 'backwardness'. Shumyatsky was keen for Soviet cinema to learn from the West, just as other spheres of Soviet industry were encouraged in the 1930s to 'catch up and overtake' the West by deploying foreign advisers.[69] In the summer of 1935 Shumyatsky headed an eight-man commission that visited the West to study film production methods in the larger studios. Shumyatsky, the Leningrad director Fridrikh Ermler and the cameraman Vladimir Nilsen visited Paris, New York, the Eastman Kodak plant in Rochester, NY, Hollywood (where they were welcomed by Frank Capra, entertained by Rouben Mamoulian and met, *inter alia*, Marlene Dietrich, Gary Cooper, Adolphe Menjou, that later scourge of 'un-American' activities, Cecil B. DeMille, G. W. Pabst and Erich von Stroheim, and watched Charles Laughton filming for *Mutiny on the Bounty)*[70] and London. Ermler and Nilsen then went on to Berlin, where they toured the UFA studios but Shumyatsky, for reasons of prudence, returned directly to Moscow.[71]

The Shumyatsky Commission concluded that 'The entire Soviet cinema is today producing fewer films than one Hollywood studio'.[72] The reason for this was, in their view, quite simple:

> When they make a film our directors are achieving a synthesis of various authors (the dramatist, the composer, the designer, etc.) but they are over-burdened with administrative and organisational functions and this turns them into 'Jacks of all trades' without proper conditions and quali-fications. This situation hinders the creative development of the director and similarly obstructs the development of the other co-authors of the film, subjugating them in administrative terms to the director.[73]

As we have seen, this was the opposite of what Shumyatsky wanted. Drastic measures were called for:

> Setting ourselves the task of producing in the first instance 300 films a year, with a subsequent expansion to 800, we conclude that there is an inescapable need to build a single cinema centre in the southern, and sunniest part of the Soviet Union, near the sea and the mountains.[74]

This project became popularly known as *sovetskii Gollivud* – the 'Soviet Hollywood' – and officially known as *Kinogorod* or 'Cine-City'.[75]

The full details of the 'Soviet Hollywood' are properly the subject for another essay. Suffice it to say here that the Shumyatsky Commission was impressed by the efficiency of Hollywood's production methods and recommended their adoption by and adaptation to Soviet cinema.[76] Above all, they were impressed by the facilities afforded to American film-makers by the climate and location of Hollywood. The decisive factor in favour of the eventual choice for a 'Soviet Hollywood' – the south-western corner of the Crimea – against competition from what we might nowadays describe as the rest of the USSR's 'sunbelt' was that it provided the closest approximation to conditions in the original Hollywood and the surroundings of Los Angeles.[77]

The relatively balmy climate of the Crimea would make location shooting possible throughout the year and liberate Soviet cinema from the rigours of the northern winter, which limited outdoor work to four or five months a year.[78] The location, the wide variety of the surrounding scenery and the opportunity to construct permanent sets that could be used over and over again for different films would obviate the need for costly filming expeditions to remoter parts the Soviet Union and lead to an overall reduction in production costs.[79]

Cine-City was only one part of the Shumyatsky Commission's plan to revitalise Soviet cinema but it was the focal point. While the production from existing studios was to be increased to 120–50 films a year through reorgan-isation, reconstruction and modernisation,[80] the bulk of the expansion in production was to be concentrated in the Crimea. Cine-City was to provide the necessary capacity to produce 200 films a year.[81] Its internal organisation was supposed to adapt the best of American practice and serve as a model for the other smaller studios.

Cine-City was to consist of four studios, each sharing certain common facilities and employing, by December 1940, around 10,000 people.[82] Each of the four studios was to be composed of ten artistic production units (Kh. P. O. or *khudozhestvenno-proizvoidstvennye ob"edineniya*) and each of these units was to comprise five filming groups (*s"emochnye gruppy*). Each unit was to be headed by a producer (or *prodyusser* – even the word was imported from Hollywood), whose function was to relieve the director and his creative workforce of the administrative and organisational burdens that had apparently 'hindered his creative development':[83]

> The producer must know everything that is going on in his filming groups, he must organise them and direct them towards their work, he must free the director from the functions that are not properly his and must render him every possible assistance in realising his creative potential . . . The producer has an enormous responsibility: he must represent the interests of the entire studio.[84]

There is an echo of the artistic production units in the creative units present in Soviet studios today through which veteran directors transmit their experience and expertise to the younger generation. A base for the filming expeditions that Shumyatsky so deprecated was constructed on the Crimean site but the rest of the project for a 'Soviet Hollywood' never progressed beyond the planning stage.

One reason for this was undoubtedly the enormous expense: the plans envisaged that construction costs would reach almost 400 million roubles for the period 1936–40.[85] Another reason was that Shumyatsky, like so many others at the time, was slipping gradually from Stalin's favour and his 'Soviet Hollywood' became an albatross around his neck.[86] Actions spoke louder than words and Shumyatsky had in the final analysis failed to produce the goods or, more precisely in this instance, the films. The production statistics were not refuted:[87]

	Planned	Completed
1935	130	45
1936	165	46
1937	62	24[88]

The financial, technical and political difficulties of Soviet cinema, many of which were beyond Shumyatsky's control, were disregarded, the enormous burden of conversion to sound ignored. All Shumyatsky's exhortations had been in vain, all the rewards for film-makers in the shape of prizes,[89] of fast cars and luxurious dachas on the Hollywood model,[90] had failed to produce their intended results.

A Soviet anecdote relates that at some time in the course of 1937, when he was already under attack in the press, Shumyatsky complained to Stalin that Soviet film-makers would not co-operate with his plans. Stalin is said to have replied, 'But they are the only film-makers we have.[91] Shumyatsky was not, however, the only administrator at Stalin's disposal. He was arrested on 8 January 1938 and denounced in *Pravda* the following day,[92] reviled as a 'captive of the saboteurs' in *Kino* on 11 January[93] and as a 'fascist cur' and a member of the 'Trotskyite-Bukharinite-Rykovite fascist band' in the film monthly *Iskusstvo kino* in February.[94] Sent into internal exile, he was executed on 29 July 1938,[95] his reputation in ruins and his name mentionable in public only as a term of abuse. But 1938 was not a very good year for reputations.

Shumyatsky's replacement, Semyon Dukelsky, was appointed on 23 March 1938[96] but sacked on 4 June 1939.[97] He was in turn replaced by Ivan Bolshakov (of whom Leonid Trauberg has said that 'He had as much connection with cinema as a policeman on point-duty'[98]), who was to survive the war to become the first USSR Minister of Cinematography in March 1946.[99]

Shumyatsky's achievement, even if not realised or fully appreciated in his own curtailed lifetime, was to have laid the foundations for a popular Soviet cinema, one that entertained, amused and attracted audiences as well as providing the agitation and propaganda that the political authorities required. He recognised that film-makers needed a certain freedom to experiment and that they needed protection both from administrative burdens and from outside financial pressures: *pace* Eisenstein, Shumyatsky is remembered now by veteran Soviet film-makers as the man who understood their needs and *let them get on with the job*.[100] He was a complex man in a complex position. But he recognised above all that cinema was a popular art form or it was nothing. A film without an audience was useless, even to the director who made it, and what a socialist film industry had to produce was encapsulated in the title of Shumyatsky's most important book: a 'cinema for the millions'.

NOTES

In these endnotes works cited frequently or by several authors are abbreviated as follows:

Babitsky and Rimberg	P. Babitsky and J. Rimberg, *The Soviet Film Industry* (New York: 1955)
ESW 1	S. M. Eisenstein, *Selected Works*, (ed. and trans. R. Taylor) vol. 1: *Writings, 1922–34* (London and Bloomington, Ind.: 1988)
FF	R. Taylor and I. Christie (eds), *The Film Factory: Russian and Soviet Cinema in Documents, 1896–1939* (London and Cambridge, Mass.: 1988).
Film Form	S. M. Eisenstein, *Film Form: Essays in Film Theory* (ed. and trans. J. Leyda) (New York: 1949)
Ginzburg	S. S. Ginzburg, *Kinematografiya dorevolyutsionnoi Rossii* [The Cinema of Pre-Revolutionary Russia] (Moscow: 1963)
Levaco	R. Levaco (ed. and trans.), *Kuleshov on Film* (Berkeley, Calif.: 1974)

Leyda	J. Leyda, *Kino. A History of the Russian and Soviet Film* (London: 1960)
LVK	*L. V. Kuleshov, Stat'i. Materialy* [L. V. Kuleshov, Articles. Materials] (Moscow: 1979)
Marchand and Weinstein	R. Marchand and P. Weinstein, *L'Art dans la Russie Nouvelle: Le Cinéma* [Art in the New Russia: Cinema] (Paris: 1927)
Pudovkin	V. I. Pudovkin, *Film Technique and Film Acting* (ed. and trans. I. Montagu) (London: 1954)
SKhF	A. V. Macheret *et al.* (eds), *Sovetskie khudozhestvennye fil'my. Annotirovannyi katalog* [Soviet Fiction Films. An Annotated Catalogue] (continuing series, Moscow: 1961 onwards)
Taylor	R. Taylor, *The Politics of the Soviet Cinema 1917–1929* (Cambridge: 1979)
Youngblood	D. J. Youngblood, *Soviet Cinema in the Silent Era, 1918–1935* (Ann Arbor, Mich.: 1985)

1. B. Z. Shumyatskii, 'Tvorcheskie zadachi templana' [The Creative Tasks of the Thematic Plan], *Sovetskoe kino*, no. 12 (December 1933), pp. 1–15.
2. *Bol'shaya sovetskaya entsiklopediya* [The Great Soviet Encyclopaedia] (3rd edn, Moscow: 1970–81), vol. 28, col. 1548.
3. See: *SKhF*, vol. 1, pp. 82–3.
4. *Pravda*, 2 February and 16 February 1926; *Kino-gazeta*, 16 February 1926.
5. *Pravda*, 6 July 1926.
6. A. V. Lunacharskii, 'O kino' [On Cinema], *Komsomol'skaya pravda*, 26 August 1925.
7. Reported in *Zhizn' iskusstva*, 24 January 1928.
8. V. Sutyrin, 'Ot intelligentskikh illyuzii k real'noi deistvitel'nosti' [From Intelligentsia Illusions to Actual Reality], *Proletarskoe kino*, no. 5/6 (May/June 1931), pp. 14–24.
9. E. Lemberg, *Kinopromyshlennost' SSSR* [The Cinema Industry of the USSR] (Moscow: 1930), p. 71.
10. E. Gabrilovich, *O tom, chto proshlo* [About What Happened] (Moscow: 1967), p. 12. See also above ch. 10, n. 8.
11. B. Z. Shumyatskii, *Sovetskii fil'm na mezhdunarodnoi kinovystavke* [Soviet Cinema at the International Cinema Exhibition] (Moscow: 1934) and *Kinematografiy millionov* [A Cinema for the Millions] (Moscow: 1935).
12. Shumyatskii, 'Signal . . ., pp. 6–7.
13. Shumyatskii, *Kinematografiya millionov*, p. 52.
14. ibid., p. 53.
15. L. V. Kuleshov, 'O zadachakh khudozhnika v kinematografe' [The Tasks of the Artist in Cinema], *Vestnik kinematografii*, no. 126 (1917), p. 15; *FF*, pp. 41–2.
16. L. V. Kuleshov, 'Iskusstvo svetotvorchestva'; *FF*, pp. 45–6.
17. Pudovkin, p. 140.
18. Preface to L. V. Kuleshov, *Iskusstvo kino* (Moscow: 1929), p. 4; Levaco, p. 41; *FF*, p. 270.
19. K. Samarin, 'Kino ne teatr' [Cinema Is Not Theatre], *Sovetskoe kino*, no. 2 (February 1927).
20. I. Sokolov, 'Skrizhal' veka' [The Table of the Century], *Kino-Fot*, 25–31 August 1922, p. 3.
21. G. M. Boltyanskii, 'Iskusstvo budushchego' [The Art of the Future], *Kino*, no. 1/2 (1922), p. 7.
22. G. M. Boltyanskii, *Lenini kino* [Lenin and Cinema] (Moscow: 1925), pp. 16–17; *FF*, p. 57.

23. B. Z. Shumyatskii, 'Rezhisser i akter v kino' [The Director and the Actor in Cinema], *Iskusstvo kino*, no. 2 (February 1936), pp. 8–9.
24. B. Z. Shumyatskii, 'Dramaturgiya kino' [The Dramaturgy of Cinema], *Sovets koe kino*, no. 7 (July 1934), p. 4.
25. B. Z. Shumyatskii, 'K chemu obyazyvaet nas yubilei' [What the Anniversary Obliges Us to Do], *Sovetskoe kino*, no. 11/12 (November/December 1934), p. 13.
26. Shumyatskii, 'Tvorcheskie zadachi templana', p. 6.
27. ibid.
28. ibid., p. 7.
29. Shumyatskii, 'Dramaturgiya kino', p. 3.
30. S. M. Eizenshtein, V. I. Pudovkin and G. V. Aleksandrov, 'Zayavka', *Zhizn' iskusstva*, 5 August 1928, pp. 4–5; translated as 'Statement on Sound' in: *FF*, pp. 234–5 and in: *ESW 1*, pp. 113–14.
31. ibid.
32. Shumyatskii, *Sovetskii fil'm*, p. 84.
33. S. M. Eizenshtein, 'Montazh 1938', *Iskusstvo kino*, no. 1 (January 1939), p. 37.
34. Denounced by Mayakovsky among others in a speech during a debate on 'The Paths and Policy of Sovkino' on 15 October 1927; *FF*, pp. 171–4.
35. I. V. Vaisfel'd and G. R. Maslovskii, 'Formirovanie sovetskoi teorii kino' [The Formation of Soviet Film Theory] in: V. V. Vanslov and L. F. Denisova (eds), *Iz istorii sovetskogo iskusstvovedeniya i esteticheskoi mysli 1930kh godov* [The History of Soviet Art History and Aesthetic Thought in the 1930s] (Moscow: 1977), p. 336.
36. Shumyatskii, 'Rezhisser i akter', p. 8.
37. Shumyatskii, 'K chemu . . .', p. 14.
38. Shumyatskii, 'Rezhisser i akter', p. 8.
39. Shumyatskii, *Sovetskii fil'm* . . ., p. 81.
40. B. Z. Shumyatskii, 'O fil'me *Bezhin Lug*' [On the Film *Bezhin Meadow*], *Pravda*, 19 March 1937, p. 3; *FF*, pp. 378–81.
41. ibid.
42. ibid.
43. *Kino*, 22 March 1934, p. 1; 28 March, p. 1; 4 April, pp. 1–2; 10 April, p. 1.
44. Shumyatskii, 'O fil'me . . ., p. 3.
45. See above, n. 14.
46. Shumyatskii, 'Rezhisser i akter'. p. 8.
47. The minutes were published as *Za bol'shoe kinoiskusstvo* [For A Great Cinema Art] (Moscow: 1935).
48. Shumyatskii, *Kinematografiya millionov*, p. 8.
49. ibid., p. 31.
50. B. Z. Shumyatskii, 'Zadachi templana 1934 goda' [The Tasks of the 1934 Thematic Plan], *Sovetskoe kino*, no. 11 (November 1933), p. 1.
51. Shumyatskii, *Kinematografiya millionov*, p. 247.
52. ibid., p. 249.
53. ibid., p. 236.
54. ibid., p. 240.
55. ibid., p. 242.
56. Shumyatskii, 'Tvorcheskie zadachi . . .', p. 11.
57. ibid.
58. *SKhF*, vol. 2, p. 67.
59. Shumyatskii, 'Zadachi templana', p. 2.
60. There is an interesting discussion of this film in I. Grashchenkova, *Abram Room* (Moscow: 1977), pp. 134–75.
61. Shumyatskii. *Kinematografiya millionov*, p. 148.
62. ibid., p. 154.
63. ibid., p. 152.

64. Cited in ibid., p. 7.
65. A. P. Dovzhenko, 'Uchitel' i drug khudozhnika' [The Artist's Teacher and Friend], *Iskusstvo kino*, no. 10 (October 1937), pp. 15–16; *FF*, pp. 383–5.
66. Shumyatskii, *Kinematografiya millionov*, p. 36.
67. ibid., p. 38.
68. ibid., p. 18.
69. Macheret's film *Men and Jobs* [1932] dealt with this theme.
70. Reports in *Kino*, 17 July 1933, p. 1, and 23 July 1933, p. 1.
71. *Doklad komissii B. Z. Shumyatskogo po izucheniyu tekhniki i organizatsii amerikanskoi i evropeiskoi kinematografii* [Report of the Shumyatsky Commission to Examine the Technology and Organisation of American and European Cinema] (Moscow: 1935), pp. 5–6. It was only after 1945 that some three dozen German films from the Nazi period went into Soviet distribution. These included the following anti-British propaganda films: *Der Fuchs von Glenarvon* [The Fox of Glenarvon, 1940; Soviet release title: *Vozmezdie* (Retribution), 1949]; *Das Herz der Königin* [The Heart of the Queen, 1940; Soviet release title: *Doroga na eshafot* (The Path to the Scaffold), 1948]; *Mein Leben für Irland* [My Life for Ireland, 1941; Soviet release title: *Shkola nenavisti* (School for Hatred), 1949]; *Ohm Krüger* [Uncle Kruger, 1941; Soviet release title: *Transvaal' v ogne* (The Transvaal in Flames), 1948]; *Titanic* [1943 but never released in Nazi Germany; Soviet release title: *Gibel' Titanika* (The Sinking of the *Titanic*), 1949]. See: M. Turovskaya (ed.), *Kino totalitarnoi epokhi 1933–1945/Filme der Totalitären Epoche 1933–1945* (Moscow: 1989), pp. 45–6.
72. *Doklad*, p. 148.
73. ibid., p. 57.
74. ibid., p. 150.
75. Rome's *Cine-Città* was also cited with approval: *Yuzhnaya baza sovetskoi kinematografii (Kinogorod)* [The Southern Base for Soviet Cinema (Cine-City)] (Moscow: 1936), p. 18.
76. ibid., p. 16.
77. *Osnovnye polozheniya planovogo zadaniya po yuzhnoi baze sovetskoi kinematografii (Kinogorod)*, [The Basic Propositions of the Planned Project for a Southern Base for Soviet Cinema (Cine-City)] (Moscow: 1936), p. 3.
78. ibid., pp. 9–10.
79. *Yuzhnaya baza*, pp. 20–6.
80. *Osnovnye polozheniya*, p. 11.
81. ibid.
82. ibid., pp. 12, 58.
83. See above, n. 99.
84. B. Z. Shumyatskii, *Sovetskaya kinematografiya segodnya i zavtra* [Soviet Cinema Today and Tomorrow] (Moscow: 1936), p. 50. This is the published text of the report delivered by Shumyatsky to the Seventh All-Union Production and Thematic Conference on 13 December 1935.
85. *Osnovnye polozheniya*, pp. 96–7.
86. As can be seen from the increasing hostility and mockery in newspaper reports appearing throughout 1937 in *Kino* and *Sovetskoe iskusstvo*, e.g.: D. Alekseev, 'Zadachi sovetskogo kino' [The Tasks of Soviet Cinema], *Sovetskoe iskusstvo*, 5 July 1933, p. 3; idem, 'Nemoshchnyi opekun' ['The Powerless Guardian', i.e. Shumyatsky], *Sovetskoe iskusstvo*, 23 July 1937, p. 3; idem, 'Vygodnaya professiya' [A Profitable Profession], *Sovetskoe iskusstvo*, 23 September 1937, p. 5, or the comments made at the First All-Union Congress of the Union of Film Workers at the end of September: see 'Na s"ezde rabotnikov kino' [At the Film Workers' Congress], *Sovetskoe iskusstvo*, 29 September 1937, p. 5. *Kino* was less outspoken, probably because Shumyatsky, as head of the State Directorate for the

Cinema and Photographic Industry (GUKF), still had nominal control over its contents. See the reports of the congress in *Kino*, 17 September 1937, p. 2; 24 September 1937, p. 2; 29 September 1937, pp. 2–3.

87. G. Ermolaev, 'Chto tormozit razvitie sovetskogo kino?' [What Is Holding Up the Development of Soviet Cinema?], *Pravda*, 9 January 1938, p. 4; *FF*, pp. 386–7.

88. To make matters worse, this figure included a number of films carried over from previous years.

89. For details of the prizes awarded in January 1935, see: *Iskusstvo kino*, no. 1 (January 1935).

90. Leonid Trauberg: interview with the author, March 1983.

91. Related to the author by a Soviet cinema historian who wished to remain anonymous, March 1983.

92. *FF*, pp. 386–7.

93. In an editorial entitled 'K novomu pod"emu' [Towards a New Advance], *Kino*, 11 January 1938, p. 1.

94. 'Fashistskaya gadina unichtozhena' [The Fascist Cur Eradicated], *Iskusstvo kino*, no. 2 (February 1938), pp. 5–6; *FF*, pp. 387–9.

95. See above, n. 2. Ironically, his old enemy from the days of the 'proletarian hegemony', Vladimir Kirshon, was shot the previous day. Both have been posthumously rehabilitated but the only biography of Shumyatsky was published in Siberia: B. Bagaev, *Boris Shumyatskii. Ocherk zhizni i deyatel'nosti* [Boris Shumyatsky. A Sketch of His life and Activity] (Krasnoyarsk: 1974).

96. V. E. Vishnevskii and P. V. Fionov, *Sovetskoe kino v datakh i faktakh* [Soviet Cinema in Dates and Facts] (Moscow: 1973), p. 116.

97. ibid., p. 123.

98. Interview with the author, April 1985.

99. Vishnevskii and Fionov, p. 170.

100. Leonid Trauberg, one of the directors closest to Shumyatsky, and Yuli Raizman in separate interviews with the author, March 1985.

11

THE COMMON PEOPLE, HISTORICAL
DRAMA AND PREPARATIONS FOR WAR

It was not only the film industries associated with totalitarian governments that turned to historical subject matter in the 1930s, and nor was the concern with the common people simply a feature of socialist filmmaking. On the contrary, these preoccupations were also evident in the United States, the United Kingdom and France in the late 1930s as they responded to both the Depression and the growing threat of fascism.

Although the Depression did not really come to an end until the United States entered the war in 1941, the film industry fared better after 1935. Most of the studios had suffered economically during the early 1930s but, by the mid-1930s, they had restructured themselves in response. Also, economic confidence was improving and consumer spending on leisure activities such as cinemagoing was on the increase. The Depression, though, was still a significant issue and Hollywood responded in two apparently contradictory ways. On the one hand, the pressing social problems required that Hollywood display a sense of social responsibility and produce films that tackled the harsh realities of the period. On the other, Hollywood also claimed to offer the exact opposite: a pleasurable escape from these harsh realities.

These apparently contradictory tendencies were rarely as opposed as one might expect. For example, Preston Sturges' comedy *Sullivan's Travels* (1941) was made at the end of the 1930s and offers a magnificently clever commentary on the period. In the film, a college-educated director plans to make a powerful commentary on the Depression in his film, *Oh Brother, Where Art Thou?* The studios want him to continue to make the light musical comedies with which he has made his name and fortune. They therefore try to convince him that, as a product of an affluent background, he doesn't 'know about trouble' and, in response, he sets out to learn about the lives of ordinary people. In the process, he discovers that many people's lives are so hard that entertainment is all that keeps them going and offers them hope. In this way, the film tackles social problems seriously while gently satirising over-earnest realism, and it celebrates entertainment while presenting it as having a vital social purpose.

Like many other films, *Sullivan's Travels* also displays a faith in New Deal reformism and a concern with the plight of the common people. It is for this reason that, looking back on the period during the 1940s and 1950s, many intellectuals argued that Hollywood films shared the same totalitarian impulses as the Stalinist Soviet Union and Nazi Germany. For intellectuals, these cinemas addressed people as masses and called for people to identify with the 'common man', an abstraction that did not address people in their individuality but through identification with that which is common to all and particular to no one.

Such a position was more complex than many of these intellectuals acknowledged. First, the 'common people' are not just seen as people in general but rather a specific section of the population. In other words, as in Soviet cinema, many of these films suggested that it was precisely the working classes that constituted the 'common people' rather than the wealthy élite. In some cases, this seemed to amount to little more than a positive affirmation of these groups, which encouraged them to accept their lot in life. In *The Wizard of Oz* (1939), for example, a young girl, Dorothy, dreams of escaping from her humdrum existence on a small Kansas farm but eventually learns that everything she ever dreamed of was already there in her own backyard. However, many depictions of the common people showed them as representing specific social values such as honesty, warmth and social community, and portrayed the wealthy as decadent and in need of reform. In these films, it is suggested that the Depression was the result of the decadence and irresponsibility of the rich and that the solution to social problems would be their re-education through contact with the common people.

This tradition is often associated with the work of Frank Capra and it can be seen in his Oscar-winning romantic comedy *It Happened One Night* (1934). The film concerns a wealthy and spoiled heiress who runs away from her family and, on her travels, meets a tough journalist. As the two travel the country, she is transformed through her contact with the common people and she falls in love with the journalist. *It Happened One Night* is also an early instance of one of the key genres of the period, the screwball comedy, and many of these films concern a similar process of transformation. In *Our Man Godfrey* (1936), a wealthy socialite learns her social responsibility for the poor and eventually uses her wealth to help solve the problems of the Depression. Similarly, in *Holiday* (1938), a decadent and eccentric family encounters a young man from a very different class background who offers them the possibility of transformation and redemption.

This concern with exchange and transformation is also central to the screwball comedy in other ways. The screwball comedy was a product of developments in scripting that followed the introduction of sound and, in these films, the set pieces are fabulous displays of verbal pyrotechnics in which characters spar with one another. Furthermore, these films were almost invariably romantic comedies in which the pyrotechnic verbal exchanges were usually the product of sexual tension between the male and female leads. However, the interplay of dialogue also suggests something else about these romantic relationships. For the verbal sparring to work, the man and the woman need to have a fairly equal status in which each can give as good as they get. As a result, the films often involve strongly independent women, and it has even been argued that if anyone is beaten down in these struggles, it is the male character. In *Bringing Up Baby* (1938), for example, the lead male is an awkward and introverted academic who is liberated by a freewheeling female to whom he eventually surrenders – but only after she has destroyed almost every aspect of his previously repressed existence.

Hollywood was not only concerned with the Depression but also the growing threat of fascism in Europe. After the First World War, the United States had become a largely isolationist country which refused to be drawn into international politics and was concerned to focus on its own interests. From the mid-1930s onwards, though, elements of the New Deal administration and the Hollywood film industry recognised that the United States might be forced to take sides in Europe and began subtly preparing the country to fight fascism. Although Chaplin faced considerable opposition to his overt satire of Nazism, *The Great Dictator* (1940), his problem was that the film industry was still trading with Germany and did not want directly to antagonise the Nazis. As a result, the preparations for war took place at a far more covert level and, during this period, the studios made a series of historical dramas that celebrated the British past and so created a sense of identification with Britain. For example, in *Captain Blood* (1935), a swashbuckler starring Errol Flynn, Dr Peter Blood is condemned to slavery by a tyrannical British king. He eventually escapes with other slaves, who form a gang of pirates and make him their leader. Eventually, he learns that the tyrant has been deposed and that a democratic king has come to the throne, and he and his men come to the aid of the state. As a reward, he is eventually made the governor of the island on which he had previously been a slave.

Although a rousing pirate story, the film also works to transform Britain from aristocratic despotism, from which the United States had fought for independence, into a democratic country that mirrors the United States itself. A similar story process takes place in *The Adventures of Robin Hood* (1938), again with Flynn, where Robin is a rebel against aristocratic tyranny. In this film, the tyrants have not only usurped power from the legitimate king but are also foreign invaders. While Robin Hood and his merry men are Saxons, Prince John and Sir Guy of Gisbourne are Norman invaders from the Continent.

These processes can also be seen in *Gone with the Wind* (1939), a lavish historical epic about the events surrounding the American Civil War, which was to become one of the biggest hits of all time. Although an epic of American history, the heroine was played by an English actress, Vivien Leigh, who was discovered in *Fires over England* (1937), a British historical film about the Spanish Armada that was itself an attempt to prepare Britain for a war with Europe. Nor was this casting incidental. It was the result of a highly publicised two-year search to find a star fit to play Scarlett O'Hara. Furthermore, the film itself concerns Scarlett's own journey as she is transformed by the destruction of the South and the privations of the American Civil War from a self-centred and naïve young girl into a powerful and determined woman. This was a subtext that did not go unnoticed in Britain during the war where the film was a sensation and its story of a way of life spectacularly destroyed by invading armies proved highly resonant.

Outside the Hollywood studios, film production was also concerned with the plight of the common people and there was a notable decline in avant-garde filmmaking around the world as interest shifted to the documentary as a practice. Even Luis Buñuel turned his hand to documentary filmmaking with *Land without Bread* (1933), a film about an impoverished region of Spain. In the United States, the Film and Photo League was established, which used cheap silent cameras to film and distribute forms of political resistance such as demonstrations and strikes. In this way, the league used the working class very differently from the Hollywood studios, of which it was highly critical; and it was largely made up of left-wing activists and figures from the avant-garde such as Paul Strand and Ralph Steiner. In 1935, the organisation was largely replaced by Nykino, which also depicted working-class resistance in films such as *Native Land* (1942), which restaged actual incidents of political confrontation.

Other documentary filmmakers turned to government support, like their counterparts in Great Britain. For example, Pare Lorentz managed to secure funding from the New Deal administration for a documentary on the dustbowl, *The Plow that Broke the Plains* (1936), and followed this success with another documentary on environmental issues, *The River* (1938), which examined the plight of the Mississippi valley. Both these films have become classics and utilised the talents of a range of figures such as Paul Strand, Ralph Steiner and Willard Van Dyke.

In Britain, there was less distance between the popular cinema of historical dramas and low musicals and comedies on the one hand, and the realist films influenced by the documentary movement on the other. Britain also differed from Hollywood in another key respect. During the early 1930s, production was largely bolstered by the 'quota quickies', a result of government regulations that required companies distributing Hollywood films in Britain to make a number of films there. Although these films were often cheap, short and despised by critics, they did provide a foundation for film production, which remained relatively healthy, even during the early 1930s when the Hollywood studios were struggling. It was only when the law was due for renewal in the late 1930s that the industry went into a period of economic uncertainty and instability.

During this period, the British film industry was dominated by two vertically integrated firms that were organised much like Hollywood studios: Gaumont-British and British International Pictures. In addition to these was a series of smaller companies such as Associated Talking Pictures run by Basil Dean, British and Dominion run by Herbert Wilcox, Gainsborough run by Michael Balcon (see Chapter 7), and London Associated Pictures run by Hungarian émigré Alexander Korda.

Although small, Korda's operation was highly significant and it produced several major historical epics of which the first was *The Private Life of Henry VIII* (1933). The film was a spectacular but restrained historical drama that sought to play Hollywood at its own game, and it was a great success in both Britain and the United States and won an Oscar for Charles Laughton. Unfortunately, Korda never enjoyed the same success with later projects although he did make a number of important historical spectaculars including *The Scarlet Pimpernel* (1934), in which a foppish eighteenth-century British aristocrat is really a dashing and brilliant adventurer fighting against European totalitarianism. In this case, revolutionary France was a clear metaphor for Nazi Germany and its star, Leslie Howard, was clearly associated with anti-Nazi propaganda. He would play the inventor of the spitfire in *The First of the Few* (1942); he narrated many key propagandist documentaries; and even mysteriously disappeared during the war, reputedly while working as a spy for the British government.

Another Korda classic is *The Four Feathers* (1939). The story concerns a young British soldier who is accused of cowardice by his friends and his fiancée, each of whom gives him a symbolic white feather. To prove his bravery, he experiences extreme suffering in order to return each feather to the person who gave it to him. The film is a stirring adventure that celebrates the qualities that supposedly made Britain superior to the rest of the world and enabled it to build its empire. It also demonstrates that vicious racism was not solely in the preserve of totalitarian countries or their cinemas.

In addition to these historical epics, the period also produced a number of significant thrillers such as Hitchcock's *The Man who Knew Too Much* (1934), *The 39 Steps* (1935) and *The Lady Vanishes* (1938). *The 39 Steps* is a simple thriller, in which a hero finds himself hunted by both the police and a secret network of spies, but it provides a wonderful blend of romance, comedy and suspense that involves an evil plot by an unnamed European power to incapacitate the British military. While *The 39 Steps* only hints at the identity of the European power, the identity of the enemy is made quite clear in *The Lady Vanishes*. In this film, a trainload of mostly British passengers join forces to foil a Nazi plot to stop a British spy from delivering vital information to the British government. Again, the film was distinguished by a light comic tone that provided a counterpoint to its darker and more suspenseful materials.

While these films were popular, the majority of British viewers claimed to dislike British films during the period. Many of these viewers were working or lower middle class, and were profoundly alienated by the middle- and upper-class characters of many British films of the time. Instead, they claimed to prefer Hollywood films that were perceived as more democratic, glamorous and ironically 'realistic'. Nonetheless, the biggest stars of the time were associated with British working-class culture. Gracie Fields appeared in a number of musicals about working-class life in which the problems of the Depression are overcome by energy, enthusiasm and pulling together. Indeed, she has been seen as embodying the values of consensus in the period, in which the solution to social problems was not class conflict but required both the working classes and industrialists to work together for the good of all.

The other major star of the period was George Formby, a well-meaning, ukulele-playing simpleton who would get into all manner of comic trouble before finally winning the girl and saving the day. He was therefore meant to represent all the virtues of working-class kindness, warmth and honesty and was often pitted against petty bureaucrats and snobbish sophisticates. Despite their centrality to British cinema during the period, these stars and their films are often marginal to, or absent from, histories of world cinema and the reason for this is that, like many popular traditions, they were not made for the international market and were rarely seen by anyone but the domestic audience. However, their relation to their domestic audience is central to these films, which were distinguished by their regional characters and by their links to popular traditions such as the music hall.

In contrast to these working-class heroes, the films influenced by the documentary movement and leftist filmmaking may have been more radical but they were much less popular with working-class audiences. Carol Reed's *The Stars Look Down* (1939), for example, not only advocated the nationalisation of coal mines but also used location filmmaking to lend a sense of authenticity to its account of coal-mining communities. While these films may have frequently spoken *about* the working class rather than *to* the working class, they cannot simply be dismissed as products of the establishment. Despite the fact that they examined the working class from a specifically middle-class perspective, the realism of these films was threatening to other sections of the middle classes. For example, the British Board of Film Censors refused to permit the filming of Walter Greenwood's *Love on the Dole* until 1940 on the grounds of its sexual and political content: one character, Sally, turns to prostitution and working-class demonstrators violently clash with the police. When it was finally made it was only on the basis of changed conditions: the war was presented as a struggle for a new postwar era in which the problems of the 1930s that were depicted in the film would never be allowed to happen again.

French cinema in the 1930s was also fascinated with working-class life but shared little of the optimism found in Britain and the United States. If the common people were a repository of positive values in the United States, and

British depictions of the working class were motivated by a desire for social reform, depictions of working-class life in 1930s France were usually fatalistic. The film industry in France was crisis ridden during the early 1930s and made up of a series of small, weak studios. However, after 1935, audiences grew and, while the vast majority of films watched by British audiences were from the United States, in France, domestic productions accounted for nearly half of the market.

Like Britain, France had its own empire films and low comedies, neither of which were made with an eye on the international market. For example, the *comique troupier* drew on popular entertainment traditions that went back to vaudeville in the 1880s, and it featured pranks played on the middle ranking military officers by their subordinates. Over forty of these films were made during the 1930s, many of them starring Fernandel, and like the films of George Formby in Britain, they displayed popular resistance to their immediate superiors but rarely challenged those in authority higher up the class hierarchy.

As a result, the use of working-class characters does not necessarily imply a socialist perspective and while French filmmakers in the 1930s displayed an interest in the working class, the political implications of this trend are far from clear. Despite their concern with the working class, the films of the period rarely concern political activism. If the working classes came to signify 'Frenchness' for a brief time, it remained a highly sentimentalised projection of middle-class imaginations that sought to associate them with tradition rather than modernity. Nonetheless, the films often depict local communities resisting external officials such as police officers who are clearly seen as alien intruders. In Julien Duvivier's *Pepe Le Moko* (1936), Pepe is a criminal who has escaped from Paris and is living in the Casbah of Algiers. Here, he is virtually immune from the police who operate in the modernised colonial city that contains but cannot control the popular world of the Casbah.

At the opening, Pepe is cynical but getting by. He does not expect too much from life and has accommodated himself to it. However, during a raid by the police, he is forced to hide out with a beautiful Parisian socialite, Gaby, with whom he falls in love. She also awakens his memories of Paris and provokes homesickness in him. Finally, in a hopeless and desperate gesture, he leaves the Casbah to return to Paris with her and, having made himself vulnerable, he is captured by the police. He asks for a moment to watch Gaby sail off towards France and, while doing so, he takes his own life.

Le Jour se lève (1939) follows a very similar pattern but is framed by a brilliantly claustrophobic narrative device. If Pepe is trapped in the Casbah, the hero of *Le Jour se lève* spends the film trapped in his apartment for a night, where he is virtually unable to move without being shot by police snipers. From within the predicament, a series of flashbacks is used to establish the circumstances that led up to this situation. Again, the lead character lives a safe working-class life until he falls in love. Although he hopes for perfect communion with the woman he loves, the affair isolates him from the community that had previously supported him and which can do nothing but watch the siege of his apartment from behind the police barricades. Like Pepe, François also commits suicide at the end of the film, and it is clear that both men are isolated and destroyed by their disastrous relationships with women. As many have demonstrated, the working-class worlds of these films are worlds of male homosocial bonding that are disrupted by woman who are as much alien intruders as the police, and possibly more destructive.

The fatalism of these films is not always so absolute. In Jean Renoir's *La Grande Illusion* (1937), the action centres on a prisoner-of-war camp during the First World War, when a French and a German officer develop a doomed relationship. Eventually, the German officer is forced to kill his friend, a death that is symbolic of the demise of their aristocratic class. However, this death also enables another pair of friends to escape, one of whom is working class and one of whom is a middle-class Jew. Although there are also tensions in this relationship, the two men are ultimately able to work together to achieve freedom. In the process, the film presents a celebration of republicanism and calls for the working and middle classes to forge an alliance against the authority of the aristocratic classes.

One of the problems with doing historical research is that the materials to which one might need to gain access are not always available. One might not have the time or money to travel to where these materials are located, or they might not even be available for scrutiny in the first place. This is the problem that faced Tino Balio when he sought to account for 'Columbia's transformation from a poverty row company to a major player within the film industry' in 'Columbia Pictures: The Making of a Motion Picture Major, 1930–1943'. In the extract, he seeks to understand Columbia as an economic organisation and, as such, he provides a business history that does not concern itself with the history of film texts, styles or movements, but rather with the changing economic strategies of a specific film company. Film has not only been important as an aesthetic form but also as a powerful economic industry, and many historical researchers have shown that it is necessary that we understand the strategies and organisational principles through which companies within the industry have sought to maintain or improve their position. Indeed, although many accounts give the impression that the studio system was a large unchanging structure for much of its history, it was actually composed of a series of highly complex companies, each of which was constantly responding both to competition from one another and to changing conditions within the economy as a whole.

Research projects such as Balio's show that while films may have specific meanings for critics and audiences, films also have meanings for the companies who develop them. Some films are made to provide exhibitors with regular pro-gramming; others are made to earn the studio prestige. However, as Balio demonstrates, even in the 1930s, before the era of the blockbuster, specific films proved financially decisive in the making or breaking of a company.

Understanding the film industry can therefore help explain how and why specific films are put together in certain ways, and even why specific projects are conceived of in the first place. Balio did not have access to Columbia's records and he therefore had to turn to other sources: 'the trade press, movie reviews and the occasional piece in business magazines'. The trade press comprises those publications such as *Variety* in the United States that provide news and commentary upon the industry for those working within the industry itself.

- Can you distinguish between the primary and secondary sources that Balio uses in his business history of Columbia Pictures?
- What strategies does Balio suggest were crucial in Columbia's rise to power?
- How might the trade press and its functions require us to be cautious when using it to create a business history?

COLUMBIA PICTURES: THE MAKING OF A MOTION PICTURE MAJOR, 1930–1943

Tino Balio

Starting out in Poverty Row, Columbia Pictures survived the battle for the theaters, the conversion to sound, and the Great Depression to emerge as a full-fledged member of the Hollywood establishment by 1934. In that year, giant film companies such as Paramount, Fox, and RKO had been dragged down by their theater chains into receivership or bankruptcy, but little Columbia won the respect of Wall Street by earning over $1 million in profits. In 1934, Columbia also won accolades from the critics by releasing two surprise hits, Victor Schertzinger's *One Night of Love*, a modern-dress operetta starring soprano Grace Moore, and Frank Capra's *It Happened One Night*, a screwball comedy starring Claudette Colbert and Clark Gable. *It Happened One Night* had the distinction of sweeping the top five Academy Awards – an achievement that has occurred only one other time in the history of the Oscars.[1]

The economic arena Columbia operated in was a virtual oligopoly dominated by the so-called Big Five – Loew's Inc. (MGM), Paramount Pictures, Warner Bros., Twentieth Century-Fox, and RKO. These companies were fully integrated – that is, they produced practically all the top-quality pictures, operated worldwide distribution networks, and owned large affiliated theater chains. Columbia, Universal Pictures, and United Artists were the Little Three. Columbia and Universal produced and distributed mostly low-budget pictures that played on the bottom half of double bills; United Artists functioned solely

Tino Balio (ed. David Bordwell and Noël Carroll), *Post-Theory: Reconstructing Film Studios* (Madison: University of Wisconsin Press, 1996).

as a distributor for a small group of élite independent producers. These eight companies constituted the majors.

Although Columbia's role in the business during the studio system era is well established, the company's entrée into the Hollywood establishment has never been fully explored.[2] A definitive account of Columbia's escape from Poverty Row must wait until the studio opens its corporate records to researchers, but even without the benefit of primary sources much can be inferred about Columbia's development from articles in the trade press, movie reviews, and the occasional piece in business magazines. Using these sources, I have isolated the goals that Columbia met in becoming a major motion-picture company, which were: volume production, national distribution, first-run exhibition, a roster of one or two stars, and a few hits.

These goals were consonant with the business practices of the American film industry as it entered the era of big business in the twenties.[3] And as Columbia's entrée into the majors will demonstrate, these goals were mutually dependent. In practice, they had to be targeted pretty much in succession. As a result, this case study has certain implications for understanding the history of the film industry. First, the major studios had no preordained right to succeed. Each company had to acquire the pragmatic skills to carve a niche for itself in the market, to stabilize its operations, and to generate profits. Second, production had to be tailored first and foremost to the paying public. Producing films to suit the personal tastes of studio moguls, boards of directors, or financiers would have ruined a company. Third, the market presented companies with an array of options. All motion-picture companies had the goal of profit maximization, but they chose different means to achieve that end.

[. . .]

Poverty Row Beginnings

Columbia Pictures got its start as CBC Film Sales Company, which was founded by Jack Cohn, Joe Brandt, and Harry Cohn in 1919 to produce and market novelty shorts.[4] Jack Cohn and Joe Brandt handled sales and managed the business affairs of the company in New York, while Harry Cohn handled the production end in Hollywood where he operated out of a rented studio in Poverty Row. The American film industry had entered the era of big business during the twenties and CBC had to expand or perish. Gradually branching out into Westerns, comedies, and even a few inexpensive features, CBC signaled its growing aspirations by incorporating as Columbia Pictures on January 10, 1924.[5] The immediate objective was to take control of its own distribution. Severing its ties to states'-rights operators, Columbia acquired its first exchange in 1925; by 1929 it had established a national distribution network and by 1931 it had branched out into foreign markets. Meanwhile, Columbia shored up its feature film production by purchasing a small studio on Gower Street in Hollywood in 1926 and by signing new directors, most notably Frank Capra, soon after.

Despite such moves, Columbia found itself in a bind. The quality of its features was not good enough to secure regular bookings in the affiliated theater chains, and the quantity of its output could not meet the needs of smaller independent theaters. That Columbia overcame these barriers to entry was largely the handiwork of Harry Cohn. Columbia underwent a management shakeup in 1931 when Jack Cohn and Joe Brandt attempted to oust Harry Cohn from the company. The details of the attempted coup are unclear, but when Columbia financier A. H. Giannini of the Bank of America threw his support to Harry Cohn, Brandt retired from the company and sold his interest to Harry Cohn. Harry Cohn took over the presidency of the company while retaining his job as chief of production, which made him the only executive in the business to hold the two posts; Jack Cohn moved up to executive vice-president in charge of distribution and remained in New York. Harry and Jack Cohn retained most of the equity and voting stock in the company and operated Columbia as a family-run business throughout the studio system era.[6]

Reorganizing Production

Columbia, with its limited financial resources, could not compete with the Big Five in important first-run situations, but it could hope to tap the low end of the market by servicing unaffiliated theaters that changed bills up to three times a week. In contrast, United Artists targeted the high end of the market by distributing high-quality independent productions. During the thirties, UA released the films of Charles Chaplin, Samuel Goldwyn, Alexander Korda, Howard Hughes, and Twentieth Century Pictures, a production company operated by Joseph Schenck and Darryl Zanuck. All specialized in 'prestige pictures,' although not exclusively. Prestige pictures, by far the most popular production trend of the decade, did not constitute a genre. The term implied production values and treatment – a big-budget special based on a presold property, often as not a literary 'classic,' and tailored for top stars.[7] For Goldwyn, prestige meant adaptations of Pulitzer Prize winners (*Street Scene* [1931]) or novels written by Nobel laureates (*Arrowsmith* [1932]); for Korda, it meant historical biopics (*The Private Life of Henry VIII* [1933] and *Catherine the Great* [1934]); for Howard Hughes, it meant spectacular action films (*Hell's Angels* [1930]). United Artists released relatively few pictures each year, from fifteen to twenty, but the pictures earned the company a reputation as the Tiffany's of the industry.

To service the low end of the market, Columbia continued its policy of marketing shorts and Westerns. Columbia's roster of shorts was immense and consisted of Walt Disney's Mickey Mouse cartoons and Silly Symphonies, Krazy Cat cartoons, Eddie Buzzell's Bedtime Stories, Scrappy cartoons, Screen Snapshots, and Sunrise Comedies, among others; its roster of Westerns included the Buck Jones and Tim McCoy series. Since the demand for these types of pictures was seemingly limitless, they provided a stable financial base for the company.

On this base, Columbia expanded feature film production. Harry Cohn modified studio operations in 1931 by converting from the central producer system to the producer-unit system and by delegating the day-to-day details of production to a group of associate producers.[8] Columbia released around thirty features a year from 1930 to 1934, when output rose to forty-three. The cause of this jump is not known exactly, but double features no doubt played a role.

Showing two pictures for the price of one was an old business practice. The shortage of talking pictures during the conversion to sound and the higher rentals they commanded stemmed the practice for a while, but the Depression gave double-featuring a boost. Independent theaters adopted the practice to break down the barriers of booking protection, which is to say, excessive clearances enjoyed by first-run theaters. Indies reasoned that if they could not present hit pictures in a timely manner to their patrons, they would offer quantity instead. Although the affiliated theater chains initially fought the practice, they too soon fell into line and by 1934, nearly every theater in competitive situations – the markets that generated the bulk of the box-office gross – showed double features. Double features essentially doubled the demand for product. Since the production facilities and talent of the Big Five limited the number of pictures they could produce, a gap existed that was soon filled by Columbia, Universal, and Poverty Row studios.

Surveying Columbia's releases from 1930 to 1934 reveals that the studio specialized in low-budget pictures having ordinary contemporary settings. Of the more than 150 features produced in this period, approximately 50 were dramas, 20 were crime/gangster pictures, 18 were mysteries, 10 were comedies, 9 were women's films, and 8 were action/adventures. In addition, the studio produced 15 Buck Jones and 7 Tim McCoy series Westerns. It is significant that the studio's roster included only 3 musicals and 2 horror films – genres that are expensive to produce because of their technical demands and special effects.

In its quest for profits, Columbia's policy was to produce economy models of class-A pictures. This meant following trends closely and relying heavily on remakes. Concerning the quality of a typical Columbia release, *Variety* had this to say: 'Nothing new in a familiar story' (*Fugitive Lady* [1934]); 'Makes no pretense of being above the split-week grade' (*The Sky Raiders* [1931]); and 'Just a western with airplanes instead of horses' (*Air Hostess* [1933]). Concerning Columbia's cost-cutting techniques, *Variety* said of *Murder on the Roof* (1930): 'The obvious inexpensive manner in which Columbia produced this all-talker won't be noticed by lay audiences. When a producing company can turn one out like this on this kind of dough, that company is bound to make money with it. So are the theatres playing it – certain theatres.' Occasionally, a Columbia picture generated special appeal. *Variety* described *By Whose Hand?* (1932) as follows: 'This Columbia [picture] is the answer to the grind house exhib's prayer. It is a vigorous melodrama, loaded with climaxes and speed, trimly played and expertly produced for the lesser grade house.'[9] Occasionally, pictures like *By Whose Hand?* might qualify as programmers, which meant they could fill either the top or bottom half of a bill, depending on the genre, location of the theater, and audience.[10]

Expanding Distribution

Expanding feature film production required an efficient distribution system, since the two areas were interdependent. Branching out into distribution after incorporating had been expensive, but Columbia no longer had to pay commissions to states'-rights exchanges. A national distribution system also meant that Columbia could coordinate domestic release patterns, control advertising and publicity at every level of die market, and set prices for its pictures – requirements if the company ever expected to release class-A pictures.

Columbia's B production operated on tight margins and it was crucial for the company to wring every possible dollar in film rentals from the market. Columbia's B features cost from $50,000 to $100,000 to produce; in contrast, the majors spent as much as $300,000 on B films and Poverty Row as little as $10,000. Regardless of cost, Columbia's routine films were sold in blocks on a flat-fee basis following industry custom.

Although block booking had been harshly attacked by federal agencies, independent theaters, and citizen's groups, the trade practice persisted throughout the thirties as a form of wholesaling which permitted studios to peddle their entire season's output to exhibitors on an all-or-nothing basis. Block booking offered distributors several advantages, among them the scale economies of selling in bulk and the guarantee that every picture released by the company would find a market regardless of quality.[11] Unlike percentage terms used for class-A pictures, flat fees prevented a distributor from capturing the extraordinary profits of an unexpected hit; on the other hand, flat fees had the advantage of generating predictable returns, so that if a studio kept costs within limits, its pictures could earn a profit. Since Harry Cohn was a notorious penny-pincher, we can assume that Columbia's conservative spending habits and its control over distribution helped secure a steady flow of financing from its principal backer, the Bank of America.

[. . .]

Strengthening Exhibition

Having acquired a studio and exchanges, Columbia's next objective was to gain access to first-run theaters. Unlike the Big Five companies, which were completely integrated, the Little Three did not own theater chains. (Universal owned a small chain for a while but was forced to sell it during the Depression.) An analysis of Columbia Pictures by *Barron's* magazine, a national financial weekly, noted that the studio's financial health in 1935 resulted partly from its steadfast refusal to own theaters.[12] The magazine made this observation during the depths of the Depression when Paramount, Fox, and RKO seemed hopelessly mired in red ink as a result of their investments in real estate. With the return of prosperity, however, the assessment of *Barron's* would no longer be valid. Ownership of theaters, first-run houses in particular, would become the tool that enabled the Big Five to maintain control of the market. Columbia, Universal, and United Artists remained in a subservient position vis-à-vis the Big Five precisely because they did not own important theater chains.

Columbia released its pictures primarily to two types of theaters. Most were subsequent-run houses, typically small independent operations; less numerous were first-run houses, typically affiliates of the majors. Since the studio had meager financial resources, it could only occasionally produce a contender and only then did the studio want access to first-run houses. (As I will discuss later, Columbia would be relegated to subsequent-run venues until it had big-name stars on its roster.) First-run playing time meant longer runs – usually a week – in large, prestigious theaters and the opportunity of renting a picture on a percentage-of-the-gross basis. Thus if a release struck the public's fancy, the studio could enjoy a substantial share of the box-office take.

United Artists had gained access to first-run houses not only because it handled quality pictures, but also because the company had indirectly gone into exhibition. Alarmed by the battle for theaters, UA's owners, with the exception of Chaplin, invested $1 million to form United Artists Theatre Circuit in 1926. With an additional $4 million from a public stock issue, the Theatre Circuit constructed and/or purchased first-run theaters in key cities. What linked United Artists to United Artists Theatre Circuit was a ten-year franchise that granted the theater chain the preferential right to exhibit UA's pictures. The maneuver worked, with the result that affiliated theater chains recognised United Artists as a forceful competitor and booked its pictures.

How did Columbia gain access to first-run theaters? Reviews in *Variety* reveal that Columbia signed a franchise agreement with RKO in 1930 granting the theater chain first call on Columbia's releases. Unlike the other members of the Big Five, RKO was a relative newcomer to the business. Founded by RCA in 1928 to complete head on with AT&T in the sound recording and playback field, RKO merged Joseph P. Kennedy's Film Booking Office, the Keith-Albee-Orpheum circuit of vaudeville houses, and RCA's Photophone sound system into a vertically integrated firm containing three hundred theaters, four studios, and $80 million in working capital.

Despite RKO's impressive pedigree, the company faced the same challenges breaking into the market that Columbia did, plus one more – choice attractions to fill the playing time of its theaters. Since the Big Five had their own interests to protect, RKO turned to independent producers and the Little Three for help. The terms of RKO's franchise agreement with Columbia are not known, but if they are similar to the terms of RKO's franchise agreements with United Artists, the deal probably went something like this. RKO agreed to exhibit a specific number of better-quality pictures each year in selected theaters and to pay a film rental for each engagement based on the production cost of the picture and on the overhead expense of the respective theater.[13] In practice,

RKO made a down payment based on a sliding scale that measured the relative production cost of the picture (the higher the production cost, the higher the down payment) and then split the box-office gross fifty-fifty after deducting the overhead expenses of the theater. These terms constituted a variation of the percentage of the gross form of rental and enabled Columbia to receive remuneration in relation to the box-office performance of its pictures.

The RKO franchise agreement may have been a turning point for Columbia. It provided both an incentive to produce higher quality pictures and a venue for their exhibition. If this assumption holds good, having a Frank Capra on the lot gains significance. A talented director, a star or two, and a few acceptable literary properties provided the leverage to lift Columbia into the majors.

After joining the studio in 1927, Capra quickly earned Harry Cohn's confidence and was awarded the task of handling the studio's occasional class-A picture. Capra responded by directing a series of inexpensive but well-received comedies. Going into the thirties, Capra's stature as a director grew with each successive release. By the time he made *American Madness* in 1932, critics were referring to him as 'one of Hollywood's best.'[14] Capra's *The Bitter Tea of General Yen* (1932) was chosen as the first feature presentation of RKO's new Radio City Music Hall in New York. After *It Happened One Night* swept the Academy Awards in 1934, Capra literally became a star and received top billing in Columbia's ads. Beginning with *The Bitter Tea of General Yen*, all the pictures Capra made for Columbia received a Music Hall send-off. Since his pictures received royal handling in New York, we can assume that a similar treatment awaited them in first-run situations around the country.

The fate of Columbia's other class-A products in this period is more difficult to assess. What is clear, however, is that simply having one Frank Capra was not enough to maintain Columbia's status as a member of the Little three. All of Columbia's competitors relied not only upon masterful directors but also upon stars. Star vehicles typically enjoyed a ready-made market, reduced the risk of production financing, and commanded the best rental terms.[15] Could a substitute be found for stars in the making of class-A pictures?

[. . .]

Acquiring Stars

Columbia therefore had no choice but to adopt the star system if it wanted to produce class-A pictures. Commenting on Columbia's star power in the period from 1930 to 1934, *Barron's* said, 'Another factor in [Columbia's] success has been the avoidance of onerous long-term contracts with stars, the long-term appeal of which is bound to be uncertain. It has followed a policy of signing artists and directors for a few pictures a year or of borrowing actors and actresses from other companies, a program that makes for economy and flexibility of production cost.'[16] This assessment needs qualification; Columbia would have been fortunate indeed to have had real stars under long-term contract. Because

Barron's assessment was likely based in part on interviews with company executives, it has the ring of a rationalization for the studio's lackluster roster.

Concerning star development, a studio had three options: (1) It could develop stars by casting players in different roles and testing audience reaction; (2) it could borrow stars from other studios; or (3) it could pretend it had stars and hope that exhibitors and the public would play along. The first option obviously consumed the most time and money; the second was feasible only for studios that had already achieved major status; the third required the most chutzpah.

During the early thirties, Columbia had the chutzpah to 'star' veteran actor Jack Holt in over a dozen pictures. A typical Holt picture was an action story containing 'love interest, melodramatics, outdoors and he-man stuff,' said *Variety*. In its review of *The Woman I Stole* (1933), *Variety* said, 'Jack Holt has been making pictures like this for years and has prospered. There's nothing especially distinguished in the output, but it is all eminently saleable material. Factory product, but factory product of a successful kind, with a ready market and satisfactory returns.'[17] Columbia's supporting male players were Ralph Graves and Ralph Bellamy. That was it. Columbia had one true female star under contract – Barbara Stanwyck – but Columbia saw her name in lights only briefly. Stanwyck got her big break as the leading lady in Frank Capra's *Ladies of Leisure* (1930). *Variety* said that Stanwyck saved the picture 'with her ability to convince in heavy emotional scenes,' but that she had 'small gifts for graceful comedy.'[18] After testing her in several roles, Columbia gave her star billing in Frank Capra's *The Miracle Woman* (1931). Her biggest hit and final Columbia release was Capra's *The Bitter Tea of General Yen* (1933). Afterward, Stanwyck departed for Warner Bros., leaving Columbia temporarily with only one female personality of any magnitude on its roster – opera singer Grace Moore.

To bolster class-A production, Columbia had to exploit the second star-based tactic: reliance on loan-outs from other studios. The majors loaned talent to one another on a regular basis. Try as they might, studios found it impossible to keep high-priced players busy all the time. Since an idle star was a heavy overhead expense, loan-outs could spread the costs. Studios devised various formulas to determine loan-out fees: the most common one was to charge a minimum fee of four weeks salary plus a surcharge of three weeks; another was to charge the basic salary for however long the star was needed plus a surcharge of 25 per cent.[19]

The Big Five, having large stables of stars, would consider loan-outs to the Little Three, including the top-ranked independent producers associated with United Artists. Myth has it that the majors used loan-outs to discipline stars and to keep difficult people in line. But this argument does not make much sense, because it implies that a studio would risk its investment in a star by allowing him or her to appear in an inferior picture produced by a second-rate company. Actually, most stars were on the lookout for challenging parts and wanted the opportunity to play them anywhere. Given Columbia's lowly status in the early thirties, most of the loan-outs to the studio were on their way down. Claudette Colbert and Clark Gable were in lulls when Columbia borrowed them from Paramount and MGM, respectively, to star in *It Happened One Night*; the picture revitalized both their careers, but their home studios, not Columbia, enjoyed most of the benefits.

Producing Hits

By demonstrating the ability to produce the occasional hit, Columbia met its final goal. Columbia could have existed as a Poverty Row studio without hits, but the company needed a winner or two each year as a major to strengthen its financial reserves, to retire its debt, and to retain the interest of Wall Street. Yet producing a box-office winner has always been a difficult task. As *Barron's* pointed out:

> Gauging the box-office appeal of a play or motion-picture before pro-
> duction has, in the long run, proved to be . . . as hazardous as guessing
> the results of a horse race. Public taste is fickle, and the mere success of a
> single 'movie' offers no assurance that its type – gangster, biography,
> musical comedy, etc. – will maintain its appeal. 'Will they buy it?' is the
> nightmare of the producer of every theatrical production, and the answer
> can never be accurately foretold.[20]

Therefore, producing hits not only generated profits, but also established a studio's credibility in the marketplace.

At Columbia, the task of producing winners fell mainly to Frank Capra. Columbia produced only three big hits from 1930 to 1934: Frank Capra's *Lady for a Day* in 1933 (Columbia's first release to make it to *Film Daily's* Ten Best pictures list), Victor Schertzinger's *One Night of Love*, and Capra's *It Happened One Night* (both in 1934). The latter two pictures enabled Columbia to generate profits of $1,009,000 in 1934, nearly equaling the company's peak pre-Depression earnings of $1,030,000 in 1929.

The question is: what strategy did the studio use to produce hits? Let's examine *It Happened One Night*. This picture and two other 1934 comedy hits – Howard Hawks's *Twentieth Century* (Columbia) and W. S. Van Dyke's *The Thin Man* (MGM) – have traditionally been regarded as initiating the screwball cycle in the thirties. However, contemporaneous sources saw *It Happened One Night* as a continuation of ongoing trends. Noting that Robert Riskin's screenplay about a runaway heiress who falls in love with a tough reporter was based on a short story in *Cosmopolitan* by Samuel Hopkins Adams entitled 'Night Bus,' *Variety*, saw the picture as 'another long distance bus story,' a variation on MGM's *Fugitive Lovers* and Universal's *Cross Country Cruise*, which had been released a month earlier.[21] Others considered the picture a 'traveling hostelry' film similar to *Grand Hotel* and such spin-offs as Fox's *Transatlantic* (1931), Paramount's *Shanghai Express* (1932), and Columbia's own *American Madness* (1932).[22] Seen from this perspective, *It Happened One Night* did not materialize out of nowhere, but from Columbia's strategy of following trends.

Capitalising on the success of *It Happened One Night*, Columbia decided to specialise in screwball comedies. Again, Capra carried most of the burden and produced three hits, *Mr. Deeds Goes to Town* (1936), *You Can't Take It with You* (1938), and *Mr. Smith Goes to Washington* (1939). If one line of screwball comedy featured the madcap adventures of wealthy heroines in comedies of remarriage, the Capra pictures, which were written in collaboration with either Robert Riskin or with Sidney Buchman, followed another line by depicting 'utopian fantasies' where the little guy always comes out on top.[23] To play the heroes of these pictures, Columbia borrowed Gary Cooper from Paramount for *Mr. Deeds* and James Stewart from MGM for the other two. Jean Arthur, Columbia's only contract star, costarred in all three.

Capra's stature as a director had grown enormously after *It Happened One Night* and, beginning with *Mr. Deeds*, Columbia placed Capra's name above the title of his pictures. The three Capra comedies were named to *Film Daily's* Top Ten and won numerous awards, including special honors for Capra. *You Can't Take It with You*, the most acclaimed of the group, was hailed by *Time* as 'the Number 1 cinema comedy of 1938' and received Academy Awards for best picture and best direction.

The returns on these pictures was another matter. Columbia budgeted $500,000 for *Mr. Deeds*, double the amount it spent on *It Happened One Night* and made a prudent investment. But Columbia permitted the budgets for Capra's subsequent productions, including his prestige picture *Lost Horizon* (1937), to escalate well beyond $1.5 million. The pictures did well at the box office, but as a group they barely recouped their production costs. Few pictures in the thirties could support such investments, with the result that Capra's pictures enhanced the reputation of the studio but earned modest profits.[24]

Columbia's other attempts at exploiting the screwball cycle fared less well. The studio borrowed Claudette Colbert from Paramount a second time to produce Gregory La Cava's *She Married Her Boss* (1935), a comic variation of the traditional 'sob-and-hanky' melodrama. The picture did only so-so business. Columbia then designed two vehicles for Irene Dunne. Dunne had previously made a name for herself at other studios performing in melodramas and musicals, but Columbia offcast her in Richard Boleslawski's *Theodora Goes Wild* (1936) and Leo McCarey's *The Awful Truth* (1937). In the former, Dunne played a 'female Mr. Deeds' opposite Melvyn Douglas in a 'distaff version' of Capra's *Mr. Deeds Goes to Town*, noted a review. In the latter, she played opposite Cary Grant in a comedy of remarriage. Neither picture made it to *Variety's* annual list of box-office champions, although *The Awful Truth* won considerable acclaim by being named to *Film Daily's* Ten Best pictures list and by winning the best direction Oscar for McCarey.

Lacking a roster of stars and a large financial cushion, Columbia was forced to concentrate mainly on one production trend as a source of its class-A pictures during the second half of the thirties. The Big Five, on the other hand, had the resources to spread risks by focusing on a range of production cycles and by producing pictures with trend-setting possibilities. And as owners of first-run theaters, the Big Five profited from any picture that struck the public's fancy regardless of which studio released it. Members of the Little Three would not secure an equal footing with the Big Five until the *Paramount* decrees went into effect beginning in 1948.

This case study has plotted a 'bottom-up' course of development for Columbia Pictures as it struggled to become a member of the motion-picture establishment. I have thereby rejected the conventional portrait of the studio era as a mature oligopoly in which Columbia, along with the other members of the Little Three, were somehow consigned by the Big Five to the second tier of the majors. In its place, this case study has offered a more dynamic account of industrial behavior depicting how one company successfully pursued a series of mutually dependent goals and objectives.

[. . .]

NOTES

1. *One Flew Over the Cuckoo's Nest*, a United Artists release, swept the top Academy Awards in 1975. Producers Saul Zaentz and Michael Douglas received the Best Picture Oscar; the other winners were director Miloš Forman, actor Jack Nicholson, actress Louise Fletcher, and screenwriters Laurence Hauben and Bo Goldman.
2. Douglas Gomery's concise overview of Columbia Pictures in *The Hollywood Studio System* ([New York: St. Martin's Press, 1986], esp. pp. 161–72) is the most authoritative account of the studio currently available; Edward Buscombe's essay, 'Notes on Columbia Pictures Corporation, 1926–1941' (*Screen* 15 [Autumn 1975]: 65–82) suggests a relationship between the financing of Columbia's pictures and the ideology of Capra's films; and Joel Finler's chapter on the studio in his *The Hollywood Story* ([New York: Crown, 1988], pp. 68–87) contains a wealth of data on the studio's releases and personnel.
3. See, for example, Halsey, Stuart & Co's prospectus, 'The Motion Picture Industry as a Basis for Bond Financing' (27 May 1927) in *The American Film Industry*, rev. ed., ed. Tino Balio (Madison: University of Wisconsin Press, 1985), pp. 195–217.
4. Gomery, *The Hollywood Studio System*, p. 162. Anthony Slide's *The American Film Industry: An Historical Dictionary* ([New York: Greenwood Press, 1986], p. 70) states that CBC was founded in 1922; David Bordwell, Janet Staiger, and Kristein Thompson's *The Classical Hollywood Cinema: Film Style and Mode of Production to 1960* ([New York: Columbia University Press, 1985], p. 403) gives 1918 as the founding date.
5. Temporary National Economic Committee, *The Motion Picture Industry – A Pattern of Control* (Washington, D.C.: U.S. Government Printing Office, 1941), p. 62.
6. Warner Bros. was the only other major that continued to be run by its founders, the others having passed into the hands of professional managers during the twenties.
7. For a discussion of the importance of the prestige film as a production trend, see Tino Balio, *Grand Design: Hollywood as a Modern Business Enterprise, 1930–1939* (New York: Charles Scribner's Sons, 1993), pp. 179–211.
8. Bordwell, Staiger, and Thompson, *The Classical Hollywood Cinema*, p. 321.
9. *Variety Film Reviews* (New York: Garland, 1983–). See the entries for the following dates: 11 December 1934; 2 June 1931; 24 January 1933; 29 January 1930; 16 August 1932.
10. Brian Taves, 'The B Film: Hollywood's Other Half,' in *Grand Design: Hollywood as a Modern Business Enterprise, 1930–1939*, pp. 317–18.

11. For a contemporaneous discussion of block booking, see Howard T. Lewis, *The Motion Picture Industry* (New York: D. Van Nostrand, 1933), pp. 142–80, and TNEC, *The Motion Picture Industry*, pp. 21–33.
12. 'Unique Motion Picture Enterprise,' *Barron's* 15 (25 March 1935): 14.
13. Balio, *United Artists*, pp. 65–6.
14. Charles Wolfe, *Frank Capra: A Guide to References and Resources* (Boston: G. K. Hall, 1987), p. 11.
15. A fuller discussion of the economics of the star system is found in Cathy Klaprat, 'The Star as Market Strategy: Bette Davis in Another Light,' in *The American Film Industry*, pp. 351–76.
16. 'Unique Motion Picture Enterprise,' *Barron's*, p. 14.
17. *Variety Film Reviews*, 4 July 1933.
18. *Variety Film Reviews*, 28 May 1930.
19. 'Less Than 2,000 Players Work,' *Variety*, 7 September 1938, p. 2.
20. 'Unique Motion Picture Enterprise,' *Barron's*, p. 14.
21. *Variety Film Reviews*, 27 February 1934.
22. Heidi Kenaga, 'Studio Differentiation of "Screwball" Comedy' (unpublished paper, University of Wisconsin, Department of Communication Arts, 1990).
23. Wolfe, *Frank Capra: A Guide*, p. 22.
24. Finler, *The Hollywood Story*, p. 75.

12

WARTIME, UNITY AND ALIENATION

With the bombing of Pearl Harbor by the Japanese in 1941, the United States entered into the Second World War. In the process, the film industry and its personnel were recruited for the war effort. Directors such as Frank Capra and John Ford were conscripted into the armed forces where they made a series of documentaries that supported US involvement. Capra, for example, made a seven-part documentary series, *Why We Fight* (1943), that was shown to all recruits to the armed forces. The series used existing footage produced by both the Allies and the Axis powers to establish the case for US involvement. Ford, by contrast, made *The Battle of Midway* (1942), in which he used 16mm cameras to capture the action and received both a medal for injuries sustained during the conflict and an Oscar for best documentary.

Hollywood was also enlisted in other ways. The Office of War Information (OWI) worked with the film industry to mobilise support for the war and maintain morale during it. In the process, a whole host of films sought to illustrate the dangers of the menace posed by the Axis powers. For example, Basil Rathbone played Sherlock Holmes in a series of films during the war years, many of which featured diabolical Nazi plots that were foiled by the brilliant detective. The OWI was particularly concerned to create a sense of national unity in which internal tensions were downplayed and the United States was presented as a diverse but unified country. In contrast, the Nazis were specifically presented as stern and repressive authoritarians who lacked individuality and required unquestioning conformity. In *All Through the Night*, a light-hearted thriller of 1942, Humphrey Bogart even persuades a group of small-time hoodlums to thwart a Nazi sabotage plot. His argument is that the

Nazis will put an end to the hoodlums' criminal activities, activities that are presented as simply a harmless and idiosyncratic characteristic of their milieu.

It is Bogart's performance as Rick in *Casablanca* (1942) that is often seen as an almost archetypal engagement with the war. When the film opens, Rick is a cynical, self-sufficient isolationist – 'I stick my neck out for nobody' – who owns a bar in Morocco. During the course of the narrative, we learn that he was once a romantic idealist who fought for the republican cause in Spain against the fascists, but had been deserted by Ilsa, a young woman who had broken his heart. Eventually, Ilsa returns and reawakens his romantic idealism and, as a result, the lonely isolationist finds the moral courage to fight the Nazis once again. In this way, it is often argued, the film not only challenges the national policy of isolationism in the inter-war years but also transforms the archetypal individualist hero of Hollywood films into an anti-Nazi.

As a result, while Hollywood contributed to the war effort, it did so through films that were still very much commercial entertainments, and the first half of the 1940s proved to be a record period in terms of box office receipts and studio profits. In addition, the audience was not simply bigger during this period but, crucially, it was structured in new ways. On a very crude level, Hollywood had to recognise that while many men had joined the armed forces, many women had been left behind. In this context, it is important to remember that cinemagoing had traditionally been intimately related to heterosexual courtship rituals and, consequently, Hollywood had to acknowledge that the structure of its audience was very different. As a result, many of its films were made with this sense of separation in mind. For example, Hollywood made a series of home-front films about women who stay behind when their men go off to war; and the ways in which they contribute to the war through their self-sacrifice, pluck and determination. Such concerns are perfectly summed up by titles such as *Since You Went Away* (1944) and *I'll Be Seeing You* (1945), but the biggest hit of the type was probably *Mrs Miniver* (1942).

Mrs Miniver starred the British-born actress Greer Garson who was one of MGM's biggest stars and represented respectability, courage and self-sacrifice. The film purports to present the lives of a typical British family living during the war but mainly concerns the plight of women suffering from the German bombing campaign while worrying about the welfare of their men. The appeal of these home-front dramas was that they pleased both sections of the audience. They dramatised the lives of the women, whose role was presented as an essential support to the men who were away, but who also presented those away from home with an image of that for which they were supposed to be fighting, offering the reassurance that home was still waiting for them on their return.

While these films were most directly addressed to those on the home front, the revue films and the combat films of the period were most directly addressed to those away from home. Revue films such as *This is the Army* (1943) and *Hollywood Canteen* (1944) usually featured a series of star turns by many of the producing studio's top stars, and these turns were held together by a thin plot that usually concerned young servicemen learning to cope with life away from home. In the process, these films not only operated like the morale-boosting USO shows that would tour military units overseas, they also promoted the studio and its talent.

The films appealed to those away from home and also reassured those at home about those who had gone away. Much the same was also true of the combat films, which were clearly aimed at a largely male audience but also idealised military personnel for the home front. Many of the combat films concentrated on platoons, or other military teams, in which the group and its dynamics operated as a metaphor for the United States. This is most clearly seen in *A Walk in the Sun* (1945), which concerns a platoon during the invasion of Italy. The platoon is made up of men from different ethic, regional and class backgrounds but they are all seen to be working together towards a larger goal. Indeed, the platoon itself is presented as one part of a larger offensive, the shape and structure of which they can only guess. Again and again, the film stresses that the platoon is unaware of the larger significance of their actions: they are just taking a little walk in the sun to capture a farmhouse somewhere in the Italian countryside, the significance of which is by no means clear. While this film tries to suggest a sense of unity in which the actions of individuals and groups are meaningful as part of something larger than themselves, the film also raises the spectre of their alienation and estrangement.

Unaware of their place in the larger conflict, the meanings of their actions as individuals or as a group are unavailable to the soldiers. They do not know what is going on around them and try to decipher the progress of the larger struggle through signs: smoke, noise and occasional encounters with others. As a result, there is the ever-present danger that instead of feeling a part of a larger whole, they will simply become alienated from their actions and perceive themselves as mere cogs in a machine, pawns in a conflict that is ordered and controlled by decision-makers far away.

This sense of alienation is central to the another key feature of wartime production: *film noir*. However, the term *film noir* is an extremely problematic one. First, it was not in existence during the period but was applied to films retrospectively by later critics. Second, the term has no precise meaning but has been used to suggest very different things by different critics. It is often suggested that these films are distinguished by an expressionist style of filmmaking that involves high-contrast lighting that, given its difference from the more common low-contrast styles employed by Hollywood, comes to signify a dangerous and alien social world. This stylistic characteristic is also associated with certain narrative patterns in which the films are seen as having labyrinthine plots, often involving complex flashbacks to the past, so that appearances are never trustworthy. As a result, it is argued that these films are distinguished by a paranoid or fatalistic atmosphere and feature flawed and/or vulnerable male heroes in tough, urban environments.

One of the problems is that few, if any, of the films associated with *film noir* share all these features. Furthermore, much of the work on *film noir* stresses the profoundly masculine nature of the category: these films are presumed to address masculine anxieties and masculine audiences. However, the period was also distinguished by another group of films that seem to share many of the same features but are seen as profoundly feminine: the paranoid woman's film. Many of these films feature Expressionist styles of filmmaking; labyrinthine plots; a paranoid and fatalistic atmosphere; flawed and vulnerable female heroines; but usually in domestic environments. Furthermore, while one of the key figures of *film noir* is supposed to be the femme fatale, an inscrutable deadly woman who threatens to destroy the hero through seduction, the paranoid woman's film often features the potentially murderous husband, an equally inscrutable and possibly deadly male who may well be out to murder the heroine with whom he is romantically involved.

The cycle followed the success of *Rebecca* (1940) and included a series of films such as *Suspicion* (1941), *Gaslight* (1944) and even *Jane Eyre* (1944). In these films, a heroine, often played by Joan Fontaine, falls for a man only to find that he has a dark and threatening secret, perhaps involving a mysterious first wife. In *Gaslight*, the heroine (Ingrid Bergman) marries after a whirlwind romance but finds that, after the honeymoon, her husband becomes distant and cruel. As the plot unfolds, it is revealed that he is a deeply disturbed murderer who is obsessed with another woman whom he killed but whose jewels he still covets. Furthermore, not only has he simply married the heroine because she provides him with access to the house in which the jewels are hidden, but he is trying to destroy her. It is never made clear whether this is simply to avoid being identified as a killer, or out of an active hatred that is the product of his psychological problems.

Thus, while the femme fatale is often explained as a masculine response to changing gender roles during the war, in which women had a far more active public life, both the deadly male and the deadly female can be seen as the product of an increasing estrangement between men and women in modern society that was intensified by the war. Like many in the war years, the leads in the paranoid woman's films often meet one another at some distance from their respective homes, engage in whirlwind romances followed by speedy marriages, and only later come to realise that their partner has a past of which they were previously unaware. Even those who have known each other before the war often find that, during their period of separation, they have both changed, so that the man who returns home, or the woman to whom he returns, does not seem to be the same person as before. In other words, the war exaggerated factors that made men and women strangers to one another.

There were also other reasons for the sense of alienation that concerned many of these films. Although the war had brought an end to the Depression, it had done so through the establishment of a Fordist system of economy in which most people were employees of large organised corporations that were managed by a scientific-technical élite. Like the soldiers in *Walk in the Sun*, this situation meant that many felt that they lacked the individual autonomy on which American liberalism was supposed to be founded, and were alienated from their labour. Of course, this was not necessarily a new situation for many, but it was a period in which sections of the middle class were experiencing this situation for the first time.

In *Double Indemnity* (1944), for example, Walter Neff is a salesman for a large insurance agency, an institution founded on the rational calculation of human life. It makes its money by turning people into statistics through which it can predict their actions. When he runs into a scheming young housewife, Phyllis Dietrichson, Neff admits that he has been longing for a way to buck the system; to assert his individualism by cheating his employers. Although he is partly seduced by Phyllis' wiles, he is clearly a man who is tired of his ordered life and longs for a way to prove his independence, and hence his manhood.

As a result, he plans to murder Phyllis' husband and defraud his insurance company by using the double indemnity clause in the insurance policy that will enable them to make the highest possible insurance claim. The crime seems to go to plan but the suspicions of Neff's closest friend, a paternal insurance investigator called Barton Keyes, are alerted. Eventually, the conspirators fall out and Neff ends up dictating his confession into an office memo recorder as he dies from a gunshot wound. In this way, the film plays out the fantasy of bucking the system but overtly punishes the criminality involved. In its place, it offers the pro-social ideal of Keyes, who rebels against his superiors and follows his own gut instincts, but does so in order to protect the corporation rather than attack it.

Double Indemnity was directed by Billy Wilder, one of the many European filmmakers and intellectuals who had moved to the United States after Hitler came to power in Germany (see Chapter 6). The influence of these intellectual émigrés on Hollywood film was profound. Technically they introduced many stylistic features from European film such as the Expressionist style that is supposed to be central to *film noir*, but they also had less direct influence. It was during this period that Hitchcock and other directors became particularly interested in Freudian psychoanalysis and surrealism. Again these two come together in *film noir*, which was often praised by surrealists for its nightmarish elements. The link is also clear in Hitchcock's thriller, *Spellbound* (1945), for which he employed the surrealist painter Salvador Dali to design the dream sequences, the interpretation of which is central to the resolution of the mystery.

It is therefore interesting that when the avant-garde re-emerged in the mid-1940s, it shared many features with *film noir*. For example, Maya Deren and her husband Alexander Hammid made *Meshes of the Afternoon* (1943), which follows a woman as she moves through various rooms and experiences a series of disjointed and unexplained occurrences. Its structure clearly draws on the dreamlike qualities of surrealism, with which it also shares a concern with the relationship between passion and violence, and the figure of the double – preoccupations that are often claimed to be central to *film noir*.

Britain faced similar problems to the United States during the war, and the Ministry of Information worked closely with the film industry. On the one hand, the British government was concerned to preserve its resources by limiting the number of films imported from the United States and, on the other, it wanted to promote a positive image of Britain and create a sense of national purpose. The films that were produced, therefore, sought to present a sense of national unity, and to give a sense of a diverse nation pulling together. *In Which We Serve* (1942), for example, tells the story of a British ship that is sunk by the enemy and provides glimpses into the different backgrounds of individual crew members as they wait for rescue. In the process, it provides an image of a diverse group of men drawn together by a common cause and a common enemy, and it purports to offer a microcosm of British social life.

While *In Which We Serve* suggests the bonds that hold together men from disparate social backgrounds, *This Happy Breed* (1944) offers an idealised picture of British domestic life in the inter-war years. It is the story of a lower middle-class family in the Southeast, and although the implicit typicality of the family is highly questionable, the film tries to give a sense of the values that Britain was fighting to defend, values that were located in the ordinary soil of the British family garden.

Unsurprisingly, given their earlier concerns, the British documentary movement was highly active during the war, presenting images of national unity. Harry Watt's *London Can Take It!* (1940), for example, presented a picture of British resilience in the face of the German bombing raids on the capital, while another of his films, *The Target for Tonight* (1941), provided an account of a British bombing raid on Germany. Although the action was not a record of an actual raid, but was staged for the camera, it provided a sense of authenticity by using the personnel who would have performed the tasks in an actual raid, rather than relying on professional actors to fill these roles. It also included a series of small personal details, a strategy taken even further by Humphrey Jennings in *Fires Were Started* (1943). This film was a portrait of the fire service that not only dealt with their professional activities during the bombing raids, but also provided a sense of their private lives as individuals through coverage of their off-duty activities.

Alternative images of Britain were also produced within the period. Powell and Pressburger produced a series of impressive colour films which not only differed from the black and white realism of the British films already discussed, but also called for a transformation of the British character. *The Life and Death of Colonel Blimp* (1943), for example, is an extravagant and humorous story of a British military officer, following him through several stages of his life and causing considerable controversy in Britain at the time of its release. The film opens with his capture during military manoeuvres during the First World War, when he is tricked by a young British soldier who doesn't play by the rules.

It therefore presents Blimp as a charming buffoon who has never quite understood life and is now an outmoded military relic.

After the opening, the film flashbacks to different moments in the officer's past, in which he is always offset by two key figures. The first is a sympathetically drawn German officer who becomes his friend but views him almost as a childlike innocent, while the second is a series of different women who are all played by Deborah Kerr and reveal both his total inability to understand the opposite sex and his inability to deal with modernity. In his relationship with the women played by Kerr, he invariably takes the role of gentlemanly protector but it is ironically one of these women, a young modern army officer, who is instrumental in his capture at the start of the film. Blimp's inability to deal with the modern world is exemplified by his inability to comprehend modern femininity.

Modernity and femininity are also central to Powell and Pressburger's *A Matter of Life and Death* (1946), made under the direction of the Ministry of Information which wanted to counter British antagonisms towards the United States. It concerns a British pilot who is forced to bail out of his plane without a parachute; before jumping, he talks to an American radio operator with whom he falls in love. Unfortunately, although he survives, he starts to have visions that involve a celestial messenger who tells him that he should have died when he bailed out, and that he must take his place in heaven immediately. The visions may be the result of a head injury or an actual supernatural experience, but the pilot makes an appeal against his death in which his love for the American radio operator is central to his case. The story is a fabulously inventive fantasy with some astonishing set pieces and an impassioned call for Britain and America to re-imagine their national identities together.

Not all the films of the war years were overt engagements with the war and some of the most popular were the Gainsborough melodramas, many of which starred Margaret Lockwood who was the biggest female star of the period in Britain. These films were period dramas that usually centred on women who chafed at the restrictions of their social worlds. In *The Wicked Lady* (1946), for example, Lockwood plays Barbara Skelton, a women who steals another woman's fiancée and, when bored with him, becomes a highwaywoman. Added to these exploits is an affair with a roguish highwayman, played by James Mason, another major British star of the period. Although the film eventually punishes Barbara for her crimes, it clearly encourages a vicarious pleasure in her actions and makes no real attempt to present the conventionally passive female characters as interesting or appealing. In this way, such films addressed a female public for whom the war had enabled relative freedom from the constraints of domestic life, but who were also required still to see themselves as preserving the homes to which the men fighting overseas would return.

Historical melodramas were also a crucial element of French production during the war, although they took very different forms given the very different circumstances of Britain and France during this period. On 5 June 1940, the

German army invaded France and within less than two weeks it had occupied Paris. This situation put a temporary halt to film production but by 1941 production had restarted. Initially, France was divided into two sections with the South administered by the Vichy government, while the North was more directly under the occupation of the German army. Ironically, the occupation forces were fairly lenient in terms of censorship and the Northern film industry suffered less from official interference than did filmmakers under the Vichy regime.

One reason for this situation was that the Germans recognised that, once they had won the war, they would need French support to rule Europe, and they also hoped to demonstrate the benefits of collaboration to other occupied countries. This situation placed filmmakers in a difficult position. On the one hand, they could present themselves as defending a tradition of French culture under occupation but on the other they could equally be accused of being mere collaborators who legitimated the occupation forces. As a result, many films sought to have it both ways. Many were historical or fantasy films that avoided any direct reference to their present, but also sought to make allegorical or coded criticism of contemporary affairs. In *Les Visiteurs du soir* (1942) the devil sends agents to corrupt a French castle but one of his agents falls in love with a princess and the devil turns them both to stone as punishment. The devil has been seen as an allegorical reference to the German invader but the film suggests no basis for resistance beyond the power of love. Furthermore, the couple's transformation into stone is ambiguous, suggesting either the eternal power of their love or the frozen impotence of French resistance.

Much the same can also be said of the most revered film of the period, Marcel Carne's *Les Enfants du paradis* (1945). The film is an epic tale of the nineteenth-century theatre and follows the fortunes of four characters: an insincere actor; a brilliant but sensitive mime artist; a young woman; and a misanthropic criminal. The relationships between the four are all treated symbolically as almost a conflict between idealism and cynicism, or authenticity and artifice. The film is also highly fatalistic with its characters destroyed by fate and circumstances, as if the playthings of cruel gods. However, the paradise of the title is not a metaphysical heaven but rather the upper balcony of the theatre, the place of the popular audience rather than the wealthier audiences of the stalls. The theatrical players are not only the darlings of the popular but also dominated by them. As a result, the film also opposes the paradise of the theatre to the criminal world of the street. However, it is unclear whether these represent two different versions of the popular mob, an object of fear within conservative French culture, or simply an opposition between the perfectible world of the theatrical arts and the corruption, disillusionment and chaos of real life.

If Balio analyses the business history of the industry, Koppes and Black examine one of the ways in which the industry is linked to political institutions in the US. The extract is a study of the Office of War Information (OWI) and its 'control over the content of motion-pictures' during the Second World War.

In this way, their work is part of a more general interest in the history of motion-picture censorship and regulation, much of which is concerned to emphasise that the study of censorship and regulation should not be restricted to the exceptional instances where films are butchered or banned. Most censorship, for example, is not formally imposed by external institutions but is rather internally imposed by cultural industries themselves. The Hays Office was not an outside body that intruded on the Hollywood studio system but actually an internal mechanism within the industry, which was run by Hollywood insiders, and was specially created to ward off the threat of external censorship. It was created to show that Hollywood could keep its own house in order without external interference. Furthermore, most censorship was not only internal but often informal. Most filmmakers did not write with one eye on the code, but worked within a taken-for-granted sense of what was 'responsible' or in 'good taste'. In other words, most filmmakers unconsciously censored their own work before the Hays Office ever became involved and, on those occasions where the Hays Office did get actively involved in the shaping of the film, it was generally to help filmmakers resolve specific problems when the general, taken-for-granted principles did not work. Nor did most filmmakers resent this situation: few wanted overtly to offend their audience or be seen as irresponsible or tasteless.

Despite the everyday quality of most censorship, the files produced by the institutions such as the Hays Office and the OWI can help the researcher not only to examine the decision-making process through which films were constructed, but also the intended meanings of film texts. This research can also examine the more complex cultural attitudes and discourses that shape individual films and filmmaking more generally. Many attempts to relate films to broader cultural attitudes fail to capture the complex negotiations between contradictory social attitudes, or the processes of mediation between general cultural contexts and specific individual texts. As a result, Koppes and Black not only demonstrate that the cultural attitudes of the OWI did not represent the nation as a whole and that, even in political circles, its attitudes were highly contested, but their work also illustrates that most censorship is rarely a matter of imposing prohibitions but usually one of careful negotiation and minor revisions. Furthermore, as such, it is often a highly creative process rather than simply a restrictive one. For example, even the common tendency to omit material through a fade-out frequently involved a subtle process of finding ways to suggest that which could not be shown.

- What primary sources do Koppes and Black use in their analysis of film censorship? Can you think of any other example of an attempt to control the content of films and how would you go about studying that example?
- What conditions might have influenced the ways in which the industry presented itself, and its products, to bodies such as the OWI, and how might this require care when examining these sources?

- Koppes and Black claim that one of the dangers with the OWI was that its attempt to control the content of films was part of a more general attempt to control how people thought. However, while Koppes and Black's research may tell us what the OWI wanted, can it tell us whether it was successful, and what sources would be necessary to examine whether films were actually understood by audiences in the ways that the OWI intended?

WHAT TO SHOW THE WORLD: THE OFFICE OF WAR INFORMATION AND HOLLYWOOD, 1942–1945

Clayton R. Koppes
and
Gregory D. Black

The uneasy relationship between propaganda and democracy proved especially troublesome during World War II. Interpreting the war as a worldwide crusade, liberals in the Office of War Information (OWI) won unprecedented control over the content of American motion-pictures. An understanding of the interaction between OWI and Hollywood sheds light on both the objectives and methods of the nation's propaganda campaign and the content of wartime entertainment films. This episode, all but ignored by historians, offers insights into America's war ideology and the intersection of politics and mass culture in wartime. Moreover, it raises the question of whether the Roosevelt administration's propaganda strategy helped undermine some of its avowed war aims.[1]

OWI, the chief government propaganda agency during World War II, was formed by an executive order on June 13, 1942, that consolidated several prewar information agencies. OWI's domestic branch handled the home front; its overseas branch supervised all United States foreign propaganda activities, except in Latin America, which remained the preserve of the coordinator of inter-American affairs, Nelson Rockefeller. Franklin D. Roosevelt instructed OWI to implement a program through the press, radio, and motion-pictures to enhance public understanding of the war; to coordinate the war-information activities of all federal agencies; and to act as the intermediary between federal agencies and the radio and motion-picture industries. OWI director Elmer Davis, a liberal radio commentator, insisted that the agency's policy was to tell the truth. But information could not be separated from interpretation, and OWI told the truth by degrees and with particular bias. In all important respects OWI met the criterion of a propaganda agency. It was an organization designed not only to disseminate information and to clarify issues but also to arouse support for particular symbols and ideas. 'The easiest way to inject a propaganda idea into most people's minds,' said Davis, 'is to let it go in through

Clayton R. Koppes and Gregory D. Black, *American Historical Review*, April 2001.

the medium of an entertainment picture when they do not realize that they are being propagandized.'[2]

Around Davis clustered a liberal staff that gave OWI one of the highest percentages of interventionist New Dealers of any wartime agency. Two assistant directors, Pulitzer-prize writers, Archibald MacLeish and Robert Sherwood, were enthusiastic New Dealers; another assistant director, Milton S. Eisenhower, though fiscally more cautious, was a New Deal veteran. The only assistant director who held the New Deal at some distance was Gardner Cowles, Jr., a moderate Republican publisher who had been recruited to give OWI an air of bipartisanship. Liberals of various hues permeated the second and third levels of the agency and included such figures as historians Arthur M. Schlesinger, Jr., and Henry Pringle, former Henry A. Wallace speech writer Jack Fleming, novelist Leo Rosten, journalists Joseph Barnes and Alan Cranston, financier James Warburg, and 'China hand' Owen Lattimore.[3]

The Bureau of Motion Pictures (BMP) in OWI was a New Deal stronghold. Its chief, Lowell Mellett, a former Scripps-Howard newspaper editor who had been a Roosevelt aide since 1939, had headed the first prewar information agency, the Office of Government Reports (OGR). 'OGRE' and 'Mellett's Madhouse' to conservative critics, OGR supervised the government film program. In response to the movie industry's offer of support in December 1941, Roosevelt told Mellett to advise Hollywood how it could further the war effort. Mellett established a liaison office in Hollywood and appointed as its head Nelson Poynter, a Scripps-Howard colleague. Poynter did not follow movies, but he shared Mellett's enthusiasms. Assisting Poynter was a staunchly liberal reviewing staff headed by Dorothy Jones, a former research assistant for Harold Lasswell and a pioneer in film content analysis.[4]

The Hollywood office became part of OWI domestic operations in June 1942 and began one of the agency's more important and controversial activities. The motion-picture, said Davis, could be 'the most powerful instrument of propaganda in the world, whether it tries to be or not.' Roosevelt believed movies were among the most effective means of reaching the American public. The motion-picture industry experienced far fewer wartime restrictions on output than most industries. Hollywood turned out nearly 500 pictures annually during the war and drew eighty million paid admissions per week, well above the prewar peak. Hollywood's international influence far exceeded that of American radio and the press; foreign audiences, which also reached eighty million per week, often determined whether a film made a profit. BMP believed that every film enhanced or diminished America's reputation abroad and hence affected the nation's power.[5]

[. . .]

Hollywood preferred to avoid issues; OWI demanded affirmation of New Deal liberalism for America and the world. When Poynter arrived in the movie capital he found the industry doing little to promote the larger issues of the war.

In the summer of 1942 Hollywood had under consideration or in production 213 films that dealt with the war in some manner. Forty percent of those focused on the armed forces, usually in combat. Less than 20 percent dealt with the enemy, and most of those portrayed spies and saboteurs. Other categories – the war issues, the United Nations, and the home front – received minimal attention. Even more disturbing to OWI, Hollywood had simply grafted the war to conventional mystery and action plots or appropriated it as a backdrop for frothy musicals and flippant comedies. Interpretation of the war remained at a rudimentary level: the United States was fighting because it had been attacked, and it would win.[6]

To help the industry 'raise its sights.' Poynter and his staff wrote a 'Manual for the Motion-Picture Industry' in June 1942 that they intended as a guide for movie makers in future projects. The manual ranks as probably the most comprehensive statement of OWI's interpretation of the war. OWI believed the war was not merely a struggle for survival but a 'people's war' between fascism and democracy, the crusade of Vice President Henry A. Wallace's 'Century of the Common Man.' The United States fought for a new democratic world based on the Four Freedoms – freedom of speech and religion and freedom from want and fear. The war was a people's struggle, BMP emphasised, 'not a national, class or race war.' Every person in the world had a concrete stake in the outcome; an Allied victory promised to all a decent standard of living, including a job, good housing, recreation, and health, unemployment, and old-age insurance – a world New Deal. The average man would also enjoy the right to participate in government, which suggested OWI's anti-imperialist stance. American minorities had not entered utopia, the bureau conceded, but progress was possible only under democracy, and the wartime gains of blacks, women, and other minorities would be preserved. A nation of united average citizens, who believed deeply in the cause of freedom and sacrificed willingly to promote victory, was the hallmark of BMP's democracy.[7]

The enemy was fascism. The enemy was not the Axis leadership nor all of the Axis-led peoples but fascist supporters anywhere, at home as well as abroad. 'Any form of racial discrimination or religious intolerance, special privileges of any citizen are manifestations of fascism, and should be exposed as such,' the manual advised. A fascist victory would entail racial discrimination, destruction of political rights, eradication of the rights of labor, and 'complete regimentation of the personal life' of the common man. 'There can be no peace until militarism and fascism are completely wiped out,' BMP warned. When victory came, the United Nations, eschewing national interest and balance-of-power politics, would build a new world expressive of the collective will. The manual enjoyed wide distribution in Hollywood; some studios reproduced the entire contents for their personnel, and many writers welcomed the bureau's interpretation.[8]

The manual reflected the intellectual ferment of the 1930s. Many intellectuals had put a premium on commitment to some large ideal or movement;

a predetermined response, not an examination of experience in its many facets, was all-important. The quest for commitment converged in the late 1930s with the search for America; the war seemed to offer that unifying commitment and it reduced intellectual content to an uncritical adulation of America and Allies. Thus, BMP reviewers in 1942 objected to the depiction of Spanish Loyalist violence in Paramount's *For Whom the Bell Tolls*, 'particularly at this time when we *must* believe in the rightness of our cause.' The bureau continued:

> Now it is necessary that we see the democratic-fascist battle as a whole and recognise that what the Loyalists were fighting for is essentially the same thing that we are. To focus too much attention on the chinks in our allies' armor is just what our enemies might wish. Perhaps it is realistic, but it is also going to be confusing to American audiences.[9]

To OWI the reality of experience threatened response.

Before the manual could have much effect, however, the bureau faced some immediate problems. Metro-Goldwyn-Mayer (MGM) wanted to re-release the 1939 film *The Real Glory*, which dealt with the United States army's suppression of the turn-of-the-century Moro rebellion, but now billed as war between American and Japanese troops. Philippine President Manuel Quezon protested vigorously, and Mellett convinced producer Sam Goldwyn to withdraw the picture. The bureau's patriotic appeals also staved off re-release of two glorifications of British imperialism, RKO's *Gunga Din* and MGM's *Kim*. When Columbia sought BMP advice on its proposed 'Trans-Sahara,' Mellett cautioned that American policy in Africa was not yet clear, and the studio dropped the project.[10]

But suggestions and patriotic persuasion had limits, OWI discovered in July 1942 when it screened Twentieth Century-Fox's *Little Tokio, U.S.A.* The film grafted a fifth-column theme to a conventional murder mystery and portrayed the Japanese-Americans – 'this Oriental bund' – as bent on sabotage and trying to takeover California. The hero-detective bullied his way into a home without a search warrant, and the police beat up Japanese 'spies' they had arrested and disarmed. These 'Gestapo methods' dismayed the reviewers, who asked, 'Did somebody mention that we are presumably fighting for the preservation of the Bill of Rights?' By the end of the film, the Japanese-Americans were marched off to detention camps; and the detective's sweetheart, converted from isolationism, appeasement, and tolerance for Japanese-Americans, implored patriots to save America. 'Invitation to the Witch Hunt,' cried BMP.

Poynter appealed to the producer, Colonel Jason Joy, to make enough changes to 'take most of the curse off.' But Joy accused Poynter of going soft on the Japanese and gave OWI an ultimatum: *Little Tokio, U.S.A.* would go out as it stood or it could be killed if it contradicted government policy. Poynter capitulated. Twentieth Century-Fox had received army approval for the film and had rushed camera crews to 'Little Tokio' in Los Angeles to shoot footage of the actual evacuation.[11]

OWI now recognized that to inject its propaganda ideas into feature films, the Hollywood bureau had to influence the studios while films were being produced; moreover, since the army was interested mainly in security not ideology, the bureau had to be the sole point of contact between the government and the industry. Accordingly, Poynter asked the studios to submit their scripts to his office for review. While he had no direct power to demand scripts, Poynter achieved some limited cooperation. He had taken an unprecedented step. The Committee on Public Information (Creel Committee) of World War I had allowed films to go abroad only if the committee's shorts went with them, but George Creel apparently had not attempted to influence the content of entertainment films directly.[12]

As studios hesitantly began submitting scripts, OWI encountered problems. Particularly sensitive was the depiction of home-front race relations. MGM's 'Man on America's Conscience' refurbished Andrew Johnson as the hero of Reconstruction; vulture-like Thaddeus Stevens fulfilled the need for a heavy. OWI passed the script to Walter White, executive secretary of the National Association for the Advancement of Colored People, who, with the black press, the *Daily Worker*, and a group of Hollywood luminaries, raised a chorus of protest. Mayer dismissed the outcry as the work of what he called 'the communist cell' at MGM. When Mellett appealed to national unity, the studio at last agreed to delete the inflammatory references to slavery and to change Stevens into a sincere, if still misguided, figure. The film, released in December 1942 as *Tennessee Johnson*, did not entirely please OWI, but it demonstrated nonetheless the influence the bureau could wield by reading scripts.[13]

Poynter seised that opportunity with one of the few scripts Paramount submitted, *So Proudly We Hail*, a $2 million epic of the seige of Bataan. He suggested that one of the army nurses headed for martyrdom might say:

> 'Why are we dying? Why are we suffering? We thought we . . . could not be affected by all the pestiferous, political spots elsewhere in the world. We have learned a lot about epidemics and disease . . . when a political plague broke out there [in Manchuria] by invasion, we would not have been willing to do something about it. We had to wait until this plague spread out further and further until it hit Pearl Harbor.'

He also outlined a Christmas sermon that traced the cause of democracy from Jesus Christ through the 'Century of the Common Man.' The studio wrote in some of Poynter's ideas, though not in his exact words, and OWI ranked it among the best of the war films.[14]

Combat films reflected OWI's influence probably as much as any type. In the bureau's ideal combat movie an ethnically and geographically diverse group of Americans would articulate what they were fighting for, pay due regard to the role of the Allies, and battle an enemy who was formidable but not a superman. In RKO's *Bombardiers* a pacifist-influenced bombardier worried about bombing innocent civilians. At OWI's suggestion the revised script introduced the concept of a just war and explained that the enemy's targets were everywhere while the Americans', although admittedly not surgically precise, were limited to military targets. Occasionally the studios became too bold for the bureau. 'War *is* horrible,' BMP acknowledged, but it nevertheless asked the studio to 'minimise the more bloody aspects' in *Corregidor.* OWI liked reality but not too much of it, which reinforced Hollywood's inclination toward avoidance. This, even more than OWI's sermonettes, vitiated the impact of many combat pictures. *So Proudly We Hail* remained chiefly a cheesecake-studded story of love on the troop carriers and in the foxholes. And 'the most sincere thing Paramount's young women did,' said Agee, 'was to alter their make-up to favor exhaustion (and not too much of it) over prettiness (and not too little of that) . . .' Few feature films approached the impact of combat documentaries, such as John Huston's *Battle of San Pietro* and especially the British *Desert Victory.*[15]

By the fall of 1942 films in all categories were showing OWI's imprint, whether through script review or application of the manual for the industry. The motion-picture bureau praised two films released in 1942 for filling in gaps on the home front. MGM's *Keeper of the Flame* dramatised native fascism. A wealthy American wanted to institute anti-labor, anti-Negro, anti-Semitic, and anti-Catholic campaigns and to exploit the people of the United States for members of his class. Universal Pictures made *Pittsburgh* to show the home front geared for war. A tempestuous love triangle composed of John Wayne, Randolph Scott, and Marlene Dietrich was resolved when labor and management united behind something greater than themselves, the war effort. Some of the speeches had been 'culled directly' from the OWI manual, the bureau observed, 'and might have been improved by translation into terms more directly and simply relating to the characters . . . in this particular film.' But OWI Hollywood reviewers urged Mellett not to miss *Pittsburgh* or *Keeper of the Flame.*[16]

If the studios chose to ignore OWI, however, they could turn out what Poynter termed 'ill-conceived atrocities.' 'Preston Sturges' giddy Paramount comedy *Palm Beach Story* carried on the Hollywood tradition of satirising the idle rich. But the BMP feared that this 'libel on a America at war,' with its blithe disregard of wartime hardships, would offend the American allies. Another Hollywood staple that disturbed OWI was the gangster film, of which Paramount's *Lucky Jordan* was representative. The hero tried to dodge the draft and swindle the army; but when the Nazi agents beat up a gin-swilling, panhandling grand-mother who had befriended him, he converted to the American cause, helped round up the Axis spy ring, and meekly returned to the army. His turnabout dramatised in specific, human terms the reality of fascism. Yet his individualistic commitment suggested to OWI reviewers that the United States had nothing ide-ological against Adolf Hitler; as the hero put it, Americans just did not like the way Nazis pushed people around. OWI wanted the hero to undergo a more profound intellectual awakening and to announce it explicitly. BMP feared, moreover, that gangster films' cynicism and lawlessness, while not particularly harmful at home, tended to support Axis propaganda abroad. The bureau asked the Office of Censorship to bar *Palm Beach Story, Lucky Jordan,* and other films it disliked from export. The censorship code was limited mainly to security information, however, and since these films hardly contained military secrets, the censor granted them export licenses. The censor, ironically, was more lenient than the advocates of free speech.[17]

Hearing increasingly bad reports on the effect of American films abroad, Davis looked for a way to keep Hollywood from putting across 'day in and day out, the most outrageous caricature of the American character.' Mellett proposed that a representative of OWI's overseas branch join BMP's Hollywood office; this official could more credibly object that certain films harmed foreign relations and could carry OWI's case to the censor. 'It would hurt like hell' if a picture were withheld from foreign distribution, Mellett pointed out. Davis agreed and appointed one of Sherwood's chief aides, Ulric Bell, as the overseas arm's representative to Hollywood. A former Washington bureau chief for the Louisville *Courier-Journal,* Bell possessed impeccable New Deal credentials and had been one of the key figures in the prewar inter-ventionist movement. Arriving in Hollywood in November 1942, he shared Poynter's reviewing staff. Bell's influence soon exceeded what Mellett and Poynter had dreamed of or, indeed, thought proper.[18]

[. . .]

By the fall of 1943 Bell had convinced every studio except Paramount to let OWI read all their scripts instead of certain selected ones, and even Paramount agreed to discuss its scripts with OWI in general terms. In 1943 OWI read 466 scripts, in 1944, 744. The 1,210 scripts reviewed in those two years represented almost three fourths of the 1,652 scripts the Hollywood office read between May 1942 and its demise in August 1945. From September 1943 through August 1944, BMP analyzed eighty-four scripts with American lawlessness or corruption as a main theme; forty-seven were corrected to its satisfaction. Racial problems were corrected or eliminated in twenty of twenty-four instances, distortions of military or political facts in forty-four of fifty-nine cases. Fifty-nine of the eighty scripts that portrayed Americans oblivious to the war were improved. During this period OWI managed to have 277 of the 390 cases of objectionable material corrected, a success ratio of 71 per cent. Yet these statistics understate OWI's influence. Many scripts already showed the influence of the 'Manual for the Motion Picture Industry' when they reached OWI readers, making alterations unnecessary. Complete statistics are not available, but from January through August 1943 – before Bell's agreement with the censor had much effect – BMP induced the industry to drop twenty-nine scheduled productions and, particularly noteworthy, to rework parts of the films already approved by the censor. Bell closed the remaining gaps of the line established by Mellett and Poynter. From mid-1943 until the end of the war, OWI exerted an influence over an American mass medium never equaled before or since by a government agency.[19] The content of World War II motion-pictures is inexplicable without reference to the bureau.

Hollywood had proved to be remarkably compliant. The industry found that its sincere desire to help the war effort need not interfere with business that was better than usual. Freedom of the screen had never been Hollywood's long suit: an industry that had feared being 'enslaved' by Mellett was already in thrall to Will Hays. As the studios learned that OWI wanted 'only to be helpful, their attitudes change[d] miraculously,' observed Robert Riskin, a Sherwood aide who had been one of Hollywood's highest-paid writers. In 'brutal honesty,' Riskin continued, the industry's 'unprecedented profits' had encouraged cooperation that surprised even the 'movie moguls.' The studios let BMP know what stories they were considering for production – some of the hottest secrets in movieland – so that the bureau could steer them into less crowded areas and thus smooth out the picture cycle. OWI's international role was especially important. Hollywood films hit the beaches right behind the American troops, provided they had OWI approval; the agency charged admission and held the money in trust for the studios. United States film makers were planning a large-scale invasion of the foreign market after the war, and OWI established indispensable beachheads. Indeed, Riskin lamented in mid-1944: 'An unsavory opinion seems to prevail within OWI that the Motion Picture Bureau is unduly concerned with considerations for commercial interests.'[20]

Although OWI and Hollywood first seemed to conflict, they eventually developed excellent rapport, for their aims and approaches were essentially compatible. The 'chief function of mass culture,' Robert Warshow has observed, 'is to relieve one of the necessity of experiencing one's life directly.' Hollywood, conceiving of its audience as passive, emphasized entertainment and avoidance of issues. OWI encouraged Hollywood to treat more social issues and to move beyond national and racial stereotypes. However, since OWI was interested mainly in response, it stressed ideology and affirmation; it raised social issues only to have democracy wash them away. Here the seemingly divergent paths of Hollywood and OWI joined: avoidance and affirmation both led to evasion of experience. Instead of opening realms of understanding by confronting experience, OWI, the propaganda agency, and Hollywood the dream factory, joined hands to deny realities. However laudable the goals of propaganda, Jaques Ellul has suggested that it creates a person 'who is not at ease except when integrated in the mass, who rejects critical judgements, choices, and differentiations because he clings to clear certainties.'[21] Through their influence over motion-pictures, the OWI's liberals undermined the liberation for which they said they thought.

NOTES

1. Film historians such as Lewis Jacobs and Paul Rotha and Richard Griffith recognise the heavy ideological emphasis of World War II movies, but do not realise the influence of the Office of War Information (OWI). Lewis Jacobs, 'World War II and the American Film,' *Cinema Journal*, VII (Winter 1967–8), 1–21; and Paul Rotha

and Richard Griffith, *The Film Till Now: A Survey of World Cinema* (London, 1967), 464–7. The most complete history of OWI restricts its film coverage to the Bureau of Intelligence. Allan M. Winkler, 'Politics and Propaganda: The Office of War Information, 1942–1945' (doctoral dissertation, Yale University, 1974). John Morton Blum accepts OWI's contention that producers should use their own judgment about wartime movie content and concludes that 'with few exceptions, *Wilson* and *Mission to Moscow* for two, films designed for the box office carried no message of purpose or idealism.' John Morton Blum, *V Was for Victory: Politics and American Culture During World War II* (New York, 1976), 25, 36. A popular account discusses OWI influence on films in a lighthearted fashion, but says that the interaction ended in mid-1943. Richard R. Lingeman, *Don't You Know There's a War On? The American Home Front, 1941–1945* (New York, 1970), 168–210.

2. Elmer Davis to Byron Price, Jan. 27, 1943, Box 3, Records of the Office of War Information, RG 208 (Federal Records Center, Suitland, Md.); Winkler, 'Politics and Propaganda'; LaMar Seal Mackay, 'Domestic Operations of the Office of War Information in World War II' (doctoral dissertation, University of Wisconsin, 1966), ch. 1–2. See also *Public Opinion Quarterly*, VI (Spring 1942); Harold D. Lasswell, *Propaganda Technique in the World War* (New York, 1938), 9; and Jacques Ellul, *Propaganda: The Formation of Men's Attitudes* (New York, 1965), x–xiv. For Elmer Davis, see Alfred Haworth Jones, 'The Making of an Interventionist on the Air: Elmer Davis and CBS News, 1939–1941,' *Pacific Historical Review*, XLII (Feb. 1973), 91.

3. Although some scholars acknowledge the presence of prominent liberals in OWI, ideology has not received the emphasis that its pivotal importance in the agency merits. See Winkler, 'Politics and Propaganda,' 13–14, 22–8, 37–41. For example, not only the questions of technique examined by Sydney Weinberg but also ideological differences fueled the 'writers' quarrel' of 1943. Sydney Weinberg, 'What to Tell America: The Writers Quarrel in the Office of War Information,' *Journal of American History*, LV (June 1968), 76, 88. For New Dealers in OWI, see Harold Gosnell to Files, Sept. 14, 1945, in 'Preparation of War Histories by Agencies: OWI, 1942–1945,' item 127, series 41.3, Bureau of the Budget Records, RG 51 (National Archives). See also Norman Markowitz, *The Rise and Fall of the People's Century: Henry A. Wallace and American Liberalism, 1941–1948* (New York, 1973), ch. 2, and Blum, *V Was for Victory*, ch. 7–9. In this essay the term 'ideology' is used not to imply 'a rigid, doctrinaire, black-and-white understanding of the world, but, rather . . . the system of beliefs, values, fears, prejudices, reflexes, and commitments – in sum, the social consciousness' of a group. See Eric Foner, *Free Soil, Free Labor, Free Men: The Ideology of the Republican Party Before the Civil War* (New York, 1970), 4.

4. Lowell Mellett and Nelson Poynter were not on OWI payroll but drew their salary from the Executive Office of the President. *Reduction of Nonessential Expenditures. Hearings before the Joint Committee on Reduction of Nonessential Federal Expenditures*, (Washington, 1942), 1140–55, 1208–25, 1308–13; Lowell Mellett, 'The Office of Government Reports,' *Public Administration Review*, I (Winter 1941), 126; Margaret Hicks Williams, ' "The President's" Office of Government Reports,' *Public Opinion Quarterly*, V (Winter 1941), 548–62; Clayton R. Koppes interviews with Poynter, Jan. 8, 1974, and Dorothy Jones, Dec. 6, 1974; Dorothy B. Jones, 'Quantitative Analysis of Motion Picture Content,' *Public Opinion Quarterly*, VI (Fall 1942), 411–27. See also Richard Dyer MacCann, *The People's Films: A Political History of U.S. Government Motion Pictures* (New York, 1973), 129–35. This essay, however, considers only OWI's attempt to influence feature films produced by the movie industry.

5. Davis press conference, Dec. 23, 1942, Box 1442. Records of the Office of War Information; *Reduction of Nonessential Expenditures*, 1213–14; *Movies at War, Reports of War Activities, Motion Picture Industry, 1942–1945*, vol. I, no. 1, pp. 1–5.

6. Jones to Poynter, 'War Features Inventory as of Sept. 15, 1942,' Box 1435. OWI Records; Gregory D. Black and Clayton R. Koppes, 'OWI Goes to the Movies: The Bureau of Intelligence's Criticism of Hollywood, 1942–1943,' *Prologue*, 6 (Spring 1974), 44–59.
7. Henry A. Wallace, 'The Price of Free World Victory: The Century of the Common Man,' *Vital Speeches of the Day*, VII (June 1, 1942), 482–5; Robert A. Divine, *Second Chance: The Triumph of Internationalism in America During World War II* (New York, 1967), 64–6; 'Government Information Manual for the Motion Picture Industry,' Summer 1942, April 29, 1943, Jan. 1944, Box 15, OWI Records.
8. 'Government Information Manual for the Motion Picture Industry,' Summer 1942, April 29, 1943, Jan. 1944, Box 15, OWI Records; Eddie Mannix to Executives, Producers, Writers, and Directors at MGM, Aug. 24, 1942, Box 1433E, OWI Records.
9. Script Review, 'For Whom the Bell Tolls,' Oct. 14, 1942, Box 3530, OWI Records; Robert Warshow, *The immediate Experience: Movies, Comics, Theatre & Other Aspects of Popular Culture* (Garden City, N.Y., 1962), 33–9; Warren I. Susman, 'The Thirties,' Stanley Coben and Lorman Ratner, eds., *The Development of an American Culture* (Englewood Cliffs, 1970), 200–6, 214.
10. Manuel Quezon to Lowell Mellett, Aug. 17, 1942, Mellett to Sam Goldwyn, Aug. 20, 1942, Goldwyn to Mellett, Aug. 22, 1942, Box 1433B, Script Review, 'Kim,' Aug. 4, 1942, Box 1438, Leo Rosten to Mellett, June 23, 1942, Box 888, Mellett to Victor Saville, Sept. 23, 1942, Box 3527, Poynter to Mellett, Aug. 25, 1942, Mellett to Poynter, Sept. 1, 1942, Box 1438, OWI Records; *Harrison's Reports*, Sept. 6, 1942.
11. Feature Review, *Little Tokio, U.S.A.*, July 9, 1942, Box 3518, OWI Records.
12. Poynter to Mellett, July 23, Sept. 2, 1942, Box 3518, Davis to Norman Thomas, Sept. 23, 1942, Box 3, OWI Records; Twentieth Century-Fox press release, 'Synopsis of *Little Tokio, U.S.A.*,' *Little Tokio, U.S.A.* file (Margaret Herrick Library, Academy of Motion Picture Arts and Sciences, Beverly Hills); James R. Mock and Cedric Larson, *Words That Won the War: The Story of the Committee on Public Information, 1917–1919* (Princeton, 1939), 142–56.
13. Jones to Poynter, Aug. 6, 1942, Walter White to Mellett, Aug. 17, 1942, Mellett to Maurice Revnes, Aug. 18, 1942, Mellett to Poynter, Aug. 27, 1942, Box 1433E, Poynter to Mellett, Aug. 25, 1942, Feature Review, *Tennessee Johnson*, Nov. 30, 1942, Mellett to Louis B. Mayer, Nov. 25, 1942, Box 3510, OWI Records.
14. Script Review, 'So Proudly We Hail,' Nov. 19, 1942, Poynter to Mark Sandrich, Oct. 28, 1942, June 22, 1943, 'Re Chaplain Speech – So Proudly We Hail,' Nov. 25, 1942, Box 3511, OWI Records.
15. Script Review, 'Air Force,' Oct. 27, 1942, Box 3515, Script Review, 'Bombardier,' Oct. 19, 1942, Box 3522, Script Review, 'Corregidor,' Nov. 21, 1942, Feature Review, *Corregidor*, March 3, 1943, Box 3515, Feature Review, *Guadalcanal Diary*, Oct. 26, 1943, Feature Review, *Desert Victory*, April 22, 1943, Box 3518, OWI Records; Manny Farber, 'Love in the Foxholes,' *New Republic*, 109 (Sept. 27, 1943), 426; Agee, *Agee on Film*, 52–3, 65; Sklar, *Movie-Made America*, 255; Jacobs, 'World War II and the American Film,' 13.
16. Feature Reviews, *Keeper of the Flame*, Dec. 7, 1942, Box 1435, *Pittsburgh*, Nov. 30, 1942, Poynter to Mellett, Dec. 2, 1942, Box 3520, OWI Records; 'Fascist Flame,' *Newsweek*, XXI (March 22, 1943), 80–1; 'Keeper of the Flame,' *Time*, XLI (Jan. 25, 1943), 86, 88; Stewart, *By a Stroke of Luck!*, 261–3.
17. Jones to Poynter, Nov. 6, 1942, Box 1433, Feature Review, *Lucky Jordan*, Nov. 17, 1942, Box 1435, Ulric Bell to Robert Riskin, Dec. 10, 1942, Box 3, Poynter to Mellett, Oct. 6, 19, 29, 1942. Office of Censorship Circular, Sept. 9, 1942, Box 1438, OWI Records. See also Michael Wood, *America in the Movies* (New York, 1975), 37–8.
18. Davis to Mellett, Sept. 7, 1942, Mellett to Davis, Sept. 9, 1942, Box 890, Davis press release, Sept. 11, 1942, Box 3510, OWI Records; William Tuttle, Jr.,

'Aid-to-the-Allies Short of War versus American Intervention, 1940: A Reappraisal of William Allen White's Leadership,' *Journal of American History*, LVI (March 1970), 840–58; Mark L. Chadwin, *The Warhawks: American Interventionists before Pearl Harbor* (New York, 1970), 51–92.

19. Bell to Lober, Dec. 15, 1943, Box 3530, 'Report of Activities of the Overseas Branch, Bureau of Motion Pictures, Hollywood Office, January 1, 1943-August 15, 1943,' 'Report on Activities, 1942–1945,' Sept. 18, 1945, Box 65, OWI Records.

20. Riskin to Bell, Oct. 22, 1943, Box 3510, Riskin to Edward Barrett, Aug. 12, 1944, Box 19 OWI Records; Koppes interview with Jones, Dec. 6, 1974; Robert B. Randle, 'A Study of the War Time Control Imposed on the Civilian Motion Picture Industry' (masters thesis University of Southern California, 1950), 85–16.

21. Warshow, *Immediate Experience*, 38: Agee, *Agee on Film*, 330: Ellul, *Propaganda*, 256.

PART II
FILM HISTORY FROM 1946 TO
THE PRESENT

13

POSTWAR CHALLENGES: NATIONAL REGENERATION, HUAC INVESTIGATIONS, DIVESTITURE AND DECLINING AUDIENCES

It is ubiquitous to state that the United States emerged from the Second World War as the international superpower but the wider effects on film history were socio-economic. In an economy lifted out of the Depression by the war and readjusting to peace in an evolving Cold War context, the industry enjoyed the last significant boom before facing a crisis in the 1950s. To begin with, the studios continued to enjoy the boom they had had during the war with film comedy, as when Paramount's Bob Hope saved Madeleine Carroll from Nazi spies in *My Favorite Blonde* (1942). In the postwar years his winning comic formula was copied by Red Skelton and the most popular postwar comic Danny Kaye. RKO's *The Bells of St Mary's* starring Ingrid Bergman and Bing Crosby was the studio's biggest success ever in 1945 and conflict itself proved a creative force with the most successful postwar films at the box office drawing on the war as a catalyst for drama, as in Britain with David Lean's almost-love story *Brief Encounter* (1945) and Carol Reed's *The Third Man* (1949). Starring Joseph Cotten, Alida Valli, Orson Welles and Trevor Howard, Reed's story of postwar racketeering, murder and intrigue was internationally acclaimed and remains iconic in its visualisation of war-torn Vienna augmented by the haunting zither playing of Anton Karas.

Despite America's auxiliary role in the Second World War, Hollywood made some of the most popular and evocative films about warfare, notably veteran director William A. Wellman's *Story of GI Joe* (1945) starring Burgess Meredith as war correspondent Ernie Pyle. William Wyler's *The Best Years of Our Lives* (1946) was the most successful hit of the immediate postwar period, telling the story of three men – army, navy and airforce boys – and their problems readjusting to civilian life; although the American landscape was physically untouched by war, the psychological trauma of the returning veteran found a sympathetic audience. The teaming of Dana Andrews and Fredric March with disabled veteran Harold Russell as Homer Parish, a naval engineer who lost his hands in a fire, delivered heartfelt insights into family and small-town reactions to returning servicemen. In one scene Al (March), the army sergeant returning to his position in a bank, is supposed to remain objective when deciding whether to grant loans to ex-servicemen; in another, newlywed Fred (Andrews) discovers that his wife loved only the glamour of his military uniform and when the only job he can find is as a soda jerk, their marriage ends. The unstable veteran would prove an enduring if disturbing figure introduced edgily in films such as *The Lost Weekend* (1945) through Ray Milland's despairing alcoholic, and epitomised by Robert Ryan's anti-Semitic soldier in Edward Dmytryk's *Crossfire* (1947) and Fred Zinnemann's *The Men* (1950).

In Britain, cinema had often been a signifier of optimism and escapist fare in wartime, with George Formby, Sandy Powell and Will Hay all 'joining up' to help the war effort. British cinema had a tradition of documentary realism during the war but it also had a strong streak of imagination as in the successful collaboration of director Michael Powell with Hungarian scriptwriter Emeric Pressburger from 1941 to 1956. Their idiosyncratic anti-realism, drawing attention to the very mechanics of film, should be noted in this context as iconoclastic and influential. Their collaboration and Powell's work alone from *The Life and Death of Colonel Blimp* (1943), the critique of the British military that thoroughly annoyed Winston Churchill, to *I Know Where I'm Going* (1945) was a slice of English surrealism with a strong sense of grounding not only in the postwar moment but in the future of cinema.

When the war ended, a primary challenge for nations devastated by war was to revive their national cinema as part of the rebuilding process. A number of American-produced film histories emphasise the destruction of film industries across Europe – Germany had lost around 60 per cent of its filmmaking facilities when Berlin was bombed – and consequent American expansion into foreign markets, releasing a backlog of films made during the war. The other side of the story of postwar international cinema is surprisingly buoyant, especially by 1948 once the Marshall Plan for Europe's economic rehabilitation began to be implemented. The postwar period included a golden age of British comedy and international respect for Italian neo-realism. Nations such as Britain established protectionist quotas to prevent their saturation with US imports. This was especially so in France where German occupation had prevented any American films being shown during the war. However, sometimes quotas were set too high for indigenous filmmakers realistically to meet targets and the quotas themselves contributed to problems for cinema industries rebuilding after the war. In Britain, for example, the government set the exhibition of British films at 45 per cent in 1947 and while it reduced the ceiling to 40 per cent, pressure to beat off American competition was too intense for a film industry struggling financially.

Measures to block American domination were largely unsuccessful. The British government levied a tax on American film imports but Hollywood responded by immediately rescinding the agreement to export. The boycott forced the government's hand and after a few months British producers found themselves struggling against an even bigger onslaught of material. J. Arthur Rank found other ways to compete. A minor film producer in the 1930s, he became a major exhibitor and producer postwar through the vertically-integrated Rank Organisation. Not only did he own the Odeon and Gaumont chains, Rank controlled cinemas overseas, in Canada, Australia and East Asia, and even secured a foothold in New York's Times Square. He became a major shareholder in Universal, ensuring that Rank pictures were distributed in America, and as a producer his successes included *Great Expectations* (1946), *Odd Man Out* (1947) and *The Red Shoes* (1948). Also in the late 1940s the phenomenal success of Ealing's comedies such as *Passport to Pimlico* (1949) and *Kind Hearts and Coronets* (1949) assured Michael Balcon's studio played out the notion of a postwar community spirit to huge popular appeal.

Japanese cinema also recovered at an amazing rate, especially considering the contradictions in the apparent democratisation of the film industry under American occupation. Problems that ensued included the monopoly of one company, Toho. With the monopoly broken by force with industry strikes, subsequent restructuring brought to international attention talented directors who had been working in Japan before the war including Ozu, Kenji Mizoguchi and Akira Kurosawa. Their work would herald an explosive New Wave of Japanese cinema in the 1950s. In the immediate postwar period, however, films such as Yasujiro Ozu's *Record of a Tenement Gentleman* (1947) caught the mood of devastation and crisis: a boy scours city streets in search of his father and a woman sets up a home for war orphans. Mizoguchi made much of the social freedoms of the postwar period in tackling the role of women in, for example, *The Love of Sumako the Actress* (1947).

Across Europe, Russia and Asia, for different reasons, a breadth of critical and popular cinematic movements brought distinctive national cinemas into the foreground. In Italy Mussolini's banning of American imports had helped provide the conditions in which a national cinema could begin to thrive, although pre-war fascists sought to control the content. In this climate Roberto Rossellini's *Rome, Open City* (1945) is a refreshing breath of political air and commonly acknowledged as the inaugurating film to be released under the neo-realist banner. Luchino Visconti's *Ossessione* (1942) was arguably the first neo-realist-style film but wrangles over copyright for the unauthorised adaptation of James. M. Cain's novel prevented it being released internationally for some thirty years. Rossellini and his collaborators on *Rome, Open City* used old film stock, filmed on location and often secretly as the Allies approached Rome and the Germans finally agreed not to destroy the city. Watched now, the film has the feel of newsreel or *cinéma vérité*.

The international influences on neo-realism included Soviet cinema of the 1920s and John Grierson's British documentary realism of the 1930s, movements which also evolved out of difficult national circumstances. The postwar situation in Italy was revitalised by new film studios, Cinecittà and the Centro Sperimentale led by Luigi Chiarini, and film journals such as *Bianco e Nero* and *Cinema*. Neo-realism was a materialist cinema which sought to portray the unexceptional and the concrete with non- professional actors, naturalistic lighting, unobtrusive editing and diegetic sound. Screenwriter Cesare Zavattini's premise for the movement stated that the cinema should 'tell reality as if it were a story; there must be no gap between life and what is on the screen'. His screenplay for *Bicycle Thieves* (1948), Zavattini's collaboration with Vittorio De Sica, often read as the representative neo-realist movie, exemplifies this credo because the film revolves around a stolen bicycle. Its theft is an apparently inconsequential fact that prevents a family rising above poverty; the father is unable to work and the mother has to pawn the family's sheets. The plot feels uncontrived and open-ended. The Rome backdrop shows evidence of urban overcrowding and the city's flea markets are the centres of barter and exchange, so much so that Andreotti worried that such sad and harsh portrayals washed Italy's dirty linen in public. Classic neo-realist films really ended with *Umberto D* (1952), a sad and quiet film in which a poverty-stricken elderly man, unable to pay the rent, ends up on the streets contemplating suicide. In its simplicity it has all the hallmarks of a Zavattini-inspired neo-realist narrative. There were later efforts to recapture neo-realism in style or theme in the cinema of Francesco Rosi and Ermanno Olmi, and notably Fellini who considered neo-realism a formative experience. But it was the immediate postwar films that influenced the important cinema movements that followed, including the British and French New Waves, and movements in India and Japan. Satyajit Ray's *Pather Panchali* (1955), for example, feels neo-realist in execution as does the early work of Japanese director Akira Kurosawa, such as *Ikiru* (1952).

The postwar context was full of contradictions. Amid cinematic celebrations of wartime patriotism and wholesome American family values, *film noir* exposed a morally dark world – an 'asphalt jungle' to borrow the title of John Huston's 1950 film (see Chapter 12). While the head of the postwar suburban Hollywood family was male, its heart was female and American cinema created good mothers (although such images were harder to sustain once Philip Wylie had coined the term 'Momism' for the maternally obsessed) and good wives (June Alyson, or Katherine Hepburn playing Spencer Tracey's wife in a raft of postwar films). Throughout the 1940s women's roles simmered with ideological tensions but the wider basis for postwar anxiety was the US' relationship with the USSR, not only in terms of the nuclear arms race but ideologically as well. In a period of right-wing anti-communist paranoia two

American political trials stood out as extreme and excessive to the rest of the world: the trial and imprisonment of Alger Hiss as a Soviet spy and the sentencing to death of Julius and Ethel Rosenberg for supposedly delivering the secret of the atomic bomb to Russia. Such events and press coverage of them fuelled the American public's anxiety over the communist 'threat'. When the government response to that threat began to focus on US film production, the blacklisting of Hollywood talent decimated the industry just as television began to impact on the movies. Lives were destroyed and careers left in tatters. Those who had turned to communism in the face of the Depression or to protest America's isolationism, and specifically the nation's neutrality in the Spanish Civil War, were to be the nation's scapegoats. Anti-communism would become venomous in Hollywood.

In the years of the communist witch-hunt, films were released exuding paranoia, pervasive corruption, human malevolence and psychological dislocation: the cinema's response to a Hollywood in crisis. In *In a Lonely Place* (1950), for example, Humphrey Bogart plays Dixon Steele, a Hollywood screenwriter believed to have raped a woman. The pressure of rumours sends Dix and those around him, notably Gloria Grahame as his girlfriend, into a heightened state of paranoia. Russia had fought with the Allies in the Second World War and a loose reflection of the positive light in which the USSR was viewed in the period was apparent in American movies such as *The North Star* and *Mission to Moscow*, both released in 1943. Postwar, however, fear and anxiety simmered and once it was understood that Russia had tested a nuclear bomb in 1949, paranoia spiralled and films such as these and others, originally thought to be patriotic and democratic, were rendered suspiciously pro-communist. Even Wyler's 7-Oscar smash *The Best Years of Our Lives* was raised as an example of a film in which a communist-style collectivism was highlighted. Ayn Rand, whose *Screen Guide for Americans* was published in 1950, retrospectively invoked New Deal ideology and the emphasis on 'the common man' as politically dangerous. Such provocation was enough to stir Samuel Goldwyn to defend his studio's massive hit. In short, New Deal liberalism had collapsed by 1950, as epitomised by Henry Wallace's failed 1948 campaign.

The Motion Picture Alliance for the Preservation of American Ideals had first invited the House of Un-American Activities Commission (HUAC) to Hollywood in 1947. HUAC was first chaired by the Republican Congressman J. Parnell Thomas (who would in 1951 find himself imprisoned for fraud) and by the early 1950s the commission had stirred up a moral panic over the 'Reds' in the Hollywood hills. HUAC aimed to indict scriptwriters who, it was believed, were responsible for inserting pro-communist propaganda into films and several of those who appeared, including Gary Cooper and Ayn Rand, swore that they could detect the stench of communism even in its most diluted forms in scripts. Of the nineteen people subpoenaed to appear in Washington in 1947, eight were writers, with Dalton Trumbo, John Howard Lawson and

Ring Lardner Jr perhaps the best known. Edward Dmytryk was the lone director among what became known as the 'Hollywood Ten' and Adrian Scott the lone producer; both were subpoenaed because they made *Crossfire* in 1947. The novel from which the movie was adapted involved the murder of a homosexual but in the film version the hate crime became anti-Semitic to get around the Production Code. With Robert Ryan as the all-American veteran who beats a Jewish veteran to death, *Crossfire* was one of the big hits of 1947 but lost out in the Academy Awards to Elia Kazan's *Gentlemen's Agreement*, a film that also took anti-Semitism as its theme.

The Hollywood Ten appealed HUAC's decision via the Supreme Court but were jailed for contempt of Congress and drummed out of Hollywood. Instrumental in this regard was the Association of Motion Picture Producers who, in a statement known as the 'Waldorf Declaration', lent their support to HUAC. While many actors and directors including John Huston, Humphrey Bogart, Lauren Bacall and Danny Kaye petitioned HUAC and flew to Washington to protest the hearings, had Hollywood producers refused to stand by the HUAC decision, it is doubtful that the purge could have continued. But, as film history shows, of the most powerful figures in Hollywood only Samuel Goldwyn (originally a 'friendly witness' but incensed by the aspersions cast on *The Best Years of Our Lives*) and Dore Schary of RKO who produced *Crossfire*, opposed the decision to disallow the Hollywood Ten from working in the industry. Blacklisting continued with a vengeance to cleanse the industry of any remaining communist sympathisers. With renewed vigour, HUAC inevitably settled on left-leaning liberals such as John Garfield who starred in both *Body and Soul* (1947) and Polonsky's *Force of Evil* (1948), the directors having already been the focus of investigation. Garfield's career was destroyed when he was asked to 'name names' and was accused of being an 'unfriendly witness'. Garfield's early death at 39, like that of Canada Lee, his black co-star in *Body and Soul*, was generally believed to have resulted from the stress of the witch-hunts. It has been variously estimated that 350 people suffered the ignominy of castigation by HUAC. Many refused to testify and left America for exile in Europe (for example, Joseph Losey, Jules Dassin, John Berry), but black-listed writers sometimes continued to work though their contributions remained uncredited. For actors (for example, Kim Hunter, Larry Parks, Zero Mostel) it was obviously more difficult to function and they faded from the screen. Although HUAC continued in one guise or another until it was officially wound up in the mid-1970s, in 1960 its directives were ignored when Otto Preminger and Kirk Douglas (as producer) credited Dalton Trumbo for his scripts for *Exodus* and *Spartacus*. Trumbo had already been awarded an Oscar as 'Robert Rich' for the screenplay of *The Brave One* in 1956 but had been unable to collect it in person.

Various films make analogous reference to the Congressional Committee hearings and the menacing question, 'Are you now, or have you ever been, a member of the Communist Party?' *High Noon* (1952) may be read, according to its writer Carl Foreman, as a parable of HUAC's attack on Hollywood, with Gary Cooper – who as a founder member of the Motion Picture Alliance first invited HUAC to town – ironically winning an Oscar in the leading role. *On the Waterfront* (1954) may also be read as a justification of director Kazan's own co-operation with the hearings as a 'friendly witness' (a member of the Communist Party, he resigned when he left Broadway for Hollywood). The rejection that Brando's Terry Molloy suffers at the hands of a mob syndicate out to break the workers is made analogous to the Communist Party: 'Keep quiet, you'll live longer.' Molloy defies corrupt union officials to testify before the Waterfront Crime Commission ('I'm glad what I done') and his testimony finally sets the union back on its feet.

The ideological emphasis on Cold War consensus permeated even the newest media and in 1950 the television company CBS followed the McCarthy line by asking potential employees to answer the questions: 'Are you now, or have you ever been, a member of the Communist Party USA, or any communist organisation?' In Hollywood while HUAC scrutinised the industry, a clutch of anti-communist or 'Red Scare' movies were released including *The Iron Curtain* (1948), *The Red Menace* (1949) and *I Married a Communist* (1949). Few had any box office clout. 'Fellow travellers' with the Communist Party, not necessarily even former members, were made to seem like fifth columnists, spying for the enemy; and, conversely, the undercover communist infiltrator (*I Was a Communist for the FBI* [1951]) and the spy became a cinematic trope of the Cold War era. Howard Hughes and John Wayne, who became vociferously anti-communist, were involved in RKO's *Jet Pilot* (1957), a bizarre film in which Wayne persuades a Russian woman (Janet Leigh) that life is much better in America, the land of free enterprise. Also in the postwar period, the Japanese film industry experienced its own form of witch-hunt while under American occupation, following the country's surrender after atomic bombs were dropped on Hiroshima and Nagasaki. The new regulating body, Civil Information and Education, with General MacArthur overseeing, expected the Japanese film unions to provide the names of 'war criminals'.

Cold War politics cannot account for all the contradictions of the immediate postwar culture. While the demonisation of communism, socialism and liberalism produced a yardstick with which to measure the political temperature of cultural productions, the film industry was also facing problems of divestiture and declining audiences. By the end of the Second World War, the big five Hollywood studios controlled 90 per cent of the movie theatres across the US but efforts to penetrate foreign markets were overtaken by problems with the domestic market. The battle over the control of first-run theatres had really begun in the 1920s but the divestiture of theatre chains from studio control finally occurred in the late 1940s. The first anti-trust suit had been filed in 1938 with the hope of destroying the oligarchic practices of the studios which included distribution control over which theatres could show first-, second- or third-run movies and what they could charge for admission. The anti-trust suits hoped to ensure the divorce of theatres from the studios, thereby breaking open the vertically integrated Hollywood system. Postponements and adjournments as well as an interim 'win' by the studios led to a petitioning of the Supreme Court and a reverse decision in favour of divestiture which the studios then appealed.

In 1948 the government finally won an anti-trust suit that divorced production from exhibition and everything in Hollywood began to change. The decision that brought about the divestiture was known as the 'Paramount decision' because Paramount Studios was the named adversary against the courts. The Hollywood studios were instructed by the Supreme Court to uncouple from their theatre chains and to terminate all joint business interests that had created a monopoly on exhibition. The studios fought against the divestiture of their theatre interests and the opening up of the industry was slow. Ratified by the Supreme Court, the decision operated as a series of decrees and just like the *Brown* decision for the integration of segregated schools in 1954, it was carried out with 'all deliberate speed', the kind of oxymoron that impeded progress rather than assured immediate impact on the five theatre circuits that had been divorced from their former 'parent' studios, or on independent exhibitors and cinemagoers. After 1948 the theatres diversified: less successful theatres were closed and different types of theatres were purchased, such as drive-ins. Some circuits expanded into film production and some theatres that had formerly shown newsreels transformed into arts theatres. Independent exhibitors gained the freedom to licence pictures singly and to bid for first-run preferences where they had previously been limited to later runs, even when situated in busy downtown areas. However, exhibitors were continuously battling for audiences.

Film audiences did not decline only because of the *Paramount* case or because of television; cinema attendance had begun falling away before 1948 and before most American homes were equipped with a television set. But, after *Paramount*, the industry found itself challenged in new and diverse ways with banks reluctant to invest in an unstable product. The consequences throughout the 1950s would include a reduction in the number of pictures produced, an emphasis on 'big' pictures to attract audiences away from their television sets, and a diversification of the venues in which films could be viewed. That television would trigger a revolution in communications had been predicted by some as early as the 1920s, just as it had been feared the movies would prove the death of the theatre in their early years, but it was in the 1950s that the new medium of home entertainment would begin to affect Hollywood's success in securing the biggest audiences. At the end of the Second World War, film audiences had hit an all-time peak – in the US in 1946 it was estimated that they reached the 80 million mark – but thereafter they declined and after the *Paramount* decrees began to take effect, independent exhibitors were hit once again, this time by the decline in B movies and low-medium budget pictures when TV series and soap operas and increasing TV rentals of films took over the market. Many small theatres closed because they could not compete with the success of the new drive-ins or with television.

Some genres succeeded in generating creative crossovers with television. The crossover between the 'women's picture', melodrama and *film noir* in the immediate postwar period was epitomised in the work of women screenwriters and directors, still largely unsung despite feminist interventions into cinema history. Catherine Turney turned James M. Cain's novel into the screenplay *Mildred Pierce* (1945) and Leigh Bracket worked alongside William Faulkner and Howard Hawks on *The Big Sleep* (1946). She continued to write for Hawks, most notably on the traditionally 'male' westerns *Rio Bravo* (1959) and *Rio Lobo* (1970). Lenore J. Coffee wrote *Sudden Fear* (1952) which provided an emotional roller-coaster of a role for Joan Crawford, and Marion Parsonnet scripted *Gilda* (1946), in which Rita Hayworth sings 'Put the Blame on Mame' in an iconic cinema moment. Actress Ida Lupino directed *The Bigamist* (1953) amongst other respected films. Finding herself described at the 1949 Oscar ceremony as the most attractive director in the business indicates what an anomaly Lupino was in a male-dominated industry. Muriel Box the British director, for whom the Second World War had provided a foothold in the industry, began by directing shorts for her husband Sidney's production company but went on to direct a clutch of features with feminist themes. Neither Lupino nor Box has yet received the attention they deserve.

In the postwar context the anxiety returning veterans felt about female loyalty had developed by the 1950s into feminine anxiety over the circum-scription of gendered roles, bound up in what the American cultural critic Betty Friedan, writing in 1963 but casting back to the 1950s, would call 'the feminine mystique'. This was the patriarchal ideology that led women to forgo college education, settle into domesticity as early as possible as wives and mothers, even with university degrees, and suffer later from 'the problem with no name', a restless desire for self-worth and autonomy. If Rosie the Riveters were seen to atrophy after their wartime contribution to the workforce, there was no collective feminist response to the problem in the 1950s, although some comedies and dramas touch on that frustration. For example, in *Calamity Jane* (1953), Doris Day successfully avoids marriage for most of the film but once caught in the romantic 'trap' swiftly sublimates her personality. In *Please Don't Eat the Daisies* filmed in 1960, again with Day, there is gentle critique of the ways in which leisure and material aspirations on the part of middle-class women should displace any political discontent they might have.

One marketing strategy that maintained its popularity across film and television through the 1940s and 1950s was the 'Woman's Film', a slippery term that gained currency in film studies after Molly Haskell used it in 1974 in *From Reverence to Rape*, her study of representations of women in the cinema. Haskell and those who followed her have pointed out that since historically there has been no mention of 'Men's Films', the studio production category refers not to genre but to the overt targeting of women as the primary audiences for productions that cross generic categories – melodrama, *film noir*, soap opera, for example, and the commodities entailed in such productions. In her materialist ethnographic study 'With Stars in their Eyes: Female Spectators and the Paradoxes of Consumption', Jackie Stacey investigates a very specific 'lost' cinema audience: British women cinema-goers in the 1940s and 1950s. She analyses their responses to Hollywood's packaging and promoting of a luxurious lifestyle through their favourite stars, and their fashions and cosmetics.

Stacey's methodological focus is on audience and its relation to film texts; in her study cinema is a social phenomenon, and she examines the act of spectatorship and the reception of – and investment in – particular stars in popular memory in the 1980s. Her context is the tastes and preferences of a broad base of (white) female respondents of a similar age (over 60) and class (lower-middle and working) who are readers of the same two women's magazines. The women respond to precise questionnaires Stacey has compiled but are also encouraged to write freely of the glamour and nostalgia that the era and its fashions stir up in their memories. Stacey's interpretation of her interviewees' comments addresses their imitation of fashions, hairstyles and stars' mannerisms and their adaptation of their preferences to local circumstances. Consequently, she posits a collective response in which the respondents through their accounts of cinemagoing become the protagonists of her study: their femininity is as much the subject of study as that of stars such as Doris Day, Lauren Bacall and Deana Durbin, and their pleasure in spectatorship and consumption the subject of detailed theorisation.

In this way, Stacey is able to argue that female spectatorship is not passive but negotiated and that the gap between American stars and British audience involves not only desire, fantasy and imitation but also considerable creativity and agency in the postwar years when economising and rationing remained significant features of British society. Returning to the postwar years in the 1980s, Stacey demonstrates a nostalgic return on the part of the women not only to their younger selves but in celebration of a period in Hollywood history and legend when 'stars were really stars'.

- How effective is Stacey's audience-led approach in opening up the problems with psychoanalytical models of cinema spectatorship and/or production-led models of consumerism?
- Assess the difficulties inherent in using fans' memories of cinemagoing forty years earlier as a basis for analysis. What other materials might Stacey have used?
- Outline and examine another historically specific example of the complex relationship between a film industry and a culturally specific audience. What materials would you use to create an equally effective case study? How important are national differences when investigating audiences?

WITH STARS IN THEIR EYES:
FEMALE SPECTATORS AND THE PARADOXES OF CONSUMPTION

Jackie Stacey

[. . .]

Shared Investments

An analysis of female spectators' memories of Hollywood stars in 1940s and 1950s Britain demonstrates the significance of the discourse of consumption to the spectator/star relationship. In addition to escapism and identification [. . .] consumption appeared frequently in spectators' accounts of their attachments to Hollywood stars at this time. That female spectators and film stars were closely connected through commodity purchase, then, can be established through the study of *both* commodity production and consumption. But the question here is what conclusions can be drawn from such connections. How do female spectators remember the significance of consumption practices and how might their accounts highlight a more contradictory relationship between spectatorship and consumption than that presented by the production studies? Did consumption simply tie women more tightly into forms of subordination, and if so, what is to be made of their pleasure and delight in such cultural practices?

In this section I examine spectators' memories of their consumption practices in terms of the importance of feminine cultural competence. The knowledge and expertise involved in such competence forms the basis of intense bonding with, and emotional, as well as financial, investment in, particular stars. In addition, connections between female spectators are formed through such shared knowledges and the use to which they may be put.

> I favoured Lauren Bacall most of all during the 1940s and 1950s and still have an interest in her . . . My colouring was the same as hers, I wore my hair in a similar style and wore the same type of tailored clothes. In the early 1940s . . . matching shoes, gloves and handbag were a 'must'. I remember Lauren Bacall always kept to this unwritten rule, and I identified with her because of that, they were my 'trademark' for years. It was surprising how quickly fashions from the films caught on. In *To Have and Have Not* Lauren Bacall wore a dogtooth check suit and small round pill-box hat, black gloves and shoes and handbag – I can remember I had one very similar with a tan pill-box . . . and my hair in a page-boy like hers. The only difference was that she wore hers without a blouse.
>
> (Kathleen Lucas)

Jackie Stacey, *Star Gazing: Hollywood Cinema and Female Spectatorship* (London: Routledge, 1994).

Here Lauren Bacall is written about within the language of product selection: she was 'favoured' above others. She is also appreciated for her enduring value: 'I still have an interest in her'. In turn, the female spectator, through her identification with the star, becomes a product herself, using the language of commodities to describe what characterised her particular personal style: her 'trademark' was the same as Lauren Bacall's in that they both shared the knowledge that matching shoes, gloves and handbags were a 'must'. Interestingly, the term 'trademark' is set in inverted commas by the respondent, as if to suggest a self-awareness, even irony, about this process of self-commodification: it is inappropriate for a woman to have a trademark, since this usually signifies a commodity, and yet it captures very well that production of self as image that is being described here.

The star is selected because of a recognition of resemblance with the spectator (Lauren Bacall had similar colouring); thus star selection involves female spectators looking for themselves (in every sense) in their star ideals. However, differences are also remembered as significant: the style and pattern of the suit is a mimetic representation, but the colour of the hat is different and Bacall's lack of blouse was obviously striking enough to be remembered. The more sexualised star is significant both in terms of national difference and in terms of the licence of Hollywood stars to present a more sexualised image than would have been acceptable for most women in 1940s Britain. Despite this difference, however, there is a strong memory of recognition and similarity. Indeed, this particular example suggests the importance of a shared feminine culture during this period based upon knowledge, expertise and 'unwritten rules'. The shared recognition in the conventions of feminine appearance produce the basis for pleasure and appreciation for this female spectator: 'I remember Lauren Bacall always kept to this unwritten rule, and I identified with her because of that'. Consumer taste, linking star and spectator, is based upon the recognition of shared feminine expertise, invisible to the 'outsider' since these rules are felt to be 'unwritten'.

Female spectators remember Hollywood stars through their connection with particular commodities and the ways in which they were worn or displayed. Typically, this association is made in relation to clothes, hair-styles, make-up and cosmetics, and other fashion accessories. It is the commodities associated with physical attractiveness and appearance that are especially remembered in connection with female stars: clothes and accessories in this case, as in most others.

The speed with which the images on the screen become images 'on the streets' is commented upon here: replications of outfits and styles are remembered as taking place swiftly after the viewing of a particular film. Another respondent offers a similar account of purchasing an outfit to copy a star after seeing a particular film:

> and I bought clothes like hers [Doris Day] . . . dresses, soft wool, no
> sleeves, but short jackets, boxey type little hats, half hats we used to call
> them and low heeled court shoes to match your outfit, kitten heels they

were called . . . as people said I looked like her [Marilyn Monroe]. I even bought a suit after seeing her in *Niagara*.

(Patricia Ogden)

The detail of the memory of particular fashions and how stars wore them in films is part of the specificity of feminine cultural competence: the colours, patterns, cut and design of clothes remains a vivid memory some fifty years later. This attests to the significance of this connection for female spectators and demonstrates the intensity of their emotional, as well as financial, investments in such details of personal appearance. Pride in having an eye for detail and the ability to recall it so many years later is expressed in the following example:

The female stars of my major filmgoing period made a big impact on me. I can see a short clip from a film and know instantly whether I've seen it before or not – and as like or not, be able to add – 'then she moves off down the staircase' or 'the next dress she appears in is white, with puffy net sleeves'.

(M. Palin)

The extraordinarily vivid memories here demonstrate the intense emotional investment in Hollywood at this time. This intensity may be because of the heightened emotional investment many young women make in feminine ideals and thus is explicable in terms of life stages. This might also be reinforced by the process of looking back and reminiscing about youthful pleasures and thus be explained in terms of nostalgia [. . .] Finally, this intensity could also be due to the feelings of recognition of the significance of Hollywood stars in the lives of respondents, after many years of little external recognition and indeed, in many cases even ridicule for their fandom [. . .]

What is striking about the two examples given by M. Palin is the way in which the memories selected both, though in different ways, focus on particular icons of femininity. The woman descending the staircase is an image from Hollywood in which female stars are typically displayed to on-lookers below, and to cinema spectators, often at moments in the film when their costumes are of crucial significance. This female icon is also significant to another respondent quoted elsewhere who remembered replicating such movement after the film screening: 'Our favourite cinema was the Ritz – with its deep pile carpet and double sweeping staircase. Coming down one always felt like a heroine descending into the ballroom' (Anon). The second image selected to exemplify the endurance of this particular respondent's memory also draws upon a particular feminine iconography: the whiteness of the dress signifies purity and virginity, the puffy sleeves an abundance of material and the net material a semi-transparency to display the female body.

Although these examples do establish a clear link between formations of female subjectivity and processes of self-commodification through con-sumption, they also demonstrate that this is by no means the only significance of consumption practices to female spectatorship. Within the world of female knowledge and expertise, consumption also importantly involved processes of (mutual) recognition between spectators, and between them and their favourite stars, and a passionate connection to feminine ideals. Thus although the end product of such emotional and financial investments in ideal and self image may be the patriarchal institution of marriage, it is important not to deny the intense pleasure and delight in forms of feminine culture reproduced between female spectators and stars in the process.

'The Intimacy Which is Knowledge'[1]

There are important forms of intimacy involved in these shared feminine identities, between spectator and star ideal, and between female spectators. The recognition of shared knowledge forms the basis for such intimacy between femininities which has tended to be ignored in existing accounts of feminine consumption.

Hollywood stars in the 1940s and 1950s were strongly remembered by female spectators for their connection with fashion, and many stars became favourites because of this association:

> The Doris Day films I used to watch mainly for the clothes – she was always dressed in the latest fashions.
>
> (Mrs D. Delves)

> The clothes and the make-up were of great interest. Bear in mind 'teenagers' had not been invented in the late 1940s, so clothes were not on the market for that age group. We seemed to go from school children to grown-ups. The fashion scene was nothing like today's mass market. We had a few outfitters and the chainstores. What was worn on the screen was of importance.
>
> (Anon)

> I loved the cool charm of stars such as Deborah Kerr . . . my childhood dream was to become like her and I used to spend hours shop window gazing and selecting what she would wear.
>
> (Judith Ford)

In these statements the role of film stars as fashion models, advertising the latest styles to female spectators, comes across clearly. In the first example, a particular star is appreciated for her up-to-date clothes in her films. The selection of Doris Day in this role occurred frequently amongst respondents: 'Doris Day was a natural star to me, when she did anything it was always 100% – everything about her is perfect, the clothes she wore and everything' (Shirley Thompson). Clothes and fashion are central here to the attainment of feminine ideals: 'clothes and everything' could be read here as clothes are everything; if you can get them right your femininity is established. There is a delight expressed here in the star who always 'got it right' which again exemplifies a shared cultural competence. Consumer taste is thus based upon forms of recognition between women which constitute a shared cultural competence (see Bourdieu, 1984).

The second example highlights the importance of 'what was worn on the screen' in relation to the transition to adult femininity. Hollywood film stars seemed to play a key role in this rather nerve-racking and treacherous journey, typically full of potential pitfalls and failures. Transition from childhood to adult femininity is signified through the transformation of the body and how it is clothed and presented. Given the centrality of physical appearance to cultural definitions of femininity, the stakes are high in this process of transformation. Film stars, representing cultural ideals of feminine beauty and charm, played a key role in these processes of identity formation. This memory draws attention to the contrast between contemporary consumer markets and those of the 1940s and 1950s. The significance of stars to spectators' knowledge of consumer fashion is reconstructed as particularly focused in the light of the expansion and diversification of fashion markets since that time.

In the final example, the spectator takes on the imaginary position of her favourite star in relation to consumption of female attire. The spectator's own identity is replaced through her imaginary identification with her ideal. This replacement of self with ideal subject position is effected through the fantasy of consumption; thus the spectator and star are linked, not through the purchasing of clothes, but through the gazing and desiring of the female spectator/consumer who imagines her ideal's choice of commodities. Cinema screen and shop window both display their spectacles: respectively, the female star and her imaginary outfits. Hollywood stars are thus linked to other com-modities by the desiring female spectator/consumer who fantasises an ideal feminine self-image through imaginary consumption. The desire to clothe your favourite star, to predict her taste and style and to imagine her in the outfit of your choice suggests an intense intimacy between female spectators and stars. Indeed, it further points to a recognition of 'self-in-ideal' in being able to predict what the star would consume.

All three examples point to the personal investments of spectators in particular stars in terms of commodities associated with female appearance. As the final one suggests, this investment may not be financial, but often took the form of fantasy and imagined identities:

> But Doris Day wore some beautifully cut clothes in some wonderful colours . . . this was in the 1940s when I first became aware of Doris Day – 'My Dream Is Yours' – need I say more!
>
> (Marie Burgess)

Here the spectator and a favourite star are linked through a common dream in which clothes are the currency of a shared femininity. The language of dreams is used frequently by respondents to describe their longings and desires in relation to Hollywood stars. The dream metaphor not only suggests the star ideal is unreachable, but also indicates a state of blissful happiness. Here the title of Doris Day's second film, *My Dream Is Yours*, is used as a self-explanatory statement in which the respondent hopes to encapsulate the exchange between spectator and star, an exchange involving particular commodities, in this case 'beautifully cut clothes in some wonderful colours'. Thus spectators are linked to stars through imagined intimacy with the Hollywood ideal; what more intimate than a shared dream?

Star Styles

In this section the connection between Hollywood stars and spectators is examined through an analysis of the construction of feminine style. The national differences between American and British femininity are especially significant to the attachment of fans to particular Hollywood stars. Differences of taste are articulated in relation to the meanings of British and American femininity at this time. Conforming to star styles in some cases could be seen as the successful reproduction of ideals of feminine appearance through consumption. This would certainly reiterate the claims made in the production studies of mutually beneficial collaboration between Hollywood and other industries (Eckert, 1978; Allen, 1980; and Doane, 1989). In other cases, however, American feminine ideals are clearly remembered as transgressing restrictive British femininity and thus employed as strategies of resistance:

> Joan Crawford looked good in suits with big shoulder pads; Barbara Stanwyck shone in diaphanous creations (it always intrigued me how dressed up they were in ordinary everyday situations).
>
> (Marie Burgess)

Many respondents used discourses of fashion to write about their favourite Hollywood stars. Some appreciated the 'fit' between fashion style and star: the semi-transparent nature of the outfit allows the star quality to shine through, for example, in the above statement: 'Barbara Stanwyck shone in diaphonous creations'. Similarly, Joan Crawford's star image as a fierce and powerful woman, rivalled only by Bette Davis, is constructed partly through her more 'masculine' costumes: 'suits with big shoulder pads'. The final comment here suggests a fascination with the incongruity of the narrativised situations and the costumes of Hollywood stars, pointing to a use of films to display women's fashions at the expense of 'realism'.

As well as remembering favourite stars through a variety of different styles of femininity, some respondents associated Hollywood stars with particular items of clothing:

> I'd like to name Deanna Durbin as one of my favourite stars. Her beautiful singing voice, natural personality and sparkling eyes made her films so enjoyable, and one always knew she would wear boleros; in one

film she wore six different ones. I still like wearing boleros – so you can see what a lasting effect the clothes we saw on the screen made on us.

(Jean Davis, Member of the Deanna Durbin Society)

In this case an item of clothing, the bolero, is remembered as Deanna Durbin's 'trademark'. The spectator takes pleasure in the fulfilment of the expectation that Deanna Durbin would appear in her films wearing this particular item of clothing. The spectator is connected to one of her favourite stars through her own purchase and wearing of this distinctive clothing sign. Again the enduring quality of these investments in star styles, replicated through commodity consumption, is striking: some forty years later the same item is worn with pleasure.

Some items of clothing were associated with Hollywood generally:

> We copied whatever we could from the stars we saw in the films. We even sent off by post to Malta and Gibraltar for Hollywood Nylons. And we got them by post.
>
> (Mary Wilson)

The use of Hollywood as an adjective here connects the cinema to the fashion industry. In particular, 'nylons' were a luxury item in Britain at this time, much sought after and extremely scarce; the connection to America would have been reinforced through the presence of American troops in Britain and their easier access to such products. In addition, nylons signify a specific form of display of the female body: the translucent covering of the leg with a fine material which emphasises smoothness and shapeliness. The display of particular parts of the female body, as I shall go on to discuss, is something which connects female spectators and stars, often a connection cemented through commodity consumption.

The connection between Hollywood and the women's fashion industry is made especially clear in the way that certain products were named after stars, not by the industries, but by the female spectators:

> I had a pair of Carmen Miranda platform shoes with ankle straps.
>
> (Vera Barford)

> The earliest film star I remembered was Shirley Temple, because I was the proud owner of a Shirley Temple style dress.
>
> (Mrs M. Breach)

Products are thus named after the stars associated with them, and female spectators purchase styles which give them a feeling of connection with their ideal:

> It was fun trying to copy one's favourite stars with their clothes, hats and even make-up, especially the eyebrows. Hats were very much in vogue at that time and shops used to sell models similar to the styles the stars were wearing. I was very much into hats myself and tried in my way (on a low

budget) to copy some of them. Naturally I bought a Deanna Durbin model hat and a Rita Haywortn one.

(Vera Carter)

Stars are inextricably linked to consumption in these examples in that their commodification extends beyond the cinema and into spectator's purchasing practices of female fashions. Stars are thus commodities within the Hollywood film industry and, in addition, their names become commodities in the fashion industry in Britain as they are used to describe particular styles.

This naming and copying of star styles was remembered in relation to hairstyles, as well as clothes and shoes:

> Now Doris Day . . . I was told many times around that I looked like her, so I had my hair cut in a D.A. style . . . Jane Wyman was a favourite at one stage and I had my hair cut like hers, it was called a tulip . . . Now Marilyn Monroe was younger and by this time I had changed my image, my hair was almost white blonde and longer and I copied her hairstyle, as people said I looked like her.

(Patricia Ogden)

Physical resemblance here links the spectator to Hollywood stars and the replication of stars' hairstyles affirms this connection further. Self-image is infinitely transformable, mirroring Hollywood ideals with new colours and styles of hair. Recognition of self in ideal shifts from star to star in an endless chain of commodification. Public recognition is crucial here; it is through other people's recognition of the spectator/star resemblance that this respondent presents her connection to particular stars (see Benjamin, 1990).

Hairstyles were an important part of the physical transformations which took place in the attempt to become more like one's ideal: whether the more 'masculine' short crop of Doris Day's down-to-earth tomboyishness or the seductive 'peek-a-boo' hairstyle of Veronica Lake:

> Doris Day is the greatest and in the 50's she had a haircut called the 'Butch cut' which I had to be like her.

(Shirley Thompson)

> I think we all liked to identify with our favourite entertainers. Why else did we copy their styles and clothes. During the forties there were thousands of Veronica Lakes walking about. Girls who copied her peek-a-boo hairstyles – long and waved over one eye.

(Mrs Patricia Robinson)

Hollywood star styles and fashions are frequently referred to in the British context in terms of representing something different, something better and often something more sophisticated or even risqué. The impact of star styles on women in Britain was so strong that it was recognised as a problem by the state, which introduced safety regulations about women's hairstyles in factories during this period (Braybon and Summerfield, 1987). It also meant frequent conflict or power struggles with authority figures such as parents:

> Girlfriends talked incessantly about stars . . . We discussed film star fashions – we were clothes mad. We wanted to dye our hair and copy the stars but we couldn't get permission from our parents.
>
> (Anon)

'Dyeing one's hair' clearly represented some kind of act of transgression or rebellion against the codes of respectable femininity in Britain at this time, since dyed hair suggested sexuality, independence and even prostitution. But it was not only sexuality that was seen as threatening, it was also the imitation of images of powerful femininity associated with stars such as Joan Crawford or Bette Davis:

> My father used to say 'don't you roll those Bette Davis eyes at me young lady'.
>
> (Patricia Ogden)

The conventions of feminine appearance are remembered not only in terms of the reassuring conformity and predictability of Hollywood stars, however, but also in terms of stars breaking with certain fashion codes:

> We were quick to notice any change in fashion and whether it had arrived this side of the Atlantic. We were pleased to see younger stars without gloves and hats – we soon copied them. Had it not been wartime we might not have got away with it, because British fashion then was very old-fashioned and rules were rigid.
>
> (Kathleen Lucas)

Hollywood stars represented fashions on the screen which were identified by spectators as transgressing restrictive codes of British feminine appearance. Indeed, Hollywood stars were considered exciting in contrast to images of femininity offered by women in everyday life in Britain:

> I liked the clothes they often wore, we talked about their hair, make-up, figures and dress. I liked stars unlike myself because in my young days they appeared much more attractive . . . Our mothers were very matronly at quite an early age.
>
> (Anon)

The reference to 'matronly' mothers here in opposition to glamorous Hollywood stars reinforces the familiar pervasive cultural dichotomy between motherhood and sexuality. The two main sources of information about femininity in the 1940s and 1950s, kinship and the cinema, are thus understood as being in opposition to each other and further reinforced by stereotypical national difference, American glamour versus British respectability.

The negotiation of idealised Hollywood femininities with mothers led to memories of intense emotional struggles:

> I was fascinated with Shirley Temple . . . she always looked perfect. I loved her curls and as I was about the same age I begged my mother to do my hair like hers with rags or tongs. But I was made to keep my plaits. As for her dresses I was envious of them. However I remember my mother receiving a second-hand dress for me which was very much like the ones she used to wear. I was thrilled and told everyone it was my Shirley Temple dress.
>
> (Muriel Breach)

The language used here suggests a strength of feeling in the attempt to copy the star ideal: this respondent felt love, fascination and envy towards her childhood idol, 'begged' her mother to copy Shirley Temple's hairstyle and was 'thrilled' when she had a Shirley Temple dress. These examples from childhood demonstrate the breadth of the impact of Hollywood stars on women in Britain during this period: it was not only regular cinema spectators with purchasing power who were addressed as consumers by Hollywood, but young girls, too, who relied on second-hand clothes for their star-like replications.

As well as being vehicles to encourage female spectators to become consumers, and to improve their appearances, then, Hollywood stars were also contested terrains of competing cultural discourses of femininity. As I have shown, they were central to challenges to what was perceived as restrictive British femininity, be it 'the dowdiness' of women in wartime Britain, the restrictions of factory regulations about hairstyles or the perceived lack of glamour of motherhood. Many respondents had vivid memories of Hollywood stars as representing an alternative to what they perceived to be these constraining forms of British femininity. In the 1950s particularly, when the purchase of fashions and cosmetics increasingly became a possibility for many women in Britain, the reproduction of self-image through consumption was perceived as a way of producing new forms of 'American' feminine identity which were exciting, sexual, pleasurable and in some ways transgressive.

The Body Beautiful

> Since women enter the market place as commodities, they are under pressure to make themselves externally presentable – to use attractive packaging to bump up their market price, or to make themselves saleable in the first place. Implicit in the image of the carefully groomed woman is an assumption that the exchange value of woman is open to manipulation, that it may be added to to give use value as an external appendage . . . Women's particular mode of socialization centres on the female body and through it the whole range of women's skills and potential competences unfolds within pre-given constraints.
>
> (Haugg, 1986: 131)

Hollywood sold its stars as icons of feminine attractiveness, whose beauty could be replicated through the purchase of particular commodities. One of the most frequent discourses through which female Hollywood stars were sold to spectators was that of the body. It is through the body that feminine identity is constructed (Haugg, 1986), and the fragmentation and commodification of the female body has been a source of much feminist debate about the specificity of women's alienation and oppression. However, as well as exploring these processes of fragmentation in the replication of ideals of feminine beauty, I shall analyse the ways in which the focus on the body, especially the face, had a different significance for female spectators in terms of the personalisation of the female star. Close-up displays of parts of the female may have functioned, not to alienate and objectify, but to produce a fascination which was remembered as a form of intimacy by female spectators. Thus, ironically, the very fetishism and fragmentation criticised within feminist film theory seems to have had a rather different meaning for spectators whose memories of such effects can be understood as a form of personalisation of the Hollywood star otherwise kept at a distance on the screen.

One striking characteristic of consumption practices amongst my respondents in relation to Hollywood stars, then, is the centrality of the female body as a key site of consumption during this period. The body was a central topic in the articulation of the relationship between female stars and spectators. Female stars were not only bodies on display providing ideals of feminine beauty – they were also used to sell products to female spectators for their self-improvement. Thus the female body was both sexual spectacle and the site of consumption:

> Rita Hayworth was a joy to watch dancing. She had a lovely square face and beautiful hair. I grew my hair as long as hers and put it up and made it bounce when I walked as hers did . . . I always bought the highest heels I could find and always copied Rita Hayworth in them.
>
> (Doreen Gibson)

Here the purchase of 'the highest heels' is closely connected to the movement of the star, and in particular the 'bounce' of her hair. Thus the purchase of a certain design of shoe produces the kind of walk which displays the hair to the best advantage: star style is copied in terms of movement and posture emphasised by high-heeled shoes.

The transformation of the body, through consumption, emerged as one of the key consumption practices that connected spectators with their favourite stars. Respondents recognised or desired a particular look or style in their favourite star which they sought to replicate in their own self-image by purchasing certain commodities:

> My colouring was the same as hers [Lauren Bacall's], I wore my hair in a similar style . . . in a page-boy like hers . . . and wore the same type of tailored clothes.
>
> (Kathleen Lucas)

> [Deanna Durbin's] . . . beautiful singing voice, natural personality and sparkling eyes made her films so enjoyable, and one always knew she would wear boleros . . . I still like wearing boleros.
>
> (Jean Davis)

The female body here is written about within the discourse of consumption in which little distinction is made between commodities and parts of the body: hair, eyes and 'colouring' are all parts of the female body which make up the whole star image, but can also be consumed autonomously, especially through the purchase of certain commodities. The whole body of the female star is a commodity, but the parts of her body (hair, legs, face) and the parts of her face (eyes, nose, mouth) and the parts of her eyes (colour, lashes, eyebrows) are also commodified. The female star's body is thus infinitely commodifiable, and, as has been illustrated above, spectators attached immense significance to particular body parts of Hollywood stars. Spectators clearly remember stars in terms of body parts they admired and, through the consumption of products, attempted to replicate their ideal through the transformation of particular body parts. The fragmentation of the female body is further commodified through the purchase of products in order to become more like star ideals.

It has been argued that the fetishisation of the female body characterised the representation of female stars in Hollywood (Mulvey, 1989). Fetishism can be related to the reproduction of feminine images both in the Marxist sense of commodity fetishism, in terms of the female body as object of patriarchal exchange, and in the more psychoanalytic sense, in terms of the fragmentation and sexualisation of parts of the female body in relation to castration anxieties, though these are not necessarily all analogous.[2] It has been argued that fetishism on the screen, in terms of the visual conventions of Hollywood during this period which fragmented and sexualised the 'woman as body', was reinforced by the kinds of consumption encouraged by female stars. The fetishised body image was accompanied by the corresponding narcissistic forms of consumption which were centred upon the improvement of self through products related to the female body.

Doane argues that women's new role in production in the 1940s 'was masked by an insistent emphasis on narcissistic consumption' (Doane, 1989a: 28). She highlights:

> the overwhelming intensity of the injunction to the female spectator-consumer to concern herself with her own appearance and position – an appearance which can only be fortified and assured through the purchase of a multiplicity of products.
>
> (Doane, 1989a: 29)

The female body is fragmented by the market, as well as by the camera, and women's bodies are broken down into component parts for the purposes of consumption:

Commodification presupposes that acutely self-conscious relation to the body which is attributed to femininity. The effective operation of the commodity system requires the breakdown of the body into parts – nails, hair, skin, breath – each one of which can be constantly improved through the purchase of a commodity.

(Doane, 1989a: 31)

The female body, in particular, can always be guaranteed to be at fault (Ewen, 1976: 39). The achievement of feminine ideals is always, to a large extent, reliant on men's approval. Since desirable ideals are always changing with new fashion trends, and feminine ideals are actually never fully realisable, the one is always contradicted by the other. Feminine insecurities about the attainment of bodily perfection are a reasonably sure bet for the endless reproduction of commodities for feminine self-improvement. The association of stars with particular products functions as the promised guarantee of the successful fulfilment of such desired progress towards feminine ideals. Thus female spectators can attempt to close the gap between self and desired feminine other through the consumption of commodities for the improvement of the female body.

However, attributing the term 'narcissistic' to forms of feminine con-sumption discussed above suggests a kind of passive self-indulgence which is misleading. This is particularly true when contrasting it with 'women's new role in production', as Doane does above: the suggestion seems to be that women's role as consumers was typically passive whilst their role as producers was more active. Narcissism has had derogatory connotations in a number of ways within psychoanalytic and other cultural discourses because of its association with femininity: it tends to be associated with a 'curiously passive desiring sub-jectivity' typical of femininity (Doane, 1989a: 31).

In contrast to this condemnation of consumption as mere feminine self-indulgence and vanity, I would argue that consumption, like female spec-tatorship, also theorised for some time in terms of its curious passivity, involves the active negotiation and transformation of identities which are not simply reducible to objectification. Narcissism needs to be rethought through in relation to its meaning as 'love of self in the ideal' and the kind of homoerotic love this may involve (see Benjamin, 1990). The gap between self and ideal, between spectator and star, continuously reproduces female subjectivity, the differences between the two endlessly deferring the fulfilment of desire. These are not just processes of objectification and self-commodification; they also (paradoxically) give rise to new and different images and identities through the selection, appro-priation and conversion of feminine ideals as self-image. Forms of recognition of the self in the idealised other, or indeed recognition of the desired self in the idealised other, inform the choices and selection of favourite stars made by spectators. What is at stake is the love for an ideal which literally embodies the desired self in an intimate negotiation between feminine images involving forms of expertise and knowledge firmly based within the culture of femininity.

Furthermore, the processes of commodification, objectification, fragmentation and fetishisation are not identical and neither are they always neatly mutually reinforcing. To regard them as unproblematically so is to construct a rather monolithic model of power and to ignore the complexity of negotiations between the production and consumption of popular images of femininity. This perspective may also underestimate the disjunctures and mismatches between the needs of the marriage market and of the commercial markets.

It is also important to point out that the female body on the screen was not only remembered through discourses of consumption. Furthermore, the forms of objectification and fragmentation were clearly not always read in ways which can be used as evidence of female self-commodification. Here too we may need to rethink the significance of the fragmentation of the body of the female star in the light of the ways in which such processes had significance for spectators. Respondents repeatedly offered detailed memories of their favourite stars' bodies and what they liked about them in ways which personalised the stars. Although the rest of the female body was occasionally commented upon, at the general level of 'enviable figures', it is the face and its features which are repeatedly the source of this feminine fascination: eyes, eyelashes, teeth and hair:

> Susan Hayward had beautiful eyes, hair and voice. Rita Hayworth was vivacious – flashing white teeth and beautiful red lips.
>
> (Anon)

> My two favourite female film stars were Loretta Young – because she had very large eyes and such lovely long lashes and a beautiful voice, and the other was Rita Hayworth – because of her ginger hair and super figure.
>
> (Mary E. Wilson)

> Technicolour was the in thing then and it couldn't have been kinder to Rita, that glorious mahogany coloured hair was shown to perfection . . . I was stunned that any human being could be that lovely.
>
> (Violet Holland)

> June Allyson always appealed to me because she had a lovely smile which always looked natural and the way she crinkled her eyes . . . She had a husky voice which always fascinated me.
>
> (Muriel Breach)

Cinema technology is remembered here as highlighting Rita Hayworth's 'glorious mahogany hair': thus changes in technology enabled new forms of feminine display and encouraged new forms of fascination. Another kind of technology which is important here is the close-up shot. The use of close-ups in Hollywood cinema emphasised the details of facial features and expressions. The details of eyebrows, lashes, teeth and so on could not have been seen by female spectators were it not for the close-up shot offering the possibility of detailed scrutiny and cataloguing. Thus the perception of stars in terms of their body parts or facial features was, in part, made possible and encouraged through particular cinematic and representational forms.

However, the technology did not only encourage the fragmentation of the female body, it also, again paradoxically, enabled a personalisation of Hollywood stars. Numerous respondents read off the type of personality of particular stars through bodily signifiers, and most especially facial details. The close-up shot has conventionally been used within cinematic practice to signify intimacy between characters within film narratives: the close-up is typically on the face and by convention encourages heightened emotional connections between stars and spectators. Respondents frequently referred to stars as friends, companions, people who have always been there. Thus, the personalisation of female stars ironically often stems from images which might also be read as depersonalising and objectifying. The same processes at the level of production that can be read as both fragmenting and objectifying the female body for consumption by the spectator can, therefore, also be seen to have produced particular forms of intimate reception in the exchange of feminine expertise about bodily appearance.

Copying a star's bodily movement, posture or gesture, as well as appearance, was frequently remembered through a bodily connection with the star:

> I was a very keen fan of Bette Davis and can remember seeing her in *Dark Victory* . . . That film had such an impact on me. I can remember coming home and looking in the mirror fanatically trying to comb my hair so that I could look like her.
>
> (Vera Carter)

Moving from cinema screen to mirror, this spectator sits in front of her own reflection trying to copy Bette Davis through this bodily connection, the hair. The replication of this gesture is clearly loaded with emotional intensity.

These forms of feminine fantasy involve intense forms of intimacy between star and spectator. The bodily connection between star and spectator, which may or may not involve consumption, is one such form of intimacy. Although the structural conclusion of such negotiations of feminine ideal images may be 'to bump up their market price' as commodities of patriarchal exchange (Haugg, 1986: 131), the meanings of desirable femininities are continuously negotiated between women and between them and their ideals. Knowledge of femininity, then, produces intimacy between women and their ideals, despite the ultimate goal of consumption of commodities in order to make oneself attractive to men.[3] Forms of intense intimacy and attachment within feminine culture, potentially separate from individual women's connections to men through heterosexuality and marriage, are thus central to understanding the role of consumption within female spectatorship . . .

NOTES

1. 'The intimacy which is knowledge' is a phrase borrowed from Gill Frith's study of female friendship in literature, originally formulated in Virginia Woolf's *To the Lighthouse* (see Frith, 1989).
2. See Marx (1976) on commodity fetishism, and Freud's 'Fetishism' (1963).
3. Much psychoanalytic theory has restricted analysis of desire to that produced by sexual difference and has ignored questions of same-sex desire, reading it within a rigidly dichotomous framework of sexual difference. See Merle Storr (1992) and Valerie Traub (1991).

WORKS CITED

Allen, Jeanne (1980) 'The film viewer as consumer', *Quarterly Review of Film Studies* 5, 4: 481–99.

Benjamin, Jessica (1990) *The Bonds of Love: Psychoanalysis, Feminism and the Problem of Domination*, London: Virago.

Bourdieu, Pierre (1984) *Distinction: A Social Critique of the Judgement of Taste* (trans. by Richard Nice), London: Routledge & Kegan Paul.

Braybon, Gail and Summerfield, Penny (1987) *Out of the Cage: Women's Experiences in Two World Wars*, London: Pandora.

Doane, Mary Ann (1989) 'The economy of desire: the commodity form in/of the cinema', *Quarterly Review of Film and Video* 11: 23–33.

Eckert, Charles (1978) 'The Carole Lombard in Macy's window', *Quarterly Review of Film Studies* 3, 1: 1–21.

Freud, Sigmund (1963) 'Fetishism', in Rieff, Philip (ed.) *Sexuality and the Psychology of Love*, New York: Collier Books.

Frith, Gillian (1989) 'The intimacy which is knowledge: female friendship in the novels of women writers', unpublished PhD thesis, Department of English and Comparative Literature, University of Warwick.

Haugg, Frigga (ed.) (1986) *Female Sexualisation*, London: Verso.

Marx, Karl (1976) 'The fetishism of the commodity and its secret', in *Capital: A Critique of Political Economy* (trans. by Ben Fowkes), vol. 1, book 1, chapter 1, section 4, Harmondsworth: Penguin.

Mulvey, Laura (1989) *Visual and Other Pleasures*, Basingstoke: Macmillan.

Storr, Merle (1992) 'Psychoanalysis and lesbian desire: the trouble with female homosexuals', paper at the Activating Theory Conference, York University, to be published in Bristow, Joe, and Wilson, Angie (eds) (forthcoming).

Traub, Valerie (1991) 'The ambiguities of "lesbian" viewing pleasure: the (dis) articulations of *Black Widow*', in Epstein, Julia and Straub, Kristina (eds) *Body Guards: The Cultural Policies of Gender Ambiguity*, London: Routledge: 305–28.

14

THE POLITICS OF POLARISATION: AFFLUENCE, ANXIETY AND THE COLD WAR

The 1950s was a decade of contradictions in society as well as cinema, a decade in which ideals such as a middle-class lifestyle, the model home, and marriage and parenthood were complicated and undermined by anxieties over gender roles and cross-generational tensions. The nuclear family ideal was of particular importance in the postwar period as a site of hope and regeneration. For example, *Marty* starring Ernest Borgnine was originally a television play but in 1955 it was the Academy's surprise choice for Best Picture. The story of the young man whose loyalty to his elderly mother slowly gives way to love and marriage in a new neighbourhood successfully tapped into a postwar ideology that linked marriage and family with civic virtues. In fact, in 1954 *Life* magazine aired a special feature on the 'domestication' of the American male. However, the rise of suburbia as a phenomenon in the 1950s also meant that middle-class wives expected to stay at home felt 'lost' in the suburbs while husbands commuted to the office. The consumer trap put pressure on both men and women to ensure that the home and family would remain perfect – even as children became teenagers in the 1950s. Out of the so-called era of conformity, there emerged an exciting cinema, with films often made by maverick outsiders, such as William Castle, Orson Welles and Roger Corman, outsiders who would come to dominate as independent directors by the end of the decade.

In the 1950s sociological studies such as David Reisman's *The Lonely Crowd* and William H. Whyte's *The Organization Man* pointed up the loss of a strong and tough masculine culture and Hollywood stepped in to fill the gap, not just with cowboys and frontiersmen but with angry young men and teenagers as disaffected anti-heroes. *Film noir* was the term coined retrospectively by French critics in the late 1950s to consolidate critically the appeal of those thrillers and melodramas that were characterised by the latent violence of a postwar *demimonde*, films which recall the stark and alienating lighting and tilted camera angles of German Expressionism and the tough content of Warner Brothers' gangster movies of the 1930s; hence, perhaps, Edward G. Robinson's ability to make the transition to *film noir*. The Kefauver Committee on organised crime was telecast in 1950–1. Tennessee Senator Estes Kefauver headed a public investigation into organised crime in interstate commerce interviewing around 600 racketeers and crime bosses across fourteen US cities. Audiences followed the mob trials in bars if not on their TV sets at home and the idea of the 'Mafia gang boss' became part of popular culture. The hearings made great television and their popularity mobilised Hollywood films in a series of fascinating movies about local crime syndicates and national corruption. From low-budget 'quickies' to blockbusters, these films included *Hoodlum Empire* (1952), *The Phenix City Story* (1955) and *The Captive City* (1952) in which Kefauver even appeared as himself. Such films were precursors to *The Godfather* in 1972.

The espionage film was another by-product of the domestic emphasis on combating crime syndicates and Cold War ideology as it affected international relations. Orson Welles' *Touch of Evil* (1958) is set on the Mexican border and in its famous opening – a three-minute uninterrupted crane tracking shot – an American businessman is blown up when a bomb explodes after he drives through the checkpoint. The film spirals into a dark and atmospheric tale of corrupt police, crime families and gangsters mired in the tension between American and Mexican investigators. Another representative example is *North by Northwest* (1959) in which a case of mistaken identity for businessman Cary Grant leads to his finding himself caught up in the machinations of a spy ring. Typically, Hitchcock refuses to specify the nature of the spy business, preferring to leave the reasons for Grant's predicament as a 'McGuffin', the term he invented to signal a device with no story behind it. In *North by Northwest* it boils down to a veiled reference to 'government secrets' that is never explained. For Hitchcock, logic was really unimportant in creating the thriller's effect of intrigue and suspense.

Janet Leigh and Eva Marie Saint who star in *Touch of Evil* and *North by Northwest* play sexually confident young women and in this period American women became very much aware that June Cleaver was not the only or best role model for women under thirty. Cinema became more daring; so much so that in the 1950s there were calls for federal censorship of the movies led by William Randolph Hearst (the subject of Orson Welles' *Citizen Kane* [1941]). Although calls for censorship focused first on what might be deemed 'communist' content, they also related to controversial content over sex and violence. In classical Hollywood women were frequently the (moral or immoral) markers in narratives that otherwise ignored them, as in John Ford's Westerns, for instance. However, by the 1950s stars exuded sexuality. Jane Russell in *The Outlaw* had been a controversial case in the 1940s: though made in 1941, the film was only officially released in 1950 because of controversy over shots of Russell's breasts in 3-D. Much more brazen cinema would follow as in the early 1950s the Production Code was tested to its limits by films like Otto Preminger's *The Moon is Blue* (1953). Although it is difficult to discern now why this pale romantic comedy should have proved such a cause célèbre on release, it was the inclusion of words such as 'virgin' and 'mistress' in conversation between a young lady and the older men who are trying to seduce her (William Holden and David Niven) that prompted the refusal of the MPAA's seal of approval. Preminger's decision to release the film anyway, without the seal of approval, provoked publicity and signalled the death knell of the outmoded Code.

The 1950s is assumed to be the decade in which America became a middle-class society epitomised by Sloan Wilson in *The Man in the Gray Flannel Suit* (1955 and filmed in 1956) and critiqued by John Kenneth Galbraith in his book *The Affluent Society* (1957). Tension between the classes became the subject of even some of the frothiest films such as *High Society* (1956) in which Grace Kelly's Tracey must choose between husbands, the upper-class and smooth Dexter (Bing Crosby) or the buttoned-up nouveau riche George (John Lund) while all the while under the scrutiny of *Spy* magazine's journalists, Frank Sinatra and Celeste Holm. In the movies working-class identity when represented at all was conflated with social deviancy, as in the motorcycle gangs of Elia Kazan's *The Wild One* (1953), while white middle-class social harmony seemed inherent in the musical genre. Most successful were comfortable comedies around courtship and marriage usually starring Doris Day, with Rock Hudson or Cary Grant often playing her executive husband. In the early 1950s, the musical took centre stage. MGM's dominance of the genre can be seen in *Seven Brides for Seven Brothers* (1954) and the success of Arthur Freed, Gene Kelly and Stanley Donen from *On the Town* (1949) to *Brigadoon* (1954). Anxieties over heterosexual gender roles and marriage are evident in all these movies. Where MGM led the way, the rest of the studios followed with equal success with Twentieth-Century Fox making *The King and I* (1956) and *South Pacific* (1958). Musicals were often seen as aspirational for women in establishing their roles as home-makers, telling as they did stories of romance turning into marriage whether within the old neighbourhood as in *On Moonlight Bay* (1951) or abroad. Even in *South Pacific*, little Nellie from Little Rock, Arkansas is finally convinced that the Frenchman she fears and desires will make a good and safe husband. In more sinister ways, representations of women also began to reflect the psycho-sexual discourse of the period, endowing them with multiple personalities, as in *The Cobweb* (1955) and *The Three Faces of Eve* (1957). In 1950 *All About Eve* made Hollywood history when all four of its women actresses were nominated for Academy Awards with a main thrust of the film being the impossibility of the career woman finding married happiness if she values career over home.

More often than not 'woman' was expressed as a problem, a source of anxiety, as were African Americans. Despite apparent economic progress in the US,

Eisenhower, who was in power for two terms from 1953 to 1961, presided over a country divided by racism and poverty. In Europe postwar anxiety initiated the collapse of the colonial project and in America the Supreme Court decision of 1954, *Brown v. Topeka Board of Education* which outlawed segregation in schools, signalled the necessity of addressing social inequities, especially in the segregated South. A raft of 'problem films' or 'message pictures' took racism as a core theme even before *Brown*. In fact, 1949–50 seemed a boom year for the 'race movie' with the release of *Pinky*, a melodrama about Jeanne Crain's 'passing' for white which, once regretted, allows her to bring the courts to bear in order to found a black clinic in the South; *Lost Boundaries*, which also tackled 'passing' with white actor Mel Ferrer in the lead role; and *Home of the Brave*, which tackled socially conscious themes in more overt ways in the arena of war. The same year saw *Intruder in the Dust*, based on Faulkner's novel about a black man falsely accused of murdering a white man, and *No Way Out* starring a young Sidney Poitier as a doctor taunted by the virulent racist (Richard Widmark) he is bound to treat. The polarisation of American society, sharply divided along racial lines, in the 1950s found particular expression in *The Defiant Ones* (1958) in which a white bigoted prisoner (Tony Curtis) and a black convict (Poitier) are chained together when they make their escape from prison. On the run, they gradually discover mutual respect and even friendship. However, the problem with the latter two films and with many social-conscience movies was that white racism and intransigence was caricatured in a bigoted individual thereby making racism somebody else's problem, that of the rabid racist, rather than implicating most Americans and all institutions.

It has been argued that the HUAC investigation was the beginning of the end of social realist themes. For example, in October 1949 in a statement in *Variety*, William Wyler called for 'men of courage' who would not be coerced or intimidated into making 'safe pictures'. Herbert Biberman's experience with *Salt of the Earth* is a case in point. Although independently financed, Biberman's film – about a peasant workers' strike in Mexico – was denied exhibition when it was made in 1954 as wholly unsuitable for distribution in the McCarthy era. Later, the 1960s would see an increase in movies focused on pointed social critique, with a host of white liberal filmmakers such as Martin Ritt, Stanley Kramer and Eric Roehmer seeking out such themes, especially as the Civil Rights Movement's struggle came to a head.

If social criticism was often masked, Hollywood still responded to the Cold War situation in some very imaginative ways. The very science and technology that signified progress postwar also instigated the threat of nuclear war that dominated societies after the atom bomb and the first H-bombs were exploded. In the US the threat was epitomised by fear of the Soviet Union, its politics and its technology, especially after the first Russian sputnik was launched in 1957 and when Vice-President Nixon and Russian Premier Khrushchev engaged in the famous 'kitchen debate' in 1959. That the latter was conducted in a model American suburban home demonstrated the capitalist and consumerist ideals that underpinned American anti-communism during the Cold War, and exhibited the shining affluence that characterised American society postwar. Nuclear technology was the harbinger of what President Truman had feared would be 'the beginning of the end' and the emphasis on civil defence strategies such as home-made bomb shelters dominated press coverage. Hollywood deployed the nuclear crisis to great creative effect especially in *film noir* and science fiction films; Allied Artists even used the image of the exploding A bomb as their logo ('a new major company explodes into action'), just as fashion designers had taken 'bikini' as the name for the new revealing swimwear to explode onto the market and targeted beautiful young women called 'bombshells' following the explosion of the hydrogen bomb in Bikini Atoll.

Cold War fears over the nuclear crisis underpin Robert Aldrich's *Kiss Me Deadly* (1955), perhaps the most effective and apocalyptic of Cold War allegories, excepting Alain Resnais' *Hiroshima, Mon Amour* (1959) and, of course, Stanley Kubrick's *Dr Strangelove or: How I Learned to Stop Worrying and Love the Bomb* (released in 1964). In *Kiss Me Deadly*, Mickey Spillane's sordid and fascistic Mike Hammer's credo is 'What's in it for me?' Private eye Hammer exists in an emotionally dead world in which the nuclear age ('Manhattan Project . . . Los Alamos . . . Trinity') has only poetry, specifically Christina Rossetti's 'Remember Me When I Am Gone Away', as a weak buffer against total destruction. The moment in which the 'radioactive giant whatsit' takes on the mythical import of Pandora's Box combines the stuff of myth with American audiences' worst nightmare. Hammer looks back from the edge of the sea at an American home enveloped in a mushroom cloud.

This apocalyptic 'end' was being told and retold throughout the early 1950s in cheaply and quickly made movies based on the comic books that animated the imaginations of young people. The 'Two-Bit' culture of paperback fiction and cheap drive-in movies prompted some of the most creative use of small budgets. The most imaginative Cold War allegories of the time were science fiction and monster films with the ubiquitous fear of aliens and the popular 'pod dramas' such as *It Came From Outer Space* (1953) and *Invasion of the Body Snatchers* (1956). In the former the aliens are accidental interlopers whose mere existence produces fear in the residents of California ('what frightens them, they're against'), and the latter may be read as a popular commentary on the threat to American individualism believed to be posed not only by communism but by bland suburban conformity. It is an idea that science fiction film plays out again and again. Such films were drive-in favourites and indicative of the polarity between low-budget films and big blockbusting historical epics and musical extravaganzas that characterised cinema for its audiences in the early years of the 1950s.

The 1950s was really the first decade in which parents and children pursued markedly different fashion styles. Although the term was first coined in the 1940s, 'teenagers' had always seemed like mini-adults and there had always been a youthful appreciation of blues and jazz. However, in the 1950s teenagers were the new market to be tapped in music, film and fashion. The shift from serving a generic 'family' audience to separate productions for children, teenagers and adults made for a more diverse if also a more divided cinematic experience. 'Adult' cinema is discussed in detail in Chapter 16 but at the other end of the spectrum children benefited from the continued quality of Disney animation (from *Alice in Wonderland* in 1951 to *Sleeping Beauty* in 1959) and also from Disney's shift into live-action features including films based on classics such as *Treasure Island* (1950). This new lease of life for Disney productions was underpinned by the weekly TV show *Disneyland* in which Disney films were promoted to children in their own homes. Disney was so successful that it has even been argued that Disney's moral stance, often dismissed as conservative, actually created something of the 1960s' counterculture's radical agenda when the postwar baby boom generation came of age as 'Sixties' hippies.

Teenagers were the movie audience that really gained from the diversification of the cinema demographic. The rise of the teenager alongside the rise of rock 'n' roll ensured that music sealed the consumer boom, as in 'Rock Around the Clock' and romantic ballads ('To Know You is to Love You' and 'Sealed with a Kiss') that 'teenpics' could employ on film soundtracks. Elvis was, of course, at the forefront of the musical teen rebellion from *Love Me Tender* (1956) in which Elvis plays a teenager during the American Civil War (!) to *Wild in the Country* (1961) where the drama of his disaffected teen on probation is so moody that it isn't even underscored with song. The 1950s also signalled a series of contradictory impulses on the British social scene. On the one hand, Prime Minister Harold Macmillan's famous declaration of 1957 that 'you've never had it so good' reflected the nation having got out from under the shadow of the war and the material hardship that followed in its wake (rationing had only ended in 1954, for instance). But, on the other hand, the teenage 'revolution' posed new challenges for postwar society.

It is axiomatic to recall that in Britain in 1955 there was an effort to ban *The Blackboard Jungle*, especially after 'Teddy Boys' went wild during a London screening. The film tells the controversial story of a Second World War veteran Dadier (Glenn Ford) who takes a job as a teacher in a New York high school where delinquent youths threaten the women teachers with rape and threaten Dadier's pregnant wife. The film's rock 'n' roll soundtrack only deepened the film's tense depiction of a rift between the generations, as epitomised by Bill Haley's 'Rock Around the Clock'. A year later, in 1956, when the film *Rock Around the Clock* was released in Britain, hordes of screaming young fans mobbed a visiting Haley and his Comets. Teenagers were becoming a 'problem' to be exploited. The 'Tammy' series of films starring Debbie Reynolds as a wholesome and virtuous girl, and *Gidget* (1959), starring 15-year-old Sandra Dee, went some way towards challenging the emphasis on teenagers as dysfunctional but 'teenpics' began as part of cinema's efforts to deal with – and exploit – social issues. The first troubled and dangerous teenager to fire the public imagination in the 1950s was, of course, Marlon Brando as the leader of the motorcycle gang in *The Wild One* and when asked what he is rebelling against, his disrespectful reply is 'Whadda ya got?' The archetypal anxiety-ridden teen on a rebellious rollercoaster ride to death has remained James Dean, who died in a car crash aged 24. In fact, Dean's own short life was exploited when it was brought to the screen very soon after his death in 1955 as the docudrama *The James Dean Story* (1957). Despite Dean's celebrity as the surly disaffected teen, the actor who really cornered the film market in troubled teens was Sal Mineo, Plato in *Rebel Without a Cause*, who starred in *Crime in the Streets* (1956) and *The Young Don't Cry* (1957) and was known as 'The Switch-Blade Kid'. Ironically and tragically, he died mysteriously in violent circumstances, stabbed to death in 1976.

The emphasis on teenage alienation from parents and institutions turned into something of a moral panic, especially when countervailing tendencies meant that distributors often tried to market films about teenagers as public service filmmaking, such as Republic's *Eighteen and Anxious* (1957), while American International Pictures (AIP) selected teenagers as its dedicated market, even operating focus groups to discover what adolescent consumers with their new discretionary spending power wanted to see on screen. AIP had taken up the story of the 'lost generation' from 1954 and teenagers became synonymous with delinquents in films such as *Teen-Age Menace* (1951) and *High School Hellcats* (1958) through to the biker teens of *The Wild Angels* (1966). Later even United Artists' multi-Oscar winning *West Side Story* (1961) stayed with the theme, an example of what Thomas Doherty has called the 'juvenalisation of American movies in the 1950s'.

The rise of the teenager was underpinned by new acting styles which proliferated through the decade. 1950s cinema saw a movement towards the method style, associated with Marlon Brando, James Dean and Montgomery Clift and with Elia Kazan who directed them all. Kazan had joined the Stanislavskian Group Theatre in 1932 and in the 1950s was a major proponent of Lee Strasberg's teaching methods, though his interest would wane in later years. In its original incarnation method acting strove for neo-realist style authenticity, a psychological realism whereby the actor 'became' the character. However, in an era in which arch theatricality and melodrama were popular, it actually and ironically evolved into something very stylised and was sometimes parodied as Brando's 'mumbling'. Nevertheless, method actors included serious students such as Paul Newman, Rod Steiger, Ben Gazzarra – and Marilyn Monroe, who was 'adopted' by the Strasbergs. The intensity devoted to character acting also allowed more risqué emotions to be expressed. This was particularly important in Kazan's *A Streetcar Named Desire* (1951) in which Blanche's (Vivien Leigh) psychological vulnerability and frustrated sexual desire is exploited by virile and cruel Stanley (Brando). Ben Gazzarra in his film début represented the conflicted teenager in *The Strange One* (1955) in which a Southern military academy (based on the Citadel) is the site of teenage anger, violence and homoerotic repression.

Across the world, cinema industries were finding their feet in the aftermath of the Second World War and responding to Cold War ideology in different ways. Increasing political stability and affluence generally ensured at least a limited success for indigenous filmmaking. In Japan, out of a strained postwar situation and despite an influx of American films while under occupation, the domestic product held sway for Japanese audiences and as the industry grew in confidence, it began to look to foreign markets, as with the phenomenal international success of Akira Kurosawa's films. If the Japanese industry recovered, at the other end of the Cold War axis, Russian power struggles stymied productivity. When Stalin died in 1953 what has popularly been called 'The Thaw' began and would go on to affect cinema throughout Eastern Europe. Khrushchev threw his support behind the cinema, and slowly filmmakers began to make critiques of the Second World War and of the Stalinist era, such as the art-cinema classic *The Cranes Are Flying* (1957). Overall the Soviet cinema situation was one of the most unsettled. Elsewhere the decline of colonialism in the years preceding 1960 ensured new national cinemas would begin to develop slowly. The collapse of European colonialism in India in 1947 was a case in point, although the ensuing partition of the country during which hundreds of thousands of people died created a traumatic rift that would not be examined in India cinema until much later, with, for example, *Garm Hava* in 1973.

The emphasis on song and dance routines that had characterised Indian cinema before the Second World War was consolidated in Bollywood's populist appeal so that India's domestic product rivalled Hollywood's: in each case the national cinema was *the* cinema of the masses. Nevertheless, Bollywood only took off internationally in the 1990s and in the postwar period Indian cinema from an international – and art house – perspective focused on the auteurs such as Satyajit Ray whose Apu trilogy of films, beginning with *Pather Panchali* (1955), won worldwide acclaim at the Cannes Film Festival, a key arbiter of international film taste and critical appreciation. Ray's intensely literate, observational and often emotional dramas contrasted markedly with Bollywood in its sunny 'golden age'. Ray's focus was often Indian social institutions and Bollywood too focused on the family and on relationships, but the overall effect could not have been more different: stars such as Raj Kapoor (an acclaimed director as well as actor), Dilip Kumar and Lata Mangeshkar, known as India's 'nightingale', could break into song as spontaneously in a family melodrama or comedy as in a musical. Often three hours in length in the 1950s, Bollywood movies were an extravaganza, often known as 'masala movies' because of the eclectic mix of entertaining ingredients that made up each film.

On the African continent, francophone African cinema began paternalistically as part of France's colonial project in West Africa with production and distribution controlled by the Bureau du Cinéma and the French Ministry for Cooperation in the region. Various film units included the Congolese ciné clubs from 1952 and French and African collaborations, such as the Fédération Panafricaine des Cinéastes from 1958. The British Colonial Film Unit had been established in 1939 with the understanding that war propaganda would encourage more colonial Africans to fight with the Allies. It was wound down in 1955, believing its postwar goal to 'educate' had been fulfilled. Charles Ambler, in the extract that follows this chapter, chooses this precise context in which to study the globalisation of Hollywood film entertainment postwar. Outside the continent, 'Africa' was exported most successfully via Safari melodramas (for example, *King Solomon's Mines*, remade in 1950) and films based on the colonial adventure stories that had fired the imaginations of imperial schoolboys in the early twentieth century. Frequently, Hollywood interventions into Africa reflected more on the racial and social situation at home than about life in modern African nations. For example, Canada Lee and Sidney Poitier starred in *Cry, the Beloved Country* based on South African Alan Paton's novel about apartheid in 1951 before Civil Rights legislation formally integrated facilities in the American South.

While much film scholarship concentrates on the deleterious representations of Africans in Western cinema or on the slow rise of indigenous film industries in African countries after the Second World War, Charles Ambler's essay, 'Popular Films and Colonial Audiences: The Movies in Northern Rhodesia', focuses on a particular place, the 'Copperbelt' mining district of Northern Rhodesia (Zambia following independence in 1964), in order to assess the circumstances in which American cinema, and by extension Western culture as constructed by the Hollywood dream factory, was consumed by a specific African audience. As in the 1920s when American silent cinema secured worldwide audiences (see Chapter 6), in the 1950s efforts were made to secure trade through the exportation of the Hollywood brand.

The Copperbelt audiences were interested in 'bioscope', the term deriving from the original apparatus projecting moving pictures, and the term was preferred to 'cinema' in southern Africa. However, their typical fare was the (non-commercial) propagandist films of the Colonial Film Unit. Masquerading as solely educational, such films were also designed to embed colonial discourse in the minds of black Africans living in a racially segregated society that considered them 'primitive' and impressionistic and therefore advocated censorship of the popular films they were allowed to see. Ambler's research shows that Copperbelt audiences responded to Hollywood films as escapist spectacle. Their appreciation of Westerns in particular gave rise to the phenomenon of the 'Copperbelt Cowboys' dressing like their Hollywood heroes. Ambler's researches reveal that this audience of African miners and their families sometimes reacted differently from their European or American counterparts by openly discussing a film during its screening. However successfully Hollywood's cultural imperialism has pervaded disparate geographical places and however coercive its global hegemony, Ambler argues that an audience assumed to have scant cultural sophistication negotiated its response to the movies and demonstrated a keen analytical grasp of cinema's power to manipulate. This was specifically evidenced by this audience's facility for co-opting film narratives to protest about local conditions in the mines.

Ambler writes against theories of spectatorship that assume that the spectator is situated by the cinema apparatus and their response determined by it. Neither does Ambler privilege key film 'texts' as the basis of his study. Instead, his methodology measures the supposed homogeneity of the cinema against the heterogeneity of its spectators. This is a specific local study of an audience in which markers such as nationality, race, place and period are salient in his conceptualisation of spectatorship. It also raises certain problems for the film historian, not least how to be assured that the sources available about an audience that existed in the past can be relied upon in the present. Ambler's case study of a pocket of spectators in colonial Africa addresses such issues in interesting ways.

- What sources does Ambler have at his disposal in order to detail the history of film entertainment, censorship and spectatorship in Northern Rhodesia in the 1940s and 1950s?
- Identify the pitfalls that might limit the film historian's ability to tell the *whole* story when trying to determine the empirical realities of exhibition and reception in a cross-cultural context.
- What sources might you use to begin a comparative study of specific British and African cinema audiences in a contemporary context? How would you specify the goals of your exploration?

POPULAR FILMS AND COLONIAL AUDIENCES: THE MOVIES IN NORTHERN RHODESIA

Charles Ambler

During the 1940s and 1950s, no visitor to the coppermining cities of colonial Northern Rhodesia (Zambia) in central Africa could escape the visible marks of the impact of American films.[1] In the vast company compounds that housed the African miners and their families on the Copperbelt, groups of African boys, 'dressed in home-made paper 'chaps' and cowboy hats, and carrying crudely carved wooden pistols,' were a ubiquitous presence running through the streets and alleys in endless games of cowboys and Indians. Others appeared 'more sinister . . . with a black mask over the eyes and a wooden dagger in the belt.' As they engaged in their mock battles, they could be heard shouting, 'Jeke, Jeke,' a local corruption of 'Jack,' the universal term among urban moviegoers in the British central African colonies for the heroes of cowboy films.[2] In the same streets, young men affected styles of dress that plainly showed

Charles Ambler, *American Historical Review*, 106(1) Feb. 2001.

the influence of westerns and gangster films – ten-gallon hats, kerchiefs, and so forth.[3]

This phenomenon of 'Copperbelt Cowboys' and its manifestation in urban areas across much of British-ruled Africa vividly demonstrates the rapid and pervasive penetration of mythic Hollywood screen imagery into even remote corners of the empire.[4] In the early 1950s, the industrial development of the Copperbelt, and the concomitant creation of urban settlements, was scarcely two decades old; even those who regarded themselves as permanent town residents still had strong ties to the countryside.[5] Yet, by the late 1930s, film shows, known locally as 'the bioscope,' were a well-established feature of life in the copper-mining towns and company compounds. Thousands of women, men, and children crowded into enclosed open-air cinemas each week to watch film programs that mixed entertainment and current events;[6] and many young town dwellers were avid bioscope fans, valuing films above all other forms of entertainment.[7] For people caught up in the dramatic development of urban and industrial communities, the popularity of films clearly represented something more than the superficial appropriation of global media jetsam. The remarkable persistence of Copperbelt audiences in their affection for cowboy films and the styles derived from them draws attention not only to the apparently inexorable dispersion of elements of Western popular culture but also to the deeper processes of media globalization.[8]

This essay takes up the history of film entertainment in Northern Rhodesia in order to explore the broad question of the transmission and reception of Western mass culture in the context of colonialism. The story of moviegoing in Northern Rhodesia places in particularly sharp relief issues defining the movement and appropriation of media images as they travel across the boundaries of culture, ethnicity, and race – in this case, the profound economic and cultural chasm that separated African residents of the Copperbelt from the centers of media production in the United States and Britain. The people who eagerly attended outdoor cinemas on the Copperbelt generally had had little if any formal education; not many had traveled outside the territory; most were little educated to the symbols, customary behaviors, and settings that context-ualised these films for Western audiences or even for relatively better-off and better-educated Africans across southern Africa. Certainly, few moviegoers had sufficient knowledge of colloquial spoken American or British English to comprehend the dialogue – even if it had been discernible in the noisy atmosphere that characterized these film shows.[9] In any case, censors had cut films shown on the Copperbelt to ensure that African audiences were not exposed to images or story lines that they imagined might inspire challenge to the white supremacist colonial order – a tall order, given the violent rituals that characterize the plot of a typical western.[10] The resulting celluloid butchery apparently left many movies devoid of discernable narrative. One official noted in 1956, 'many films which you may have seen are sadly lacking in continuity.'[11] Most members of the audience could therefore make little sense of film plotlines and consequently experienced these movies in quite different ways than did moviegoers in North America. If censorship and noise obscured plots and dialogue, what was it, then, that drew African filmgoers to Hollywood westerns, and how did these filmgoers comprehend or consume these films across the sharp cultural and class divide between filmmaker and filmgoer?

Movies emerged as popular entertainment in Northern Rhodesia at the same time that social critics in the United States and Western Europe began to give serious attention to the impact of films on 'impressionable' audiences – chiefly youths, immigrants, and the urban poor. Scholars linked to the Frankfurt School argued that movies constituted a kind of trivial mass deception;[12] while in more concrete terms, studies like those of the Payne Fund on 'Motion Pictures and Youth' accumulated data to document charges that movies encouraged antisocial behavior among young people, sustaining debates about the impact of media that still thrive.[13] The rise of movie attendance in the 1930s inspired many white residents of the Copperbelt and more than a few prominent Africans to express similar concerns – about what they saw as the negative and potentially dangerous effects of the products of Hollywood on the impressionable African youths who festooned themselves with cowboy gear.[14] Because censors in both South Africa and Northern Rhodesia had reviewed and often cut the films that were approved for African audiences, such worries were presumably exaggerated.[15] But if attempts to link filmgoing to criminality, a decline in deference, the erosion of traditional values, and sexual violence strain credulity, the popular passion for these films that persisted among urban youths for several decades was nevertheless a remarkable sign of the strong engagement of urban audiences with films. Yet scholars have largely ignored the complicated interplay between African audiences and popular films.[16]

[. . .]

Empirical observations about the experience of watching movies in Northern Rhodesia converge persuasively with a new scholarship that argues for a radical rethinking of the complicated relationship between viewer and subject that would embed the reception of 'film texts' in specific historical circumstances. Locating the history of the bioscope in this way implies shifting the perspective from the films themselves, and the objectives of those controlling their distribution and exhibition, and instead focusing attention on audiences. Such an emphasis on spectatorship requires in turn exploring the 'cultures' of film viewing and extending the meanings of a film in networks of information transmission beyond the theater; cinema becomes, in other words, 'a particular public sphere . . . a space where viewing communities are constructed in a way that involves both acculturation to social ideals and the affirmation of marginality.'[17] This new literature on spectatorship, rooted in feminist scholarship, is strangely silent, however, on issues of race, culture, and class.[18] The work that purports to explore the racial dimensions of spectatorship is in fact mostly concerned with isolating stereotypical imagery in films whose subject matter is identifiably race rather than reading the reception of mass-audience films in race-conscious or culture-conscious terms.[19] Still, the impulse that has led scholars to feminist readings of audience engagement with horror films holds considerable promise for analysis of the often raucous outdoor film showings that were regular features of the urban landscape of Northern Rhodesia during the 1940s and 1950s.[20] Just as women and men may experience the apparently misogynist themes and images of horror movies in ways that confound confident assumptions, so, too, African audiences seem to have appropriated elements of westerns and other action movies in ways that subverted the narrative and racially defined principles of censorship. The recent and dramatic growth of the distribution of imported videocassettes across Africa has attracted a few scholars to the complex phenomenon of audience response to popular films.[21] Whether exploring the popularity of Indian movies among audiences in northern Nigeria or the appeal of romance films to secluded Muslim women on the Kenya coast, this work focuses attention on the com-plicated processes through which films are seen across cultural divisions.[22] Likewise, audiences on the Copperbelt in the 1930s, 1940s, and 1950s were by no means passive consumers of cinema. They absorbed exotic images and discussed the actions and motivations of characters, but they also appropriated and reinterpreted film images and action in their own terms. To the young women and men who flocked to film shows on the Copperbelt, the often disjointed and exotic images of the 'Wild West' that Hollywood films conveyed comprised a crucial repertoire of images through which to engage notions of modernity – a vital concern for residents of this industrial frontier.[23]

In the networks of film distribution, the Northern Rhodesian mining district lay on the extreme margins, a distant outpost for a South African distributor.[24] The introduction and spread of film entertainment in Northern Rhodesia followed rapidly on the development of the copper mining industry in the late 1920s, as colonial officials and mine management sought to provide 'appropriate' leisure activities for an African work force that was for the most part unaccustomed to the temporal and spatial constraints of industrial employment. After the first public film showing in 1928, the bioscope spread steadily across the Copperbelt.[25] By the mid-1930s, tens of thousands of Africans lived in municipal African townships and mining company residential compounds in the mining district, and cinema shows had become a commonplace feature of town life.[26] Through the 1930s, British and American silent films dominated screens, but by 1935 the paucity of silents in distribution had forced the mine companies to introduce sound.[27] World War II brought a rapid expansion of film showings across the British Empire under the aegis of the Colonial Film Unit, as imperial officials strove to mobilize support for the war effort.[28] In 1942, the Northern Rhodesia Information Service began a mobile cinema service in the countryside.[29] In 1944, when the African population of the entire territory numbered about 1.3 million, approximately 17,000 Africans saw films each week in the established municipal and mine-company cinemas; in addition, the mobile cinema van reached about 80,000 people during the year.[30] By 1947, the film library had expanded to 650 titles, and six mobile units and fifteen outdoor theaters provided films to Africans in Northern Rhodesia; seventeen private exhibitors also showed movies from time to time.[31] Thus, by the 1950s, a large segment of the African population in Northern Rhodesia had some knowledge and experience of films, and an established audience of filmgoers had emerged in towns.[32]

The government recognized the development of a local movie audience by launching 'The Northern Spotlight,' a 35-millimeter current events magazine series, and by permitting the establishment of film societies and film showings in clubs.[33] These efforts to reach an influential segment of the African population coincided with the emergence of bitter opposition among Africans in Northern Rhodesia to the amalgamation of Northern and Southern Rhodesia and Nyasaland into a Central African Federation dominated by white settlers, with a broader campaign by the mining companies and the state to nurture a privileged class of relatively well-paid and well-educated African workers.[34] Commercial indoor movie theaters in Northern Rhodesia, however, remained reserved for whites, and regulations thwarted even private showings of films for groups that included both whites and Africans, until all public facilities were desegregated in 1960 in anticipation of majority rule.[35]

The mythology of the birth of film celebrates stories of spectators screaming and running from auditoriums in terror at the destruction of the distinction between the real and imaginary that motion-pictures putatively represented. Film historian Tom Gunning has argued that vivid and exaggerated early accounts, and the persistent theoretical assumptions drawn from these stories, have typically portrayed early film showings as the dramatic confrontations of naifs with a frightening unknown force, replicating 'a state usually attributed to savages in their primal encounter with the advanced technology of Western colonialists, howling and fleeing in impotent terror before the power of the machine.'[36] Gunning effectively situates these early film shows as a 'cinema of attractions' in a history of spectacle. He persuasively rereads the myths of reactions to moving images of onrushing trains 'allegorically rather than mythically,' arguing that 'screams of terror and delight were well prepared for by both showmen and audience.'[37] Audiences in the mining compounds and at rural film shows experienced films in much the same way as European audiences at the turn of the century. The movies shown in Paris and New York at that time aimed to amaze – like the magic shows that preceded them – not to tell stories. By 1905, narrative films had entirely supplanted this early genre, but, exported to Northern Rhodesia and shown in censored form, mainstream movies were often perceived viscerally as a disconnected series of exotic, exciting, and frighteningly pleasurable images and special effects. At film shows on the Copperbelt, the audience members continually engaged in the action: 'men, women, and children rose to their feet in excitement, bending forward and flexing their muscles with each blow the cowboys gave. The shouting could be heard several miles away.'[38] Accounts of film showings invariably emphasize the enthusiasm of audiences, but they provide little evidence of the existence of 'primitive' machine terror.[39] African audiences may have had no specific experience of magic attractions, but they could nevertheless locate films in an indigenous tradition of plays and other kinds of performances and enjoy them in the context of a storytelling tradition that was by no means rooted in linear narrative.[40]

If audiences seem in fact to have rapidly accommodated film technology, colonial cinema policy (not to mention modern cinema scholarship) remained rooted in deeply held assumptions about the powerful, emotional effect of films on Africans. Even as late as 1960, when the colonial government was attempting, against considerable settler resistance, to engineer a transition to majority rule, many white colonial officials remained absolutely convinced of the continued need to censor films on a racial basis. When Harry Franklin, longtime director of information in Northern Rhodesia, had the temerity to argue, 'the idea that the white female leg or the safe blowing crackman shown on the screen encourages Africans more than any other people to immorality or crime is outmoded,' the official reviewing the memorandum penciled in defiantly, 'But it's still true.'[41]

Ironically, it was educated people, both European and African, rather than the general African audience, who were most dazzled by the medium and convinced of its powerful potential for harm and good. In 1960, an African government official could still aggressively defend racial censorship in public testimony, citing the deleterious impact of 'scenes of crime or violence being shown to the unsophisticated, uneducated mass of the African people.' He went on to assert: 'such films have an adverse effect emotionally . . . The primitive African is always being told of the advantages of assimilating Western Civilisation, but when he sees Europeans in a film indulging in sexual and criminal misbehavior doubts are raised in his mind.'[42] Even if, in retrospect, it seems laughable that the state would have found it necessary to protect African audiences from *Fitness Wins the Game* or *The Lavender Hill Mob* (1951),[43] the assumptions that sustained such actions and the criticisms of them inscribe critical debates about the relationship between the nature of film media on the one hand and on the other the evolution of class and race difference. Moreover, the practice of censorship had a direct, material effect on the actual experience of film attendance, while the ideas that shaped the practice provide an essential context for reading the accounts of African filmgoing – texts that were largely the product of white officials and observers and that often took the form of ritualised encounters of 'the primitive' and technology.[44] Thus a white businessman proposing the establishment of commercial cinemas for Africans in the 1950s noted casually that, 'from a health point of view,' it was essential such film shows be in the open air.[45] Similarly, a description of mobile cinema shows in Northern Rhodesia in 1950 contained the warning that 'on no account should an attempt be made to give a demonstration in a confined space unless the attendance can be effectively controlled. The larger the space the better.'[46] These concerns about space reveal plainly the imminence of danger that Europeans saw in film shows for Africans, where it was imagined that emotional surges provoked by moving images might inspire irrational, immoral, or criminal acts.[47]

From the very beginning of film showing in the early 1930s, government officials insisted on some form of race-defined censorship; in the late 1930s, as the number of film showings increased quickly, they created a special board to censor films for African audiences.[48] The principles that governed the board's actions flowed from a number of sometimes contradictory formulations of the interplay between African audiences and film. Employers and many government officials held that only 'action' could hold the interest of African spectators and that settings and meaningful plotlines were often irrelevant.[49] Such officials regarded action movies as 'healthy amusement' for urban workers and could be contemptuous of those who saw the entire genre as lacking in value or even as dangerous.[50] By contrast, the activities of the Bantu Educational Cinema Experiment (BECE) and subsequent experiments with educational film were rooted in an opposing perspective.[51] As early as 1932, the report of an investigation of conditions on the Copperbelt sponsored by the International Missionary Council waxed rapturous on the possibilities that Soviet media campaigns had demonstrated for Christian education and development through film. Mesmerised by the power of film, and in particular the power of film over 'primitive' audiences, those involved in the BECE and its successors like the Colonial Film Unit believed deeply in the educational and development potential of film and were profoundly disturbed by what they believed to be the economic and social consequences of the popularity of commercial movies.[52] During its brief existence between 1935 and 1937, the Carnegie-funded BECE concentrated on the production of didactic 'entertainment' films with local settings and actors that would be shown especially in rural areas in British East Africa and central Africa.[53]

The development of programs of educational film distribution in Northern Rhodesia and other British African colonies incorporated a distinctly imperial theory of African visual cognition that surfaced repeatedly in the pages of the official periodical, *Colonial Cinema*. An article published in 1943 emphasised that, to gain and maintain the attention of the African audience, a filmmaker had to employ a 'technique which is skillfully related to the psychology of the African.' That meant that images had to be 'needle sharp' and subjects correspondingly straightforward. Above all, it was critical that 'tricks' used in filmmaking to convey elapsed time or to shift scene be avoided:

> visual continuity from scene to scene should be sustained. Every new shot without a visual link with its predecessor starts another train of thought which may exclude everything that has gone before . . . To the illiterate

such a technique leads to utter confusion; their minds are not sufficiently versatile to comprehend these swift and sudden changes.[54]

Similarly, films that framed a distance shot of a moving boat with a swaying tree branch closer up would supposedly confuse African filmgoers, who would focus on the moving branch rather than the boat.[55] Certainly, the BECE placed particular emphasis on the importance of using recognizable film settings and avoiding exotic locales, a perspective maintained by the officials of the Colonial Film Unit: 'Fun and games in the snow do not look so funny to an audience which thinks snow is sand and wonders how it sticks together.'[56] The enormous popularity of American westerns – in which such techniques were commonplace – would seem effectively to dispose of these theories.[57] But perhaps not. The evaluation of the effects of film techniques invariably made narrative comprehension the measure of a movie's quality; but in a cinema of attractions, individual sequences and powerful imagery supersede questions of narrative and continuity.

If whites in Northern Rhodesia debated the dangers and entertainment value of ordinary Hollywood fare, virtually all agreed that certain categories of films and film images were inappropriate for Africans to view. No statutory guidelines governed censorship decisions, but the definition of what was suitable for African audiences remained consistent over time, although political concerns seem to have become more prominent after 1945.[58] Scenes 'invariably cut from films' in 1946 included women in swimsuits or other scanty attire, 'women of easy virtue, manhandling of women, prolonged embraces, fights between women, crimes readily understood by Africans [and] scenes of drunkenness.'[59] A list dating from 1951 used those same categories but stressed the censorship of scenes involving violence, laying special emphasis on those ritual scenes in which American Indians captured and tied up white pioneers. Objections were also raised to films that included scenes of war atrocities, violent battles, arson, masked men, or rioting and demonstrations.[60] A 1956 summary of the Censorship Board's criteria for cutting or banning films added 'deliberate murder, wanton killing, and knife scenes,' as well as any films 'with religious references which might be misunderstood and thereby reflect poorly on any church.'[61] By the mid-1950s, the board reviewed as many as 200 films a year and cut scenes from perhaps half. A number of films were banned outright for African audiences.[62]

The public discourse on censorship imputed a powerful relationship between moving images of violence and sexuality and impulsive, aggressive, and violent forms of behavior on the part of male, working-class Africans. This preoccupation expressed itself especially in terms of the repression of black male sexuality and a defense of white womanhood. Any kind of display of white women's bodies or of female sexuality, it was argued, undermined Africans' respect for (white) morality. A defender of tight censorship maintained that 'the safety of the [white] women and girls in Northern Rhodesia hangs upon their being respected by the Africans.'[63] Perhaps more to the point, the security of white male authority required that respect. Censorship was in fact defined essentially as a male domain. White women were included on the Censorship Board beginning in the 1930s, but only reluctantly, because it was difficult to find men with the spare time to devote to a task that, despite the rhetoric, was regarded as essentially frivolous. Moreover, officials privately argued that the presence of a woman member would 'disarm criticism' if any 'unpleasant crime by natives in this area should be attributed to anything seen on the films.[64] The message was clear: this (male) official did not really believe that any such connection was likely to exist. The token female members of the Censorship Board were meanwhile tolerated as ineffectual observers of base imagery, as it was argued that they did not recognize scenes of 'rank indecency' readily identified by their male counterparts.[65] The all-white board was very eager, however, to include male African members, arguing that such men would bring a special insight into what was for many whites an unfathomable world of African taste.[66] By 1945, two of the ten unofficial board members were Africans, whose perspectives differed little from 'moderate' white members in their concentration on the impact of film on urban youth.[67] Interestingly, none of the series of commissions appointed to investigate urban discontent and labor activism on the Copperbelt made mention of movies as a source of urban criminality or aspirations.[68]

Actions taken on which films to pass or ban often struck perplexed observers as arbitrary or even ludicrous. In the late 1950s, a letter to the governor on the subject questioned permitting the distribution of a film on the Indian Ocean slave trade, *West of Zanzibar* (1954), which included a scene of African slaves throwing overboard 'slick Indian lawyers and a villainous Arab dhow captain,' while at the same time the board banned *Frontier Trail* (1928), a silent western that followed a 'half caste American Indian sneaking through the snows and conifers of Canada to ambush a posse of 'Mounties.'[69] If the proposition that African audiences would be more likely to identify with a slave mutiny than American Indians defending their land seems obvious, the banning of *Frontier Trail* possessed a certain tortured logic in the provincial and racially charged context of Northern Rhodesian censorship: the Mounties were, after all, British Empire policemen, and they were white; the slavers were Arabs, and they were represented as criminals.[70]

White residents of the colony often emphasised the dangers they saw in exposing Africans to typical cowboy movies with their scenes of lawlessness and violence, including violence that pitted 'one bunch of Europeans against another.'[71] Some censors were even uneasy about films depicting combat during World War II or resistance to the Nazis.[72] A film like *Town Meeting of the World* might be banned for the dangerous democratic and internationalist sentiments it was likely to convey, but much more threatening was the American western that included a train hijacking and seizure of weapons, 'poisonous stuff' in Northern Rhodesia when increasingly bitter conflict over political power challenged the race hierarchy and threatened order.[73] Many whites saw all popular films as intrinsically dangerous – they eroded the fundamental culture of deference by encouraging 'the idea that to stand and speak to anyone with hands in pockets, lounging, and possibly giving the hat – firmly on the head – an insolent backward tilt is to show a high degree of sophistication.'[74]

In an interview conducted in 1990, the South African actor John Kani described his childhood encounter with Hollywood films: 'Just to sit in this dark place, and magic takes place on the wall. For a moment, we forgot apartheid, we forgot there was another world that wasn't good, we sat there and were carried away by the dream of these American movies.'[75] As the actor Djimon Hounsou, from Benin, has very recently recalled, going to the movies in African cities differed strikingly from the experience in the United States or Europe. The film was usually a dated western, but 'it was amazing . . . We'd climb the walls to get in, and you'd see people packed in . . . Here, people refuse to sit in the first row of the theater. In Cotenou [Benin's capital] there were kids pressed up against the screen.'[76] Children in Ghanaian cities would pool their change to raise enough money to buy a single movie ticket for the one boy or girl who could be counted on to absorb the film and describe in detail the hero's dress and gait and repeat his memorable phrases.[77] Elderly Zambian city-dwellers hold similar memories of escapist pleasure in their recollections of the bioscope. One African woman became particularly animated as she recounted hours spent watching westerns. She did not care for the other important diversions that town life had offered her; she did not drink or attend dances: 'I only liked the bioscope. Horses, cowboys, big hats, America.'[78]

Film attendance in Northern Rhodesia grew rapidly during the 1940s – the same time that the movies reached their peak as an attraction in North America and Britain. Many thousands of Africans were paying a small admission to see films each week, and with 'African cinemas well equipped and supervised, especially in the Copperbelt, a generation of regular 'film fans' is in the making.'[79] The campaign of the various information arms of the imperial state to develop a base of support for the war effort brought film to a much wider area of the country at the same time that the intensifying movement between rural home areas and urban industrial employment spread knowledge about the character of urban life and its amenities, such as the cinema.[80] This was by no means, however, the same cinema that attracted many millions of patrons in Europe and the United States. Simple outdoor amphitheaters or mobile cinema vans or barges stood in for luxuriously appointed movie palaces. And whereas marquees and posters attracted spectators in North America and Britain from shopping streets in urban business districts into an enclosed world, in Northern Rhodesia it was the setting up of apparatus and the gradual transition from dusk to dark that drew people into the film world. In both urban and rural areas until well into the 1950s, Africans saw movies almost exclusively out of doors. At the Roan Antelope Mine in the mid-1950s, two thousand or more would gather for weekly film shows that were social events as much as entertainment:[81]

> At seven o'clock on a clear evening, adults and children lined up for their tickets – 'thruppence' (three pennies) for adults and a penny for children – at the large, unroofed white stone amphitheatre connected with the mine Welfare Hall . . . As the theater began to fill up, friends greeted each other, some young men attempted to make assignations with young women, children jostled and pushed each other and were told to be quiet and to make way for their elders. There was a continuous hubbub. The large audience spilled over into the center aisle, sitting on the steps of the inclined floor. Late-comers stood by the walls. Talk, laughter, and a sense of expectation pervaded the theater.[82]

Cinema shows attracted mainly children and young adults, although older people were certainly found among the audiences. A survey of film attendance conducted on the Copperbelt in the 1950s suggests that a majority of town dwellers attended movies at least occasionally and that a sizable minority went to film shows on a weekly basis. Males clearly predominated, but substantial numbers of young women were also dedicated moviegoers. Copperbelt residents with more education and better jobs were more likely to go to movies than their less educated counterparts and probably more likely to be dedicated fans, but it was still working-class male youths with relatively little education who made up the core of film audiences.[83]

The program typically began with 'The African Mirror,' a magazine series that showed elements of African life such as first-aid teams at a mine, traditional dancing, and commercial agriculture. This was followed by 'The Northern Spotlight,' the government-sponsored newsreel, and then British news. Animal cartoons, called *kadoli*, favored by small children, preceded the main feature, usually a dated or 'B' cowboy film or occasionally a *Superman* film. Although each week brought a new feature, the cheap westerns that dominated film shows for three decades were generally instantly recognizable to audiences. In film after film, cowboy heroes faced brutish outlaws and badmen in a series of confrontations. Sometimes, the hero himself was disguised as an outlaw, or the villain was a supposedly respectable citizen, or stereotypically bloodthirsty Indians were called upon to take to the warpath in opposition to the heroes. Although major Hollywood westerns became increasingly complex and sophisticated during the 1940s, the 'B' movies that dominated the Copperbelt outdoor cinemas remained remarkably consistent, offering uninterrupted series of vignettes of fights, chases, and horse-back stunts.[84] By the time the chase was over and the hero victorious, it was 9:30, the show was over, and the audience drifted home on foot and bicycles.[85]

Even as African audiences became more accustomed to film entertainment and some became regular moviegoers, the film experience in Northern Rhodesia still involved aspects of the wonder and amazement that were characteristic of first encounters with motion-picture technology. The imperial mythologies of natives struck dumb by moving images and disembodied voices emanating from black boxes may have been largely products of Europeans in the thrall of the medium, but film shows did provide novel and sometimes thrilling experiences as darkness fell and the images and sounds brought familiar scenes to the screens or exposed audiences to exotic, incomprehensible settings. Europeans argued that the lack of understanding of the technologies that produced these films meant that Africans regarded movies in the 'same category with the miracle of an airplane.'[86] But audience behavior reveals no more sense of such mystery and alienation than that of Americans today confronting baffling cyber technologies.

In the Roan Antelope mine compound in the early 1950s, 'going to the movies was a social experience . . . There was an excitement in being part of a movie audience of more than a thousand people, constantly commenting to each other, shouting their pleasure and booing their displeasure.'[87] In place of the regimented and reverential silence imposed on filmgoers in North America and Europe, African film shows were characterized by the noise, commentary, and engagement typical of spectacles.[88] Scenes of mine workers produced loud commentaries on the quality and energy of the workers; portrayals of 'trad-itional' dances led to debates on changing mores; a newsreel on Kenya produced discussion of mountains in the tropics and memories of war service; but the greatest and most enthusiastic involvement was reserved for the featured western.[89] The dynamic of these film shows underscores Lawrence Levine's argument that, in nascent industrial communities, 'people enjoyed popular culture not as atomised beings vulnerable to an overpowering external force but as part of social groups in which they experienced the performance or with which they shared it after the fact.'[90] Although the characters and plots varied, Northern Rhodesian audiences always called the hero 'Jack.'[91] This convention, at odds with American and British preoccupations with particular characters and the actors who portrayed them, symbolises a deeper divide in film spectatorship.

African audiences in Northern Rhodesian for the most part seem to have ignored or dismissed plots, made murky in any case by the unfamiliar language or accents, the crowd noise, and the censor's shears.[92] Moviegoers watched the films for the stock scenes that amused and delighted, in one form or another, in film after film: the characteristic stride, the fighting style, the memorable phrase. These elements were observed and appreciated according to well-defined standards of action taste, at least according to young male viewers. As one satisfied patron noted when a film came to an end, 'this is the kind of Jack we want.'[93] Although whites were often dismayed by films that portrayed holdups and murders, descriptions of film shows suggest that audiences viewed and appropriated elements of these in isolation from the narrative or plot. In a protest to the Northern Rhodesian Department of Information during the mid-1950s, one employer charged that showing cowboy action films was 'nothing less than criminal folly.' The concern was well placed in the sense that audiences focused on the scenes of stagecoach holdups and various murders in isolation, paying little attention to the fact that the heroes eventually brought the villains to justice: 'With two thirds of the cast galloping all over the place at breakneck speed . . . I can promise you,' this critic wrote, 'that the plot was not understood by the audience. I have taken the trouble to make quite sure of this fact by questioning the one more intelligent individual, a bricklayer, who did attend. What *was understood*, was the fact that the film portrayed utter lawlessness and indiscriminate use of revolvers and rifles.'[94] But it is equally clear from audience response that these scenes conveyed general styles of masculine bravado, rather than literal models of behavior.[95]

Fight scenes drew especially favorable responses, with one man describing how he liked 'to see cowboys run after one another on horses, and the fighting. Jack beats his friends skillfully, and it pleases me to see him plant blows on other men's faces.' Another liked 'best the cowboy films, because they teach us how to fight others and how to win lovers.' A young, educated man explained that he felt 'as if I am fighting. I always want to see how strong Jack is and whether he can be knocked out early. But I expect the hero, Jack, to beat everyone and to win every time.'[96] Such reactions often perplexed whites. To a researcher in the 1950s, the connection that a group of teenagers made between the appearance of Superman with his cape and a Roman official in a toga in a movie about the Crucifixion demonstrated an inability on the part of African viewers to understand the representational nature of film.[97] But to audiences who watched films as a disconnected series of scenes, with close attention paid to styles of clothing and action, such comparisons made perfect sense. Similarly, such an appreciation of movies as intrinsically disconnected from the linear and the real partly explains the apparent overwhelming preference of African audiences for black and white films when color films were initially introduced.[98] The first color movies shown tended to be locally made and didactic, but the preference apparently went beyond that to an assertion that color films were not 'natural-looking.' The conjunction of the use of color and the introduction of local settings also took films in the direction of the mundane, where plainly they did not belong. The anthropologist Hortense Powdermaker reported a deep reluctance among schoolchildren and some adults to accept that films were staged, and claimed that audiences reacted with irritation when an actor, shot dead in a previous film, turned up alive in another.[99] But the very conventions of naming the hero Jack and analyzing and comparing the stock sequences argues for a fine appreciation of films as fantasy.

Audiences invariably responded insistently and angrily to the occasional attempts of paternalistic officials to vary programs and broaden local film taste.[100] In 1953, the white managers at the Luanshya municipal residential compound experimented with a showing of *Cry, the Beloved Country* (1951). Shown on a program that included a *Superman* movie, the film drew a very large audience. The screening was preceded by a synopsis in a local language,

Chibemba, and three educated African men were asked to mingle with patrons and collect reactions. The audience engaged with the film in typical fashion, making general comments and holding open discussion, rather than sitting in the reverential silence that Europeans expected for serious movies. People in the audience continually complained about the film and demanded 'cowboys.' Uproarious laughter greeted the scene in which the wealthy white landowner Mr. Jarvis is informed of the murder of his son, and audience members were 'visibly delighted when Mrs. Jarvis was grief-stricken at the news of the death of her son.' The appearance of the murderer's father, Reverend Kumalo, elicited loud and derisive comments like 'church,' 'Christianity,' and 'we want cowboys.'[101] Such seemingly callous responses might be represented in part as 'oppositional' statements. Certainly, the reaction to Kumalo conveyed some of the resentment that working-class African men felt toward the church leaders and other 'respectable' men in their community; but it is unlikely that antipathy to white domination, however bitter, would translate into derision of the emotional grief of a white mother and father over the loss of their son. Unable or unwilling to comprehend the dialogue, audience members largely ignored character development and plot, and probably in this case reacted to extreme facial expressions. They experienced or 'read' the film as they would have the cowboy movie they had anticipated seeing – as a series of action scenes. In a slow-moving and rather pretentious film like *Cry, the Beloved Country*, there was little 'action,' and audiences reacted viscerally to the few scenes that stood out. As the report of the showing makes clear, a substantial proportion of the audience demonstrated their boredom simply by walking out.[102]

The world of films, and especially cowboy films, spilled out into the popular culture of Northern Rhodesian urban communities and followed filmgoers into the streets and their homes and eventually back to their rural home villages. When members of the audience got back to their rooms or houses or met friends at work or at other social occasions, films were often the subject of discussion.[103] As in Ghana, youths talked over the films in the days that followed, paying particular attention to the styles of dress and fighting techniques that were central to the appeal of westerns. Oral recollections reveal the same flow of Hollywood imagery into Cape Town's District Six community. There, people waiting in line for tickets could be overheard sprinkling their conversation with terms like 'pardner' and 'howdee,' and motifs drawn from films often surfaced in the costumes of the annual New Year carnivals.[104] Certainly, in rural areas of Northern Rhodesia, the mobile cinemas left a great many images in their wake for audiences to savor and rehearse before the van returned, even if many of the residents had in fact spent considerable time in towns and would have been somewhat familiar with film shows.[105]

A film show in a remote rural area was, of course, much more of a special event, since mobile cinemas did not reach a given village or town much more often than once or twice a year in the 1940s or once a month in the 1950s. The entertainment began with the arrival of the van, and crowds began to assemble in the afternoon to watch and assist in setting up the projector and screen, eventually numbering from one hundred to three thousand people. Before the film show itself, members of the mobile cinema staff gave educational talks illustrated with film strips on topics like malaria eradication; they tuned in the national radio station and piped it out to the crowd on loudspeakers; and they sold various books and newspapers.[106]

Consistent with the noncommercial, educational mission of the mobile cinema, the main program did not include 'unsuitable' westerns or other adventure movies. But the staff was careful to alternate 'entertainment' films with more didactic ones. The program usually began with 'one or two amusing films, followed by an instructional film. The next film is usually something else of particular interest, not necessarily comedy. It might be a short film on game or a 'musical' with catchy tunes.' If ten reels were shown, half would be solely for entertainment, three 'really educational,' and the remaining two general interest films and regionally oriented newsreels.[107] By the 1950s, rural audiences had become substantially more sophisticated in their film tastes, as the mobile cinema program expanded and more people spent time in the urban areas. Local, 'respectable' men and women shared the distaste of the mobile cinema staff for cowboy films, regarding them as a dangerous influence; but younger people who had visited the towns were increasingly caught up in cowboy craze that had taken root in the Copperbelt, even though westerns were still not usually shown by the mobile cinema that served remote rural areas.[108]

African audiences often disturbed European officials by the ways they used material from films to make judgements about the outside world, the nature of imperialism, and the character of European culture. Seemingly innocuous footage of healthy cattle in Southern Rhodesia, for example, inspired commentary from Northern Rhodesian moviegoers in the 1950s on racial segregation and the inferiority of the diet of Africans in comparison to whites. A Northern Rhodesian newsreel showing the dedication of a home for the aged elicited comments in the crowd that these had to be for whites: 'do you think they can build houses for Africans like that?'[109] Depictions of whites engaged in manual labor invariably inspired sarcastic, critical commentary.[110] Although the white settlers who actively promoted censorship often advanced the shibboleth of black sexuality to defend the need to subject films to close scrutiny, colonial officials were much more concerned – and quite correctly so – that scenes of half-dressed and philandering white women would become the evidence for critical judgements on white morality.[111] Scenes of kissing or scantily clad women were more offensive than sexually provocative. A discussion of a scene of courtship in a European café led one man to ask, 'are these proper ladies or are they clowns?' Another responded, 'It is the behavior of white ladies. They are not ashamed.' Men and women swimming together was denounced: 'I do not like it. It encourages immorality.' But at the same time, movie patrons paid careful and detailed attention to a distinctively modern style of dancing that might be reproduced later at a local party.[112]

As the cowboy phenomenon makes plain, film made its most distinctive impact on local youth culture. During the 1930s and 1940s, when primary schooling was not yet entrenched in urban areas, young boys often were at loose ends. They roamed around in gangs, whose leaders gave themselves names like 'Jeke,' after the cowboy hero, and 'Popeye.' Among the main occupations of these gangs were 'cowboy games' where rivals pretended to shoot each other. By the early 1950s, all children were expected to attend school, and many more organized activities had become available.[113] But filmgoing was still very popular, and that popularity was reflected in the styles of dress of school-age boys as well as young men.[114] 'Respectable' Africans along with whites generally found these styles reprehensible, associating them in their minds with insolent attitudes if not outright criminality.[115] In the industrial areas of South Africa, local hoodlums often appropriated the names of film stars or notorious characters from westerns or gangster movies.[116] In 1947, a prominent member of the Northern Rhodesian African Representative Council demanded to know in debate whether the government was aware that 'the films shown to African children in bioscopes at present are harmful to their characters?'[117] In Dar es Salaam, it was claimed that 'the cult of cowboy clothes is the safety-valve of the dangerous mob element.[118] Fear of the spread of such behavior certainly motivated many of the paternalistic believers in educational cinema. Indeed, it was almost an article of faith that if good films could be effective tools of education and development, bad ones would produce the juvenile delinquents that many saw as a growing Copperbelt problem.[119] What whites and others in positions of authority feared, of course, was that African town-dwellers would appropriate immoral and criminal behavior from cowboy and gangster movies. Official files on film censorship contain a report from the late 1940s that appeared to justify such fears. A group of six young African men, convicted of robbing and beating a man in the mining town of Mufulira, claimed in their defense that they had seen similar acts in films and wanted to copy them. Whether or not exposure to cowboy movies inspired criminal activities, these young hoodlums were resourceful enough to play on stereotypes by rationalizing their actions in terms of film allusions. It is possible, too, that they hoped paternalistic officials might go easy on unsophisticated youths who were believed to be highly susceptible to the power of film imagery.[120]

For young crooks, as for the mass of Copperbelt youth, film offered a repertoire of images, characters, and behaviors that could be drawn on to define and navigate modern urban life. Descriptions of audience behavior draw attention not only to the enthusiasm that filmgoers showed for fights and other action sequences but also to the close attention the people paid to the material content of films. Notwithstanding the efforts of the Colonial Film Unit, audiences showed little patience for films that depicted rural life and the potential for the development of agriculture. Movies represented an escape from the harsh realities of urban life, especially in an increasingly repressive South Africa; despite the exotic locales of gunfighter epics, film also provided a kind of guide to urban modernity and sophistication. Published memoirs of urban black South Africans reveal the powerful and romantic appeal of Hollywood products, yet it is clear as well that audiences drew the characters into urban southern Africa, weaving their own practices of witchcraft and kinship politics into discussions of the meanings of particular sequences. As one filmgoer from the Copperbelt noted, 'the cowboy has medicines to make him invisible . . . Cowboys show respect. And Jack is also the son of a big man.'[121]

Those men and women who regarded themselves as mature often dismissed the bioscope as a trivial pastime appropriate only to children. One Copperbelt woman in her thirties defined films as a distinctly urban phenomenon only appealing to those who had been raised in the city: 'Cinema shows and radio are there to entertain youth. We people of old age cannot attend such things where small boys go. Our form of entertainment is beer . . . How can I develop the habit of going to cinema now? The people who enjoy it are those who have been born here.'[122] In the urban areas of central and southern Africa, the divide between those who self-consciously remained oriented toward their rural homes and those who took up a distinctively modern worldview surfaced visibly in leisure activities: people who conceived of themselves as 'modern' participated in church activities and organized sports and were bioscope enthusiasts, while those who rejected modernity dismissed such pastimes and generally preferred to spend their leisure time in informal socializing and drinking.[123]

In the last, bitter years of colonial rule in Northern Rhodesia, some Africans and their liberal white allies directly challenged the censorship of films on racial lines, as part of a broader assault on the color bar.[124] Some of the younger and better educated town residents, in particular, found the bioscope unappealing and were eager to see more sophisticated and varied movies in more sedate surroundings.[125] In 1957, the chairman of the interracial Capricorn Africa Society drew attention 'to the fact that large numbers of educated Africans are profoundly dissatisfied with the programs being shown on the African locations. They wish to see the films that Europeans, Indians and Coloureds are seeing but the decisions of the Board are preventing them from doing so.[126] When the board chose to ban African viewing newsreels that depicted the resistance of Hungarians to the Soviet invasion and the demonstrations that followed in various European cities, the controversy reached the floor of the British House of Commons. There, a government spokesman vigorously defended censorship with the assertion that 'Africans were more likely to be impressed by moving pictures.'[127]

The opening of a multi-racial cinema in 1957 in Lusaka provided an opportunity for Africans to see a wider range of films in the more genteel atmosphere of an indoor theater, but the continued application of censorship rules meant that educated African patrons still risked being turned away at the door if a particular film had not been passed for African audiences.[128] For this small but highly influential group, the humiliation of being forbidden to see films that had been approved for viewing by whites, including children, was a stark reminder of the continued ascendancy of racial hierarchy and made a mockery of promises of 'racial partnership' and non-racialism.[129] Yet, as late as 1960, on the eve of the legislated desegregation of public facilities in Northern Rhodesia, Roman Catholic bishops still vigorously defended racial censorship: 'Material reasons like uniformity of treatment, economy, convenience and such ought not be allowed to weigh against the need to safeguard from evils of the moral order of the African people, the vast majority of whom have . . . primitive ideas of morality affecting public order and decency.'[130]

This tenacious devotion among whites in Northern Rhodesia to the specter of film's power over Africans reveals not only a deeply entrenched racial order but an unquestioning confidence as well in the powerful force of the medium of film as an instrument of cultural subversion. The claims advanced in colonial Northern Rhodesia and across colonial Africa that movies, and popular culture generally, undermined traditional authority and custom belongs to a powerful intellectual tradition of modern imperialism enshrined in administrative terms by the British in the form of the doctrine of indirect rule and more broadly in the ideal of trusteeship.[131] The strong attraction of African audiences to a vision of Europe and North America inscribed in Hollywood westerns and other action movies subverted cherished colonial notions of Africa as Britain's 'Wild West.'[132] This colonial antipathy to the global consumerism of urban Africans, decried as evidence of dangerous 'detribalization' or 'westernization,' has survived in postcolonial discourse in the context of debates over cultural imperialism. Ranging across the ideological and disciplinary spectra, scholars and critics lament the disruption of societies, characterized variously as traditional or backward, and in particular stress the role of mass media in projecting the ideological messages of international capitalism and demand for global consumer commodities at the expense of traditional values and practices.[133]

Ariel Dorfman and Armand Mattelart's influential study of Disney cartoons in the Third World, *How to Read Donald Duck*, drew on dependency theory to argue that such hugely popular but seemingly innocent media products in fact have extended American global hegemony by conveying to unsophisticated readers principles that bolster capitalist values and thus restrict the emergence of genuine consciousness.[134] In their confident analysis of the meanings of mass-media products and assumptions of the power of those products to persuade, Dorfman and Mattelart and other critics of global information flows not only share common ground with liberal critics of global cultural homogenization but also betray a perverse intellectual debt to alarmist imperial rantings against the nefarious influence of Hollywood films. In each case, 'Third World' peoples or audiences are assumed to lack the sophistication to resist popular media images or to engage them critically.

The moviegoing experiences of Africans in Northern Rhodesia challenge such assumptions, suggesting that the meanings of films and other pieces of mass media are elusive and contested, and that audiences continually appropriate and re-appropriate such media and subject them to various and fluid readings. The cowboys who populated westerns emerged from screens on the Copperbelt as characters rooted as much in urban Northern Rhodesian communities as in the American West, and the ways that audiences drew on and referred to film images varied as widely as confident official and scholarly pronouncements on their meaning. Seemingly bizarre audience responses to a film like *Cry, the Beloved Country* made perfect sense in terms of local expectations for film shows and constructions of film character behavior. Certainly, highly politicized informal audience commentaries on film depictions of life in African colonies demonstrated a keen appreciation on the part of African moviegoers of the manipulative power of film. Although very little research has directly addressed the global appeal of popular media, the work that has been done, especially that exploring the seemingly inexplicable universal popularity of the American television program 'Dallas' (1978–91) and its supposed glorification of wealth, has suggested how 'naïve and improbable is the simple notion of an immediate ideological effect arising from exposure to the imperialist text.'[135] Like movie patrons in colonial Northern Rhodesia, viewers of 'Dallas' sometimes drew on the program to criticize American excess, or saw in the program a guide to style, or simply responded to the basic morality plays that drove the series. But reliance on immediate reactions in controlled circumstances very much limits the validity of this kind of audience research, no matter how stimulating the findings.[136] The Copperbelt audiences who filled the seats of noisy outdoor cinemas analyzed and debated the elements of films while they watched them, adopted and modified film modes of dress, speech, and behavior, and then took those sensibilities back to the theaters in a process that was difficult to capture at the time and now, in the age of video, resembles in popular memory a kind of quaint nostalgic relic. Yet, as the fragmentary evidence of audience response suggests, moviegoers sought in films not only entertainment and sources of style but also an opportunity to engage and critique the colonial order they inhabited and to appropriate and synthesise notions of modernity that they believed would facilitate urban life.

The process of decolonization that culminated in 1964 in an independent Zambia swept aside any open assertion of racial discrimination and merged race-based claims of the impact of movies into broader debates about the effect of popular culture on children. In postcolonial Zambia, the introduction of television and more recently the proliferation of small video dens and individually owned videocassette recorders has effectively pushed the bioscope – formal film showings – to the margins of entertainment. The current popularity of martial arts and other contemporary action movies has overshadowed the deep affection for the cowboy genre exhibited by several generations of viewers in the industrial towns of the Copperbelt and elsewhere in east, central, and southern Africa. But if the encounter of African audiences with film during the 1940s and 1950s lacked the complexity of the diverse and fragmented circulation of media that is characteristic of Zambia and the rest of southern Africa today, it is apparent that the critical process through which audiences consume visual media developed on a diet of horse operas.[137] As Hortense Powdermaker observed of Copperbelt film shows in the 1950s, 'whatever was seen was commented on, interpreted, criticized. Questions were asked.[138]

Notes

1. The British colony of Northern Rhodesia became Zambia at independence in 1964. During the 1950s, Northern Rhodesia was linked with Southern Rhodesia (Zimbabwe) and Nyasaland (Malawi) in a Central African Federation dominated by white settler interests.

2. H. Franklin, 'The Central African Screen,' *Colonial Cinema* 8 (December 1950): 85. 'Jack' was supposedly a tribute to the actor Jack Holt. Also see 'The Cinema in Northern Rhodesia,' *Colonial Cinema* 2 (June 1944): 22.

3. R. J. Allanson to Director, Department of Information, Lusaka, January 27, 1956, National Archives of Zambia (hereafter, NAZ), Sec. 5/16, I, no. 88.

4. According to a 1956 survey, in Dar es Salaam 'there has grown up, as elsewhere in East Africa, the cult of the cowboy . . . The young man . . . soon acquires the idioms of tough speech, the slouch, the walk of the 'dangerous' man of the films; the ever-popular Western films teach him.' J. A. K. Leslie, *A Survey of Dar es Salaam* (London, 1963), 112; and see Rob Nixon, *Homelands, Harlem and Hollywood: South African Culture and the World Beyond* (New York, 1994), 31–5.

5. For an introduction to the large literature on the history of the Copperbelt, see Jane L. Parpart, *Labor and Capital on the African Copperbelt* (Philadelphia, 1983).

6. Already by the early 1930s, twice-weekly film shows at the Roan Antelope Compound in Luanshya drew an average attendance of more than a thousand. Charles W. Coulter, 'The Sociological Problem,' in *Modern Industry and the African*, J. Merle Davis, ed. (London, 1933), 72.

7. Hortense Powdermaker, *Copper Town: Changing Africa; The Human Situation on the Rhodesian Copperbelt* (New York, 1962), 227. In the District Six neighborhood of Cape Town, movies were 'unquestionably the most popular form of paid entertainment in the inter-war years.' Bill Nasson, ' "She Preferred Living in a Cave with Harry the Snake-catcher": Towards an Oral History of Popular Leisure and Class Expression in District Six, Cape Town, c. 1920s–1950s,' in *Holding Their Ground: Class, Locality and Culture in Nineteenth and Twentieth-Century South Africa*, Philip Bonner, Isabel Hofmeyr, Deborah James, and Tom Lodge, eds. (Johannesburg, 1989), 286.

8. The globalized power of the media and its role in transmitting American culture is probably more assumed than it is studied. For an exception, see Peter Manuel, *Cassette Culture: Popular Music and Technology in North India* (Chicago, 1993), esp. 2–18. In practice, the study of media 'development' in Africa has been shaped by assumptions associated with modernization theory. See, for example, Graham Mytton, *Mass Communication in Africa* (London, 1983), 4–18; and Robert L. Stevenson, *Communication, Development, and the Third World: The Global Politics of Information* (New York, 1988). For critical evaluation of debates about media globalism, see John Tomlinson, *Cultural Imperialism: A Critical Introduction* (Baltimore, 1991), 34–67; and Jonathan Friedman, *Cultural Identity and Global Process* (London, 1994), 195–232.

9. Powdermaker, *Copper Town*, 259.

10. NAZ, Sec. 2/1121, 'Censorship of Films for Natives, 1932–48,' and subsequent files.

11. Response to Mr. R. J. Allanson, February 28, 1956, NAZ, Sec. 5/16, no. 88.

12. Alan O'Shea, 'What a Day for a Daydream: Modernity, Cinema and the Popular Imagination in the Late Twentieth Century,' in *Modern Times: Reflections*

on a Century of English Modernity, Mica Nava and O'Shea, eds. (London, 1996), 243–5.

13. See, for example, Herbert Blumer, *Movies and Conduct* (New York, 1933). The tendency to look for sources of violence and antisocial behavior in the media is noted in a recent analysis in the *New York Times*, 'Rampage Killers: A Statistical Portrait,' April 8, 2000.

14. Franklin, 'Central African Screen,' 87.

15. NAZ, Sec. 2/1121, 'Censorship of Films for Natives, 1932–48,' and subsequent files.

16. Although not centrally concerned with film, Debra Spitulnik, 'Anthropology and Mass Media,' *Annual Review of Anthropology* 22 (1993): 293–315, provides an effective introduction to some of the theoretical assumptions shaping media studies on Africa.

17. Judith Mayne, *Cinema and Spectatorship* (London, 1993), 8–9, 17, 65. Also see Miriam Hansen, *Babel and Babylon: Spectatorship in American Silent Film* (Cambridge, Mass., 1991), 3–5.

18. Linda Williams, ed., *Viewing Positions: Ways of Seeing Film* (New Brunswick, N.J., 1995). But see the essays in the section on 'Black Spectatorship,' in *Black American Cinema*, Manthia Diawara, ed. (New York, 1993), 211–302. Some of the work on early film audiences in North America and Europe has focused attention on perspectives of working-class and immigrant audiences. See Judith Thissen, 'Jewish Immigrant Audiences in New York City (1907–1914),' in *American Movie Audiences: From the Turn of the Century to the Early Sound Era*, Melvyn Stokes and Richard Maltby, eds. (Bloomington, Ind., 1999), 15–28; and Roy Rosenzweig, *Eight Hours for What We Will: Workers and Leisure in an Industrial City, 1870–1920* (Cambridge, 1983), 191–221.

19. For example, E. Ann Kaplan, 'Film and History: Spectatorship, Transference, and Race,' in *History and Histories within the Human Sciences*, Ralph Cohen and Michael S. Roth, eds. (Charlottesville, Va., 1995), 179–208. Also see Stuart Hall, 'Cultural Identity and Cinematic Representation,' *Framework* 36 (1989): 68–81.

20. For example, Carol J. Clover, *Men, Women and Chain Saws: Gender in the Modern Horror Film* (Princeton, N.J., 1992); and Barbara Creed, *The Monstrous-Feminine: Film, Feminism, Psychoanalysis* (London, 1993). The issues raised by these scholars have not yet made their way into studies of filmgoing in Africa. The special issue of *Matatu* 19 (1997) devoted to 'Women and African Cinema' includes no article that explores the female film audience or interprets spectatorship in gendered terms.

21. For the role of imported videos in local cultures, see Minou Fuglesang, *Veils and Videos: Female Youth Culture on the Kenyan Coast* (Stockholm, 1994); and Brian Larkin, 'Indian Films and Nigerian Lovers: Media and the Creation of Parallel Modernities,' *Africa* 67 (1997): 406–40. Most of the work on video concentrates on local production and distribution and on the analysis of video film content. The most important studies are Onookome Okome and Jonathan Haynes, *Cinema and Social Change in West Africa* (Jos, Nigeria, 1995); and Jonathan Haynes, ed., *Nigerian Video Films* (Jos, 1997).

22. Martin Allor, 'Relocating the Site of the Audience,' *Critical Studies in Mass Communication* 5 (1988): 217–33, traces the development of theoretical approaches to the relationship between medium and audience.

23. According to Leo Charney and Vanessa R. Schwartz, 'Cinema, as it developed in the late nineteenth century, became the fullest expression and combination of modernity's attributes.' 'Introduction,' *Cinema and the Invention of Modern Life*, Charney and Schwartz, eds. (Berkeley, Calif., 1995), 1; also, 1–3. For a stimulating analysis of ideas of 'the modern,' see Nestor Garcia Canclini, *Hybrid Cultures: Strategies for Entering and Leaving Modernity* (Minneapolis, 1995 [Spanish edition, 1989]). The reception of film images was linked as well to the

development of a mass-consumption economy. See Timothy Burke, *Lifebuoy Men, Lux Women: Commodification, Consumption, and Cleanliness in Modern Zimbabwe* (Durham, N.C., 1996).

24. Spearpoint, Compound Manager, Roan Antelope Mine, Luanshya, to General Manager, October 2, 1935, 'Films for Compound Bioscope,' RACM WMA/94, 204.2, Zambia Consolidated Copper Mines, Archives, Ndola (hereafter, ZCCM); and 'Film in Northern Rhodesia,' *Colonial Cinema* 11 (December 1953): 81.
25. Powdermaker, *Copper Town*, 255.
26. Commissioner, Northern Rhodesia Civil Police, to Chief Secretary, August 22, 1932, NAZ, Sec. 2/1121, no. 1; and 'Cinema in Northern Rhodesia,' *Colonial Cinema* 2 (June 1944): 22. The Copperbelt became the site of intensive social scientific research carried on by scholars affiliated with the Rhodes Livingstone Institute, including A. L. Epstein, J. C. Mitchell, J. A. Barnes, and Gordon Wilson. See Epstein, *Urbanization and Kinship: The Domestic Domain on the Copperbelt of Zambia, 1950–1956* (London, 1981).
27. Spearpoint, 'Films for Compound Bioscope.'
28. The Colonial Film Unit,' *Colonial Cinema* 5 (June 1947): 27–31; and African Film Library Purchasing Committee, List of Films Purchased, 1942, NAZ, Sec. 2/1122, 84/1.
29. Note for Finance Committee, May 29, 1945, NAZ, Sec. 2/1121 (5), no. 245; and 'Cinema in Northern Rhodesia,' 22.
30. 'Cinema in Northern Rhodesia,' 22.
31. *Colonial Cinema* 6 (September 1948): 56–57.
32. Extract, January 6, 1956, ZCCM, RACM WMA/94, 204.2 (2).
33. 'Film in Northern Rhodesia,' 82. For discussion of the development of clubs generally, see Charles Ambler, 'Alcohol and the Control of Labor on the Copperbelt,' in *Liquor and Labor in Southern Africa*, Jonathan Crush and Ambler, eds. (Athens, Ohio, 1992), 352.
34. District Commissioner Mufulira to Provincial Commissioner, Ndola, December 23, 1954, NAZ, Sec. 5/16 (3), no. 53/1. Frederick Cooper connects these local policies to broad questions of labor and decolonization in *Decolonization and African Society: The Labor Question in French and British Africa* (Cambridge, 1996), 336–48.
35. Extract from *Central African Post*, November 5, 1956, NAZ, Sec. 5/16, no. 107A; Rev. George Shaw (Member, Film Censorship Board), February 23, 1960, and J. V. Savanhu (Parliamentary Secretary to the Minister for Race Affairs), March 18, 1960, in Enclosed File, 'Film Censorship: Evidence Submitted to Federal Working Party, 1960,' NAZ, Sec. 5/15, 16.
36. See Tom Gunning, 'An Aesthetic of Astonishment: Early Film and the (In)Credulous Spectator' [1989], rpt. in L. Williams, *Viewing Positions*, 114–33, 115.
37. Gunning, 'Aesthetic of Astonishment,' 129.
38. Powdermaker, *Copper Town*, 258.
39. 'Cinema in Northern Rhodesia,' 22.
40. Harry Franklin (former Director, Northern Rhodesia Information Service), February 12, 1960, 'Film Censorship: Evidence Submitted to Federal Working Party,' NAZ, Sec. 5/15, 16. Vanessa Schwartz argues in a study of early film audiences in Paris that 'cinema's spectators brought to the cinematic experience modes of viewing which were cultivated in a variety of cultural activities and practices.' 'Cinematic Spectatorship before the Apparatus: The Public Taste for Reality in "Fin-de-Siècle" Paris,' in Charney and Schwartz, *Cinema and the Invention of Modern Life*, 298.
41. Franklin, February 12, 1960, 'Film Censorship: Evidence Submitted to Federal Working Party,' NAZ, Sec. 5/15, 16.
42. J. V. Savanhu, March 18, 1960, 'Film Censorship: Evidence Submitted to Federal Working Party,' NAZ, Sec. 5/15, 16.

43. African Film Library Purchasing Committee, List of Films Purchased, 1942, NAZ, Sec. 2/1122, no. 84/1; and extract from *Northern News*, May 9, 1957, NAZ, Sec. 5/16, no. 170.

44. Louis Nell, 'The Mobile Cinema in Northern Rhodesia,' *Colonial Cinema* 6 (June 1948): 44.

45. H. Stelling, Chingola to Committee for Local Government, March 16, 1955, NAZ, Sec. 5/16 (3), no. 69/1.

46. W. Sellers, 'Mobile Cinema Shows in Africa,' *Colonial Cinema* 9 (September 1950), 80.

47. These concerns, of course, resemble fears inspired by immigrant, working-class, and youth audiences in the United States and Europe. See Rosenzweig, *Eight Hours for What We Will*, 191–215. Recent public debates about theater location and selection of films in contemporary American cities reveal the persistence of assumptions about the effects of movies on racially and age-defined audiences. *New York Times*, December 28, 1998, and January 31, 1999.

48. District Commissioner Kitwe to Provincial Commissioner, November 25, 1937, NAZ, Sec. 2/1121 (2), no. 54/1.

49. Letter from Interested Citizens, February 8, 1960, 'Film Censorship: Evidence Submitted to Federal Working Party,' NAZ, Sec. 5/15, 16; and Memorandum on Native Film Censorship, December 12, 1947, Sec. 2/1121 (7), no. 348.

50. J. D. Cave, Native Welfare Officer (and Film Censorship Board member), to District Commissioner Kitwe, August 7, 1940, NAZ, Sec. 1/1121 (3), no. 130/4.

51. Rosaleen Smyth, 'The British Colonial Film Unit and Sub-Saharan Africa, 1939–1945,' *Historical Journal of Film Radio and Television* 8 (1998); 'Movies and Mandarins: The Official Film and British Colonial Africa,' in Curran and Porter, *British Cinema History*; 'The Development of British Colonial Film Policy, 1927–1939, with Special Reference to East and Central Africa,' *Journal of African History* 20 (1979). Also see Thomas August, *The Selling of the Empire: British and French Imperialist Propaganda, 1890–1940* (Westport, Conn., 1985), 101–02.

52. J. Merle Davis, 'The Problem for Missions,' in Davis, *Modern Industry and the African*, 323.

53. Smyth, 'British Colonial Film Unit'; Smyth, 'Movies and Mandarins'; and L. A. Notcutt and G. C. Latham, eds., *The African and the Cinema: An Account of the Work of the Bantu Educational Cinema Experiment during the Period March 1935 to May 1937* (Edinburgh, 1937).

54. 'Films for African Audiences,' *Colonial Cinema* 1 (June 1944): 1–2.

55. *Colonial Cinema* 1 (May 1943): 1.

56. *Colonial Cinema* 1 (December 1942): 3.

57. 'Films for African Audiences,' 1–2.

58. See Philip Corrigan, 'Film Entertainment as Ideology and Pleasure: A Preliminary Approach to a History of Audiences,' in *British Cinema History*, James Curran and Vincent Porter, eds. (Totowa, N.J., 1983), 29.

59. Acting Chief Secretary to Government Secretary, Mafeking, March 8, 1946, NAZ, Sec. 2/1121 (6), no. 297.

60. Minutes of a Meeting of the Native Film Censorship Board, August 31, 1951, NAZ, Sec. 5/16, no. 12A.

61. Memorandum on Film Censorship, n.d. [1956], NAZ, Sec. 5/16, no. 121.

62. Memorandum on Film Censorship, no. 121.

63. Mr. Shaw, Lusaka, July 28, 1959, 'Film Censorhip: Evidence Submitted to Federal Working Party,' NAZ, Sec. 5/15.

64. District Commissioner Kitwe to J. D. Cave, Native Welfare Officer, August 6, 1940, NAZ, Sec. 2/1121 (3), no. 130/3.

65. Cave to Kitwe, Nkana, August 7, 1940, NAZ, Sec. 2/1121, no. 130/2.

66. Censorship Board, Lusaka, minute, June 20, 1945, NAZ, Sec. 2/1121, no. 246.

67. General Notice 596 of 1945, September 16, 1945, NAZ, Sec. 2/1121, no. 269.

68. Notably, Great Britain, Report of the Commission Appointed to Enquire into the Disturbances in the Copperbelt [Russell Commission] (Lusaka, 1935).

69. H. A. Fosbrooke, Rhodes Livingstone Institute to Governor Arthur Benson, March 5, 1957, NAZ, Sec. 5/16, no. 147.

70. Similarly, the director of information argued in clear racial terms for banning the movie *Huckleberry Finn*. Director of Information to Chief Secretary, December 8, 1940, NAZ, Sec. 2/1125, no. 19.

71. R. J. Allanson to Director, Department of Information, Lusaka, January 27, 1956, NAZ, Sec. 5/16, no. 88.

72. 'Guiding Principles for the Use of Native Film Censorship Board,' n.d., NAZ, Sec. 5/16, no. 121.

73. Rev. George Shaw, February 23, 1960, 'Film Censorship: Evidence Submitted to Federal Working Party,' NAZ, Sec. 5/15, 16.

74. Allanson to Director, January 27, 1956.

75. Quoted in P. Davis, *In Darkest Hollywood: Exploring the Jungles of Cinema's South Africa* (Athens, Ohio, 1996), 23.

76. *New York Times*, December 7, 1997.

77. Emmanuel Akyeampong, personal communication with the author, January 1998.

78. Interview by the author, Mrs. W., Kamwala, Lusaka, July 5, 1988.

79. 'Cinema in Northern Rhodesia,' 22.

80. Capt. A. G. Dickson, 'Effective Propaganda,' *Colonial Cinema* 3 (December 1945): 82–5.

81. Roan Antelope Mine Welfare Office, Annual Report, 1952–1953, September 26, 1953, ZCCM, RACM 1.3.1C.

82. Powdermaker, *Copper Town*, 255–6.

83. Powdermaker, *Copper Town*, 337–8.

84. George Fenin and William K. Everson, *The Western, from Silents to the Seventies*, rev. edn. (New York, 1977), 31–12, 199.

85. Powdermaker, *Copper Town*, 258.

86. Powdermaker, *Copper Town*, 228–9.

87. Powdermaker, *Copper Town*, 256; also see Michael O'Shea, *Missionaries and Miners: A History of the Beginnings of the Catholic Church in Zambia with Particular Reference to the Copperbelt* (Ndola, Zambia, 1986), 246.

88. J. H. G., 'My First Visit to the Cinema,' *Colonial Cinema* 8 (September 1950): 60–1.

89. Powdermaker, *Copper Town*, 256–8.

90. Lawrence W. Levine, 'The Folklore of Industrial Society: Popular Culture and Its Audiences,' *AHR* 97 (October 1992): 1396.

91. Powdermaker, *Copper Town*, 261; 'Cinema in Northern Rhodesia,' 22; and Franklin, 'Central African Screen,' 85.

92. M. O'Shea, *Missionaries and Miners*, 245–6; and Powdermaker, *Copper Town*, 259.

93. Powdermaker, *Copper Town*, 258.

94. Allanson to Director, January 27, 1956, italics in original.

95. See Yvonne Tasker, 'Dumb Movies for Dumb People: Masculinity, the Body, and the Voice in Contemporary Action Cinema,' in *Screening the Male: Exploring Masculinities in Hollywood Cinema*, Steven Cohan and Ina Rae Hark, eds. (London, 1993), 230–44.

96. Powdermaker, *Copper Town*, 260–1.

97. Powdermaker, *Copper Town*, 264.

98. Powdermaker, *Copper Town*, 260. In contrast, George Pearson, director of the Colonial Film Unit, claimed it was evident that 'coloured films help tremendously in getting a story across to Colonial peoples . . . We know from the reactions of the audiences there that these films are greatly appreciated.' Quoted in David

R. Giltrow, 'Young Tanzanians and the Cinema: A Study of the Effects of Selected Basic Motion Picture Elements and Population Characteristics on Filmic Comprehension of Tanzanian Adolescent Primary School Children' (PhD dissertation, Syracuse University, 1973), 17. Giltrow's own study showed audience preference for color but no real difference in didactic terms, p. 15.

99. Powdermaker, *Copper Town*, 263–4. In the 1960s, Tanzanian schoolchildren who had rarely attended films had little trouble identifying objects and actions represented on screen. Giltrow, 'Young Tanzanians and the Cinema,' 132.

100. Roan Antelope Mine Welfare Office, Annual Report, 1952–1953.

101. Welfare Officer, Luanshya Municipal Board to Chairman, African Film Censorship Board, November 6, 1953, NAZ, Sec. 5/16, no. 44/1.

102. South African black intellectuals had criticized the book on which the movie was based for its negative view of urban life and the 'religiosity, deference, and the urban incompetence' of the central character, Reverend Kumalo. Nixon, *Homelands, Harlem and Hollywood*, 27.

103. J. H. G., 'My First Visit to the Cinema,' 61.

104. Nasson, ' "She Preferred Living in a Cave," ' 289.

105. Tony Lawman, 'Information Research: An Experiment in Northern Rhodesia,' *Colonial Cinema* 10 (September 1952): 59–61.

106. *Colonial Cinema* 4 (September 1946): 64–5; and Nell, 'Mobile Cinema in Northern Rhodesia,' 43–6.

107. Nell, 'Mobile Cinema in Northern Rhodesia,' 45.

108. Lawman, 'Information Research,' 56–61.

109. Powdermaker, *Copper Town*, 257.

110. Powdermaker, *Copper Town*, 269.

111. Powdermaker, *Copper Town*, 168, 267; Rev. George Shaw, February 23, 1960, 'Film Censorship: Evidence Submitted to Federal Working Party,' NAZ, Sec. 5/15; and Lawman, 'Information Research,' 59.

112. Powdermaker, *Copper Town*, 267.

113. Powdermaker, *Copper Town*, 196–7.

114. Franklin, 'Central African Screen,' 85; 'Cinema in Northern Rhodesia,' 22; and Allanson to Director, January 27, 1956.

115. Lawman, 'Information Research,' 56–61.

116. Nixon, *Homelands, Harlem and Hollywood*, 12, 31–5; and Don Mattera, *Sophiatown: Coming of Age in South Africa* (1987; Boston, 1989), 75.

117. Nelson Namulango, African Representative Council Debates, July 1, 1948, excerpted in NAZ, Sec. 2/1121, no. 346.

118. Leslie, *Survey of Dar es Salaam*, 112–13.

119. Powdermaker, *Copper Town*, 198.

120. Extract from Mufulira Monthly Police Report, 1947, *Rex vs. John Kandu and Five Other Africans*, NAZ, Sec. 2/1121, no. 346/1. In the end, however, each received a punishment of twelve strokes.

121. Film spectators quoted in Powdermaker, *Copper Town*, 263; also see 256–9. Among a number of memoirs, see, for example, Bloke Modisane, *Blame Me on History* (1963; New York, 1986), which refers repeatedly to the allure of cinema and its importance in constructing elements of cosmopolitanism.

122. Powdermaker, *Copper Town*, 298.

123. Philip Mayer, *Townsmen or Tribesmen: Conservatism and the Process of Urbanization in a South African City* (Cape Town, 1961), esp. 111–17.

124. Film censorship had a parallel in the regulations that restricted African consumption of European-type alcohol. Africans were forbidden to consume spirits until late in the colonial period. See Michael O. West, ' "Equal Rights for All Civilized Men": Elite Africans and the Quest for "European" Liquor in Colonial Zimbabwe, 1924–1961,' *International Review of Social History* 37 (1992): 376–97.

125. A few private clubs sponsored by mining companies provided relatively privileged

Africans the opportunities to see films not approved for African audiences. Memorandum on Film Censorship, Cinema Officer, n.d. [c. 1956], NZA, Sec. 5/16, no. 121.

126. Mr. Kemple, Chairman, Capricorn Africa Society, to Native Film Censorship Board, Lusaka, March 10, 1957, NAZ, Sec. 5/16.

127. Extract, *Central African Post*, May 10, 1957, NAZ, Sec. 5/16, no. 171a.

128. H. A. Fosbrooke to Governor, March 5, 1957, NAZ, Sec. 5/16.

129. Kemple to Native Film Censorship Board, March 10, 1957.

130. Northern Rhodesia Bishops Conference, Secretary General, March 9, 1960, 'Film Censorship: Evidence Submitted to Federal Working Party,' NAZ, Sec. 5/15.

131. Mahmood Mamdani, *Citizen and Subject: Contemporary Africa and the Legacy of Late Colonialism* (Princeton, N.J., 1996), 62–90.

132. Barbara Bush, *Imperialism, Race and Resistance: Africa and Britain, 1919–1945* (London, 1999), 28–38.

133. Tomlinson, *Cultural Imperialism*, 1–33.

134. Ariel Dorfman and A. Mattelart, *How to Read Donald Duck: Imperialism Ideology in the Disney Comic*, David Kunzle, trans. ([1972]; New York, 1975). See also Dorfman, *The Empire's Old Clothes: What the Lone Ranger, Babar, and Other Innocent Heroes Do to Our Minds* (New York, 1983). This critique is drawn from Tomlinson, *Cultural Imperialism*, 35–45.

135. Tomlinson, *Cultural Imperialism*, 47. Note especially Ien Ang, *Watching Dallas: Soap Opera and the Melodramatic Imagination* (London, 1985).

136. Tomlinson, *Cultural Imperialism*, 50–7.

137. Debra Spitulnik, 'The Social Circulation of Media Discourse and the Mediation of Communities,' *Journal of Linguistic Anthropology* 6 (1997): 161–87.

138. Powdermaker, *Copper Town*, 270.

15

CINEMATIC SPECTACLES AND THE RISE OF THE INDEPENDENTS

The 1950s saw the breaking up of the studio system in the new age of television and a refining of the cinematic experience. Technologies that were pioneered in the 1920s, such as zoom lens and widescreen, found their niche in the cinema of the 1950s. It is not a coincidence that the 1950s is associated with a series of technological innovations in cinema. As television began to take off outside the studios' control, audiences for theatre-based entertainment declined. Hollywood made both bold and sometimes outlandish attempts to bring them back. By the end of the 1950s, widescreen entertainment had become entrenched as a Hollywood staple and film producers and exhibitors were even competing for the best way to pipe smells around an auditorium. In the meantime events like the *Paramount* decision of 1948 and resistance to having to qualify for the MPAA seal of approval for films with controversial content contributed to the rise of independent producers and directors.

In a decade in which leisure became a market, cinema was only one of a panoply of options for entertainment; driving and camping holidays, and home improvement, for example, provided a veritable democracy of consumption. The emphasis on families spending time together and the rise of the suburbs in the 1950s speaks to a general disinclination to travel downtown to the cinema on a regular basis. The venue had to change and the suburban shopping mall with a new cinema complex and drive-in movies just outside town succeeded in coaxing back sections of the audience. Drive-ins had existed in small numbers since the Depression of the 1930s but after the *Paramount* decision thousands began to operate huge screens on the edges of towns to provide cheap family entertainment until there were estimated to be around 5,000

---

drive-ins in the US by 1956. Owners tried to provide a family experience with hot food and drinks delivered to cars by carhops circling the audience. Some drive-ins extended their facilities to include nurseries for young children, miniature golf and zoos to entertain older children, and even motels for family sleep-overs. However, while drive-ins remained popular in the summer months, families were not enamoured of the cold, or the rain affecting picture quality, or the generally very poor sound facilities. The cinema in the suburban shopping mall was far more successful and continues to be most American patrons' preferred venue to this day.

As the vertically integrated studio system collapsed, a significant by-product was the rise of the independents and the consequent critical emphasis on the director as author or *auteur*. In America, the *Paramount* decision and its prohibition of block theatre booking finally began to foster healthy competition in the 1950s. Freedom of choice in production and exhibition led to the breakdown of certain established features of the film industry, such as the Production Code (see Chapter 16). To begin with there was a concerted push to release more films but this calmed in the 1950s when it became apparent from market research that cinemagoers were becoming selective. The regular visit to the movies was replaced by more infrequent visits to enjoy big-budget spectacles and star vehicles. Employment became more precarious for actors and writers. Fewer big names were kept 'under contract' and by the 1960s filmmaking would be almost entirely an independent concern with the studios actually producing more and more television and selling studio space and finance to independents. This situation seemed to reflect precisely the cultural change that United Artists had hoped for in the 1920s and ironically the change was fostered by the studios themselves.

The studios responded to the new climate in various ways, including becoming creative in their strategies for competing with television which affected the cinema industry as a whole. RKO was the first studio to diversify into television. RKO had struggled to make an impact with films released under Howard Hughes' management after 1948 and many believed he was more interested in routing out communism than making films. Hughes rented RKO's film archives to TV in 1955 and RKO was bought out in 1957 by Desilu, the TV production company owned by Desi Arnaz and his wife Lucille Ball. Ironically, Ball had herself been one of RKO's biggest stars and in *I Love Lucy*, one of five TV series in which she starred, she played a bored housewife trying to break into television show business.

Some actors successfully forged new dual careers in both film and television in the 1950s and they were not always the most successful in Hollywood's stable. The crossover between film melodrama and TV soap opera animated the careers of Dorothy Malone and Robert Stack, for example. She had won an Academy Award for her role as Marylee Hadley in Douglas Sirk's *Written on the Wind* (1956) and Stack was nominated for the same film. They were among the most successful crossover stars: Malone played Constance Mackenzie in the long-running TV version of *Peyton Place* and Stack was G-Man Eliot Ness in TV's *The Untouchables*. More generally, moving successfully in and out of different media was the province of Frank Sinatra. Famed as 'The Voice' and co-star (usually with Gene Kelly) in a string of musical comedies in the 1940s, he suffered a setback in the early 1950s when CBS suddenly cancelled his TV show. But, as Maggio in *From Here to Eternity* (1953) he won an Oscar for his first film role and when other roles followed (in *The Man with the Golden Arm* [1955] and *The Joker is Wild* [1957]), Sinatra the dramatic actor succeeded in balancing this new career with record-breaking sales for Capitol records and a new TV lease of life.

Films about television are an interesting source for gauging Hollywood's reaction to the new medium. They were few to begin with. In fact, Jack Warner declared that there would be no scenes in any Warner Bros. films which included a television set. However, those films that began to comment on the success of the new medium did so in revealing ways. *Dragnet* (1954), actually a Warners' release, was the first film based on a television drama series, whereas *A Face in the Crowd* (1957), which starred Andy Griffith as a megalomaniac radio-television personality, functioned as a critique of mass culture in its new and sometimes pernicious forms. In Britain, Muriel Box's *Simon and Laura* (1955) captured something of the mood of the industry in its exploration of a husband-and-wife team on a television a soap opera. By the 1960s the enactment of breaking news on the television screen – civil rights struggles, assassinations, the Vietnam War – would secure television's place as the chief family leisure activity and provide advertisers with the scope to target consumers. The studios continued to negotiate their relationship with the major TV companies (NBC, CBS and ABC) for some time, largely haggling over the distribution of movies. Hiring films for screening on television took off in Britain when writers and directors persecuted by HUAC fled to Britain and others, like Ring Lardner Jr who stayed in the US, began writing for British television. *The Adventures of Robin Hood* starring Richard Green was the first popular UK success, not without its ironies considering the man who supposedly robbed the rich to feed the poor had been deemed 'communist' and therefore subversive during the McCarthy witch-hunts.

From the sidelines, studios saw what was lucrative about joining with the enemy to exploit its new audiences and 'Warner Bros. Presents' began in 1955 on the ABC network. Not only did studios begin to release their archives as RKO had, but they began to sell post-1948 films for exhibition in the nation's homes, as when Warner Bros. sold the rights of some 800–1,000 feature films. By 1960 after a number of sometimes difficult scrimmages, Hollywood successfully diversified into television so that TV 'dream factories' (Screen Gems – founded in 1952 by Columbia – Desilu, MGM and CBS) were scattered across the Hollywood hills and it would be only another smaller step in the 1960s and 1970s to begin to produce TV movies. Rivalry between cinema and TV faded into mutually convenient and financially secure mergers, and the 1960s and

1970s would see leading directors emerging from apprenticeships in television – Martin Ritt, Arthur Penn, John Frankenheimer and Steven Spielberg – to take up significant careers as film directors in a Hollywood renaissance.

The major way in which Hollywood attempted to consolidate its place at the pinnacle of mass entertainment in the 1950s was through emphasising the spectacular. The spectacle of colour and widescreen cinema was a key phenomenon of the period. In 1952 Cinerama had been introduced, demonstrating stereophonic sound and deploying three separate cameras to film and, therefore, needing three separate projectors to exhibit the film perfectly on a huge curved screen. However, few cinemas could risk installing the new projection facilities, especially when a single projector was still favoured by other widescreen systems. The innovation caught the imagination of the public, though. The documentary *This is Cinerama* (1952), showcasing the wizardry of the technology, ran for two years in New York City and other Cinerama-effect films, usually travelogues, grossed more than $30 million in profits and remained popular through the 1950s. Cinema was becoming special while television was securing the quotidian leisure market in the same way that in the 1920s talking pictures had reinvigorated the theatre by making it play on its unique qualities.

Technical innovation would revitalise the cinema. Experiments with various widescreen formats, 3-D techniques and zoom lenses had coincided with the innovation of synchronised sound in the late 1920s, as in *The Four Feathers* (1929), but by the 1930s such experimentation had dissipated. Innovations were partly a result of the movie theatre experience becoming more professional and lavish. However, the investment in sound equipment generally prohibited spending on other technologies, so the coming of sound remained the first major technological development. It was followed by the change from optical to stereophonic sound (where sound appears to be emitted from its exact source on screen, as with the speakers hidden behind and at either side of the CinemaScope screen). This change in sound was, ironically, much 'quieter'. The magnetic sound system had been introduced after the Second World War but declining audiences then meant that it did not create the impact that otherwise might have been expected. The classic silent film had always been delivered in the ratio 1.33:1, almost a square, and was modified in 1930, but CinemaScope changed the aspect ratio to an amazing 2.55:1 for the new giant widescreen experience.

In 1953 *The Robe* was the first movie shot in CinemaScope but only those theatres with the technology to show films with such innovative improvements in sound and vision reaped the benefit; in some theatres *The Robe* looked and sounded like any other movie. Nevertheless, it was Twentieth-Century Fox's baby and once the studio's financial investment in the technique became clear, theatres followed suit so that the second CinemaScope release, *How to Marry a Millionaire* (1953) with Marilyn Monroe, became a box office smash. By 1955 around half of US theatres had installed the required equipment and the cinema experience had become spectacular and 'new'. Widescreen enlivened every genre from the horror *House of Wax* (1953) and the CinemaScope western *Shane* (1953), to the musical *Oklahoma* (1955). *Around the World in Eighty Days* (1956) used the most expensive Todd-AO system whereby six separate soundtracks were incorporated into the widescreen experience. It should be noted that while Fox acquired the patent in 1952, CinemaScope was sometimes known as the 'Chrétien process' in France, after Henri Chrétien who in the 1920s had originally invented the anamorphic lens process that he sold to Hollywood.

In the late 1950s, some news editorials asserted that the Hollywood studios only really continued to exist because of 'tricks' like widescreen or 3-D, with detractors joking that widescreen was perfect if you wanted a shot of a train but most objects, including people, did not 'fit' the frame to best effect. Directors were more imaginative, however, and Hitchcock decried 'pictures of people talking' as boring cinema, experimenting with widescreen and sometimes with 3-D, as in *Dial M for Murder* (1954). Individual directors who used the widescreen format in creative ways included Anthony Mann, Samuel Fuller and Vincente Minnelli. CinemaScope could convey spectacular shots of land, sea and sky, panning across the monumental American landscape, as in the case of the desert in John Sturges' *Bad Day at Black Rock* (1955) that so effectively emphasises the alienation of the stranger (Spencer Tracy). Its only real rival for a while was VistaVision which was sharper in definition (as shown to good effect in *White Christmas* [1954]) but was more expensive and did not use the standard anamorphic 35mm film that CinemaScope still employed with a single projector.

The European film industries developed versions of CinemaScope, such as Francoscope as seen to effect in Jean-Luc Godard's *Le Mépris* (1963) which actually makes widescreen cinema the butt of many of its satirical comments. CinemaScope had become the widescreen standard bearer of the 1950s, despite competition, until, in fact, the end of the 1960s when Paramount's Panavision took over. Some features of the race for special cinematic effects bordered on the ludicrous. Even the names of the brands Smell-O-Vision and AromaRama now seem a clear sign that the idea of sensory cinema would never take off. In 1959 Michael Todd (of Todd-AO) and Walter Reade Jr battled with their respective brands. Smell-O-Vision was the most expensive option for theatres but neither solved the problem of the effect of accumulated sense sensations hanging in the theatre space; by the end of a particularly 'smelly' film the audience could be overwhelmed. In less strange but similarly entertaining fashion, 3-D was supposed to boost the cinema's appeal as a visual extravaganza. It was actually inaugurated in an independent production with the suggestively exploitative title *Bwana Devil* (1952) with the publicity promising 'a lion on your lap'. Nevertheless, it had only gimmicky success with audiences sporting special Polaroid glasses that would integrate separate projected images into one to create the impression of multi-dimensions. All the same, in an industry chasing the next special effect, Warner Bros. brought out

House of Wax with its tag line '3-D Action! 3-D Color! 3-D Sound!' in the hope that patrons would feel caught up in the action on screen. 3-D, however, never made further inroads into mainstream cinema and remained a seldom used technique, although it was sometimes used to effect in exploitation cinema.

Traditional B and genre films, with small budgets telling stories of 1950s containment culture, were animated by special effects: *The Thing from Another World* (1951), *Invasion of the Body Snatchers* (1956), *The Day the Earth Stood Still* (1951) and a host of sci-fi films began as small-budget but succeeded as spectacle. As the decade progressed, the science fiction film's reliance on written narrative models in the form of pulp fiction stories would develop into an emphasis on the visceral audience reaction to startling special effects such as alien creatures and aerial invasions. *The War of the Worlds* won the 1953 Academy Award for Best Visual Effects and the award was the third for producer George Pal who, with Ray Harryhausen, was at the forefront of special effects wizardry in the 1950s. This was the 'Atomic Age' of science fiction technical know-how and its special effects experts continued to develop effects technology into the 1960s with Harryhusen woking on the fantasy *Jason and the Argonauts* (1963) and the *Sinbad* film series in the 1970s. Stanley Kubrick's *2001: A Space Odyssey* (1968) would be seen as a definitive masterpiece of special effects technology, poetic in its evocation of space and shot in Cinerama-style, using anamorphic lenses and 70mm film to create the widescreen effect.

The new letterbox format opened up the horizontal field of the viewing experience and especially enriched the production values of the epic or historical saga with sweeping landscapes and thousands of extras, so it is not surprising that by the late 1950s the epic had become the blockbuster of the day. In 1959 *Ben-Hur* was remade by William Wyler who had worked on the original silent spectacle. It stormed the Academy awards to win a historic eleven Oscars. It was the most expensive film Hollywood had made to date, a spectacle costing around $15 million in which the chariot race sequence became the distillation of all that was thrilling and visually stunning about cinema; and the actor Charlton Heston, as Judah Ben-Hur, whose feud with Messala fuelled the movie's melodrama, became the personification of the epic hero. Hollywood's penchant for epics continued into the 1960s with Charlton Heston again playing the eponymous hero in *El Cid* (1961), John the Baptist in *The Greatest Story Ever Told* (1965) and General Gordon in *Khartoum* (1966). It should be noted that the most successful of the epics were sometimes remakes (*Quo Vadis?* [1951]), often biblical stories (*The Ten Commandments* [1956]), or interventions into Greek history (*Alexander the Great* [1955]) or Greek mythology (*Helen of Troy* [1956]). The 1920s met the 1950s when Cecil B. DeMille decided to remake his own silent spectacle *The Ten Commandments*. His final film was another smash, with classic epic scenes such as the parting of the Red Sea sealing the spectacle's popular appeal. Epics became part of cinema history, even intertextually: in *Sunset Boulevard* (1950), one of the most cinematically allusive films ever made,

DeMille is actually working on another biblical epic, *Samson and Delilah* (1949), when Norma Desmond, played by his former protégée Gloria Swanson, visits him on the studio lot.

In the 1950s, the visually spectacular epic held such sway that when Otto Preminger made *Saint Joan* (1957) he deliberately stylised it as an anti-epic, shooting the film with monochrome stock in a standard format because he believed that colour and widescreen would detract from the intense emotions of actress Jean Seberg and from Graham Greene's script. While the widescreen format opened up the horizontal field, and even Cinerama had one last attempt in 1963 with *How the West was Won*, it impacted detrimentally on the depth of field when the edges of the frame moved out of focus. The staging of shots had to change and it could even be said that film style reverted, as Jacques Rivette argued in *Cahiers du Cinéma*, to the lateral staging typical of very early cinema. The intimate close-up, a staple of modern cinema, seemed to be in danger for some devotees to classical cinema, but as Jacques Rivette also argued, the 'cardinal virtues' of CinemaScope were magisterial landscapes, vivid colour, long takes and, in short, letting the air into the cinema. The opinions of *Cahiers'* critics influenced British and American criticism of film style in the 1950s. The effects on *mise-en-scène* captured so crisply in *Citizen Kane* (1941) and in the cinematography of Gregg Toland were re-evaluated.

Had television not impacted on cinema so seriously, technological developments might have moved at their own pace, but in the 1950s they became vital in the studios' strategy to differentiate the panoramic Technicolor cinema experience from the fuzzy black-and-white television screen. For example, colour pictures shot up to around 50 per cent of the US industry's output at the beginning of the 1950s as the result of Technicolor colour production, originally pioneered in the 1930s, and Eastman Color stock which CinemaScope used. Technicolor seemed to have the edge and in the 1970s it was discovered that Eastman stock had a tendency to fade. Nevertheless, colour had arrived and was used to garish effect in the British horror film, for example, as directed by Terence Fisher (*The Curse of Frankenstein* [1957] and *The Mummy* [1959]) which made blood-red use of colour technology. Dependence on colour film was such that when films were released in monochrome – *On the Waterfront* (1954), *From Here to Eternity* (1953) and *Psycho* (1960) – they created a different cinematic effect. In the case of *Psycho*, Hitchcock's aesthetic attachment to monochrome horror lent much to its cult status.

It is axiomatic to state that the decline of the studios, despite their investment in special effects, was partly the result of the onset of television, but it is doubtful that alone the new medium would have impacted so seriously on the studio system. The anti-trust lawsuit which forced the studios away from exhibition also meant that theatres manoeuvred out from under their control. Independence of exhibition allowed independent producers to get a foothold in the industry and book their own pictures into theatres so that there was a huge shift from mass production by the major studios to individual productions by established directors working autonomously within the Hollywood system. Studios had, of course, witnessed the rise of independents within the studio structure, as in the case of Arthur Freed at MGM whose unit functioned to all intents and purposes as an independent champion of those who became the big names in directing musicals, such as Gene Kelly and Stanley Donen, and Vincente Minnelli. Orson Welles was another case in point. Let go by RKO in 1942, he went on to produce and direct *The Lady from Shanghai* (1947) and *Touch of Evil* (1958) and to continue experimentation with deep focus, long takes and overlapping dialogue, techniques for which *Citizen Kane* had been celebrated. In fact, in Europe independents had been enjoying a certain autonomy since the war years, as with Powell and Pressburger's company The Archers, founded in 1943.

In Britain, independents had made very important inroads into the cinema industry, by either controlling studios or working at the edges. Michael Balcon is a good example. Ealing comedies peaked with *The Ladykillers* in 1955 before a financial oversight on the part of panicky investors brought about Ealing's end in the same year. Balcon continued to champion independent productions even after the golden era of the English studio was over. It could be said that government decisions and corporate unease really led to the demise of Rank and Balcon, the nearest rivals Britain had to the Hollywood producer moguls. There was also the more limited success of independent producers like Alexander Korda from whom the new National Film Finance Corporation (NFFC) accepted bids that financed various successes such as Carol Reed's *The Third Man* (1949) and other collaborations with writer Graham Greene, which led to Reed being knighted in 1952. Failures sapped the NFFC, though, and the situation became more precarious. Britain tried levying production subsidies, such as the 1950s Eady levy, as independents sought creative ways to fund domestic cinema.

In France, the situation was made interesting by the return of directors who had worked successfully in Hollywood in the preceding years such as René Clair, Jean Renoir and Max Ophüls. New young independent directors would also go on to influence the French New Wave, such as Jean Cocteau whose *Orphée* (1950), based on the Greek myth, demonstrated a richly poetic and personal realism. Among the independents whose work came to prominence in the postwar period were the bizarre comedian Jacques Tati, who directed and starred in *Jour de Fête* (1948) and *Monsieur Hulot's Holiday* (1952), and Robert Bresson who could not have been more different in his quiet approach to religious subjects. Together they illustrate something of the diverse styles that could co-exist outside studio production. But by the mid-1950s, French cinema critics, notably those writing for *Cahiers du Cinéma* founded by André Bazin in 1952, were beginning to celebrate certain US independents as cult figures. Much of the appeal initially derived from a new critical appreciation of US popular culture epitomised in the films of director Jean-Pierre Melville. Melville – who took his professional name from Herman Melville – explored

American mass culture and paid homage to popular culture in witty and experimental films that combined *film noir* with tropes of the gangster movie, as in *Bob le Flambeur* (1955).

In America, United Artists (UA), founded in 1919 and sold in 1951, was revitalised when it became clear after the *Paramount* decision that good quality 'little' dramas were needed by theatres who had lost their cheaply produced B movies. UA began to entertain ideas from independent producers and directors and released fifty films in 1949, the year following the *Paramount* decision. Samuel Goldwyn and Walt Disney had, of course, broken away to establish studios of their own and there had been directors who succeeded in making a living as independents in the 1940s (Hunt Stromberg and Edward Small, for instance) but Otto Preminger is perhaps the best representative figure if we wish to study the iconoclastic independent in the movement away from the studio system.

Preminger had worked for Max Reinhardt, the theatrical producer, in Berlin in the 1920s and on arrival in America directed plays on Broadway before working for Twentieth-Century Fox. At Fox, his creativity was often stymied by the legendary Fox boss, Darryl Zanuck, a man he admired but who, for example, first asked John Ford and later Elia Kazan to direct the 1949 social conscience drama *Pinky* when it was Preminger who had discovered the story. From 1953 when he released *The Moon is Blue*, Preminger went it alone. Neither *The Moon is Blue* nor *The Man with the Golden Arm* were granted the MPPA Seal but their release through UA and sufficient new independent theatres ensured that both were popular smashes, the latter involving a ground-breaking portrayal by Frank Sinatra of drug addiction. The film was a strong moral lesson, according to its director, that broke an old Production Code taboo. Withholding that seal from Preminger initially meant that theatres could not book his films as part of their block booking system but it also led to their popular success when released independently through United Artists. In America sex caught the censors' attention, rarely violence, and Preminger caught the attention of censors more often than any other director. It was a mark of his independence. *Anatomy of a Murder* (1959), in which the words 'panties' and 'contraceptive' were used, caused a furore on release despite the words being uttered by a stalwart and slightly embarrassed James Stewart. Old cinema institutions like the MPPA were losing ground to maverick and talented independents whose individual enterprise – Preminger found stories, turned them into screenplays, produced, directed, cast his films and sometimes even organised publicity – was matched only by the audience's appetite for taboo-breaking stories. Directors such as Elia Kazan, Hal Wallis and Stanley Kramer all became producers in the 1950s.

Hitchcock was one of those popular 'genre' producer-directors revalorised as *auteurs* by the critics who came together in *Cahiers du Cinéma*. The New Wave of art cinema in Europe in the late 1950s was at the centre of film criticism which advanced a counter thesis that actually Hollywood cinema should be considered as art and which re-evaluated popular genres such as *film noir* and directors including Nicholas Ray, Howard Hawks and Alfred Hitchcock as *auteurs*. Hitchcock was part of a transatlanticism that characterised the shift from the 1950s into the 1960s though his *oeuvre* is often divided into his 'British' and 'American' periods and he became a US citizen in 1955 – a transnationalism that was reinforced in interview with François Truffaut. Auteurism or *les politiques des auteurs* has proved a tremendously durable concept in film studies and it is still sometimes difficult to shift the idea that a director's personality *is* a film's authority in order to encompass an industrial and collective understanding of cinematic production, that is to say the conditions under which directors worked, and the complexity of the film industry. This is not to say that directors (Griffith, Buñuel, Murnau, Welles) had not been recognised as creative forces in film culture before the 1950s and the rise of independents. Creative difficulties within the studio system were legion. However, *Cahiers* critics resituated critical discussion of independents by lauding directors who had traditionally been seen as 'popular' and therefore less aesthetically important than a pantheon of 'greats': Minnelli, Howard Hawks, Robert Aldrich, the former journalist Samuel Fuller. The *Cahiers* critics also extended discussion of *mise-en-scène* as a specific and consistent mark of authorship, even for those directors who moved in and out of different genres like Hawks. The New Wave in French criticism influenced other journals such as *Movie* (founded in 1962 in the UK) and changed the debates going on in *Sight and Sound*. *Cahiers* published strong position pieces with which other film critics could engage, including Truffaut's 'A Certain Tendency of French Cinema' (1954), and their clearest sphere of influence was French cinema itself. Although Bazin died in 1958, his younger disciples went on to consolidate the French New Wave or *nouvelle vague* which brought to French cinema a prominence it hadn't enjoyed since the 'golden age' of the 1930s (see Chapter 16).

The 1950s signalled the end of classical Hollywood and although some individual directors continued to succeed working within classical traditions – Minnelli in his transforming of the stage musical, for instance – the studio era had largely given way to an emphasis on independent filmmaking. Minnelli too branched out to make two biting satires of the Hollywood system that couldn't have been further from his musical extravaganzas: *The Bad and the Beautiful* (1952) and *Two Weeks in Another Town* (1962). Frequently, independent directors made films that critiqued aspects of American society, as in Ray's *Rebel Without A Cause* (1955), Stanley Kubrick's *Paths of Glory* (1957), a visually distinctive anti-war film, and Douglas Sirk's *Written on the Wind* (1956). Certain established actors too made the most of the post-studio changes in cinema culture, notably Kirk Douglas and Burt Lancaster, the former producing the epic *Spartacus* in 1960 in widescreen and Technicolor with an all-star cast and crediting HUAC casualty Dalton Trumbo for his contribution (see Chapter 13). Lancaster forged what was then a unique relationship with his agent Ben Hecht allowing him autonomy in picking film projects and when the pair teamed later with scriptwriter James Hall who scripted, for example, the Lancaster vehicle *Apache* (1954), the successful combination ensured creative success until the end of the 1950s.

Of the host of Euro-American director-independents, Douglas Sirk, like Preminger, is a fascinating case study of the shift from studio-driven to independent filmmaking. His film career traversed Germany, the Netherlands and America. He began work in the 1920s as a theatre director, and then found that in working at UFA he had a taste of the autonomy a director could know when in control of the story and the production values. Once he moved to the US, Sirk suffered the vagaries of Hollywood studio production when working under Harry Cohn at Columbia, not surprising when it is remembered that Cohn had ruled the studio since 1924. Cohn's refusal to allow Sirk to direct as he wanted pushed him toward independent status. Sirk was a righteous independent but a complex one, especially because the influence of producers such as Albert Zugsmith and Ross Hunter remains a noticeable variable in evaluating his work; in interview Sirk often refers to his own films as 'a Zug film' or part of 'the Hunter cycle'.

Sirk has been celebrated largely for the melodramatic vision with which he imprinted 1950s cinema. Melodrama as a form and a genre has successfully crossed centuries, largely because of its topicality, its emphasis on the social setting and on questions of modernity, and its rendering of society as morally legible. Barbara Klinger's study of the reception of Douglas Sirk draws out the different meanings that Sirk's films can take on for audiences depending when and how they were encountered. There are very precise differences between encountering a Sirk film on the television on a Sunday afternoon and at a film festival or as part of an arts theatre revival. Klinger's methodology foregrounds audience and reception studies but she does not try to account for actual audiences in an ethnographic sense, as Jackie Stacey does in the extract that follows Chapter 13, but as a means of studying the material and cultural conditions according to which critical distinctions were made.

Klinger begins by focusing on the release and exhibition of Sirk's films in the 1950s before turning to examine retrospective reclamations of Sirkian cinema in the 1970s. Her focus is film reviewing and journalistic discourse as it supplies added value to the descriptions of the films as first determined by the filmmaker and the studios. In this way, she reveals shifts in cinema culture and its consumption across two dissimilar decades through an examination of 'tastemaking' and the web of interrelated factors that influenced the reception of Sirk's films and that transformed Sirkian criticism.

- Summarise the methods and materials Klinger deploys in order to assess how Sirkian melodramas were received in the 1950s and 1970s.
- Distinguish between the role and function of the epiphenomena that surround a film and which identify film as a commodity. (Consider editorials,

press releases, star features and so on that form the intertextual relay around a chosen film and its director.) What are the gains and risks of considering this material as a film historian?

- Are there other materials the film historian might use, besides those Klinger focuses on, to examine tastes and distinctions?

TASTEMAKING: REVIEWS, POPULAR CANONS, AND SOAP OPERAS

Barbara Klinger

The denial of lower, coarse, vulgar, venal, servile – in a word, natural – enjoyment, which constitutes the sacred sphere of culture, implies an affirmation of the superiority of those who can be satisfied with the sublimated, refined, disinterested, gratuitous, distinguished pleasures forever closed to the profane. That is why art and cultural consumption are predisposed, consciously and deliberately or not, to fulfill a social function of legitimating social differences. (Pierre Bourdieu)[1]

[. . .]

Arthur Knight and Lee Rogow of *The Saturday Review* were two of the few critics of the time who had anything charitable to say about Sirk's melodramas. Of *Magnificent Obsession*, Rogow wrote, 'The remarkable thing about the film is the proof that these great cheap formulas can touch the fringes of real emotion.' Similarly, Knight conceded that Zuckerman's screenplay for *Tarnished Angels* 'retained a surprising amount of the raw emotion of the book,' while *Imitation of Life* presented audiences with 'life as they would like to believe it, and it makes good movie material – at least for a matinee.'[2]

Albeit with somewhat grudging praise, each critic redeemed these films based on the reigning aesthetic for drama by emphasizing their apparent adherence to an *emotional* realism. Most other critics found a destructive tension between any realism offered by these films and the fakeries of the culture industry, personified by a combination of soap opera formulas and Hollywood commercialism.

Reviewers consistently traced a lineage between Sirk's narratives and mass-circulated soap operas in magazines and on the radio as a means of illuminating their eclipse of realism. As early as 1944 James Agee commented that Sirk's adaptation of Chekhov's *The Shooting Party* for *Summer Storm*, 'looks as if Mr. Sirk had wanted to be faithful to something plotty, melodramatic, and second-grade, with psychological possibilities in it which he, or his actors, failed to make much of . . . most of it had for me, the sporty speciousness of an

Barbara Klinger, *Melodrama and Meaning: History Culture and the Films of Douglas Sirk* (Bloomington and Indianapolis: Indiana University Press, 1994).

illustrated drugstore classic.' Parodying a line from one of these 'classics,' Agee writes, ' "Speaking of women," ' murmured the Baron, toying with his aperient.'³ Although meant in a playful sense, in bringing together women and aperients (that is, laxatives), Agee's imaginary quotation foregrounds an association between women and the debasing effects of mass culture that continued to underwrite assessments of Sirk's work.

For example, Crowther later evaluated *All That Heaven Allows* (1955) as 'one of those doleful situations so dear to the radio daytime serials.' In this 'frankly feminine fiction,' Crowther wrote, 'solid and sensible drama plainly had to give way to outright emotional bulldozing and a paving of easy clichés.' *Time* referred disparagingly to the film as a woman's picture, lamenting the fact that the 'the characters talk *Ladies' Home Journalese* and the screen glows like a page of *House Beautiful*. The moviegoer often has the sensation that he is drowning in a sea of melted butter, with nothing to hang on to but the clichés that float past.'⁴

Commonweal put these sentiments in somewhat stronger terms in its review of *Magnificent Obsession* (1954). Its reviewer suggested that

> Perhaps there is some defense for soap opera on radio: at least a woman can go about her work as she half-listens and day-dreams over their pre-posterous stories. But soap operas in the movies are something else again. Even a handsome Technicolor opus like [this] . . . gets tiresome as its characters . . . go through one empty situation after the other – situations that have almost no relation to real life.⁵

Although later champions of Sirk, the British in the BFI's *Monthly Film Bulletin* criticised all of his melodramas on the basis of their relation to the artifice of soaps and Hollywood. A critic called *All That Heaven Allows* 'a complacent reconstruction of a thirties magazine serial world which is as laboriously predictable as it is fatuously unreal . . . Rock Hudson manfully imposes sense where possible on the sentimental proceedings.' *Written on the Wind* was 'Hollywood moonshine of the slickest vintage. A streamlined piece of magazine fiction, mounted with superb physical gloss.'

The *Monthly Film Bulletin* saved its harshest criticism for *Imitation of Life*, of all Sirk's films perhaps the one with the most obvious relation to social problems. Noting Hollywood's penchant for 'high-class pulp fiction' which has 'led to many a confession tale and glossy family saga,' the reviewer argued that 'when their novelletish emotional entanglements are coupled with a fashionably 'liberal' theme, the result can be eminently dislikeable . . . Its onslaught on the emotions is almost entirely synthetic . . . its attitude toward its racial problem is debased and compromised.'⁶

The question of style added to the problems Sirk's films had in reproducing a realist aesthetic to the satisfaction of reviewers. *Written on the Wind's* decor was 'luxurious and the color is conspicuously strong, even though it gets no closer to Texas – either geographically or in spirit – than a few locations near

Hollywood.'[7] Reviewers continually registered this kind of negative association between Sirk's mise-en-scène and Hollywood artifice. *Newsweek* called *Imitation of Life* 'a picture rich in decor but lacking in imagination and restraint'; while *Catholic World* resented the combination of a 'theatrical atmosphere and success story . . . full of phony glamour' without relation to 'anything that ever happened in real life' with a story about racial prejudice. What aroused the reviewer's particular indignation was the fact that the studio hoped to attract an audience for the film based on 'its lavish color production, its tearjerking qualities, and the irresistible circumstance that Lana Turner wears more than one million dollars worth of jewelry and a wardrobe of equal opulence and bad taste.'[8]

The polar opposition between soap plotting and Hollywood commercialism, on the one hand, and social and dramatic integrity on the other, licensed reviewers to conduct unapologetic parodies of the dramatic structure and situations of the films in question. As just one example, John McCarten of *The New Yorker* wrote of *Magnificent Obsession*,

> Although he doesn't seem to be the brightest fellow in the world, there are really no flies on our hero mentally, and at length he becomes a brain surgeon as sure with a scalpel as a shad boner in Fulton Fish Market. Sawing away on his sweetheart's head – I believe he is trying to clear up a slight case of astigmatism – the man knows real peace of mind. But it's movies such as this that prevent me from feeling likewise.[9]

Thus, although Sirk's films shared many characteristics with adult melodramas, including serious social content, melodramatic story lines, and an often elaborate style, they were more often subject to wholesale condemnation by periodical reviewers. For reviewers, Sirk's films so embodied the antirealism and aesthetic liabilities of soaps and Hollywood greed that they generally refused to admit them to the realist canon. At every point, critics opposed the Sirk film to relevant subject matter, plausible dramatic situations, psychological realism in character, and a style that would function as expressive support. Instead, his films supported the mass cultural dream machines by offering their audiences tacky, sensationalistic formulas and cheap emotionalism. Further, the Sirk soap was clearly linked to a leisured domestic female audience whose taste, in reviewers' minds, signified the debasement of art into sentimentality and cliché. Reviewers castigated the 'fatuous' unreality of the soap opera through a visible antipathy to the feminine. The best one could hope for in these formulas is that someone would 'manfully impose sense where possible.'

While the realist canon played an important role in determining the meaning and value of these films in the postwar era, it is unlikely that realist preoccupations alone could explain the intensity of Sirk's aesthetic ostracism, particularly its peculiar gender dimensions. In fact, reviews reflected prevalent, often vituperative, attitudes toward mass culture that characterized intellectual discussion in the 1940s and 1950s. Sirk's critical status during this time was determined additionally by more general cultural prejudices that perceived affiliations between his melodramas and the negative capabilities of mass culture.

As we have seen, Sirk reviews chronicled the generic relation of his films to a number of soap opera predecessors: magazine fiction, radio soaps, and 'high-class' pulp fiction (that is, best-sellers). Although not mentioned by name, these reviewers were referring generally to such popular 1940s radio soap operas as 'The Goldbergs,' 'Stella Dallas,' 'Woman in White,' and 'Guiding Light,' as well as to the omnipresence of romantic fiction in women's magazines like *McCall's*, *Ladies' Home Journal*, and *True Story*. More specifically, Sirk's films were sometimes based on the work of best-selling authors like Lloyd C. Douglas (for *Magnificent Obsession*) and Fanny Hurst (for *Imitation of Life*), authors whose popularity sometimes stood in the way of serious critical attention.

Given these affiliations, one could say that Sirk's melodramas lacked the appropriate patrimony. Except for *Tarnished Angels*, which was based on William Faulkner's 'Pylon,' Sirk's melodramas lacked the prestigious ancestry of a Tennessee Williams or a Pulitzer Prize-winning play by William Inge. For critics, Sirk's melodramas had *matrilinear* roots in forms explicitly regarded as feminine in substance and appeal. As some recent theorists have pointed out, the feminine did not fare well in past debates about the nature and effects of mass culture. Critics writing from the 1930s through the 1950s defined mass culture's aesthetic bankruptcy and even endangerment of *real* art through the feminine metaphor of passivity; they invoked this trait to describe the susceptibility, mindlessness, and sheer capacity for manipulation that the culture industry relied on to dominate cultural production and reception.[10] The judgements against Sirk's films were heavily freighted by this kind of implicit equation of things female with the threatening and debilitating potentials of mass culture.

Soaps, Totalitarianism, and Taste

During the Cold War era, as intellectuals began to shun Marxism and radical politics because of their public association with communism, the realm of mass culture assumed a special importance. As Richard Pells argues, intellectuals 'no longer assailed their traditional enemies – the capitalists, the political bosses . . . with the old ideological fervor. But if they wished to preserve a little of the radical heritage, they could concentrate on popular tastes and values as the new opiates of their countrymen.' By assailing the media, 'writers might demonstrate their dislike for the quality of American life without having to challenge the nation's political or economic institutions as well.' In this way, the critique of the media often strategically displaced more direct assaults on the government, while preserving the image of the socially committed liberal intellectual.[11]

The exponential growth of mass culture during the postwar years provided a provocative terrain for this alternative cultural mission. Intellectuals saw the expansion of mass culture which had begun in the pre-World War II era as heralding a new cultural 'democracy.' This democracy was characterized, on the one hand, by the mounting popularity of forms associated with the average individual, such as television shows, best-sellers, magazine fiction, paperbacks, comic books, radio soaps, 'B' movies, and hit music. On the other hand, more pervasive networks of dissemination for cultural products had arisen, resulting in the wide availability of a variety of fictional types. Television, for example, had the ability to deliver programming to a large number of households, while changes in print distribution found material from the great novels to comic books to pinup magazines, ready for purchase in drug or candy stores. Many felt the dominance of popular forms in combination with mass diffusion would result in a forever changed relationship between mass and literate cultures, wherein the former would subsume the latter, determining what was valuable through the sheer act of consumption.

As Andrew Ross has pointed out, two general positions toward this new, apparently more democratic state developed among Cold War liberals. The first stemmed from Theodor Adorno and Max Horkheimer's antifascist critique of mass culture as exercising a form of social control. Dwight MacDonald, for example, compared mass culture's enforcement of the same standards for everyone with fascism, totalitarianism, and communism. From this perspective, capitalist culture, represented by the endless, profit motivated production of formulaic products, was the enemy of true democracy, obliterating social differences and empowering a protofascist mob of common people. The second position rejected a blanket condemnation of mass culture. Popularity was no longer a sign of fascism, but a mark of how well a fictional type responded to deep social needs (for example, in Robert Warshow's discussion of the western, the genre provided a serious cultural orientation toward violence). Ross argues that this therapeutic argument was an important moment in Cold War liberalism because of its attempt to disassociate capitalism from the specter of totalitarianism. By stressing the potentially benevolent effects of mass culture on diverse populations, U.S. society appeared as an order that assisted, rather than obstructed, the development of human potential.[12]

Among intellectuals on both sides of this debate, postwar developments in mass culture also aroused particular concern about the standards of public taste. In 1953, for example, *The Saturday Review* ran a series on the 'Common Man' and the 'temper of taste in America today,' in the face of changes brought about by mass communications. On one side of the discussion stood the negativists. Increasingly dissatisfied with the intellectual quality of what was being purveyed, they asked, 'Can we have the Age of the Common Man without an Age of the Common Denominator?'[13] These writers equated democracy with a 'tyranny of mediocrity' that would 'seriously displace or possibly annihilate literate culture.' The standardization and proliferation of texts within the culture industry led to 'a 'democracy' of taste,' which meant a 'practically unanimous demand for Grade-B movies.'[14] Modern culture was thus characterized by a 'new democratic snobbery' that preferred the popular arts to the classics and, in its confusion of the best with the most generally acceptable, revealed 'a spiritual confusion which is subtle and insidious.'[15] For these writers, the strong links between popular objects of mass culture and their audiences threatened a permanent displacement of good taste by a powerful self-congratulatory mediocrity.

However, in the same series, there were those who defended mass culture as a potential democratic culture. While admitting that mass culture could cause a vulgarisation of taste, they argued that mass communications also exposed more people to the very best of world literature and substantive films, and that such exposure could actually help raise the level of public taste.[16] Critics such as Gilbert Seldes held out hope that the producers of mass culture would assume their social responsibility and develop better programming to elevate the audience's sensibilities. While both negativists and hopefuls were committed to concepts of a literate culture, the latter openly advocated the potential virtues of modern cultural production.

The growing defenses of mass culture in both political and aesthetic discussions led to analyses that claimed the worth of certain of its artifacts, including western pulp fiction, science fiction, comic books, and genre films. However, even within this more generous climate, critics continued to invoke soap operas as embodying the worst kinds of corruption of spirit and taste that the culture industry could produce.

Adorno and Horkheimer's passing references to soap operas in their 'Culture Industry' essay established the genre as exemplary of the totalitarian operations of mass culture on art and subjectivity. The dramatic formula of most mass cultural artifacts, built on the housewife's 'getting into trouble and out again . . . embraces the whole of mass culture from the idiotic women's serial to the top production.' The endless repetition of such clichés not only threatens to engulf the authentic work, but stunts the 'mass-media consumer's powers of imagination and spontaneity.' Further, women's serials co-opt subjectivity and emotion through their explicit relation to states of inwardness: emotion appears as 'mere twaddle . . . an embarrassingly agreeable garnish, so that genuine personal emotion in real life can be all the more reliably controlled.'[17] Bernard Rosenberg, a writer very much in this camp, wrote similarly in 1957 that 'sleazy fiction, trashy films, and bathetic soap operas,' are among forms that threaten 'not merely to cretinize our taste, but to brutalize our senses while paving the way to totalitarianism.'[18] In their popular formulaic structure and artificial relation to emotions, soaps signified the mark of the beast of fascism in its desire to control aesthetics, subjectivities, and political mentalities.

Soaps also played a role in discussions of taste among the hopefuls. In 1948, Paul Lazarsfeld and Robert Merton questioned assumptions of the blanket social control exercised by media, while being concerned about the conformism and 'narcotizing dysfunction' the media could produce. However, within a framework designed to temper fears about the depraved effects of the media on public taste, they nonetheless asserted that 'the women who are daily entranced for three or four hours by some twelve consecutive "soap operas," all cut to the same dismal pattern, exhibit an appalling lack of aesthetic judgement.' Calling for an analysis of this state of affairs, they ask, 'What is the historical status of this notoriously low level of popular taste?'[19] Gilbert Seldes agreed with this position when he singled out 'neurotic daytime serials' as that which the broadcast industry had to move away from to assume the role of raising public taste.[20] Even researchers and critics who had some faith in the promises of a mass democratic culture believed that soaps and their female audiences hampered mass culture's more utopian possibilities by representing its potential for aesthetic depravity and automated reception.

As we can see, then, reviewers' reception of Sirk's melodramas in the 1950s was influenced by a host of interrelated factors, both critical and cultural. In terms of specific review standards, Sirk's films affronted the realist canon by their perceived relation to the artifice characteristic of Hollywood commercial imperatives and soap opera formulas. These evaluations in turn took place within broader circumstances, in which the mass culture debates of the Cold War period fingered soaps as the incarnation of mass media evil. But while we can see what climates of opinion helped shape and justify critical opinion toward Sirk, it remains to ask what was at *stake* in these judgements, what was ultimately at issue in their particular equations of Sirk and soap operas with bad taste.

Recalling the epigraph for this chapter taken from Bourdieu, the case of Sirk and soap operas stands as a classic instance of critics' tendencies to reject 'lower, coarse, vulgar, venal, servile – in a word, natural – enjoyment' as a means of insulating themselves from the 'commoners' who allegedly identify with the spectacles offered by popular representations. In their 'disgust at the facile,' nowhere better represented than in the parodic recounting of soap plots or moralistic condemnations of their formulaic pleasures, critics claimed a superior status for themselves as cultural watchdogs of taste. At the same time, they created a debased image of the masses as aesthetic incompetents and threats to a civilized world. Critical canons of good taste could be ventured and sustained, in fact, only by constituting a heathen underclass of tasteless consumers to serve as a radical, aesthetic Other. Since these consumers were primarily perceived as women in the case of soaps, the fallout of such social and aesthetic hierarchization may have subtly aggravated deeply held convictions about sexual difference, which figured a certain disdain for women at the same time as it assisted their social and moral marginality.

The 1950s did not provide, however, the last word on popular Sirk criticism. Completely transfigured in many ways by the 1970s, the critical establishment had another significant opportunity to judge the work of this director.

The 1970s: Retrospectives

After their original release, Sirk's melodramas, like the work of so many other directors, reappeared publicly via retrospectives from the 1970s through the

1980s. In New York City, a prime location for such activities, screenings invariably took place in museums, theaters wholly or partially devoted to revivals, and other institutions associated with public intellectual life. Specific revival enterprises for Hollywood films in New York included the Museum of Modern Art, Theater 80, St. Marks, Carnegie Hall, the Bleecker Street Theater, the Regency, the Thalia, and the New York Film Festival.

Such forums differed from mainstream commercial theaters in presenting old films as part of enlightened culture, edifying for an urban cognoscente, rather than as simply entertainment for the average moviegoer. Assisting this enterprise were a cadre of film reviewers often similarly situated within an alternative framework, whether *The Village Voice* or *The Soho Weekly News*. Within this context of exhibition forums and presses, Sirk's films earned sustained, appreciative reviews for the first time in a mass cultural environment. Reviewers praised and defended his films, making their past degraded status appear as the product of a sorely misguided critical mentality.

The growth of exhibition site as archive clearly aided the critical rewriting of past products of the film industry. But the radical shift in perspectives on Sirk and other directors owed to at least two other factors that likewise encouraged a valorization of 'Old Hollywood' during this time. The first of these concerned the nature of the critical canon of the 1970s, shaped by heated discussions of the 'New American Cinema.' Within these discussions, the 'Old' in many cases appeared as better and more authentic than the 'New.' This preferential treatment was not simply a product of journalistic whim; it was part of the overall thrust toward nostalgia that marked public discourse and popular culture during the 1970s. The second, and perhaps more patently obvious, of these factors was the penetration of academic auteurism into journalistic writing on film. The combination of nostalgic revisionism and auteurism helped the Sirks of the film world to emerge as revered talents in review journalism during this time.

The New versus the Old

> And seeing *Psycho* again is rather like visiting a historical monument or a national shrine; when one approaches the legendary staircase where Martin Balsam was stabbed . . . you're awed to think that this is where it happened, as though you were surveying one of the battlefields of the Civil War.[21]

In the 1960s, the term New American Cinema reflected, on the one hand, the economic and organisational differences in filmmaking after the demise of the studio system, with a rise in corporate takeovers and independent film production. On the other hand, it was a catchall phrase used to describe various types of films being made through the 1970s. Most now familiarly associate the label with the bold generic and stylistic experimentation carried out by filmmakers such as Robert Altman in *McCabe and Mrs. Miller* (1971), Terrence

Malick in *Badlands* (1973), and Woody Allen in *Annie Hall* (1977), whose films broke with past traditions of style and construction. But reviewers of the time also applied the label to commercial blockbusters such as *Star Wars* (1977) and *The Deep* (1977), which crystallized the economic conservativeness of corporate Hollywood, as well as to more humble offerings like *Rocky* (1976) and, farther on the fringe, *Jackson County Jail* (1976), which seemed to purvey a low-budget honesty in the face of flashy or commercial projects. The New American Cinema could be by turns innovative, crass, or refreshingly simple.

But no matter what the nuance, as Robert Ray has pointed out, the New American Cinema was heavily indebted to the Old. Besides a flurry of nostalgia films such as *The Way We Were* (1973), *American Graffiti* (1973), and *That's Entertainment* (1974), Hollywood incessantly replayed generic formulas of the past, often with parodic overtones.[22] Thus, *The Pink Panther* (1964), *Bonnie and Clyde* (1967), *Little Big Man* (1970), *Star Wars*, and *Jackson County Jail* were among a great number of contemporary films that reworked, respectively, the conventions of the comedies, gangster, westerns, science fiction serials, and 'B' movies of the preceding decades.

What is of interest here is not so much the details of this ultra-reflexive development, but rather how reviewers' responses to this aspect of the New American Cinema shaped an aesthetic – an aesthetic that had ramifications for determining the merits of classic Hollywood. Inevitable comparisons between the two eras arose which were laden with 'value judgements.'

'The system' provided one of the arenas in which the New was constantly brought into association with the Old. Articles in *The New York Times* and elsewhere discussed how the business contrasts between the studio system and the contemporary corporate megalith affected filmmaking aesthetics. In one such article, Garson Kanin praised the old studio heads with whom he had worked as both director and screenwriter, saying that they might have been 'pirates and barracudas, but however crass, cruel and ruthless they were, they were simply crazy about making movies. I don't find that true about the present generation of tycoons.' He continued, 'I can't believe that the head of Trans America is any more interested in movies when he buys out United Artists than he is in, say, automobiles, when he buys out Budget Rent a Car.' Kanin bemoans the loss of both the old studio heads' personal touch and the 'individual imaginations of a Lubitsch or a Ford or a Preston Sturges.' Imagination is sacrificed within the 'strictly commercial' and businesslike aspects of contemporary filmmaking, where producers 'seem intent on calculating what will appeal to the widest possible audience. Instead of trusting their own instincts, they tend to opt for the proven, the tried, the familiar . . . blockbusters, sequels, repeat formulas.' Kanin then concludes, 'Goldwyn would hate it. He'd say you can't hold the public with sensationalism, you can only hold them with good stories.'[23]

Reviewers for *Film Comment's* issue on the 1970s seemed to sum up such sentiments when they complained about the conservatism of the film industry: 'The generation that grew up on *The Graduate* took over Hollywood and went into plastics,' and 'Instead of making *Star Trek II*, why don't they give $10 million each to David Lean, Sergio Leone, Joseph L. Mankiewicz, and Orson Welles?'[24]

Such pieces participated in relandscaping the past, depicting bygone eras as simpler and less corrupt. Here, what was at one time perceived as the seat of capitulations to mammon – the studio system – is nostalgically redefined as an artisanal culture that provided a safe haven for individuality, personal craftsmanship, and ingenious creativity; this in contrast to the perceived eviscerating effects of large-scale, postindustrial corporatism on artistic enterprise.

Specific aesthetic arguments echoed this perspective when reviewers contrasted the films of both eras. Some criticism remained relatively content to trace the total indebtedness of New to Old, that is, how *The Electric Horseman* (1979) presents us with 'an exact, perfectly restored specimen of the 1930s Frank Capra populist-political comedy – a *Mr. Smith Goes to Washington* with Frye boots and videotape.'[25] David Ehrenstein of *Film Comment* argued similarly that *Coming Home* (1978) was 'more than reminiscent of *Written on the Wind*.' Citing correlations between the characters played by Bruce Dern and Robert Stack – the gun under the pillow, the self-destructive neurosis – as well as the romantic triangle and a dance to compare with Dorothy Malone's 'Temptation' number, Ehrenstein insists that despite its political trappings, *Coming Home* 'practically *is Written on the Wind*, refurbished and updated – a melodrama.'[26]

The implicit contention that the contemporary was often nothing more than an imitation of the past typically, however, had a more critical partisan edge. One reviewer complained that the 1970s was 'a modish antique store of a decade that pilfered issues and styles from more vital times.'[27] Chief among offenders in this regard was Brian de Palma. In 'The Man Who Would Be Hitchcock,' a review of de Palma's latest venture, *Obsession* (1976), Walter Goodman wrote that 'to compare Alfred Hitchcock, even at his second or third best, with Brian de Palma is not fair sport; it's like putting Muhammad Ali in the ring with Andy Warhol.'[28]

Alternative sources agreed. Andrew Sarris's reviews in *The Village Voice* frequently condemned contemporary films for so unsuccessfully attempting to 'repackage the past.' Sarris noted as early as 1964 a strong 'deficiency of newer films in comparison to older,' criticising *The Pink Panther* for borrowing from *Duck Soup*, *The Awful Truth*, and Hitchcock's *Foreign Correspondent* and *To Catch a Thief*. In treating the same issue in later years, he cited the imitativeness of *Smokey and the Bandit* (1977), *Star Wars*, and *Sorcerer* (1977), excoriating the last of these as a rip-off of H. G. Clouzot, John Huston, and David Lean. None of the contemporary manifestations of old traditions could 'come close to matching their craftsmanship.'[29]

Hence, critics faulted some of the generically recycled films of the newer era as lackluster imitations of more glorious examples of artistic integrity and originality. As in the case of business comparisons, reviewers engaged in historical revisionism to create their canonical objects, obscuring how commercially oriented and formulaic classic Hollywood cinema had been as well. As the quotation at the beginning of this section suggests, films from the past could even attain the kind of sacred, enduring monumentality usually reserved for epic historical events.

This penchant for rewriting the past at the expense of the present was no doubt supported by the intense romanticizing of earlier periods of history that marked the 1970s. If, as historians tell us, widespread nostalgia tends to appear at times of social discontent with the present, then this decade was a prime candidate for the nostalgic sensibility.[30] Those writing about the 1970s experienced it as a time of profound social dislocation, a founding sentiment for what many referred to as the period's nostalgia wave or 'boom.'

This sense of dislocation was partially instigated by the legacy of the 1960s. Vietnam, the King and Kennedy assassinations, Kent State, racial violence, Civil Rights, hippies, gay liberation, and feminism challenged notions of 'natural' and rightful orders that had operated for decades.[31] Besides inheriting troubling features from the recent past, specific events occurred during the 1970s that caused a painful 'rediscovery of limits' within the exercise of U.S. global and domestic power. These included the failure of the Vietnam War, the rise of the OPEC cartel and ensuing energy shortage, and our decreasing hold on outer space with the collapse of Skylab, as well as Watergate, Three Mile Island, and a host of other internal social problems such as rising unemployment, high interest rates, divorce, and inflation.[32] In each of these instances, the decade seemed to have no positive character of its own. Rather, its events aggravated a public sense of sheer social instability, a disintegration of 'simple' national values, as well as decisive U.S. power, under the influence of advanced capitalism and increasingly complex world affairs.

Public dissatisfaction with the decade was often expressed through a drama of historical comparisons, wherein the present was judged as a 'departure from superior past realities.'[33] To play this role, the past had to be sanitized of serious social strife, a sleight of hand engineered by the nostalgic imagination. The querulous social sensibilities of the 1970s willfully and wishfully reconstructed bygone eras as pre-industrial and pre-corporate utopias, where traditional values of individuality, creativity, home, and family reigned. Prior historical moments were thus neatly packaged by the therapeutic urge for stability that underpinned such revisionism. The past, then, served primarily as a reactive, escapist alternative to the pressures and chaos of an incipient postmodernity. While conservatives celebrated the nostalgic sentiment, radicals criticized its whitewashing tendencies and neglect of contemporary social conditions.[34]

The 1970s commitment to the past was evidenced in such diverse phenomena as the reincarnation craze, postmodern architecture's 'pastiching' from preceding styles, and the huge historical preservation movement, which attempted to save historic sites and communities from the bulldozers of urban renewal. But it was more properly in popular culture that relations to the past attained a strongly nostalgic component. Cultural manifestations of this phenomenon included renewed interest in the 1950s, pre-television Hollywood musicals, romantic comedies of the 1930s, the radio serials of the 1930s (which had been so thoroughly trashed a few decades earlier), fashions of the World War I era, swing bands, F. Scott Fitzgerald, and even a revived Beatlemania toward the end of the decade. In addition, tributes to bygone eras constituted a substantial percentage of media productions. While the New American Cinema was replaying key classic genres, big Broadway musicals featured *Hello, Dolly* and *Grease*, while television sported 'Happy Days' (1974–1984) and 'Laverne and Shirley' (1976–1983), which, like *Grease*, revisited the 1950s.

The social malaise of the 1970s thus gave birth to a nostalgia that helped create a reverence for the past in compensation for a disjointed and dysfunctional present. In this context, film reviewing appears as one more cultural voice calling out in the 1970s wilderness. The critical regard for the old masters of Hollywood cinema, as well as the pessimism about current trends, serves as another indicator of the dynamics of the 1970s nostalgic imagination. Reviewers created an aesthetic hierarchy that confirmed alienation from the present through a vision of classic filmmaking free of corporate taint and full of the individuality, originality, and vitality found lacking in contemporary industry products.

By itself, however, the nostalgic tone of the 1970s cannot explain why classic films attained such canonical heights; the forces of auteurism had a more visible hand in this process. However, the substantial yearning for yesterday during the period created an agreeable cultural environment for the revisionist work of the *auteur* critics, which relied so heavily on the celebratory rewriting of historical persons and artifacts into the contemporary script.

Public Auteurism

During the 1960s and 1970s, newspaper and magazine articles devoted to classic directors abounded, a fact assisted by the continuing productivity of many of these directors. Essays titled 'John Huston: I Want to Keep Right on Going,' 'Nicholas Ray: Still a Rebel with a Cause,' and 'It's a Wonderful Life, but . . . New Light on the Darker Side of Frank Capra' provided the means of attesting to the creative genius of these directors. These articles documented their past glories working in the Hollywood system and their often negative appraisals of contemporary commercial Hollywood.[35] Thus, interviews with directors served as a prime site for the articulation of the split between New and Old and the kind of nostalgic sentimentality about the studio system and individual creativity characterizing aesthetic hierarchies of the time.

Sirk's public authorization owed in part to this drama of comparison. Along with Fritz Lang, Max Ophuls, and others, critics invoked Sirk as an exemplar of the foreign director working within the Hollywood system as a means of discussing the relative successes of contemporary transplanted foreign directors such as Roman Polanski and Miloš Forman. Naturally, the reviewer concluded that it was easier to make the 'transfer' when Hollywood was an organized system, rather than the big commercial venture it was in the 1970s.[36]

But in terms of judgements established through an interplay of Old and New, Sirk's stature as a director was enhanced by his links to the New German Cinema – a foreign cinema widely canonized during this time. Jean-Luc Godard and Rainer Werner Fassbinder had both written essays on Sirk in the early 1970s that journalists later used to validate Sirk's authorship for the public via the aura of foreign artistry. But it was more properly Fassbinder's review of Sirk's work in a reprint of his 'Six Films by Douglas Sirk' in *Film Comment* and his frequent proclamations of indebtedness to Sirk in his own work that helped the latter to gain validity.[37]

Fassbinder's discussion of six of Sirk's melodramas, among them *All That Heaven Allows* and *Written on the Wind*, ends with the lines: 'I have seen six films by Douglas Sirk. Among them were the most beautiful in the world.'[38] Fassbinder's euphoric admiration demonstrated, as did most *auteur* criticism of the time, that the apparently hokey exteriors of Sirk's melodramas housed a social criticism of the United States, articulated visually through a self-reflexive mise-en-scène that pointed to the flawed materialism of the bourgeoisie. The fact that such statements were made by a foreign director closely identified with political filmmaking, and in particular with the overt political transformations of melodramatic material in films such as *The Merchant of Four Seasons* (1971), lent an authority to this kind of appraisal.

Fassbinder's remake of *All That Heaven Allows* in *Ali, Fear Eats the Soul* (1974) paid further homage, as did the particular character of his melodramas. His films seemed to simulate Sirk by using melodrama as a platform for social criticism. Stylistically, Fassbinder employed a baroque mise-en-scène complete with the Sirk trademarks of mirrors and doorways as distancing devices. While the content of the New German director's work was played out in a more overtly incendiary fashion, the parallels nonetheless reinforced the sense that Sirk's films had been a significant influence on a significant cinema.

The Fassbinder connection, then, served a double purpose: it resuscitated Sirk for a contemporary audience through association with a prestigious foreign cinema, at the same time that it placed Fassbinder's films within more accessible Hollywood generic traditions. In addition, the European roots of both Sirk and Fassbinder dovetailed nicely with the 'anti-Americanism' of 1970s criticism in relation to the corporately produced works of the New American Cinema.

While this particular discourse on the Old and the New contributed to Sirk's authorisation at the time, journalism's *auteur* critics provided detailed inter-pretations of his films that went further in giving Sirk a public profile as an artist. Creating value for objects of mass culture in the public sector relied as much as academia did on establishing the aesthetic worth of their authors. As mentioned, most public critical commentary on Sirk was initiated by retro-spectives beginning in the latter half of the 1970s. This commentary was marked by a blend of Andrew Sarris's conservative auteurism and the more politicised perspectives of the left-thinking *Screen* and other academic journals, which often found an ideologically agreeable climate in newspapers affected by 1960s alternative culture. More directly, those affiliated with academic auteurism sometimes wrote these reviews.

In introducing Sirk to the cultured masses for the first time, revivals often replicated the 'discovery' phase in academics in the early 1970s [. . .] At the Carnegie Hall Cinema in 1976; the Museum of Modern Art in 1977; and the largest retrospective, sponsored in 1979 by Columbia University's School of Art, the Museum of Modern Art, the Goethe Society, and the Thalia Theatre to celebrate Sirk's return to the United States after a twenty-year absence, retrospectives presented films outside the pantheon of his 1950s melodramas. These included Nazi era films such as *Final Chord* (1936) and *La Habanera* (1937), as well as later U.S. films such as *Hitler's Madman* (1943), *Sleep, My Love* (1948), *Thunder on the Hill* (1951), *Has Anybody Seen My Gal?* (1952), and *Sign of the Pagan* (1954). In addition, in keeping with the rhetoric of discovery, reviews rehearsed Sirk's autobiography as a means of substantiating his artistic credentials, and defended him rigorously against prior criticism that had derided him on the basis of his association with 'tearjerkers.' However, programs consistently included Sirk's renowned melodramas, as well as the perspectives that had created their special status, revealing that revival institutions were well aware of Sirk's canonization in academia.

George Morris's review of the 1979 retrospective for *The Soho Weekly News* demonstrates how important academic interpretations were to popular reviewing at this time. Morris credited the early auteurists with recognizing that 'Sirk's work was unified by one of the most dazzling personal visual styles in the American cinema.' He then established the director as someone who, like fellow émigré directors Preminger and Lang, was 'fascinated by the contradictions within American society and culture.' Sirk used the 'hoary clichés and exhausted conventions of the so-called "woman's picture"' to explore these contradictions 'with irony and detachment.' On a deeper level, 'he was questioning the basic assumptions and ideals that were supposedly sustaining this country during the Eisenhower era. Sirk actually subverts and ruthlessly criticises the middle-class values that his films superficially endorse.' For elements of Sirk's visual signature that support their subversive intents, Morris mentioned mirrors that 'splinter reality,' and 'oppressive objects and decor' that 'externalise the inner tensions of the story.'[39]

Morris's interpretation provides a particularly detailed example of the penetration of the early *Screen* and *Monogram* projects into review discourse, especially the work of Paul Willemen, Jon Halliday, and Thomas Elsaesser. The reviewer depicted Sirk as a director who redeemed a questionable genre, launched a social critique of middle-class conceits of the Eisenhower era 'beneath the surface,' and employed self-reflexive and symptomatic imagery.[40]

This penetration was clear even in writers who had previously interpreted Sirk's films apolitically. Fred Camper, who had written about Sirk for *Screen* in the early 1970s without *Screen*'s characteristic left perspective on the director, now defended him as someone who revealed 'an understanding of America far more subtle and profound than that of almost any other filmmaker.' Among other things, Camper described how *Written on the Wind's* mise-en-scène – 'an exploration of a labyrinthine set of possible relations between people and costumes, people and objects, people and decor' – critiqued the materialism of U.S. life.[41] Similarly, for Andrew Sarris, Sirk's perverseness 'consisted of gilding fables for the masses until they meant the opposite of what they seem.'[42] In referring to Sirk's style as 'artfully artificial,' 'relentlessly reflective,' and ironical, Sarris's reviews were tinged with a sense of textual politics absent in his earlier comments on Sirk in *The American Cinema*.[43]

While few reviewers actually cited academic sources, academic interpretations were absorbed into the system of certain magazines and newspapers, acting as a ready-made stash of meanings upon which the reviewer could draw. Review discourse differed from academic in shunning theoretical 'jargon'; but these critics nonetheless rendered academic readings more accessible to the public.

This is not to say, however, that all critics responded reverently to prior schooled interpretations. These interpretations often appeared as so immersed in their own lofty logic that they lost purchase on reality. For example, MOMA's retrospective of four of Sirk's German films in 1980 prompted Jonathan Rosenbaum to applaud Sirk's 'consummate craftsmanship' but question the presence of a Brechtian subtext or social criticism in his films. He noted that there is a 'curious unresolved split between Leftist and campy readings,' made even greater by the fact that audiences rarely see the former and seem to revel in the latter.[44] Academia still serves as a point of departure here. But Rosenbaum questions its position on the director in the face of reception, sensing that academics ignore mass audience response because such response contradicts aesthetic propositions required to make Sirk a political *auteur*.

More recently, we can see a rare example of a marriage (rather than 'an unresolved split') between left-oriented academic and camp readings in Sirk criticism. J. Hoberman's review in *The Village Voice* of *Written on the Wind*, shown at the Public Theater in 1987, focuses on the artifice of the film in such a way as to fuse academic insights with camp. Quoting Halliday and Fassbinder, Hoberman shows himself to be a critic conversant with academic readings. Citing Sirk's background as a European intellectual, Hoberman recognises how the artifice – the excess of the film with its exaggerated colors, decor, and use of mirrors – renders a 'distanced antinaturalism,' that self-reflexively critiques the brash consumption of the petit bourgeois in this 'quint-essential American movie of the 1950s.'

At the same time, his review treats the film's excesses in an appreciative yet parodic manner aligned with a camp aesthetic. Here, exaggeration is revered for its own sake by those savvy enough to recognize the alternative pleasures embedded in its departure from the conventional aesthetics of good taste. *Written on the Wind* is 'trash on an epic scale, it's a vision as luridly color-coordinated, relentlessly high-octane, and flamboyantly petit-bourgeois as a two-toned T-Bird with ultrachrome trim.' The film is 'meta-trash' focusing on 'the vanity of trash' itself.

Hoberman's understanding of the film rests, then, on its transcendence of schlock through its strange combination of lurid style and self-reflexive social critique. This combination is especially clear in his response to Malone's 'Temptation' dance. He remarks, 'One cares for the grotesque Malone because her continually thwarted sexuality poses the greatest threat to the patriarchal order . . . in the film's most hilarious excess, her inflamed strip-mambo literally knocks the father dead.'[45]

This review provides a fitting finale to review discourse on Sirk's films for several reasons. *Written on the Wind* maintains its academic identity as a self-reflexive critique of the petit bourgeois and patriarchy through its exaggerated mise-en-scène and use of color. At the same time, by so thoroughly embracing the campy, overdrawn aspects of the film, Hoberman addresses the 'repressed other' of interpretation. That is, he poses a reading of Sirk's melodramas based on their implausibility and 'bad taste' that auteurists had all but stifled, and 1950s New York critics had used to condemn his work. But instead of taking this latter tack, Hoberman gives the film a rave review through a camp reading that celebrates its unconventional artifice. Thus, we see a blending of past comprehensions of Sirk's melodramatic excess that includes academia's self-reflexive and symptomatic readings, as well as accusations of bad taste by past critical establishments, now repossessed as a sign of quality by a 'hip' camp aesthetic.

In sum, whereas Sirk had almost no status as an artist in the 1950s, 1970s nostalgia helped create the conditions for his public embrace as an old master, while journalistic auteurism enthusiastically granted him an aesthetic status by offering a relatively stable set of interpretations, domesticated from their academic sources and offered to an urban cognoscente. In each case, review journalism assigned meaning and value to Sirk's films in relation to a series of existing canonical ideals, that is, realism in the 1950s and nostalgic auteurism in the 1970s. These ideals were themselves fueled by social developments, ranging from postwar film production to post-1960s alienation.

If I stopped my analysis here, we might well be left with the impression that this 'revolution' in Sirk's public profile signified the vast differences between 1970s and 1950s critical establishments. In fact, there are fundamental consistencies between the two that would belie such an impression.

During both periods, reviewers based their evaluations on a conception of Hollywood as a crass, commercial, formulaic, hence aesthetically and even morally bankrupt institution. I argued that in the 1950s, through their affiliation with industry commercialism and its association with corrupted mass cultural formulas, Sirk's soap operas helped represent a kind of zero-degree cinema, against which other films could be judged as successful. Critics constructed the 'realist' film, with its perceived platform of social content supported by dramatic plausibility and a suitably expressive style, as an antibody to the common Hollywood virus represented by Sirk.

Similarly, 1970s critics, particularly of the alternative presses, treated certain films of the New American Cinema as negative aesthetic benchmarks on the same grounds. *Star Wars*, a *Voice* cinematic whipping boy of the time, was no more than a 'sensationalistic factory product.' It stood as an example of pure commercialism, which created escapist fantasies tinged with reactionary politics and manipulated the audience into passive consumption. For Sarris, the 'lowest common denominator has become the magic number for success stories in the industry.'[46]

From this nucleus, a constellation of films with less overt commercial ambitions and perceived greater complexity emerged as aesthetically superior. There were 'Heroes and Villains in the Arts,' with filmmakers like Andrej Wajda occupying the former role, George Lucas the latter.[47] Foreign films, particularly those by Wajda, Godard, and filmmakers of the New German Cinema, merited attention on almost everyone's ten-best lists, as well as numerous awards from the New York Critics circle. Such U.S. box-office failures as *New York, New York* (1977) and *Pennies from Heaven* (1981) became critical successes in the *Voice* based on their departure from 'the melancholy trend of infantilism' characterising the mainstream in films such as *The Deep* and *The Other Side of Midnight* (1977).[48] Small-scale ventures like *Heartbeeps* (1981) or *Handle with Care* (1977) were championed because of the affiliations their directors (Allan Arkush and Jonathan Demme) had with independent filmmaking, and their knowing use of film conventions coupled with a lack of inflated ambition.

Critics valued all of these different kinds of films for their opposition to the evils of the film industry: its official optimism and lack of complexity, ambiguity, and realism, as well as its catering to what Molly Haskell (borrowing from Siegfried Kracauer) referred to as an updated 'shop girl' mentality – a naïve, emotional, and ultimately passive subscription to the desires of the culture industry.[49]

Despite positive changes in critical attitudes toward the mass media given the adversarial and alternative function many served in the 1960s, Adorno and Horkheimer's position toward mass culture still occupied a central role in the more recent reviewers' manner of constituting aesthetic hierarchies. Whereas in the 1950s Sirk's films had been generally reviled as the seat of a 'mindless,' totalitarian mass culture represented by Hollywood, now some films of the New American Cinema occupied that place. What changed between the two eras of film criticism was not the fundamental manner of creating critical canons; it was rather the *identity of the specific films* that would play the necessary *bête noire* role of Hollywood aesthetic bankruptcy and defilement of audience mentalities. Instead of Sirk, Lucas.

In this way, review journalism in alternative presses maintained the basic structure of aesthetic hierarchies from the past, spun from a notion of a corrupt mass culture. Sirk's appreciation at the time was a product not only of a shift in cultural and critical winds via nostalgia and auteurism; he was also the indirect legatee of a fundamental feature of review aesthetics, which simply required more recent films to represent the zero degree.

There is, finally, one other parallel between the two critical establishments that works against a sense of their absolute differences. While the more contemporary attitudes toward Sirk underwent radical change from the past, this change did not include appreciation of any cathartic pleasures Sirk's melodramas might offer as soap operas. I have suggested that 1950s critics segregated themselves from the masses by repudiating the 'natural' enjoyment afforded by products of mass culture through judgements based on a refined sense of realism. What Bourdieu would call such a Kantian 'taste of reflection' is as applicable to those in charge of Sirk's later aesthetic salvation. In most critics championing his films' social critique, self-reflexivity, and, in particular, distanciating effects, there is still a refusal of the 'vulgar' enjoyments suspected of soap operas. This refusal again functions to divorce the critic from an image of a mindless, hedonistic crowd he or she has actually manufactured in order to definitively secure the righteous logic of 'good' taste. It also, as Haskell's remark about shop girls suggests, perpetuates negative notions of female taste and subjectivity. Critiques of mass culture seem always to invoke a disdainful image of the feminine to represent the depths of the corruption of the people.

The process of tastemaking in both historical periods operated, then, to create hierarchical differences between the aesthete and the masses through the construction of canons and aesthetic positions antithetical to the perceived unrestrained and tasteless pleasures of the crowd.

NOTES

1. Pierre Bourdieu, *Distinction: A Social Critique of the Judgment of Taste*, Richard Nice, trans. (Cambridge: Harvard University Press, 1984), 7.
2. Lee Rogow, *The Saturday Review*, July 31, 1954: 36; Arthur Knight, *The Saturday Review*, Jan. 25, 1958: 27, and April 11, 1959: 28. See also, for example, Pauline Kael's later very qualified praise of *Tarnished Angels* as 'it's the kind of bad movie that you know is bad – and yet you're held by the mixture of polished style and quasi-melodramatics achieved by the director,' in *5001 Nights at the Movies* (New York: Holt, Rinehart and Winston, 1982), 580.
3. James Agee, *Agee on Film* (New York: McDowell, Obolensky, Inc., 1958), 105, Originally appeared in *The Nation*, July 22, 1944.
4. Bosley Crowther, *The New York Times*, Feb. 29, 1956: 35; *Time*, Mar. 26, 1956: 104.
5. Philip T. Hartung, *Commonweal*, July 23, 1954: 388.
6. 'All That Heaven Allows,' *Monthly Film Bulletin*, Oct. 1955: 151; 'Written on the Wind,' *Monthly Film Bulletin*, Nov. 1956: 139; 'Imitation of Life,' *Monthly Film Bulletin*, May 1959: 55.
7. Bosley Crowther, *The New York Times*, Jan. 12, 1957: 12.
8. *Newsweek*, Apr. 13, 1959: 118; Moira Walsh, *Catholic World*, Aug. 1959: 154–5.
9. John McCarten, *The New Yorker*, Aug. 14, 1954: 59.
10. See, for example, Patrice Petro, 'Mass Culture and the Feminine: The Place of Television in Film Studies,' *Cinema Journal* 25.3 (Spring 1986): 5–21.

11. Richard H. Pells, *The Liberal Mind in a Conservative Age: American Intellectuals in the 1940s and 1950s* (Middletown, Conn.: Wesleyan University Press, 1989), 218.
12. Andrew Ross, *No Respect: Intellectuals and Popular Culture* (New York: Routledge, 1989), 53–4.
13. Joseph Wood Krutch, 'Is Our Common Man too Common,' *The Saturday Review*, Jan. 10, 1953: 8.
14. D. W. Brogan, 'The Taste of the Common Man,' *The Saturday Review*, Jan. 28, 1953: 50.
15. Brogan, 48; Krutch, 36.
16. Edward C. Linderman, 'The Common Man as Reader,' *The Saturday Review*, May 9, 1953: 11–12, 47–8; Gilbert Seldes, 'Radio, Television, and the Common Man,' *The Saturday Review*, Aug. 29, 1953: 11–12, 39–41.
17. Theodor Adorno and Max Horkheimer, 'The Culture Industry: Enlightenment as Mass Deception,' *Dialectic of Enlightenment* (1944; New York: Herder and Herder, 1977), 152, 126, 144.
18. Bernard Rosenberg and David Manning White, eds., *Mass Culture: The Popular Arts in America* (Glencoe, Ill.: The Free Press, 1957), 9.
19. Paul Lazarsfeld and Robert Merton, 'Mass Communication, Popular Taste, and Organized Social Action,' *Mass Culture* (Rosenberg and White), 464–6.
20. Seldes, 'Radio, Television, and the Common Man,' 39–40.
21. Nora Sayre, 'Films That Still Have the Power to Panic,' *The New York Times*, July 31, 1977: 85.
22. Robert B. Ray, *A Certain Tendency of the Hollywood Cinema, 1930–1980* (Princeton: Princeton University Press, 1985), 247–95.
23. Michiko Kakutani, 'Garson Kanin Recalls Hollywood's High Times,' Nov. 18, 1979, *The New York Times Encyclopedia of Film*, Gene Brown, ed. (New York: Times Books, 1985).
24. Richard Corliss, 'The New Conservatism,' *Film Comment*, Jan.–Feb. 1980: 34–5 and 45.
25. Roger Angell, *The New Yorker*, Dec. 31, 1979: 52.
26. David Ehrenstein, 'Melodrama and the New Woman,' *Film Comment*, Sept.–Oct. 1978: 59.
27. Russell Baker, quoted by Richard Corliss in 'The Seventies,' *Film Comment*, Jan.–Feb. 1980: 34.
28. Walter Goodman, 'The Man Who Would Be Hitchcock,' *The New York Times*, Aug. 8, 1976: II, 11.
29. Andrew Sarris, *The Village Voice*, July 26, 1977: 41; June 11, 1964: 13; July 18, 1977: 37.
30. For a source that thoroughly discusses the nature of the phenomenon of nostalgia and its different historical manifestations, see David Lowenthal, *The Past Is a Foreign Country* (New York: Cambridge University Press, 1985).
31. Fred Davis, 'Nostalgia, Identity, and the Current Nostalgia Wave,' *The Journal of Popular Culture* 11.2 (Fall 1977): 421.
32. Peter Clecak, *America's Quest for the Ideal Self: Dissent and Fulfillment in the 60s and 70s* (New York: Oxford University Press, 1983), 43.
33. Ibid., 44.
34. See Fred Davis, *Yearning for Yesterday: A Sociology of Nostalgia* (New York: The Free Press, 1979), 104–7.
35. In *The New York Times Encyclopedia*: Andrew H. Malcolm, 'John Huston: I Want to Keep Right On Going,' *The New York Times*, Dec. 11, 1979; Vincent Canby, 'Nicholas Ray: Still a Rebel with a Cause,' *The New York Times*, Sept. 24, 1972A; Morris Dickstein, 'It's a Wonderful Life, but . . .' *American Film*, May 1980: 42–7.
36. 'Can a Director Grow on Foreign Soil?' *The New York Times*, May 2, 1976A, *The New York Times Encyclopedia*.

37. Rainer Werner Fassbinder, 'Fassbinder on Sirk,' Thomas Elsaesser, trans., *Film Comment* 11.6 (1975): 22–4; Andrew Sarris, 'Fassbinder and Sirk: The Ties That Unbind,' *The Village Voice*, Sept. 3–9, 1980: 37–8.

38. Fassbinder, 'Fassbinder on Sirk,' 24.

39. George Morris, 'Sirk's Imitations of Life,' *The Soho Weekly News*, Dec. 13, 1979: 40.

40. Program notes written in conjunction with the various series similarly demonstrated an absorption of academic values, rendered more accessible. The Thalia's notes were composed, for example, by James Harvey, a professor at the State University of New York–Stony Brook, who had previously published work on Sirk in *Film Comment*. Harvey refers to Sirk's 'famous ironical sub-text,' arguing that although his films elicit ambivalent responses from audiences unsure as to whether they are watching sheer tackiness or a critique of it, the films support an ironical reading through devices like the unhappy end. 'A Thalia Series in Honor of Douglas Sirk's First Visit to America in Twenty Years,' 1979.

41. Fred Camper, 'Sirk's Masterworks,' *The Soho Weekly News*, Aug. 5, 1976: 21.

42. Sarris, 'Fassbinder and Sirk: The Ties That Unbind,' 37–8; see also Sarris, *The Village Voice*, Dec. 17, 1979: 54–5.

43. Sarris, *The Village Voice*, Nov. 21, 1977: 44.

44. Jonathan Rosenbaum, 'Sirk's Works,' *The Soho Weekly News*, Aug. 27, 1980: 44, 48.

45. J. Hoberman, 'Twister,' *The Village Voice*, Oct. 27, 1987: 70; reprinted in Hoberman's *Vulgar Modernism: Writing on Movies and Other Media* (Philadelphia: Temple University Press, 1991), 248.

46. Andrew Sarris, *The Village Voice*, Dec. 30–Jan. 5, 1982: 26, 36; see also Molly Haskell's critique of George Lucas as a reactionary in 'May the Force Shut Up!' *The Village Voice*, July 4, 1977: 37.

47. J. Hoberman, 'Heroes and Villains in the Arts,' *The Village Voice*, Dec. 30–Jan. 5, 1982: 26.

48. Haskell, 'May the Force Shut Up!' 37.

49. Ibid.; see also on the *Voice*'s attitudes toward the mass audience, Andrew Sarris, 'Smart Movies, Dumb Audiences,' in which he laments the popularity of *The Jerk* over *Pennies from Heaven*, blaming the audience for its lack of discrimination, *The Village Voice*, Dec. 30–Jan. 5, 1982: 36.

16

NEW WAVES, SPECIALIST AUDIENCES AND ADULT FILMS

An examination of art films and adult cinema reveals a changing film industry at the end of the 1950s and into the 1960s as cinema's role as classic family entertainment was lost to television. Films diversified to attract different audiences, including young Americans for whom sci-fi, horror and titillation at the drive-in would guarantee a great evening out, and more specialist 'art house' screenings for American audiences for whom European imports held the intellectual high ground. The art house cinema circuit was typically the neighbourhood theatre in big cities where revivals of European classics such as Jean Renoir's *The Rules of the Game* (1939) and appreciation of more recent films such as Hiroshi Inagaki's *Samurai* (1954) consolidated art house cinema, differentiating it from the mass cultural products that were seen as typical of 'American' cinema in the 1950s. The rise of the art house as an outlet for a more diverse cinema product coincided with new cinema movements, or 'New Waves,' that would wash through cinema culture and change it.

In the same period, the Production Code largely administered by the studios was no longer easily enforceable. Some independent producers turned to exploitation movies, especially since in 1952 the Supreme Court extended the rights of free speech enshrined in the Fifth Amendment to the cinema in order to bring the institution in line with other media such as news. The Production Code that had contributed to the internal regulation of explicit sexual and violent content in Hollywood cinema would be continually modified until it was finally overturned to allow the representation of subjects previously deemed controversial which had, in any case, already entered mainstream cinema. In wider 1950s society, birth control was not widely available in the pre-Pill days of the 1960s and abortion was still illegal in most American states. Sex remained a taboo except between husband and wife so it is difficult to believe now that by the end of the 1950s only scenes of sexual 'perversion' (usually a coded way of referring to homosexuality but also a way of alluding to women's sexual agency) remained beyond the pale, and that the 1960s would see this change too with much more explicit representations of a newly 'permissive' society. In 1952, for example, the Cinematograph Act in Britain had introduced the X-Certificate film, largely to regulate continental European films where the sexual content was more daring. By 1966 the code had been thrown out by new MPAA head Jack Valenti who favoured for the US a rating system like Britain's as a guide to parents and to audiences in general. This liberal move also served to differentiate the controversial X-rated films from the rest and helped to secure an 'adult' audience for violent and erotic movies by the 1960s, from Hershell Gordon's 'bloodfests' and Russ Meyer's soft porn to classic thrillers such as *Rosemary's Baby* (1968). The rating system would successfully differentiate between 'adult' and 'other' audiences until the 1970s when movies such as *Deep Throat* (1972) and *The Exorcist* (1973) would throw even the rating system into turmoil.

The late 1950s and early 1960s was arguably the richest period of international cinema to date, largely as the result of 'New Waves' in cinema that reflected the push toward national sovereignty and identity following the end of the Second World War. New Waves were predominantly those that were revered and publicised so the initial publicity surrounding a new movement in cinema generally issued from success at an international film festival or exhibition abroad in arts cinemas rather than acclaim at home. For example, US arts theatres celebrated Rossellini's *Rome, Open City* (1945) on release. Many arts theatres had been established in the 1920s (see Chapter 8) and after the Second World War newsreel theatres also converted into art house cinemas and not only survived but increased admissions. This was largely due to the success of imported foreign films. For example, the 1952 decision to extend the First Amendment to film as well as books and newspapers came about because of Rossellini's *The Miracle* (1948), filmed from Federico Fellini's first original screenplay, which the Legion of Decency declared blasphemous. In the film, a simple Italian peasant (Anna Magnani) meets a tramp (Fellini). When she discovers she is pregnant, she comes to believe that he is Joseph and that she may be the Virgin Mary. The Supreme Court case surrounding the film, *Burstyn vs. Wilson*, was the first case about movie censorship that had come before the Supreme Court since 1915 and *The Birth of a Nation*.

Joseph Burstyn's success in overturning objections to the film's screening in New York opened up opportunities to represent areas of society that had previously been regulated off the screen by self-censorship as well as the Production Code. It also signalled a broadening of cinema's remit following the *Paramount* decision which allowed for a wider distribution of more diverse cinematic fare. That a foreign film could be the controversial test case also signalled a shift in the American public's awareness of international cinema and, by extension, of European cinema's more comfortable and explicit treatment of women as sexual beings in all their complexities. Fellini, who began directing in 1950, would be credited with contriving an entire Fellini-esque universe in *The White Sheik* (1951), *I Vitelloni* (1953) and *La Strada* (1954), and the sexually explicit *La Dolce Vita* (1960), a burlesque, tragic and often surreal and magical world, with the 'melos' to Fellini's drama supplied by Nino Rota. Rota's theme to *La Strada*, known as 'Gelsomina's theme', sold millions of copies around the world, largely due to the art house theatre crowds. Fellini, whose interest in the gaudy and tawdry often involves the sexual and sordid, had by the 1960s become a huge influence on filmmakers. Fellini and Antonioni who both began as postwar neo-realists had become progressively more avant-garde, Antonioni dispensing with realist narrative for a more high-modernist random sequencing. *L'Avventura* (1960), for example, was initially criticised for its seemingly aimless 'plotting' and lack of resolution, but was soon celebrated as an art house classic, as were his other films – *The Red Desert* (1964) and *Blow-Up* (1966) – which were taken to represent a frustrated search for meaning in contemporary society.

Although the French New Wave typically dominates discussions of this period, Britain and Poland both preceded France in revolutionising national cinema. In Poland, a dark and foreboding Romantic national cinema evolved, epitomised by the work of director Andrzej Wajda. He was lauded at the Cannes Film Festival in 1957 for *Kanal* while his *Ashes and Diamonds* (1958), set at the end of the Second World War, includes the classic scene in which communist resistance workers and the bourgeoisie discover that their lives are ironically and tragically interwoven. Political filmmaking also characterised the filmmakers of the British New Wave – Tony Richardson, Karel Reisz and Lindsay Anderson also had backgrounds in documentary filmmaking. They had been focal in the postwar 'Free Cinema' movement of the 1950s which decried the detachment to which Italian neo-realism aspired, and advocated a personalised visual evocation of social problems in short documentary form, as in Anderson's *O Dreamland* (1953). Their shift to feature films by the 1960s retained something of the same ethos and also drew on literary and theatrical sources (novels by Alan Sillitoe, John Braine and Stan Barstow and plays by John Osborne and Shelagh Delaney) in which anger and youthful hopes are thwarted.

Social problems receiving attention in 1950s Britain included issues of class, gender and racism. Britain was divided by class and generational conflict and by region: the affluent South was seen to be undervaluing the industrial North and failing to see the poverty at the heart of the southern cities such as London. Demonstrations against the invasion of Egypt in 1956 and the CND (Aldermaston) marches of 1958 lent Britain's youth an air of protest that underpinned the popular response to classic 'New Wave' films like *Look Back in Anger* (1959), Tony Richardson's adaptation of John Osborne's play with Richard Burton as Jimmy Porter, the first 'angry young man'. These young British directors made stars of previously unknown young male actors including Tom Courtenay, Richard Harris and Alan Bates. A clutch of similar films followed: *Room at the Top* (1959), *Saturday Night, Sunday Morning* (1960) with Albert Finney as a frustrated factory worker, *A Taste of Honey* (1961) based on Delaney's play, *The Loneliness of the Long Distance Runner* (1962) and *This Sporting Life* (1963). Lindsay Anderson and John Schlesinger were the most important of the filmmakers to emerge out of British New Cinema, as epitomised in *If . . .* (1968), Anderson's satire on the public school system, and Schlesinger's *Darling* (1965), a satire of the upper classes which brought Julie Christie to public attention. Schlesinger would remain a controversial filmmaker, going on in 1969 to direct the American 'Sixties' classic *Midnight Cowboy*. By the 1960s, socially conscious British cinema had expanded to include much more edgy topics, moving from Muriel Box's feminist *The Truth about Women* (1950) to *Sapphire* (1959), a study of racism and films about industrial disputes such *The Angry Silence* (1960) with Richard Attenborough, albeit sometimes taken to comedic extremes as in *I'm All Right Jack* (1960).

In France the New Wave in cinema was very much the collective vision of different indigenous film styles and filmmakers who were all critics and cinéphiles. After the war, French film critic André Bazin had enthused about Luchino Visconti's *La Terra Trema* (1947) which had impacted less favourably in Italy but which Bazin recognised as a personally informed neo-realist vision. He felt it was imbued with a love of cinema that the French New Wave directors he influenced would come to exemplify in the late 1950s and 1960s, as in François Truffaut's *The 400 Blows* (1959), a cinéphile's memories of childhood. While neo-realism had always veered toward the sentimental in its focus on the individual's plight, Visconti captured something of the evolving critical sense of the author or artist at work, stamping the film with his personality, and it would be an idea that the *Cahiers du Cinéma* critics led by Bazin would evolve (see Chapter 15). In France in the 1950s cinema was incredibly buoyant commercially and critically and attendance would not be affected by the rise of television until the very end of the decade – and even then the French love of art films (Cocteau's *Orphée* [1950] and Bresson's *A Man Escaped* [1956]) secured audiences ready for the *Cahiers du Cinéma* critics: a new generation who would crash through what they considered the constipated 'cinéma de papa'.

The French New Wave directors were young, energetic and often experimental, favouring location shooting, improvisation, long takes and jump cuts and privileging *mise-en-scène* over the technique of montage they associated with previous generations. Their brand of film authorship in which the director was the key would be labelled *auteur* theory by American critic Andrew Sarris. The 'nouvelle vague' comprised François Truffaut, Eric Rohmer, Alain Resnais and other intellectual filmmakers but most notably, the iconoclastic Jean-Luc Godard who would become the 1968 generation's favourite director (see Chapter 17). His *A Bout de Souffle* (1959) is characterised by a love of popular culture, and is itself a remake of the popular American thriller *Gun Crazy* (1950), and Godard's

Alphaville (1965) recalls *Kiss Me Deadly* (1955). The French New Wave is too often presented as a masculine endeavour which risks overlooking the talents of Agnès Varda who directed *La Pointe Courte* (1956) when she was 25 years old. The film prefigures much of the movement's ethos. Varda would go on to direct *Cleo from 5 to 7* (1961) and *Happiness* (1965) as well as a film study of the American Black Panthers.

In all its facets the French New Wave would influence filmmakers as different as Arthur Penn and Woody Allen. The semi-documentary style was also popularised by the development of lightweight, portable camera equipment and sychronised sound equipment. New Waves took to the streets as in the case of Robert Drew shooting *Primary* (1960) by following John F. Kennedy and Hubert Humphrey electioneering during the Wisconsin primary in a fly-on-the-wall evocation. This and other films often privileged the role of the cinematographer over that of the director in capturing 'life as lived' in 'authentic' cinema as championed first in France by Jean Rouch and Edgar Morin in their *Chronicle of a Summer* (1961), a self-conscious film in which non-actors were expected to engage with the act of filmmaking by asking questions and becoming involved with film as ethnography. French cinema was a beacon in the period for such experimentation, especially via Rouch and Chris Marker, but Robert Drew and others pioneered American *cinéma vérité* (as it was known in France) or 'direct cinema' (as it was often called in the United States) with Drew going on to make further films with and about Kennedy, even filming his funeral in the short film *Faces of November* (1963). Drew Associates released a number of their films on television but in general this was not the case and often the documentary-style films made in 16mm failed to secure a general cinema release. When this happened their main outlet was often arts cinemas and college campuses.

In America, New York became a centre for independent avant-garde filmmaking. The 'New York School' used hand-held cameras to make avant-garde semi-documentaries that took off in the mid-1950s on the back of art cinemas, with Jonas Mekas and Shirley Clarke coming to prominence with *Guns of the Trees* (1961) and *A Cool World* (1963) respectively. Their aesthetic experimentation was influenced by Italian neo-realism and, most notably, the French New Wave and Mekas was also editor of the journal *Film Culture*, so there was a distinct sense in which new movements in filmmaking were underpinned by the filmmakers' immersion in film history and film culture. The best-known director in New York was John Cassavetes whose improvised film *Shadows* (1959) was acclaimed. He financed his independent filmmaking by his work as a serious actor and successfully balanced the two until his death in 1989. By the mid-1960s, what became known as the 'New American Cinema' was established, with figures such as Jack Smith and Gregory Markopoulos. Markopoulos espoused the avant-garde and was compared to modernist writers such as Joyce and Proust in his creation of 'thought-images'. He wrote 'Toward a new Narrative Film Form' in 1963, a manifesto that recalls the film culture of the 1920s as much as it reflected the 'New Waves' of the 1960s. 'New American Cinema' would push even further into the esoteric and reach its apogee with Andy Warhol's *Sleep* (1963), a film of a person sleeping, and *Empire* (1964), in which a static camera is held on the Empire State Building for the entire eight hours that the film lasts.

The Swedish director Ingmar Bergman was really the archetypal art house director, professing no interest in commercial cinema and refusing rather than failing to appeal to mass audiences. Bergman's *The Seventh Seal* (1957) became an art house classic based on memorable symbolic sequences, like that in which Death and the Knight play chess, enhanced by Gunnar Fischer's black-and-white cinematography. In fact, the film is a series of set pieces or scenes in which a vision of medieval life is incrementally created. Bergman's very personal – even autobiographical – anguished vision and his trademark poetic parables made him the ultimate 'serious' filmmaker for cinéphiles in the 1950s and after. But that is not to say that there was not a rich choice of alternatives. In 1951 *Rashomon*, a film directed by Akira Kurosawa, had stormed the Venice International Film Festival and became a smash hit bettered only by the same director's *Seven Samurai* in 1954. It is ironic perhaps that *Rashomon*, a complex narrative that provides multiple perspectives on a rape, should have made such an international impact when it was probably its director's least successful film at home. Nevertheless, Kurosawa brought Japanese cinema to centre stage with work by Yasujiro Ozu and Kenji Mizoguchi acclaimed in a Japanese New Wave that included Kurosawa's *Yojimbo* (1961) and that would continue into the 1970s. Actor Toshiro Mifune became an international phenomenon, at the centre of Kurosawa's films for decades. The Japanese New Wave would include the work of independent director Susumi Haru whose *Bad Boys* (1960) is made in a pseudo-documentary style using inmates from a young offenders' prison as actors in the story of a delinquent boy. It is an example of what Nagisa Oshima would call 'the new subjectivity' and like his own film, *Cruel Story of Youth* (1960), it is typical of the Japanese New Wave that would insert a youthful energy into Japanese-filmmaking: a tale of disaffected, alienated youth.

Rebellious youth had been a money spinner since the 1950s. Boys like working-class Plato (Sal Mineo) with whom middle-class Jimmy Stark (James Dean) associates in *Rebel Without A Cause* (1955) conveyed the young as exciting, if dangerous and anti-social. Similarly, another box-office sell-out was sensuality and sexual promiscuity. Even in mainstream cinema the body was being celebrated. The male body was caressed by the camera in *Ben-Hur* (1959) and *Spartacus* (1960) and even skinny Frank Sinatra became the archetypal swinging playboy figure living out married men's fantasies in *The Tender Trap* (1955) and in more sordid fashion in *Pal Joey* (1957). Representation of women's sexuality was becoming much more raw and raunchy recalling a few rare early films such as Ida Lupino's *Hard, Fast and Beautiful!* (1951) and Shelley Winters as *Playgirl* (1954): 'There's a price tag on her kisses and trouble was never so cheap.' First in Italian and later in US cinema there was Gina Lollobrigida and

Sophia Loren, 'La Lollo' formidable as Sheba in *Solomon and Sheba* (1959) and Loren as Cleopatra in *The Two Cleopatras* (1952). But the real love goddess was Marilyn Monroe who exuded sensuality. She had first come to notice in John Huston's *The Asphalt Jungle* (1950) and by 1961 had made her final film. She was found dead at home in 1962 aged 36. Monroe was one of the last studio stars and an accomplished comic too. Directed by Howard Hawks in *Gentlemen Prefer Blondes* (1953) and by Billy Wilder in *The Seven Year Itch* (1955), she was the symbol that inspired Hugh Heffner, who launched his multi-million dollar empire with Monroe as the centrefold of the first edition of *Playboy* in December 1953. Monroe had become the stuff of popular legend by the end of the 1950s (as she famously said, 'I'm not interested in money. I just want to be wonderful') and in *The Seven Year Itch* Tom Ewell fantasises about Monroe's character precisely because he first saw her in a magazine.

Monroe has become iconic over the decades, as first validated by Andy Warhol's silk screens in the 1960s. She is the subject of numerous films and of books by strikingly different writers such as long-standing feminist Gloria Steinhem and the masculinist Norman Mailer. Cast as a fantasy figure, the enigma that is Monroe in the film history of this period lies in the purity which directors and fans believe radiates in each performance and in its contrast: the very 'adult' story of her rape at age nine, her role as victim of male desire, the sexy star's rise through Hollywood due as much to the casting couch as talent, and the conspiracy surrounding her death. The mass production of popular cultural celebrities such as Elvis and Monroe which began in the 1950s prefaced the wider consumerist trend. The Barbie doll first appeared on shelves in 1958, for example, its hour-glass figure and perfect wardrobe recalling Monroe and celebrating if domesticating her image. Monroe epitomises the way in which sex and sexuality permeated American cinema in the 1950s and her domestication ensured that none of her films was ever denied an MPAA seal.

It is important to note the crossover between New Waves and adult films in this period, as signalled by *The Miracle* and by French director Roger Vadim's *. . . And God Created Woman* which was released in the US in 1957. Starring Brigitte Bardot, it was heavily censored and in many states, especially in the South where censors such as Lloyd Binford in Memphis made sure it was impossible for segregated black audiences to see a white 'sex kitten' cavorting on screen, it was not shown at all. Nevertheless, it was an art house smash, made Bardot an international star, and made Americans more aware of a 'continental' easiness about sex. The same art house/'adult' crossover was played out over and over again in films released in the early 1960s. *Psycho* (1960), for example, is Hitchcock's most 'adult' film and his aesthetic attachment to monochrome is a nod to the New Wave. Similarly, the liberal attitude to sex which characterised the European New Wave is evident in Hitchcock's very 'American' movie. There are, of course, numerous suggestive scenes in many of Hitchcock's films and the prospect of sex is 'interrupted' by a train going through a tunnel in *North by Northwest* (1959), but in the Gothic thriller *Psycho* Marion Crane (Janet Leigh) is made the object of male desire from the opening daring shots as the camera swoops in through the window of the seedy hotel where she is having a lunchtime rendezvous; it was the first time that a women in a brassiere had been shown in American film. Nevertheless, as cinema culture manoeuvred out of the censors' grasp, another much more blatant side of 'adult' cinema would be apparent in the softcore pornography of cult director Russ Meyer as epitomised in *Faster, Pussycat! Kill! Kill!* (1965) with its exploitation movie title.

The Catholic Legion of Decency, founded in 1934 to help 'purify' the cinema and protect youth from any negative influences, was frequently demanding cuts in movies into the 1950s, despite the MPAA's internal regulation. The legion, far more conservative than any regulatory body, quite often used its category C rating to 'condemn' films it believed to be immoral or to label those it saw as objectionable in some way (rating B), as with Otto Preminger's *Forever Amber* (1953). However, it was becoming harder to control foreign films such as Marc Allégret's *Lady Chatterley's Lover* (1955) which was seen to represent adultery as a positive life choice. It is ironic that in the novel *Forever Amber* on which Preminger's film is based, the protagonist enjoyed more than twenty lovers and the film is such a strait-laced adaptation. Debate over whether a film should be awarded a seal caused controversy in itself and publicity for what audiences felt would be an 'adult film' with adult themes – as in the case of Elia Kazan's *Baby Doll* (1956) based on a Tennessee Williams play which Catholic censors described as 'dirty' and 'carnal', thereby securing an audience for the story of a child-bride even before Geoffrey Shurlock, Breen's more liberal or realistic successor, gave it the MPAA's seal of approval. A Production Code seal from the MPAA was shown to be obsolescent when even comedies like *The Tender Trap* (1955) began to include risqué scenes and when films denied a seal because of supposedly unacceptable content could draw big audiences for that reason alone. *Peyton Place*, Grace Metalious' taboo-busting novel which had ripped the lid off steamy small-town America, was filmed the following year and turned into a long-running – if much more tame – TV serial.

The career of Jane Fonda exemplifies the shift into adult themes that would permeate the cinema of the 1960s. Beginning at the Actors Studio, she débuted on Broadway and her first film in 1960, *Tall Story*, was a clean-cut drama combining sport and romance; but she followed it with *Walk on the Wild Side* (1962) set in a brothel, before moving to France where she was 'made' by director Roger Vadim into a 'sex kitten,' to rival his first successful starlet, Brigitte Bardot, and his third, Catherine Deneuve, who would become a star of the New Wave in Luis Buñuel's *Belle de Jour* (1967). Vadim's *Barbarella* (1968) was the sexy, frothy sci-fi fantasy that, though panned by critics on release, became a cult hit in the years that followed. By the end of the decade, returning to America after a visit to India, Fonda began to channel her beliefs into a radical counter-cultural agenda and even visited North Vietnam during the Vietnam War, a decision that left her sidelined by Hollywood for some time.

In the battle against television, films exploring controversial issues and taboo subjects were a significant draw. Their subject matter was seen as unsuitable for television and the 'adult' tag earned them audiences they might not otherwise have enjoyed. *Baby Doll*, for example, is famous for its dedicated marketing: the billboard of Carroll Baker lying seductively in a baby's crib sucking her thumb was an incredibly successful exploitation of the film's theme. American International Pictures (AIP), founded in 1954 by Sam Arkoff and Jim Nicholson and renowned for its focus on the 'teenpic' (see Chapter 14), was incredibly successful at exploiting the adult market and in providing its primary adolescent market with its first cinematic forays into risqué subjects. Roger Corman is a representative director who in films such as *Teenage Doll* (1957) and *The Trip* (1967) achieved phenomenal success. He began with AIP but became an independent producer-director releasing an autobiography that sums up his success: *How I Made a Hundred Movies in Hollywood and Never Lost a Dime* (1990). *Teenage Doll* was a violent shocker dealing with gang warfare which was released in two versions to get past the censors. Its disparaging *Boxoffice* review sums up its appeal as violence for the sake of violence. *The Trip* explored what it would be like to take an LSD trip and like AIP's *The Wild Angels* (1966) before it, which had been a cult exposé of the Hells Angels, it was lambasted for exploiting the problems of the drug culture, although it was clever camp, going on to gross $4.5 million at the box office. Trade advertisements marketed how much the film was grossing around the country in its first two weeks of exhibition, promising 'Groovy Gravy' for distributors.

The popularity of exploitation movies in the 1950s rivalled their appeal in any previous decade, with independent producers successfully churning out cheap productions such as Ed Wood's *Plan 9 from Outer Space* (1956) and huge hits such as *The House of Usher* (1960) which began Roger Corman's film cycle based on Edgar Allen Poe's stories. The biggest grossing exploitation film before this period had been *Mom and Dad* (1944) but it was only licensed for general release in New York a decade after its initial release in 1956. Such wrangles with censors are indicative of the power of exploitation movies to disturb not only the cultural status quo but the legal system.

The term 'exploitation' was originally based less on the manipulation of controversial subject matter and more on the marketing techniques used to promote the film, reflecting the fact that such movies were shot cheaply with finance ploughed into their promotion. However, between 1945 and 1960 exploitation films had settled comfortably into forbidden topics: sexual disease, abortion, adultery, teenage pregnancy, miscegenation (the American pseudo-scientific neologism for interracial relations in a segregated society). They became what Eric Schaefer calls Hollywood's 'shadow cinema'; from the first exploitation movies made as early as 1914 they had supplied the exquisite nausea that derives from supposedly 'gross' imagery.

In *Bold! Daring! Shocking! True!* (1999), Schaefer traces that shadow cinema in counterpoint to mainstream Hollywood from 1919 to 1959. He shows that what is seen as socially peripheral is often symbolically central. In the extract, his conclusion to that groundbreaking study, he maps the field and nuances a sea change in cinema culture whereby a combination of factors, including the rise of independents such as Otto Preminger and Roger Corman in a post-studio set-up, would contribute to the making of a new and more diverse American cinema in the 1960s and 1970s.

This kind of film history presents a series of interesting challenges and a few problems. It is difficult to map the terrain covered by exploitation cinema when many of the films never received cinema release or have been lost, and this leaves the film historian dependent on other sources. These may be anything from interviews with those who made the movies, or who remember seeing them on release, to newspaper accounts, fanzines and the press kits that were the epitome of exploitation tactics. Schaefer exploits myriad interdisciplinary sources in telling the exploitation story and he succeeds in compiling a narrative film history where none had existed before. Although there had been studies of individual producers and directors and studies of cult films, from a disparate and fragmented resource base, Schaefer teases out the movie trends and the historical changes that evolved into the exploitation industry. He also sets the scene for the rise of 'sexploitation' films in the 1960s and 'blaxploitation' in the 1970s.

- Assess the sources Schaefer deploys in his study. Can you differentiate between his primary and his secondary sources?
- Schaefer's study involves rediscovery of material about films that are lost as well as the authentication of a tradition in film history subsumed in much film scholarship. What are the problems one faces in reconstructing this kind of film history?
- New Wave and adult cinemas grew up as part of a 'post-studio' system. What other sources might you use to tell the story of these developments?

The End of Classical Exploitation

Eric Schaefer

[. . .]

The first factor in the decline of classical exploitation can be traced to the physical deterioration of those who had made a consistent living with

Eric Schaefer, *Bold! Daring! Shocking! True!: A History of Exploitation Films, 1919–1959* (Durham, NC and London: Duke University Press, 1999).

exploitation films for up to forty years. Samuel Cummins, in his sixties, began to withdraw from the business. S. S. Millard died in the late 1950s. J. D. Kendis, who remained an active producer into the early 1950s, died in 1957 at seventy-one. Willis Kent, who continued to produce films well into his seventies, called it quits in the late 1950s and died at age eighty-seven in 1966. Dwain Esper had gradually moved away from the business after World War II, finally retiring in 1962. George Weiss coasted through the transition from exploitation to sexploitation with some nudist pictures and initiated the popular 'Olga' series about a dominatrix in 1964, but 'America's Fearless Young Showman,' Kroger Babb, was never able to duplicate the phenomenal success of *Mom and Dad*. His efforts rapidly deteriorated into rants against pay television and a whacky market research-cum-pyramid scheme called 'The Idea Factory.'[1] The first generation of great exploiteers was passing from the scene.

Censorship on the Wane

Just as the original exploiteers were moving out of production, the grand old men of Hollywood – Zukor, Cohn, the Warners, Ford, and Capra – were retiring, being forced out of the business, or dying. The same was true of those who had held the reins of censorship for decades. That censorship underwent tremendous changes in the postwar period that affected both Hollywood and the exploiteers is a given. Those changes affected, and were in part the result of, the exploitation business, as well as relaxing moral standards and shifts in the industrial conditions that had given rise to and sustained the exploitation film since the late teens. The *Paramount* decision of 1948 and the subsequent consent decrees rocked Hollywood. The court decision, coupled with decreased movie attendance resulting from the effects of suburbanization, the G. I. Bill, the baby boom, and the diffusion of television, led to the release of contract talent and a reduction in the number of films produced by the large studios. In an effort to offer an alternative to the family-oriented programming on television, many of the movies emerging from the studios took on a decidedly more mature quality. The cycle of 'adult' westerns including *The Gunfighter* (1950), *High Noon* (1952), and those directed by Anthony Mann were joined by sophisticated contemporary dramas including *A Streetcar Named Desire* (1951), *A Place in the Sun* (1951), *From Here to Eternity* (1953), *Baby Doll* (1956), and *Anatomy of a Murder* (1959). When a spate of articles with such titles as 'The Big Leer' and 'Movies Are Too Dirty' commented on the surge in screen sex in the early 1960s, the objects of attention were generally not nudist films or racy French movies but pictures from the majors such as *The Apartment* (1960), *Butterfield 8* (1960), and *Walk on the Wild Side* (1962) that dealt with prostitution and adultery.[2]

The Production Code had been enforceable because of the lock the five majors had on first-run exhibition. Films lacking a Code seal could not play in affiliated theaters. Barred from the lucrative first-run market, it was economic suicide for the majors to make films that could not be granted Production Code approval. But after divestiture, the equation was altered. Producer/director Otto Preminger's *The Moon Is Blue* (1953) and *The Man with the Golden Arm* (1955) were both released by United Artists without Code approval and achieved critical and financial success. Although denied a Code seal, *The Man with the Golden Arm* was accorded a B rating by the Legion of Decency – the first film not given a seal that was not also condemned by the Legion.[3] Upon his retirement in 1954, Joe Breen was replaced as head of the PCA by Geoffrey Shurlock. Shurlock was not the rigid ideologue Breen had been, nor did he have Breen's close ties to the Catholic Church. The long-standing unanimity among the PCA, the Legion of Decency, and state censors began to fracture. *Baby Doll*, released by Warner Bros. in 1956, was vigorously denounced by the Legion of Decency but given approval by the PCA.[4] The Legion's power was effectively broken by the incident, and the Code underwent substantial revisions in 1956, eliminating the ban on miscegenation and loosening the prohibitions on depiction of narcotics, abortion, prostitution, and kidnapping.[5] As suggested earlier, self-regulation was imposed to some extent as a means of eliminating unacceptable films made outside the mainstream industry. Yet the Code was being eroded from within by movies released by the majors just as much as it was being damaged by outside sources.

Companies outside the mainstream played an equally important role in the decline of censorship. In *United States vs. Paramount Pictures*, Justice William O. Douglas wrote, 'We have no doubt that moving pictures, like newspapers and radio, are included in the press whose freedom is guaranteed by the First Amendment,' opening the door for a challenge to motion-picture censorship. That challenge came in *Burstyn vs. Wilson*, commonly known as *The Miracle* decision.[6] The 1948 Italian film, directed by Roberto Rossellini, concerned a simple-minded peasant woman who is seduced by a wanderer she thinks is Saint Joseph. She believes that her resulting pregnancy is a miracle, and after being driven from her village, she gives birth in a secluded church in the hills. Initially passed by New York censors, the film's license was withdrawn on the grounds that it was 'sacrilegious' following complaints and pickets by Catholic organisations. In 1952 the United States Supreme Court reversed lower court decisions that had upheld the censorship board's action. The Court held that movies were constitutionally protected under the First Amendment and that the New York law that allowed the banning of films on the ground that they were 'sacrilegious' was too broad. Although the Court's opinion did not decide the question of whether the state had the power to 'censor motion-pictures under a clearly drawn statute designed and applied to prevent the showing of obscene films,' *Burstyn vs. Wilson* seriously compromized the concept of prior restraint. A series of per curiam opinions followed that rejected 'immoral,' 'tending to corrupt morals,' 'harmful' or 'conducive [to] immorality [or] crime' as criteria for banning films.[7]

Also in 1952, *Latuko*, an exotic shockumentary about an African tribe that played the exploitation circuit, was confiscated by the Newark, New Jersey, director of public safety prior to a showing. The nakedness of the women from the waist up and the full-frontal nudity of the men proved to be the nub of the controversy. The American Museum of Natural History, which held the rights to the film, and the theater owner brought suit against the public safety director, seeking an injunction to prevent his interference in public showings. The injunction was granted by the Superior Court Chancery Division, the judge holding that 'there is nothing suggestive, obscene, indecent, malicious or immoral in the showing of the Latuko aborigines in their normal living state.'[8] Although the decision did not have immediate fallout, it did signal that the courts were beginning to take a more liberal stand on nudity – long the primary source of spectacle in exploitation films.

Representatives of the six states that maintained censorship boards met and issued a call 'for new statutes to prevent the exhibition of "obscene and immoral" films and to justify their [the boards'] continued existence.'[9] Hugh M. Flick, the head of New York's censorship board, was most concerned about exploitation films, claiming in 1954 that 'the most offensive movies were made by independent producers,' consisting 'largely of "girly shows" and borderline subjects such as sex hygiene, drug addiction, and clinical subjects including operations and childbirth.' Echoing the age-old fear of the professional censor, Flick worried that without some form of government censorship, 'these films would be able to prey on the more susceptible elements of the community.'[10] But a series of court decisions opened the door for an almost unrestricted flow of exploitation films to the nation's screens by the end of the decade.

Following years of wrangling with the New York censor board, *Mom and Dad* was finally licensed in 1956 when the Appellate Division of the State Supreme Court overturned the board, deciding that human birth was not 'indecent.' That same year, in *Excelsior Pictures Corp. vs. Regents of the University of the State of New York*, the New York Court of Appeals upheld a lower court order that had annulled the censorship board's ruling finding *The Garden of Eden* 'indecent' and ordered it licensed, in effect stating that nudity without sexual behavior was not obscene. The Maryland Court of Appeals found in 1957 that aboriginal nudity was not 'obscene or pornographic' in and of itself in *Maryland State Board of Motion Picture Censors vs. Times Film Corporation*, a suit involving *Naked Amazon* (1954). When Hallmark appealed the Pennsylvania censorship board's third refusal to license *She Shoulda Said 'No'!* in the Court of Common Pleas of Philadelphia, the court reversed the board's order and declared the Pennsylvania Motion Picture Censorship Act unconstitutional. The decision was upheld by the Supreme Court of Pennsylvania, finally ending censorship in that state. Other state and municipal censor boards began to fall like dominos. By the mid-1960s, the remaining boards had become anachronisms, if not embarrassments. The increasingly ineffectual Production Code and the fall of prior censorship led to the film rating system, introduced by the MPAA in 1968.

Teenpics and Art Films

If the *Paramount* decision undercut the power of the Production Code and paved the way for *Burstyn vs. Wilson*, it also helped expand the competition for product among theaters. As Thomas Doherty has observed, the blockbuster mentality compelled the majors to direct their resources toward fewer, more elaborate films that could yield higher domestic box office and greater returns from the increasingly important international market.[11] B units were shut down; the studios that had specialized in low-budget westerns and some programmers, such as Republic, sold their movies to television and closed up shop. As theaters were cut loose from production companies, exhibitors vied for product in a more competitive environment. Many sought salvation aboard the technological bandwagon, installing 3-D systems, widescreen, and stereo. A few even succumbed to harebrained schemes like Smell-O-Vision and AromaRama. Large chains quickly sold off their weak houses, and many theaters were closed for good. Still others turned to new, specialized product and the audience that came with it.

Some exhibitors, especially those who ran neighborhood theaters that depended on subsequent runs and double bills, felt abandoned by the majors. According to Doherty, by the mid-1950s, 'they were "wide open and hungry" for indie product that was cheap, regular, and exploitable.'[12] The movies that low-budget outfits such as Allied Artists, DCA, Howco, and above all, AIP made were often referred to as exploitation films, but as Doherty has pointed out, they were 'all but indistinguishable' from traditional B pictures.[13] And even though this new breed of film was cheap to produce – often under the $100,000 mark – they ranked as more polished than the classical exploitation pictures being made at the time, which, as a rule, continued to come in under $25,000.[14] What set these new 'exploitation' films apart was that they were geared toward the largely untapped teenage market, which by the early 1950s made up the most loyal and regular segment of the moviegoing audience. With increased mobility and millions in disposable income, teenagers became a marketer's dream come true. Teenpics were similar to classical exploitation films insofar as their advertising promised more than the films actually delivered; AIP's *Day the World Ended* and *Phantom from 10,000 Leagues* combo was billed as 'The Top Shock Show of All Time!'[15] Hardly. The films themselves were narratives in the strict classical Hollywood cinema mode, eschewing the educational or titillating spectacle that had differentiated classical exploitation from Hollywood product. In fact, Sam Arkoff, who cofounded AIP with James Nicholson, described himself and his partner as 'pretty old-fashioned': 'We weren't necessarily trying to break new ground in areas like violence and sex.' Although AIP had the occasional scrape with the Legion, none of the company's films was ever rejected by the Code.[16] Classical exploitation films continued to be pitched for adults only, a policy that would have prevented a large segment of the audience for AIP movies from attending.

The teenpics succeeded in drawing one specialized portion of the movie audience; the 'art film' became another alternative for exhibitors anxious to stay in business but who were either unable or unwilling to compete for the smaller number of movies issued by the majors. In fact, the art cinema had more in common with traditional exploitation than the prepackaged double bills being cranked out by Arkoff and Nicholson. The line between art cinema and exploitation was often a thin one, and this confusion played a greater role in the decline of the classical exploitation film than the advent of the so-called exploitation pictures made by AIP and similar low-end operations.

Following World War II, there was a sharp rise in interest in foreign, or art, cinema. New theaters opened and others converted to an 'art house policy,' showing films that were made outside the United States. As Douglas Gomery has written, art houses not only showed movies that differed from those offered by run-of-the-mill theaters, they provided a much different environment. Popcorn and candy were replaced by coffee, tea, and pastries. An air of seriousness pervaded the art house and was reflected in higher admission prices.[17] The spread of art houses has been linked to American travel during and after the war, increasingly refined audience tastes, a reduction in isolationist sentiment, the location of the United Nations in New York City, and a general rise in interest in cultures beyond U.S. borders.[18] Patrons of such theaters have usually been described as more 'sophisticated' and 'educated' than the average moviegoer, and this may have been the case to some degree. However, foreign films had had a history in the United States in the twenty-five years prior to the end of World War II that was closely tied to the exploitation film.

[. . .]

Critics sought to make distinctions between the 'entertainment' provided by American films and the 'art' of foreign pictures. A review of *Ecstasy* in the *New York Post* claimed, 'True, the picture is, like many of its "arty" cousins, un-Americanly frank, yet typical of those ventures of certain foreign studios to which the cinema is a true art itself.'[18] The *Philadelphia Exhibitor* considered the film 'a distinct tonic to the art theaters' – the few that existed at the time – and commended its direction, photography, and casting.[19] On the other hand, in condemning the film, the Legion of Decency blasted its 'heavy handed symbolism.'[20] Foreignness, art, and obscenity were conflated. Because foreign films spilled over categories, because they were narratives, because they contained the spectacle of exploitation films, because they employed symbolism and made use of modernist techniques, because they could play in the few existing art theaters as well as Main Street houses that specialized in exploitation films, they were not contained within traditional boundaries and thus were obscene.

When increased numbers of foreign films were released in the United States after World War II, precedent for selling them to skeptical American audiences had already been set. Arthur Mayer, who with Joseph Burstyn would bring many of the classics of Italian neo-realism to U.S. shores, recalled, 'The only sensational successes scored by Burstyn and myself in the fifteen years in which we were engaged in business were the pictures whose artistic and ideological merits were aided and abetted at the box office by their frank sex content. These we were able to exhibit profitably in big theaters as well as small.'[21] According to Mayer, *Open City* (1945) was usually advertised with a misquoted line from *Life* magazine that read, 'Sexier than Hollywood ever dared to be,' coupled with 'a still of two young ladies deeply engrossed in a rapt embrace, and another of a man being flogged, designed to tap the sadist trade.'[22] Advertising for *Paisan* (1946) featured a young woman undressing while a male visitor lounged on a couch. The most highly lauded neorealist film presented something of a problem for exhibitors: '*The Bicycle Thief* [1948] was completely devoid of any erotic embellishments, but exhibitors sought to atone for this deficiency with a highly imaginative sketch of a young lady riding a bicycle. This was not good, or bad, enough, and in spite of the critics' rave reviews it did far less business than either of the others.'[23]

Mayer also recalled that although better 'art' product usually died everywhere outside New York, 'films of a highly sexy nature like *Manon* and *Latuko* were, in territories unencumbered by censors, holding them out in long queues at the so-called art theaters. Simultaneously, *Bitter Rice* was breaking records set by *Open City* and *Paisan*. It had no cinematic merit but it had a bountifully proportioned leading lady, Silvana Mangano.'[24] *Bitter Rice* (1949) was sold with Mangano's physical assets. Her figure and skintight, skimpy attire caught the eye of audiences, reviewers, and the Legion of Decency, as did story elements about childbirth and abortion. Indecorous costuming, nudity, and reproductive health were the topics of exploitation films; to their audience, the source of a film or its intent meant little. Although not an exploitation film, the similarities between *Bitter Rice* and typical grindhouse fare brought down the wrath of moralists. Legion officials found *Bitter Rice* 'a serious threat to Christian morality and decency,' and William Mooring, writing in *Tidings*, attempted to tie the film to the International Communist Conspiracy.[25] Illustrating how powerful the sex angle could be, *Variety* indicated that the average foreign film made 60 percent of its revenues in New York, whereas 'sexacious pix or those with a good exploitation angle garner 25% from Gotham and the balance from the hinterlands.'[26]

Friedman has noted that during the 1950s there were two markets for candid films, 'one for the select, sophisticated white-wine-and-canapés crowd, the other, and much larger one, for the less discriminating, cold-beer-and-grease-burger gang. As diverse as the two audiences were, both were intent, oddly enough, on viewing pictures in which human female epidermis was exposed.'[27] During this period, exploitation items such as *Latuko* played in the growing number of art houses as well as grindhouses. Foreign films slipped from venue to venue as well. Ingmar Bergman's *Summer with Monika* (1953) was screened by exploitation mogul Kroger Babb, who, according to Friedman, 'saw pronounced profit possibilities in [Harriet] Andersson's bare behind by eschewing the artsy orbit and bringing the movie to the hoi polloi.'[28] The film's ninety-five-minute running time was chopped to sixty-two minutes (retaining the crucial nude swim sequence), dubbed in what Babb called 'American' English, supplied with a new score by the popular Les Baxter, and renamed *Monika, the Story of a Bad Girl*.[29] Advertising art that displayed the title character's bare behind was concocted, along with Friedman's tag line, 'A Picture for Wide Screens and Broad Minds,' which played on the 1950s' big-screen phenomenon but had nothing to do with the film's aspect ratio. *Monika* also played the art house circuit in its original form. Other movies such as Roger Vadim's *And God Created Woman* (1957) moved from art house to grindhouse with no alternation.

By the early 1960s, the terms art theater and art film had become synonymous with nudity, completing the cycle begun with *Ecstasy*.[30] Exploitation director Barry Mahon could claim, 'So-called exploitation pictures originally started with the idea that it's European, therefore it's artistic and consequently it's risqué.'[31] In his classic 1968 study of film censorship, Richard S. Randall reasoned that, 'though the art film does not inherently press against the limits of acceptability as does the exploitation film, its potential for becoming a source of censorship of one kind or another remains. "Artistic sovereignty," taken seriously by many art film proprietors, is an uneasy companion to self-restraint, if in fact the two elements can coexist at all.'[32] The early sexploitation distributors and producers were willing to press the limits of acceptability in the name of art if that meant reaching a broader audience. Have a foreign film that wasn't risqué enough? A little doctoring gave audiences what they expected to see on the screen. New York-based distributor William Mishkin regularly added inserts of nudity and soft-core sex to the films he imported, as did Radley Metzger for his company, Audubon Films. *Variety* later described the process for a Cambist Films release: 'Original version of [*The Female*] was directed by Torre Niellson and was Argentina's official entry at Cannes in 1961 and a winner the same year at the San Sebastian fest. [Lee Hessel, president of Cambist Films,] bought the U.S. rights, re-edited to speed up the slow pace and added sex scenes. Result? A dirty art house playoff. This combination of art and sex is particularly effective in smaller situations where people will flock to see the same film at an art house they would not go near in a sex house.'[33] Adding sex scenes after a film had been imported was also a way of avoiding problems with U.S. Customs. A number of the theaters that had oscillated between art films and exploitation in the postwar period gradually began to specialize in one form or the other by the end of the 1950s. According to Friedman, Louis K. Sher's Art Theatre Guild, headquartered in Columbus, Ohio, was one chain that made the switch from an art cinema policy to adult films when Sher discovered that it was the skin that was bringing the audiences in.[34]

Sexploitation

The combination of nudity, more daring story lines, and the association with 'art' helped films such as *The Twilight Girls* (1961), *The Fourth Sex* (1962), and *Sexus* (1964) push old-line exploitation out of the picture. They were being imported by a new breed of exploiteer, Radley Metzger, for example, looking for fresh terrain. In turn, those films found competition in increasingly daring homegrown productions. Consequently, distributors such as Mishkin and Metzger turned to production by the mid-1960s. Production of what was coming to be known as 'sexploitation' began in the United States around 1960 and, in combination with more daring European product and factors mentioned above, put the final nail in the coffin of classical exploitation.

The film most often credited with inaugurating the sexploitation era, and the first of the nudie-cuties, was Russ Meyer's *The Immoral Mr. Teas* (1959). Meyer had been an Army Signal Corps photographer during World War II. During the postwar years, he made industrial films and shot cheesecake photographs and early *Playboy* centerfolds. He also did the cinematography for Pete DeCenzie's burley film, *French Peep Show* (1950), and the abortion picture *The Desperate Women* (1954), in which his wife, eventual coproducer, and sometime star, Eve Meyer, had a role. In 1958, DeCenzie asked Russ Meyer to make a nudist film. Reluctant to work in the genre, allegedly because of its noneretic context, Meyer made *The Immoral Mr. Teas* with DeCenzie for $24,000. It has been described as *Monsieur Hulot's Holiday* with naked women. David K. Frasier has observed that 'in content and theme *Teas* is a literal translation of what [Meyer] had been doing for *Playboy*, a movie version of the girlie magazine.'[35] The loose story follows Bill Teas, one of Meyer's old army buddies, a modern Everyman. Teas delivers false teeth on a bicycle and in his travels comes across a series of women who wear low-cut blouses and dresses. Teas also spends some time peeping on a stripper at a burlesque show. While under sedation to have a tooth removed, he fantasizes that the dentist's attractive female assistant is nude. Teas continues to fantasize about naked women on and off the job. The narration asks, 'Has pressure of modern living begun its insidious task of breaking down the moral fiber of our indomitable Mr. Teas?' Teas visits a psychiatrist, but when he imagines her nude as well, he happily resigns himself to his condition.

Its title notwithstanding, *The Immoral Mr. Teas* was not particularly immoral, and despite Meyer's objections to the lack of eroticism in the nudist genre, *Mr. Teas* was no more arousing than the run-of-the-mill volleyball games and sunbathing in those films. Still, the movie proved to be significant for two reasons: first as a decisive break from classical exploitation and second as a compass that pointed to the trajectory of sexploitation. On the surface, *Mr. Teas*'s questions about modern life and its sexually frustrated protagonist appear to tie it to the critique of modernity found in the classical exploitation films of Esper and others. Yet *Mr. Teas* is played for ironic laughs throughout, setting it apart in tone and ideological stance from classical exploitation. Moreover, *Mr. Teas* and the sexploitation films that followed seldom made use of a prefatory square-up. The lack of a square-up was perhaps the greatest point of divergence between classical exploitation and sexploitation and a clear indicator of the changed moral climate. Sexploitation films can best be described as exploitation movies that focused on nudity, sexual situations, and simulated (i.e., nonexplicit) sex acts, designed for titillation and entertainment. Such films no longer required explicit educational justification for presenting sexual spectacle on the screen – although they often made claims of social or artistic merit as a strategy for legal protection.

The postwar economic boom, driven by uninhibited consumption, furthered the transition from a production-based economy to one fueled by consumer activity. By the early 1960s, sexual desire, especially male sexual desire, was economically legitimate. *Playboy* and its imitators, *The Immoral Mr. Teas* and the dozens of nudie-cuties that followed provided, at one and the same time, an escape from the rigors of the 9-to-5 grind and the breadwinner ethic and a headlong plunge into the consumption that was the end result of the job. As Barbara Ehrenreich has written, 'For all its potential disruptiveness, *Playboy* was immune to the standard charges leveled against male deviants. You couldn't call it anti-capitalist or unAmerican, because it was all about making money and spending it.'[36] If the new sexploitation films did not wax philosophical about consumption in the same overt way that *Playboy* did, they were still a manifestation of the economic changes that had increasingly expanded the acceptable sphere of desire.

The expansion of that acceptable sphere of desire would escalate in the 1960s. Sexploitation films would diversify, with subgenres including 'roughies' and 'kinkies' by the middle of the decade as well as a number of cycles: the suburban exposé, the costume picture, the campus film, the hillbilly movie, and so on. Of particular significance was the growing recognition of the desire of women, younger people, and those deemed to be in some way 'deviant.' In acknowledging the legitimate sexualization of the Other, sexploitation films contributed to an increasing 'democratization.' Lawrence Birken notes that 'sexualization appears apocalyptic because it is symbolic of the extension of the democratic model of society to its furthest limit.'[37] This active period of democratisation, generally referred to as the sexual revolution, was marked by a moral panic unmatched since the early part of the century. Sexploitation reigned from about 1960 to a point in the late 1970s when its content, like classical exploitation before it, was absorbed into mainstream movies – *Summer School Teachers* (1975), *Porky's* (1981), and others – and hard-core features gained a firm foothold in the theatrical market. With the advent of theatrical hard-core, the spectacle that classical exploitation could only hint at through nudity and the aftereffects of sex was finally on the public screen.

[. . .]

NOTES

1. Kroger Babb, 'We've Got the Ball!' *Hallmark of Hollywood Pipeline*, extra ed. (Hollywood: Hallmark, 1971).
2. See, for example, 'The Big Leer,' *Time*, 9 June 1961, 55–6; John Crosby, 'Speaking Out: Movies Are Too Dirty,' *Saturday Evening Post*, 10 November 1962, 8–10; Don Wharton, 'How to Stop the Movies' Sickening Exploitation of Sex,' *The Reader's Digest*, March 1961, 37–40; Bosley Crowther, 'Sex in the Movies,' *Coronet*, June 1961, 44–8; 'Sex and Celluloid,' *Newsweek*, 11 December 1961, 57. Among the other major films evoked in the articles were *The Dark at the Top of the Stairs* (1960), *Elmer Gantry* (1960), *Psycho* (1960), *Breakfast at Tiffany's* (1961), and *Go Naked in the World* (1961).
3. Edward de Grazia and Roger K. Newman, *Banned Films: Movies, Censors, and the First Amendment* (New York: Bowker, 1982), 91.
4. Ibid., 93–4.
5. Ibid., 92.
6. For those unfamiliar with all the details of this important case, see de Grazia and Newman, *Banned Films*, 77–83, and Ellen Draper, ' "Controversy has probably destroyed forever the context": *The Miracle* and Movie Censorship in America in the Fifties,' *The Velvet Light Trap* 25 (spring 1990): 69–79.
7. See de Grazia and Newman, *Banned Films*, 83–4.
8. Ibid., 234–5.
9. Ibid., 84.
10. Quoted in ibid., 85.
11. Thomas Doherty, *Teenagers and Teenpics: The Juvenilization of American Movies in the 1950s* (Boston: Unwin Hyman, 1988), 29–30.
12. Ibid., 34.
13. Ibid., 36.
14. Take, for example, Klaytan W. Kirby's *A Virgin in Hollywood* (1952), which cost $17,000 even though it featured a 'name' in Dorothy Abbott, a regular on TV's *Dragnet*.
15. Sam Arkoff with Richard Trubo, *Flying Through Hollywood by the Seat of My Pants*. (New York: Birch Lane Press, 1992), 46.
16. Ibid., 66–7.
17. Douglas Gomery, *Shared Pleasures: A History of Movie Presentation in the United States* (Madison: University of Wisconsin Press, 1992), 186.
18. Review of *Ecstasy*, *The New York Post*, 25 April 1936, n.p.
19. Review of *Ecstasy*, *Philadelphia Exhibitor*, 15 May 1936, 49.
20. Review of *Ecstasy*, *National Legion of Decency*, 21 May 1936, n.p.
21. Arthur Mayer, *Merely Colossal* (New York: Simon & Schuster, 1953), 233.
22. Ibid.
23. Ibid., 233–4.
24. Ibid., 234.
25. James M. Skinner, *The Cross and the Cinema: The Legion of Decency and the National Catholic Office for Motion Pictures, 1933–1970* (Westport, CT: Praeger, 1993), 94.
26. 'Sexacious Sellin Best B.O. Slant for Foreign Language Films in U.S.,' *Variety*, 9 June 1948, 18.
27. David F. Friedman with Don De Nevi, *A Youth in Babylon: Confessions of a Trash-Film King* (Buffalo, NY: Prometheus Books, 1990), 100.
28. Ibid., 101.
29. Ibid.
30. See, for instance, 'The Nudeniks,' *Time*, 23 June 1961, 51.

31. Gordon Hitchens, 'The Truth, the Whole Truth, and Nothing but the Truth about Exploitation Films with Barry Mahon,' *Film Comment* 2, no. 2 (1964): 10.
32. Richard S. Randall, *Censorship of the Movies: The Social and Political Control of a Mass Medium* (Madison: University of Wisconsin Press, 1968), 219.
33. 'N.Y. Over-Seated for Sex,' *Variety*, 3 July 1969, 70.
34. David F. Friedman, personal interview, 14 April 1994.
35. David K. Frasier, *Russ Meyer – The Life and Films* (Jefferson, NC: McFarland, 1990), 5.
36. Barbara Ehrenreich, *The Hearts of Men: American Dreams and the Flight from Commitment* (New York: Anchor Books, 1984), 50.
37. Lawrence Birken, *Consumer Desire: Sexual Science and the Emergence of a Culture of Abundance, 1871–1914* (Ithaca, NY: Cornell University Press, 1988), 12.

17

RADICALISM, REVOLUTION AND COUNTER-CINEMA

The success of the postwar art cinema reawakened an awareness of the possibilities of cinema, and created a sense of dissatisfaction with established cinematic traditions, particularly those of Hollywood. The second half of the 1960s, therefore, saw a surge in alternative filmmaking around the world. This period also witnessed the growth of left-wing radicalism as revolutionary struggles in the Third World inspired one another and motivated student radicalism in Europe and the United States.

Stylistically, this radicalism manifested itself in two main ways. On the one hand, there was an interest in both realism and documentary, in which filmmakers sought to engage audiences politically by exposing social processes and conditions. On the other hand, there was an interest in avant-garde strategies that were designed to challenge audiences' perceptions and question the ideological workings of cinema itself. While these two trends were often opposed to one another in rhetoric, they were rarely as distinct as this rhetoric might suggest. The realists and documentary filmmakers were often highly experimental while the avant-gardists often tackled overtly political content.

For example, *The Battle for Algiers* (1965) is often presented as a key impetus in the development of Third World cinema. Although directed by an Italian director, Pontecorvo, it was made by the Algerian government as a way of celebrating its independence from France after a long and bitter struggle. The film, therefore, tells a story of inspirational fighters within the Franco-Algerian war, and it employs a documentary style to create a sense of realism and authenticity. Despite its clear sympathies and allegiances, the film refuses to become mere propaganda but constantly demonstrates the complexity of the anti-colonial struggle and of people's situation within it. It is also continually concerned to emphasise the unreliability of visual reality.

One of the most fascinating figures in the film is therefore not one of the revolutionaries but rather the vicious French officer sent in to stamp out the rebellion, and the film makes great efforts to understand its enemy, rather than present him as a caricature. He is also visually distinguished by his dark sunglasses, an image that has become commonplace now but emphasises his implacable investigating gaze. His job is to reveal that which is hidden, to root out the ringleaders from the mazes of the Algerian city, while they hide in its busy narrow streets and, in one scene, literally are concealed behind a false wall. The Algerians also use disguise against their enemy in other ways, and in one of the most discussed scenes in the film, young Algerian women dress up in Western clothing so that they can infiltrate the French colonial city where they launch a bombing campaign.

While Algeria turned to a European director to tell its story, Latin America began to call for a cinema that rejected Western models of filmmaking. The most influential Latin American movement was Cinema Novo, which emerged in Brazil after its failed attempt to create a postwar commercial cinema. Although Brazilian filmmakers were initially influenced by Italian neo-realism and the French New Wave, many started to call for the creation of indigenous forms of filmmaking. It was often claimed that Latin America was *under*-developed rather than *un*developed, by which it was meant that the problem was not that it had failed to catch up with the West, but rather that its exploitation by the West had forced it into a position of dependence that had corrupted it. Furthermore, the filmmakers called for an end to not only economic dependence but also cultural dependence.

It is therefore significant that while Cinema Novo began during a period of political liberalism and economic prosperity, a military coup soon transformed the country and, ironically, intensified the radicalism of filmmakers associated with the movement. The coup blocked liberal hopes and forced filmmakers into a more strident position. It also blocked a sense of national possibility and led increasingly to identification with Latin America as a whole, and even the Third World in general.

One of the key filmmakers of the movement was Glauber Rocha whose now classic essay, 'An Esthetic of Hunger', called for filmmakers to see their own scarce resources positively insofar as that scarcity enabled them to develop new techniques and so assert their difference from Western models. He called for 'sad, ugly films' that would 'ultimately make the public aware of its own misery'. As a result, his films demonstrate a fascination with the folk cultures of the impoverished Brazilian communities outside the modern cities. *Barravento* (1962), for example, concerns the exploitation of a small fishing community, while *Black God, White Devil* (1964) concerns an assassin who is hired by business interests to kill a local bandit in the Brazilian outlands. This story is continued in *Antonio de Mortes* (1969), which is set thirty years after the murder when the assassin is forced to realise that the killing of the bandit has not improved the region but only enabled the business interests to intensify their exploitation of it.

While the radicalism of Brazil was a reaction to political repression, the radicalism of Cuba was the product of popular revolution in the late 1950s. The revolution also made Fidel Castro's Cuba the object of intense political opposition from the United States, which supported an abortive counter-revolution known as the Bay of Pigs in 1961 and brought the world to the brink of nuclear war during the Cuban missile crisis of 1962. The revolutionary government saw cinema as one way of chronicling the revolution and spreading its message to a largely illiterate population and it invested heavily in film production. By the end of the decade, Cuban cinema had proved highly productive and enjoyed an impressive reception in international art cinema.

Internationally, the most celebrated Cuban film is almost definitely Tomas Gutierrez Alea's *Memories of Underdevelopment* (1968), which concerns an intellectual, Sergio, who has refused to flee Cuba for the United States but who cannot commit himself to the revolution. In the process, he is rendered politically and emotionally impotent, and finds himself intellectually unproductive. Consequently, the film concerns the classic alienated bourgeois intellectual of European art cinema, but it also mixes fictional storytelling with documentary footage to create dramatic contrasts and to challenge the audience. The ending, for example, cuts between footage of the Cuban missile crisis and Sergio's penthouse to emphasise the relationships and disjuncture between the two. The film is, therefore, far from simply realist but actually encourages audiences to compare and contrast various different types of filmmaking and the politics of representation that they involve.

Much the same is also true of the Argentinian film, *Hour of the Furnaces* (1968), which is both documentary and avant-garde in its techniques. In other words, the film is largely constructed out of documentary and found footage but it involves a complex process of montage that suggests that truth does not lie in the meaning of any one visual image but rather in the relationship between them. In one particularly celebrated moment, for example, the film alternates between commercials for soft drinks and the slaughter of a bull (the Argentinian economy was largely based on the export of its beef products to the United States and Europe). In this way, the film actively encourages its audience to think about the relationship between different images: it even encourages audiences to take breaks in which to discuss the issues raised by the film. As the film announces at one point: 'Now it's up to you to draw conclusions, to continue the film. You have the floor.'

One must be careful assessing these films, given that their reputation is largely based on their reception by international art cinema audiences. Many claims have been made about their formal features but little exists on how they were actually consumed, if at all, by indigenous popular audiences. There is also the problem of deciding how representative they were. It is clear from reviews of *Memories of Underdevelopment* in the United States that it was largely well received because critics saw it as a film about bourgeois alienation that was similar to the films being produced in European art cinema. Even more significantly, while *Hour of the Furnaces* is actually a three-part documentary, it is rarely shown in its entirety. It is the first part that presents a critique of neo-colonialism that is shown most often, while the second two parts that concern the Argentine more specifically are seldom screened. The first plays well to Western guilt about exploitation of other countries, but Western audiences seem to show little interest in the specifics of the countries that they exploit.

This is also a problem when assessing the history of African cinema. As we have seen, while there was very definitely a film culture in Africa prior to the 1960s, it largely revolved around the consumption of films from Europe and the United Sates and, in many African countries, it was only after independence that indigenous film industries began to emerge. Even then many countries did not have the resources for a film industry and, as a result, African cinema is often identified with the work of Ousmane Sembene. In fact Sembene was largely trained outside Africa and is often celebrated because he fits Western notions of authorship. His career started in France where he began publishing fiction in French, but with the independence of his home state, Senegal, he decided that cinema was a more appropriate way of addressing the largely illiterate population of that country. He received his film training in the Soviet Union and, on his return to Senegal, made a series of films that dealt with neo-colonial exploitation including *Black Girl* (1966), *The Money Order* (1968), *Xala* (1974) and *Ceddo* (1977). *Black Girl* tells the story of a young girl who works as a maid for a French family and is driven to suicide, while *Xala* concerns the fate of Senegal after independence. It starts with the expulsion of French business interests which return to Senegal in the form of advisors and corrupt the newly independent Senegalese businessmen. One such businessman celebrates his new-found wealth by taking a new wife but discovers that he has been cursed with impotence. In the process, his life gradually unravels and he loses everything. Finally, he has to debase himself in order to be free of the curse.

Unlike the Latin American filmmakers, Sembene's style is very traditional and he uses neither their documentary nor their avant-garde techniques. Elsewhere the period was a golden age for documentary. In the early 1960s, as we have seen, Jean Rouch had pioneered *cinéma vérité*, and direct cinema had grown out of the work done by Drew and Associates for Time-Life (see Chapter 16). These films were followed by a series of documentaries later in the decade, such as those associated with D. A. Pennebaker, who used the new lightweight cameras and synchronised sound for *Don't Look Back* (1967), a film that followed Bob Dylan's tour of Britain in the mid-1960s, and *Monterey Pop* (1968), a film that documented a rock festival of the late 1960s.

Another key documentary director of the period was the American Frederick Wiseman, whose films largely concentrated on institutions such as hospitals.

Rather than telling the stories of individuals or structuring his films around a central problem or crisis, he tried to give a sense of the institution by moving between different scenes with different participants. While it is easy to view these films as attempting to attain objectivity with the filmmaker as simply recording an objective reality, Wiseman and others were often explicit in their view that their films were aesthetic creations devised according to specific principles and, therefore, they created a world that did not exist before the film. It is not that they played fast and loose with the worlds that they represented, but rather that they were self-conscious about the processes of representation that they used. While we might criticise those processes, it cannot be on the grounds that they lacked self-consciousness.

In addition to these films and filmmakers, the documentary form was also used for a series of political ends, particularly in opposition to the Vietnam War. Its aesthetics were also used by fiction filmmakers such as Ken Loach, whose highly political films of the late 1960s often deployed non-professional actors and other techniques to create a sense of documentary realism. In *Kes* (1969), Loach explored the brutalisation of the British working class through the story of a young boy who becomes attached to a kestrel, a bird of prey that is eventually killed out of spite by the boy's own family. The politics of the family is also central to Ken Loach's *Family Life* (1971), which draws on the radical psychotherapy of R. D. Laing, and tells the story of a young woman's psychological breakdown. Haskell Wexler's *Medium Cool* (1969), on the other hand, was highly praised in the period for its mingling of fiction and documentary footage to examine the politics of representation in 1960s America. The film concerns a documentary filmmaker who is filming the turmoil surrounding the 1968 National Convention of the Democratic Party. Although he starts out with a purely professional attitude to his craft, he becomes increasingly aware of the politics of his representational practices.

If the period therefore witnessed an upsurge of dissent in the Third World, the United States and Western Europe, dissent was also a key feature of cinema from behind the Iron Curtain. For a time, it even seemed that the Eastern bloc would see the end of the old regimes bolstered by the Soviet Union. The Prague Spring of 1968 exemplified these changes, although this brief period of reform was brutally suppressed by the Soviet military in August of the same year. In this period, political liberalisation was accompanied by the blossoming of the Czech New Wave of which Milos Forman was a key figure. His most famous film, *The Firemen's Ball* (1967), is a comedy that revolves around the retirement party for a departing fire chief, which descends into chaos and so exposes greed and corruption.

In Yugoslavia, Dušan Makavejev became known for his surreal films concerning sex and sexuality. *W. R. Mysteries of the Organism* (1971) used documentary footage and presented itself as a biography of the radical sexual theorist Wilhelm Reich, but it is essentially a wild, libertarian attack on Soviet communism. Despite the importance of sexual liberation to the early agenda of Soviet communism, and its continual significance within left thought throughout the century, Makavejev attacked the Soviet communism of his day and the film called for a properly libertarian socialism. As one woman in the film claims, 'Communism without free love is a wake in a graveyard.' None of Makavejev's surrealism could prepare one for Sergei Paradzhanov's *The Colour of Pomegranates* (1968), a magnificently visual and experimental film that is based on the life of the Armenian poet Sayat Nova. Rather than present a traditional biography of the poet's life, the film attempts to capture the author's poetic imagery and creates something unique and quite extraordinary. Unfortunately, although it was made in 1969, the authorities suppressed the film for two years and even then the director was imprisoned in 1974 on a series of charges.

The undisputed international star of experimental cinema in the late 1960s was Jean-Luc Godard. Although he had started as a figure of the French New Wave, he came into conflict with figures such as Truffaut and broke with classical narration. He developed a self-reflexive style that continually disrupted and examined the established forms of cinema. For example, he frequently used direct address (in which actors spoke to the camera) in order to shatter the illusion that the audience was watching an objective reality and, through devices such as these, he sought to force audiences to become aware of the ideological nature of film language. Although such techniques may seem strange today, Godard was taken very seriously at the time – he had huge intellectual cachet and was as 'cool' as any contemporary director. He was the product of a very particular intellectual climate that was to reach a climax in May 1968 when students and workers took to the streets. Inspired by revolutionary movements abroad, there was a genuine sense that revolution was inevitable. Furthermore, influenced by structuralist and Marxist theory, they believed that the key to revolution was the disruption of all cultural systems of meaning, of which film language was a particular example.

Another important context was the influence of Maoism during the late 1960s. Many shared the feelings expressed in the Eastern bloc countries that Soviet communism no longer offered a desirable alternative to capitalism, and turned to Mao Tse Tung's China for such an alternative. Furthermore, China was currently going through the Cultural Revolution and, while it would later be revealed to have been deeply problematic, this movement seemed to offer the model of a truly revolutionary rethinking of all institutions and ideologies, a truly revolutionary rejection of established systems of authority. Maoism was therefore the subject of Godard's 1967 classic, *La Chinoise*, in which a group of Maoists debate politics and make declarations on the state of contemporary society and culture. The film lacks almost any narrative or any sense of engagement with the participants, and it is therefore unclear how their politics is to be judged. Are they just middle-class students, self-indulgently performing politics in a protected environment that is disconnected from the world beyond, or do they offer a fundamental challenge to established ideologies?

Moreover, is the film unconcerned with the content of what is said or simply a formal exercise that forces the spectator to confront the nature of cinematic conventions?

Similarly, *Weekend* (1968) is a bizarre depiction of social breakdown in which a middle-class couple take a weekend break. Bourgeois life is ridiculed and condemned throughout the film, which is famous for its lengthy portrayal of an extremely bloody and absurd car wreck. Again, the insubstantial narrative is continually disrupted by figures unconnected with the narrative, who give speeches to the camera claiming to be characters from fiction, and even God. In the second half, the action shifts to a revolutionary group who seem to have 'gone native' in the woods and in rejecting bourgeois society, engage in all manner of fantastic activities, even cannibalism. Quite what this says about Godard's attitude to the 'primitive' is not clear, but one of the key features of Godard's cinema is its attempt to challenge spectators and force them to work to make sense of his films rather than engage in the forms of passive consumption that he associated with mainstream cinema.

At one level, Godard's influence has been huge, and figures such as Tarantino still reference him. However, few have actually taken his avant-garde techniques much further. Laura Mulvey and Peter Wollen claim to be highly indebted to him but they are still better known for their film theory than for *Riddles of the Sphinx* (1977), a film that explores many of the issues that Mulvey also tackled in her now classic essay, 'Visual Pleasure and Narrative Cinema'. In other words, the film looks at the way in which the figure of woman is constructed as an image, an object of narrative desire rather than its subject. Similar issues are also explored in Sally Potter's *Thriller* (1979), in which the heroine of *La Bohème*, returns from the dead to explore how things might have been different had she been the subject rather than the object of the opera's narrative.

It is Chantal Ackerman's *Jeanne Dielman, 23, Quai du Commerce, 1080, Bruxelles* (1976) that is probably the most significant example of avant-garde feminism. The film follows its central character through one day in her life as a housewife, and spends its 225 minutes in detailing the minutiae of the daily domestic tasks that most films exclude. In this way, it challenges the narrative priorities of most cinematic narrative but it also details the gradual breakdown of her routines, which eventually results in the stabbing of her client: for Jeanne is not just a housewife but also a prostitute, and the film suggests that both are virtually interchangeable forms of economic and sexual exploitation. It is also interesting in that while many films of the period examined the violence of oppressed groups and celebrated that violence as a liberating and moral rejection of oppression, the violence in Ackerman's film is a reaction to the tiny details of Jeanne's everyday life and is not directed at a clearly identified enemy. As the film suggests, the forces that oppress women are integral to the fabric of everyday life and, as a result, far more difficult to identify and oppose.

One of the problems with film history is the inevitable focus on those cinemas, such as Hollywood, that dominate world markets, and Randal Johnson's study of Cinema Novo is part of an attempt to counter this problem. It is also part of a larger history of Brazilian cinema that is outlined in the introduction to the groundbreaking collection, *Brazilian Cinema*, that he edited with Robert Stam. It therefore represents an absolutely indispensable kind of research, which is a pre-condition for later research: the mapping of the key historical shape of an under-researched area of cinema. In the process, Johnson sets out to provide a sense of the main historical and cultural contexts for Brazilian cinema and its development, and to map the key films and tendencies. Given the nature of his subject, this also involves a political history in which the political conditions that shaped Cinema Novo are explored along with the politics of this movement itself.

For Johnson, Cinema Novo needs to be understood in relation to the situation of economical dependence which Brazil experienced as a result of its exploitation by more powerful economies, particularly that of the United States. This situation radicalised its Brazilian intellectuals, which included its filmmakers, and led to a cinema that sought to challenge and oppose the dominance of the United States both economically and culturally. As a result, he is concerned to demonstrate that the difference between the aesthetics of Cinema Novo and Hollywood was not one in which Cinema Novo should simply be judged as inferior but that, on the contrary, Cinema Novo embraced its difference from Hollywood models to which it attempted to offer both an alternative and a critique.

Inevitably this kind of research largely involves the accumulation and synthesis of existing information, and therefore rarely involves much primary historical research, but this should not be seen as a lower form of historical analysis. First, good synthetic research should always go beyond simply bringing existing accounts together, and should seek to work through the conflicts and contradictions between them. In other words, this involves a literature survey that transforms existing understandings of the field by placing contradictory accounts in relationship to one another and trying to resolve the oppositions between them. Second, one can only begin to do more focused historical research once one has a sense of the general shape of the history within which any focused project is located, even if only so that one can dispute assumptions about the general shape of that history. In other words, research that maps areas through synthetic methods is indispensable, so long as we remember the limits and dangers of such work. For example, this work necessarily focuses on key moments, or highlights, within the history and cannot capture the complexities and details of that history. Such limits are not necessarily problems so long as the researchers remain clear that they are constructing a picture in broad strokes; after all, as we have seen, no history can ever hope to be a complete and full account.

- Johnson suggests that Cinema Novo was a political cinema that was not simply the mouthpiece of the state. Can you think of another cinema that could be seen as political in this way?
- What dangers might there be in concentrating on the key points or highlights within a history rather than on the 'ordinary' and the 'everyday'?
- Can you think of other examples where it is worth demonstrating that a certain tradition of filmmaking is different from, rather than inferior to, another, and how might you go about analysing this tradition?

CINEMA NOVO

Randal Johnson

[. . .]

Cinema Novo (and similar movements in theater and popular music) grew out of a process of cultural renovation that began in the early fifties and was strengthened with the election of Juscelino Kubitschek as president in 1955. The period of his presidency was somewhat atypical in terms of the general tendencies of Brazilian political life since the Revolution of 1930 when Getulio Vargas took power, atypical, especially, in its relative stability. Kubitschek was the only civilian president in the 1930–1964 period to remain legally in office throughout his designated term. His administration, characterised by economic expansion and industrialization, was stable for several reasons but primarily because he managed to unite the Brazilian people behind a common ideology: developmentalism.

Developmentalist ideology was, by its nature, riddled with contradictions. A powerful catalyst for popular mobilisation, it was also an effective way of controlling and defusing social and political conflict. The government fanned nationalist sentiment, but at the same time based its economic policy on foreign investment. The administration's open-handed generosity to foreign investors increasingly alienated the left, and the end of Kubitschek's presidency was marked by vocal opposition from many sectors. By 1959, virtually all governmental crises revolved around economic questions such as inflation – one result of developmentalist policies – and the role of foreign capital in the nation's economy. The middle class became increasingly politicized, and power became consolidated in the hands of the industrial bourgeoisie. In the northeast Peasant Leagues led by Francisco Julião pressed for agrarian reform.[1]

We are dealing, then, with a period of apparent economic expansion based on foreign investment, a period of political militancy, strong nationalist

---

Randal Johnson (ed. Robert Stam and Randal Johnson), *Brazilian Cinema* (New York: Columbia University Press, 1995).

sentiments, and increasing social polarization. The Kubitschek years and the early sixties were essentially optimistic: Brazil, it was felt, was on the verge of escaping underdevelopment. The ultra-modern architecture of Brasília symbolizes the euphoric mentality of the period. The optimism and nationalism of the period continued through the 1960 election of Jânio Quadros, his resignation after less than seven months in office, and the presidency of João Goulart until the 1964 military coup that brutally unmasked an already existing structural crisis.

For the purposes of this general overview, we will break down the Cinema Novo movement into several phases, each corresponding to a specific period of Brazilian political life. After a preparatory period running roughly from 1954 to 1960, we see three main phases: a first phase going from 1960 to 1964, the date of the first *coup d'état*; from 1964 to 1968, the date of the second *coup*-within-the-*coup*; and from 1968 to 1972. After 1972, it becomes increasingly difficult to speak of Cinema Novo; one must speak, rather, of Brazilian Cinema. The period leading up to the present is marked by esthetic pluralism under the auspices of the state organ Embrafilme. While such *a posteriori* divisions are artificial and problematic, they are also broadly useful, because they illustrate the inseparable connection between political struggle and cultural production. While on one level Cinema Novo remained faithful to its initial project – to present a progressive and critical vision of Brazilian society – on another, its political strategies and esthetic options were profoundly inflected by political events.

The first signs of a new awakening in Brazilian cinema occurred several years before the official beginnings of the movement, coinciding, ironically, with the bankruptcy of the Vera Cruz Studios. Although Brazilian cinema, out of economic necessity, had always been predominantly non-industrial in its form of production, in the post-Vera Cruz period filmmakers began opting for independent, artisan forms as a matter of esthetic and political choice. Alex Viany's *Agulha no Palheiro* ('Needle in the Haystack,' 1953) attempted for the first time to put the lessons of Italian Neo-Realism into practice in Brazil: films made in natural settings with non-professional actors, popular themes, and a simple, straightforward cinematic language. Even more important was Nelson Pereira dos Santos's *Rio 40 Graus* ('Rio 40 Degrees'). By its independent production and critical stance toward established social structures, this film marked a decisive step toward a new kind of cinema. It is difficult to overestimate the contribution of Nelson Pereira dos Santos to Brazilian cinema. His practical contribution to the formation of Cinema Novo includes, besides *Rio 40 Graus*, the film *Rio Zona Norte* ('Rio Northern Zone,' 1957), the production of Roberto Santos's *O Grande Momento* ('The Great Moment,' 1958) and the editing of several early Cinema Novo films like Rocha's *Barravento* (1962) and Leon Hirszman's *Pedreira de São Diogo* ('São Diogo Quarry,' 1961), which was incorporated into the feature length *Cinco Vezes Favela* ('Favela Five Times,' 1961), an early landmark of Cinema Novo produced by the leftist Popular Center of Culture of the National Students' Union. More important, dos Santos became a kind of generous presiding spirit, the 'conscience,' in Glauber Rocha's words, of Cinema Novo.

The initial phase of Cinema Novo extends from 1960 to 1964, including films completed or near completion when the military overthrew João Goulart on 1 April 1964. It is in this period that Cinema Novo cohered as a movement, that it made its first feature films and formulated its political and esthetic ideas. The journal *Metropolitano* of the Metropolitan Students' Union became a forum for critics like David Neves and Sérgio Augusto and for filmmakers like Rocha and Diegues. The directors shared their opposition to commercial Brazilian cinema, to Hollywood films and Hollywood esthetics, and to Brazilian cinema's colonization by Hollywood distribution chains. In their desire to make independent non-industrial films, they drew on two foreign models: Italian Neo-Realism, for its use of non-actors and location shooting, and the French New Wave, not so much for its thematics or esthetics, but rather as a production strategy. While scornful of the politics of the New Wave – 'We were making political films when the New Wave was still talking about unrequited love,' Carlos Diegues once said – they borrowed its strategy of low-budget independently produced films based on the talent of specific *auteurs*. Most important, these directors saw filmmaking as political praxis, a contribution to the struggle against neo-colonialism. Rather than exploit the tropical paradise conviviality of *chanchada*, or the just-like-Europe classiness of Vera Cruz, the Cinema Novo directors searched out the dark corners of Brazilian life – its *favelas* and its *sertão* – the places where Brazil's social contradictions appeared most dramatically.

The most important films of the first phase of Cinema Novo include *Cinco Vezes Favela*; the short *Arraial do Cabo* (1960) and the feature *Porto das Caixas* (1962) by Paulo César Saraceni; *Barravento* (1962) and *Deus e o Diabo na Terra do Sol* ('Black God, White Devil,' 1964), by Glauber Rocha; *Os Cafajestes* ('The Hustlers,' 1962) and *Os Fuzis* ('The Guns,' 1964), by Mozambican-born Rui Guerra; *Ganga Zumba* (1963), by Carlos Diegues; and *Vidas Secas* ('Barren Lives,' 1963), by Nelson Pereira dos Santos. The films of this phase deal typically, although not exclusively, with the problems confronting the urban and rural lumpen-proletariat: starvation, violence, religious alienation, and economic exploitation. The films share a certain political optimism, characteristic of the developmentalist years, but due as well to the youth of the directors, a kind of faith that merely showing these problems would be a first step toward their solution. *Barravento* exposed the alienating role of religion in a fishing community. *The Guns* and *Barren Lives* dealt with the oppression of peasants by landowners, while *Black God, White Devil* demystified the twin alienations of millennial cults (the black god) and of apolitical *cangaceiro* violence (the white devil). *Ganga Zumba* memorialized the seventeenth-century slave republic of Palmares and called, by historical analogy, for a revolt of the oppressed against their oppressors. Made *for* the people by an educated middle-class radical élite, these films occasionally trans-mitted a paternalistic vision of the Brazilian masses. In *Barravento*, as critic Jean-Claude Bernardet points out, political salvation comes from the city; it is not generated by the community. Esthetically, these 'sad, ugly, desperate films' showed a commitment to what Rocha's manifesto called 'An Esthetic of Hunger,' combining slow, reflexive rhythms with uncompromising, often harsh, images and sounds.

The second phase of Cinema Novo extends from 1964, the year of the first *coup d'état*, through 1968, the year of the *coup*-within-the-*coup* that handed power to even more reactionary sectors of the army. These two events, taken together, constituted an historical cataclysm that left democratic institutions and a political style – populism – in ruins. Democratic forms were replaced by authoritarian military rule; the social gains of the previous era were reversed; laws were signed assuring foreign corporations high profits; and North American capital flowed into Brazil. Many filmmakers, not surprisingly, poked around the smouldering ruins of democratic populism in an attempt to dis-entangle the causes of a disaster of such magnitude. If the films of the first phase were optimistic, those of the second phase are anguished cries of perplexity; they are analyses of *failure* – of populism, of developmentalism, and of leftist intellectuals. Paulo César Saraceni's *O Desafio* ('The Challenge,' 1966), Rocha's *Terra em Transe* ('Land in Anguish,' 1967), Gustavo Dahl's *O Bravo Cuerreiro* ('The Brave Warrior,' 1968), and dos Santos's *Fome de Amor* ('Hunger for Love,' 1968) all dissect the failures of the left. Gustavo Dahl, writing of his own *Bravo Guerreiro*, sums it up:

> In *O Desafio*, in *Land in Anguish*, and in *The Brave Warrior*, there wanders the same personage – a petit-bourgeois intellectual, tangled up in doubts, a wretch in crisis. He may be a journalist, a poet, a legislator, in any case he's always perplexed, hesitating, a weak person who would like to tragically transcend his condition.[2]

Although the left, unprepared for armed struggle, was politically and militarily defeated in 1964, its cultural presence, paradoxically, remained strong even after the *coup d'état*, exercising a kind of hegemony despite the dictatorship. Marxist books proliferated in the bookstores, anti-imperialist plays drew large audiences, and many filmmakers went from left reformism to radical critique. One senses in these films an angry disillusionment with what Roberto Schwarz calls 'the populist deformation of Marxism,' a Marxism that was strong on anti-imperialism but weak on class struggle. The contradictory class-alliances of left populism are satirised in Rocha's *Land in Anguish*, where pompous senators and progressive priests, party intellectuals and military leaders, samba together in what Rocha calls the 'tragic carnival of Brazilian politics.'

If the films of the first phase displayed – Glauber Rocha being the obvious exception – a commitment to realism as a style, the films of the second phase tend toward self-referentiality and anti-illusionism. While the films of the first phase tended to be rural in their setting, films of the second phase were predominantly urban. Luiz Sérgio Person's *São Paulo S.A.* (1965), with its punning title – S.A. means both 'Incorporated' and 'Anonymous Society' – deals with alienated labor and alienated love in São Paulo; Leon Hirszman's *A Falecida* ('The Deceased,' 1965), explores the spiritual torments of the urban middle class; and Carlos Diegues's *A Grande Cidade* ('The Big City,' 1966) treats the fate of impoverished northeasterners in Rio de Janeiro. At the same time, many films were drawn from Brazilian literary classics, notably: Andrade's *O Padre e a Moça* ('The Priest and the Girl,' 1966), based on a poem by Carlos Drummond de Andrade: Walter Lima Jr.'s *Menino de Engenho* ('Plantation Boy,' 1966), based on a novel by José Lins do Rego; and Roberto Santos's *A Hora e Vez de Augusto Matraga* (Matraga, 1966), based on a short story by Guimarães Rosa.

During the second phase of Cinema Novo, filmmakers realised that although their cinema was 'popular' in that it attempted to take the point of view of 'the people,' it was not popular in the sense of having a mass audience. Although the policy of low-budget independent production seemed sound, nothing could guarantee the film's being *shown* in a market dominated by North American conglomerates. If the masses were often on the screen, they were rarely in the audience. The filmmakers linked to Cinema Novo, consequently, began to see the making of popular films as, in Gustavo Dahl's words, 'the essential condition for political action in cinema.'[3] In cinema as in revolution, they decided, everything is a question of power, and for a cinema existing within a system to which it does not adhere, power means broad public acceptance and financial success.

In their efforts to reach the public, Cinema Novo adopted a two-pronged strategy. First, with producer Luiz Carlos Barreto, they founded a distribution co-operative: Difilm. Second, they began making films with more popular appeal. Leon Hirszman's *Garota de Ipanema* ('The Girl from Ipanema,' 1967), the first Cinema Novo feature in color and the first to attempt the new strategy, explored the myth of the sun-bronzed 'girl from Ipanema' in order to demystify that very myth. Joaquim Pedro de Andrade's *Macunaíma* (1969), however, was the first Cinema Novo film to be truly popular in both cultural and box-office terms, offering a dialectical demonstration of how to reach the public without compromising a left political vision of Brazilian society.

Macunaíma is generally classified as part of the third phase of Cinema Novo, the so-called 'cannibal-tropicalist' phase.[4] Tropicalism in the cinema begins around the time of the 1968 *coup*-within-the-*coup* and the promulgation of the Fifth Institutional Act (initiating an extremely repressive period of military rule) and extends roughly to the end of 1971. Because of rigorous censorship, the films of this period tended to work by political indirection, often adopting allegorical forms, as in Andrade's *Macunaíma*, Rocha's *Antônio das Mortes* (1968), dos Santo's *Azyllo Muito Louco* ('The Alienist,' 1969), Guerra's *Os Deuses e os Mortos* ('The Gods and the Dead,' 1970), Diegues's *Os Herdeiros*

('The Heirs,' 1969), dos Santos's *Como Era Gostoso Meu Francês* ('How Tasty Was My Little Frenchman,' 1970), and Jabor's *Pindorama* (1971). An artistic response to political repression, Tropicalism, at least in the cinema, developed a coded language of revolt. *The Alienist*, for example, made subversive use of a literary classic. Based on *The Psychiatrist* by Machado de Assis, it tells the story of a mad psychiatrist-priest who constantly changes his standards for placing people in the local madhouse, a story with obvious implications for military-ruled Brazil. *How Tasty Was My Little Frenchman*, a kind of anthropological fiction, suggested that the Indians (i.e., Brazil) should metaphorically cannibalise their foreign enemies, appropriating their force without being dominated by them. At the same time it criticized the government's genocidal policies toward the Indian as analogous to seventeenth-century massacres.

Tropicalism, a movement that touched music and theater as well as the cinema, emphasised the grotesque, bad taste, *kitsch*, and gaudy colors. It played aggressively with certain myths, especially the notion of Brazil as a tropical paradise characterized by colorful exuberance and tutti-frutti hats à la Carmen Miranda. The movement was not without its ambiguities. Roberto Schwarz, a Brazilian intellectual then living in Paris, interpreted the movement in an article published in *Les Temps Modernes*, 'Remarques sur la Culture et la Politique au Brésil, 1964–1969.' Tropicalism, he suggests, emerges from the tension between the superficial 'modernization' of the Brazilian economy and its archaic, colonized, and imperialized core. While the Brazilian economy, after 1964, was becoming integrated into the world capitalist economy, the petit bourgeoisie was returning to antiquated values and old resentments. 'The basic procedure of such a movement consists in submitting the anachronisms (at first glance grotesque, in reality inevitable) to the white light of the ultra-modern, presenting the result as an allegory of Brazil.'[5]

Concurrent with the third phase of Cinema Novo, there emerged a radically different tendency – *Udigrudi*, the Brazilian pronunciation of 'Underground.' As Cinema Novo decided to reach out for a popular audience, the Underground opted to slap that audience in the face. As Cinema Novo moved toward technical polish and production values, the Novo Cinema Novo, as it also came to be called, demanded a radicalisation of the esthetics of hunger, rejecting the dominant codes of well-made cinema in favor of a 'dirty screen' and 'garbage' esthetics. The Underground proclaimed its own isolation in the names they gave their movement: marginal cinema, subterranean cinema. Although they were intentionally marginal, identifying socially downward with rebellious lumpen characters, they were also *marginalized*, harassed by the censors and boycotted by exhibitors. The movement nurtured a love–hate relationship with Cinema Novo, at times paying homage to its early purity, while lambasting what it saw as its subsequent populist co-optation. In *The Red Light Bandit*, Rogério Sganzerla symbolically puts to flame the St. George triptych from *Antônio das Mortes*, while he spoofs the multi-layered soundtrack of *Land in Anguish*. Some of the important names and titles in this diverse and prolific movement are: Rogério Sganzerla (*O Bandido Da Luz Vermelha*; 'The Red Light Bandit,' 1968); Júlio Bressane (*Matou a Familia e ao Cinema*; Killed the Family and Went to the Movies,' 1970); João Trevisan (*Orgia ou o Homen Que Deu Cria*; 'Orgy, or the Man Who Gave Birth,' 1970); Andrea Tonacci (*Bangue Bangue*; 'Bang Bang,' 1971); André Luiz de Oliveira (*Meteorango Kid: O Herói Intergaláctico*: 'Meteorango Kid: Intergalactic Hero,' 1969); José Mojica Marins (*À Meia-Noite Encarnarei No Teu Cadáver*; 'At Midnight I Will Incarnate Your Corpse,' 1967); Ozualdo Candeias (*A Margem*; The Margin,' 1967); Neville Duarte d'Almeida (*Jardim de Guerra*; 'War Garden,' 1970); and Luiz Rosemberg Filho (*America do Sexo*; 'America of Sex,' 1970).

Toward the end of what we have called the Tropicalist phase, Cinema Novo entered into a politically engendered crisis of creativity that reached its nadir in 1971–1972. As censorship and repression worsened Glauber Rocha, Rui Guerra, and Carlos Diegues left Brazil for Europe. As funding became more problematic, several directors undertook co-productions with other countries or completely financed their projects abroad. Joaquim Pedro de Andrade's *Os Inconfidentes* ('The Conspirators,' 1972) was produced by and for Italian television. Nelson Pereira dos Santos's *Quem é Beta?* ('Who Is Beta?' 1973) was a co-production with France. Gustavo Dahl's *Uirá, um Indio a Procura de Deus* ('Uirá, an Indian in Search of God,' 1973), was a co-production with Italian television.

Around this time, a flood of vapid erotic comedies – *pornochanchadas* – rushed into the vacuum left by political censorship and departing filmmakers. Taken together, these films offer a cinematic portrait of the sexual alienation of the Brazilian petite-bourgeoisie; they exalt the good bourgeois life of fast cars, wild parties, and luxurious surroundings, while offering the male voyeur titillating shots of breasts and buttocks. Their titles give some indication of their vulgarity; *Um Soutien Para Papai* ('A Bra for Daddy'), *Essas Mulheres Lindas, Nuas e Maravilhosas* ('Those Beautiful, Naked, Marvelous Women'), *Mais ou Menos Virgem* ('More or Less Virgin'), *As Secretárias . . . Que Fazem de Tudo* ('Secretaries . . . Who Do Everything'), and *A Virgem e o Machão* ('The Virgin and the Macho'). Sexist and reactionary, these films are also anti-erotic and moralistic. Rather than deliver on the erotic promise implicit in their titles, they offer instead frequent nudity and perpetual *coitus interruptus*. The military regime, phenomenally alert to violations of 'morality' in the films of the more politicized directors, has hypocritically tolerated, indeed encouraged, these productions.

[. . .]

NOTES

1. For a discussion of this period see Maria Victória de Mesquita Benevides, *O Governo Kubitschek: Desenvolvimento Econômico e Estabilidade Política* (Rio de Janerio: Editora Paz e Terra, 1976).
2. From the Difilm Distribution notes to *O Bravo Guerrerio*.

3. Gustavo Dahl et al., 'Situation et Perspective du Cinéma d'Amerique Latine.' *Positif* 139 (June 1972): 2.
4. The cannibalist metaphor goes back to the Brazilian modernist movement of the twenties. 'Only cannibalism unites us,' proclaimed modernist poet-novelist-dramatist-critic Oswald de. Andrade, 'Tupi or not Tupi – that is the question.' Through the metaphor of cannibalism, Brazilian artists thumbed their nose at their own 'palefaces' and at over-cultivated Europe, while heeding surrealism's call for 'savagery' in art.
5. Roberto Schwarz, 'Remarques sur la Culture et la Politique au Brésil: 1964–1969,' *Les Temps Modernes* 288 (1970): 52.

18

MODERNISM, NOSTALGIA AND THE HOLLYWOOD RENAISSANCE

During the late 1960s and early 1970s, the United States was torn by internal conflict as divisions between young and old, black and white, and left and right became increasingly polarised. As a result, it is hardly surprising that the Hollywood cinema of this period displayed so many tensions and contradictions. While this can be seen as the period of Hollywood modernism, in which a series of films and filmmakers displayed the influence of the international art cinema, it can also been seen as one in which Hollywood cinema incorporated other cinemas, containing their threat by absorbing that which was threatening. In political terms, this can also be seen as both an era of political radicalism in which a whole series of aspects of American culture and society were criticised and as one of conservatism in which there was an attack on the claims and gains made by the left.

In the mid-1960s, the industry was threatened by a series of costly financial failures such as the musicals *Dr Doolittle* (1967) and *Star!* (1968). As a reaction to its declining audiences and in the aftermath of some major hits such as *The Sound of Music* (1965), the industry had invested heavily in a series of big budget productions many of which seriously underperformed and by 1969, the industry as a whole was in serious financial difficulty. In 1968, MGM even saw itself acquired by Kirk Kerkorian who stripped the company and sold off its assets.

In this climate, the industry went through a major rethink of its strategy. Previously it had courted the family market and even though it didn't expect members of the family necessarily to see films together, it made films on the understanding that the films should be able to play to children and not just adults.

However, after the financial success of films such as *Who's Afraid of Virginia Woolf?* (1966), the code, which was supposed to guarantee that the films made were suitable for the family audience, was replaced by a rating system. This meant that films were freer to court adult audiences through adult material, although this often meant that they courted youth audiences with previously taboo materials such as drugs, sex and violence. Furthermore, the success of a series of counter cultural hits such as *The Graduate* (1967), *Bonnie and Clyde* (1967) and *Easy Rider* (1969) consolidated these developments. Indeed, these films are often seen as marking a Hollywood renaissance, although it is never quite clear what was being revived, although the implication was that this period rekindled an interest in the artistic possibilities of the cinema. In *The Graduate*, Ben's sense of despair at the prospect of becoming like his parents leads him into an affair with an older woman, but when he falls in love with her daughter, he and his young love reject the middle-class life from which they come and to which they are being directed. In *Bonnie and Clyde*, two young outlaws go on a rampage but are destroyed by a cold and inhuman system of law. Finally, *Easy Rider* concerns two bikers who travel across America, engage in different types of counter cultural activities, and are eventually shot by Southern 'rednecks'.

All three are also associated with a supposed genre revisionism within the late 1960s in which established genres were transformed, often involving a critique of their original meanings. For example, there was a spate of westerns, such as *Little Big Man* (1970), in which the Native Americans are presented as the victims of a brutal and oppressive white civilisation, but such a claim tends to imply that genres had a stable meaning in the first place. Indeed, films featuring sympathetic Native Americans and an unsympathetic white civilisation can be found in the 1950s and earlier.

Nonetheless, Peckinpah's *The Wild Bunch* (1969) was a western that proved consonant with counter cultural values with its outlaws who find themselves unable to find a place in a modernising America and its vivid depiction of violence as a disturbing but potentially liberating expression of the oppressed. Similarly, Altman's *M*A*S*H* was a war film that did not concentrate on the heroics of war but on its absurdity. The film concerned a medical unit during the Korean War and, like many other Altman films, it had a large ensemble cast that played a motley collection of offbeat characters that the film observes from a detached and distant point of view. However, the complex interplay of ingredients that were a feature of Altman's films was most evident in his use of sound, which involved a highly complex mixing of elements.

Less commercially successful but often praised as a key American modernist was John Cassavetes. Although he was probably better known as an actor in film such as *Rosemary's Baby* (1968), Cassavetes also directed a series of films that were inspired by his love of jazz and employed largely improvisational acting and filming techniques to create a rough but compelling immediacy. His films also featured a small group of players including his wife Gena Rowlands, and friends Ben Gazzarra and Peter Falk. The film that established him was, as we have seen, *Shadows* (1960) but his key moment of productivity was the late 1960s and early 1970s when he made *Faces* (1968), *Husbands* (1970), *A Woman under the Influence* (1974) and *The Killing of a Chinese Bookie* (1976).

This was therefore a period in which the borders between Hollywood and the avant-garde seemed to be breaking down: Marlon Brando appeared in Bertolucci's *Last Tango in Paris* (1972); Antonioni made *Zabriskie Point* (1970) for Hollywood, and cast Jack Nicholson in *The Passenger* (1975); and Polanski made *Rosemary's Baby* and *Chinatown* (1974) in Hollywood. No doubt part of this process was an attempt by Hollywood to capitalise on the critical and commercial success of the European art cinema. But it was also due to art cinema's own increasing ambition within a now large and lucrative international market for art cinema. The period therefore saw a number of large international co-productions featuring a range of international players. For example, Italian director Luchino Visconti made *The Damned* (1969), the story of a German family of industrialists during the Nazis' rise to power that features a cast of major international players. Similarly, Bertolucci made *1900* (1976), an epic six-hour marathon concerning the rise and fall of fascism in Italy and starring a cast of players that included Robert De Niro, Gerard Depardieu and Donald Sutherland.

Some small art films were still being made, including *The Spirit of the Beehive* (1973), an allegorical study of Spanish society and culture under Franco. The film is set during the civil war and concerns a young girl who protects a soldier who is hiding from the authorities, under the mistaken belief that he is her favourite movie character, Frankenstein's monster. However, the main source of small (although not necessarily short) art films in the period was Germany. The New German cinema, as it came to be known, was a loose movement that was part of a more general radicalisation of Germany in the late 1960s and 1970s, when the generation coming of age began to ask serious questions about the Nazi past that their parents had repressed. Added to this was a more general sense of ambivalence about the German economic miracle of the postwar period, and the values that it involved.

Nonetheless, the directors of this movement still had an awkward relationship with Hollywood. Wim Wenders has frequently attacked the supposed colonisation of the German mind by Hollywood, both in his films and in print, but his films have remained fascinated with American popular culture and draw heavily on it. *Kings of the Road* (1976), for example, borrowed from the Hollywood road movie while *The American Friend* (1977) was not only an adaptation of a novel by Patricia Highsmith who had written Hitchcock's *Strangers on a Train* (1951), but starred Dennis Hopper from *Easy Rider*. Wenders has also found the pull of Hollywood irresistible and, despite his complaints about the making of *Hammett* (1982), which he directed for Coppola, he returned a few years later to make *Paris, Texas* (1984).

At the time, Herzog was often seen as a far more serious and important director, although his career self-destructed at the end of the 1970s. Again, for all his art house credentials, Herzog's films were imbued with a highly individualistic sensibility and concerned visionaries whose flouting of convention was presented as a heroic non-conformism that was clearly paralleled with the director's own sense of self-importance. Although often moving and powerful, this strand reaches ridiculous extremes in Herzog's doomed project *Fitzcarraldo* (1982) in which the protagonist of the title plans to build an opera house in the Latin American jungle and is obliged to carry a boat over a mountain to attain his ambition. Everybody tells him that he is mad but he battles against impossible odds to realise his vision regardless. The Herculean efforts of the protagonist were clearly a mirror image of those of Herzog himself and a fascinating documentary was made about the disastrous history of the production, *Burden of Dreams* (1982).

In retrospect, it is Rainer Werner Fassbinder who remains the most interesting figure from this historical moment, and although he died young, he left an extraordinarily extensive legacy of films including the fifteen and a half-hour television epic, *Berlin Alexanderplatz* (1979–80). Fassbinder's films deal with the outsiders in German society, such as prostitutes, drug addicts and homosexuals, but he was also heavily influenced by Hollywood. Rather than an avant-gardist who sought to distance or detach the emotions, Fassbinder wanted to engage them and drew inspiration from Hollywood weepies: *Fear Eats the Soul* (1974), for example, borrowed from Douglas Sirk's *All that Heaven Allows* (1955) and concerns an affair between a Moroccan guest worker and a German woman who is twenty years his senior.

The start of the 1970s also saw the emergence of a new generation of filmmakers in Hollywood, many of whom had come through film school and displayed not only a deep admiration for the art cinema but also a nostalgia and affection for the classical cinema. If the late 1960s is often seen as a reaction to and critique of the Hollywood cinema, the early 1970s displayed a fascinating ambivalence about this period. Far enough away from the age of the studio system, many now saw it as a golden age that they had studied and celebrated in film school; Coppola even made a failed attempt to create his own studio with the establishment of Zoetrope in the late 1960s. However, while he admired the studio era, Coppola was also hoping to make art films at Zoetrope as *The Rain People* (1969) makes clear. As a result, he was initially horrified by the idea of filming *The Godfather* (1972) but eventually ended up making a film that was a commercial success which drew a great deal on the art cinema. Furthermore, he used the money from this success to finance *The Conversation* (1974), an extraordinary thriller in which a surveillance expert uses the most complex technological devices to spy on a couple but misinterprets the meaning of what he records. The film's stark, bleak and paranoid world is as alienating and fascinating as anything from the art cinema.

The true darling of this generation was, in the early 1970s, Peter Bogdanovich who used black and white for both *The Last Picture Show* (1971) and *Paper Moon* (1973), both of which were period dramas that evoked a deep nostalgia for the classical period, while also using a range of modernist techniques and devices. The first film concerns the coming of age of two young men whose loss of idealism is mirrored by the declining fortunes of the local cinema in their small Texas hometown. Alternatively, his comedy, *What's Up Doc?* (1972), was celebrated for its attempt to recreate the screwball comedies of classical Hollywood, although the film has not dated well and now clearly displays the problems that beset his career later in the decade.

Like Bogdanovich, many other directors from this era have seen a profound change of fortune. John Milius was a figure of immense prestige and power in the period, both as a writer and a director, and his aggressively masculine adventures were often brilliantly realised. Not only did he invent *Dirty Harry* (1971) and write *Apocalypse Now* (1979), but he also produced two outstanding films. *The Wind and the Lion* (1975) is an epic adventure in Morocco. Set around the same time as *The Wild Bunch*, it features a Berber bandit rather than bank-robbing outlaws. His next film, *Big Wednesday* (1978), follows the fortunes of three surfers from their early idealism to the aftermath of Vietnam and, like the earlier film, has an epic grandeur and poetry that is quite exceptional. His career has fared less well since the 1970s. *Conan the Barbarian* (1982) was a commercial success but lacked the mythic grandeur of his earlier films, and while *Red Dawn* (1984) came some way to recapturing his former glories, its story, which concerned American school kids resisting a Russian invasion of the United States, still makes the film seem uncomfortably propagandist despite its considerable merits.

In contrast, Brian De Palma started out as the 'American Godard' in the 1960s before concentrating on a series of Hitchcockian horror films in the 1970s and 1980s – *Sisters* (1973), *Phantom of the Paradise* (1974), *Carrie* (1976), *The Fury* (1978), *Dressed to Kill* (1980), *Blow Out* (1981), *Scarface* (1983), *Body Double* (1984) – and then moving on to blockbusters in the late 1980s and 1990s – *The Untouchables* (1987) and *Mission Impossible* (1996), *Mission to Mars* (2000). The Hitchcockian horror films were known for their dazzling set pieces, often involving overt references to earlier films, and for their vividly violent imagery. Both *Sisters* and *Dressed to Kill*, for example, are almost structured through their debts to *Psycho* (1960), and concern psychological driven killers. Debate rages over whether De Palma's films are all style and no substance, or whether they represent a highly self-reflexive cinema.

Friedkin's career has been much like that of Bogdanovich. After a brief period of prestige, he quickly found it difficult to make films and when he did, they were neither critically nor commercially successful. His breakthrough was with *The French Connection* (1971), a gritty realistic detective film that features one of the most stunning car chases in film history. The film was a major hit and he went on to make *The Exorcist* (1973), another major success that maintained the gritty, realistic feel despite the spectacular fantasy plot in which Catholic priests battle to save a young girl who has been possessed by the devil. His career became troubled when he made the remarkable error of attempting to remake the French classic, *Wages of Fear* (1953/1977). Not only was this critically almost doomed from the start, given that the idea of remaking the film was considered virtually sacrilegious, but it was also hugely expensive yet failed to appeal to audiences. He then followed it up with *Cruising* (1980), a thriller in which Al Pacino hunts a serial killer through the homosexual underworld and is apparently corrupted by the process. As a result, the film was not only attacked as profoundly homophobic but also brought to a head worries about Friedkin's politics. Although a part of the moment of Hollywood modernism, many still consider his films to be closer politically to a strain of supposedly right-wing filmmaking within the era. Ironically, Friedkin is actually more conservative than this implies. *The Exorcist*, for example, is virtually a diatribe against the liberalisation of the Catholic Church during the 1960s and a re-affirmation of the need for traditional notions of good and evil.

Alternatively, the allegedly right-wing films of the 1970s are complex and ambiguous. It is claimed that the 'vigilante' movies such as *Dirty Harry* and *Death Wish* (1974) violently oppose the liberalisation of society during the 1960s and call for the vicious repression of subordinate groups. In *Dirty Harry*, Clint Eastwood plays Harry Callahan, a San Francisco detective who complains that the justice system favours the rights of criminals over those of the victims. It is therefore claimed that he stands for traditional conservative values and implicitly justifies the repression of minorities who had made gains in the 1960s and 1970s, particularly African Americans and women. Similarly, *Death Wish* concerns a liberal businessman who turns to vigilante violence when his wife is murdered.

These movies are more complex than a description of their plots would indicate. Both overtly reference westerns and explore many of the concerns with modern America found in supposedly radical westerns such as *The Wild Bunch* and even *Easy Rider*, in which modern America is a bureaucratic nightmare that has no place left for individualism and non-conformity. Claims about the conservatism of *Dirty Harry* usually ignore crucial elements of the film and its central character. For example, the film features a jazz score and while jazz is often used to suggest a dangerous urban environment through its racial associations, it was also well known that Eastwood is a fan of jazz and would later direct a biography of Charlie Parker. Furthermore, both Harry and the film are composed out of a complex series of countercultural signifiers. Harry's clothing and hair styling all suggest an association with rebellious 1950s youth cultures and, while he clashes with the liberal establishment, he often shares a sense of mutual understanding and admiration with the criminal underworld that he polices. In other words, both cop and crook in this film share an opposition to the bourgeois establishment. The only exception is the perverse killer who is Harry's nemesis and is clearly associated with the bourgeois establishment and uses the law to protect himself.

As a result, despite its problems, the film can be seen as less a diatribe against women and African Americans than a critique of American bureaucracy. Much the same can also be argued about the series of disaster films such as *The Poseidon Adventure* (1972), *The Towering Inferno* and *Earthquake* (both 1974). Again, these films are often claimed to depict a crisis which demonstrates the need to accept the authority of experts, but more usually the reverse is true. In *The Poseidon Adventure*, a group of individuals are forced to battle their way to the hull of an ocean liner when it is capsized by a tidal wave. Although they follow a maverick priest, he emphasises that God cannot save them and that they must rely on one another to escape. The ship is also capsized due to the greed of the shipping line and the captain's failure to stand up to his bosses. Similarly, in *The Towering Inferno*, it is economic greed that is responsible not only for the fire that rages through a massive tower block but the very hubris that builds skyscrapers in the first place given that, as the fire chief points out, there is really no way of fighting a fire over the first few floors. If experts do save the day, it is only after the death of corrupt builders and politicians, and the film eventually ends with the professional architect demonstrating that he is willing to learn from the blue-collar fire chief. Similarly, in *Earthquake*, Charlton Heston's corrupt architect is swept away in a flood of biblical proportions and so leaves it up to a street cop to rebuild a devastated Los Angeles. Furthermore, the cop is played by George Kennedy, who is the one actor who reappears throughout most of the *Airport* series where he again represents the most blue-collar of the characters, the engineer.

These themes are clearly in evidence in the conspiracy thrillers made during the period, most of which are seen as key examples of the radical modernist cinema and include not only Polansky's *Chinatown* but a series of films directed by Alan J. Pakula: *Klute* (1971), *The Parallax View* (1974), *All the President's Men* (1976) and *Rollover* (1981). They can also be found in films of the modernist period as diverse as *Network* (1976) and *One Flew Over the Cuckoo's Nest* (1975), which concern corrupt institutions that exploit or threaten individuality. In the conspiracy thrillers, American society has become a nightmare of control by large-scale organisations, in which all truth is manufactured to disguise the actual processes in operation. In *The Parallax View*, for example, Warren Beatty plays a small-time journalist who begins to investigate the death of a series of witnesses to a political assassination that clearly suggests the killing of President Kennedy. Although the assassination is dismissed as the act of a lone individual, Beatty's character unearths a massive conspiracy involving the Parallax Corporation. Before he can reveal the truth, his contacts are killed and he finds that he has been manipulated into a situation where he will be the patsy for the latest political murder which can again be blamed on yet another lone individual – himself.

Similar concerns also preoccupy the science fiction films of the period in which contemporary social processes are shown to lead to social and/or ecological catastrophe. In *Soylent Green* (1973), for example, a population explosion and the callous exploitation of the world's resources has created a dystopian society in which most live in squatter camps, and an élite live in luxury apartments where beautiful young women are provided as 'furniture'. When one of the élite is murdered, Charlton Heston's cop investigates and with the help of an old timer (Edward G. Robinson in his last role), finds that the victim has been murdered to maintain the secret of Soylent Green, a highly desired processed food that, it is finally revealed, has to be made from human flesh because the ecosystem can no longer sustain life.

Cannibalism is also a feature of George Romero's *Night of the Living Dead* (1968), which was not only a cult hit but also received critical acclaim for its director. However, although it too has been linked with the avant-garde in a number of ways, it was not a highbrow modernist document like Cassevetes' films, nor even a mainstream classic like those of Coppola or Bogdanovich. It wasn't even a popular genre film such as *The Poseidon Adventure* or *Soylent Green*. Instead it was a micro-budget exploitation horror film.

One of the effects of changing audience demographics was to alter the meanings of certain sites of cinemagoing or to change the economic significance of certain sections of audience. As suburbia expanded as a result of so-called 'white flight', for example, African Americans were one of the few sections of the audience that continued to attend inner city cinemas regularly. This not only made them increasingly important to these exhibitors but also changed the meaning of the cinemas themselves. On the one hand, like the inner cities themselves, these cinemas acquired an aura of danger and perceived threat for many sections of white middle-class suburbia, but, on the other, it was this very aura that made them seem fascinating and exciting to many white youths from the suburbs for whom they symbolised exotic otherness.

This led film companies to cater for African American audiences through the development of blaxploitation, but it also led certain white youth audiences to celebrate such films as 'cult' cinema. *Night of the Living Dead* was made before the advent of blaxploitation but it was clearly made with an awareness of the inner city audience, as was a whole host of other horror movies of the time. This period was therefore a rich one in the history of the genre and produced an number of *auteur* directors: Larry Cohen (*It's Alive* [1974], *It Lives Again* [1978]); Wes Craven (*Last House on the Left* [1972], *The Hills Have Eyes* [1977]); David Cronenberg (*Shivers* [1975], *Rabid* [1977]); Tobe Hooper (*The Texas Chainsaw Massacre* [1974]); and George Romero (*Night of the Living Dead*, *Martin* [1977]), and so on.

Blaxploitation emerged after the success of Melvin Van Peeble's small budget *Sweet Sweetback's Baad Asssss Song* (1971), and a series of studios cashed in on the phenomenon with films such as *Superfly* (1972), in which an African American drug dealer tries to escape control by 'the Man', and *Shaft* (1971), in which a black detective takes on crime, corruption and racism. The cycle created a number of black stars including Richard Roundtree and Pam Grier, who appeared in a number of action-oriented but female-centred blaxploitation movies.

In addition to cult horror and blaxploitation, the period also saw the emergence of sexploitation cinema. In the 1950s and 1960s, one of the key features that distinguished the art cinema from the mainstream was its sexual explicitness. Before the end of the code, Hollywood films had made films that could be suitable for children and had real problems with sexual material. However, with the end of the code, not only was Hollywood able to deal with issues much more explicitly but also cinemas began to appeal to audiences in search of increasingly explicit material. For example, *Midnight Cowboy* (1969) became a major studio hit although its story concerned the relationship between a male prostitute and a 'low-life'. The period saw the massive success of films such as *Last Tango in Paris* (1972), *Emmanuelle* (1974) and *Deep Throat* (1972). It is interesting that of these films, the first two were not just sex films but also had associations with the art cinema. Indeed, sexual material had often been the sign of artistic filmmaking, and one of the complaints lodged against the Hollywood mainstream was its inability to deal with sex and violence in 'adult' terms. Consequently, there was a close relationship between the art cinema and pornography, which remained strong until well into the 1970s when the liberalisation of censorship ironically saw the two begin to diverge.

Horror, blaxploitation and pornography all demonstrate the growing significance of cult exploitation cinema within the period. Another important feature was martial arts cinema and particularly those films made in Hong Kong. In 1958, the Shaw Brothers moved to Hong Kong, where they built a large production complex, Movietown, which formed a key element in their vertically integrated empire. This development massively increased the productivity of the Hong Kong film industry, and made the Shaw Brothers dominant within it. It also led to a situation in which Hong Kong cinema would become virtually synonymous with martial arts.

In the late 1960s, one of the Shaw Brothers' prodigies, King Hu, moved to Taiwan where he made martial arts epic of unparalleled scale and sophistication, *A Touch of Zen* (1971), and Raymond Chow, their head of production, left to found Golden Harvest, which was crucial in the opening up of international markets, particularly in the United States. To achieve this end, Chow used Bruce Lee, who already had an established career in Hollywood where he had worked in films and even starred as the hero's sidekick in the television series, *The Green Hornet*. The films that Lee made at Golden Harvest before his untimely death have become classics – *The Big Boss* (1971), *Fist of Fury* (1972) and *Way of the Dragon* (1972) – but, in 1973, he was loaned out to the United States where he made the film that would confirm his international star status and become the inspiration for a worldwide martial arts craze, *Enter the Dragon*. Lee's films were distinguished by a greater sense of authenticity in the fight sequences than previously, which were filmed to emphasise the relative lack of special effects. His death in the mid-1970s left a void in the industry until the emergence of Jackie Chan in the 1980s. Chan's films also relied heavily on authenticity, and the credit sequences at the end of many of his films pay homage to this authenticity by running out-takes of the often painful mistakes made during filming – Chan even broke his back on one project. However, despite his phenomenal international stardom, Chan is very different from Lee. While Lee was taut and intense, Chan's films often feature light comedy and even the fight sequences are usually played as highly choreographed and acrobatic slapstick. Like the star Hong Kong directors of the 1980s, Tsai Hark and John Woo, Chan would begin to work in Hollywood in the 1990s, but in the 1980s, he was very much the star of an international cult cinema that had its roots in the 1970s.

Work on reception has often tended to focus on marketing, critical reception or audience ethnography, and to a lesser extent on the practices of exhibition, but one area that still remains relatively under-researched is the practices of distribution. This area of research is not only valuable in itself but it can also help one to examine the exhibition of specific films. This kind of research can be seen in Kevin Heffernan's 'Inner-City Exhibition and the Genre Film: Distributing *Night of the Living Dead*', which uses the film to open up a series of issues about distribution in the late 1960s. *Night of the Living Dead* has become a 'cult' film, praised for its supposedly political and formal radicalism. On the one hand, its black hero is often used to anchor a series of claims about its politics and, on the other, it has been associated with the avant-garde in formal terms. However, much of this reputation is due to the ways certain critics were mobilised to defend the film in response to a moral panic at the time of its initial release. As Heffernan demonstrates, not only was this panic a reaction against long-term distribution policies that resulted in *Night of the Living Dead* being shown as a children's matinée, but much of what critics have seen as radical about the film was not a break with earlier horror films, as is often suggested, but rather the consummation of long-established tendencies.

In this way, Heffernan makes it clear that distribution is not just a neutral process in which films are made prior to distribution and then are simply brought to exhibitors by distributors. Instead, distribution companies are often involved with the very production process itself. Even when films are made without the initial involvement of a distribution company, these companies may shape the meanings of films. For example, distributors assign meanings to films through the ways in which they are released to different markets. As Heffernan shows, the distribution company Continental presented different films in different ways. Some were released to cinemas that catered to inner-city African American audiences, others were sold to cinemas as children's matinées and others were identified as specialised product aimed at art cinemas. Furthermore, distribution companies assigned meanings to films through the ways in which they were packaged with other films as double bills, or were released at specific times of year such as Halloween.

In the process, Heffernan looks at a variety of sources including the trade press and local advertising campaigns in the Pittsburgh area in order to identify specific patterns of distribution, and the ways in which these patterns determined the ways that films were presented to the public. Finally, he looks at the various generic tendencies and intertexts of *Night of the Living Dead* to re-examine the relationships between generic trends and distribution strategies. In the process, he provides a rich account of generic trends within the under-researched period of the 1960s, and of the complex relationships between art and exploitation cinema.

- Heffernan tries to place *Night of the Living Dead* within certain tendencies in distribution during the 1960s. What sources does he turn to to identify these tendencies?
- Heffernan's account may tell us a lot about how the practices of distributors can shape the meanings of films but to what extent can his research reveal how audiences made sense of these films?
- Heffernan demonstrates that distributors had different strategies that were meant to target films at particular audiences. Can you think of any examples where the same film might have been distributed to different audiences, and these different patterns of distribution might have affected its meaning?

Inner-City Exhibition and the Genre Film: Distributing *Night of the Living Dead* (1968)

Kevin Heffernan

[. . .]

For the second summer, Walter Reade Theatres in New York and New Jersey towns will play the annual Vacation Movie shows for children, under official school and Parent-Teacher Association sponsorship. Mr. Reade says the wonderful public and community relations that accrued from last year have made it easy to organize the series again. (*Motion Picture Herald*, May 15, 1954[1])

Night of the Living Dead . . . casts serious aspersions on the integrity and social responsibility of its Pittsburgh-based makers, distrib Walter Reade, the film industry as a whole, and exhibs who book the pic. (*Variety*, October 16, 1968[2])

It is now almost forgotten that *Night of the Living Dead* was released theatrically in 1968 by art-film distributor Continental Releasing. However, the controversy surrounding the release of the film, recounted in J. Hoberman and Jonathan Rosenbaum's *Midnight Movies* and in many histories of the horror film, is now very well known.[3] Unleashed by Walter Reade theater chain subsidiary Continental onto unsuspecting kiddie-matinee audiences in October

Kevin Heffernan, *Cinema Journal* 41(3) Spring, 2002.

1968, the film was excoriated in *Variety* for hawking a 'pornography of violence' and lambasted by Chicago reviewer Roger Ebert in a piece that was later reprinted in *Reader's Digest*. Ebert's essay, which is somewhat of a surprise for modern readers who are familiar with his defense of exploitation films and his screenwriting duties for nudie-king Russ Meyer, begins with a description of the theater, the film, and the audience:

> It was a Saturday matinee in a typical neighborhood theater. There were a few parents, but mostly just the kids – dumped in front of the theater for a movie called *The Night of the Living Dead*. There was a cheer when the lights went down. The opening scene was set in a cemetery (lots of delighted shrieks from the kids) when a teenaged couple are placing a wreath on a grave. Suddenly a ghoul – looking suitably decayed and walking in the official ghoul shuffle – attacks. The boy is killed, and the girl flees to a nearby farmhouse. (More screams from the kids. Screaming is part of the fun, you'll remember.)[4]

Ebert goes on to describe the film's escalation of outrages and recounts the stunned and terrified silence of the children in the theater at the end of the film, after the hero is gunned down by redneck vigilantes who have mistaken him for a ghoul. 'I felt real terror in that neighborhood theater,' he writes. 'I saw kids who had no sources they could draw upon to protect themselves from the dread and fear they felt . . . What are parents thinking,' demanded Ebert, 'when they drop their children off to see a movie called *Night of the Living Dead*?'[5]

A different question might be, What were theaters thinking when they booked such a film into their afternoon-matinee slot? The case of *Night of the Living Dead's* initial theatrical playoff illustrates both the changing audiences for genre films in the late 1960s as well as the efforts of neighborhood theaters and nonmajor distributors like Continental to negotiate massive changes in the distribution and exhibition branches of the film industry. Many of the theaters that showed *Night of the Living Dead* were in the inner city and served a predominantly African American audience, and several changes in the film marketplace over the previous twenty years had placed these neighborhood theaters (or 'nabe houses,' in trade paper jargon) in a precarious position. The major distributors had cut back on the annual number of releases and adopted a 'blockbuster policy' of releasing fewer and costlier movies. Confiscatory rentals and extended first runs in large suburban theaters meant that last season's hits began their subsequent runs in the inner city virtually played out. Many theaters faced severe product shortages for their three-times-a-week changes[6] and tried to fight back with an eclectic mix of programming that included not only subsequent runs but kiddie matinees, huge multitheater saturation openings of genre films, and films from the nascent 'adults-only' distribution network. The controversy surrounding the initial release of *Night of the Living Dead* was the result of Continental's misguided efforts to place the film in the inner-city nabe, horror-matinee, and multiple-opening situations simultaneously.

The film's Philadelphia playoff was fairly typical of the patterns of distribution Continental used in major markets. Continental employed what had become a common strategy for the release of horror films by the late 1960s. *Night of the Living Dead* was released in the slow Halloween season and was booked into a dozen or more neighborhood theaters, which split the cost of a huge saturation advertising push on radio and television and in local newspapers. In many cases, theaters showing the film first run in the evening carried it over into their Saturday-matinee slot. For this article, I consulted the Friday movie listings in the *Philadelphia Inquirer* for the theaters, cofeatures, and show times for the 1968 Philadelphia-area playoff of the film. For its evening and matinee runs, I will focus on five theaters in the predominantly African American Northeast and West Philly: the Pearl, Fans, Uptown, Leader, and Nixon.

Distribution, Exhibition, and the Inner-City Theater

The controversy surrounding *Night of the Living Dead* was only the most recent in a long series of skirmishes that Walter Reade and Continental faced as they tried to carve out a profitable niche for themselves in the movie marketplace. While circuit owner and Theater Owners of America president Reade worked hard to establish good community relations for his houses and the exhibition branch in general, in his role as head of Continental Distributing, he sought to serve the market with product clearly differentiated from that of the major studios. In 1963, Reade asserted that the days of the movie with universal appeal was over and that distributors and exhibitors now had to tailor their product to one of a number of possible audiences.[7] In lieu of pre-sold product that would appeal to a wide range of moviegoers, Continental mined the disparate strands of the art house, the product-hungry neighborhood theater, and the inner-city movie house that served the African American community.

For most of the 1960s, Continental had been associated with the distribution of films for the art-theater circuit. In fact, Continental's parent company, the Walter Reade theater chain, owned some of the New York area's most successful art houses, including the Baronet in New York City. Continental had courted controversy with a series of challenging films for the high-class adult audience, including a trio from the 'Kitchen Sink' or 'Angry Young Man' school in England. *Room at the Top* (1959) was both condemned by the Legion of Decency and banned in Atlanta.[8] *Expresso Bongo* (1960) was also condemned by the Legion,[9] and *Saturday Night and Sunday Morning* (1961) was both condemned by the Legion and banned in Kansas City.[10] One of the company's most controversial releases was the drama *The Mark* (1961), about a man's efforts to rebuild his life after his release from the psychiatric ward of an Irish prison, where he served time for child molestation.

Continental's success in importing features led the company into limited partnerships in film financing. One such effort was *Black Like Me* (1963), the adaptation of John Howard Griffin's autobiographical account of his travels in the South disguised as an African American. The film, with James Whitmore in the lead and featuring a cast of unknowns,[11] was part of a trend in the early to mid-1960s for independent producers to make low-budget topical films about U.S. race relations. Other films in this subgenre included Roger Corman's *The Intruder* (1961), Shirley Clarke's *The Cool World* (1963), Ossie Davis's *Gone Are the Days* (1963), and Michael Roemer's *Nothing but a Man* (1965). These films were marketed at both neighborhood theaters in African American communities and to the wider market through appeals to the exploitation audience. An unnamed producer told a trade journal in 1963, 'We are budgeting our picture so that, if necessary, we can recoup our costs in just the Negro market, even while aiming at as broad a market as possible.'[12]

Continental released *Black Like Me* in the summer of 1964 on a double bill with the horror import *The Hands of Orlac* (1960), a metamorphosis narrative that bore more than a passing resemblance to *Black Like Me*, and opened it in a multiple-run exploitation playoff. In Philadelphia, the *Black Like Me/Orlac* combination played for a week at the downtown Stanley Warner Palace grind house, following American International's *Black Sabbath/Evil Eye* package, before opening wide at inner-city neighborhood theaters and suburban drive-ins the following week.[13]

In this double-feature package. Continental was combining two types of films that were most popular with the African American audience, the horror movie and the race-themed topical feature. The motion-picture industry was no different from other sectors of the culture industry in the 1960s in trying to reach the growing African American market through specialized products and specialized promotions of standard products. By 1967, *Variety* estimated that black moviegoers represented 30 per cent of first-run movie patrons while numbering only 10 to 15 per cent of the general population.[14]

By the late 1960s, the exhibition branch of the industry was finally learning to exploit the growing suburbanization of the white middle-class movie audience through new theater construction and changing distribution patterns. At the same time, downtown picture palaces and inner-city neighborhood theaters enjoyed proximity to a large percentage of the black movie audience and were developing strategies to serve the communities near those theaters. An African American supporting player often became the central attraction featured in a film's publicity. For example, the Leader theater, at 41st and Lancaster Streets in Philadelphia, featured ads for the 1965 subsequent-run engagement of *The Cardinal* by heralding 'A Big Cast with Ossie Davis'[15]; the Pearl, at 21st and Ridge, announced 'Woody Strode in *The Professionals*' in 1967[16]; and, later that year, Simon of Cyrene became the bible's biggest star when the Leader advertised 'Sidney Poitier in *The Greatest Story Ever Told*.'[17]

Horror films were very popular with African American audiences; in fact, on the rare occasions when neighborhood theaters in African American neighborhoods in Philadelphia played first-run films, it was often for mass openings of horror combinations such as Fox's releases of *Dracula, Prince of Darkness* and *Plague of the Zombies* in 1966 and *Frankenstein Created Woman* and *The Mummy's Shroud* in 1967. As in the case of the *Orlac/Black Like Me* combination, some of these genre pictures were double-billed with black-themed Hollywood and independent films in wide openings or subsequent runs in inner-city theaters. The Fans on Market Street supported the 1962 sub-run engagement of AIP's *Premature Burial* with the backstage musical *Swinging Along*, which featured a performance by Ray Charles, touted in the theater's newspaper ads. At the Pearl, *The Cool World* was cofeatured with the Bert Gordon sci-fi comedy *Village of the Giants* in 1965, the Leader supported *The Cool World* with Fox's *Curse of the Fly*,[18] and the Poitier western *Duel at Diablo* was paired at the Pearl in its multiple opening with the Amicus horror import *The Psychopath* in 1966.[19]

There was heated debate in industry circles about whether films about 'the race issue' were best sold as prestige problem pictures or as exploitation items. For example, one of the films financed by Pathé-America's brief foray into feature distribution was Corman's *The Intruder*,[20] in which William Shatner plays a racist agitator sent to a small southern town by a right-wing group to thwart integration, The film did not receive wide bookings until 1965, when Alabama huckster M. A. Ripps retitled it *I Hate Your Guts!* and issued it to the exploitation circuit through his Cinema Distributors of America.[21]

Just five months after Continental's release of *Black Like Me*, Cinema V faced a similar quandary over its handling of *The Cool World*, Shirley Clarke's drama of Harlem life. Cinema V's initial publicity emphasised the film's action and exploitation angles, and at first it played only in grind houses specializing in action fare and in theaters in African American neighborhoods in Washington, D.C., and Philadelphia. Unsolicited promotion from a San Francisco disc jockey helped the film cross over to both black and art-house audiences in its successful run at the Vogue. This crossover success was elusive, however. The producer of *The Cool World*, noted documentary filmmaker Frederick Wiseman, remarked that many theater owners were wary of black-themed topical films because 'they think if they show a movie about Negroes, they'll have a riot on their hands.'[22]

Crossover success was also thwarted by anti-integration sentiments on the part of exhibitors. Theaters in Washington, D.C., resisted booking *Black Like Me* because, in the words of the film's incredulous producer, Julius Tannenbaum, they were concerned that '*Negro patrons might get into the habit of attending their theaters.*'[23]

At the same time that Continental was negotiating the often-conflicting demands of the various markets for these race-themed pictures, changes in the film marketplace were leading the company to broaden its usual roster of releases beyond art-house product into general-release films for a mass audience. Continental's parent company, the Walter Reade Organization, had merged with syndicator Sterling Television in 1961.[24] Reade-Sterling had enjoyed success in the TV market for several years, but the roulette wheel of public whim was increasingly landing on the wrong color for Continental. In 1964, Walter Reade-Sterling posted a $491,000 loss, largely due to 'disastrous results from artie releases,' according to *Variety*. The following season, the company enhanced its release schedule with more overtly commercial items. Telling the trade press that 'you can't take good reviews and awards to the bank,'[25] Reade and Continental issued *Agent 8 3/4*, a James Bond spoof that was very successful in a number of large cities early in the summer.

For its big turnaround in 1965, Continental released the Japanese giant-monster import *Ghidrah, the Three-Headed Monster* in the slow fall period in a mass territorial opening with saturation advertising. The 'class-to-mass' strategy was highly successful: *Agent 8 3/4* racked up more than a million dollars in rentals, and *Ghidrah* surpassed $1.3 million and played many theaters that had never before played Continental product.[26] The following year, Continental balanced its art-house entries, which Reade now called 'specialized product,' including *Kwaidan*, *The Gospel According to St. Matthew* (a surprise hit, it turned out), and *Time of Indifference*, with the British science-fiction import *Dr. Who and the Daleks* and the Japanese animated feature *Gulliver's Travels beyond the Moon*.[27] TV revenues and increased rentals of its more commercial product enabled Reade, which had shown a $500,000 loss in 1964, to record a similar-sized profit in 1965.[28]

The success of Continental's mass-appeal features *Ghidrah*, *Dr. Who*, and *Gulliver* in their saturation openings continued in what was one of the most important subsequent-run markets for horror and science-fiction films in this period, the afternoon-matinee circuit. In 1966, *Variety* noted that in the first half of the decade 'the revenues from kiddie matinees have mushroomed and more than a dozen indie companies and several major distributors vie for prime playing time during the peak tot school season.' From the perspective of the local theater owner, these children's matinees provided programming supported by a large advertising push, the cost of which was amortised over a large number of theaters, as well as an opportunity to enjoy lucrative concession sales. The three largest suppliers of specialized kiddie-matinee programming were Edward Meyerberg's New Trends Associates, Inc.[29]; K. Gordon Murray, whose Mexican import feature *Santa Claus* was an enormous seasonal hit for more than five years[30]; and Childhood Productions, whose success led it into runaway production and a public stock offering in 1967.[31] These three companies arranged for saturation advertising campaigns in major television markets and opened their films in as many as one hundred houses. *Santa Claus* alone earned $500,000 a week nationwide in the 1964 holiday season.[32] Murray, New Trends, and Childhood Productions demonstrated that with the children's matinee market, 'the normal 'hit-or-miss' rules of film distribution do not apply.' These companies provided films whose fantasy and fairy-tale qualities did not appear to date with the passing of time, and, in the words of a trade journal, 'the 3-to-10-year-old age group to which [these distributors] aim their product is being constantly replenished.'[33]

In addition to the multiple openings of specialized kiddie product from Childhood, Murray, and New Trends, nabe owners often programmed double features of horror, fantasy, and science-fiction films for a slightly older matinee audience of six to twelve year olds. As genre film historians like Thomas Doherty and William Paul have shown, the target audience for the horror film, like the movie audience generally, had drastically declined in age since the 1950s.[34] Because this audience was also constantly turning over and the purpose of the Saturday matinee was to give children a chance to leave the house and the watchful eyes of their parents for a few hours, which films were shown in these double features was often of secondary importance. Parents could drop their children off at the theater for a few hours of quiet, and the children enjoyed an afternoon of snacks, scares, and laughter with members of their own age group. For the theater owner, these engagements were a very low cost source of programming, often rented for a flat fee and bicycled between houses in a circuit-wide playoff over several weeks. A five hundred-seat theater, charging thirty-five to seventy-five cents admission, could bring in more than $200 at the box office, a small portion of which went to the distributor, and keep all the concession profits for itself. For the distributor, these engagements represented pure profit, since prints circulated through local exchanges and still generated income ten to twelve years after their initial theatrical runs. Distributors like American International, Continental, Allied Artists, and some of the majors could therefore keep almost-shredded prints of their already-televised features in circulation for hundreds of engagements every weekend. (For young horror fans in the mid-1960s, the kiddie matinee was only one component of an explosion of horror-related media and merchandising that included Aurora plastic model kits, playing cards, LP records of radio horror shows, 8mm home-movie versions of the Universal classics, monster magazines, and reprints of 1950s horror comics.[35])

Between 1965 and 1967, Continental divided its release schedule into three categories: mass-appeal features destined for wide openings, 'specialized product' for art theaters, and prestige roadshow attractions like the Soviet import *War and Peace* and the James Joyce adaptation *Ulysses*. In attempting to showcase films like *War and Peace* and *Ulysses* as roadshow attractions, Continental was following a trend that the majors had instituted very lucratively; the high ticket prices for Fox's roadshow engagements of *The Sound of Music* (1965) had enabled the Julie Andrews musical to break the decades-old box-office record of *Gone with the Wind* (1939) as all-time rental champion. In fact, the U.S. Department of Commerce asserted in 1967 that the increasing annual revenues of the motion-picture industry were largely the result of higher admission prices and predicted that increasing revenues would continue to depend on the growing number of roadshow attractions released annually.[36]

Continental's prestige program was inextricably linked with Reade's efforts to fight censorship and age classification in both distribution and exhibition. The $3 million box-office success of *Ulysses*, partly the result of censor-baiting publicity,[37] was necessary to compensate for the great disappointment of *War and Peace*. Acquired from Mosfilm in 1967 for an almost bank-breaking $1.5 million, *War and Peace* was simply too long, at almost six hours (each unit of the two-evening program carried a $7.50 admission price),[38] to become a successful roadshow release.[39] Continental also was courting the African American audience in 1967 with a black-themed topical, the screen adaptation of LeRoi Jones's play *The Dutchman*.[40] Then, in 1968–1969, the company released both the Theater Guild's production of the Herbert Biberman-directed *Slaves*, with Ossie Davis and Dionne Warwick, and a low-budget horror film from Pittsburgh with an African American protagonist, *Night of the Living Dead*.[41]

Night of the Living Dead *and the Changing Genre Film*

Night of the Living Dead marks a crucial turning point in the history of the low-budget horror film, and its tremendous influence makes some of its most startling elements invisible to modern viewers. The absence of stars and the movie's marginal place in the network of 1968 horror-film production and distribution led the filmmakers to seek a particular type of product differentiation that emphasized graphic violence, bleak social commentary, and a downbeat ending. This formed the basis of its initial rejection by critics and the traumatisation of its initial audiences at weekend-afternoon matinees as well as its eventual critical recuperation as a visionary and subversive work. The film recounts one night in the lives of seven people trapped in an isolated farmhouse while, outside, an amassing horde of recently dead, radiation-infected cannibal zombies attempts to break into the house. As the number of zombies increases, the internal struggles of the human survivors become more lethal; Ben, the African American protagonist, serves as protector to catatonic survivor Barbara, whose brother, Johnny, is murdered by a zombie in the opening of the film. Ben and Barbara are mirrored by Harry and Helen Cooper, a middle-aged married couple keeping watch over their zombie-infected daughter, Karen, and by Tom and Judy, a teenaged couple. After Tom and Judy are killed in a fiery death while attempting to flee the house (we see the zombies devouring the couple's cooling entrails in the most famous scene in the movie), Ben shoots Harry Cooper in a struggle over the locked front door, the now-dead Karen kills and devours her mother, and Ben boards himself in the basement, which Harry had insisted was the only place they could survive. Discovered by a redneck posse in the morning, Ben is mistaken for a ghoul and shot in the head. The film ends with Ben's body being dragged into the morning light and incinerated in a bonfire with the dead zombie who killed Johnny in the opening scene.

In *Night of the Living Dead*, Continental had a product that was suited to the well-tested playoff of the genre film. It was released at Halloween, during the slow period of the fall-release schedule. Further, Continental linked subsequent-run houses and drive-in theaters in a multiple-opening campaign supported by saturation advertising in newspapers and on radio and television.

Some ads for the film used a gambit copied from former schlockmeister William Castle, by 1968 a respected producer at Paramount: 'If 'Night of the Living Dead' Frightens You to Death,' screamed the ads, 'you are covered for $50,000!'[42]

The film contained elements from the company's successful combination of *Black Like Me* and *Hands of Orlac* all in one package. The proven success of horror in the inner-city market was now enhanced by a film with an intelligent and resourceful black hero. In addition, *Night of the Living Dead* featured a perfect 'Mr. Charlie' foil to Duane Jones's Ben, the fidgety, balding middle-class patriarch Harry Baldwin.

In the intervening years, many critics have praised *Night of the Living Dead* for introducing a particularly sophisticated form of bleak social commentary into the low-budget horror film. Evidence in the film to support this claim includes the fascistic Bull Conner-like police chief McClellan, as well as the crowd of zombies amassed among the flames outside the farmhouse that shelters the interracial duo of Ben and Barbara. Ben remarks, 'There's bound to be a lot *more* of them as soon as they find out about *us*.'

In fact, many of the elements that writers emphasize in their interpretation of the film had been important components of horror and science-fiction movies for years. Hoberman and Rosenbaum assert that Romero and screenwriter John Russo were 'inspired by Richard Matheson's 1954 *I Am Legend*,' an apocalyptic novel about an army of enfeebled blood-starved ghouls besieging the last uninfected man boarded up in his house, but more likely the feature was inspired by the book's 1964 adaptation, American International's *The Last Man on Earth*, directed by Sidney Salkow and starring Vincent Price. On the most obvious level, the gaunt, disheveled, 'feeble-minded' swarms of ghouls with cadaverous blackened eyes in *Night of the Living Dead* bear an uncanny resemblance to their counterparts in *The Last Man on Earth* (in Matheson's novel, the vampires are capable of sprinting after their victims). The repeated scenes in *Night of the Living Dead* of zombies reaching through doors and windows after the protagonists is derived from the way similar scenes were blocked in *The Last Man on Earth*. Also, a key subplot of Romero's film, the Coopers' death watch over their daughter, is a major component of the second act of *The Last Man on Earth*. Most important, at the end of the 1964 adaptation, Robert is sought out by fellow 'survivor' Ruth and captured by her fellow 'mutations,' who, although infected by the vampire virus, remain alive and seek to rebuild a fascist although (therefore?) human society. Before Robert can be executed by his captors, Ruth brings him poison capsules so he can cheat his executioners and die by his own hand. *The Last Man on Earth* ends with a furious chase through the ruins of the city to a church where Robert is staked like a vampire, while screaming at his murderers, 'You're all freaks! Mutations! I'm a man. The last man!' This ending, in which the solitary human survivor is executed like a monster, would be directly transposed to *Night of the Living Dead*.

The overt social commentary in Matheson's 1954 novel and Salkow's film was part of a major component of pop-culture dystopias of the Cold War era. In fact, Alfred Hitchcock's *The Birds* (1963), often seen as a progenitor of a particular kind of claustrophobic, family-based apocalyptic terror, appeared near the end of a cycle of what I call end-of-the-world films. The postnuclear microcosm of human society was the setting of several 'serious' problem pictures of the 1950s, including *On the Beach* and *The World, the Flesh, and the Devil* (both 1959). On the low-budget end of the film industry, American International weighed in with Corman's *The Day the World Ended* (1956) and Ray Milland's directorial debut, *Panic in Year Zero* (1962).

The Day the World Ended combined the terrors of radiation-induced cannibal mutation with the infighting of a group of people trapped in a survivalist's mountain shelter in the days following a nuclear war. The survivalist, Maddison, is a stern, bible-quoting patriarch who oversees the requisitioned food and water with his automatic pistol and seeks to protect his daughter, Louise, from the advances of a gangster named Tony, trapped in the house with his stripteaser girlfriend, Ruby. Also in the house is Radek, a radiation-infected survivor who may be turning into a cannibal mutant and who has a mysterious telepathic connection to a huge three-eyed monster who lurks outside in the swirling radioactive fog. At the end of the film, only Louise and the stock character of the young geologist Rick survive; the others have been destroyed by the monster outside or in internal power struggles.

Much in *The Day the World Ended* prefigures the narrative of *Night of the Living Dead*, from the struggle over the gun and the patriarchal authority it represents to the human greed and lust and unnatural radiation-induced cannibalism. However, *Panic in Year Zero* is an even less disguised social allegory. The Baldwin family – parents Harry (Ray Milland) and Ann (Jean Hagen) and their teenaged children, Rick (Frankie Avalon) and Karen (Mary Mitchell) – leave home in Los Angeles at 4:00 A.M. to go on a weekend fishing trip. While they are in the mountains of Northern California, Los Angeles suffers an all-out nuclear attack. The film details the efforts of the family to survive the anarchy and lawlessness that follow, particularly the repeated attacks of a group of violent and rapacious delinquents, Carl, Mickey, and Andy. The beginning of the film, when the Baldwins are unaware of the apocalypse, shares much with *Night of the Living Dead*. There are also parallels between the (perpetually off-screen) external threats of enemy missiles, radiation, and roving bands of miscreants and survival-obsessed consumers.

At the center of the concerns in *Panic in Year Zero* is the patriarch, Harry Baldwin, who must negotiate the demands of survival and the need to remain 'civilized' and human after the collapse of society. The film takes a highly ambiguous view of his actions. Ann constantly expresses horror at Harry's ruthlessness, remarking at one point, 'You're not the man I married,' and, after Mickey and Carl rape Karen, Harry shoots both men in cold blood. It is also suggested that the well-scrubbed Rick develops a taste for violence when he remarks regretfully that, had his mother not pulled his rifle away, he 'could have blown [Andy's] head off.'

During the climax of the film, as the Baldwin family drives a wounded Rick toward an uncertain future, an unseen group of threatening, heavily armed men suddenly stop them, shine bright flashlights in their faces, and appear ready to murder them and take their car. In fact, the men are in an outpost of the National Guard and are about to escort Rick and the family to safety. The film ends with normality and faith in authority restored as the escort departs down the lonely highway. *Night of the Living Dead* reverses the terms of this climax and resolution 180 degrees.

In Romero's film, the elaborate construction of audience sympathy for Ben and Barbara is responsible for one of the film's most audacious uses of stock characters from the end-of-the-world genre: the patriarch Harry Cooper, his wife, Helen, and their wounded daughter, Karen, set in motion the events that insure the destruction of all the human protagonists. Thus, the protagonists in *The Day the World Ended* and *Panic in Year Zero* (indeed, Harry and Karen Cooper even have the same names as the father and daughter in Milland's movie) are presented as potential threats to the characters who serve as figures of the audience's sympathy. In fact, it is precisely by introducing Harry Cooper in this fashion that the film begins progressively to undermine the patriarchal authority that would have been his birthright in the earlier films. Helen Cooper is a bitter, chain-smoking foil for her petty and bullying husband, and she exhibits none of the surprised dismay at his actions that characterize the long-suffering Ann Baldwin. The unmistakable – but largely unspoken – racial implications of both the antagonism between Harry and Ben and Ben's eventual fate at the hands of the vigilantes recall a passage in the novel *I Am Legend*. One of Robert Neville's drunken interior monologues concerns what he calls the 'minority prejudice' against vampires:

> Are his deeds any more outrageous than the deeds of the parent who drained the spirit from his child? The vampire may foster quickened heartbeats and levitated hair. But is he worse than the parent who gave to society a neurotic child who became a politician? Is he worse than the manufacturer who set up belated foundations with the money he made by handing bombs and guns to suicidal nationalists? Is he worse . . . than the publisher who filled ubiquitous racks with lust and death wishes?[43]

Hoberman and Rosenbaum, Tony Williams, and Robin Wood, whose writings on 1970s low-budget horror canonised films like Romero's, were certainly onto something in their analysis of the downbeat ending of *Night of the Living Dead* as foreboding the racial apocalypse seemingly on the horizon in 1968. However, much of the dystopic fantasising of the 1950s and early 1960s had contained a strong element of social commentary that is relevant in analysing *Night of the Living Dead*. The aforementioned end-of-the-world genre, particularly Stanley Kramer's *The World, the Flesh, and the Devil*, which featured Harry Belafonte, contained African Americans as (secondary) protagonists. The final images of *Night of the Living Dead*, of Ben's body being dragged into the dawn sunlight to be immolated with the remains of the zombies, is part of a strain of such imagery that is characteristic of the genre. The penultimate image in the film, a close-up of the dead faces of Ben and the first zombie in repose, recalls one of the final ruminations of *I Am Legend's* Robert Neville, who, 'with an inward shock that he could not recognise in the rush of the moment . . . realised that he felt more deeply toward the vampires than he did toward their executioners.'[44]

Thus, *Night of the Living Dead* shared a number of traits with the horror and science-fiction films of the previous fifteen years. These generic traits helped the film fit into programming strategies for the matinee. That is, many staples of the horror-matinee circuit were a decade old and had been in rotation on television for years. In the spring of 1966, for example, the Towne Theater in Levittown, Pennsylvania, was playing a double feature of American International's *The Screaming Skull* (1958) and *I Was a Teenage Frankenstein* (1957).[45] Two weeks later, the Nixon was running Allied Artists' *Frankenstein 1970* (1958) and *Caltiki, the Immortal Monster* (1959),[46] while in May 1966, the inner-city Uptown, at Broad and Dauphin, featured a double bill of the Jerry Lewis comedy *Who's Minding the Store* (1963) and Ed Wood's ten-year-old *Bride of the Monster*.[47]

A comparison of weekly television schedules in the *Philadelphia Inquirer* with that paper's movie listings suggests that exhibitors remained unconcerned about or even oblivious to day-and-date competition with television. In July 1966, the Uptown ran a double feature of Allied Artists' *Castle of Blood* and *Monster from the Ocean Floor*, although the latter had been on television the previous Tuesday,[48] and in 1967 Philly's Route 309 Drive-In showed AIP's *Queen of Blood* (1966) twenty-four hours before it showed up on Channel 48's *Double Chiller Theater* under its TV title, *Planet of Blood*.[49]

Difficulties often plagued neighborhood theaters that were subsisting on the eclectic mix of subsequent-runs, matinees, and exploitation films. Far from atypical were the weekends of June 11, 1966, when the Leader featured a kiddie-horror matinee of *Blood of Dracula* (1958) and *Captain Sinbad's Magic Voyage* (1963) while in the features in the evening were Audubon Film's racial sexploitation drama *I Spit on Your Grave* (1965) and the mondo sexploiter *Ecco* (1963).[50] Six months later, another inner-city house, the Pearl, showed *I Married a Monster from Outer Space* (1958) and *Hey, There, It's Yogi Bear* (1963) in the daytime, while evening patrons were treated to a first-run double feature of *The Pink Pussycat* and *Unsatisfied*.[51]

Some theaters attempted to show the same movie at the matinee and in the evening: First-run multiple engagements of *King of the Grizzly* at the Pearl[52] and *Fireball 500* at the Avenue on Lehigh[53] (both July 1966) and Disney's *Bullwhip Griffin* at the Center City Broadway and the Norris in Norristown (both March 1967)[54] could easily perform matinee service. Other evening combinations were more problematic fits. In March 1967, the Capital in West Philadelphia carried *For a Few Dollars More* in the matinee slot,[55] the Leader showed its regular evening program of *The Dirty Dozen* and *Thunder Alley* as the matinee the following September,[56] and the Nixon used its matinee to continue the regular first-run multiple opening of Fox's Hammer double feature *Frankenstein Created Woman* and *The Mummy's Shroud* later that month.[57] One of the reasons for this practice was the increasing control that the major distributors were attempting to exert over the nabe box office. Both Edward Meyerberg of kiddie distributor New Trends Associates and Marshall Fine of the National Association of Theater Owners lambasted the practices of distributors who either insisted on exclusivity in the runs of their evening pictures or on inserting clauses in film rental contracts entitling the distributors to a percentage of the entire day's gross receipts. Both these practices often had the unintended effect of forcing neighborhood theaters, in the rare cases when they were enjoying first-run status as part of a wide multiple opening, to show the adult-oriented evening picture at the matinee.[58]

In Philadelphia, the multiple-break, or mass-territorial, opening for *Night of the Living Dead* utilized twenty neighborhood theaters and drive-ins, including the Leader and the two drive-ins that often specialized in horror fare: the Airport, in southwest Philadelphia, and the Ridge Pike Drive-In, in Conshohocken. For inner-city theater owners, the film appeared to be exploitable in both horror-matinee and evening slots. In the afternoon, *Night of the Living Dead* could be shown with a years-old AIP or Allied Artists black-and-white programmer (with which, as I have shown, *Night of the Living Dead* shared a number of traits). In the evening, the film could be highlighted on a double bill with a second feature designed to appeal to the African American audience. At the Merben, on Frankford Avenue, *Night of the Living Dead* played its first-run engagement with the Poitier prestige drama *For the Love of Ivy*. This combination showed up the following week at the Nixon and the Eric Terminal, at 69th and Market. The Eric, in suburban Fairless Hills, played Romero's film on a double bill with the Jim Brown caper *The Split*. At the Astor, on Girard Avenue, *Night of the Living Dead* played with the Dean Martin and Robert Mitchum western *Five Card Stud*. Finally, at the Mount Holly, in New Jersey, the film was part of a double feature with the Toho giant-monster import *King Kong Escapes*.

At the Eric Terminal, Eric Fairless Hills, Mount Holly, and Astor, these double features, including Romero's film, were carried over into the matinee slot. At the Nixon, the management wisely substituted an AIP double feature of *Invasion of the Saucer Men* (1957) and *Circus of Horrors* (1960).[59] The management's wisdom was born of bitter experience. In 1964, Nixon manager George Norcutt had been fined $1,000 by a grand jury for 'giving and advertising an obscene show' and 'contributing to the delinquency of minors' for featuring the 'obscene, sadistic, and perverted' Herschell Gordon Lewis *Blood Feast* at an April Saturday matinee.[60] By 1968, the protracted scenes of zombie extras, some partially or completely nude, munching on chocolate syrup-soaked entrails in the black-and-white *Night of the Living Dead* equaled or surpassed anything in Lewis's groundbreaking Eastmancolor gore classic.

It was under a similar set of circumstances that Ebert witnessed the onslaught of *Night of the Living* in inner-city Chicago. After the unexpected end of the second act, when the teenaged couple and would-be protagonists Tom and Judy are incinerated and devoured by the ghouls, 'the mood of the audience changed,' according to Ebert. 'Horror movies were fun, sure, but this was pretty strong stuff. There wasn't a lot of screaming anymore. The place was pretty quiet.' At the end of the movie, the theater was silent:

> I don't think the younger kids really knew what hit them. They'd seen horror movies before, but this was something else. This was ghouls eating people – You could actually see what they were eating. This was little girls killing their mothers. This was being set on fire. Worst of all, nobody got out alive – even the hero got killed.[61]

At the end of Ebert's tirade, he appealed to the recently adopted MPAA age-based classification system and noted that the Walter Reade Organisation and Continental did not subscribe to the ratings.[62] Reade's theaters began using the MPAA classification system in late 1968, but the company steadfastly refused to submit Continental releases to the board for classification.[63]

Conclusion

Night of the Living Dead did not meet Reade's expectations of a million-dollar gross in the first year of release. However, thanks to the unremitting success of the film at midnight screenings and campus film societies in the U.S. and its excellent box-office returns in Europe and Japan, the gross far exceeded that figure.

To Romero's horror, the film seemed to pass into the public domain after Continental folded in the 1970s. The film's working title had been *The Night of Anubis*, after the jackal-headed Egyptian god of mummification and the underworld, but when Continental changed the title card on release prints to the more commercial *Night of the Living Dead*, it neglected to include a copyright notice. In the 1980s, at the dawn of the video era, the film turned up in virtually every public-domain video catalog. The years of lost revenue attributable to this oversight were responsible for the filmmakers' decision to regroup for a color remake in 1990 and a rescored DVD release of the original black-and-white version in 1999.

The influence of *Night of the Living Dead* is incalculable. It established on-screen cannibalism as *the* horror motif of the 1970s, spawned two Romero-directed sequels and countless imitations in Europe, and inspired homages in films as disparate as *Pink Flamingos* (1972) and *They Came from Within* (1975). The film was even screened at the Museum of Modern Art.

Its artistic elements anticipate many trends in the low-budget horror and blaxploitation genres of the 1970s. When it was released in 1968, however, it shared both generic traits and marketing elements with the horror and science-fiction genre films of the 1950s and the low-budget race-themed topical dramas of its time, both of which were crucial programming elements in the doomed efforts of theaters serving the inner-city neighborhood market to adapt to the changing movie marketplace. In the ensuing years, Hong Kong-produced martial arts films and the blaxploitation cycle of 1971–1974, which contained a strong current of horror-genre hybrids like *Blacula* (1972) and *Abby* (1974), created interest at the inner-city nabe box office. By the end of this cycle, in the mid-1970s, though, Philadelphia's Pearl, Nixon, Uptown, and Leader theaters had closed their doors for good.

The case of *Night of the Living Dead* illustrates how issues of audience, text, and industrial context intersected during a period of immense change in both popular culture and the American film industry. A thorough and nuanced history of the horror film in the decades following the breakup of the Hollywood studio system must chart the changing commercial and cultural functions of the horror genre against the background of historical issues touched on in this essay. These issues include the changing relationship between the distribution and exhibition branches of the film industry, the rise of independent production and television syndication, and the growing importance of overseas markets and international coproduction.

NOTES

I would like to thank Don Crafton, Paul Ramaeker, and Rick Worland for many helpful comments on the several drafts of this essay.

1. 'Reade Starts 2nd Vacation Movie Series,' *Motion Picture Herald*, May 15, 1954, 45.
2. Rev. of *Night of the Living Dead, Variety*, October 16, 1968.
3. See J. Hoberman and Jonathan Rosenbaum, *Midnight Movies* (New York: Harper and Row, 1983), 110; Robin Wood, 'George Romero: Apocalypse Now,' in *Hollywood from Vietnam to Reagan* (New York: Columbia University Press, 1986), 115; Andrew Tudor, *Monsters and Mad Scientists: A Cultural History of the Horror Movie* (Oxford: Basil Blackwell, 1989); and David J. Skal, *The Monster Show: A Cultural History of Horror* (New York: Penguin Books, 1993), 307–09.
4. Roger Ebert, 'Just Another Horror Movie – Or Is It?' *Chicago Sun-Times*, January 5, 1969.
5. Ibid.
6. In 1953 and later in 1956, the Senate Small Business Committees held hearings to investigate possible restraint of trade on the part of major distributors. While many small exhibitors complained of a shortage of product, excessive first runs, and confiscatory rentals, their requested solution, binding arbitration of film rentals, was not adopted in the committee's final report. See *Motion Picture Distribution Trade Practices – 1956*, Hearings before a subcommittee of the Select Committee on Small Business, 83rd Congress, 2d sess., 1956. Many of the changes in the sixties film distribution and exhibition landscape are outlined in Gary Edgerton, *American Film Exhibition and an Analysis of the Motion Picture Industry's Market Structure, 1963–1980* (New York: Garland, 1983).
7. Walter Reade, Jr., 'Recipe for Getting and Maintaining the Film Audience,' *Motion Picture Herald*, April 3, 1963, 9.

8. See 'Continental Plans to Refile Damage Action on "Room,"' *Motion Picture Herald*, May 20, 1961, 12.
9. 'Legion of Decency Condemns "Expresso,"' *Motion Picture Herald*, May 7, 1960, 13.
10. 'Legion Condemns "Saturday,"' *Motion Picture Herald*, May 13, 1961, 15, and 'Britain's "Saturday Night" Banned in Kansas City,' *Motion Picture Herald*, July 1, 1961, 16.
11. See '$273,000 Budget on Reade-Sterling "Black Like Me."' *Variety*, July 17, 1963, 3.
12. 'Race to Film Race Issues,' *Variety*, July 17, 1963, 20.
13. Movie listings, *Philadelphia Inquirer*, June 3, 1964, 31, and Movie listings, *Philadelphia Inquirer*, June 10, 1964, 30.
14. 'One Third of Film Public: Negro,' *Variety*, November 29, 1967, 3.
15. Movie listings, *Philadelphia Inquirer*, October 11, 1965.
16. Movie listings, *Philadelphia Inquirer*, January 21, 1967.
17. Movie listings, *Philadelphia Inquirer*, March 25, 1967.
18. Movie listings, *Philadelphia Inquirer*, September 28, 1965.
19. Movie listings, *Philadelphia Inquirer*, June 25, 1966.
20. 'Pathé-America's 1962 Financing of 12-to-18 Indie Features,' *Variety*, December 27, 1961, 3.
21. 'Let 'Em Ripps: Dixie & Pixie; Fink, Trash, Guts as Typical Sell,' *Variety*, August 4, 1965, 5.
22. 'Puzzle Re Clarke's "Cool World,"' *Variety*, November 11, 1964, 23.
23. 'Dixie Shy of 'Black Like Me,' *Variety*, February 17, 1965, 7.
24. See 'Reade, Sterling TV in Merger,' *Broadcasting*, December 25, 1961, 47.
25. 'Nice Notices Not Negotiable; Reade's Policy Now Hard-Nosed,' *Variety*, September 15, 1965, 7.
26. 'Bettered Outlook at Continental Co.,' *Variety*, November 8, 1965, 5, 21.
27. See Continental trade ad, *Variety*, January 8, 1966, 87, and 'Pasolini's "St. Matthew" for Reade; New Range of Product Ups Quarter,' *Variety*, November 24, 1965, 7.
28. 'Reade-Sterling Turns Around From 491G Loss in '64 to 505G Profit,' *Variety*, May 4, 1966, 12, and 'Walter Reade/Sterling Shows 1965 Fiscal Profit,' *Broadcasting*, April 20, 1966, 78–9.
29. 'Woes of Special Matinees; Kids Dates Hit, Indie in Blast,' *Variety*, April 13, 1966, 24.
30. 'Source of U.S. Kidpix: Mexico,' *Variety*, December 16, 1964, 7.
31. 'Kiddie Matinee Economics; Timeless Pics, With Pitfalls,' *Variety*, October 25, 1967, 13.
32. 'Source of U.S. Kidpix,' 24.
33. 'Kiddie Matinee Economics,' 13.
34. See Thomas Doherty, *Teenagers and Teenpics: The Juvenilization of American Movies in the 1950s* (Boston: Allen and Unwin, 1988), and William Paul, *Laughing/Screaming: Modern Hollywood Horror and Comedy* (New York: Viking, 1994).
35. Skal devotes an entire chapter to this phenomenon, which he calls 'The Graveyard Bash.' See *The Monster Show*, 263–86.
36. U.S. Department of Commerce, Business and Defense Services Administration, *U.S. Industrial Outlook 1968* (Washington: U.S. Government Printing Office, 1967), 85–6.
37. See 'Reade in L.A.; Non-Theater Pix Up; "Ulysses" at $3-Mil; TV Insures "War & Peace,"' *Variety*, November 20, 1968, 26.
38. 'Showmanship Links U.S.–U.S.S.R.: Soviet and Reade on "War & Peace,"' *Variety*, April 17, 1968, 5.
39. 'Reade's "W & P" Sell: Tix Going By Installments,' *Variety*, July 5, 1968, 7, and 'Saxton Strong on Reade Regardless of Rutland Deal,' *Variety*, October 30, 1968.
40. 'After Gamy "Ulysses," It's Inter-Racial "Dutchman" For Reade Distribution,' *Variety*, February 1, 1967, 24.

41. See Continental trade ad, *Variety*, October 9, 1968, 18,
42. See Movie listings, *Philadelphia Inquirer*, October 23, 1968, 27.
43. Richard Matheson, *I Am Legend* (New York: Walker and Company, 1954), 15–16.
44. Ibid., 113.
45. Movie listings, *Philadelphia Inquirer*, May 21, 1966.
46. Movie listings, *Philadelphia Inquirer*, June 25, 1966.
47. Movie listings, *Philadelphia Inquirer*, May 28, 1966.
48. Movie listings, *Philadelphia Inquirer*, July 30, 1966.
49. Movie listings, *Philadelphia Inquirer*, October 13, 1967.
50. Movie listings, *Philadelphia Inquirer*, June 11, 1966.
51. Movie listings, *Philadelphia Inquirer*, February 4, 1967.
52. Movie listings, *Philadelphia Inquirer*, June 18, 1966.
53. Movie listings, *Philadelphia Inquirer*, July 23, 1966.
54. Movie listings, *Philadelphia Inquirer*, March 18, 1967, and March 25, 1967.
55. Movie listings, *Philadelphia Inquirer*, March 25, 1967.
56. Movie listings, *Philadelphia Inquirer*, September 2, 1967.
57. Movie listings, *Philadelphia Inquirer*, September 16, 1967.
58. 'Theatres Warned to Retain Matinee Rights for Kidpix,' *Variety*, April 27, 1966, 7, and 'Woes of Special Matinees,' 13.
59. Movie listings, *Philadelphia Inquirer*, November 1, 1968.
60. ' "Blood Feast" Arrest; Hold House Manager on "Delinquency" Angle,' *Variety*, April 1, 1964, 8.
61. Roger Ebert, 'Just Another Horror Movie – Or Is It?,' *Chicago Sun-Times*, January 5, 1969.
62. Ibid.
63. See 'Sans Allies, Reade Complies.' *Variety*, December 18, 1968, 3.

19

FROM MOVIE BRATS TO MOVIE BLOCKBUSTERS

If the late 1960s and early 1970s witnessed a fascination with the art cinema within the Hollywood mainstream, the late 1970s is often seen as a ruthless reassertion of the supposed conservatism of commercialism and entertainment. However, it was the new generation of largely college-educated 'movie brats' who had been central to the modernist Hollywood of the previous period who were central to the shift from the modernist art cinema to blockbuster fantasies. Furthermore, while this moment is often associated with a nostalgic reference to the Hollywood past, as has already been pointed out, the modernist moment was itself ironically infused with a reverence for the golden age of classical cinema.

Despite this shift, the period from 1975 to 1980 is also distinguished by another feature. The importance of the director as a figure had grown dramatically in the late 1970s and during this period successful directors acquired considerable power. This was also exacerbated by a situation in which the studios were increasingly reliant on a few hit films a year to cover costs. By the end of the decade, though, many directors had developed a reputation for reckless extravagance and self-indulgence.

One figure who is often seen as especially representative of these processes was Stephen Spielberg. Originally, emerging from television, Spielberg's first break in films was with *Duel* (1971), in which a car driver is menaced by a large truck while travelling cross-country. The film was originally made for television and based on a short story by Richard Matheson, a key figure in 1950s horror whose stories had been staples of shows such as *The Twilight Zone* and who had written key scripts for Roger Corman's Poe adaptations. Despite being made for television, the film received a successful theatrical release, and was followed by *Sugarland Express* (1974), a small road movie in which a young couple kidnap a highway patrolman and force him to drive them across country so that they can reclaim their baby, which the state has taken into care. Stylistically, and in terms of its subject matter, the film was clearly reminiscent of a series of counter cultural and modernist films from the period, particularly *Bonnie and Clyde*.

Spielberg's next film was to be quite different. *Jaws* (1975) was a calculated studio blockbuster that was to become a cinematic phenomenon and representative of many of the changes transforming the industry. The studio had bought the rights to the original novel before publication and was therefore able to use the book to promote the film and vice versa. In this way, the film was the centre of a careful and complex marketing campaign that made it into a runaway hit. Interestingly, the film also worked through very careful references to the cinematic past, such as 1950s monster movies and particularly *The Creature from the Black Lagoon* (1954).

The film turned Spielberg into a star and gave him the industrial clout to make the monumental science fiction epic, *Close Encounters of the Third Kind* (1977). It was also a magnificent hit and a special effects extravaganza. The film is suffused with a sense of imagination, wonder and awe, which it associates not only with children but also with the films of Spielberg's own past. The film even features a performance from François Truffaut, the French New Wave director whose own breakthrough film was *400 Blows* (1959), which recounted his own childhood and his own love of the cinema.

Despite these successes, Spielberg's next film was a massive flop, a colossally overblown slapstick comedy about the panic that gripped Los Angeles in the aftermath of Pearl Harbor, *1941* (1979). The film did considerable damage to the director's reputation, which was only rehabilitated by the success of *Raiders of the Lost Ark* (1981) and *ET: The Extra Terrestrial* (1982). *Raiders of the Lost Ark* was a large action adventure in which archaeologist Indiana Jones travels the globe and encounters countless dangers as he tries to prevent the Nazis capturing a legendary religious relic that will enable them to dominate the world. Again the film was filled with references, particularly to *The Ten Commandments* (1956) and *Citizen Kane* (1941), but although it was a big-budget blockbuster, Spielberg made a great play of the economy and discipline of his filmmaking, which enabled him to bring it in on time and on budget. He then made a point of turning his back on big budget filmmaking for the production of *ET*, a modestly budgeted film about a boy's relationship with an alien, a film that ironically went on to become one of his biggest and best loved hits.

Although directed by Spielberg, *Raiders of the Lost Ark*'s posters emphasised that it was produced by George Lucas, who is also seen as representative of transformations within the industry during this period. Unlike Spielberg, Lucas was very much a product of film school and, at the start of his career, he was the most avant-garde of all the movie brats. He was fascinated by experimental cinema, and his college film was a strange avant-garde science fiction piece that was later converted into cinema release under the title *THX1138* (1971). The film portrayed a future world run by robot policemen where the population is kept docile through drugs. His next film was a classic of the modernist cinema, *American Graffiti* (1973), which concerned a young man spending his last night in his small Californian hometown before leaving for college the next day. The film is a loving recreation of the sights and sounds of the early 1960s that casts it all in a nostalgic glow. Although the story examines the loss of innocence, a key modernist concern, there is still a strong sense that Lucas is less interested in the content than in the formal features of the film, the play of different sounds and images that pre-occupied his early experimental work.

This becomes even more emphatic in a fantasy adventure that he made as a labour of love, despite the lack of support from the studios: *Star Wars* (1977). Again the film is concerned with childhood innocence and the powers of imagination, and is a virtual recreation of the kind of fantasy adventure serials that he had loved in his childhood. The film does contain themes common to the 1970s, with its individualistic rebel heroes battling a cold and authoritarian empire that has replaced a democratic republic, but Lucas seemed much more interested in the stylistic recreation of earlier entertainments and the technological elements (sound and visual effects) that he used to modernise and intensify the original materials.

Indeed, after *Star Wars*, he became less interested in the job of director, and became more heavily involved in the technical side, which would result in Industrial Light and Magic, his special effects studio, which remains at the cutting edge of technological transformations in the industry to this day. As a result, the sequel to *Star Wars*, *The Empire Strikes Back* (1980), not only became more oriented around special effects but was also directed by Irvin Kershner, rather than Lucas who produced the film.

Another key feature of the *Star Wars* series was that it became a merchandising goldmine and encouraged the industry to develop products that were designed to have spin-offs such as toys, novels, games, tie-ins with fast food companies and so on, a trend that is often disparaged by those who see this as rampant commercialism that has nothing to do with film aesthetics. While *Star Wars* was a stark example of how lucrative such merchandising initiatives could be, it was not itself responsible for the growth of merchandising. One of the key factors was the increasing conglomeration of the movie industry during the late 1960s and 1970s. As the industry went into recession, it was ripe for acquisition by media empires that sought to add the industry to their portfolio of other entertainment companies, and hopefully create cross-media products that would enable different entertainment sections to promote one another.

A classic example of this was *Saturday Night Fever* (1977), which represented a major shift in the musical. The music used was largely non-diegetic, pre-recorded music by artists working in the music industry. *Saturday Night*

Fever, for example, was famous for its use of the Bee Gees. The film was also produced by Robert Stigwood, a music industry figure who used the film to promote their music, even as the music promoted the film. Film and soundtrack were therefore mutually supportive products and, like *Jaws* and *Star Wars*, the film had numerous different spin-offs.

In the analysis of the changing function of films within the industry, many critics make the same mistake of which they accuse the industry and its audiences – they forget the films themselves – and *Saturday Night Fever* is interesting because it is both more conventional than is often acknowledged and more unconventional. As a musical, it is actually very reminiscent of many classic backstage musicals insofar as it concerns the story of a young man with a talent for dancing whose talent offers him the possibility of social mobility. He yearns to break free of his working-class roots but he lacks the courage and rejects the cultural pretensions of other social climbers. Its style and content, however, also distinguish it from earlier musicals insofar as its depiction of working-class life draws heavily on the modernist cinema. The film deals with material that was often taboo in a musical, particularly sexual material, and it features a very disturbing rape. Indeed, the film is so dark that once the hysteria surrounding the film took hold, the studios had to produce an edited version that could play to those in the pre- or early-teens who were desperate to see the film.

Part of the reason for this desperation was the handling of male sexuality, and its male star, John Travolta, not only became an overnight star but did so largely due to the extreme eroticisation of his body. Though many film theorists claimed that the woman was the privileged object of the look within Hollywood cinema of the time, it would be hard to establish in this case. This is not to suggest that the film is an example of feminist cinema but simply that the film revolved around the eroticisation of its male star and no female within the film comes anywhere near diverting the gaze from his body.

The period also became preoccupied with fantasy cinema. Although science fiction was dominated by big-budget special effects features, horror was also an important genre of the period and it was dominated by small-budget productions. Certainly, the horror boom was partly a response to the massive success of big studio productions such as *The Exorcist* and *The Omen*, but these themselves were attempts to cash in on the success of the low-budget horrors of which *Night of the Living Dead* and *The Texas Chainsaw Massacre* are examples. The key horror film in this period remains *Halloween* (1978), a story about three schoolgirls who are targeted by an unstoppable psycho-killer. The film was directed by John Carpenter and was praised for its brilliant stylistic features and its clever and self-conscious referencing. Indeed, the film is a brilliant synthesis of elements from psycho-killer movies such as *Psycho*, which it cleverly references through a range of features including its casting of Jamie Leigh Curtis, the daughter of *Psycho*'s first victim, Janet Leigh.

The film, and the cycle of 'slasher films' that followed its success, has also been heavily attacked as an anti-feminist film that punishes sexually active women.

However, this position has also been attacked on a number of grounds, and it has even been pointed out that key features of these films are actually the lack of positive and effective male figures and the presence of a strong female lead or 'final girl' who is the one who engages the killer most effectively and usually dispatches the killer at the end. The figure of the killer is also significant in that while it blends elements of the demonic possession films such as *The Exorcist* and *The Omen* with the psycho-killer of *Psycho*, *The Texas Chainsaw Massacre* and *Black Christmas* (1974), it is also an example of the blank, unstoppable killers such as the shark in *Jaws* and the creature in *Alien* (1979). Indeed, the key detail about the killer, Michael Myers, is his eyes, which are described in a speech that bears strong similarities to Quint's famous monologue about the shark in *Jaws*.

In addition to the major success of the slasher movie cycle that ran from 1978 to 1982 and included *Friday the 13th*, *The Shining* and *Terror Train* (all 1980), the period also saw a series of science fiction horror monsters such as the bio-engineered killer fish in *Piranha* (1978), the chemically enlarged sewer dweller in *Alligator* (1980), and the shape-shifting creature in *Alien*. *Alien* itself has not only become a film franchise that survives until the present day, but it has also received considerable critical acclaim. In narrative terms, it is little more than a science fiction slasher movie, in which an alien creature kills off the crew of a spaceship one by one until it is eventually killed by the film's own final girl, Ellen Ripley. However, the critical reception was largely due to the film's impressive visual style and its clear contrast to the lighter, less adult science fiction on offer. It was directed by Ridley Scott and established him as a major director, and it was written by Dan O'Bannon, who had worked with John Carpenter on the brilliantly witty cult science fiction classic, *Dark Star* (1974), in which a group of bored and seemingly stoned hippie spacemen travel the universe until they are forced to discuss existentialism with a talking bomb in order to persuade it of the futility of exploding.

In addition to low-budget slashers, the period also saw a series of low-budget teen comedies that were usually distinguished by their deliberate bad taste. The cycle began after the success of *Animal House* (1978), a comedy about a fraternity in the early 1960s that rejects the repressive values of other fraternities and rebels against the college authorities. There is no sixties political idealism here. The rebellion is purely hedonistic and is clearly presented as completely doomed to failure. It is merely an orgy of anarchic energy. The film was directed by John Landis, who became a major comedy director of the late 1970s and early 1980s with films such as cult classics *The Blues Brothers* (1980) and *An American Werewolf in London* (1981).

Although *Animal House* was a major studio release, the films that followed it were largely small-budget films such as *Meatballs* (1979) and *Porky's* (1982) that were more focused on sexual humour. The anarchy of *Animal House* was mostly defined through the causal attitude to sex and implicit lack of repression, but the films that followed largely revolved around the misadventures of a group of teenage boys in their awkward attempts to satisfy their sexual urges.

Despite the rise of the special effects blockbuster and low-budget horror and comedy, the modernist impulse was not dead by the mid-1970s. As we have seen, the blockbusters often emerged from the modernism of the late 1960s and early 1970s, but it was also the case that the modernism of this earlier period also became the stuff of blockbusters itself. Indeed, as the success of *The Godfather* demonstrates, the two had never been that far apart, and in 1979 Francis Ford Coppola would release another epic modernist blockbuster, *Apocalypse Now*.

During the Vietnam War, the country had been polarised into those who supported and opposed military intervention and Hollywood had largely shied away from tackling the problem, but with American withdrawal in 1976, filmmakers began to tackle the conflict. In Coppola's grand, almost surreal epic, which is an adaptation of Joseph Conrad's novella *Heart of Darkness*, an army assassin (Martin Sheen) is sent up the Mekong River on a small patrol boat to kill the renegade General Kurtz (Marlon Brando). As he journeys up river, the war becomes increasingly chaotic and surreal until he reaches Kurtz's camp, which seems to have descended into primitivism and mysticism. The production of the film became legendary and was beset by all manner of disasters, some natural and some induced by its sheer excess. It therefore kept running over budget and over schedule and Coppola kept having to sink more and more finance into the venture. Eventually, however, it proved a major artistic and commercial success, a favourite of college and cult audiences for years after, even if it gave Coppola a reputation for irresponsibility and self-indulgence within the industry.

The same was not true, however, of Michael Cimino's *Heaven's Gate* (1980), which not only virtually destroyed Cimino's career but also bankrupted a studio, United Artists. Cimino had started out as a scriptwriter before directing Clint Eastwood in *Thunderbolt and Lightfoot* (1974). He then took on *The Deer Hunter* (1978), an epic story of three steelworkers and the impact of Vietnam upon their lives. The film initially won immense critical praise and was a major commercial success, but stories started to emerge about the liberties that it had taken with history and the film was even accused of overt racism. By the time that Cimino's next film came out the critics seemed eager to make the film pay for their excessive praise of the previous film. Added to this, *Heaven's Gate* was an absolutely monumental film with a massive budget that came to represent the hubris of contemporary filmmakers. The film was therefore not only panned by the critics but spectacularly failed at the box office. Although the film also takes liberties with the history that it recounts, *Heaven's Gate* is actually a quite remarkable film, if rather unclear and confused. It recounts the history of a range war between settlers and cattle barons, and aspires to a poetic grandeur that it often achieves, even though its attempt to emulate the art cinema's ambiguous characterisations often makes it frustrating, unsatisfying and obscure.

The one director of the period who was influenced by the art cinema but escaped accusations of irresponsibility and self-indulgence was Martin Scorsese. This was partly because he made much smaller-budget films, and because they were seen as highly personal films that suggested an autobiographical dimension, even if Scorsese himself wasn't actually a hoodlum, a psychotic vigilante or a prizefighter. His first major film was *Mean Streets* (1973), the story of a small-time Italian American hoodlum who is searching for redemption and believes that it cannot be earned in the Catholic Church but only on the streets. His search for redemption goes horrifyingly wrong and ends tragically. The film featured stunning performances from Harvey Keitel and Robert De Niro, and a magnificent soundtrack largely made up of 1960s pop classics such as 'Be My Baby'.

His next film was *Taxi Driver* (1976), in which De Niro plays a psychotic veteran of the Vietnam War, Travis Bickle, whose alienation from American society on his return home leads to violence and mayhem. Lost and searching for a purpose, Bickle becomes obsessed with a teenage runaway (Jodie Foster) who is working as a prostitute for a pimp (Harvey Keitel). Bickle decides to rescue her from this life through a psychotic outburst of violence. The film borrows heavily from John Ford's classic western *The Searchers* (1956) and features a disturbingly ironic end in which it is Bickle's violence that finally leads to his redemption: it makes him into a hero and so enables him to be assimilated into the society from which he had previously been alienated.

Scorsese's next film also concerned male violence and became the subject of some debate over the handling of its subject matter. *Raging Bull* (1980) was a biography of prizefighter Jake La Motta, but while Jake's violence makes him a success in the ring, he does not know how to function in everyday life. Verbally and emotionally inarticulate, he is overwhelmed with sexual paranoia in his relationships with women, particularly his long-suffering wife. Some critics were concerned about the film's fascination with male violence and particularly violence against women, but for most it was a brilliant analysis of violence. Indeed, *Raging Bull* continues to be seen by many critics as one of the greatest movies of all time for its uncompromising and unflinching portrayal of La Motta and for its endless stylistic invention.

As should be clear, many of the classics of the Hollywood Renaissance and its aftermath were highly masculine, but those films associated with Jane Fonda were exceptions. Fonda's career goes back to the 1960s when she was originally known for her sex appeal, although her image began to change as she joined the protests against the Vietnam War, and became known as 'Hanoi Jane'. In the first half of the 1970s, she made a number of key films, particularly *Klute*, one of Alan J. Pakula's best paranoid thrillers, and *Julia* (1977), a key women's film of the period that strongly emphasised its political credentials and has therefore often been celebrated as a major feminist achievement. The film is a biographical story that concerns the relationship between the left-wing writer Lillian Helman (Fonda) and a female friend from her childhood. This relationship is told against the background of twentieth-century politics, particularly the rise of Nazism and the witch-hunts of Cold War America.

In the second half of the 1970s, Fonda not only worked as star of her films, but also produced them, and she made a series of political films. *Coming Home* (1978), for example, tells the story of a middle-class housewife who starts to do volunteer work while her husband is away in Vietnam, and falls for a wheelchair bound veteran through whom she learns about the realities of the war. Her next film, *The China Syndrome* (1979), concerns a local newswoman who starts investigating a nuclear power plant and reveals corruption that could endanger the planet. The 'China Syndrome' of the title is a reference to the possible outcome of a nuclear accident, in which a reactor would create radioactive matter that would burn its way through the earth and keep going until it reached China, on the other side of the world from the United States. The topicality of the film was further enhanced by an incident at a nuclear plant on Three Mile Island that happened close to the release of the film. Although Fonda also went on to make other films, such as the self-consciously feminist comedy *Nine to Five* (1980), she became better known in the 1980s for her exercise videos than for her films, many of which became largely self-serving vehicles that lacked the political or dramatic values of her earlier films.

Despite Fonda's critical reputation, it was Barbra Streisand who was the most important female star of the 1970s in commercial terms. Fonda gets more attention because of her closeness to the masculine aesthetics of the Hollywood Renaissance, through her appearances in films such as *Klute* and her production of art cinema influenced films such as *Coming Home* and *The China Syndrome*. Streisand demonstrates that one of the problems with existing histories of the 1970s is the tendency to concentrate on films that are distinguished by their artistic credentials rather than their industrial significance or importance to audiences. As a result, in David Cook's mammoth history of the period, *Lost Illusions*, the film *The Way We Were*, which featured Streisand and Redford, is dismissed in a few sentences, despite being the fourth highest earner of 1973, and *A Star is Born* is only mentioned in passing on a couple of occasions, despite being the second highest earner of 1976. Nor are the values that privilege Fonda over Streisand unique to Cook, whose history at least mentions these stars and their films. On the contrary, these values are central to most discussions of the period. Indeed, it is only in the late 1970s, when Streisand became a director and made a series of bids for seriousness, that she started to be written about in more detail, but this period was far less commercially successful. In his account, Cook dismisses *The Way We Were* as too glossy and romantic to be taken seriously as a discussion of the American left from the radical 1930s through to the Cold War of the 1950s. It is therefore interesting that if Streisand's films were seen as too feminine, critics had more time for the small number of women's films that tried to tackle feminism in the period. Some of these starred Fonda but others, including *Alice Doesn't Live Here Anymore* (1974), *An Unmarried Woman* (1978) and *Girlfriends* (1978), all in different ways, deal with women learning to live with independence, even if many eventually seem to find happiness with a male lover.

The late 1970s also saw the emergence of Australia as a major film producer. Although films had been made in and by Australia before this period, the 1970s saw the establishment of the Australian Film Development Corporation, later renamed the Australia Film Commission, which provided government support for film production. The initiative proved highly successful and the late decade saw a series of international successes. One interesting feature of the Australian film industry during this period was that it did not try to emulate the European art cinema. Although the films were often marked as quality productions, they were not directed at the art market but were unashamedly examples of popular generic filmmaking that sought to compete with Hollywood. For example, Peter Weir's first feature was *The Cars that Ate Paris* (1974), a weird horror film in which a small town, off the beaten track, has been preying on unsuspecting motorists. Eventually the cars of their victims that have been freakishly transformed by the predators turn on the town and destroy it. This was followed by *Picnic at Hanging Rock* (1975), in which sexual tensions in a girls' school erupt when an inexplicable incident befalls a school trip to Hanging Rock, a natural monument heavily associated with the Australian nation, in much the same way as the Grand Canyon is associated with America. In *The Last Wave* (1977), American actor Richard Chamberlain plays a man whose investigations lead him into the world of Aboriginal myth, and the film ends with a magnificent apocalyptic vision of a great wave that has been called forth by Aboriginal magic to wipe the continent clean and free it from the corrupt Western civilisation that has colonised it. Gillian Armstrong also emerged as an important director with *My Brilliant Career* (1979), the film version of a literary classic in which a women is eventually forced to reject the love of men so that she can achieve independence as a writer. The film was celebrated as a major feminist film at the time and made stars of both Judie Davis and Sam Neill.

It was the career of George Miller, though, that would prove most successful financially, if not always critically, and it started dramatically with the release of *Mad Max* (1979), a hybrid of the vigilante film, road movie, horror film and post-apocalypse science fiction. Society is falling apart; gangs roam the highways and a small group of brutal police are the only hope for law and order. Max is one of these policemen but when the gangs kill his wife and child, he goes on the rampage in revenge. The film was visually inventive and brilliantly realised, despite its small budget, and it went on to become a major box office success, even in the United States, where it had to be redubbed from Australian into American! It made a star of its leading man, a very young Mel Gibson, and was followed in 1982 by an Australian made, but Hollywood financed sequel, *Mad Max 2* or *The Road Warrior* (1981), which took the strengths of the first film but extended them into a magnificent epic. Indeed, the story is told by a narrator in a future that recounts a mythic story of the primitive pre-history of his own society in which the foundation of that society depends upon, but must also reject, Max's heroic action.

The analysis of film industries has much to tell us about the ways in which films get made. However, most of this work concentrates on the strategies of those responsible for organising and managing the processes of production rather than those involved in the actual creative processes being organised and managed. This does not mean that those involved in management do not have creative agendas or make creative decisions, but it does stress the necessity of making a distinction between management and cultural practitioners (actors, directors, set designers and so on), if only because the perception of a difference is so central to these organisations. Managers spend much of their time trying to discipline and control creative workers, who are often seen as irresponsible and as having no interest in the economic bottom line; while creative workers spend much of their time complaining about interference from management, who are seen as tasteless bureaucrats with no interest in aesthetic issues.

While most research on creative workers is through textual analysis, in which the intentions of filmmakers are simply deduced from an analysis of the text, Gianluca Sergi represents an alternative approach, which examines the decision-making processes of filmmakers through an analysis of their own accounts of these processes. The extract that follows analyses the sound design of *Star Wars*, a film that was pivotal within the industry through its exploration of the 'dynamic potential' of new sound technologies. It draws on traditions in historical poetics, such as those represented by the extract from Janet Staiger on scripting in Chapter 4, in which historical researchers have attempted to outline the aesthetic norms that practitioners used within their creative practices. In this work, the notion of the aesthetic norm does not imply a rule but rather a guiding principle or 'rule of thumb', which does not require strict adherence but establishes the normal practice from which creative deviation becomes meaningful. Lucas and his associates transformed practices of sound design but within terms that redefined, but did not reject, established norms of Hollywood storytelling. Sergi shows that these transformations were possible because of Dolby sound, which had been introduced to enhance sound quality but also created the opportunities for a new approach to film sound.

The continuing tendency in film studies to ignore film sound impoverishes the discipline. Indeed, a focus on sound can seriously challenge assumptions about film as a medium that are made solely in relation to the image. For example, theories of spectatorship still focus on the image – as the very term itself makes clear – and often continue to see spectatorship as being based on a radical separation from, and distance between, the spectator and the object of their gaze. However, as Sergi's research makes clear, sound design has been working in entirely the opposite direction since *Star Wars*. Indeed, the development of surround sound, as its name implies, was created in order to immerse the audience within the world of the film and to approximate the experience of being placed within the action rather than outside it.

Sergi uses different materials from those who deal with earlier historical periods and therefore do not have access to the cultural practitioners themselves. He is able not only to examine the norms that practitioners use but also the decision-making process within which these norms are put into operation. Like Staiger, he looks at manuals and guides to gain a sense of the norms in which practitioners are trained and he examines the trade press to explore the ways in which these are talked about within the industry. However, he draws many of his findings from an analysis of interviews with creative practitioners within a range of publications, although, in later work, he also conducts his own interviews with creative practitioners.

- Sergi provides an account of the ways in which the filmmakers associated with *Star Wars* sought to use new sound technologies. What are the primary sources that he consults in order to produce this account?
- Even in those situations where we are confident that filmmakers are being open and honest about their actions, or the reasons for those actions, why should we be careful about the ways in which we interpret their accounts?
- In what sources, to which you have access, do filmmakers provide accounts of their creative activities and how might the nature of these sources influence the ways in which they talk about these activities?

TALES OF THE SILENT BLAST: *STAR WARS* AND SOUND

Gianluca Sergi

It is often difficult to talk about film sound. The problem is of a cultural nature. On a critical level, a vocabulary of film sound is still to be agreed upon. Some scholars, such as Michel Chion and Rick Altman have attempted to form a basic skeleton for others to use. However, when it comes to sound, our existing film vocabulary still operates more in terms of exclusion than inclucion. From descriptions of film as a 'visual medium' and the 'moving picture' to descriptions of filmmakers as 'visionary directors' and 'masters of light,' it appears clear that our way to 'narrate' films does not include the sound aspect.[1]

This discriminatory approach toward sound in films has conditioned our basic attitude toward thinking and talking about movies in two main ways. On the one hand, we are neither equipped for nor used to articulating our thinking on film sound beyond harmful generalizations. In exemplary fashion, writing on *Star Wars* in the early days of its release, Pauline Kael reduces the complexity of one of the most innovative soundtracks in film history to one expression: 'the loudness' (708). On the other hand, we have also come to regard the topic of film sound as of a lesser value or even as damaging to the 'true' nature of cinema: the image. As Tom Levin correctly points out,

Gianluca Sergi, *Journal of Popular Film and Television*, 26 (1) Spring, 1998.

The history of the development of cinema sound can be treated as an oscillation between its difference [from the image] understood as supplement and its difference understood as a threat. (63)

This cultural inadequacy, both in linguistic and critical terms, is amplified by the tremendous development that the art of film sound has accomplished in the last 20 years. The availability of new technologies (most important, the Dolby Stereo sound system) and experimentation with multi-track mixers (as in Robert Altman's 1975 film *Nashville*) have provided filmmakers with a unique possibility to employ multilayered and multichannel sound.

This freedom to depart from prior constrictions, particularly the limiting choice between (optical) monophonic sound and expensive (magnetic) stereo, has given birth to a very sophisticated sound architecture.[2] From a limited number of tracks layered with an approach that had to deal with the real limitations imposed by mono reproduction in film theaters, soundtracks moved quickly into a new arena in which complex structures were achievable. As sound designer Walter Murch, among others, noticed, Coppola's *The Godfather* (1972) was produced and exhibited in the early 1970s following virtually the same criteria employed in 1939 for *Gone with the Wind*. Yet, new technologies allowed him to employ a radically different approach only a few years later in the film *Apocalypse Now* (1979).

In the case of surround sound, to quote but one important example, pre-Dolby soundtracks were rather 'shy' in its use, thus limiting its dynamic potential. It is only in the last 20 years that the surround sound channel has been employed with a clear realization of its potential, both as an independent sound channel and as a means to originate creative tension with the front channels. In a way, it is as though filmmakers were finally allowed to explore not only what lay immediately to the sides of the screen but the whole off-screen space, extending the aural space of the audience well beyond the confines of a two-dimensional viewing experience.[3]

George Lucas's 1977 space epic *Star Wars* (Twentieth-Century Fox) was the film that, more than any other, signaled this change – its soundtrack went further into exploring the potential of the newly available technology. It represented the most successful example of the collaboration between a new generation of sound technicians and sound-conscious directors whose formation was deeply rooted in the 1960s rock (and aural) revolution.[4] The result of that collaboration is a soundtrack that meant a breakthrough in both sound production and exhibition and that provided audiences with a new array of aural pleasures. From sound architecture to spatial awareness, from sound texture to detail, from mixing to editing, from voice characterization to physical sound, the film suggests a concept of sound that is willing to abandon its traditional shyness and move forward to challenge the primary role of the image.

Yet, this brave new approach to sound has received insufficient critical attention, Kael's reductive approach being but one example. My article aims to put the balance right, especially in lieu of the film's twentieth-anniversary theatrical re-release. First, however, for this analysis it is necessary to recognize the soundtrack as an indivisible body made of four distinct elements. Those elements – effects, music, silence, and dialogue – are significant only if seen as working in a system of collaboration, that is, as a soundtrack, with no element claiming primacy over the others. Although gifted with individual qualities, it is their fusion into a carefully balanced soundtrack that frees them from their original frame (be it music, literature, or other) and confers on them filmic significance. In a way, this should also emphasize the importance of approaching a film's soundtrack not only from its literal or musical meaning but also from its everyday quality (some notes, some words, some noise, some silence). It is with that thought in mind that we can now take a closer look at *Star Wars* and its ingenious use of sound.

A Point in Time: Historical and Institutional Considerations

Although the success of *Star Wars* is not directly imputable to one single element, a combination of economic and institutional factors can help us understand why it was such a breakthrough in film sound. First, the technological developments described above took place at a time when filmmaking practices were undergoing significant changes in Hollywood. Lucas himself was in the mold of a new emerging figure of filmmaker, one that, though floating adrift of Hollywood in a geographical and political sense, still kept the same shores firmly in sight. As Steve Neale observed, this somewhat paradoxical figure was in fact 'dedicated to the aesthetics and values of the studio-based, classical Hollywood movie, dedicated to narrative, action, spectacle, identification – and genre' (37). Thus, the so-called movie brat generation was not so much attempting to replace existing Hollywood production patterns but, rather, was exploring their boundaries, often in the light of recent technological developments. Sound was one of those boundaries.

In the case at hand, Lucas and his producer Gary Kurtz demonstrated this new attitude by approaching film sound not at a postproduction stage, as was customary (and to a certain extent still is today), but as an integral part of the creative process from the very beginning. In particular, three main changes can be identified. First, and perhaps most important, Lucas and Kurtz approached Dolby Laboratories as early as 1975 to discuss the film's philosophy toward sound. This move signaled Lucas's intention to consider sound in terms of not only production but also exhibition, always the weak link in the sound chain. The specific film genre, science fiction, was quickly seen by Dolby as a great opportunity, especially considering that previous efforts in sound innovation had mainly concentrated on musicals, such as *Nashville* (1975) and *A Star is Born* (1976). As Ioan Allen comments, 'From Dolby's point of view the subject matter would allow them to show their wares in a way more demonstrative than was common' (748). This relationship allowed Lucas to employ confidently both 35 mm and 70 mm prints after Dolby's reassurance that its new technology would be available in both formats (70 mm prints were to employ a new type of encoding designed to emphasize sub-bass response). Moreover, Dolby engineers visited the sets of *Star Wars* before shooting began in an attempt to optimize results in the production stage.

Second, Lucas hired Ben Burtt, a man who was to become the key figure in the creation of the new sound universe that Dolby hoped for and relied on for its success: Ben Burtt. As Burtt himself remembers, '[Lucas and Kurtz] just gave me a Nagra recorder and I worked out of my apartment near U.S.C. for a year, just going out and collecting sound that might be useful' (45). Lucas hired Burtt virtually at the same time that he was negotiating with Dolby, a clear indication of the correlation of interests between Lucas and Dolby. His move to hire Burtt was a direct response to the need to showcase not just a new sound system but also a new type of soundtrack whose impact would not have been experienced before. Burtt delivered exactly that by creating a whole new range of recorded sounds rather than simply employing existing sound libraries. As a result, he was awarded an unprecedented Academy Award for Special Achievements in Sound.

However attentive Lucas and his collaborators were in terms of production, the key factor in their innovations was their belief that here was a unique opportunity to change radically sound exhibition, as evidenced in their decisions during production and distribution. In the former case, all stages of sound recording (including Foley, effects, dailies, and ADR) were Dolby-encoded, and sound recordists were asked not to boost high frequencies (a practice usually employed to improve dialogue intelligibility but at the expense of dynamic range) to improve distortion levels during playback in Dolby-equipped theaters that employed wider dynamic ranges than standard theaters. As for distribution, *Star Wars* was to be released in Dolby Stereo format in over 50 per cent of theaters during its first release wave. That is to say, Lucas intended audiences to hear the difference as it had been planned and carefully orchestrated during production so that '[f]or the first time ever, the sound heard in the theater should to all intents be identical to that heard by the director during the mix' (Allen 761).

Such innovative practices and thinking were light-years from the classic Hollywood approach to sound, though the film still adhered to Hollywood's overall system of signs. As Neale has pointed out, speaking of Steven Spielberg's 1981 film *Raiders of the Lost Ark* (for which Ben Burtt won another Academy Award): 'It uses an idea [the signs] of classical Hollywood in order to promote, integrate and display modern effects, techniques and production values in order to attract a modern audience' (38).

Thus, Lucas's break with studio practices, though only partial, is significant, particularly because it had a positive effect in creating fertile ground for other filmmakers to depart from institutionalized practices when creating soundtracks, especially by employing new technologies.[5]

Hollywood as an industry was also being reshaped. New technologies apart from sound, such as cable television, satellites, pay TV, and videos were redesigning the relationship between Hollywood and other major entertainment industries, forming new alliances and opening up new avenues for revenue. In sound terms, *Star Wars* contributed to the change mainly by boosting the diffusion of the Dolby Sound System. Indeed, Dolby's sales, already significant in the music industry, in which its system of noise reduction was rapidly becoming a standard, were to skyrocket from this point on, until Dolby Sound became a standard in the film industry. A further measure of the formidable power of the alliance between the film industry and Dolby Sound can be found in its institutionalization by the Academy of Motion Picture Arts and Sciences: Since *Star Wars*, all Academy Award winners in the two sound categories have been Dolby-encoded soundtracks.

A further significant change in the period was represented by the increase in film production costs. These were significantly on the rise (the average cost increased from $2 million to $10 million during the 1970s), thus delineating a clear need to maximise profit and attract new audiences. Most crucial, in this sense, was the realisation by Lucas and his collaborators that the possibility of breaking with the low-fidelity monophonic soundtracks that had become the industry's standard during the late 1960s and early 1970s could have an impact not only on production techniques but also on audiences. The affordable Dolby stereophonic system, available to the vast majority of theaters through a relatively simple and economical installation, resuscitated the meaning of the word *stereo* for cinema audiences by dissociating it from very expensive, road-show 70 mm prints, mostly affordable only for film theaters in large city centers. More than anyone before, Lucas understood that he could confidently target the hi-fi generation emerging from the late sixties and early seventies and bank on and consolidate Hollywood's young, under-30 audience (Steve Neale's 'modern audience'), which had replaced the formerly dominant family audience.

A Sound Architecture of Change

The awesome yellow planet of Tatooine emerges from a total eclipse, her two moons glowing against the darkness. A tiny silver spacecraft, a Rebel Blockade Runner firing lasers from the back of the ship, races through space. It is pursued by a giant Imperial Stardestroyer. Hundreds of deadly laser bolts streak from the Imperial Stardestroyer, causing the main solar fin of the Rebel craft to disintegrate.[6]

The few lines above describe the opening sequence of *Star Wars*. The information given is overwhelmingly visual. Indeed, no word is directly related to sound: There is no 'deafening sound,' no 'roaring engines,' or 'squeaky metal noises.' This should not surprise us too much: In a book on screenwriting, Robert Berman identifies screenplay terminology as follows:

Fade in, fade out, angle on, another angle on, wide angle, close on, insert of, back to scene, point-of-view, reverse shot, dissolve to, cut to, tight

> angle on, pull back to, reveal, off camera, off screen, voice-over, slow pan to, in the foreground, in the background, reaction. (22)

Thus, an early consideration, as obvious as it is revealing, is that sound people and sound-literate directors often have an uphill struggle, having little or no direct indication as to what the film should 'sound like.' The process of visualisation, intended here as the translation of a screenplay's visual instructions and dialogue into images, is undoubtedly aided, if not guided, in the screenplay's passage. But the equivalent process for sound, which I will call 'audilization,' is not.[7]

As the opening titles of *Star Wars* disappear into the background at the top of the screen, the musical score does not simply fade out to allow the effects in; it is, rather literally, blasted away by an explosion (the only sound clearly indicated in the screenplay): Desperately fleeing the Imperial destroyer, the rebel ship squeaks, alarm sirens fill the air, and violins are drowned in a flood of laser bolts. From here on, the music is as though dwarfed by the power and exceptional quality of the effects, to become not a major star, but merely one of the elements of a soundtrack. In terms of sound architecture, the spatial revolution is also defined immediately: one hears starships flying overhead; ships move from right to left; and blasts are heard around the auditorium. *Star Wars* explores a universe of sound where there is not only a loud and soft, but also an up and below, a right and left, a behind and in front, and all this in little more than four minutes. This awareness of issues such as three-dimensionality and directionality goes beyond a mere understanding of technical qualities: It demonstrates a confidence in the creative use of sound not witnessed before.

It is in such a confident approach to sound that the major change is to be found. Unlike his predecessors, Lucas sensed that this was no 'freak' experiment. This was not a film whose soundtrack employed technology unavailable to other filmmakers; nor was the technology going to be available only to a handful of first-run, big-time theaters. It was quite clear that Dolby's compatibility with existing reproduction apparatuses would give it a decisive head start in the competitive arena it had just entered.

In creative terms, Lucas's confidence is constantly emphasised through a series of choices that can be summarized in a few brief considerations. The first point, as we have already seen, is that both music and dialogue are challenged by effects from the very first moments of the film, demonstrating the filmmakers' willingness to explore the full potential of a soundtrack by rejecting the well-established hierarchy that gives preference to dialogue and music over effects and silence. The possibility of employing a wider frequency range than ever before for optical tracks, thanks to Dolby's noise reduction system, certainly aided this decision.

Following this first departure from convention, a starship is distinctly heard flying overhead (itself a novelty), while another one, of a different sound signature, follows immediately afterward. This constituted too clear a departure from conventions not to be noticed by critics. Although in a symptomatically inadequate fashion, Jane Morgan's review of *Star Wars* states, 'Heraldic music accompanies the roar of a spaceship zooming onto the screen pursued by another dwarfing the first, frightening and thrilling' (437).

Indeed, Lucas's use of the surround channel, as demonstrated in the example above, is most certainly the first noticeable step toward today's aesthetics of surround, wherein the channel is less a means to provide music and some rare ambiance effects than a source of primary sound information.[8] Its former limited use, possibly a legacy of the use of the 'extra' channel employed in musicals (examples range from *West Side Story* to *My Fair Lady*, from *Oklahoma!* to *Hair*) and epics (such as *Julius Caesar, Spartacus*, and most of David Lean's films), is turned upside down in *Star Wars*, a clear signal of Lucas's confidence. When one considers that musicals and epics were the main arenas in which stereophonic sound was employed, it is easier to understand why those two sound genres had affected the use of surround sound until *Star Wars*.

A further innovation in *Star Wars* is to be found in the use of 'physical sound.' The deep and rumbling sound that the huge Imperial craft produces, achieved through an active use of sub-frequencies, is a sign of the crucial understanding that audiences can be 'reached' by sound and made to participate not only visually or orally but also *physically*, in a literal sense. Although this was hardly news to Hollywood, again Lucas shows a degree of awareness never shown before, exemplified in the opening sequence by the earth-rattling Imperial ship. The film also redefines the issue of 'sound texture' through an amazing array of various sound blasts and laser bolts: The sounds are significantly different from one another (see below). Speaking on Burtt's achievements in *Raiders of the Lost Ark*, Marc Mancini correctly identifies the impact that Burtt's work was to have in the years to come by emphasizing that '[h]is insistence on completely original or refurbished classic sounds counters the numbness we all have to recordings heard a thousand times, hence, his new sound creations can become "fresh events" ' (Burtt 45). Burtt's work has left a permanent legacy, clearly visible in many later films, from the submarine pings in *The Hunt for Red October* to the amazing array of different sounds of rain in *Forrest Gump*.

Moreover, directionality also presented room for interesting innovations. The choice of having the rebel craft sound as if it were flying from screen right to front left to rear left emphasizes the filmmakers' awareness that it was now possible to employ multichannel technology 'on the drawing board,' knowing that it would not be confined to a handful of theaters. They used sound to expand the film into off-screen space, not only to the sides of the screen, but also toward the auditorium and the audience. The spectator is immersed in a sound universe that was unknown and unavailable before, and his or her way of listening to a movie is changed forever. Indeed, in the years that followed *Star Wars* this trend has been consolidated: from sound tied to the screen image to sound free to 'fly' across the auditorium. As Michel Chion humorously emphasises, this multifaceted approach to sound has also had important consequences on the relationship between sound and the image. Today, 'sound operates on two, three, four layers of equal presence, and the image is nothing but another layer, not anymore the principal one. In this vast sonic aquarium, the image comes floating, a poor small fish' (Chion 28; my translation).

Hearing the Falling Tree: Audilization in Star Wars

Notwithstanding the technological awareness and crafting prowess described above, the main achievement of *Star Wars* lies in the successful translation of outstanding technological innovation into a powerful storytelling tool. One can tackle this aspect by looking more closely at the film's narrative and the way it was 'audilized.'

Briefly, with its villains and heroes, helpers and victims, the narrative of *Star Wars* closely follows well-known parameters. As a trilogy, *Star Wars* narrates the attempt of a small group of freedom fighters to rebel against an evil Empire. The Empire has taken over the previous Republic by exterminating its custodians and moral pillars, an order of knights called the Jedi. As the story unfolds, the rebels eventually manage to destroy the Empire's most powerful weapon (the *Death Star*), kill the evil Emperor, and turn back to goodness the Empire's chief enforcer, Darth Vader. By the end of the trilogy, the small rebellion has grown strong enough to challenge the remains of the Empire and restore the Republican order with the help of a new order of Jedi knights, led by Luke Skywalker. In short, good wins some, loses some, and eventually triumphs.

An element that needs to be established clearly, if the story is to work, is the mismatch of forces and means between the powerful Empire and the small, weaker rebellion. This element, which effectively appeals to our capacity to support the underdog and paves the way for our taking sides with the rebels, needs to be established at the beginning of the story. And it is here that the work of the film's sound designer starts.

As we have seen, the screenplay details to a certain extent the visual action taking place at the film's beginning: 'a tiny silver spacecraft' is pursued by 'a giant Imperial Stardestroyer.' The size of the two crafts engaged is unmistakably defined, and the mismatch established. However, the screenplay does not indicate what sound should be used in the same scene, let alone its quality. To put it simply, the screenplay calls for what may be defined as a 'silent blast,' a sound that is expected but whose quantity and quality are unknown and unspecified.

When we see the two starships (emphasized by the famous overhead shot of the Stardestroyer), we are asked to use elementary geometrical reasoning (i.e., big menacing triangle meets small chunky polygon; big triangle swallows up small polygon). However the sounds that the ships make can neither follow a similarly effective reasoning (a louder sound may not necessarily convey a feeling of superiority over a softer sound) nor be immediately associated with any 'real' sound (ever hear a starship before?). As soundman Claude Beaugrand correctly points out, 'The sound universe of a film finds its source in the transformed reality of the sound editor's auditory memory and his recollections' (32; my translation).

The problem here is that *Star Wars* ventures into the future, that is, a place that cannot possibly yield any auditory memories. Thus, it is not a tree that we have heard fall before. Although this was in some way an advantage for both Lucas and Dolby, insofar as it allowed the former to be creative and innovative and Dolby to show off the new sound system, it created more than just a headache for sound people, for the vast majority of sounds required in the film were not immediately available either as a concept or as actual recordable event. Hence the problem: How to make audible the mismatch between the ships? Perhaps the key is to be found not in a visual approach to sound but in an aural one. In other words, the relationship that lies at the core of the process of audilization in *Star Wars* is one that does not necessarily follow the usual top-down, image-sound hierarchy but rather one that, while following closely the overall narrative drive, starts with sound.

Star Wars shares well-known themes with Hollywood tradition and with the western film in particular. Whether chasing or being chased, firing or being fired at, future human and machine need to share as close and effective a relationship as that of man, horse, and gun in westerns. Thus, the technology associated with each of the characters bears significance to, the characters themselves and their role in the film. The sound design in *Star Wars* seems to follow this narrative device closely. As this is an unknown (unheard) world, the soundtrack must provide the audience with a structuring element, a recognizable pattern that can function as a 'lead' in a world of unknown sounds. This lead, which needs to be a splinter from our everyday life (and therefore immediately recognizable), is not so much represented by any given sound but by the sonic relationship between father and child.[9] This strategy appeals to our experience in recognizing an elementary difference: The 'father sound' holds a deep quality emphasized by its ability to reach low frequencies; the 'child sound' has a higher frequency and thus is less full bodied and more fragile. This kind of aural reasoning is embodied in the expression that a boy's voice 'has broken,' which clearly indicates our tendency to associate sounds of a higher pitch and frequency with something fragile and in a precarious state.

In *Star Wars* this 'guiding principle' is applied to both the characters and the technology at their disposal, in particular, to their flying machines. In the aforementioned opening sequence, two main characters, on opposite sides of the fight, are introduced: Darth Vader (David Prowse, with the voice of James Earl Jones) and Princess Leia (Carrie Fisher). Princess Leia's ship does not reach low frequencies to produce a deep-quality sound; rather, it is the source of a high-pitched, shrilling sound. In this it mirrors all the peculiarities pertaining to the child sound. Meanwhile, Vader's ship reaches very deep frequencies, emphasized by its earth-rumbling properties.

Coherently, the sound design follows this principle to its logical conclusion as the characters' own voices reflect the balance: When Leia and Vader finally meet on board the captured rebel craft, Leia's attempt to impose her voice (thus, her version of events) is immediately interrupted and overpowered by Vader's deep baritone voice. Indeed, this first exchange is aurally very similar to an encounter between a naughty child and her upset father – perhaps not surprisingly considering that, as it is revealed later in the trilogy, Vader *is* Leia's father.[10]

This mismatch (also mirroring that between the strength of the Empire and the relative helplessness of the rebellion) is not an accident but a carefully planned device. Vader's voice, so pivotal to the success of the film, was achieved by Burtt through manipulating Hollywood's most famous voice, that of James Earl Jones.[11] The end product is a fascinating mixture of two opposite aspects: an extremely captivating, operatic quality (especially the melodic meter with which he delivers his lines) and an evil and cold means of destruction (achieved mainly through echoing and distancing the voice). One may even argue that that is probably how a child would experience such a verbal exchange with a towering, black-robed, angry father!

The same audilising approach to characters and their role in the film is present throughout. Luke Skywalker's (Mark Hamill) vehicle, a landspeeder, reflects its owner's youth by being capable of producing only high-pitched frequencies. This is matched by the characteristics of Luke's voice: impatient (staccato quality), inexperienced (interrupting/interrupted – i.e., not yet knowing its place in the sound balance as in life), youthful (high pitch). In the case of Han Solo (Harrison Ford), the only main figure in the film to be neither a father figure nor a child, Burtt had to accommodate Solo's greater age and life experience. Hence his ship produces a much more 'grown-up' sound than either Leia's or Luke's by reaching deeper bass frequencies. Once again, this is mirrored in Solo's voice: Although at times impatient (his meter often changes, proving incapable of the same stability in tone and meter of the more mature voices of Ben Kenobi, played by Alec Guinness, and Vader), it nonetheless provides a rather 'experienced' sound at a considerably lower pitch.

This aural dictotomy is often played against opposite characteristics to a creative effect. The first encounter between the *Millennium Falcon* and an Imperial fighter is, perhaps, the best example. As the smaller Imperial craft desperately tries to avoid the *Falcon*, it emits a sound whose envelope and texture closely resemble that of a fearful child's cry for shelter and comfort. In fact, the fighter is rushing toward its mother ship, the *Death Star*. In contrast to this, later in the film, the rebel X-wing and Y-wing fighters attacking the *Death Star*, though small, emit a wider range of frequencies, ranging from the high to the low (piloted as they are by men of different ages and experience), suggesting their ability to succeed (as they eventually will do), even though clearly mismatched.

[. . .]

Conclusion

The brave new world of sound has its foundations in the extension of audience space in which filmmakers are to create new daring sound constructions for the audience to be actively and pleasurably engaged. The field of science fiction constituted the ideal terrain to test those foundations because it provided filmmakers with only the constraint of verisimilitude, not an exact reference: The sounds did not have to match known parameters, for they were not present in our world, and those existing from previous science fiction films were being reshaped by Burtt and his collaborators.

Most crucially, this interpretation of sonic spectacle should still ring a warning bell, 20 years later, regarding our understanding of the role of sound in the creation of filmic pleasure. *Variety* wrote in 1977 that '[the] use of Dolby Sound enhances the overall impact.' But sound as it is deployed in *Star Wars* does not act as a mere amplifier; rather, it is part of the original 'signal,' part of the 'impact.' Indeed, pleasure does not originate somewhere outside sound, in a reiteration of the discourse of exclusion highlighted above; on the contrary, a film's sound is an integral part of the production and reception of pleasure. This reasoning was brought to the fore in dramatic fashion by *Star Wars*, and the film's greatest achievement lies exactly in having helped to elevate and establish film sound from an instrument to diffuse pleasure originating somewhere else in the film apparatus, to an instrument to produce pleasure, requiring an altogether different approach from critics and audiences alike.

NOTES

1. In this sense, it is depressing that the most important institution for the study and promotion of cinema in the United Kingdom, the British Film Institute, should endorse this attitude so wholeheartedly as to embed it in its motto: 'Celebrating the moving image.'
2. In the 1970s, 70 mm magnetic stereo prints cost on average seven times more to produce than an optical monophonic 35 mm version.
3. It is perhaps worth remembering that the creative use of off-screen space was explored from the very inception of film sound in excellent films such as Hitchcock's *Blackmail* (1939).
4. Lucas himself has often pointed out that the young average age of those involved in the production of *Star Wars* was mid twenties.
5. This 'pioneering' role has been further qualified during the years by Lucas's decision to base his operations outside Hollywood (near San Francisco), the creation of Skywalker Ranch, and the inception of the THX and TAP programs.
6. George Lucas, *Star Wars: Episode IV. A New Hope*, revised fourth draft, Jan. 1976, Lucasfilm Ltd.
7. As defined in the 1993 edition of *The New Shorter Oxford Dictionary*, 'audile' is a person 'responding to perceptions more readily in terms of audile imagery than in tactile or visual terms.'
8. For two excellent examples of modern use of surround, see the opening sequence of *The Fugitive*, directed by Andrew Davis (Warner Brothers, 1993) and *Speed*, directed by Ian De Bont (Twentieth-Century Fox, 1994).

9. Of course, this may well open a series of justified questions on its rather sexist approach, considering that there is no 'mother sound' and that Princess Leia (Carrie Fisher) is the only significant female voice in the film.

10. It has often been noted that *Vader* in Danish means *father* and that *Darth* is suspiciously close to *dark*.

11. Interestingly, Jones was also chosen to be the official voice of another 'empire,' Ted Turner's CNN.

Works Cited

Allen, Ioan. 'The Dolby Sound System for Recording *Star Wars.' American Cinematographer* 58.6 (July 1977): 748.

Beaugrand, Claude. 'Entendre l'arbre qui pousse.' *24 Images* 60 (spring 92): 32–3.

Berman, Robert. *Fade In: The Screenwriting Process*. Studio City, CA: M. Wiese Productions, 1988.

Burtt, Ben. Interview. 'Sound Thinking.' With Marc Mancini. *Film Comment* 19 (1983): 40–7.

Chion, Michel. 'Révolution douce . . . et dure stagnation.' *Cahiers du cinéma*. 398 (July/Aug. 1987): 26–32.

Kael, Pauline, ed. *5001 Nights at the Movies*. New York and London: Marion Boyars, [1982] 1993.

Levin, Tom. 'The Acoustic Dimension: Notes on Cinema Sound.' *Screen* 25.3 (May/June 1984): 55–68.

Magid, Ron. 'An Expanded Universe.' *American Cinematographer* (Feb. 1997): 60–70

Morgan, Jane. *Films in Review* 28.7 (Aug. – Sept. 1977): 437.

Neale, Steve. 'Hollywood Corner.' *Framework* 19 (1982): 35–40.

Variety. Rev. of *Star Wars*: 25 May 1977.

20

THE EXHIBITORS STRIKE BACK: MULTIPLEXES, VIDEO AND THE RISE OF HOME CINEMA

After over a quarter of a century of declining audiences, the cinema of the 1980s saw not only the stabilisation of audience numbers, but also the creation of new audiences. One of the main reasons for this was the emergence of new forms of film exhibition. The late 1970s and early 1980s saw the emergence of home video as a new form of domestic technology. One use of the video was to time-shift the viewing of television programming by taping its transmission and playing it back at another point. It also allowed the distribution of films on video that could be viewed in the home.

The studios initially reacted with horror at the technology, which was viewed as a major threat to cinema exhibition, but it was soon discovered that video reawakened interest in film in general and not only did cinema attendance start to grow once more but, by the mid-1980s, over half the revenue from feature film production came from video. In other words, just as the studios had previously operated the zone-run-clearance system, the contemporary film industry was able to use a video release to prolong the life of a film once it was played out at cinemas and hence it could continue to generate income from it. Indeed, since the mid-1980s, video has become even more important than the cinema financially (although it is being replaced by DVD) so that it is often claimed that cinema exhibition is no longer the key medium for Hollywood but now operates as a means of promoting the film prior to its release in other media.

It was not only the studios who were anxious about video and, in 1984, it became the focus of a national campaign in the United Kingdom that led to government legislation to regulate video. The intrusion of video into the home, it was claimed, meant that material that was unsuitable for children might fall into their hands. As a result of the majors' opposition to video and their reluctance to release their major films in the format during the early 1980s, the market was open to a series of independents so that the market became flooded with an eclectic series of materials from different sectors of the international film industry. Violent and sexual material, which could be marketed as different from traditional cinema fare, was particularly prevalent and these items, lumped together under the term 'video nasties', became the focus of the campaign. However, when looked at more closely, the video had largely become the focus of broader struggles over the family at a time when the right-wing government was opposed to the liberalism of the 1960s and 1970s and calling for a return to 'traditional family values'.

While the government might have opposed the video nasties, the campaign turned the films collected under this term into a new form of cult cinema and one classic nasty, the hilariously hyper-violent *The Evil Dead* (1981), launched the career of Sam Raimi, the director of *Spiderman* (2002). The video nasties were only a small portion of the material available on video, and the openness of the market also made the period fertile for cult and independent movies. In addition to low-budget horror and science fiction, the period not only enabled the emergence of directors such as David Lynch, John Sayles and the Coen Brothers, but also was particularly distinguished by the presence of women directors such as Amy Heckerling, Susan Seidleman, Donna Deitch, Kathryn Bigelow and Lizzie Borden.

Lynch first became known through his cult classic *Eraserhead* (1977), a surreal and disturbing film in which a young man is left to raise a monstrous child in a nightmarish apartment building. His next film, *The Elephant Man* (1980), continued his interest in monstrosity though the story of a hideously deformed but sensitive and articulate man, who becomes a celebrity in nineteenth-century London. This was followed by *Dune* (1984), a massive science fiction epic based on the classic novels by Frank Herbert; but although it was visually brilliant, it was also completely obscure and seemed to have finished Lynch's career until he came back with *Blue Velvet* (1986), one of the most celebrated films of the 1980s.

If Lynch's career started just before this period, the Coen Brothers' career took off towards the end. They initially started out working with Raimi on *The Evil Dead*, and on the basis of this got to make *Blood Simple* (1984), a stylish and violent example of the *film noir* homages that were popular in the period. This was followed by *Raising Arizona* (1984), a zany comedy of family life that drew heavily on cartoon action such as that featuring Roadrunner and Wily Coyote; and *Miller's Crossing*, a homage to the gangster films of the 1930s that emphasised its debt to writers such as Dashiell Hammett from whom they had borrowed the term 'blood simple' for their first film. Since then they have won prestigious prizes at international festivals and have a career that is still going strong although there is still some debate over their significance. Their films are always visually inventive but they seem to swing between genuinely entertaining genre filmmaking and infuriating pretension and incomprehensibility.

Sayles also continues to make films, although they are very different from either Lynch or the Coen Brothers. Sayles has always presented himself as an independent filmmaker with a political agenda. Originally a novelist, he started writing scripts for low-budget films such as *Piranha*, *The Lady in Red* (1979) and *Alligator* and used the money to fund *The Return of the Secaucus Seven* (1979), a film about a reunion of friends from the 1960s that he directed and from which Laurence Kasden got the idea for his own 1980s *Zeitgeist* film, *The Big Chill* (1983).

Many want to present Sayles' involvement with low-budget genre filmmaking as merely a means to an end, but the quality of his early scripts contradicts this, as does Sayles' continuing fascination with genre filmmaking thereafter: *Baby, It's You* (1983) is a teen romance through which he explores class conflict; *Brother from Another Planet* (1984) is a science fiction adventure in which he explores social and racial prejudice; *Matewan* (1987) is a western about the bloody conflict between capital and labour in the early twentieth century; *Eight Men Out* (1988) is a sports movie through which he explores economic exploitation; and *Lone Star* (1996) is a western through which he explores the politics of race relations in contemporary America.

It is this relationship to popular cinema that he shares with the new women directors of the period. Amy Heckerling came to fame as the director of *Fast Times at Ridgemont High* (1982), an off-beat teen comedy that deals with topics often elided by its rivals and launched the careers of a whole host of key actors including Sean Penn and Jennifer Jason Leigh. Similarly, Susan Seidelmen became known for her kooky romantic comedies. Following the success of *Smithereens* (1982), the story of a young woman's involvement in the Greenwich Village punk scene, she had a major hit with *Desperately Seeking Susan* (1985), a romantic comedy again set in the New York punk underground and at least as interested in the relationship between its two female leads (Rosanne Arquette and Madonna) as it was in their relationships with men. The lesbian suggestions of Seidleman's film were made explicit in Deitch's *Desert Hearts* (1985) in which the central character comes to Reno for a divorce and becomes fascinated by a lesbian on the ranch where she is staying.

Interestingly, despite their early promise, none of these three continues to have prominent careers as directors. Heckerling did direct the magnificent teen comedy *Clueless* (1995), which later became a long-running television series, and she created the *Look Who's Talking* series, which is often despised by critics. Similarly, while Seidelman and Deitch have continued to work in film, they have actually had at least as much success in television. Significantly, Seidelman was used as a director on the first series of *Sex and the City*, while Deitch has worked heavily on Steven Boccho-produced series such as *Murder One* and *NYPD Blue*. For whatever reason – scheduling commitments or the material that they deal with – these directors have often found television more conducive a medium to work in than film.

It is also interesting that it is Kathryn Bigelow, a director of tough action cinema, who has achieved long-term success in film. A brilliant stylist, her first film was an arty biker drama, *The Loveless* (1982), which was quickly followed by a dazzling cowboy-vampire-road movie, *Near Dark* (1987), and *Blue Steel* (1990), the story of a tough woman cop who becomes the target of a psychotic stalker. Even Lizzie Borden, the female director of the period with the clearest art cinema credentials, turned to science fiction for *Born in Flames* (1983). The film is set in the aftermath of a socialist revolution in which its female characters turn to violence when they realise how little they have gained.

In addition to video, the multiplex also emerged as a new site of exhibition within the period. Instead of inner-city cinemas like the picture palaces, these were located in shopping malls in North America and were therefore part of the everyday world of suburban families. In Europe, they were often built as part of leisure complexes situated out of town, near the intersection of major roads which meant that they could be accessed by car from a considerable distance. These cinemas created a renaissance in cinemagoing as a form of family entertainment. In the early 1980s, there was a vogue for fantasy films that picked up on the success of *Star Wars*, but had a clear fairytale dimension. The Indiana Jones films were also part of a larger interest in adventure films suitable for the whole family, although *Indiana Jones and the Temple of Doom* (1984) did provoke some concern over its violence given the audience at which it was directed. *ET* was also part of another trend. While there was a series of films, including *D.A.R.Y.L.* (1985), in which American families encountered and befriended lonely and abused aliens, androids and so on, *ET* was also explicitly about a fatherless home.

A series of family films therefore concerned the rites of passage of children (predominantly male children) who must learn to grow up without a father. In *The Karate Kid* (1984) films, which were major hits of the period, a young boy living with his mother learns how to be a man through a relationship with an Oriental martial arts trainer. The guidance that he is offered is clearly distinguished from the violent and oppressive masculinity that a rival martial arts instructor teaches his students. While these movies were aimed at children who were being taken to the cinema by adults, the location of the multiplex also made the cinema a place that older teenagers frequented too. During the early 1980s, Coppola made two adaptations of S. E. Hinton's novels of teenage life that were more reminiscent of 1950s teen movies than the teen movies of the mid-1980s. But they did introduce a series of young actors who would become major stars over the next few years: Matt Dillon, Emilio Estevez and Tom Cruise.

However, the key figure associated with the teen movie of the 1980s is, without question, John Hughes. Hughes wrote, directed and/or produced a whole series of teen movies often set in suburban Illinois and featuring a company of teen actors. In *The Breakfast Club* (1985), Molly Ringwald, Judd

Nelson, Emilio Estevez, Ally Sheedy and Anthony Michael Hall find themselves on a Saturday detention and while initially hostile because of the high school cliques that each represents, they eventually learn to identify with one another and develop a firm bond. In *Ferris Bueller's Day Off* (1986), on the other hand, Matthew Broderick plays Ferris, a fast-talking opportunist who decides to play truant from school and takes himself and two friends on a wild trip to Chicago. Ferris is an almost unstoppable figure who gets to live out his every fantasy, but like many of Hughes' films there is a darker current under the surface. While often dismissed for lacking the radicalism or rebellion of earlier youth cinema, Hughes' films nonetheless emphasise his teenage characters' profound sense of dissatisfaction and alienation, and their sense of powerlessness and dread at the prospect of becoming like their parents.

The anarchic comedies of the period formed another key trend in the films that appealed to teenage audiences. John Landis' films had often drawn upon figures such as John Belushi and Dan Ackroyd who had come from the television show *Saturday Night Live*. During the 1980s, a series of other comedians from the show would become major stars, particularly Chevy Chase, Bill Murray and Eddie Murphy. In *Caddyshack* (1980), Chevy Chase ridicules and outrages the uptight members of a golf club while Bill Murray's moronic groundsman is continually outwitted by a gopher that he is trying to exterminate. The film was a big success and became a cult favourite of college audiences, but *Ghostbusters* (1984) become a major blockbuster of the period. In the film, Bill Murray, Dan Aykroyd, Harold Ramis and Ernie Hudson play psychic researchers who are fired from their university positions and start a freelance practice. While being continually harassed by uptight civil servant William Atherton, they discover that a skyscraper threatens the world with demonic power. Rather than greet this confrontation with the seriousness one might expect in a horror film, Murray approaches it with the same insolence and irresponsibility with which he treats women and bureaucracy. Much the same is also true of Eddie Murphy's cop in *Beverley Hills Cop* (1984), in which he plays an inner-city cop from the east who causes havoc in Los Angeles when he goes there to investigate a crime and runs into uptight white cops who behave like bureaucrats.

Such comedies have been associated with the individualism of Reaganite America. Reagan's victory in the presidential election of 1980 marked a fundamental shift in American politics, economics and culture. He was explicitly opposed to the liberalism of the 1960s and 1970s, and had strong support from the religious right. However, he was also opposed to state regulation of the economy and championed free-market capitalism. Furthermore, after a brief period of cautious collaboration between the United States and the Soviet Union in the 1970s, Reagan's era was associated with the renewal of the Cold War and a new arms race.

As this description should make clear, the period was more complex than is often acknowledged. A significant portion of the American population were opposed to Reagan and even Reaganism itself was a contradictory movement.

The religious right wanted an end to the permissiveness of the 1960s and 1970s, and this came into conflict with the anti-regulatory and individualistic economic policy. Reaganism was a movement that held in balance two opposed tendencies. As a result, the Hollywood cinema of the period cannot be reduced to a simple Reaganite formula. Not only is there ample evidence that Hollywood was especially anti-Republican, it was also deeply divided. Thus while a series of films such as *Red Dawn* and *Invasion USA* (1985) presented America as being threatened by Soviet aggression, many successful films of the period, such as *War Games* (1983) and *The Terminator* (1984), presented the American military defence systems themselves as the real threat.

The problems of seeing early 1980s Hollywood as simply a Reaganite cinema are also highlighted by its relationship to gay audiences. While gay rights was one of the chief targets of the Reaganite religious right, Hollywood actively targeted gay audiences at the time. During the 1970s, the gay community had proved itself to be a very important and valuable market, and Hollywood explored a number of strategies for tapping that market. For example, the early 1980s saw a number of films addressing gay issues such as *Making Love* (1982) and *Partners* (1982), while both John Sayles' *Lianna* (1982) and Robert Towne's *Personal Best* (1982) addressed lesbianism. There was also a small cycle of movies about cross dressing which attempted to challenge perceptions of sex and gender, such as *Victor/Victoria* (1982) and *Tootsie* (1983). The different types of films had varying levels of critical and commercial success, and their handling of issues ranged from the genuinely interesting, to the vaguely sympathetic, the exploitative and even the downright homophobic. But they did represent a genuine attempt to acknowledge and respond to cultural change, and while the impetus may have been economic for some (although by no means all), it demonstrates that Hollywood was not simply a reflection or stooge of Reaganite politics.

The availability of exhibition outside the inner cities also made cinema more attractive to female audiences, once the cornerstone of the Hollywood film industry. Suburbanisation was partly a response to, and partly contributed to, the changing meaning of inner cities, which became increasingly seen as dangerous and threatening places, particularly to women. The malls within which the new multiplexes were located were, however, specifically designed to feel safe and attractive to female consumers. As a result, the period also saw Hollywood's growing recognition of the female audience and two massive romantic hits – *An Officer and a Gentleman* (1982) and *Dirty Dancing* (1987) – helped to rejuvenate Hollywood interest in the romantic comedy as a form. Indeed, *Dirty Dancing* was a massive success on video that confirmed the importance of women in domestic film consumption. *Dirty Dancing* was in addition a musical and there was a series of successful musicals at this time: *Fame* (1980), *Flashdance* (1983) and *Footloose* (1984).

The period saw the rise of a series of powerful women in Hollywood. Meryl Streep emerged as a major star of Oscar-winning quality dramas such as

Kramer vs Kramer (1979), *Sophie's Choice* (1982), *Silkwood* (1983), *Falling in Love* (1984), *Plenty* (1984) and *Out of Africa* (1985), and her surname is even used in some critical writing to describe a particular kind of acting. To 'do a Streep' means to turn in a performance that seeks to draw attention to itself as complex and difficult. In other words, while highly regarded by some, others found her performances pretentious, mannered and self-important. She was also particularly known for the accents that she adopted in a bid for authenticity, accents that some found hilariously overdone.

A less obvious power player was Goldie Hawn. Originally a TV star in the 1960s, she moved into cinema in the 1970s when she appeared in a number of significant films, particularly *Shampoo*, an important social satire of the early 1970s. However, she still played dizzy blondes, a persona that did not fit well with the image of the movie mogul that she became during the 1980s after the success of her self-produced comedy, *Private Benjamin* (1980). The reason that Hawn is often ignored is that she specialised in kooky romantic comedies, which were often dismissed as either trivial or conservative by both male critics and feminists. Even when she did tackle material with more respectability, critics reacted harshly: her particular femininity was seen as inappropriate to such material. The film in question was *Swing Shift* (1984), a romantic drama that tackled the issues raised by the feminist documentary *The Life and Times of Rosie the Riveter* (1980), about women's experience of working in traditional male industries during the Second World War. The film was directed by Jonathan Demme, a male director who is often seen as sympathetic to feminism, and when a battle broke out between director and producer, it was Demme's account that was accepted. The male director was associated with political and aesthetic integrity and its female producer was seen as a threat to both.

The final new mode of exhibition that emerged over the period was the cable channels such as Showtime and Home Box Office. Again, these provided the studios with yet another opportunity for revenue generation but they also began to produce and finance their own productions. Like video, they were also largely intended for domestic consumption, although they also created opportunities for other types of private consumption. One effect of private film consumption was that it allowed films to be used not only to create moments of family togetherness but also other types of intimacy. For example, the period witnessed a change in the handling of sexual material in film. There was a developing interest in the *film noir* thriller of the past, tales of steamy illicit affairs that result in murder, but filmmakers were able to be much more explicit in the depiction of sexual affairs. Some of these were remakes, such as *The Postman Always Rings Twice* (1946/1981) and *Against All Odds* (a remake of *Out of the Past* [1947/1984]), but others were new attempts to recreate the feel of older films such as *Body Heat* (1981). Rather than simply titillating male tastes, these films were often directed at couples in which the sexual material both distinguished these films as adult entertainment that was distinct from the family entertainment available elsewhere, and operated to create a sense of excitement and intimacy.

These transformations in exhibition also had their impact on the art cinema, which was dramatically transformed over the period. In the late 1970s and early 1980s, Andrzej Wajda made two key films that challenged the communist authorities in Poland, but these represented the end rather than the continuation of a particular tradition of art cinema. *Man of Marble* (1977) is the story of a student who is making a documentary that investigates the life of a worker constructed as a hero by the communist propaganda of the past. As she strips away the propaganda, she finds an alternative history in which he heroically opposed his own mythologisation. *Man of Iron* (1981) followed on the success of the earlier film but concerned Solidarity, the organisation of workers who opposed the Polish authorities of the period. Although the international success of these two films enabled Wajda to make a big international co-production, *Danton* (1983), these films did not set a trend for other art cinema filmmakers.

Similarly, Andrei Tarkovsky made a series of key films in the late 1970s and early 1980s in the Soviet Union, but was eventually forced to leave in the early 1980s, after which he made two key films before his death in 1986. Tarkovsky's career had started in controversy with his epic drama of medieval Russia, *Andrei Rubelov* (1966), which was denounced by the authorities for its nudity and violence, but he then made *Solaris* (1972), a film that remains a classic to this day and was recently remade by Steven Soderberg and George Clooney. The film concerns a space station that is orbiting the planet Solaris that seems able to give flesh to the repressed guilty pasts of the inhabitants of the space station. The film's vision of the future is therefore highly bleak, suggesting that technology will not save us from the painful emotional problems of human existence.

His next film, *Mirror* (1975), however, reconfirmed him as a problem for the Soviet establishment. As a director, he rejected the political filmmaking favoured by the authorities and remained committed to a religious interpretation of the world. In his next film, *Stalker* (1979), his characters escape a bleak alienating industrial world and travel into 'the zone', an area transformed by some unspecified event. The journey through the zone is an obscure process of navigation in which the protagonists are forced to decipher the terrain in bizarre ways, and like many of his films, much of the film is made up of extremely long takes, in which we seem literally to watch objects as they are transformed by the passage of time. Finally, he left the Soviet Union to make *Nostalgia* (1983) in Italy and *The Sacrifice* (1986) in Sweden, both of which displayed the religious and stylistic features of his previous films. Like Wajda, whatever the quality of Tarkovsky's films, his status in the 1980s was largely due to his reputation as a director of conscience who was opposed to Soviet authority. In other ways, his films seem remarkably (although not necessarily undesirably) different from the dominant trends in the art cinema of the period.

Elsewhere, new modes of exhibition, and the possibilities for finance that they created, led to the emergence of a more traditional style of filmmaking.

In Britain, the early 1980s promised a renaissance of the film industry that seemed to be represented by the phenomenal success of *Chariots of Fire* (1981) at both the box office and the Oscars. The film was a costume drama about two athletes struggling against the British establishment to achieve success at the Olympic Games. It created a vogue for other costume dramas, particularly a series of films about the British in India such as *Gandhi* (1982) and *A Passage to India* (1984). The aesthetic values of these films harked back to an earlier moment of British filmmaking as is made clear by their directors: Richard Attenborough and, returning to filmmaking after a long absence, the director of numerous historical epics, David Lean.

This trend was further consolidated with the emergence of Channel 4, a new television channel that, in the early years, heavily branded itself through its association with the art cinema and consolidated this reputation by providing funding for a number of British films in return for screening rights. One of the main recipients of this initiative was the filmmaking partnership of Ishmael Merchant and James Ivory, an Indian and an American who had been making quality dramas with literary associations since the 1960s. After the success of *A Room with a View* (1985), which was funded by Channel 4, they made a series of films, often based on the novels of E. M. Forster, which studied the English middle classes during the first decades of the twentieth century. These films are strangely contradictory entities. They are 'art films' that avoid experimentalism in favour of middlebrow production values; and they are critical of the British establishment while visually worshipping its styles, designs and fashions.

Another key mode of filmmaking that was funded by Channel 4 was that associated with the director Peter Greenaway. Originally Greenaway's films sought to emphasise the debt to other aesthetic systems. *The Draughtsman's Contract* (1982), for example, was filmed to look like the eighteenth-century artworks that it concerned, while also encouraging the reader to see the visual image as a complex puzzle to be deciphered. Although the films suggested that the puzzle might be insoluble, it was the puzzle which was significant, not its resolution.

Finally, Channel 4 also funded *Angel* (1982), a film by the Irish writer Neil Jordan, which used a thriller plot to investigate the Troubles in Northern Ireland. Instead of using a realist and documentary style, as did most others dealing with the same material, as its title suggests, Jordan's thriller is a strange magical fantasy. Like Jordan's later work, it is willing to use popular genres but will not be constrained by them. Indeed, many of Jordan's films involve abrupt shifts between generic systems, as in the case of *The Crying Game* (1992), where a story of the Troubles suddenly shifts into a tale of sexual confusion and uncertainty.

Janet Wasko's 'Talkin' 'Bout a Revolution: Home Video' is another example of industrial analysis, but while Balio's extract is a business history of Columbia, and Sergi's research an examination of cultural practitioners, Wasko provides a political economy of the industry. In other words, while Balio attempts to outline the organisation and business strategies of a single company, Wasko seeks to explain the industry and its practices in terms of its structural conditions as a capitalist industry. In the process, she is overtly critical of the economic relationships on which the industry is founded and within which it is organised.

For Wasko, capitalist industry is based on certain structural economic relations, in which not only is there a division between capital and labour, but labour is organised as a commodity; and these relations exert specific limitations and pressures. Consequently, her account is not interested in the texts themselves, except to the extent to which she claims that these relations create a pressure to limit diversity and for a number of key players to dominate the industry. Instead, she is interested in the larger economic process in which individual films are largely irrelevant, even for those within the industry. Her account doesn't even focus on the industry's production of films but rather the ways in which they are made available to the public.

The extract concerns the industry's response to the introduction of home video as a technology, and the ways in which the key players in the film industry shifted from seeing this technology as a threat, to using it as a means of consolidating their power. While the dominant figures within the industry were initially fearful of the impact of off-air taping on cinema attendance, they found ways of using video rental and retail not only to massively increase revenue but also to stimulate interest in cinemagoing. Furthermore, while the initial reticence of key players meant that the early video market provided space for a variety of different sections of the international film industry, the key players soon re-established and even extended their dominance, forcing out competition and diversity. To construct this analysis, Wasko engages in two main tactics. First, she presents a narrative of the industry's relationship to video and, second, she breaks the industry up into a series of sectors. It should be clear that Wasko's interest is not in providing a narrative history – what happened when – but rather a structural history of the underlying economic structures that explain this process of development. She examines the industry trade press and more general economic commentary, as well as political and legal documents such as court records that detail policymaking and issues such as copyright law. From these sources, she is able to identify what policies were made both by the industry and the state, and the reasons given for these policies. The result is a fascinating story of a key moment of transition within the industry, which demonstrates that while great changes took place, they did not fundamentally alter the structuring economic relations but rather intensified the power of capital.

- What sources does Wasko use to examine changing attitudes towards video technology in the film industry?
- While cultural industries may try to control how the technologies and texts that they produce are consumed, other factors may also affect their

consumption. For example, the video machine became a feature of British homes more quickly and more broadly than it did in the US (that is, a higher percentage of British homes had a video machine than US homes). What factors might account for this difference in the diffusion of this technology?

• Can you think of any other moments of transition in which the industry has had to adjust to a social, economic or technological change, and how might you go about examining this example?

TALKIN' 'BOUT A REVOLUTION: HOME VIDEO

Janet Wasko

Home video has had a revolutionary effect on the entertainment habits of the nation.

1991 International Television and Video Almanac

Videocassettes are the new opiate of the people.

G. D. and O. H. Ganley, *Global Political Fallout:*
The VCR's First Decade

By the beginning of the 1990s, home video machines were in over 70 per cent of the television homes in the USA. Over 30,000 video stores, devoted primarily to the rental or sale of videocassettes, dotted the urban and rural landscape, while video sales or rentals were common features in a wide variety of businesses, from bookstores, record shops and large department stores, to small grocery stores and gas stations. The video industry claimed that 300 million tapes were rented from video stores each month, and three times as many people rented videos as attended motion-picture theaters.[1]

This 'video revolution' has been accompanied by its own assortment of promises, both for the industry and the public. Consumers are said to have more control over the time and location of viewing a wider range of entertainment and information. They can even create their own entertainment using home video cameras and recorders. A. M. Rubin and C. R. Bantz conclude simply that 'VCR technology allows the audience more choice, participation and control.'[2]

In terms of the entertainment business, independent film and video makers have been offered new, less expensive outlets for the distribution of their products. And new video distribution activities and rental outlets have provided new sources of entrepreneurial activity. Thus, video was another opportunity for competition in the entertainment industry.

Janet Wasko, *Hollywood in the Information Age: Beyond the Silver Screen* (Cambridge: Polity Press, 1994).

Hollywood again has projected a schizophrenic attitude towards this new technological innovation. On the one hand, the popularity of home video has been a competitive threat, not only to the film industry (especially the exhibition sector), but also to broadcasting, cable and other leisure time activities. In 1990, consumers spent $14.9 billion renting or buying videocassettes, outpacing theatrical box office revenues by nearly $10 billion.

On the other hand, home video has become yet another market for Hollywood films, and an extremely lucrative one. Out of total home video revenues of $11.3 billion for 1989, $4.1 billion went to the suppliers of video programming – mostly the Hollywood majors.[3] By 1992 an estimated 35–40 percent of distributors' total revenues for new films were derived from worldwide video distribution.[4]

If home video represented simply another outlet for motion-pictures, why did Hollywood panic and Jack Valenti depict video as the biggest threat facing the film industry?[5] Why did Hollywood companies spend millions of dollars challenging viewers' right to record video signals in their home? And then, only a few years later, why were the same people embracing home video as though they couldn't live without it, with Valenti exclaiming, 'If ever there was a union of interests, it is electronics and movie-making'?[6]

And what about those promises offered by home video technology – is there really more diversity, independence, and competition?

To answer these questions, it is necessary to look more closely at the growth and structure of this new branch of the entertainment and information business.

[. . .]

The Evolution of Home Video Software/VCR use

The growth of home video must be considered, however, in light of factors other than the availability of the hardware and assumed market demand. The perfection of home video technology at costs affordable to many households had been accomplished by the early 1980s – but for what use? Why would a consumer want to purchase a video recorder or playback machine?

Basically, there are at least three possible uses for video recording or playback equipment:

1 to *record* from other sources, especially off-the-air television programs, or *time-shifting*.
2 to *play back* pre-recorded video material.
3 to *produce* video tapes, or direct recording.

To Record and (Maybe) to Play Back

Early promotion of VCRs by manufacturers emphasized time shifting. So it may not be surprising that for the first few years, taping programs from television was the most popular use of home video technology.[7] However, the emphasis on taping programs off the air did not escape the attention of the Hollywood majors, some of the most important suppliers of television programming.

Universal v. Sony/Betamax case

The first major response to home video recording by the film industry was prompted by Sony's advertising campaign in September 1976 for Betamax as a way to time-shift television programming. Universal and Disney filed a lawsuit in November 1976, challenging the copyright law pertaining to fair use. At Universal's initiative, all the majors were asked to join, but only Disney agreed to be co-plaintiff.[8]

Disney's lawyer expressed the sentiments of both companies when he explained simply that 'the videotape machine would be used to steal our property.' However, the other studios, represented in the amicus curiae brief submitted by the MPAA, were less interested in the case. As Sid Sheinberg, head of Universal at the time, noted: 'It's a constant problem in this industry that most people in high places are not worried about what might happen ten years down the road. They're worried about getting to the Polo Lounge.'[9]

Although Sony suggested a royalty fee on machines and cassettes as a compromise, MCA was not listening. As Sony's US representative observed, 'I don't think it was accidental that the company that took the lead in fighting the videocassette was the company that held all the patents on the videodisc.'[10]

The trial started on January 30, 1979, and was tried by Judge Warren Ferguson, US District Court, Central District of California. The case received a great deal of public attention and revealed the film industry's attitude toward home video at the time, as well as serving as a test for the standards of fair use described in the new copyright legislation. More specifically, the 1976 law delineated fair use as:

1 the right to reproduce the work in copies;
2 the right to distribute those copies;
3 the right to prepare derivative works (such as translations and drama-tisations) based upon copyrighted works;
4 the right to perform or display the work publicly.[11]

While interpretation of these rights was pivotal for the defendants, several other issues also were emphasised during the trial. First, it was argued that revenue would be lost from the sale of movies to network TV. In addition, television networks and stations would lose advertising revenue because viewers would not be watching at specific air times. Despite the claim that the studios (specifically, Universal, MCA, and Disney) had encouraged Sony's development of home videotape recorders, MPAA President, Jack Valenti, called the Betamax a 'parasitical' device.

Finally, in October 1979, Judge Ferguson decided that the concept of fair use was applicable, as home taping was done in private homes, and the film companies had 'voluntarily' transmitted their works over public airwaves: 'Home-use recording from free television is not copyright infringe-ment, and even if it were, the corporate defendants are not liable and an injunction is not appropriate.'[12]

Although the hardware manufacturers breathed a sigh of relief, their triumph *was* short-lived, as the plaintiffs pursued the case to the US Court of Appeals, Ninth Circuit, which ruled on October 20, 1981, that home video recording was an infringement, and Sony was responsible. The response to the con-troversial decision was widespread and immediate, as cartoonists, editorialists, and comedians envisioned a 'Video Police State.'

According to James Lardner, 'In the long history of its offenses, that much-maligned branch of government, the judiciary, had probably never issued a decision that attracted more abuse and less sympathy.'[13]

The decision prompted several bills in Congress, introduced by Reps Parris, DeConcini, and Mathias. Meanwhile, the film industry – although pleased about the reversal – also responded to the widespread criticism by preparing an alternative to the home recording ban. A provision for royalties on VCRs and blank tapes was proposed as 'a compromise which would preserve the interests of consumers and creators simultaneously.'[14]

Thus, the battle raged on. In March 1982, Rep. Mathias added royalties for audiotaping as well as videotaping to his bill, as well as giving copyright owners the exclusive right to authorize rental of pre-recorded tapes – an issue which, as we shall see in the next section, was becoming increasingly more important as a video rental system emerged.

Meanwhile, Sony enlisted assistance from the Electronics Industry Association, forming the Home Recording Rights Coalition. They also found support from video dealers, who in addition to resisting tape royalties, wanted to fight the added rental provision.

The battle lines were drawn between the 'Home Recorders' and the 'Copyrightists,' as numerous PR and lobbying firms were hired by both sides. Debates took place in the press, through direct mail campaigns, and on television talk shows. Charles Ferris (former FCC commissioner) was hired as a spokesman for the Home Recorders, and became the rival of Jack Valenti, spokesman for the Copyrightists, who called VCRs 'millions of little tapeworms' eating away at the core of the American film industry.

A Home Taping bill was eventually introduced in the House and hearings were held in April 1982.[15] Much of the Congressional activity was placed on hold in June 1982 when the Supreme Court decided to hear the Betamax case. But as a landmark 27 amicus curiae briefs were filed with the Court, the hearings and debates continued. In 1983 *Variety* reported that the struggle was 'reaching new heights of acrimony.'

As Lardner observed:

> By the middle of 1983 the two lobbying coalitions had assembled
> between them a vast Washington brain trust which included two former

cabinet-level officials; four former top advisers in the Carter White House; two former senators; five former representatives; two former chairmen of the Federal Communications Commission; two former White House economists; and two former chief counsels to the Senate Judiciary Committee. Hardly any issue facing the nation in recent memory had engaged the attention of a more formidable array of elder statesmanhood.[16]

On the other hand, there was a great deal of skepticism and derision of these activities. 'It's corporate pigs versus corporate pigs,' was one Congressional aide's assessment. 'So you sort of watch it like a pig fight. All these people running around with five-hundred-dollar suits and three-dollar cigars. You walk into the hearing rooms and it's wall-to-wall pinstripes.'[17]

Then, on January 17, 1984, the Supreme Court, with a vote of five to four, reversed the District Court's decision:

> One may search the Copyright Act in vain for any sign that the elected representatives of the millions of people who watch television every day have made it unlawful to copy a program for later viewing at home, or have enacted a flat prohibition against the sale of machines that make such copying possible.[18]

While the majors had lost their eight-year battle, they were, at the same time, busily jumping into the video market. Indeed, the arguments made during the Supreme Court case often referred to the majors' increasing profits from home video ($400 million in 1983). Another example of Hollywood's schizophrenic attitude towards video is offered by Lardner, who explains that Disney even made a deal with Sony to distribute its videocassettes before the case was settled. A Disney executive was said to soothe his worried Sony colleague by telling him, 'Look, the people who are suing you are a different division of the company. If this makes economic sense for both of us, why should we let the lawsuit stand in our way?'[19]

So, viewers had 'won' the right to tape at home. And despite the fears of the film and broadcast industry, and the claim that VCR owners were 'independent entertainment seekers,' early research by Mark Levy indicated that 'most VCR households record and playback much the same programs which are watched and enjoyed by the mass audience.'[20]

Levy further concluded that, for the short term, at least, the TV networks would be the principal beneficiaries, since the prime source for recordings was network-affiliated stations. Yet, Levy also hinted at long-term effects on broadcast audiences. Later research revealed that while viewers used VCRs for time shifting, the process was actually incomplete, as recordings were made, but often not replayed.[21] The important point, however, was that the popularity of VCRs at the time was related to the time-shifting convenience. This, again, partially explains the popularity of VCRs over videodisc players.

Levy's research also indicated that, at least for the first few years of home video growth, recording movies was the most frequent time-shifting/recording activity.[22] So it seems that the growth of home video also was related to the availability of films on TV, especially offered by pay-cable channels such as HBO.

With the popularity of time-shifting activities, the growth in blank tape sales also expanded rapidly: retail sales grew from around 24 million in 1982 to nearly 300 million in 1986.[23] One indication of the growth in tape sales was the announcement by Eastman Kodak that the traditional film supplier would enter the video tape business in 1984. The explanation? 'We believe that our entry into the videotape field is properly timed to match these new business opportunities,' stated a Kodak executive.[24]

Yet, by the time that the Universal/Sony case was settled, the time-shifting novelty was gradually wearing off. One study noted that by 1986, the primary reason most people gave for purchasing a VCR was to view rental movies.[25] According to another estimate, only 30 per cent of VCR viewing by 1987 was watching tapes recorded from television or cable, and the majority of VCR activity centered on watching pre-recorded videos.[26] By mid-1988, it was reported that the average VCR owner spent only two-and-a-half hours recording tapes, but almost four hours playing tapes.[27]

Later indications were that there was probably less time shifting than reported, as consumers seemed to have some difficulty in actually programming their VCRs. A series of solutions was proposed and introduced, including easier programming procedures by manufacturers as well as various devices (such as bar codes) linked to television schedules. One popular system, accepted by many VCR manufacturers, was VCR Plus+, a device that automatically taped programs which were pre-assigned numbers listed in TV schedules.

Pre-recorded Videos: To Sell or to Rent?

The use of home video technology for pre-recorded tape playback had grown more slowly, as this activity depends to a great extent on the availability of such tapes. As home video machines became more popular in the late seventies, direct sales were emphasized, but at high prices. Only about one million cassettes sold annually. The most prevalent types of pre-recorded tapes available at first were pornography or X-rated films, often selling for $60–125 each. (Some were even as high as $300.)[28]

According to some reports, the earliest effort to distribute pre-recorded tapes of major motion-pictures was by Andre Blay, an 'industry outsider' who had formed Magnetic Video in Farmington Hills, Michigan, in 1969. Blay contacted the majors about obtaining rights to sell their films on video.

And, while some people at the studios were considering video distribution, none had made the move. At first, the studios' interest seemed related only to time shifting, and focused on Universal's Betamax case. However, the ultimate concern was losing control over product, whether it was expressed as fear of time shifting, direct sales, or piracy. Consequently, the majors were hoping that the 'right' video technology would prevail, in other words, videodiscs, which did not allow recording or copying. But, videodisc systems quickly lost ground to VCR systems; thus, the market was ripe for pre-recorded programs on videocassettes.

Apparently only Twentieth Century Fox was interested in Blay's proposal to buy the rights to films for sale on videotape. In 1977, Blay purchased the non-exclusive rights to 50 Fox films, which had already appeared on network TV. His agreement with Fox involved a $300,000 advance, plus a minimum of $500,000 a year against a royalty of $7.50 on each cassette sold. Blay chose (from a list offered by Fox) films such as *M*A*S*H, Patton*, and *Sound of Music*, and sold them to retailers for $37.50, or to individuals for $49.95 each through a direct-mail operation, called the Video Club of America.

> Fortuitously the Fox titles went on sale just as RCA and Sony were going head to head with their pre-Christmas ad campaign and just as a new competitiveness – spurred by the arrival of models that bore the Zenith, Sylvania, and Magnavox labels – brought prices under $1,000. As the number of VCRs grew, so did the demand for pre-recorded cassettes.[29]

By March 1978, Blay had sold 40,000 cassettes, to retailers and Video Club members. By the end of the year, he had sold 250,000 tapes, and started buying additional titles from independents (Avco Embassy, Viacom, etc.), as most of the majors were still reluctant to offer their films for sale.[30]

About the same time, a few enterprising individuals began to rent copies of movies purchased from companies like Magnetic. But the legal status of such activities seemed unclear. As companies began selling their films on tape, their contracts specifically prohibited rental. But, was it actually illegal to rent video copies of films after purchase?

One of the early pioneers in video rentals, George Atkinson, again an 'industry outsider,' received the following advice from his lawyer (according to Lardner): 'You can't copy it, you can't publicly exhibit it – that's a violation of copyright. But yes, you can rent it, you can eat it, you can destroy it. You bought it. It's your property.'[31]

The First Sale Doctrine, a provision of the Copyright Act of 1976, allows the legitimate buyer of a copyrighted work to dispose of the copy as he or she wishes.[32] In other words, after a cassette has been *sold* to a retailer, no further royalties can be claimed, and the copyright owner loses control of that copy.

While the studios philosophically supported a rental system as a more appropriate system of distributing their films on video, they certainly did not care for the First Sale Doctrine, and, thus, tried to prevent rentals via contractual restrictions, as well as pushing a direct sales rather than a rental market.

Nevertheless, video entrepreneurs, such as Atkinson, obtained copies and continued to rent, as well as starting others in the video business through franchises (Atkinson's franchises were called Video Stations). By the end of 1978, a rental system was emerging, despite the reluctance of the major distributors. As Lardner notes,

Over the next few years the VCR and the pre-recorded videocassette set hearts on fire in entrepreneurial breasts all over the land. Americans from every imaginable walk of life cracked open their nest eggs, remortgaged their homes, and put the arm on their parents, siblings, and in-laws in order to become the proud proprietors of Video Castles, Connections, Corners, Hutches, Huts, Palaces, Patches, Places, Shacks, Sheds, Sources, Spots, and Stations. It was as if someone had hung a classified ad in the sky: 'Retail Oppty. – Lo Cash/EZ Startup.'[33]

While the majors still tried to prohibit rentals in their contracts, they eventually yielded to the popularity of rentals, and did not enforce the restrictions. They also started releasing more of their films on video.

Fox and Warner were the first of the majors to enter video distribution, but by 1981 all of the large Hollywood distributors had their own video divisions (even MCA, which had hesitated because of the Sony suit), or they combined with another company to distribute their films in video form (i.e. RCA/Columbia, CBS/Fox).[34]

However, the business was still expected to develop as direct sales, and so the film distributors priced their cassettes at $79.95. This would allow a royalty of about $10 – 'a handsome return if multiplied by millions of individual purchasers, but a far less attractive one when multiplied by ten or fifteen thousand video store owners, each of them free to take a cassette which had cost, say $50 wholesale, and rent it out a hundred times or more at $5 a shot.'[35]

As the rental system emerged, the studios wanted more, arguing that they were not receiving their 'creative share' when video store owners were not required to pay them a percentage of each rental transaction. Though they continued releasing films on video, they also initiated a series of challenges from 1980 to 1982 (called 'the rental wars' by Lardner), in an attempt to get more of their share from rentals.

Several different proposals were offered by the studios around this time. In 1980, Disney proposed a two-track marketing system, featuring rental-only and sale-only cassettes. During 1981, the Warner Home Video Rental Plan was introduced, with leased cassettes on a weekly basis. In addition, Fox and MGM/CBS proposed different rental plans. And, in 1982, Warner's Dealer's Choice offered rental terms of four to six weeks, for A and B titles.

The distributors claimed that the retailers could actually make more money by agreeing to these schemes. But,

> [h]owever the studios explained the rationale behind their plans, it looked to the dealers as if the underlying purpose were to capture a bigger share of the take from each rental. They felt like colonists who had been through a few tough winters and were about to harvest a bumper crop only to learn that the mother country was going to raise their taxes.[36]

Thus, each plan was resisted by the retailers, who responded by forming two national organizations in 1982 at the Las Vegas Consumer Electronics Show.

The Video Software Retailers Association (VSRA), the more militant group, even proposed a boycott. ('Let's pull their booth apart,' 'Rip their catalogs apart, and throw them in their faces.') The Video Software Dealers Association (VSDA) was more moderate, but still would not accept the studio's proposals. They pointed out that not only would they potentially lose money, they would also lose control over their business, and especially, their inventory, which provided the basis for bank loans, etc. 'The reason people go into small business is to have some control,' pointed out one dealer. 'If you look at the history of Hollywood, it's been a history of trying to have disproportionate control – complete vertical control.'[37]

By mid-1982, the new rental plans had been scrapped. One studio executive moaned, 'We couldn't fight the tide,' while others attributed the lack of cooperation by retailers to their immaturity. 'Immature they might be. Ineffective they weren't. Their ability to mount a coordinated campaign of resistance from coast to coast was a source of amazement and annoyance to the studio people.'[38]

As previously discussed, the majors turned to legislative efforts to change the First Sale Doctrine, especially after the Supreme Court's Betamax decision. Bills introduced during the 98th Congress received the majors' full attention, as they waged one of their typical Washington campaigns. Although well-paid and influential lobbyists called on legislators to help out their Hollywood friends, and a few powerful allies, including the White House, were enlisted, the 'Home Recorders' ultimately were able to rally video dealers around the country and squash the legislation.[39]

Hollywood lobbyists also tried to get a royalty tax on rentals and sales of copyrighted movies, but failed. In 1986, the industry tried another tactic: pushing legislation that would require manufacturers to install anti-copying devices in all VCRs. As Jack Valenti explained in his testimony, 'Unauthorized back-to-back copying is a malevolent threat to the creative future.' As he went on to compare the practice to 'a deadly virus,' it appeared that creativity was not the only issue, and perhaps not even the most important one: 'Every unauthorized copy made from a pre-recorded videocassette potentially displaces a sale or rental of a pre-recorded videocassette.'[40] The virus continued, but the legislation failed.

During 1987–8 the introduction of pay-per-transaction (PPT) was another attempt by the majors to work around the First Sale Doctrine. Video copies of films were to be leased to retail outlets at prices much lower than outright sale, and a percentage of each transaction (50 per cent) then paid to the supplier and distributor – 'a revenue-sharing plan,' noted *Variety*, 'which splits the actual dollars consumers spend.'[41] The plan also involved computer systems which recorded each transaction, and, of course, could be accessed by the suppliers. Orion was the first program supplier to offer all retail outlets PPT deals. But one of the largest retail chains, National Video, also pushed the program, claiming that it would solve the retailers' problem of depth of copy, or the number of copies of a specific title. Eventually pay-per-transaction was killed by the retailers' less than enthusiastic reaction (cries of 'big brother' and 'capitulation to Hollywood's dictates' were common), but also by the studios' reluctance to push a scheme that most retailers resisted. Although pay-per-transaction died a slower death than the previous schemes, the retailers had again resisted the dominating force of the Hollywood majors.

There have been other schemes to gain more control over the rental business. One system kept track of the number of times a cassette had been played through a built-in counter.[42] Thus, the supplier could charge the dealer per transaction, but also the dealer could charge consumers for the number of times the cassette was played. A few years later several companies, including Polaroid, developed cassettes that destroyed themselves after a specific number of plays, reminiscent of the self-destructing taped assignments in the *Mission Impossible* television series. Another version was a cassette that automatically erased after 25 plays.[43]

The Birth of the Video Industry

Meanwhile, rentals grew and direct sales diminished. According to a Nielsen report, the proportion of VCR owners who rented tapes for playback increased from 37 per cent in 1984 to 45 per cent in 1985.[44] In a 1985 Nielsen report, 74 per cent of VCR owners had rented a pre-recorded cassette at least once, while 67 per cent were active renters and rented at least once per month.[45] One study reported that 42.5 per cent of VCR owners rented in 1987 and 44.3 per cent in 1988.[46]

The home video business was growing, with a distinct industrial structure emerging. And the retail revenues doubled. And doubled again. In 1983, sales and rentals of videos totaled $1.06 billion. Revenues of $2.04 billion were reported in 1984, and $4.5 billion in 1985. By 1987, revenues were $7.46 billion, far exceeding theatrical box office receipts.[47]

In addition to their efforts to persuade Congress to change the First Sale Doctrine or provide another form of 'relief' for the film industry, the majors gradually dropped their retail prices to encourage the sell-through market. In 1984, Paramount offered *Top Gun* (including a Pepsi commercial) for $26.95. By the end of 1987, nearly 3 million units had been sold, and according to *Variety*, '. . . re-established the viability of low-priced blockbuster films and made sure the industry's first major experiment with a commercial on a film cassette was a huge success.'[48] In 1988, Nelson Entertainment went even further and launched a new sell-through product line at $14.98, the lowest price at that time for top films from a program supplier.[49]

Around the same time (1986), however, the video companies announced that they would increase their prices to wholesalers from $79.95 to $89.95 or $99.95, thus raising retailers' prices far beyond the standard $50.[50]

So, the marketing of pre-recorded cassettes has gone through three phases:

1 1975–8: emphasis on sell-throughs at high prices;
2 1979–84: mostly rentals;
3 1985–present: mix of rentals and sell-throughs at lower prices.

Home video has proven to be an extremely lucrative business, attracting attention from the popular press and jealousy from other entertainment sectors. But this success cannot be attributed only to consumers' fascination with a new technology and the declining prices for VCRs. Home video has become popular in the USA because of the availability of software, or pre-recorded tapes, especially Hollywood movies, and the development of a popularly accepted distribution system (rentals). In other words, the home video market has become yet another profitable market for theatrical motion-pictures.

Despite the early resistance, Hollywood has not only accepted home video but has embraced the new distribution outlet. Various observers have attributed this acceptance to the inability of the studios to challenge or lobby away the First Sale Doctrine, to successful box office receipts from 1988 through the end of the decade, and to the realization that home video distribution of films provided not only another outlet for their films but an extremely profitable one, with extremely low distribution expenses involved.[51] Thus, by 1988, the head of Walt Disney Studios, Jeffrey Katzenberg, was calling video retailers 'Hollywood's ambassadors,' and noting that video and theatrical distributors are not as much competitors as 'synergistic allies.'[52]

To further understand Hollywood's turn-about, as well as its involvement with this new distribution medium, we need to look more carefully at the business of home video. The following sections of this chapter will describe the production, distribution and retailing arrangements for motion-pictures on video.

[. . .]

A Video Revolution?

Home video has become a way of life in millions of homes around the world. The convenience and ease of viewing entertainment at any time of day or night has been accepted and celebrated by millions of VCR owners. How can one quibble with this technological breakthrough?

After considering the development of home video in this chapter, we can conclude that, similar to media technologies in the past, some very familiar patterns have emerged with this 'revolution.'

There is no question that the consumer has gained more independence from the schedules of those who control cultural and informational output. But, again, there is still nearly total dependence on that output. In other words, home video recorders for the most part are used to record and playback information and entertainment *created for* audiences. Though the technology is available, audience members have not been encouraged to develop truly two-way communication via new video equipment. Again, communication and culture have been conceived as one-way processes.

An interesting development of the video revolution has been the use of home video recording equipment, but camcorders and other video systems have been used by the public mostly as a replacement for still cameras and 8 mm film equipment to document family activities. Nevertheless, there is still some hope that video can become a new medium of communication and art. For instance, video artist Nam June Paik envisions 'a channel devoted solely to video art showcasing the best of the millions of videotapes made by consumers every year.'[53] So far, however, the type of activity we have seen in the USA is represented by ABC's *America's Funniest Home Videos*, which became the number one prime-time television program in the USA in March 1990. The show relies on audience members to send in funny videos, but chooses mostly those that capture people (or animals) in awkward or embarrassing moments. Another notable (and sometimes disturbing) use of camcorders has been for recording crimes or unlawful activities, thus turning ordinary citizens into video vigilantes. It remains to be seen whether or not the 500-channel universe will provide the opportunity and impetus for other uses of video technology.

While the convenience of home video is hailed by those pointing out the inconveniences of going to a theater, it still seems remarkable that the public has adapted to a rental system that actually does take them out of their home, not once, but twice, to pick up and return rented cassettes. Certainly, the cost of renting a film and sharing it with the rest of the family or a few friends is appealing. But, again, we are isolated from larger groups of people and increasingly experience culture in our homes. Culture increasingly is narrowed to a private rather than a public experience.

And there are those who also bemoan the quality of the viewing experience with video. As Steven Spielberg once stated, 'Movies should be seen in dark, hallowed halls.'[54] There is no doubt that encountering a film on a 20-inch box via electronic technology is a qualitatively different experience than viewing a film on a large screen via celluloid technology and more sophisticated audio systems. The conversion to video involves a loss of picture size and quality, thus the original intention of the creators may be virtually lost when viewed on even the best video systems. And then there's the difference in the viewing environment: a theater should provide a more ideal setting to view a film, uninterrupted by household noises and telephones (unless you happen to sit next to someone who brings their cellular telephone to the theater). The special nature of 'going out' to a movie also may contribute to the experience of theater viewing (although there are those, of course, who might argue that in many urban environments, it is increasingly dangerous and risky to venture outside the security of one's home for any reason).

But there have been signs that the VCR has not been such a hit with the entire population for other reasons. As the sales of video equipment started declining in 1989, there were widespread reports of a decline in the amount of time spent using a VCR after its initial purchase. Some even admitted that the technology had 'limited utility.' An EIA representative explained: 'There are a lot of people out there who simply don't want to buy a VCR, either because it's too difficult for them to operate, or because they don't watch much TV, or some other reason.'[55]

Another reason may be that those without the resources to purchase a video recorder – those who may have chosen in the past to view a film when it is presented on over-the-air commercial television – may not have that option, as the film may never even appear on network or syndicated television, with cable and video options more lucrative to distributors. Perhaps it is a small problem, but might there be an 'entertainment' or 'cultural' poor, in addition to an information poor?

In essence, home video has been yet another communication technology developed primarily as a commodity. Those corporations involved with entertainment, especially, have echoed the sentiments of Madison Square Gardens, when they explained the creation of their home video label as 'a *natural* extension of our core business.'[56] Indeed, the truly *revolutionary* characteristics of home video – control over the creation and retransmission of information and cultural creation – has been overshadowed by the acceptance of the technology as a *natural* developmentent of the commodified form of information and entertainment and consequently, control of home video's development has remained in the hands of those corporations which previously dominated these activities.

Again, we have seen the potential for more competition and diversity developing around home video technology. Yet, again, as with most other areas of cultural production, concentration and consolidation have been apparent, and perhaps inevitable, in light of the corporate and industrial character of home video's development. And it follows for many that the consolidation of the home video industry has meant less diversity, at least among those voices heard. As one writer for *Video Business* simply stated, 'In a universe of fewer players, there will be fewer programming choices.'[57]

While there are still advantages for alternative and truly independent production through less expensive and more accessible video formats, there is still the age-old problem of distribution. Even if an independent producer successfully gets a film to the video stage, how is it possible to reach audiences when video stores accept a Hollywood 'blockbuster' mentality, an attitude which is (not too surprisingly) picked up by consumers. The result? Audiences equate home video to yet another, sometimes more convenient, outlet for Hollywood products.

But what is the big problem? Are we not still offered hundreds, possibly thousands, more films to choose from, to view in the convenience of our home? Yes, of course, but those products available in our local video stores are the same products which have been available in the past, only in a different form. On the one hand we are getting simply more of the same, but on the other hand, we are also getting less of the same. As noted earlier, the number of new Hollywood films has decreased rather than increased, despite high box office and video revenues.

Yes, there still are exercise and documentary videos on some of the shelves of video stores and retail outlets. Yes, it is possible to find videos for a wider audience (children's programming, for instance). But, for the most part, the home video industry is fueled by, dominated by, driven by Hollywood products. And, increasingly, *BIG* Hollywood products.

And who benefits? Audiences are offered more entertainment – for a price – and a great deal of money is made through the sale of video equipment and the video release of films, both new and old. One might ask why that seems to be such a problem. After all, that is capitalism. And it is also the commodification of culture. The point is that there is not so much really new here, despite those who want us to believe that there has been a revolution.

NOTES

1. 'Homevideo Track,' *Variety*, 13 July 1988, p. 40.
2. A. M. Rubin and C. R. Bantz, 'Utility of Videocassette Recorders,' *American Behavioral Scientist*, May/June, 1987, p. 472.
3. *1991 International Motion Picture Almanac*, New York: Quigley Publishing, 1991, p. 603.
4. *Standard & Poor's Industry Surveys*, 11 March 1993, p. L21–2.
5. 'President of MPAA Describes Film Industry's Biggest Threat . . . including Home Video Recorders,' *New York Times*, 5 May 1985, Sec, II, p. 1.
6. 'MPAA's Valenti Offers Truce in CES Keynote Speech,' *Video Business*, 20 January 1989, p. 6, cited in Daniel Moret, 'The New Nickelodeons: A Political Economy of the Home Video Industry with Particular Emphasis on Video Software Retailers,' unpublished MA thesis, University of Oregon, March 1991, pp. 85–6.
7. See Mark R. Levy, 'Program Playback Preferences in VCR Households,' *Journal of Broadcasting* 24, no. 3, Summer 1980; Mark R. Levy, 'The Time-Shifting Use of Home Video Recorders,' *Journal of Broadcasting* 27, no. 3, Summer 1983; Donald E. Agostino, Herbert A. Terry, and Rolland C. Johnson, *Home Video: A Report on the Status, Projected Development and Consumer Use of Videocassette Recorders and Videodisc Players in the United States*, FCC Network Inquiry Special Staff, November 1979.
8. The Betamax cases include: Universal City Studios, Inc., et al. v. Sony Corp. of America Inc., et al., 480 F. Supp. 429 (C.D. Cal 1979); Sony Corp. of America, Inc. et al. v. Universal City Studios, Inc., et al., 659 F. 2d 963 (9th Oct. 1981); and Sony Corp. of America, Inc., et al. v. Universal City Studios, Inc., et al., 464 U.S. 417, 104 S. Ct. 774 (1984).
9. James Lardner, *Fast Forward: Hollywood, the Japanese and the Onslaught of the VCR*, New York: W. W. Norton, 1987, p. 34.
10. Ibid., p. 36.
11. See Title 17 U.S.C. Section 106.
12. See 480 F. Supp. 429.
13. Lardner, *Fast Forward*, p. 204.
14. See US House, H.R. 4783, 97th Cong., 1 Sess., 20 October 1981; US House, H.R. 5705, 97th Cong., 1st Sess., 3 March 1982; US Senate, S. 31, S. 32, S. 33, 98th Cong., 1st Sess, 26 January 1981.
15. US House, Committee on the Judiciary, Subcommittee on Courts, Civil Liberties, and the Administration of Justice, *Home Recording of Copyrighted Works, Part 1*

and Part 2, Hearings on H.R. 4783, H.R. 4794, H.R. 4808, H.R. 5250, H.R. 5488, and H.R. 5705, 97th Cong., 1st Sess and 2nd Sess, 12–14 April, 24 June, 11 August, 22–23 Sept. 1982. Hearings also took place in the Senate: US Senate, Committee on the Judiciary, *Copyright Infringements (Audio and Video Recorders)*, Hearings on S. 1758, 30 November 1981, and 21 April 1982. Also see 'Home Truths for Hollywood,' *The Economist*, 30 July 1983.

16. Lardner, *Fast Forward*, p. 250–1.
17. Ibid., p. 253.
18. 464 US 417, 104 S. Ct. 774.
19. Lardner, *Fast Forward*, pp. 274–5.
20. Mark R. Levy, 'Program Playback Preferences,' p. 335.
21. Mark R. Levy, 'The Time-Shifting Use,' pp. 267–8.
22. See Bruce A. Austin, 'The Film Industry, Its Audience and New Communications Technologies,' in Austin, ed., *Current Research in Film*, vol. II, Norwood, N.J.: Ablex Publications, 1985.
23. Aaron Foisi Nmungwun, *Video Recording Technology: Its Impact on Media and Home Entertainment*, Hillsdale, N. J.: Lawrence Erlbaum Publishers, 1989, p. 161; statistics also cited by the International Federation of Phonogram and Videogram Producers, London, reported in *Variety*, 14 January 1987.
24. William A. Koch, 'Eastman Video Tape and Future Imaging Technologies,' *American Cinematographer*, March 1984, p. 83.
25. Study cited in Terry L. Childers and Dean M. Krugman, 'The Competitive Environment of Pay-Per-View,' *Journal of Broadcasting and Electronic Media* 31, no. 3, Summer 1987, pp. 335–42.
26. 'Sales of VCRs are Slowing Down,' *Register Guard*, 15 January 1989.
27. David Lachenbruch, 'Here, Buy Another,' *Channels/Field Guide 1989*, p. 126.
28. Lardner, *Fast Forward*, p. 184.
29. Ibid., p. 174.
30. Blay's enterprise was so successful that in 1978 Fox bought Magnetic for $7.8 million. Ibid., pp. 172–3; George Rush, 'Home Video Wars,' *American Film*, April 1985, pp. 61–3.
31. Lardner, *Fast Forward*, p. 176.
32. Title 17 U.S.C. Section 109: Limitations on Exclusive Rights: Effect of Transfer of Particular Copy or Phonorecord, reads: 'the owner of a particular copy or phonorecord lawfully made under this title, or any person authorized by the owner, is entitled, without the authority of the copyright owner, to sell or otherwise dispose of the possession of that copy or phonorecord.'
33. Lardner, *Fast Forward*, p. 180.
34. Rush, 'Home Video Wars.'
35. Lardner, *Fast Forward*, pp. 188–9.
36. Ibid., p. 197.
37. Ibid., p. 201.
38. Ibid., p. 202.
39. See US House, Committee on the Judiciary, House Report 98–987, 31 August 1983; and US Senate, Committee on the Judiciary, Senate Report 98–162, 23 June 1983.
40. US Senate, Committee on the Judiciary, *Home Video Recording*, Hearing on Providing Information on the Issue of Home Video Recording, 99th Cong., 2d Sess., 23 September 1986. Also see Robyn Norwood, 'VCR Anti-Copying Device Urged,' *Los Angeles Times*, 24 September 1986.
41. 'Rentrak Tests P-P-T Outside,' *Variety*, 10 August 1988, p. 33.
42. The system known as Playcount was tested in Australia, but was partially owned by Capital Cities/ABC Video Enterprises. Al Stewart, 'Depth Deals Get Shallow Start,' *Billboard*, 13 August 1988, p. 89.
43. Jennifer Stern, 'The Case of the Missing Movies,' *Video Review*, October 1988, pp. 23, 26; 'Pay-per-view Tapes Expected on Market,' *Register-Guard*, 5 May 1991.

44. Michael Wiese, *Home Video: Producing for the Home Market*, Westport, CT: M. Wiese, 1986, p. 23; Miriam Furman, 'VCR Prices Decline,' *Leisure Time Electronics*, January 1986, p. 46.
45. Wiese, *Home Video*, p. 25.
46. Tom Bierbaum, 'Distrib Upheavals Cloud Industry,' *Variety*, 20 July 1988, p. 71.
47. Wiese and others have relied on data from the Fairfield Group for these revenue estimates.
48. *Top Gun* cost around $17.5 million to produce, but brought in $270 million in ticket sales and another $50 million in video sales by 1988. See 'Home Video Had a Spotty 1987,' *Variety*, p. 96; Joe Handese, 'Hollywood's Top Gun,' *Marketing and Media Decisions*, March 1988, pp. 109–14.
49. 'Home Video Had a Spotty 1987,' *Variety*, p. 89.
50. Dennis Hunt, 'Gods Must Be Crazy Tops the Foreign-Film Survey . . .,' *Los Angeles Times*, 28 November 1986.
51. Mark Christiansen, Vice-President, Western Division Manager, MGM/UA Distribution Co., lecture at the University of Oregon, November 1990; Daniel Moret, 'The New Nickelodeons: A Political Economy of the Home Video Industry with Particular Emphasis on Video Software Retailers,' unpublished MA thesis, University of Oregon, March 1991, p. 86.
52. Jim McCullaugh, 'A Title Business is A-1 for Sales,' *Billboard*, 20 August 1988, p. 5.
53. Frank Spotnitz, 'What's Next?' *American Film*, January/February 1989, p. 32.
54. Meigs, 'E.T. Comes Home.'
55. 'Sales of VCRs are Slowing Down,' *Washington Post*, 15 January 1989.
56. Frank Beerman, 'Madison Square Garden to Start HV Label,' *Variety*, 13 July 1988, p. 39.
57. G. Ptacek, 'Making it into the Minors,' *Video Business*, 3 November 1989, pp. 26–7, cited in Moret, 'The New Nickelodeons,' p. 98.

21

POSTMODERNISM, HIGH CONCEPT AND EIGHTIES EXCESS

The 1980s are often thought of as a period defined by excesses of style and consumption, a 'postmodern' moment where the aesthetics of consumer culture – typified by the promotional flow of music video on television channels such as MTV – came to the fore. It is in this period that Hollywood film assumed a particular style that movie executives would label 'high concept'. Responding to key industrial developments in the 1980s, such as the widespread adoption of marketing research and the growth of ancillary markets (such as music soundtracks), high concept movies were often based on pre-sold elements such as a best-selling book or a comic strip, and emphasised a distinctive style, conveyed in sleek images and music, which were integrated with their marketing. According to Justin Wyatt, the marketing 'hook' functioned alongside the stylistic 'look' within the spectrum of high concept. Whether soundtrack-driven movies such as *Flashdance* (1983), *Top Gun* (1986) or *Dirty Dancing* (1987), teen genre films such as *The Lost Boys* (1987) or *Young Guns* (1988), or high-budget blockbusters like *Dick Tracy* (1990), high concept films mobilised bold images and music, and the marketability of particular stars, to maximise their presence and appeal.

The most significant figures to popularise high concept filmmaking in the 1980s were the producers Don Simpson and Jerry Bruckheimer. Making a stream of hits for Paramount, their films were defined by a powerful blend of visual imagery and popular music, a rock video style of filmmaking that often relied on extended montage sequences cut to music. These elements were often carefully extracted for marketing purposes. For example, *Top Gun* included a lengthy scene of fighter pilots playing beach volleyball to one of the soundtrack numbers by Kenny Loggins, 'Playing with the Boys'. The sequence is shot in the style of a music video: glistening male bodies are captured in slow motion and with strong backlighting. While the lyrics bear loosely upon character action, the sequence has no obvious narrative function. However, it did help promote album sales of the film soundtrack that, in turn, helped identify the film's high concept image, essentially combining the star presence of Cruise with adrenalin-fuelled aviation spectacle.

While *Days of Thunder* (1988) – described in typical high concept style as 'Top Gun on wheels' – arguably saw the exhaustion of Simpson–Bruckheimer's stylised mode of filmmaking, high concept signalled a growing impulse in Hollywood to 'brand' film in ways that could enable profits to be leveraged in ancillary markets such as theme parks, video games, merchandise and music. While this kind of 'synergy' would become a virtual orthodoxy in the entertainment industry during the 1990s, its roots were planted in the 1980s. Pioneered by executives at Disney and Paramount, it was also exploited by Hollywood majors such as Warner Bros. For example, the studio's high concept blockbuster *Batman* (1989), given a striking Gothic makeover by Tim Burton, was able to project its brand logo into numerous ancillary markets. While the movie division of Warner Bros. saw profits generated from box office receipts and licensed consumer products, its recorded music division reaped revenue from the soundtrack album by Prince. Meanwhile, television and publishing divisions saw profits increase through renewed commercial interest in the popular history of the Batman character, for which Time Warner owned the comic book rights. The case of *Batman* demonstrates the way that movies were increasingly designed to create self-reinforcing revenue streams, linked to the transition in Hollywood from producing 'film' to that of a more broadly defined idea of 'filmed entertainment'.

Studios were not always the most significant players in the formulation of movies in the 1980s, high concept or otherwise. Talent agencies played a crucial role, with agents and lawyers becoming pivotal industry power brokers. The industry's three leading talent agencies were William Morris, Creative Artists Agency (CAA) and International Creative Management (ICM). These operated as an effective cartel, controlling access to stars, directors and material, and frequently assembling packages that could be sold to studios. By winning major names such as Sean Connery, Tom Cruise, Robert De Niro, Al Pacino, Dustin Hoffman, Robert Redford and Sylvester Stallone, CAA could entice studios with projects such as *Rain Man* (1988), a film put together entirely through its in-house talent reservoir. The ability of agents to steer projects in this way, and to negotiate deals on behalf of their clients, led figures such as Michael Ovitz of CAA to a position at the very top of Hollywood's power élite.

As well as reducing the power of studio executives, the agencies helped fuel the enormous salaries of major stars. Agents would receive a 10 per cent commission on salaries negotiated for their clients. As such, salaries escalated in a period where star power was in the ascendant. This added greatly to the inflationary cost of filmmaking, pricing all but the major studios out of the market for blockbusting, star-driven fare. While male stars such as Jack Nicholson and Tom Cruise were able to command the highest salaries (Nicholson receiving $50 million, including profit participation, for his role as The Joker in *Batman*), female stars such as Julia Roberts exercised considerable power within the context of the industry's 'talent oligopoly', able to command $20 million per picture. Excess was not simply a question of style in the 1980s, but also one linked to disproportionate hikes in star salaries and movie and marketing budgets.

While overspending created disquiet and anxiety in the film industry, little was done to arrest the huge costs of movie blockbusters, which continued to escalate precipitously. Indeed, the average costs of producing, marketing and distributing a mass-audience film rose from $14 million in 1980 to $60 million in 2000, with megapictures such as *Titanic* (1997) costing upwards of $200 million.

If excess became a defining feature of high concept filmmaking in the 1980s, then display of the excessive masculine body became one of its aesthetic signatures. While expressed in the maverick cop action films of *Die Hard* (1988–95) and *Lethal Weapon* (1987–98), produced by Joel Silver, it reached its apotheosis in the male body films of Sylvester Stallone and Arnold Schwarzenegger. For Stallone, one of the decade's most bankable stars, this came in 'hard body' pictures ranging from the *Rocky* (1976–90) and *Rambo* (1982–8) films, to movies such as *Cobra* (1989) and *Over The Top* (1987). For Schwarzenegger, flexing his way to a major screen career, it included post-*Terminator* (1984) action films such as *Commando* (1985), *Predator* (1987) and *Red Heat* (1988). In each case, the male body became a source of screen spectacle. It also encouraged both actors to spoof their star personae in films that also parodied their bulk, however, with Stallone remodelling his grunt action hero in *Tango & Cash* (1989) and the dire comedy *Stop! Or My Mom Will Shoot* (1992) and Schwarzenegger branching into the family market with *Twins* (1988) and *Kindergarten Cop* (1990). Demonstrating the degree to which cinema and video were still addressed as different markets at the end of the 1980s, Jean Claude Van Damme and Steven Seagal became the major action stars for the rental markets, appearing in martial arts body films such as, respectively, *Kickboxer* (1989) and *Hard to Kill* (1989).

While the 1980s are often associated with the muscular bodies of Stallone and Schwarzenegger, it is worth remembering that both started out in modernist and independent films such as *The Lords of Flatbush* (1974) and *Stay Hungry* (1976). *Rocky*, although clearly influenced by the modernism of its time, is often read as a key film in the transformation from 1970s radicalism to the supposedly conservative feel-good entertainment of the 1980s. Stallone's repertoire of hard body action heroes is subsequently linked to a right-wing militaristic tendency within cinema. In certain production cycles, a latent Cold War politics did reflect Reagan's own stance of anti-communist militarism. The Rambo series was a notable celebration of American power against demonised enemies in Afghanistan and Southeast Asia, enacting hard-body heroics in the name of victory against the threat of communism. A film such as *Rambo: First Blood Part 2* (1985) is more complex than is often assumed, however. Like other films that we have looked at, it is more an attack on bureaucracy than anti-war sentiment, and clearly positions Reagan's portrait behind the corrupt bureaucrats who, more than the Soviets or the Vietnamese, are Rambo's real enemy and target. He may kill a phenomenal number of opposition forces, but it is largely so that he can fulfil his revenge against the American military officials who have betrayed him.

This is not to claim in any sense that it is really a liberal film, but the complexity of the period is perhaps best illustrated by James Cameron's position. Not only did the *The Terminator* feature its own body star, Schwarzenegger, who plays the cold, destructive extension of Reagan's 'defensive initiative', but Cameron co-wrote and was asked to direct *Rambo*. Furthermore, the Cameron script for *Rambo* was not about Vietnam but Latin America, and it was Stallone who wrote a new story around some of Cameron's action sequences. In other words, the politics of the body films is much more fluid and ambiguous than is often suggested.

While films of the 1980s were rarely unmitigated, or at least uncomplicated, right-wing fantasies, a large body of films directly challenged conservative visions of America during the period. For example, the making, reception and commercial success of Oliver Stone's *Platoon* (1986) were all clearly a reaction against the comic book heroism of *Rambo* and the supposed attack on the 1960s opposition to the war that it entailed. The film made a star of its director, and was at pains to emphasise the significance of the class and race of the soldiers sent to fight. In tandem with films like Stanley Kubrick's *Full Metal Jacket* (1987) and Barry Levinson's *Good Morning Vietnam* (1987), Stone's film engaged with the troubled legacy of America's involvement in Vietnam, rehabilitating the portrayal of the Vietnam soldier while questioning the motivations and brutality of the war.

Stone would extend his social critique of contemporary America in *Wall Street* (1987), a film more deliberately attuned to the corporate excesses of the period. If the Reagan era was defined by the unfettered promotion of big business and defence spending and the rollback of welfare infrastructures, *Wall Street* offered a morality tale about insider trading and the 'greed is good' philosophy of Gordon Gecko. Played by Michael Douglas, Gecko is a ruthless corporate raider who at first seduces and is then undone by a gullible broker (Charlie Sheen) struggling to remake his identity in and between the influence of Gecko and his own blue-collar father, a union representative played by Martin Sheen. The figure of the Yuppie, or at least the entrepreneurial culture of the 1980s, would also be taken up in films such as *The Secret of My Success* (1987), *Bright Lights, Big City* (1988) and *Doc Hollywood* (1991), all drawing centrally upon the youthful star image of Michael J. Fox. Not limited to films that dealt with business in direct terms, the critique of corporate excess in the

1980s was expressed in other less obvious genres. In James Cameron's science fiction films *Aliens* (1986) and *The Abyss* (1989), for example, the former makes sport of the baddie played as Yuppie, while the latter uses computer-generated special effects to stage an underwater drama that makes a point of attacking the military-industrial complex. In a decade characterised for its 'remasculinising' tendencies, it is not insignificant that female characters are notably empowered in each case.

The negotiations of female identity were expressed in a variety of film cycles in the 1980s. While muscular heroines such as Sigourney Weaver in *Aliens* and Linda Hamilton in *The Terminator* moved to the centre of action narrative, incorporating the physical vulnerabilities and strengths of their male counterparts, developments in the representation of female identity were also expressed in thrillers and comedies, helping to establish the careers of Meg Ryan, Julia Roberts and Sharon Stone in the process. The seductions and dangers of sexuality, for example, were marked in a number of erotic thrillers that focused on predatory female characters. In a climate marked by the spectre of AIDS, erotic thrillers such as *Jagged Edge* (1985), *Fatal Attraction* (1987) and *Basic Instinct* (1992) gave sexual relationships a particularly graphic and fraught treatment, centring on the revivified figure of the femme fatale. This differed in part to the new romantic comedy where, in films such as *Moonstruck* (1987), *When Harry Met Sally* (1989), *Green Card* (1990) and *Pretty Woman* (1990), the transformative nature of gender relations took precedence. While Julia Roberts plays a prostitute called Vivien in *Pretty Woman*, for instance, questions of female identity are consumerist in nature rather than about the exploitations of sexual power. *Pretty Woman* is largely concerned with the female as consumer. Remaking her identity through the experience of shopping, Vivien is transformed through costuming, a process that helps Vivien realise her 'true' self and thereby rescue the emotional life of a suave corporate raider.

Rather than replicate ideological positions in any uniform or straightforward manner in the 1980s – whether consumer materialism, Cold War militarism, or patriarchal capitalism – Hollywood responded to the period's cultural and economic concerns in disparate and ambiguous ways. As a means of maximising its audience base, Hollywood mixed ideological messages in individual films while at the same time investing in a broad mix of genres and production cycles. Indeed, more prominent than hard body action films, so often seen as the epitome of 1980s filmmaking, were those in traditional genres such as fantasy and science fiction. These ranged from thrillers by Paul Verhoeven, including *Robocop* (1987) and *Total Recall* (1990), to family-oriented movies such as *Back to the Future* (1985), *Honey, I Shrunk the Kids* (1989) and *Who Framed Roger Rabbit?* (1988). Together with science fiction, the horror genre also spiked in the late 1980s, moving from the violence of *The Texas Chainsaw Massacre 2* (1986) to hybrid horror films such as *The Fly* (1986). Particularly significant in each genre were film serials such as *Star Trek* (1979–98) and *A Nightmare on Elm Street* (1984–91), part of a growing impulse in the film industry towards the movie franchise. Rather than a coherent mouthpiece for corporate and political ideology, Hollywood film remained polyvalent in the 1980s and even became wrapped in renewed debates about its own cultural legitimacy.

Conflicts over the moral content of film have recurred in charged ideological periods and the 1980s were no different in this respect. Indeed, they witnessed particular agitation by the powerful coalition of the New Right over Hollywood's representation of sex, race, violence, family values and homosexuality. The increasingly explicit depiction of sex during the 1980s, within both the porn industry and mainstream films such as 9½ Weeks (1986), led to an unusual political alliance between right-wing Christian fundamentalists and anti-porn feminists of the left. Other issues saw blunt divisions between left and right, however. Virulent protests by the Christian Right against Martin Scorsese's The Last Temptation of Christ (1988), largely on the grounds of its perceived blasphemy, generated stark oppositions over questions of censorship. The result of these struggles over Hollywood's supposed moral torpor came in adjustments to the ratings system by the Motion Picture Association of America (MPAA), creating the categories of PG-13 in 1984 and NC-17 in 1990, designed to replace the previous X category. While Hollywood became more graphic in representational terms during the 1980s, this did not occur without expressions of outrage and the portrayal of the entertainment industry, to quote right-wing critic Michael Medved, as 'an all powerful enemy, an alien force that assaults our most cherished values and corrupts our children'.

Resistance to the form and content of Hollywood film came in a number of discrete directions, both nationally and internationally. This was less a question of moral complaint than one of maintaining a difference in cinematic and political style. Documentary filmmakers such as Errol Morris and Michael Moore used the legacy of cinéma vérité as an alternative to fictional film, refashioning the techniques of direct cinema with self-conscious and obtrusive documentary styles. While Morris' The Thin Blue Line (1988) addressed the miscarriage of justice surrounding the murder of a Dallas policeman, Roger and Me (1989) was based on a strident and personalised account of the closure of General Motors factories in Michael Moore's home town of Flint, Michigan. The film is based on Moore's pursuit of CEO Roger Smith, intent on showing him the devastating social and economic consequences left by General Motors' move to cheap factory labour in Mexico. Documentary in the 1980s frequently combined an agenda of social activism with continuing experiments in formal technique. This was exemplified in the documentary and avant-garde work of Trinh T. Minh-ha, a Vietnamese-born American immigrant who in Reassemblage (1982) and Surname Viet, Given Name Nam (1989) constructed disruptive works that investigated questions of knowledge and representation, especially as they came to bear on the understanding of people beyond North America and Europe.

Internationally, attempts to compete with Hollywood's financial and cultural power emerged through strategies of regional alliance. In the late 1980s, initiatives were taken by the European Community to provide new forms of international film funding as a means of developing the continent's audiovisual industries. In 1987, the European Community founded MEDIA, a programme that helped fund EC productions through loans. This functioned alongside the European Film Distribution Office, which offered financial incentives for national distributors to handle imported films, and a commission called Eurimages that backed films such as *Cyrano de Bergerac* (1990) starring Gérard Depardieu. Attempts to create a distinct 'Film Europe' market first emerged in the 1920s, but the late 1980s saw renewed attempts to create cultural and economic conditions that might enable the European film industry to challenge Hollywood's industrial hegemony (see Chapter 6).

The power of Hollywood remained firm, however. Indeed, only 5 per cent of European films recouped their investment in theatrical runs and 80 per cent were never seen outside their country of origin. Meanwhile, Hollywood remained vigorous in attempts to press into international markets, the MPAA (steered by Jack Valenti) resisting legislative efforts by the EC to contain and restrict the presence of American film. This was especially felt in the early 1990s during negotiations over the General Agreement of Tariffs and Trade (GATT). While the French scored a minor victory in establishing protectionist measures against the encroachments of Hollywood – maintaining subsidies and tariffs to enable domestic products to compete with international imports – this could not prevent the increasing penetration of American film into overseas markets.

Despite the pressure exerted by Hollywood, European cinema did produce a number of directors who would develop distinct styles and identities. The Polish director Krzysztof Kieslowski, for example, would explore the lives of three different women in his *Three Colours* trilogy (1993–4), a portrait of contemporary Europe inspired by the colours of the French flag and its principles of liberty, equality and fraternity. While Kieslowski's work was humanistic and art house in tone, European cinema also had affinities with high concept and its fashion-inspired video style. If postmodernism is often associated with the surfaces of consumer culture, this was not simply an American affair. It was also absorbed by a young generation of French filmmakers who, influenced by New Hollywood *auteurs* such as Francis Ford Coppola, developed a style that French critics labelled the *cinéma du look*. This involved chic imagery inspired by advertising and television commercials, and stories that were frequently youth-oriented. Typified in the films of Luc Besson, whose work included *Subway* (1985), *The Big Blue* (1988) and *Nikita* (1990), the *cinéma du look* incorporated mass cultural aesthetics in films that had a slick, stark feel. It was also a style that distinguished the work of Tamil director Mani Ratnam, whose films *Agni Nakshatram* (1988) and *Anjali* (1990) took on a certain MTV quality in the way they used song, lighting, diffuse camera work and quick editing to tell popular love stories.

While associated with the aesthetics of consumer culture, postmodernism could also describe more political methods of representational style and subject. In Europe, this was expressed in a move towards accessible and experimental art cinema. The Spanish director Pedro Almodóvar was distinguished by his blending of melodrama and sex comedy in films such as *Matador* (1986), *Women on the Verge of a Nervous Breakdown* (1988) and *Tie Me Up! Tie Me Down!* (1989). Almodóvar's work was based on the creation of faintly erotic films that helped invigorate the Spanish film industry after the cultural restrictions of Franco's regime. *Tie Me Up! Tie Me Down!*, for example, told the story of a former porn star kidnapped by a psychiatric patient, a love story based around kinky sex and bondage. While not without its risks in the marketplace, Almodóvar's work was popular at home and abroad, and helped launch the career of Antonio Banderas.

Meanwhile, British director Peter Greenaway inspired the revival of experimental art cinema in works that incorporated numerical themes such as *Drowning by Numbers* (1988) and *Prospero's Books* (1991). While far removed from the high concept principles shaping key parts of Hollywood's output, and differing in style from the fond but also bruising realism of *Distant Voices, Still Lives* (1988), Terence Davies' film about working-class Liverpool, the work of both directors embodied an alternative notion of the postmodern. In Almodóvar's case, this was reflected in particular thematic interests in camp and sexual marginality. With Greenaway, it was associated with narrative experimentation, self-consciously playing with traditions and boundaries of literary and historical representation.

Within North American independent cinema, directors pushed representational conventions to more extreme limits. David Lynch came to encapsulate this in a series of works that explored the sexual and psychological disquiet of American life in films such as *Blue Velvet* (1986), *Wild at Heart* (1990) and the television series *Twin Peaks* (1990–1). Creating hallucinatory and surreal effects within narratives about the violence and repressed obsessions buried in suburban communities, Lynch's films were based on the unsettling exploration of an apparent, and frequently murderous, normality. *Blue Velvet* introduced many of Lynch's core themes, exploring the savagery and evil repressed within the cheery façade of suburban America. Including a chilling performance by Denis Hopper, playing a psychopath called Frank Booth, the film creates a stylistically noxious feeling of the grotesque, introduced from the outset by a disturbing close-up of rioting ants in the lawn of a suburban garden where a man has just had a seizure and collapsed.

If Lynch's work relied on surreal atmospheres, the films of Jim Jarmusch often relied on the quirky interlinking of stories. While *Mystery Train* (1989) interweaves three stories set in a Memphis hotel, linked by the presence of Elvis Presley, *Night on Earth* (1991) tells five separate character tales through taxi rides on the same night in Los Angeles, New York, Paris, London and Helsinki. Together with the much discussed work of Québecois director Denys Arcand, whose *The Decline of the American Empire* (1986) and *Jesus of Montreal* (1989) cleverly unravelled bourgeois and spiritual pieties, independent cinema sought to explore, in a rich variety of surreal, spare and satirical film techniques, the underlying depth and complexity of human relationships.

This was drawn in more specific political directions when it came to the depiction of marginalised peoples and subcultures. The representation of gay and lesbian identity was a particular subject to emerge within European and American avant-garde film of the 1980s, with works in the 'New Queer Cinema' showcased at the inaugural New York Gay and Lesbian Experimental Film Festival in 1987. Associated with filmmakers such as Derek Jarman and Isaac Julien, marginal identity was celebrated in films that explored the history and community of gay, lesbian and ethnic minorities. Isaac Julien's *Looking for Langston* (1988), for example, investigated the homophobic legacy of black nationalism in the United States. Related to the history of New York at the time of the Harlem Renaissance in the 1920s, *Looking for Langston* probed the difficulties of the black gay community in both the present and the past and was indicative of a climate where 'identity politics' was coming to the fore.

This described the struggle to represent, and make visible, groups that had been historically marginalised within dominant (that is to say white, male, heterosexual) culture. Identity politics would underpin the American 'culture war' debates that emerged in the late 1980s and early 1990s, describing a series of battles over cultural representation within art, media and education. These would provide a backdrop to mainstream films that sought to reclaim forgotten or abused histories, including the likes of *Glory* (1989), focusing on the first black regiment to fight in the American Civil War, and *Dances with Wolves* (1990), Kevin Costner's sentimental epic about a soldier who befriends Sioux Indians. Despite these expressions of historical and cultural plurality, conservatives warned against the threat, or excess, of multiculturalism, suggesting that diversity would challenge national values and ideas of tradition.

For independent cinema, culture war debates had an effect on government funding opportunities. The National Endowment for the Arts was reluctant to fund projects that were unsupportive of conservative values. In Britain, funding opportunities for small-scale filmmaking were also drastically cut, although not generally as a result of culture war politics. While government subsidies had previously supported offbeat work, film funding in the UK virtually ceased under Margaret Thatcher's Conservative government. This represented a more general trend where the extension of privatisation into the cultural industries moved funding sources from national governments and individual investors to media conglomerates, private investment groups and banks. Filling the vacuum were financing bodies in television such as Channel 4 that helped fund innovative and often controversial films such as *My Beautiful Launderette* (1985), a film about interracial gay love in 1980s London. However, funding opportunities outside the major studios and film companies remained bleak. While Hollywood was defined by corporate excess, those on the outer margins had to scrape for funds and often struggled for opportunities to produce and distribute their films.

In his essay, 'The Formation of the "Major Independent": Miramax, New Line and the New Hollywood', Justin Wyatt examines two key film companies that came to prominence in the late 1980s, shaping marketing and investment strategies in ways that would influence the major studios and the commercial environment for independent film. While Paramount developed high concept rosters in the 1980s, leading to lucrative franchises such as *Beverley Hills Cop* (1984–94) and *Star Trek*, Wyatt suggests that a similar principle of franchising became the lynchpin of New Line's success as an independent distributor. This was demonstrated by its transformation of low-budget exploitation films such as *Nightmare on Elm Street* and comic book characters such as *Teenage Mutant Ninja Turtles* (1990–3) into valuable commercial properties. Meanwhile, Miramax demonstrated the marketing leverage to be gained by associating art house film with media controversy. Moving beyond the analysis of high concept movies that Wyatt, in earlier work, equates with 1980s filmmaking, Miramax and New Line provide a means of complicating the picture of how films were marketed and advertised in the late 1980s. This is situated within an analysis of the uncertain shakedown and incorporation of the independent sector.

In methodological terms, Wyatt provides an example of business history. Rather than concentrate on aesthetic or ideological questions, he concentrates on the industrial factors that shaped the marketplace, and how particular companies sought to navigate its competitive waters. Rather than simply describe the corporate history of New Line and Miramax, Wyatt situates his analysis within wider frameworks of industrial power, projecting forward to the meaning and implications of corporate ownership that would come with media conglomeration. While the early business success of New Line and Miramax can be located in the 1980s, their story carries significance for developments in the film industry throughout the 1990s.

In terms of evidence, business history is sometimes constrained by the reluctance of companies to share information about their operations, finances and processes of decision-making. However, there remains a wealth of corporate information that businesses are either obliged to publish (publicly listed companies such as Time Warner, for example, must write annual reports that are freely available) or that is frequently reported in the media. Wyatt draws significantly on the latter, using the business sections of newspapers such as the *Los Angeles Times* and trade magazines like *Variety* to map the evolution and significance of New Line and Miramax in their move from independent distributors to 'major independents'.

- As a primary source, what perspectives are enabled by Wyatt's use of trade papers such as *Variety* and *Hollywood Reporter*?
- How far can the impact of a film be judged from box office information, and what else might you need to consider in judging a film's apparent 'success' or 'failure'?

- In economic terms, how significant would you say the film business is to the global media companies that own today's major film studios? What source material might you draw upon to investigate this?

THE FORMATION OF THE 'MAJOR INDEPENDENT': MIRAMAX, NEW LINE AND THE NEW HOLLYWOOD

Justin Wyatt

While much of the economic film history of the New Hollywood has focused on the conglomeration of the industry and the globalization of media production, the industrial structure has changed not just for the major studios, but also for those distributors on the margins, the independent film and video distributors. In this chapter, I intend to analyse how the marketplace for independent film (films not released by the majors) has shifted in the past two decades by considering the development of the two largest independent companies, New Line Cinema and Miramax Films. The case studies of New Line and Miramax illuminate the diverse distribution, marketing and advertising methods developed and co-opted by the independents to weather an increasingly competitive economic climate. Perhaps strongest evidence of the two companies' success in traversing the marketplace can be seen by the recent mergers between these independents and major companies which have provided both New Line and Miramax with substantial financial backing.

[. . .]

New Line Cinema and Franchising

Formed in 1967 by Robert Shaye, New Line Cinema began as a non-theatrical distributor focusing on the market for 'special events' on college campuses. Through such films as *Reefer Madness* (1936) and *Sympathy For the Devil* (1970) and a lecture series representing among others William Burroughs, Norman Mailer and R. D. Laing, New Line maintained a constant presence until 1973 when Shaye decided to open a theatrical distribution arm.[1] Shaye targeted his product narrowly, distributing, as described by *Variety*, 'arty and freak' films. 'Arty' translates to films by Lina Wertmuller (*The Seduction of Mimi* (1974)), Claude Chabrol (*Wedding in Blood* (1973)) and Pier Paolo Pasolini (*Porcile* (1969)), while 'freak' would include *Reefer Madness, The Texas Chainsaw Massacre* (1974) and *Pink Flamingos* (1972). Shaye opened some of these films, such as *Pink Flamingos*, in a midnight screening pattern, followed by a larger theatrical release. By 1974, the New Line Cinema

Justin Wyatt (ed. Steve Neale and Murray Smith), *Contemporary Hollywood Cinema* (London and New York: Routledge, 1998).

distribution slate mixed foreign, sexploitation, gay cinema, rock documentaries and 'midnight specials' reserved exclusively for midnight exhibition. The intent behind these choices was to tap those markets which would be ignored by the majors, and to maximise the difference of New Line's product from more traditional commercial film.

In 1978, New Line began a limited policy of film production inspired by two major factors. As the market for art films became more established, a greater number of distributors entered the marketplace and competition became more intense within this market. As a result, 'the bidding auction' for film distribution encouraged the price to rise. New Line had already begun to advance money (albeit the small amount of $150,000) in pre-production deals to acquire the completed pictures for distribution.[2] Shaye's decision to enter production was facilitated by access to a fresh source of production funds: Chemical Bank and a group of private investors supplied a $5 million loan based on New Line's consistent track record.[3] Vowing to limit budgets to under $2 million, Shaye maintained that his decision to enter production was also motivated by the growing availability of money from television, syndication, foreign territories and other subsidiary markets.[4]

Over the next decade, New Line continued to augment their distribution slate with pickups, often forming long-term alliances with production companies. For example, New Line signed an exclusive three-year deal with the British company Working Title Productions giving New Line all North American rights, excluding home video.[5] Even more significant from a financial standpoint, New Line entered into a distribution partnership with Carolco Pictures, under which New Line agreed to release lower-budget Carolco features separate from their features for TriStar Pictures.[6] During the decade, New Line also managed to translate the low-budget exploitation film *A Nightmare on Elm Street* (1985) into a wildly profitable six-part series by developing the iconic value of Freddy Krueger. Breaking from the expected decay from film to film in a series, *Nightmare III* (1987) grossed $15 million more than *Nightmare II* (1985) and *Nightmare IV* (1988) grossed $7 million more than *Nightmare III*. Revenue from the franchise was funnelled back into the company rather than into hasty and sizeable production and distribution expansion; as Shaye commented, 'We are a highly efficient operation with significantly low overhead. One *Elm Street* annually suffices to pay for it. We do not need to make pictures merely to support our distribution apparatus, so we can be selective in our judgements'.[7]

The *Nightmare* franchise was augmented by New Line's most successful film – the most successful independent film ever made – *Teenage Mutant Ninja Turtles*, grossing $135 million in 1990. The film moved New Line from a loss position in 1989 to a $5.3 million profit for the first half of 1990.[8] Picking up the completed film, New Line's share of ticket sales amounted to only 15 per cent, yet this figure, added to the *Nightmare* franchise, transformed the company.[9] Based on a comic book about crusading radioactive reptiles, the film possessed a wide level of awareness given the comic book and a host of assorted merchandised items: in 1989, a year prior to the film's release, over 100 companies licensed *Turtles* merchandise totalling approximately $350 million. Immediately on release, New Line executives began referring to the Turtles as a franchise – *Turtles II* was released a year after the first film and *Turtles III* two years later. The lag on the third film did not lower the box office revenue. As New Line marketing and distribution president Mitchell Goldman described at the release date of *Turtles III*, 'There's no question that we knew the turtles weren't what they once were. However, there's a second generation of children who are 3 or 4 years old and who love the turtles. We knew the videocassettes, TV show, and toys were still selling well.'[10]

New Line's franchises recall Paramount's adherence to 'tent pole' movies: in the mid-1980s, Paramount built their release schedule around commercial tent poles, like the *Indiana Jones, Star Trek* and *Beverly Hills Cop* movies, which could support less viable projects.[11] For New Line, the franchise permitted two developments: the creation of a home video division and a separate distribution arm, Fine Line Features, devoted to more specialised, hard-to-market films. While many New Line films had been distributed through RCA/Columbia Pictures Home Video, the benefits of retaining video rights were clear: control of another window of release and the advantage of further coordination of the theatrical-video release programme.

As early as 1983, New Line announced that they would split their product into mainstream and speciality items.[12] Ira Deutchman, former marketing and distribution president of independent distributor Cinecom, was chosen to be the president of Fine Line Features, the specialised division of New Line launched in 1990. Distancing himself from the failed 'classics divisions' of the major studios, Deutchman highlighted the market appeal of the potential Fine Line films: 'We're looking for films that perhaps take a little more immediate special attention to launch them into the marketplace, a little more time to find their audiences, but they have more market, more crossover potential than classics-oriented films.'[13] The move has allowed New Line to produce more commercial fare and to hire stars as insurance for their films. Most conspicuously, in 1994, New Line's product included two Jim Carrey vehicles, the comedy/special effects movie *The Mask* and another film for which they paid $7 million for his talents, *Dumb and Dumber*. Ridiculed in the press at the time (Carrey had appeared in only one successful film, *Ace Ventura: Pet Detective* (1994), when the deal for *Dumb and Dumber* was signed), both films became blockbusters, with *The Mask* making $119 million and *Dumb and Dumber* $127 million domestically.[14] Fine Line Features enjoyed early success with the art house hit by Robert Altman, *The Player* ($21.7 million) in 1992, but their track record since has been less auspicious: top grossers for each year include Altman's *Short Cuts* ($6.1 million in 1993), the documentary *Hoop Dreams* ($7.8 million in 1994), *The Incredibly True Adventure of Two Girls in Love* (a dismal $2.2 million in 1995), and finally a breakthrough hit with *Shine* at the end of 1996 ($36 million). Shaye vowed to concentrate on acquiring distribution rights for Fine Line Features, rather than being an active producer.[15] This decision was motivated by the lower revenue potential associated with specialised art house films. By separating product between the two arms, Shaye has been able to create a market identity for each company and to allocate advertising/distribution expenditures consistent with each film's potential pay-off.

Miramax Films and Marketing Media Controversies

Miramax Films, run by Harvey and Bob Weinstein, also started by mining the college audience, through booking rock concerts and roadshow concert movies.[16] Their experience in film distribution began with acquiring distribution rights to films which, at the right pickup price, would enable them to reap at least a small profit. Consider Billie August's *Twist and Shout* (1986): with the North American rights acquired for $50,000, Miramax was able to nurture the film to about $1.5 million at the box office.[17] *I've Heard the Mermaids Singing* (1987), *Working Girls*, (1987) and *Pelle the Conqueror* (1988) were all successes for Miramax in the mid-1980s.

Miramax became more visible with the acquisition of Steven Soderbergh's *sex, lies and videotape*, which they advanced $1.1 million for the North American theatrical rights alone. Appropriately enough the film was produced through pre-selling the video rights to RCA–Columbia Home Video. Winning the Audience Award at the Sundance Film Festival and the Palme d'Or at Cannes, *sex, lies* was sold by Miramax as a sexy and intense comedy about relationships: ad images displayed Peter Gallagher and Laura San Giacomo embracing, and James Spader and Andie MacDowell about to kiss. Highlighting the critical acclaim also, Miramax realised a gross of over $26 million domestically. The film's success can be attributed to its topicality: many critics considered the film as primarily centred on the relationship between culture and technology in the age of 'safe sex'. With Graham (James Spader) videotaping interviews by women talking about their sex lives and his professed total reliance on masturbation as a sexual outlet, the film represents the intersection of the latest 'new technology' with sex, or rather with a form of sex that is completely safe. As Karen Jaehne astutely noted, 'Soderbergh wants Graham to explode the neo-conservative Eighties with video the way David Hemmings did the swinging sixties with photography in *Blowup*.'[18] Soderbergh's technique was to start by exploring the limited sexual boundaries available in the 1980s, a move that was calculated to some extent by the director. When queried on the difficulty of the project in terms of funding, Soderbergh explains, 'Well, on the one hand, it may seem like a risk. On the other, remember that we've got four relatively young people drenched in sexuality in a film that can be made for $1.2 million.'[19] Given the critical triumph, prizes and aggressive marketing by Miramax, the gross destroyed the previous benchmark for an art house hit. Independent marketing executive

Dennis O'Connor, who has worked at Strand Releasing and Trimark Pictures, believes that the marketplace for independent or specialized film has changed drastically since the time of *sex, lies and videotape*. In terms of box office, whereas the mark of an independent success used to be a gross of about $3 million, the figure currently is closer to $10 million.[20] Perhaps because of his film's role in this phenomenon, Soderbergh now has mixed feelings:

> The positive aspect is that it shows that 'art movies' can be a viable commercial product. They don't have to remain ghettoized as an art film. The bad thing is that it's established an unrealistic benchmark for other films. That's unfortunate. All you have to do is look at the Sundance Festival in the following years after *sex, lies* won, and you see films which may have been passed over since 'it's just not another *sex, lies*.' I actually think that my next two movies (*Kafka* and *King of the Hill*) will hold up better over time. I just feel that *sex, lies* is so much the beneficiary of being of that time that it's become so dated, like a Nehru jacket![21]

The experience with *sex, lies* has been replicated on many occasions by the company – more specifically, selling a product which lends itself to media-induced controversy. Repeatedly Miramax has maximized the publicity created by challenging the MPAA ratings system: Miramax films *Scandal* (1989), *The Cook, The Thief, His Wife and Her Lover* (1989), *Tie Me Up! Tie Me Down!* (1990) and *You So Crazy* (1994) all received X (or NC17) from the ratings board, with Miramax publicly announcing the injustice of the ratings system for independent companies compared to the majors.[22] While in some cases, cuts were made to obtain the R rating, most often (*Cook, Tie Me Up!*) Miramax chose to release the film unrated. Despite this fact, Miramax wagered often lengthy campaigns – all heavily reported in the media – against the 'arbitrary and capricious' ratings system which would assign an X to, for example, *Tie Me Up!*[23]

This ratings battle also has occurred with Miramax's advertising, with the company receiving reprimands from the Classification and Rating Administration of the MPAA.[24] After releasing Peter Greenaway's *The Cook, The Thief, His Wife and Her Lover* unrated – yet foregrounding the letter X in the ad copy, 'X as in . . .' – Miramax sought to advertise Greenaway's *Drowning By Numbers* (1987) through a silhouette of a naked man and woman embracing matched with a critic's quote stating, 'Enormously entertaining. No, no one gets eaten in this one.[25] The MPAA believed that the combination was too suggestive for widespread advertising. Amid wide coverage in industry trades, Miramax surrendered the R rating for the film, rather than alter the advertising.

Enormous publicity was generated by the campaign for *The Crying Game* which, unlike the original British ad campaign, centred on a shot of supporting actress Miranda Richardson with a smoking gun. For its North American opening in November 1992, the tag line proclaimed 'Play it at your own risk. Sex. Murder. Betrayal. In Neil Jordan's new thriller nothing is what it seems to be.' By January, the ad line was replaced with the following: 'The movie everyone is talking about, but no one is giving away its secrets.' Miramax wanted to stay away from the film's political elements and instead position it as a thriller based around a core secret (the gender of the character Dil, played by Jaye Davidson, revealed halfway through the film). This major secret was responsible for the film's cross-over success; due to the barrage of publicity and press coverage growing from the secret, an amazing $62.5 million was grossed by this film which would seem to be firmly within the boundaries of the art cinema.[26] As *Variety* describes Miramax's marketing campaign, 'Miramax sold the film as an action-thriller with a big "secret". If it had been realistically pegged as a relationship film with gay connotations, it might never have broken beyond the major cities.'[27]

As with *sex, lies and videotape*, *The Crying Game* benefited from engaging its audiences in current and timely issues – in this case, the national debate over homosexual rights, specifically the proposal to end the ban on gays serving in the military.[28] In many ways, the film's thriller plot line is secondary to the romance between Dil and Fergus (Stephen Rea) which addresses the blurry line between attraction and repulsion, not to mention constructed and essential differences across sexual, gender, class and national lines. As with the 'gays in the military' issue, the film confronts the fears of straight men being considered a sexual object by someone of the same gender. Less commented on during the release were the sexual politics inherent in such a position. While Jordan does feature an unlikely 'romantic' pairing of IRA member with a transvestite hairdresser, the film does nevertheless embody many clichés and stereotypes of gayness: the in-the-closet relationship, the continual drug-taking and night-clubbing, and the mental/psychological instability invoked by the character of Dil. Therefore, while the gimmick certainly placed and maintained the film in the domestic market, the cross-over popularity of the film must be considered in terms of its ideological stance. *The Crying Game* simultaneously allowed viewers to engage the subject of gayness while reinforcing 'traditional' and discriminatory views, all within the larger genre of the thriller.

The strategy of refocusing an advertising campaign also surfaced with Miramax's highest grossing film, *Pulp Fiction*. The campaign was designed to cross over as soon as possible from an art house audience to a wider action-thriller clientele. The trailer demonstrates this approach: the preview begins solemnly by announcing that the film has won the Palme d'Or at the Cannes Film Festival and that it has been one of the most critically acclaimed films of the year. Suddenly gunshots appear through the screen, and a fast-paced barrage of shots from the film stressing the action, sexuality and memorable sound bites. Through the trailer, Miramax has been able to sell to the art house audience through the film's credentials, but, more significantly, an image was created of the film as being full of action, comedy and sex. This approach no doubt broadened the film's audience without alienating those drawn by the critical acclaim. This strategy can also be evidenced in *Pulp Fiction*'s one-sheet which defines the term 'pulp fiction' for those unfamiliar – a process clearly aimed at educating the masses who might have been alienated by an 'obscure' title.

[. . .]

Life under Conglomeration

If Miramax and New Line represent the most ambitious and seasoned independents, their current claim to the label 'independent' is much more tenuous. In May 1993, Disney acquired Miramax, while the Turner Broadcasting Corporation merged with New Line. Paying close to $60 million for Miramax, Disney acquired the Miramax film library (over 200 features) and the talents of the Weinsteins who signed contracts for a five-year period.[29] Disney agreed entirely to finance the development, production and marketing of Miramax's features. The benefits for the Weinsteins include better ancillary deals in markets such as home video and pay television. The brothers estimate that by aligning with Disney they will be able to extract in excess of $750,000 to $2 million per film. Bob Weinstein cites the example of two Miramax children's films – *Arabian Knight* (1993) and *Gordy* (1995) – which failed theatrically but were saved by aggressive selling at the video window by Disney: 'We were rescued by Disney in home video. Now, that's a clear case of synergy.'[30] Ted Turner acquired New Line Cinema, along with Castle Rock Entertainment, to provide fresh programming for Turner's television networks, TBS and TNT.[31] New Line/Fine Line was acquired for about $600 million, while Castle Rock cost Turner $100 million in cash and about $300 million in assumed debt.[32]

The intent for both Disney and Turner was to leave New Line and Miramax as separate from the allied companies. In this manner, both New Line and Miramax would be able to maintain some autonomy. This position is significant given the lessons learned from the 'classics' divisions of the major studios in the early 1980s. Established to distribute specialized product, the classics divisions, such as Triumph Films (Columbia) and Twentieth Century Fox International Classics, entrusted distribution for their films to the studios' domestic distribution arm.[33] Focusing their energy on the mainstream (and more costly) films, domestic distribution bungled release after release from the classics divisions. New Line and Miramax have retained control of distribution and marketing for their releases. The most impressive difference given their new affiliation was a greater access to funds and more latitude in production decisions.

Indeed, these major independents, Miramax and New Line, have served to polarise the market for independent film. Miramax, in particular, has become even more aggressive in buying distribution rights to completed films, with their efforts increasing the price for product. As Ira Deutchman of Fine Line comments, '[The Disney era] Miramax has definitely affected the marketplace. People are buying films earlier and earlier, and paying more and more.'[34]

Marcus Hu of the independent company Strand Releasing repeats this observation: 'It's tough when you find a Miramax buying up stuff like *Clerks*. If *Crush* had come out this year, a bigger company would have snapped it up.'[35] Even executives at Miramax admit that this syndrome is problematic: acquisitions vice-president Tony Safford comments, 'We think other people have overpaid. We are all having to make strategic decisions that may involve overpaying because of lack of product.'[36]

Since the mergers in 1993, against professed intentions, corporate domination has somewhat constrained both Miramax and New Line despite their greater access to capital. With Miramax, the policy of marketing through media controversy has occasionally created friction with Disney. In 1995, this conflict was evidenced with the releases both of *Priest*, a British film directed by Antonia Bird about a conservative gay priest fighting inner and outer battles to gain peace, and *kids*, Larry Clark's exposé of debauched youth in New York. In a move that was described by William A. Donohue, president of the Catholic League, as placing 'salt on the wounds of believers', Miramax scheduled the release of *Priest* for Good Friday. Miramax, expressing surprise at the vehemence with which the film was being protested, shifted the release date amid a great deal of publicity. A representative headline over the incident read, 'Protest Delays Wide Release of Priest; Miramax Bows to Catholic Group and Reschedules Controversial Film's General Distribution Till After Easter'.[37] Advertising maximized the controversy: the title carried the letter 't' in the shape of the cross, while the ad line referenced both the gay priest's secret and the secondary tale of incest which the priest must expose: 'In the world of rituals, in a place of secrets, a man must choose between keeping the faith and exposing the truth.' Given Miramax's affiliation with Disney, the effects persisted though: several stockholders, including the Knights of Columbus and Senator Bob Dole's wife Elizabeth Dole, sold stock in Disney soon after the *Priest* scandal. The Knights of Columbus, selling $3 million of Disney stock, cited the company's ties to Miramax and *Priest*, while a Dole spokesman commented, 'Mrs. Dole was surprised to learn that Disney owned Miramax and Hollywood Records and has decided to sell her stock.'[38]

kids was able to maintain an almost consistent flow of publicity and promotion from its appearance at the Sundance Film Festival in January 1995 through its release in July. Ostensibly a cautionary tale, *kids* follows a day in the life of 17-year-old Telly, a 'virgin surgeon' whose mission in life is to seduce virgins. One of his earlier conquests, Jennie, discovers that she is HIV-positive and, while Telly is pursuing more girls, Jennie tries to find Telly to tell him the news. Playing into the media's most florid depiction of forgotten urban youth, the film's *cinéma vérité* style furthered the critics' and reviewers' beliefs that Clark was depicting only a thinly veiled reality: as *New York* magazine titled their cover story on the film, 'What's the Matter with *kids* Today?'[39] *kids* received an NC17 rating (for 'explicit sex, language, drug use, and violence involving children') from the Motion Picture Association of America.

Contractually Miramax, as a subsidiary of Disney, cannot release NC17 films. Thus the Weinsteins were forced to form another company, Shining Excalibur Pictures, just to release *kids*. Although some industry analysts viewed this move as an attempt by the Weinsteins to distance themselves from Disney, the brothers denied any such intention.[40]

Whereas Miramax has been able to continue its strategy of marketing through controversy, albeit with occasional institutional difficulties, New Line's fate under the Turner regime has been more precarious. The long-term differences in their life under conglomeration can be appreciated by contrasting two releases from 1996, Miramax's *Trainspotting* and Fine Line's *Crash*. *Trainspotting*, a mixture of hyperbolic music video visuals with a downbeat tale of heroin addiction among a set of friends in Scotland, became the second most popular British feature in UK box-office history and was adopted by Miramax for North American release. The Weinsteins partly dubbed the film to make the Scottish accents more comprehensible and sold it more along the lines of disillusioned youth than on heroin addiction. The trailer shifted the narrative trajectory to the heist of the last third of the film, limiting mention of drugs to an absolute minimum, while the print ad positioned the film in terms of lifestyle choices for the young ('Choose life. Choose a job . . .' through to 'Choose rotting away at the end of it all'). While the film's advertising diminished the role played by heroin in the narrative, a secondary level of publicity detailed the 'heroin chic' culture of emaciated and drugged fashion models and the rise of heroin use among the young. The result was a solid gross of $16.5 million, not a cross-over hit, but certainly a respectable art house box-office figure.

David Cronenberg's *Crash* describes a subculture of people sexually aroused by car accidents, following a young couple's descent into this world after their own crash. Admittedly, the subject matter strictly limited the film to art house exhibition, but New Line's owner Ted Turner reportedly delayed the release of the film after finding it distasteful: the release date was moved from October 1996 to March 1997, putting *Crash*'s American release after many other territories, including Canada and France. Turner's intervention in his subsidiary companies over 'difficult' projects had already impacted Anjelica Huston's television film *Bastard Out of Carolina*, depicting the rape of a 12-year-old by her stepfather. Huston's film was dropped from Turner's TNT cable network after Turner called the film 'extraordinarily graphic' and 'inhumane'.[41] Apart from shying away from controversy, the merger of Time Warner with Turner Broadcasting in 1996 further complicated New Line's position through making New Line directly compete with Warner Bros. for feature films. By mid-1996, industry trade papers reported that New Line was for sale by Time Warner as a result of this conflict of interest.[42] Around the same time, the Weinsteins extended their deal with Disney for another seven years.[43]

While historically New Line and Miramax were able to develop strategies – franchises and aggressive marketing/publicity – to maintain a consistent market presence, their merger with the larger companies has created a curious hybrid, the 'major independent'. The major independents have fragmented the marketplace for independent film further and further – through producing films parallel to the majors and through stressing art house acquisitions which have the potential to cross over to a wider market. While New Line and Miramax have gained financial backing through their affiliations, the remaining unaffiliated companies have experienced greater difficulty in acquiring product at a reasonable price. The net effect is a contraction in the market for independent film, bolstering the status of the majors and major independents, and creating an increasingly competitive market for those smaller companies. This movement towards the major independent as a market force constitutes a key shift in the industrial parameters of independent film, studio moviemaking and the New Hollywood. These two companies, seemingly on the margins of Hollywood, actually illustrate a number of the ways through which the New Hollywood has been refigured in industrial, aesthetic and institutional terms.

NOTES

1. 'Arty and "freak" films packaged to theatre trade by New Line; sex, too', *Variety*, 4 July 1973, p. 6.
2. 'Negative pickups a new policy for N.Y.'s New Line Cinema', *Variety*, 11 August 1976, p. 26.
3. 'Pickup costs, other factors propel New Line to enter production', *Variety*, 28 June 1978, p. 6.
4. Ibid.
5. 'New Line, Working Title in 3-year deal', *Variety*, 31 May 1989, p. 21.
6. Claudia Eller and Max Alexander, '*Turtles* vid heads for sell-through as New Line catches screen sequel', *Variety*, 18 July 1990, p. 3.
7. Myron Meisel, 'New Line's nightmare spurs ambitious expansion program', *The Film Journal*, April 1986, p. 37.
8. Judy Brennan, 'Turtles a hero for New Line in first Half', *Variety*, 1 August 1990, p. 27.
9. Ronald Grover, 'Nightmares, turtles – and profits', *Business Week*, 30 September 1991, p. 52.
10. Martin Grove, 'New Line's future is filled with franchises', *The Hollywood Reporter*, 25 March 1993, p. 5.
11. For an analysis of Paramount's strategies in designing these commercial tent poles, see Justin Wyatt, 'High concept as product differentiation', *High Concept: Movies and Marketing in Hollywood* (Austin: University of Texas Press, 1994), pp. 104–7.
12. 'New Line restructured for 24-pic annual goal', *Variety*, 29 June 1983, p. 4.
13. Claudia Eller, 'New Line forms new label for specialty releases', *Variety*, 10 December 1990, p. 5.
14. Data on domestic New Line and Miramax grosses have been supplied by Entertainment Data, Inc.
15. Claudia Eller, 'New Line forms', p. 5.
16. Anne Thompson, 'Will success spoil the Weinstein Brothers?', *Film Comment*, July/August 1989, p. 73.
17. Ibid., p. 75.
18. Karen Jaehne, Review of *sex, lies and videotape*, *Cineaste*, vol. 17, no. 3 (1990), p. 38.
19. Harlan Jacobson, 'Truth or consequences', *Film Comment*, July/August 1989, p. 23.
20. Dennis O'Connor, telephone interview, 19 May 1995.
21. Steven Soderbergh, telephone interview, 26 October 1994.

22. Miramax sold off distribution rights to *You So Crazy* to the Samuel Goldwyn Company in March 1994. As a subsidiary of Disney, a Motion Picture Association of America member, Miramax was forbidden to release the film without a rating.
23. Richard Huff, 'Shackles on *Tie Me Up?*: Kunstler calls X rating arbitrary', *Variety*, 27 June 1990, p. 10.
24. Will Tusher, 'Distrib forfeits R on *Numbers* due to ad flak', *Variety*, 27 May 1991, p. 3.
25. Ibid.
26. Caryn James, '*The Crying Game* wins at gimmickry', *The New York Times*, 31 January 1993, p. H11.
27. Michael Fleming and Leonard Klady, ' "Crying" all the way to the bank', *Variety*, 22 March 1993, p. 68.
28. A month before the release of *The Crying Game* in North America, President-elect Bill Clinton announced that he planned to reverse the bans on homosexuals in the military as his first policy decision. For a chronology of events and issues leading to this point, see Scott Tucker, 'Panic in the Pentagon', *Humanist*, vol. 53 (June 1993), p. 41. The national furore over this proposal is covered in Bruce B. Auster, 'The Commander and Chiefs', *U.S. News and World Reports*, 8 February 1993, pp. 37–40.
29. Claudia Eller and John Evan Frook, 'Mickey munches on Miramax', *Variety*, 3 May 1993, p. 60.
30. Claudia Eller, 'The synergy between unlikely partners Miramax and Disney has surprised many – including Miramax and Disney', *The Los Angeles Times*, 1 December 1995, p. D1.
31. Anita Sharpe, 'Turner film ventures gets mixed results', *The Wall Street Journal*, 11 August 1994, p. B1.
32. Claudia Eller, 'Media's mega-deal makers', *The Los Angeles Times*, 18 July 1996, p. D6.
33. Alicia Springer, 'Sell it again Sam', *American Film*, March 1983, p. 55.
34. John E. Frook, 'Call Harvey Mickey Mouth', *Variety*, 29 November 1993, p. 75.
35. Mary S. Glucksman, 'The state of things', *Filmmaker*, Fall 1994, p. 29.
36. John Brodie, 'Harvey's hefty cash lends fest some flash', *Variety*, 23 May 1994, p. 63.
37. John Dart, 'Protest delays wide release of *Priest*', *The Los Angeles Times*, 25 March 1995, p. Metro 1.
38. 'Disney link to assailed movie spurs Dole's wife to sell stock', *The Los Angeles Times*, 3 June 1995, p. A16.
39. Lynn Hirschberg, 'What's the matter with *kids* today?', *New York*, 5 June 1995, pp. 36–41.
40. Elaine Dutka, 'Miramax circumvents *kids* controversy', *The Los Angeles Times*, 29 June 1995, p. Calendar 2.
41. Warren Berger, 'A harsh story finally avoids a harsh fate', *The New York Times*, 15 December 1996, p. H37.
42. Turner's reported pricing of New Line stalled some potential bidders for the company; see Dan Cox and Martin Peers, 'New Line goes back in time', *Variety*, 10 April 1997, p. 1.
43. Claudia Eller, 'Miramax's production duo extending run with Disney', *The Los Angeles Times*, 10 May 1996, p. 5.

22

CULTS, INDEPENDENTS AND 'GUERRILLA' FILMMAKING

Despite Hollywood's consolidation of power, and the centrality of the mass-audience blockbuster to the economics and aesthetics of contemporary filmmaking, there remained enough flexibility in the film industry for alternative models of cinema to exist, and in some cases flourish, beyond the exclusive control of the major studios. This was related in no small part to occasional funding sources and specialised forms of institutional support that emerged for independent film. The video market, in particular, became a crucial source of funding through cassette presales. Similarly, broadcast industries in Europe, such as Channel 4 in Britain and ZDF in Germany, were eager to purchase low-budget niche American films for their burgeoning programming schedules. These provided valuable funding streams for independent film.

At the same time, international film festivals such as Cannes, Venice, London, Berlin, Toronto, Hong Kong and Pusan were becoming an important showcase for raising public awareness of films produced outside Hollywood. Frequently mixing filmmakers, producers, industry personnel, scholars, journalists, archivists and ordinary fans, film festivals would attract a broad spectrum of participants in a jamboree atmosphere that could make or break new films, especially foreign (meaning non-US), marginal or 'difficult' films. Festivals came to represent an alternative distribution network in the 1990s, crucial to the success of movies ranging from *Cinema Paradiso* (1989) to *The Wedding Banquet* (1993).

While an international festival circuit emerged after the Second World War, it proliferated in the 1980s and 1990s, leading to events of varying size, duration and prestige. The most prestigious, or 'A list', festivals were accredited by the International Federation of Film Producers Associations (FIAPF), and frequently held prize competitions. These would represent a crucial source of publicity for low-budget films. Developing into a global distribution network, certain festivals developed special interest and regional profiles during the 1990s. For example, San Francisco's Tranny Fest became a significant platform for feminist and gay filmmakers. In the United States, however, Robert Redford's Sundance Film Festival became the key venue for independent film, inaugurated in Park City, Utah, in 1990. Increasingly attractive to Hollywood agents and distributors seeking 'breakout' hits – such as Steven Soderbergh's *sex, lies, and videotape* (1989) that took the top prize at Sundance and went on to gross $100 million worldwide – Sundance played a part in bringing independent film into the mainstream. Robert Redford explained this function in positive terms, suggesting that the festival seeks to 'eliminate the tension that can exist between the independents and the studios', enabling independent filmmakers to make contacts and strike deals. This is especially important for independent film where selling a movie, or rather its distribution rights, can be enabled by festival 'buzz'.

Occasionally, festivals launched films that went on to spectacular success, buoyed by strategic marketing campaigns by the likes of Miramax, as described by Justin Wyatt in the previous chapter. The key to Miramax's success in the early 1990s was undoubtedly Quentin Tarantino, forging cult status through his début film *Reservoir Dogs* (1992) and the enormous independent success of *Pulp Fiction* (1994). Winning the Palme D'Or at Cannes in 1994, *Pulp Fiction* cost $8 million to make and grossed $200 million worldwide. Moving from the violent caper of *Reservoir Dogs*, Tarantino's follow-up played inventively with cross-plots and overlapping character stories in a movie that mixed elements of the gangster, outlaw and prize-fight film. As a self-confessed movie geek, Tarantino peppered his films with myriad pop cultural references and cinematic borrowings, specifically drawn from the 1970s. Just as Tarantino's third main feature, *Jackie Brown* (1997), drew upon a seventies blaxploitation aesthetic, giving a lead role to Pam Grier, *Pulp Fiction* revitalised the career of John Travolta in its own retro fusion of past and present.

While Tarantino has been widely fêted for his personal flair as a filmmaker, it is important to recognise the rich mix of influence on his work, in particular the debt to Hong Kong filmmaking. Tarantino's representation of brutal violence, for example, was especially influenced by the work of John Woo. Adapting martial arts choreography to contemporary crime thrillers in the late 1980s and early 1990s, John Woo used kung fu acrobatics in gun-toting spectacles defined by their ultra-violence. From *A Better Tomorrow* (1986) to *Hard Boiled* (1992), Woo developed an aesthetic of violence based on stylised gunfights, explosions and action stunts, and often involving prolonged action sequences that used multiple and abrupt camera angles and quick adjustments in the speed of shots. This gangster-hero cycle ultimately projected him towards Hollywood. Indeed, the cross-cultural dialogue between film styles of East and West was centrally expressed in the developing relationship between Hollywood and Hong Kong, Woo eventually bringing his talents to bear in Hollywood blockbusters such as *Face/Off* (1997) and *Mission: Impossible 2* (1999).

Hong Kong cinema was multi-faceted. Alongside vehicles for action stars like Jackie Chan and Jet Li, came more lyrical and intricate art films. Wong Kar-wai's *Chungking Express* (1994), for example, was made up of a series of meditative scenes bearing on different couples and their hopes, investments and attitudes towards time and love. In narrative terms, the film was distinguished by its controlled handling of two disparate storylines, one concerning a jilted cop's encounter with a female heroin trafficker, and another based on a waitress's obsession with another police officer. Targeted at the festival circuit, this was more successful internationally than it was in local markets. Like the work of John Woo, however, it would have a discreet bearing on Western directors such as Tarantino.

The influence of Hong Kong cinema in the 1990s was underpinned by a surge in regional film production that occurred prior to the handing back of Hong Kong to China in 1997. It was also linked to the growing international distribution, and festival success, of film from the Pacific Rim more generally. The year before *Pulp Fiction* won the Palme d'Or, for instance, the coveted prize was shared by Jane Campion's period drama set and filmed in New Zealand, *The Piano* (1993), and Chen Kaige's epic drama about two Peking opera singers set across fifty years of Chinese history, *Farewell My Concubine* (1993). In the same period, festival success was also bestowed on new Taiwanese cinema, Hou Hsiao-Hsien winning the Golden Lion at the Venice Film Festival for his film about a Taiwanese family's postwar experiences, *City of Sadness* (1989), and Ang Lee winning the main prize at Berlin for his comedy about the contemporary clash of Eastern and Western cultures in *The Wedding Banquet*. It was in response to the increasing vibrancy and profile of Asian film culture that the Pusan film festival was established in South Korea in 1996, becoming a major showcase for work from the Pacific Rim.

Regional cinema became increasingly visible to filmgoing publics in the 1990s, signalled by the international success of large-scale European films such as *The Last Emperor* (1987) and *Cyrano de Bergerac* (1990), as well as by films from Asia. As with the independent sector, this did not signal any lessening of Hollywood's power. Creating classics divisions to handle foreign and independent titles, the major studios used independent as well as regional film to serve distinct audience subsets. Hollywood not only incorporated indie films within its larger stable of products, for example, it often used them as a way of identifying niche markets. In this sense, Richard Linklater's *Slacker* (1991) identified a market for 'Generation X' movies that would later be serviced by *Reality Bites* (1994), a star-driven treatment of overeducated, underemployed 'Gen X-ers' searching for meaning in their working lives and personal relationships.

While rarely autonomous in industrial terms, independent film continued to produce original and creatively uncomfortable work. Danny Boyle's fast-paced exploration of heroin addiction in *Trainspotting* (1995), for example, combined harrowing and bleak depictions of drug abuse with funny, soundtrack-driven, episodes covering the disintegrating friendships of four Edinburgh youths. In a quite different depiction of male relations, Kevin Smith's micro-budget film *Clerks* (1994) was based on frank discussions about videos, food and mainly sex in a New Jersey convenience store. Together with films such as *Poison* (1990) by Todd Haynes and *Spanking the Monkey* (1994) by David O. Russell, which dealt respectively with issues of male sex and incest, a number of small-budget films in the early 1990s achieved notoriety and success through their frank and often uneasy treatment of contemporary life and youth identity.

While such films assumed cult credentials, independent filmmakers did not simply make low-budget fare, or hawk their wares on the festival circuit. While *Henry: Portrait of a Serial Killer* (1986) had established a documentary fascination with the cinematic representation of mass murderers, Jonathan Demme's *The Silence of the Lambs* (1991) and David Fincher's *Se7en* (1995) revisited the territory in popular films defined by their atmospheric tension and visual style. While these films are sometimes generically coded as 'horror' and 'noir', they capture a notable fluidity in the way that a film's identity may be produced, marketed and consumed. In the aforementioned examples, each film combined the status of any one of art film, horror, thriller and quality drama. They are not easily defined by genre, just as they are not categorically defined as 'mainstream' or 'independent' in their visual style or direction.

While there is a tendency to celebrate 'independent film' as something free-standing, it must be understood in terms of Hollywood as the dominant system. The films of Oliver Stone and Spike Lee were especially significant in mapping this relational dynamic onto sensitive and overlooked social themes. Associated with social-problem filmmaking, Stone became a key Warner Bros. director after independent success with *Platoon* (1986). Exploring manifestations of military, political, financial and media power in American life, Stone made a number of controversial films in the early 1990s, including *JFK* (1991) and *Natural Born Killers* (1994). These were frequently propelled by Stone's jarring stylistic tendencies and anti-establishment positions. While *JFK* fused historical footage and fictional drama in its rendering of the Kennedy assassination, *Natural Born Killers* used a number of disruptive cinematic styles in its exploration of media-fuelled serial killing. This included the use of rapid cuts, jolting camera movements, and the mixing of colour and black and white footage. In each case, Stone's 'independence' was defined through his challenging cinematic style and aggressive liberal politics rather than from any necessary position outside the Hollywood system.

Spike Lee also occupied a position within and yet askance to the Hollywood system, mapping socio-political concerns about race in the United States onto various kinds of documentary, drama-musical and epic biography. Lee came from a tradition of independent black cinema seeking to explore and project alternative representations of black identity from that offered by dominant cinema. This was forged in early pictures such as *She's Gotta Have It* (1986), a romantic comedy about three black men pursuing a sexually liberated black woman. Playing upon African American slang and musical idioms, and using to-camera monologues and montage sequences, the film made $30 million in domestic theatrical grosses and sent Lee on his way to a studio career from which he continued to examine the pressures, as well as the pleasures, of black identity.

Race in America became an especially charged and divisive issue in the early 1990s, producing a tense racial climate fed by a series of incidents given wide coverage in the mainstream media. This included the Rodney King beating and the Los Angeles riots, the trial of O. J. Simpson, the Million Man March, and a conservative backlash against both affirmative action policies in higher education and the social influence of gangsta rap and gun crime. At the same time, Hollywood began to look with renewed interest to the heterogeneous and potentially profitable black audience as a means of insuring against white, big-picture flops. Spike Lee's move from independent to mainstream cinema was situated in this mix of cultural and economic forces.

While *Do the Right Thing* (1989) offered a portrayal of racial and sexual tension in Harlem in a single day, experimenting stylistically with vivid colour schemes and a striking hip-hop soundtrack, Lee's biographical *Malcolm X* (1992) was staged as an event movie. If the former was principally made as a black audience film, the latter was designed with crossover appeal, part of a cycle of 'ghettocentric' films in the early 1990s that focused on the violence and social politics of inner-city black ghettos. Lee framed this topic as one theme of a panoramic biography of the Black Muslim leader. The cycle was fully realised, however, in films by Mario Van Peebles such as *New Jack City* (1991) and by John Singleton in *Boyz N The Hood* (1991).

Boyz N The Hood was an independent film that adopted mainstream elements. Indeed, it was sold as a male-focused action/crime picture. Set in the South Central district of Los Angeles, and engaging themes of gang warfare and black-on-black killing, the film turns on the despair and hopelessness of the urban African American experience. At the same time, if offers a narrative of escape for the main protagonist Tre (played by Cuba Gooding Jr). Analysing the complex position of black masculinity in a culture of racial and economic division, *Boyz N The Hood* also raised questions about its arguably dismissive representation of women and reliance on social solutions that stressed individual betterment rather than radical, collective action.

In bringing black themes to mainstream cinema, black filmmakers sometimes drew accusations of co-option. This describes the way that Hollywood can exert pressure on those who work within its systems, containing ideas that may challenge dominant culture by using familiar genres or thematic conventions. However, this underestimates the significance of directors like Lee and Singleton. Lee, in particular, was instrumental in articulating African American cultural and political themes in stylistically daring and politically challenging films. Ideas of co-option also downplay the tangled relationship between independent and mainstream cinema, especially the fact that financing black films can represent challenges of its own. In trying to crack the discriminatory insider networks of Hollywood, Spike Lee became an advocate of 'guerrilla cinema'. This spoke of techniques of funding and production that could challenge the investment ceilings of Hollywood studios. When funding ran out for *Malcolm X*, Lee appealed to prominent black figures such as Bill Cosby and Oprah Winfrey for money to complete the picture, raising millions of dollars as a result. These insurgent strategies played with and against Hollywood's infrastructure, in Lee's case moving towards progressive filmmaking that could place race more centrally on Hollywood's agenda.

Guerrilla tactics were not the exclusive preserve of black cinema. Neither were they limited to questions of finance. Guerrilla techniques were also adopted by young directors whose lack of budget became a selling point in movies that relied on a low-tech and purposely amateurish look. One of the most celebrated examples was *El Mariachi* (1992) by Robert Rodriguez, apparently made for $7,000. This was a gun-toting Mexican action film that utilised a minuscule cast and crew, employed resourceful camerawork and swift cutting, and was based on videotape editing that Rodriguez carried out while living and working at home. While a certain romance is often attached to such 'do-it-yourself' filmmaking, this can belie the true costs involved. In reality, *El Mariachi* cost significantly more than $7,000 to get to screen, as Rodriguez signed a deal during the filming process that enabled him to complete the picture and cover its substantial distribution and exhibition costs. This amounted to hundreds of thousands of dollars, taking it closer to the conventional definition of a 'microbudget' film, meaning anything under $2 million.

The early 1990s is often characterised as a renaissance for independent filmmaking. This was associated with a new clutch of young directors, but also with established *auteurs* such as Joel and Ethan Coen, Tim Burton, Gus Van Sant and John Sayles. While the Coen brothers developed quirky projects such as *Barton Fink* (1991) and *Fargo* (1996), Burton made a number of idiosyncratic films such as *Edward Scissorhands* (1990) and *Ed Wood* (1994). Meanwhile, Gus Van Sant moved from his exploration of seventies drug life in Portland, Oregon, in *Drugstore Cowboy* (1989), to the more experimental treatment of gay subculture in *My Own Private Idaho* (1991). This film drew upon hallucinatory dream sequences and *cinéma vérité* confessions with male hustlers, and was notable for playing Keanu Reeves against type. If the Pacific North West became a backdrop for Van Sant, John Sayles' *Lone Star* (1996) offered a textured account of American multiculturalism as set in a small Texan border town. While a cycle of films in the early 1990s looked ambiguously at the victim status of the white male – in particular associated with Michael Douglas in *Falling Down* (1993) and *Disclosure* (1994) – more poignant explorations of marginalisation and struggle were contained in films such as

Lone Star and also *Thelma and Louise* (1991), contributing to ongoing debates about ethnicity and gender in the United States.

Texas became an important narrative backdrop for the rape-revenge narrative of *Thelma and Louise*. Similar to films like *The Silence of the Lambs* and *Terminator 2: Judgment Day* (1991), it put forward the figure of the independent woman as heroine. Refashioning the traditionally male genre of the road movie, *Thelma and Louise* became a focal site for debates about the oppression and empowerment of women. Running from the police after Louise (Susan Sarandon) shoots a man trying to rape Thelma (Geena Davis), the film unfolds as a narrative of transformation and self-discovery, symbolised in part by the heroines' self-sufficient handling of guns. The representation of female identity in Ridley Scott's film differed in part to the more psychotic depictions of women also evident in the period. This was notable in films such as *The Hand that Rocks the Cradle* (1992) and *Single White Female* (1992), focusing respectively on the nanny and lodger 'from hell'. While some criticism has been quick to dismiss the compromised or demonised representation of the female subject in each of these films, this belies the complex means by which identity is forged within the terms of popular cinema, responding variously to the pleasures and generic legacies of, in this case, the road movie and the psychological thriller.

Despite the resurgence of independent film, it should not be forgotten that the early 1990s was also a period where Hollywood powerfully reaffirmed the blockbuster. Sometimes, these were made by *auteurs* such as Michael Mann who developed a reputation for stylish dramas focusing on heroic and often conflicted male protagonists. From Daniel Day-Lewis' frontiersman in *The Last of the Mohicans* (1992) to the gripping standoff between Robert De Niro and Al Pacino in *Heat* (1995), Mann developed intelligent and visually striking portrayals of masculine bravura in a range of historical and contemporary settings. These differed from blockbusters that were more cartoonish in their style and address. While 1994 saw the release of films such as *Clerks* and *Pulp Fiction*, it should also be remembered that this was the year of *Speed*, *True Lies*, *The Lion King* and *Forrest Gump*. Action spectacles and calculated family-adventure movies dominated the box office, creating a challenging market environment for independent film.

In certain cases, independent film sought to compete by adopting an explicitly commercial slant. For instance, the success of the British export *Four Weddings and a Funeral* (1994) was largely due to its market positioning as a 'date' movie rather than as an art house film from director Mike Newell. With the target audience focused on the 18–40 age range, the American distributor Gramercy downplayed the film's independent status, and established it as a mainstream romantic comedy. This was enabled by the fact that *Four Weddings and a Funeral* was formally and thematically conventional in style, relying for its niche identity on a performed 'Britishness', typified by the accent and antics of Hugh Grant. Its key formula would be replayed in a cycle of British romantic comedies, tailored for the American market and all starring Grant. Produced by the British company Working Title, this cycle would include *Notting Hill* (1999), *Bridget Jones's Diary* (2001) and *Love Actually* (2003).

Despite the force of mainstream Hollywood, various attempts were made in the 1990s to challenge industrial norms with alternative forms of cinematic style, financing and marketing. Strategies that worked against the pull of dominant cinema were not limited to the West. In China, a politically subversive film movement emerged, based around a youthful film and video underground. For much of the 1980s, a new generation of filmmakers from the Beijing Film Academy (known as the Fifth Generation) had challenged reigning ideas of cinematic realism that were linked, ideologically, to Chinese political culture. Reacting against the Cultural Revolution, Fifth Generation filmmakers such as Chen Kaige explored the restrictive nature of rote learning in education, together with other forms of cultural and intellectual proscription. During the late 1980s, however, the Chinese government began to tighten control against the 'bourgeois liberalisation' it associated with student-led calls for political reform. While this led to more accessible and commercial work by Fifth Generation filmmakers, violent suppression of pro-democracy protest in 1989, culminating in the Tiananmen Square massacre, led to its decline as a coherent movement.

While Chen Kiage continued to direct films using foreign financing, including *Farewell My Concubine*, and Zhang Yimou won international acclaim for *Raise the Red Lantern* (1991), a story about the repression of women in 1920s China, a Sixth Generation emerged domestically. Made up of independent directors, unattached to sanctioned Chinese studios, Sixth Generation directors invariably made films without a distribution or exhibition permit. These were known as 'illegal films'. Concerned thematically with young people and social problems, Sixth Generation cinema ranged from films about Chinese rock culture (*Beijing Bastards*, 1993) and gay cruising (*East Palace, West Palace*, 1996) to new forms of video documentary exploring the impact of Tiananmen Square (*I Graduated!*, 1992).

If guerrilla cinema can be understood more explicitly in particular national and political contexts, Iranian filmmakers had to negotiate a censorious clerical establishment in the 1980s and 1990s. The theocratic regime of Ayatollah Khomeini drove out foreign cinema and condemned traces of Western influence in Iranian film. To receive an exhibition permit in the Iranian film industry, all films had to undergo a four-stage approval system that scrutinised a film's synopsis, screenplay, cast and crew. This was designed to codify Islamic values and encourage the production of quality films. Despite its restrictive parameters, many imaginative films emerged from this system, winning acclaim at international film festivals. For example, the work of Abbas Kiarostami in *Where is my Friend's House?* (1987) and *Through the Olive Trees* (1994) deals respectively with the simple drama of a school expulsion, and with a romance that ensues off-screen during the production of one of Kiarostami's earlier films.

With different degrees of poetry and self-reflection, both draw upon the rugged Iranian landscape, offering in the latter case a tribute to the inhabitants of Iran's earthquake-ravaged northlands.

While facing huge financial crisis, exacerbated by Iran's war with Iraq between 1980 and 1988 and the Persian Gulf War in 1990 to 1991, the Iranian film industry grew steadily in the period, encouraged by the government's Farabi Cinema Foundation that poured money into production. Indeed, cinema was not opposed by the clerical regime but its 'misuse' was monitored, with frameworks established to prevent the 'corruption' and 'subjugation' of Iranians by Western influence. This led to a regulated industrial climate for Iranian filmmakers, but one that had its advantages, specifically in not having to compete in the domestic theatrical market with (banned) American film.

In Middle-Eastern and Pacific Rim countries where American film and financing were not restricted, the fortunes of independent and art house cinema were often tied to government support agencies and their promotion of local film production. While tax incentives for film production in New Zealand wound up in 1984, a number of directors made their international mark in the early 1990s, often locating their work specifically in New Zealand. For example, Jane Campion's *The Piano* examined relationships of communication between a woman (Holly Hunter) who has given up speech and her lover played by Harvey Keitel. While using American and Australian stars, the film is set in New Zealand and draws purposely on local Maori dialect. In a different vein, Lee Tamahori's *Once Were Warriors* (1994) deals with ghetto Maori life and the trials of urban impoverishment. Meanwhile, Peter Jackson would use a true story in New Zealand's recent past as the basis of *Heavenly Creatures* (1994), a film that would also launch the career of Kate Winslet. Of these, Jackson in particular would help invigorate the New Zealand film industry, dramatising the landscape in future projects including the *Lord of the Rings* trilogy (2001–3), and through regional post-production units established in the mid-1990s such as the digital workshop WETA.

In Australia, the Film Finance Corporation (FFC) was established in 1988 to provide funding and promote greater commercial visibility for Australian films in the art house market. While tax concessions for investors had spurred Australian film production in the 1980s, leading to hits such as *Crocodile Dundee* (1986), the FFC established a dedicated film fund, investing in such as Baz Lurhmann's romantic comedy *Strictly Ballroom* (1992). This was one of a number of films that moved away from outback fantasies and stories of the bush, to more complex and plural visions of Australia, captured in films ranging from the drag queen road movie *The Adventures of Priscilla, Queen of the Desert* (1994) to the musical biography *Shine* (1996). As was the case in the United States, debates about multiculturalism – combined with the growing importance of niche markets – led to an increase in gay, feminist and ethnic themes.

And yet, the FFC was inspired less by the need to project alternative images of Australia than in generating success in domestic and international markets.

While claiming minor triumphs like *Strictly Ballroom*, international success really came in the form of co-productions using a combination of Australian and American film financing. When the FFC budget was cut by the conservative Liberal-Nationalist coalition in 1997, co-productions became more common, resulting in films such as Baz Lurhmann's *William Shakespeare's Romeo + Juliet* (1996) and *Moulin Rouge!* (2001). This reduced the number of films addressing local themes, but did create a boost for the Australian film industry in terms of investment. For national cinema, and within independent filmmaking more generally, success continued to be linked inextricably with Hollywood's industrial and distribution muscle.

Taking *Bram Stoker's Dracula* (1992) as a case study, Thomas Austin's essay '*Gone with the Wind* Plus Fangs', examines the particular means by which film in the early 1990s was distinguished by what he calls 'industrially motivated hybridity'. This describes the means by which film creates appeal not through any singular or unified style, as might be implied with the marketing theories of high concept, but through 'promotional and conversational processes of fragmentation, elaboration and diffusion'. Examining the means by which film texts are addressed to, and understood by, different kinds of audience, Austin loosens some of the more rigid categorisations that shape critical under-standings of genre. Crucially, this is linked in his argument to the 'taste formations' that construct and reconstruct the meaning of texts. Austin con-centrates on questions of genre, but the idea that there is nothing innate about the identity of film, that its status relies on particular 'discursive formulations', also has a bearing on the definitional fluidities of 'cult', 'independent' and 'mainstream' cinema. Indeed, the figure of Francis Ford Coppola, who directed *Bram Stoker's Dracula*, is particularly interesting in clouding these distinctions.

Rather than simply examine the production, or the marketing, or the reception of *Bram Stoker's Dracula*, Austin takes a multidimensional approach to film history; he uses different methodologies in order to demonstrate the complex means by which films are made, positioned and understood. Unlike film analysis that might see production, marketing and reception as discrete stages, or that focus singularly on one aspect, Austin demonstrates how they inform one another as processes. By interlinking industrial and audience methodologies, Austin is better able to examine the different meanings and 'invitations to view' that coalesce around a text.

Such an approach relies on a wide variety of primary evidence. Together with industrial information drawn from trade magazines and film production notes, Austin examines reviews in broadsheet newspapers and popular and specialist film magazines. This is further matched with a questionnaire designed to elicit response to the film by viewers. Austin examines the diverse appeal and meaning of *Bram Stoker's Dracula* through an equally diverse range of source material. While his case study is strategic, concentrating on a purposely ambiguous film in generic terms, his conclusions about industrially motivated hybridity, and its relation to classification, typology and taste, stretch beyond the film and the period in question.

- To what degree is Austin's research method simply a case of putting three different ways of analysing film (i.e. production, marketing and reception) side by side?
- To what extent can general conclusions about audience response be drawn from Austin's questionnaire sample, and what might be done to expand the picture of film reception?
- Do you think genre hybridity is a contemporary phenomenon? How would you test this claim?

'GONE WITH THE WIND PLUS FANGS': GENRE, TASTE AND DISTINCTION IN THE ASSEMBLY, MARKETING AND RECEPTION OF BRAM STOKER'S DRACULA[1]

Thomas Austin

Bram Stoker's Dracula (1992) is a particularly overt example of contemporary Hollywood's 'commercial aesthetic' of aggregation.[2] The film is a combination of diverse textual components subsequently disaggregated and promoted through marketing, media exposure and merchandising. These procedures mobilised a series of sometimes conflicting promises about the film. It was variously advertised, reviewed and consumed as the latest creation of an auteur, a star-vehicle (for any of four stars), a reworking of a popular myth, an adaptation of a literary 'classic', as horror, art film or romance, or as a mixture of these genres. In other words, *Bram Stoker's Dracula* was organised as what I have termed a 'dispersible text'. This is a package designed to achieve commercial, cultural and social reach, by both facilitating and benefiting from promotional and conversational processes of fragmentation, elaboration and diffusion. The dispersible text is not unstructured or infinitely open to interpretation, but its multiple address to a coalition of audience fractions is readily amplified through advertising, publicity and merchandising.[3] The dissemination of images, characters, songs, stars and interpretations of the film extends its presence in the social arena of potential viewers.[4] With no single, unified identity in the marketplace, *Bram Stoker's Dracula* was designed and positioned to 'touch base with all the sectors of the audience'.[5] Its industrially motivated hybridity and ultimate commercial success foreground issues of genre and taste.[6] In this article I interrogate how discursive formulations and categorisations of audiences are produced, and how distinctions are made between them, in three imbricating fields of activity: industrial practices,

Thomas Austin (ed. Steve Neale), *Genre and Contemporary Hollywood* (London: BFI, 2002).

publicity and media commentary, and the behaviours of film viewers. In the process, I shall reconsider some assumptions of orthodox genre theory as it has developed in film studies.

The procedures of film assembly and marketing target audiences by anticipating patterns of consumption and 'piggybacking' on established tastes, including those for stars, story properties, music and visual styles. The production and advertisement of generically identifiable films constitutes one such attempt to manage demand, minimise risk and secure a stable market by promising 'guaranteed' pleasures.[7] Genre typologies also facilitate the segmentation and classification of film audiences according to perceived spending habits and the standardisation of product via a system of regulated difference.[8] For genres to function successfully, not only does the industry have to 'institutionalise . . . expectations, which it will be able to fulfil',[9] but audiences have to play – and pay – their part in such 'contractual' propositions as well. In this way, the genre system operates in the circuit of production, distribution and consumption by mediating between industry and audiences. However, as my research will demonstrate, there is no guaranteed fit between business intent and consumer response, despite the tacit assumptions to this effect which underpin many studies of film genres.[10]

I concentrate on taste conflicts fought out over the generic classification of *Bram Stoker's Dracula* and its corresponding assumed audiences, which were variously championed and disparaged by industry representatives, published observers and viewers. I track two conflicting tendencies in the marketing of the film: first, the commercial aim of disseminating it across multiple taste formations and, second, the hierarchisation of textual components, and the audiences for which they bid, according to their perceived economic significance. These procedures of dispersal and stratification were mediated and sometimes contested by the actions of commentators and individual viewers.

In 1984, Alan Williams asserted that: 'Genre studies' notion of the film audience will not stand up to examination: audiences are not uniform masses, reacting with uniformity and consistency.'[11] Despite two significant interventions, to which I shall soon turn, Williams's reproach remains apposite. Audiences' participation in the genre system is too often taken for granted, rather than subjected to sustained scrutiny. One of my aims is to address this blind spot by demonstrating how film viewers make use of ideas of genre, in part to construct their own discursive distinctions between audience groups. Rather than argue that genre is an invalid or redundant concept, I investigate its usages for a range of different agents engaged in the processes of formulating cultural and social categorisations. I consider the contingent and fluid nature of genres as collective understandings and the power relations that structure the demarcation and circulation of genre taxonomies. In taking this approach, I am building on James Naremore's concept of the 'genre function', which foregrounds the discursive productivity of genre naming.[12] Naremore shows how generic labels can be reworked according to critical and industrial

515

imperatives. Rick Altman has developed a line of inquiry in his seminal analysis of 'genrification' – that is, the ongoing discursive construction and reconstruction of film genres. Altman shows how genres are always in process and subject to the interventions of producers, critics (both popular and academic) and (potentially) audiences.[13] However, Naremore focuses exclusively on institutional factors in the naming and policing of genres, and Altman's work on audience engagements with genre remains largely speculative. By contrast, I investigate both how genre headings and hierarchies are mobilised through commercial procedures and how they are reproduced or rewritten not only by press commentators, but also by individual viewers. The restoration of the audience enables a fuller understanding of the role which genre plays in the production, distribution and consumption of popular film, not least by facilitating a comparison between industrial, critical and 'ground-level' perspectives on audiences for particular genres.

Differentiating Bram Stoker's Dracula from Previous Versions of the Vampire Myth

Bram Stoker's Dracula was the first release in a short-lived Hollywood production cycle of big-budget 'classic' costume horrors which included Mary Shelley's Frankenstein (1994) and Mary Reilly (1996). Bram Stoker's Dracula was made for Columbia Pictures, while the other two films – both commercial disappointments – were made for its sister studio, TriStar Pictures.[14] Warner Bros.' successful adaptation of Anne Rice's cult novel Interview with the Vampire (1994) can also be seen as part of the cycle.[15] All three later films followed the lead of Bram Stoker's Dracula in targeting 'mainstream' and infrequent cinemagoers, especially women, beyond a 'core' horror audience perceived as predominantly male. This strategy can itself be seen as an attempt to replicate the success of The Silence of the Lambs (1990), an Oscar-winning 'upmarket' horror/crime thriller hybrid featuring a 'strong' female protagonist.[16]

As 'quality' films, costume horrors were aimed at broader markets than the 'low horror' slashers and gore films which served the video sector in the late 1980s and early 1990s. The new cycle consisted of opportunistic combinations of pre-sold literary properties, familiar horror character-types, expensive production values and major stars associated with non-horror genres such as Robert De Niro in Mary Shelley's Frankenstein and Julia Roberts in Mary Reilly. Despite Warners' success with Interview with the Vampire, the relative failure of TriStar's two costume horrors, and of other updated horror properties such as Wolf (1994) and Vampire in Brooklyn (1995), presaged the end of the cycle.[17]

I have been tracing here moments in the continual redefinition of the horror genre – in this instance, via the decisions of film producers. Subsequent rewritings of horror from producers' perspectives have included the boom in teen horrors which followed the success of Scream (1996) and the popularisation of documentary stylings initiated by the Blair Witch Project (1999). The fluidity of genres does not make them simply interchangeable, however.

The genre system still functions to demarcate different film types, even if the boundaries between such categories are mobile and variously defined. Thus the concept of a genre hybrid as a recognisable combination of distinct genres still has theoretical and practical validity, as will become clear. The point is that a genre needs to be recognised as such by some agents in the process of genrification. By writing about a 'costume horror cycle', I am of course acting as just such an agent myself, constituting a filmic category by including certain titles and excluding others. It is such acts of generic definition, their conditions of production, their implications, their reproduction and their contestation, that I trace around *Bram Stoker's Dracula*.

Production, marketing and reception contexts for *Bram Stoker's Dracula* were complicated by the sedimentation of previous incarnations of the vampire and Dracula myths. More than 600 films and a hundred television programmes from around the world were listed in *The Illustrated Vampire Movie Guide*, itself published to coincide with the UK release of *Bram Stoker's Dracula*.[18] Accordingly, the film had to be differentiated from the extensive constellation of Dracula and vampire texts. Jon Anderson, director of advertising and publicity at the UK distribution arm of Columbia/TriStar Films, acknowledged this: '*Dracula* was in many respects a "Pre-Sold" title, so our job was making it a special event that people would want to see.'[19] In this way, *Bram Stoker's Dracula* provides a particularly clear case of Hollywood's simultaneous standardisation and variation of its products.

The title presented *Bram Stoker's Dracula* as a faithful adaptation of the novel and distinguished it from its predecessors. (Screenwriter and co-producer James Hart's script was originally subtitled 'The Untold Story'.) The film was also sold as unique via its allegedly unprecedented inclusion of the novel's gothic romance (a claim disputed by some commentators on the grounds of both fidelity and novelty). As Altman has argued, the production of popular film is a process of innovation and imitation shaped in part by producers assaying previous hits and recombining their components in new forms that they hope will be successful.[20] In interviews Hart declared just such an intention, to reproduce the broad appeal of the book and so capture a hitherto untapped audience of women:

> For *Dracula* to be done right on the screen, it needed a magnificent production on an epic scale, and a reading that reached to the heart of the character's seductiveness. Women more than men have tended to read *Dracula* and other vampire stories, and to understand the vampire's attraction.[21]

> To me, it's like *Gone with the Wind* with sex and violence.[22]

The claim to distinction made on behalf of the film here is rhetorical rather than reliable, however. Hart exaggerates the romance elements in the book and effectively rewrites a number of earlier screen versions. In fact, the film merely amplifies romantic and erotic elements already present in pictures such as *Dracula* (1958), *Count Dracula* (1973) and *Dracula* (1979). Nevertheless, the commercial opportunity presented by the female audience can be seen as a crucial reason why Hart's script – initially due to be filmed as a cable television movie – was picked up and developed by Coppola's company American Zoetrope and by Columbia. From the outset of the production, the strategy of widening the film's address was envisaged in terms of a generic and gendered mixture. Lester Borden, vice president of merchandising at Columbia's parent, Sony Pictures, commented: 'It's a very exciting story to tell, and it's also a male/female thing – a very romantic love story.'[23] Thus, to quote Robert E. Kapsis, 'which genres finally get made depends on how organisational gatekeepers at various stages of the film production process assess the potential product in relation to their perception of the audience's future tastes'.[24]

In the event, industry figures suggest that 50 per cent of the film's cinema audience in Britain was female.[25] The assumption that all these women were attracted to the film simply because of its high-profile romantic elements must be avoided, however. As will become clear, some of the female audience were habitual consumers of horror, who did indeed enjoy *Bram Stoker's Dracula*, but not because it was safely 'beyond' the horror category.

Hart's script rewrites the novel by introducing a prologue in which Romanian knight Vlad the Impaler (Gary Oldman) becomes a vampire following his wife's suicide. More than 400 years later, as Dracula, he finds that Mina (Winona Ryder), the fiancée of Jonathan Harker (Keanu Reeves), bears a strong resemblance to his wife, and he comes to London in the guise of Prince Vlad to find her. Employing Rick Altman's terminology, it is possible to trace in the film syntactic and semantic elements traditionally associated with both horror and romance.[26] Any such analysis effectively assumes more agreement on the recognition of 'romance' and 'horror' codings than is likely to exist among real, heterogeneous audiences, however. As Altman notes, 'disparate viewers may perceive quite disparate semantic and syntactic elements in the same film'.[27] It is nevertheless clear that the development of a romance between Dracula and Mina provided Columbia with a counterbalance to the story's well-known horror content that could be pushed aggressively in the advertising campaign. The poster tagline 'Love Never Dies' was intended to attract women viewers to a genre traditionally perceived as selling to male audiences.[28] The complex generic identity of the film was thus established not just by (nor is it simply readable from) its intratextual components. It was also constructed via extratextual advertising, publicity and merchandising. For example, the range of publicity stills put into circulation foregrounded codings of horror and romance, period costumes and settings, spectacular monster effects and a number of star images.

Casting decisions extended the appeal of *Bram Stoker's Dracula* across age, gender and taste boundaries. A roster of stars supplemented the uncertain commercial potential of the adaptation. The presence of pin-ups Winona Ryder (as Mina) and Keanu Reeves (as Harker) was intended to hook into a mixed-gender youth market labelled the 'MTV audience'.[29] In the role of the vampire hunter Van Helsing, Anthony Hopkins combined a background in British theatre and art-house cinema with a mass-market profile gained from *The Silence of the Lambs*. As Dracula, Gary Oldman was the source of some anxiety at Columbia, never having played the romantic lead in a major Hollywood production before. However, the familiar story and strong star line-up ensured that his name did not have to carry the film alone. The presence of Coppola as star-director added to the list of attractions: 'The legend appeals to the broad market; the Coppola name appeals to the sophisticates.'[30] Thus, rather than standing in opposition to commercialism in popular cinema, the discourse of auteurism is readily incorporated within industry logics.[31]

Released in the United States to tap into the 1992 Thanksgiving and Christmas market, *Bram Stoker's Dracula* opened in Europe the following January and February. In Britain, Columbia/TriStar made multiple promises about the film across a range of satellite texts. The narrow horror market remained in some ways taken for granted, while mainstream audiences were targeted more enthusiastically. Beyond the specialist horror press, cast and crew members took steps to distance *Bram Stoker's Dracula* from the genre. In the press pack circulated to journalists, Ryder categorised the film as 'very romantic and sensual and epic, a real love story . . . It's not really a vampire movie.'[32] Questioned on *The South Bank Show*, Hart commented: 'This is not Freddy Krueger Goes to Transylvania.'

The bid to win incremental markets risked upsetting horror enthusiasts, but for Columbia this was a risk worth taking to reach a wider audience. However, the campaign did take some steps to persuade horror fans that the thrills they wanted had not been entirely displaced. Production information, personnel interviews and publicity stills were made available to horror and fantasy publications, which gave the film extensive coverage even while often expressing doubts about its overall quality. The reassurance of horror fans was also attempted through the bloody lettering of the ubiquitous title. The main poster mixed generic codings, however, showing Oldman and Ryder in an embrace below a gargoyle and combining the film's rubric with the romantic tagline.

The diversity of market segments that *Bram Stoker's Dracula* was intended to capture was echoed in its spread of licensed merchandising. In the publishing sector, the UK rights to the title logo and artwork were sold to Pan Books, which used them for a range of products: a novelisation of the script, a 'moviebook' containing script, behind-the-scenes information and lavish illustrations, and a paperback edition of *Dracula*. Further merchandise in the United Kingdom included an 'official graphic novel',[33] a licensed board game, a video game and a music soundtrack. The last two items are examples of the much-touted synergy which consumer electronics giant Sony enjoyed after its $3.4 billion purchase of Columbia and TriStar Pictures in 1989.[34] While

Columbia Pictures made the film, Sony Imagesoft brought out the video game and Columbia Records released the soundtrack album.

Judging by both cultural profile and commercial performance, the assembly, marketing and merchandising of *Bram Stoker's Dracula* were largely successful in making the film an 'event' and encouraging a proliferation of possible avenues of access to it. Such strategies of dispersal also brought about some audience disappointments and clashes between disparate taste publics, however. These conflicts can be traced in both published accounts of the film and through audience research, and they were often played out via the discursive construction of generic taxonomies.

Distinctions in Press Commentary

Press commentary mediated *Bram Stoker's Dracula* by inserting it into a number of different interpretive frames and writing its generic identity in various ways. Reviews discriminated between the film's heterogeneous components and the diverse implied audiences addressed by these elements. While the details vary, the rhetorical strategy of differentiation and the selective ratification of taste fractions is a common one.

One vector of the film's multiple address was towards a 'cultured' audience. Borrowings from literature and painting, and the use of costumes designed by Japanese artist Eiko Ishioka endowed it with an aura of 'good taste'.[35] High art references to Klimt and Cocteau, in particular, were flagged in the press pack and 'moviebook'.[36] These gestures towards élite culture were largely ignored by the youth press and popular tabloids, but were picked up and elaborated upon in the so-called 'quality' press.[37] Coppola's status as an *auteur* – certified in 'middle-market' and 'up-market' publications – further elevated the cultural standing of the film.[38] On occasions, commentators asserted distinctions between 'knowing' audiences who could recognise the film's high-art citations and the 'base' tastes of less elevated viewers. In a *Sunday Telegraph* review freighted with a number of assumptions and judgements, Anne Billson wrote: '[The film] runs aground on the lovey-dovey scenes, which are not just inept but boring. By turning the bogeyman into a Mills & Boon heart-throb, screenwriter James V. Hart has drained the story of most of its plasma.'[39] The film's romance elements are rejected here through their association with a culturally denigrated 'female' genre, that of 'lowbrow' romantic fiction. Billson erected a second axis of distinction in rejecting another 'common' taste formation, that of an implicitly Americanised youth culture: 'Those of you with deliciously shivery memories of Christopher Lee or Bela Lugosi will not be disposed to look favourably upon *Bram Stoker's Dracula* . . . Coppola's film is a Dracula for the Nineties, aimed not at classicists but at a fang-de-siècle generation weaned on MTV.' The inclusion of Lee, a star of the often-derided Hammer horror cycle, under the heading of 'classic horror' testifies to the flexible borders of such critical categories across time. When Billson considered positive effects of the film's 'feminisation', she mobilised an 'up-market' image of the female spectator: 'This has all the makings of a classic Accessory Film: one ought never to underestimate the cumulative aesthetic effect of all those nice scratchy fountain pens, pebble-lensed spectacles and pearly earrings.' In this (admittedly playful) review, three target audiences are stratified and only one is legitimated – that made up of adult, middle-class, art-loving, female spectator-consumers. Whereas Columbia's strategy was to appeal to both teenagers and adults, to 'élite' and 'common' tastes,[40] Billson makes a clear distinction between the terms of each couplet. This is an instance of the 'refusal' of the preferences of the 'other' which, according to Bourdieu, places tastes in mutual opposition.[41] Those who share Billson's taste draw on cultural capital provided by education and class background, and are thus differentiated from the 'masses'.

In the specialist horror press, commentators often took on the role of gatekeepers of the genre, judging the film by its fidelity or otherwise to the norms of horror. Those deeming *Bram Stoker's Dracula* successful allowed it entry to the generic corpus as a worthwhile innovation sometimes labelled 'epic' horror.[42] Other writers rejected the film because it was too different, citing the incursion of romance. Oppositions between an informed horror audience and ordinary cinemagoers ignorant of the genre structured reviews in the British horror magazines *The Dark Side* and *Sambain*. In contrast to Hart's approving comparison, the reference to *Gone with the Wind* (1939) here stands as a measure of the film's failings:

> Instead of Murnau's 'symphony of Horror' we have Coppola's pop promo of Horror, or even, a rather unwieldily modified *Gone with the Wind* plus fangs.[43]

> It's a horror movie that never once exudes or creates fear, menace or terror. It's a love story without a remotely believable scenario . . . Mills and Boon Gothic at best.[44]

Like *The Sunday Telegraph*, these reviews characterised the film through its association with juvenile and 'lowbrow female' tastes. All three commentaries rejected perceived commercial priorities in proposing alternative taste hierarchies. To unpack further the differentiations made in the horror press, I shall draw on Sarah Thornton's theory of 'subcultural capital'.[45] This modification of Bourdieu's model of cultural capital is designed to take account of the accumulation of 'additional' cultural resources beyond those derived from education and family background. Displayed in record collections, fashionable haircuts – or knowledge about films – subcultural capital 'confers status on its owner in the eyes of the relevant beholder'.[46] Its differential distribution underpins taste distinctions such as 'cool' youth's disparagement of 'mainstream' culture. In opposing sanctioned versions of the Dracula myth with Columbia's offering, horror reviewers display subcultural capital (implicitly held by their readers, too) and establish dichotomies between an authentic horror culture and 'mainstream' Hollywood, which sells inferior

products to easily pleased audiences. The horror fan subculture in which publications such as *Samhain* and *The Dark Side* circulate is commercial, but often
represents itself as less so than the 'blind commercialism' of 'mass-market'
Hollywood. Horror fans are at the very least differentiated as more discerning
consumers than the cinemagoing crowd, whose preferences render them 'tasteless'. In all the reviews considered so far, 'average' and 'inauthentic' audiences
are characterised as 'inferior' not just through their tastes, however, but also via
marks of age, gender and/or class. In the process, *Bram Stoker's Dracula* is
implicitly infantilised, feminised and/or banalised in contrast to tastes ratified
by cultural or subcultural capital. The critical reception of the film thus
foregrounds the articulation of taste conflicts with social and cultural identities.
It succeeded commercially not by resolving these ongoing conflicts and
assembling a unified or homogeneous mass audience, but by selling to an
aggregation of different taste formations. This objective is not endangered by
taste disputes, as long as enough audience segments find that a part of the film
package speaks to them.

Audience Responses

How did viewers respond to the multiple address of the dispersible text? How
did they classify the film generically? In what terms was its perceived success or
failure expressed? What distinctions did individuals make between its different
audiences? In this section, I draw on questionnaires handed out to cinemagoers
attending my local multiplex shortly after the film's first screening on terrestrial
television.[47] The questionnaire included both open-ended and more specific
questions. Of 250 questionnaires given out, a total of forty-nine were returned.
The vast majority of this self-selected sample was white, with ages ranging from
sixteen to forty-eight. Twenty women and eleven men had seen the film in
some format.

I asked respondents to state their preferences for, and dislikes of, film types
and genres. Gender is the sociological factor that is usually assumed by
industry personnel and commentators to correlate most closely with genre
preferences, and on occasion it was employed here as a mark of difference in
taste. The correspondence between gender identity and genre preference was
not always as neat as stock assumptions would imply, however. While some
favoured films did conform to stereotyped 'female' and 'male' tastes, others
confounded these and sometimes cut across 'incompatible' genre categories.
For instance, one woman listed as her favourites 'Disney, true stories, murder,
action'. Some respondents did not adhere to received genre typologies at all,
but organised films under more idiosyncratic headings such as (for likes)
'clever', 'well directed' and 'intelligent cool films' or (dislikes) 'stereotyped' or
'most British films after 1970'. This kind of taxonomy appears to coexist with
an awareness of more familiar classifications, while effectively overwriting
them. I have been tempted to employ a 'public'/'private' dichotomy here, but
it is somewhat problematic. What I might have termed 'private' typologies are

less likely to be picked up by the media or otherwise endorsed in the public domain and so lack the institutional consolidation which marks and constitutes a film genre. But they, too, contribute to viewers' self-perceptions and can be 'converted' into a limited social currency through peer group interaction.[48] Moreover, all (institutionally sanctioned) genres are 'privatised' to the extent that individuals are able to recognise and deploy them. Indeed, genres rely on such shared recognitions to function successfully – even while viewers variously refashion, reconfigure and valorise or denigrate them in the process. It is clear that established film genres may also be entirely rewritten into idiosyncratic groupings such as those above. Some such groupings are even endorsed more publicly. Although 'clever', 'well directed' and 'intelligent cool films' are not as yet installed as fully fledged genres, similar categories are often proposed in critics' top tens or in scheduling decisions for televised film strands such as BBC 2's *Moviedrome*. By employing these terms, informants may be drawing upon such public discourses and presenting themselves as 'experts' with knowledge, taste and the ability to evaluate films across a range of genres. Viewers and commentators will of course disagree about the films to be included and excluded from any such corpus, but, as this article demonstrates, similar border skirmishes occur around more familiar, established genres.

Audiences approached *Bram Stoker's Dracula* anticipating pleasures that were shaped both by prior viewing experiences and awareness of diverse attractions flagged through advertising, publicity and ancillary products. There was no simple consensus about the film's generic status. Instead, it was ascribed various identities, including 'sensual, sad, romantic', a 'gothic-horror-love story', 'a thriller' and a 'normal Dracula movie with a bit more sex'. Horror fans[49] of both genders judged the film against favoured examples of the genre. Some rejected *Bram Stoker's Dracula* as a 'mainstream' mishandling of horror, so prioritising generic fidelity over mass appeal and implying alternatives to Columbia's operative taste hierarchy. The primary complaint was a failure to frighten. In characterising the film's ideal audiences as lacking in generic knowledge and subcultural capital, the following informants implicitly distinguished themselves from these less 'educated' taste publics, much as press commentators had done:

> Why I watched the film – the story is a classic, scary . . . [The film was] Crap. I simply was not scared enough.
> [Who do you think *Bram Stoker's Dracula* appeals to most?] Those uneducated in film.
> (*17: anon. female. Charity worker, age 22. Part two; Q.35.)

> [Who do you think *Bram Stoker's Dracula* appeals to most?]
> People who mistakenly believe that Hammer = hammy. Fans of style over content.
> (*3: anon. male. Media worker, age 26. *Sambain* sample. Q.35.)

Some respondents had strategically lowered their expectations in anticipation of concessions to 'other' tastes:

> Didn't want to see it because I was sure they'd butcher it. Saw ½ of it on TV recently.
> [Who do you think *Bram Stoker's Dracula* appeals to most?]
> 13-year-olds, girls who wear itty bitty backpacks, fools.
> (*19: anon. male. Student, age 23. Part two; Q.35.)

Not all horror fans were so disappointed, however:

> I thought the Gothic atmosphere was portrayed excellently. The make-up effects on Gary Oldman were good, and his portrayal of dracula was quite moving.
> The 'long lost love' angle . . . was more interesting than the usual blood and gore type of vampire film.
> (*10: anon. female. Biomedical scientist, age 33. Part two.)

This account evinces a dislike of 'gratuitous' gore, an enjoyment of involving characterisation and a sympathy for the dilemma of the vampire, all of which echo some of Brigid Cherry's findings about female horror fans.[50] Cherry's research points to women's pleasurable investments in the relationships between vampires and to a wider affinity for the monsters and 'outsiders' portrayed in the horror genre. While no simple and clear-cut gendered division emerged in my project, such pleasures were less likely to be mentioned by men in the sample.

Some informants' statements effectively corroborated Hart's claims about the sexual appeal of the film for female viewers. It is notable that these women also enjoyed being scared:

> I'm an avid fan of horror – books and films alike, so there was no way I was going to miss *Dracula* . . . I do remember getting the impression that the film was rather sexual in a subtle way. I think I got a bit aroused by it!
> (*11: Evonne. Female student, age 21. Part two.)

> I watched it because I quite like horror films and I thought it would be quite erotic and beautifully filmed. I was interested in the type of imagery used. I like being scared.
> (*9: Anon. female. Student, age 21. Part two; Q.35.)

Brigid Cherry's suggestion that vampire films may function as a 'form of erotica for some women',[51] providing the opportunity for sexual fantasy along with pleasurable tension and suspense, is borne out here. Among respondents, more women than men found the film erotic. In a rare admission of sexual pleasure, a male *Samhain* reader wrote:

> I appreciate the way Hart and Coppola attempted to give the novel more resonance by adding the 'eternal love' aspect . . . by trying to appeal to

two separate audiences: the horror fan, who wants to be scared, and those who find the vampire idea sexy as hell, there were two disparate avenues it could have explored. Unfortunately, Coppola tried both, and fell between them. As a viewer who wanted both aspects in my film, I was a bit happier than most . . . I loved it.
(*3: anon. male. Media worker, age 26. Part two.)

What is striking here is the coexistence of a conception of the film-makers' commercial imperatives (the appeal to two markets) alongside a high degree of personal investment in the film. Such a dual perspective on the valued artefact has been located in other studies of fans' engagements with mass-media products.[52] Elsewhere in the sample, viewers less happy with the film typically attributed its failure to 'Hollywood-isation' – a phrase used to imply crass commercialism, Americanisation and simplification of the original material. Whatever their final opinion, many horror fans evaluated *Bram Stoker's Dracula* according to their 'rules' of the genre and favourite instances of this film type. Such judgements were similar, but less public, than those made in specialist publications. In this way, generic regimes may be policed privately by audience members as well as publicly by reviewers.

Despite attempts to sell the film to audiences wary of horror, it was expressly defined as such by some people – particularly women – for whom the term was clearly pejorative. The following account draws upon a popular 'folk theory' of media influence to express concern about horror films:

Disliked it. Not my kind of film. I get nightmares very easily. I think horror films (cinema or TV) deaden one's sensibilities and make one less sensitive to, and hence less caring about, the real horror in the real world.
(*21: Anon. female. Tax consultant, age 35. Part two; Q.12.)

By contrast, enthusiastic viewers often perceived the film to be addressed to audiences shaped in their own self-images:

[Who do you think *Bram Stoker's Dracula* appeals to most?]
Young, imaginative people.
(*11: Evonne. Female student, age 21. Part two; Q.35.)

Audiences are able to read markers of genre in advertising and publicity as one set of a series of 'publicly distributed orientations'[53] offering patterned ways of preparing for and responding to a film. They may participate in the contractual transactions which film genres propose (to which they bring payment and knowledge, and from which they expect a pleasurable combination of the familiar and the novel). Or they may read generic markers not as incitements to consume, but as reasons to avoid a film. In all cases, potential viewers are mediating industrial procedures of production, advertising and publicity, mobilising assumptions about the nature of a film and its target audience by drawing on extratextual materials and their experience of films similarly classified. Exactly how (non)viewers perceive a genre – its value, boundaries, pleasures and audience – will vary according to their different competencies, repertoires and orientations. As Gemma Moss puts it, the exact places users construct for a genre are shaped by their socially specific 'histories of engagement'.[54] In the process, they are also asserting something about themselves. In watching a film or declining invitations to do so, individuals use markers of cultural preference to negotiate their own sense of self. Identity is constructed and (re)asserted both through positive self-images (as 'imaginative', knowledgeable or tasteful, for instance) and by distinguishing oneself from those with 'invalid' tastes – for example, 'girls', 'boys', 'fools' or horror consumers with deadened sensibilities.

Conclusion

Accounts of genre in film studies need to examine in more detail audiences' differentially distributed knowledges of, and participations in, the generic regimes of Hollywood and other popular cinemas. As a first step, I hope to have demonstrated how this turn to the audience can produce new understandings of the interplay between industrial and critical logics and audience activities of discrimination and self-definition. Viewers may enjoy belonging to taste publics (commonly invoked in reviews and advertising campaigns) based on shared patterns of consumption, such as a preference for horror films or for appearances by Keanu Reeves or Winona Ryder. These communities are more often imagined or implied, rather than convened in a literally shared space.[55] But they can nevertheless offer consumers a powerful sense of identity. So can the symbolic rejection of such taste formations. Both positions were evinced in the affiliations and distinctions found in informants' accounts. In deploying generic markers, audiences are not simply accepting commercially and critically recognised categories in a passive fashion, but are taking them up and making them work for their own purposes. In the process, they shape the meaning, value and frontiers of established genres according to their diverse tastes and motives. Respondents' decisions about whether or not to classify *Bram Stoker's Dracula* as 'horror' suggest some variance over the definitions and contents of traditional genre categories. It seems that individuals can maintain ensembles of preferences which are not necessarily coterminous with industrial and critical typologies, while simultaneously knowing that they are addressed as members of institutionally constituted and demarcated constituencies through production, marketing and reviewing strategies. Such personal 'taste maps' may incorporate institutionalised categories such as horror, as well as groupings such as 'intelligent cool films' which cut across more established generic headings. It is not time to jettison the familiar taxonomies proposed by film genres. But it is necessary to recognise that they are subject to constant rewriting – by audiences in addition to producers and reviewers – and that they exist alongside, and their members are always being (re)arranged into, discursive categories which are yet to attain institutional consolidation.

NOTES

1. An earlier version of this argument appeared in *Framework, The Journal of Cinema and Media*, vol. 41 (1999). An extended version is included in Thomas Austin, *Hollywood, Hype and Audiences* (Manchester: Manchester University Press, 2002). Thanks to those involved in both publications for permission to reproduce this piece here. Thanks also to Mark Jancovich, Matthew Hills and Charlotte Adcock for their helpful comments.
2. The term is Richard Maltby's. See Richard Maltby and Ian Craven, *Hollywood Cinema: An Introduction* (Oxford: Blackwell, 1995), pp. 30–5. The extent of textual aggregation does, of course, vary from film to film.
3. My concept of the dispersible text builds on the work of Barbara Klinger in her 'Digressions at the cinema: reception and mass culture', *Cinema Journal*, vol. 28, no. 4 (1989), pp. 3–19.
4. Assembling films as composite goods targeted at diverse audiences is not new. However, this mechanics of aggregation has intensified since the 1970s, driven by developments in Hollywood's economic organisation and operational procedures.
5. Duncan Clark, Columbia/TriStar's senior vice president of international marketing, quoted in Ana Maria Bahiana, 'Tooth and nail', *Screen International*, 13 November 1992, p. 12.
6. *Bram Stoker's Dracula* grossed $82 million in the United States and Canada, and $110 million in overseas markets.
7. See Steve Neale, *Genre and Hollywood* (London: Routledge, 2000), pp. 231–42.
8. See Steve Neale, *Genre* (London: BFI, 1980), pp. 22–3; Richard Maltby, ' "Sticks, hicks and flaps"; Classical Hollywood's generic conception of its audiences', in Melvyn Stokes and Richard Maltby (eds), *Identifying Hollywood's Audiences: Cultural Identity and the Movies* (London: BFI, 1999), pp. 23–41.
9. Neale, *Genre*, p. 54.
10. See also Rick Altman, *Film/Genre* (London: BFI, 1999), p. 16.
11. Alan Williams, 'Is a radical genre criticism possible?', *Quarterly Review of Film Studies*, vol. 9, no. 2 (1984), p. 124.
12. James Naremore, 'American film noir: the history of an idea', *Film Quarterly*, vol. 49, no. 2 (1995/6), pp. 12–28.
13. Altman, *Film/Genre*, especially pp. 30–82.
14. *Mary Shelley's Frankenstein* grossed $22 million in the US. *Mary Reilly* grossed a mere $6 million in the US.
15. The film grossed $105 million in the US.
16. See Mark Jancovich, 'Genre and the audience: genre classifications and cultural distinctions in the mediation of *The Silence of the Lambs*', in Melvyn Stokes and Richard Maltby (eds), *Hollywood Spectatorship: Changing Perceptions of Cinema Audiences* (London: BFI, 2001), pp. 33–45. The film grossed $130 million in the US.
17. *Wolf* grossed $65 million in the US, on a budget of $70 million. *Vampire in Brooklyn* grossed $20 million in the US.
18. Stephen Jones, *The Illustrated Vampire Movie Guide* (London: Titan Books, 1993).
19. Jon Anderson, letter to the author, 19 July 1993.
20. Altman, *Film/Genre*, pp. 41–7. Of course, this process cannot guarantee success.
21. James V. Hart, 'The script that wouldn't die', in Francis Ford Coppola and James V. Hart, *Bram Stoker's Dracula: The Film and the Legend* (New York and London: Newmarket Press/Pan Books, 1992), pp. 6–7.
22. Suzi Feay, 'Staking reputations', *Time Out*, 28 October 1992, pp. 18–19.
23. Bahiana, 'Tooth and nail', p. 12.
24. Robert E. Kapsis, *Hitchcock: The Making of a Reputation* (Chicago: University of Chicago Press, 1992), p. 6.
25. Cinema Advertising Association.

26. The 'semantics' of a genre are its 'building blocks': familiar settings, props, costumes and character-types. 'Syntax' refers to the meaning-bearing structures in which semantic elements are arranged. See Rick Altman, 'A semantic/syntactic approach to film genre', *Cinema Journal*, vol. 23, no. 3 (1984), reprinted in Altman, *Film/Genre*.

27. Altman, *Film/Genre*, p. 207.

28. Anderson, letter to the author.

29. Bahiana, 'Tooth and nail', p. 12.

30. Anderson, letter to the author.

31. See Timothy Corrigan, 'Auteurs and the new Hollywood', in Jon Lewis (ed.), *The New American Cinema* (Durham, NC: Duke University Press, 1998), pp. 38–63.

32. Columbia Pictures, *Bram Stoker's Dracula: Production Notes*, 1992, p. 5.

33. Roy Thomas, Mike Mignola and John Nyberg, *Bram Stoker's Dracula* (London: Pan, 1993).

34. Sony acquired CBS Records for $2 billion in 1987.

35. The film won an Oscar for best costume design.

36. See Coppola and Hart, *Bram Stoker's Dracula*, pp. 39, 70.

37. Anthony Quinn, 'Absolutely ravishing', *Independent on Sunday*, 31 January 1993, p. 19.

38. Ibid.; Jonathan Romney, 'At the court of Coppola', *The Guardian*, 21 January 1993, G2, pp. 2–3.

39. Anne Billson, 'Vlad the Mills & Boon hero', *The Sunday Telegraph*, 31 January 1993, Arts section, p. xv.

40. Cinema Advertising Association figures suggest that 54 per cent of the film's British cinema audience were from classes ABC1 and 46 per cent were from classes C2DE. 44 per cent of the audience were under twenty-four, and 22 per cent were over thirty-five.

41. Pierre Bourdieu, *Distinction: A Social Critique of the Judgement of Taste*, trans. Richard Nice (London: Routledge, 1984), especially pp. 31–4.

42. Frederick S. Clarke, editorial comment, *Cinefantastique*, vol. 23, no. 4 (December 1992), p. 3.

43. Ian Calcutt, '*Bram Stoker's Dracula*', *Samhain*, 37, March–April, 1993, p. 38.

44. Stefan Jaworzyn, '*Bram Stoker's Dracula*', *The Dark Side*, 29, February 1993, p. 9

45. Sarah Thornton, *Club Cultures: Music, Media and Subcultural Capital* (Cambridge: Polity Press, 1995).

46. Ibid., p. 11.

47. ITV, Saturday, 24 October 1996, 10 p.m. *Samhain* magazine had already published a request for readers to write to me. The reaction was disappointing: three letters and one subsequent questionnaire.

48. On 'conversion', see Roger Silverstone, *Television and Everyday Life* (London: Routledge, 1994), pp. 130–1.

49. By this term, I mean respondents who identified themselves as such or listed horror among their favourite genres.

50. Brigid Cherry suggests that women fans may not reject gore or violence per se, but that they are more often concerned with the way these elements are used in horror. Cherry, 'Refusing to refuse to look: female viewers of the horror film', in Stokes and Maltby (eds), *Identifying Hollywood's Audiences*, p. 196.

51. Ibid., p. 196.

52. See for example, Daniel Cavicchi, *Tramps Like Us: Music and Meaning among Springsteen Fans* (New York: Oxford University Press, 1998), pp. 83–5. Thanks to Matt Hills for pointing me towards this book.

53. The phrase is from Martin Barker and Kate Brooks, *Knowing Audiences: Judge Dredd, Its Friends, Fans and Foes* (Luton: University of Luton Press, 1998) p. 142.

54. Gemma Moss, 'Girls tell the teen romance: four reading histories', in David Buckingham (ed.), *Reading Audiences: Young People and the Media* (Manchester: Manchester University Press, 1993), pp. 119, 133.

55. See Altman, *Film/Genre*, pp. 156–65.

23

FROM CINEMAS TO THEME PARKS: CONGLOMERATION, SYNERGY AND MULTIMEDIA

During the 1980s, nearly all the Hollywood majors became subsidiary divisions within giant corporations seeking to diversify their investments. While some film studios remained untouched by this emerging corporate pattern, a new burst of takeovers and buyouts in the mid- to late 1980s saw the remaining studios acquired, often by non-US buyers. In 1985, the News Corporation, owned by Australian publisher Rupert Murdoch, purchased Twentieth-Century Fox; in 1989, the Japanese electronics company Sony bought Columbia Pictures from Coca-Cola; and in 1990, Universal was acquired by Japan's Matsushita Electronic Industrial Company. Only Disney remained autonomous in corporate terms. Amidst this business activity was an emerging picture of consolidation in media industries. Gradually getting rid of non-film and media interests, conglomerates began to streamline their operations and consolidate their power around the core business of entertainment and communications.

One of the most significant examples of media conglomeration came in 1989 when the publishing company Time Inc. merged with Warner Communications Inc. in a $14 billion deal. Followed by subsequent mergers with Turner Broadcasting in 1996 and America Online in 2000, the market worth of the conglomerate had reached $96 billion by the start of 2000. It had combined stakes in publishing, cable, music, film, video, television, the Internet, professional sports teams, retail outlets, studios, cinemas and theme parks. Linking old media and new media, Time Warner was committed to the creative synergy of its multi-media investments and to ever-deepening global market expansion. It became the largest of several colossal vertically integrated media conglomerates to emerge in the 1990s, also including the News Corporation, Disney, Bertelsmann and Viacom.

As a concept, synergy is best described as a principle of cross-promotion whereby companies seek to integrate and disseminate their products through a variety of media and consumer channels, enabling 'brands' to travel through an integrated corporate structure. While much discussed, synergy has practical difficulties that are often ignored in criticism of global media power. The decentralised nature of Time Warner, for example, has often set different corporate divisions against each other rather than bringing them together. Nevertheless, synergy became a powerful concept for media operations in the 1990s, Disney becoming its arch corporate practitioner. As a media company, Disney both was centralised in structure and had an established range of powerful entertainment brands that it could market through film, video, cable television, merchandise, studio stories and theme parks. From Mickey Mouse to Simba the Lion, Disney transformed brands old and new into rich streams of revenue.

Disney had been cross-promoting its products for decades. However, the management team of Frank Wells, Michael Eisner and Jeffrey Katzenberg accelerated the principle of synergy in the 1980s and 1990s, dramatically increasing production of filmed entertainment and pursuing an aggressive policy of brand licensing. In this context, animated features such as *Beauty and the Beast* (1991) and *The Lion King* (1994) were successful not only as theatrical films, but also in their transformation into merchandise, home videos, television series and Broadway productions. Even modest box office performers such as *Hercules* (1997) would vastly exceed their production costs through an array of promotional tie-ins. Produced for $70 million, *Hercules* made $245 million in worldwide box office revenue before the ancillary profits were even calculated. While hardly competing with the reported profit of $1 billion generated by *The Lion King,* Disney's animated features remained hugely profitable.

If animation sold especially well to the family audience, Disney's success was replicated in digitally animated films such as *Toy Story* (1995) and *Monsters Inc.* (2001). Using computer generated technology, animated characters in these films were gradually built through software tools and data scanned from sculpted models, creating three-dimensional animated graphics. In particular, the technology company Pixar developed CGI techniques in progressively ambitious films. Having tackled human movement in *Toy Story*, Pixar's next film *Monsters Inc.* focused on the more difficult process of representing fur. Meanwhile, *Finding Nemo* (2003) based the spectacle of digital animation upon the highly complex representation of water. Released under the Disney banner, the success of Pixar's animated features demonstrated the creative force, and potential influence, of digital companies that worked outside the studio system.

In a competitive market environment, the inventive use of CGI offered a platform not only for companies like Pixar but to new studios like Dreamworks SKG. This was the first movie studio to be set up in more than seventy years, established in 1994 by Steven Spielberg, Jeffrey Katzenburg (who left Disney acrimoniously) and David Geffen. Making a varied roster of hits, animation enabled the studio to distinguish itself through innovative production spectacles like *Shrek* (2001). A 40 per cent interest having been purchased in the computer animation company Pacific Data Images, *Shrek* was made by 275 animators, all using digital technologies to create a richly textured fairytale world. The story of a swamp monster's determination to reclaim his swamp and his love from the evil Lord Farquaad, *Shrek* was voiced by stars such as Mike Myers and Eddie Murphy and found a balance of humour that not only lent itself especially well to the lucrative market in children's entertainment, but also held pleasures for parents as well.

The family audience became central to Hollywood in its production of blockbusters in the 1990s. Broadening appeal beyond a core audience of teenagers and young adults, the family-adventure movie defined many of the industry's megapictures, including live action films such as *Jurassic Park* (1993), *Titanic* (1997) and *Star Wars: Episode One – The Phantom Menace* (1999), all of which grossed over $300 million in box office revenue. Sold globally, and marshalling all of the synergistic and promotional energies of the major studios, megapictures were at the heart of Hollywood's production activities in the 1990s. Costing upwards of $100 million, such high-risk financial ventures could be sustained only by conglomerates, able to maintain profitability by offsetting box office failures against other corporate divisions or, more often, recouping a film's costs through ancillary markets.

The extension of profits in ancillary markets was especially linked to the franchise film, encapsulated by Steven Spielberg's *Jurassic Park* and its sequels. A franchise describes an entertainment property owned by a studio or corporate parent where copyright is controlled. It can therefore be sold or licensed as a brand. *Jurassic Park* not only became a global brand for Universal – its dinosaur logo appearing on merchandise and video games and at theme parks all over the world – the film would reflect on this status in quite explicit ways. This included panoramic shots of the Jurassic Park gift shop, and discussions about the value of family entertainment. In a series of ways, *Jurassic Park* helped construct, foreground and even comment upon its own brand potential, foreshadowing the extension of the T-Rex logos that would unify licensed products in a diverse range of cultures and markets across the globe.

The inclusion of a gift shop in *Jurassic Park* was not incidental. Indeed, the creation of studio stores and theme parks became instrumental to the synergistic designs of media conglomerates. These helped transform entertainment properties into physical tourist attractions. Warner Bros., Universal and Disney all established movie theme parks in the 1990s, operating in the United States, Western Europe, Australia and Japan. These mixed entertainment and consumption in very explicit ways, delivering visitors from rides into associated gift shops, eating places and hotel accommodation. Theme parks were in many ways the prime expression of entertainment synergy.

While theme park rides were often based on studio movies, they could also provide the basis for films themselves, Disney's *Pirates of the Caribbean* (2003) beginning life as a theme park attraction. This was suggestive of the cross-pollination of cultural and media forms more generally. In harnessing the enormous popularity of video games, for instance, an increasing number of films were based on characters inspired by the lucrative gaming market. While *Lara Croft: Tomb Raider* (2001) capitalised directly on the success of the buxom video game heroine, the German crime drama *Run Lola Run* (1998) assumed a video game aesthetic in its frenetic replaying of Lola's attempt to find the money that would save her boyfriend from drug runners.

The pursuit of synergy created new kinds of entertainment spectacle, but also gave rise to crossover stars that could bridge the divide between different media. Will Smith was an example in kind. Achieving success in the music industry in the late 1980s as The Fresh Prince, half of a rap/hip-hop act, Smith became a television star in the series *The Fresh Prince of Bel Air* (1990–6). His crossover potential was quickly identified and exploited by the film industry, however. While Smith's unthreatening persona was seen to attract audiences across racial boundaries, he also represented commercial possibilities for film–music synergy. While early films such as *Bad Boys* (1995) and *Independence Day* (1996) relied on Smith's persona of charm, wit and exuberant cool, *Men in Black* (1997) and *Wild Wild West* (1999) tied this to the revival of his music career. Performing title hits from each film, Smith demonstrated the degree to which synergy could be orchestrated around the enduring brand significance of star power.

With a different sense of crossover appeal, Jackie Chan's Hollywood breakthrough in the mid-1990s represented the increasing significance of export markets to the major studios. One of the biggest Asian film stars, Chan's success in films such as *Rumble in the Bronx* (1995) and *Rush Hour* (1998) was tied to the increasingly circular flow of stars, visual styles and modes of storytelling between global Hollywood and its Asian counterparts. The influence of the East Asian martial arts film, in particular, was pronounced in the late 1990s. Directors such as John Woo and Tsui Hark, actors such as Chow Yun-fat and Jet Li, and martial arts choreographers such as Yuen Wo-ping and Corey Yuen, all made their mark in films such as *Face/Off* (1997), *Lethal Weapon 4* (1998), and *The Matrix* (1999). While most also continued to work in the Hong Kong film industry, a more explicit degree of transnational borrowing took place between US and Asian film industries in the late 1990s, a result of the growing importance of global markets and the need for a wider sense of crossover market appeal.

While calculated franchise events characterised the pursuit of cultural synergy in the 1990s, not all franchises were mega-budget investments. They continued to offer strategic opportunities for 'independents' like Miramax and New Line. The *Scream* (1996–9) franchise, for example, became a lucrative property for Dimension, the exploitation division of Miramax. Reviving the career of Wes Craven, the *Scream* franchise reinvented the slasher genre in ways that self-consciously explored its own techniques of fear and suspense. Drawing attention to the 'rules' of the slasher film while maintaining its ability to scare, *Scream* focused on a media-literate youth audience. The same was also true of New Line's *Austin Powers* franchise (1997–2002), starring the Canadian actor Mike Myers as the eponymous 'international man of mystery'. Similar to Myers' previous comic outing in *Wayne's World* (1992–3), these films were highly self-conscious about their generic identity. While youth-oriented franchises such as *American Pie* (1999–2003) represented a fairly straight revival of teen 'gross out' comedy, many others assumed an ironic and 'knowing' relation to their status as media texts.

This reflexive tendency cut across genres. In thematic terms, it was especially apparent in films that assumed a 'retro' quality in their concern with the cultural and cinematic past. From Paul Thomas Anderson's portrait of the 1970s porn industry, *Boogie Nights* (1997), and Gary Ross's meditation on 1950s America, *Pleasantville* (1998), to remakes such as *Starsky and Hutch* (2004), retro films used stylistic codes of media, music and fashion to create period 'feel'. In their stylistic fusion of past and present, they typified what Jim Collins terms the 'eclectic irony' of 1990s filmmaking. This was also matched by what he labels a counter tendency towards 'new sincerity'. Indeed, the retro film differed from a concurrent move to the past in costume pictures and period dramas. Suited to the mid-range budgets of the independents, costume pictures became the hallmark of Merchant Ivory productions, specialising in literary adaptations such as *Howards End* (1992) and *The Remains of the Day* (1993). They also distinguished Miramax films such as the *The English Patient* (1996) and expensive co-productions such as Nikita Mikhalkov's *The Barber of Siberia* (1998), a Russian film about the Tsarist past made with stars of American, Russian and British cinema.

The past became a rich source of subject material and stylistic recycling within nineties filmmaking. This signalled the importance of historical and cultural memory in both independent and mainstream cinema. Within different cinemas, this was drawn around particular kinds of period or event. German cinema, for example, returned variously to the fall of the Berlin Wall. While Margarethe Von Trotta's *The Promise* (1995) reckoned with questions of national division and personal identity after unification, Wolfgang Becker's *Goodbye Lenin* (2003) staged the comic reconstruction of East German life by the children of a dedicated socialist mother, recently awakened from a coma. Meanwhile, the Second World War became a mark or staging point for a number of popular Italian films about reminiscence (*Cinema Paradiso*, 1989), romance (*Il Postino*, 1994) and tragedy (*Life is Beautiful*, 1997).

Within mainstream Hollywood, the turn to the past was signalled most distinctly by Steven Spielberg's preoccupation with historical memory in *Schindler's List* (1993), *Amistad* (1997) and *Saving Private Ryan* (1998). While the first of these grew out of Spielberg's own identification as an American Jew, and concerned the appalling history of the Nazi Holocaust, *Amistad* addressed the forced passage of slaves from Africa to the United States. Based on a slave revolt that led to legal struggles over the definition of freedom and rights, *Amistad* took on America's own history of racial persecution. As with *Saving Private Ryan*, historical memory was cast in relation to European and transatlantic sites of trauma.

Spielberg witnessed a change in his relationship with the blockbuster in the 1990s, developing a self-styled 'seriousness' in his treatment of the historical past. This demonstrates that studio films were never simply about blockbusting spectacle, even in the canon of its arch practitioner. Spielberg's movement between mega-budget blockbusters and more sober 'artistic' work reflected other hybrid tendencies in the shape and making of the studio picture. In particular, directors experiencing success outside of the studio domain were increasingly recruited by Hollywood. While this included the likes of British theatre director Sam Mendes, whose début *American Beauty* (1999) won a clutch of Oscars for its portrayal of midlife crisis in suburban America, it more often saw the recruitment of 'indie' directors. Steven Soderbergh's triumph with *sex, lies, and videotape* (1989), for example, led to a directorial career that would veer between aspiring art films such as the *The Limey* (1999), *Traffic* (2000) and *Solaris* (2002), and slick studio pictures such as *Out of Sight* (1998), *Erin Brockovich* (2000) and *Ocean's Eleven* (2001). Working at the nexus of mainstream, independent and popular art cinema, Soderbergh's rich body of work helped develop the screen career of George Clooney. Not only did Clooney star in numerous Soderbergh films, the two men established a production company called Section Eight that, according to Clooney, sought to 'push an indie sensibility within the Hollywood mainstream'.

While it is difficult to define this sensibility, Hollywood film in the late 1990s was keen to exploit the hip credentials of filmmakers drawn from the independent sector. This was related to the profit-making potential of indie film that had been demonstrated so powerfully by the success of *Pulp Fiction*. While David Fincher would follow his independent thriller *Se7en* (1995) with the millennial *Zeitgeist* movie *Fight Club* (1999), made for Twentieth-Century Fox, Larry and Andy Wachowski moved from the lesbian *noir* film *Bound* (1996) to the blockbusting heights of the Warner Bros. trilogy *The Matrix* (1999–2003). Meanwhile, David O. Russell mixed generic and cinematic styles in another Warner Bros. film, *Three Kings* (1999).

The last of these is interesting for the way it secretes its 'indie sensibility'. Playing with its status as a caper movie, *Three Kings* changed pace from an action-adventure set in Iraq after the first Gulf War to a melodrama about the suffering of dissident Iraqi families and their escape as refugees. Stylistically, the film used brisk pace, inventive stylistic shifts and the star power of George Clooney to transform a caper movie into an indictment of American policy in Iraq under George Bush Sr. Even within the blockbuster economics of Hollywood, controversial studio films could be made if they marshalled the right combination of star elements and stylistic experimentation and disguised their politics.

Along with Clooney, *Three Kings* starred Spike Jonze. Having developed a reputation as a music video director, Jonze joined with scriptwriter Charlie Kaufman to make the innovative comedies *Being John Malkovich* (1999) and *Adaptation* (2002). Both turned self-reflexively on the place and nature of film itself, the former based on a dark tunnel that leads inside the head of Hollywood actor John Malkovich, and the latter focusing on the travails of a scriptwriter called Charlie Kaufman (played by Nicholas Cage). Like Michel Gondry's *Eternal Sunshine of the Spotless Mind* (2004), these represented a highly self-referential strain of independent filmmaking in the early 2000s, playing experimentally with narrative space, time and characterisation. The outright fragmentation of narrative, linked to themes of memory and amnesia, also defined Christopher Nolan's *Memento* (2000). Focusing on a character unable to remember or make links between present and past, the film played with non-linear narrative to create an acute feeling of temporal disorientation. As with Soderbergh, Fincher, Danny Boyle and others, Nolan would later translate his 'indie' pedigree to studio pictures such as *Insomnia* (2002) and *Batman Begins* (2005).

The movement of hip indie filmmaking into the mainstream would give studio pictures a new credibility, but its stars and style would also influence traditional action blockbusters. The new action films of Jerry Bruckheimer, for example, were notable for the way they eschewed traditional action stars. While *The Rock* (1996) remade the quirky persona of Nicolas Cage into an action hero, *Con Air* (1997) matched Cage once again with indie stalwarts such as John Malkovich, Steve Buscemi and John Cusack. In effect, Bruckheimer moved towards action films that were at the same time knowingly trashy yet inveterately cool.

If there was fluidity in the boundaries between mainstream and independent film, there was also flexibility in the places and spaces where the encounter with film took place in the 1990s. The centrality of domestic film consumption, aided by video, digital and cable technologies, meant that movie theatres, in particular, had to renew the appeal of 'big screen' viewing. While alternative exhibition venues such as IMAX theatres promised massive projection systems that could play specially tailored films, the multiplex gave way in many cities to what trade journals called the 'megaplex'. Situated in urban centres, rather than suburbs, these brought together a host of leisure attractions in a single entertainment complex, cinema luring audiences through the promise of stadium seating, advanced projection systems, digital sound and expansive concession stand facilities.

In visual and aural terms, the moviegoing experience was characterised in the 1990s by the impact of digital technology. In 1992, the introduction of Dolby Digital and the rival sound formats of DTS and SDDS standardised digital sound in the production and exhibition of studio blockbusters. Creating sound of spectacular clarity, movies such as *The Phantom Menace* made full use of surround technologies in their creation of effects. These combined with visual technologies used to create new kinds of spectacle, underpinning a cycle of disaster films in the late 1990s – including *Independence Day*, *Titanic*, *Deep Impact* (1998) and *Armageddon* (1998) – that all used digital technology to visualise dramatically the destruction of ships, buildings, cities and entire nations. While in generic terms these films pulled in different directions (towards melodrama, science fiction and the buddy film), they were all based on the spectacle of digitally enhanced destruction.

To pioneers of digital technology such as George Lucas, whose effects company Industrial Light & Magic remained at the cutting edge of digital developments, computer generated imagery opened up new creative possibilities. Notably, *The Phantom Menace* used CGI technology to create vast battle scenes and an unprecedented array of creatures and characters. In aesthetic terms, digital technology represented challenges to traditional ideas of cinematic realism, at least as it was associated with photographic, celluloid-based filmmaking. The rise of digital morphing techniques and other forms of electronic manipulation created new benchmarks for special effects and possibilities for movie representation. At the same time, however, digital technology created particular kinds of anxiety. In the political satire *Wag the Dog* (1997), for instance, digital technology is used to create realistic news images of a fake war, serviceable to an American president needing to divert media attention from a brewing scandal involving a young girl. In its exploration of media power, the film raised indicative questions about the cultural and political effects of digital 'hyperreality'. The capacity to invent convincing new realities opened new creative avenues, but also, for some, threatened to collapse the status of 'the real' in cinematic representation.

Anxieties about digital cinema should not be overemphasised. Notwithstanding the historical contingency of what audiences find 'convincing', digital technology was taken up as swiftly within cinema professing a new relation to the real as it was in cinema generally understood to portend its collapse. Notably, the avant-garde manifesto sketched by Danish filmmakers Lars von Trier and Thomas Vinterberg, known as Dogme 95, was a call for purity in filmmaking, setting out 'an indisputable set of rules' for a new kind of avant-garde film. These rules were based on a concept of authenticity: films should be shot on location and in colour; they should use hand-held cameras and direct sound; and they should use no forced conventions, whether those of genre, action or effects.

In the creation of a spontaneous or 'chaste' mode of filmmaking, digital video became the preferred mode because of its highly compact and unobtrusive nature. Vinterberg's *The Celebration* (1998), winner of the Jury Prize in Cannes in 1998, was in this context defined by loose camerawork and collaboration between director and performers in the construction of scenes, establishing a raw and emotional narrative based on the damaged history between a father and his children. Dogme 95 launched an international film movement in the late 1990s that used digital technology to create a supposed *absence* of effects. Experimentation with digital video technology similarly distinguished the later work of Abbas Kiarostami. Notably, his in-car drama *Ten* (2002) was based on ten car journeys that a young woman takes through modern Tehran, each vignette filmed by a digital video camera mounted on the dashboard. For both Vinterberg and Kiarostami, technology was used to help jettison cinematic conventions of narrative and performance, creating the feeling of life captured unawares.

Not restrained to avant-garde filmmaking, the phenomenal success of *The Blair Witch Project* (1999) by Eduardo Sanchez and Daniel Myrick illustrated the 'guerrilla' potential of digital and web-based technology. An independent film made on a shoestring budget, the film was reliant on unsteady hand-held cameras. Made as a faux documentary, it focused upon three teenagers searching for the truth behind a witch in woods outside Burkittsville, Maryland. More remarkable than the film itself was the shrewd Internet and word-of-mouth marketing campaign that embellished the Blair Witch legend, helping to create its own cult momentum. This do-it-yourself marketing was based on the 'authenticity' of the horror; it suggested that the documentary had simply been found, and that the fate of the people (rather than the actors) had been chillingly caught on digital video camera.

Digital technology was not simply a question of aesthetic effects. It also had implications for the circulation and distribution of film. In one sense, the use of web-based and digital technologies helped create new possibilities for independent filmmaking, sidestepping the formidable industrial and representational power of the studio majors. In a different sense, the advent of digital technologies such as DVD proved an enormous windfall to the film majors. Gaining penetration in the late 1990s and early 2000s, DVD began to replace videotape as a mass-market product. Storing information digitally on a disc, DVDs were a new opportunity for studios to release classic and contemporary products; films could be refreshed and made distinct as products by incorporating a host of 'extras' such as film trailers, documentaries and cast commentaries.

DVDs accompanied new developments in home entertainment such as widescreen televisions, high-definition (plasma) screens, and surround sound technology. As the move from big to small screen became ever more sophisticated and technically 'wired', so the entertainment industry began to look towards a future of media convergence. This describes the attempt to blur media realms so that cable television, wide-band telephone lines and computer networks converge in their function of delivering entertainment to potential consumers. In this scenario, film would be digitally piped along cable lines and across satellites to awaiting computer screens and interactive televisions. While in its developmental stage, the possible convergence of DVD, Internet and other computer-based media led to initiatives to compress and decompress information in processes that would enable filmed entertainment to be 'streamed' over the web.

While difficulties in video streaming such as network congestion and poor resolution limited early experiments with this process, the prospect of entirely digitised movies remained attractive to the majors. Indeed, it promised a way of bypassing theatres and rental stores altogether, selling film 'on demand' to those willing to pay for its delivery through cable and Internet lines. However, the fear of media piracy remained a potent and realistic threat, potentially undermining the majors' hold on distribution. Inspired by music file-swapping sites such as Napster, users could prove adept at swapping the latest mass-audience movies. In 2000, the MPAA estimated that 275,000 movies were being downloaded each day, rising to one million by 2002. In this regard, the prospect of a multi-media future became a mixture of promise and peril for media conglomerates seeking to maintain control over, and maximise revenue from, profound changes in the production, distribution and exhibition of film.

If contemporary film is defined by the migration of texts across media and cultural and geographic sites, Josh Stenger concentrates on the means by which 'Hollywood' has been taken up and thematised within urban space. In his essay 'Return to Oz: The Hollywood Redevelopment Project, or Film History as Urban Renewal', he examines the means by which the city of Los Angeles has appropriated images from Hollywood's past in the name of urban renewal. Analysing the way that real-estate developers and city officials in the 1990s sought to exploit the myth of Hollywood to renew strategic areas of the city's landscape, Stenger provides a detailed case study of the Hollywood Redevelopment Project. From studio stores to theme parks, consumption space in the 1990s not only drew upon the commercial popularity of movie brands, but also sold the movie industry *as* a brand. The Hollywood Redevelopment Project enables Stenger to ask questions about this process, analysing the degree to which the project's 'spatial logic makes concrete the triangular relationship between LA, Hollywood, and hegemonic consumerism'.

The analysis of space is central to Stenger's methodology. Rather than examine film history from an industrial or textual perspective, he examines the sites and environments that have been organised around the idea, and the iconography, of filmed entertainment. Hollywood, in this case, is shown to have a particular bearing on cultural geography, describing the forms of (city) space where movies have an imprint; where its myths and fantasies have been used by property developers and local politicians to create new sites of consumption. In the case of the Hollywood Redevelopment Project, this is especially geared towards tourism. While Stenger concentrates upon a billion dollar development project in Los Angeles that may be seen as atypical, his analysis is nevertheless suggestive of the means by which forms of urban space in metropolitan and regional cities have been transformed into themed (entertainment) spectacle.

In terms of evidence, Stenger draws less upon source materials produced by the film industry than on city records and council ordinances. In particular, he draws upon documents relating to Los Angeles' Community Redevelopment

Agency (CRA). If the cultural geography of film is a question of analysing the spatial fantasies that emerge in cities and regions around the world – from local multiplex developments to major theme parks – this is necessarily linked to the history of property development and to policy debates about the use of space and landscape. Stenger co-links this material in a critical discussion of how film history has been used commercially in the 1990s in the figurative move from cinemas to theme parks.

- What key documents does Stenger use to construct his argument, and what or whose 'voice' do they represent?
- To what extent can urban policy decisions help us understand the way that people use and engage with forms of city space, and what research might you undertake to analyse this?
- Can you think of other projects or developments that you know, or have visited, that are based on the experience of cinema? In what specific ways might you examine these as spatial fantasies?

RETURN TO OZ: THE HOLLYWOOD REDEVELOPMENT PROJECT, OR FILM HISTORY AS URBAN RENEWAL

Josh Stenger

In 1986, the Los Angeles City Council decided to answer a question George Cukor had posed over fifty years before. The question: *What Price Hollywood?* The answer: $922 million. This was the amount allocated by the LA City Council to the Community Redevelopment Agency (CRA) to finance a thirty-year campaign in Hollywood, known simply as the Hollywood Redevelopment Project.[1] The Hollywood Redevelopment Project is currently one of twenty-nine redevelopment zones administered by the CRA, the agency which oversees city-funded renewal programs in Los Angeles. With one of the biggest budgets in LA's urban planning history, the Hollywood Redevelopment zone includes roughly 1,100 residential and commercial acres, making it second in size only to the CRA's fifty-year-old campaign to redevelop Bunker Hill and the Central Business District in LA's downtown. Alongside its formidable surface area and dizzying price-tag, one can add the statistic that within the zone reside 37,000 people who reportedly speak over eighty languages, making the Hollywood Redevelopment Project the most populated and heterogeneous redevelopment zone in LA history.[2] In this chapter, I will provide a brief account of how the CRA's approach to redevelopment in Hollywood contributes to LA's long history of aligning itself with the spectacle, glamour, and cultural purchase of

Josh Stenger (ed. Mark Shiel and Tony Fitzmaurice), *Cinema and the City: Film and Urban Societies in a Global Context* (Oxford: Blackwell, 2001).

the movies. Specifically, I am interested in calling attention to how the CRA is working to incorporate an idealized version of Hollywood's perceived 'Golden Age' into the contemporary urban landscape, staging the recovery of film history as a viable form of urban renewal.

The relationship between Los Angeles's cultural mythology, urban landscape, and Hollywood film is hardly new, nor is the enlistment of cinematic representations of LA to obfuscate and elide real racial, cultural, and socio-economic tensions. As David Thomson remarks of the place in 'Uneasy Street,' 'Los Angeles became a city through the act of seeing its industrial transmission all over the world . . . Its great urban and civic problems may slip past if it plays well.'[3] Indeed, both materially, at the level of the built environment, and symbolically, at the level of its cultural mythology, LA has for over a century promoted itself as a singular form of urban fantasia, a utopian space characterised by beauty, fame, leisure, and conspicuous consumption. As the film industry began to play a defining role in the production and distribution of LA's cultural mythology, it became increasingly difficult to distinguish the city's cultural geography from that of its cinematic doppelgänger, rendering Los Angeles and Hollywood as interchangeable spaces and interchangeable signs.

Attempting to solidify this bond, which has been strained of late, Los Angeles and the CRA intend to reclaim Hollywood's lost luster for their own, gambling nearly one billion dollars that an economic and cultural resurgence in Hollywood will, like the tide that lifts all boats, benefit the entire city. There is, of course, an irrefutable ideological project at work in Hollywood's (and now the CRA's) conflation of 'city' with 'fantasy' – hegemonic versions of city history and urban space exist at the obvious expense of other, marginal histories and less idyllic built environments. In the case of the Hollywood Redevelopment Project, this takes on at least three dimensions, all of which reify the dominant ideological myth of a paradisaical Los Angeles. First, there is the casting of film history in the role of urban renewal, a process wherein the CRA hopes to build a future by resurrecting Hollywood's imagined past. Second, there is the attempt to create a geography where before there was only a set of signs, invoking the fame, leisure, and lifestyle of conspicuous consumption associated with Hollywood as a way to cement at the broadest level the city's association with the whole historical map of Hollywood cinema; in doing so, the CRA can build a virtually instant, and instantly nostalgic commercial landscape. Third, there is the prioritisation of projects that thematise urban histories and circumscribe consumption, spectatorship, and tourism as the preferred forms of urban experience.

In *America*, Jean Baudrillard remarks of Los Angeles that it

> seems to have stepped right out of the movies. To grasp its secret, you should not, then, begin with the city and move inwards to the screen; you should begin with the screen and move outwards to the city. It is there that

cinema does not assume an exceptional form, but simply invests the streets and the entire town with a mythical atmosphere.[4]

In order to begin with the screen and move outward to the city, then, I would like to briefly describe the beginning of two films, *Hollywood Hotel* (1938) and *Pretty Woman* (1990), for these films neatly illustrate the imbrication of the cinema, the city, and fantasy in LA, while establishing Hollywood Boulevard as the *locus classicus* of that imbrication. The opening scenes of each announce plainly that these are films of different genres, different eras, different industries, and, to be sure, different Hollywoods. Moreover, each in its own way documents a particular moment in time wherein lived experience in Hollywood and LA is definable by, indeed reducible to, the liminal space of Hollywood Boulevard.

Hollywood Hotel opens at St. Louis Airport with Benny Goodman and his orchestra serenading friend and saxophonist Ronny Bowers (Dick Powell) with 'Hooray for Hollywood.' Bowers has landed a ten-week contract in Hollywood and, though skeptical about finding fame and certain he'll rejoin his friends at the end of his term, receives a hero's send-off. After Bowers takes off, with 'Hooray for Hollywood' still playing insistently, the film cuts to a montage of Hollywood's many famous place-names. 'Hollywood', as the film depicts it in this sequence, is a utopian landscape – one that is made possible by the movies and offered exclusively for the spectator's consumption, for Bowers is still on the airplane and does not have diegetic access to this onslaught of images.

Beginning with an establishing shot of a Hollywood Boulevard street sign, the brief montage sequence guides the spectator through a tour of the city's most recognizable 'Hollywood' landmarks, all of which appear to exist in the imaginary space of a seemingly boundless Hollywood Boulevard. Moving quickly from the Hollywood Bowl to the Brown Derby, the Café Trocadero, Sardi's, the Vendôme, the Ambassador Hotel and Cocoanut Grove, and the Hollywood Hotel, the montage vigorously asserts Hollywood Boulevard as the spatial epitome of film production, exhibition, and consumption. The final images of the sequence show maps to the stars' homes for sale, Grauman's Chinese Theater, film crews shooting on location, and an aerial view of the First National/Warner Bros. studios. During this montage, and throughout the film, *Hollywood Hotel* shows us Hollywood Boulevard in its heyday, a place where dreams come true and where stars are born. And yet, the film's version of Hollywood Boulevard is not simply expansive, it is downright fantastical: the Hollywood Bowl is several miles north on Highland Avenue, while the Ambassador and Cocoanut Grove are even further away in the mid-Wilshire district near Downtown. Still, the fact that half of the images featured in the montage are either historical anachronisms or geographical inaccuracies notwithstanding, Hollywood Boulevard as depicted here is the street LA's boosters had taken to promoting as 'The Great White Way of the West.'

In stark contrast to the Hollywood Boulevard depicted in *Hollywood Hotel*, *Pretty Woman* goes some way to illuminating the need for redevelopment in Hollywood by 1990. No longer the 'Great White Way,' *Pretty Woman* shows us the 'Boulevard of Broken Dreams,' a place where teenage runaways peddle drugs, where prostitutes mark their turf by the stars on the Walk of Fame, and where the glamour of the klieg lights has surrendered to a garish neon reality. Whereas *Hollywood Hotel* reveals a thriving commercial and entertainment district that is inseparable from the movies, *Pretty Woman* represents a more nocturnal, predatory urban habitat in which the cultural purchase of Hollywood appears less as a unifying principle than as an occasion for satire. However, no matter how far into neglect it may have sunk, *Pretty Woman*'s Hollywood Boulevard remains a site of fantasy, for it is on this street that the film's lovers – Vivian, the titular Pretty Woman (Julia Roberts), and Edward, her knight-errant (Richard Gere) – will meet, crossing paths just as we are reminded that 'everyone who comes to Hollywood's got a dream.' As it turns out in this fairytale, the 'Once-upon-a-time' of Hollywood Boulevard is quickly exchanged for the 'and-they-lived-happily-ever-after' of Beverly Hills and Rodeo Drive. The moral of the story? Even when the community of Hollywood disappoints, Hollywood the culture industry reminds spectators – potential tourists and consumers all – that the LA landscape can be read most conveniently as a series of consumer-cultural metonymies.

I mention these films because they reveal rather nicely the dialogic relationship between LA's urban landscape and Hollywood film, the former always already mediated by the latter. Indeed, films like *Hollywood Hotel* and *Pretty Woman* provide a complex map of an imaginary and recombinant Los Angeles. Each in its own way contributes – whether through reinforcement or subversion – to what Mike Davis, in his seminal 'excavation' of Los Angeles, *City of Quartz*, calls LA's 'city-myth,' which, according to him, 'enters the material landscape as a design for speculation and domination.'[5] Broadly, one might understand this myth as embodying the hegemonic sentiment that LA is essentially a simple equation of sunshine, beaches, palm trees, and a uniformly classless yet always upwardly mobile consumer society. Davis credits the city's early boosters with giving form and function to the city-myth, but even its originators could not promote the illusion as well as Hollywood could. To be sure, while LA has a long history of vigilant boosterism, the 'fairy-tale' side of Los Angeles has never been given better, more persistent representation than in the flickering half-light of the movie theater.

Baudrillard and Davis approach the city with decidedly different agendas and from decidedly different perspectives, yet each reminds us in one way or another that to live in Los Angeles is in many ways to live according to the metaphors made available by the film industry. Inside this place of 'pleasure domes decreed,' Davis argues, the perspective of the LA resident is like the projected image, depthless and inauthentic: 'To move to Lotusland is to sever connection with national reality, to lose historical and experiential footing, to surrender critical distance, and to submerge oneself in spectacle and fraud.'[6] Perhaps the same might be said of the CRA's Hollywood Redevelopment Project, for it too asks us to surrender critical distance. It too is deeply submerged in and organized around the spatial and cultural logic of the spectacle.

Typically, the CRA's primary objective in a redevelopment zone is to act as the catalytic agent for the tangible and expeditious improvement of the quality of life for residents and commercial tenants within the neighborhood and/or community.[7] The aim in Hollywood, however, seems substantively different, with an increased emphasis given over to the cultivation of entertainment-related and entertainment-themed businesses whose goal is to generate greater profits for the area from tourists and local consumers. Given that over 37,000 people live within the 2 square miles of the Hollywood Redevelopment zone, one might reasonably conclude that improving living conditions and community services for these residents would constitute major goals of the project. While state law requires the CRA to spend at least 20 per cent of the $922 million in redevelopment funds to construct new, and improve existing, housing for very low-, low-, and moderate-income families, the lion's share of the money has been earmarked for the subsidy and development of commercial projects designed to foreground the entertainment industry and intended to court tourists and their money back to Hollywood.

According to CRA reports, the agency anticipated spending $7 million on housing from 1994 to 1999, while almost $20 million was slated to underwrite entertainment-related business loans, the construction of the Hollywood Entertainment Museum and the improvement of parking lots and streetlights in commercial areas.[8] These numbers are lopsided enough by themselves, yet they fail to account for the $90 million the CRA has committed to the Hollywood-Highland project, the crown jewel of Hollywood's redevelopment, a subject I will return to shortly. While the disparity between these figures goes some way toward revealing the business-oriented approach to redevelopment favored by the CRA, the agency is more explicit in its 1998 'Progress Report' on its five-year implementation plan. Although this CRA report insists that the 'preservation and expansion of housing and the meeting of community needs of area residents' constitute primary redevelopment objectives, the top three priorities listed – '(1) [to] encourage economic and commercial development; (2) [to] promote and retain the entertainment industry; and (3) [to] revitalize the historic core' – do little to address the 'needs of area residents.'[9]

Indeed, in order to accomplish these aims, the CRA has prioritized the stimulation of entertainment and retail businesses in order to attract tourists, consumers, and moviegoers – the distinction between these roles being blurred whenever possible. As I mentioned, the promotion of entertainment landmarks and of studio-era Hollywood's fabled past is central to the CRA's strategy for spurring redevelopment in Hollywood. In its attempts to recover the spirit of Hollywood's Golden Age, the CRA has approached urban renewal as a kind of film adaptation. Armed with a blockbuster-size budget, the CRA is planning to bring the world 'Hollywood: The Sequel,' wherein a kind of crude spatialization of Hollywood film history will act the part of genuine material revitalization. In 1996, *LA Times* writer Duke Helfland described the situation quite succinctly: 'For the 1990s remake [of Hollywood Boulevard], investors and boosters are betting Hollywood's future on its storied past. They believe that preserving and capitalizing on a bygone elegance will satisfy hungry tourists who flock to the movie capital expecting to be dazzled . . .'.[10] To be sure, the CRA's strategy for economic recovery in Hollywood hinges largely on its ability to successfully merchandise film history as a form of consumer nostalgia.

One important mechanism in this strategy is the reassertion of Hollywood Boulevard's status as a center of film exhibition or, more accurately, to reposition exhibition as the bridge between the Boulevard's halcyon past and the anticipated success of the area's future. In other words, in order to ensure the large-scale economic success the CRA has promised the city, the film industry, and the business community, Hollywood must foreground itself as a preferred site of movie*going* if not of movie*making*. In an early move to do just that, the Hollywood Chamber of Commerce jumped on the 'redevelopment' bandwagon in June 1991, designating a new Cinema District along an eight-block stretch of Hollywood Boulevard. The new district, comprising six different theaters – the Ritz, the Vogue, Pacific's El Capitán, the Chinese, the Galaxy Theater, and the Egyptian – touted moviegoing as Hollywood's stock-in-trade.[11]

The announcement of the Cinema District was timed precipitously to coincide with the high-profile reopening of the newly renovated El Capitán Theater, which became the first major effort to exploit the purchase of Hollywood-past as a way to resuscitate the Boulevard's future when it reopened in June 1991. That the El Capitán was to be the new West Coast flagship for Disney releases was key to the CRA's goal of attracting other investors to the area. As the *LA Times* reported, 'City officials saw the grinning mouse's squeaky-clean image as a boon to any urban renewal plans. If Disney was willing to set down amid sex shops and pizza parlors, the logic went, Hollywood must be good for the whole family.'[12] Although it may be difficult to gauge at this point how directly Disney's presence affected other development projects within Hollywood, the El Capitan's successful restoration did little to discourage the CRA from pursuing its initial hunch – namely, that the recovery of Hollywood's 'bygone elegance' would either fulfill or replace the mandate to redevelop the area. And although the El Capitán did not receive CRA funds, its successful reopening did help pave the way for the second major renovation effort along the Boulevard – the CRA-subsidized recovery of the Egyptian Theater.

The first movie palace in Hollywood, the Egyptian opened in 1922 on Hollywood Boulevard, several blocks east of the future sites for the El Capitán and the Chinese Theater. However, by the early 1990s the theater had become defunct and was finally shut down in 1992 in the face of dismal attendance and extensive structural deficiencies. Following the success of the El Capitán, the

City of Los Angeles purchased the Egyptian Theater in that same year to ensure its preservation. But the Egyptian's fate was far from decided, for when the Northridge earthquake struck in January 1994, the theater suffered significant structural damage and was condemned.[13] In 1996, the CRA agreed to sell the Egyptian to the American Cinemathèque – a non-profit organization – for $1, and offered to help renovate the time-addled theater by contributing $5 million of the $13 million needed for the restoration. The remaining funds were raised through the contribution of public and private donors.[14]

When the Egyptian reopened on 4 December 1998, it not only provided a home for the American Cinemathèque – whose charter involves hosting retrospectives of classic Hollywood, *avant-garde* and foreign cinemas – it marked another strong connection to Hollywood's cinematic past with which the CRA was so enamored. Yet problems persist, for not only is the American Cinemathèque still heavily in debt following ballooning restoration costs, but the organization's agenda seems to have shifted in order to meet its financial obligations.[15] Hoping to draw more moviegoers, the Cinemathèque, which had formerly been a reliable place to escape the industry's stranglehold on movie culture in the area, is 'now focused on bringing in mainstream Hollywood,' going so far as to feature a James Cameron retrospective in order to 'broaden its appeal.'[16] Such a shift is indicative of the impact of place, for Hollywood Boulevard, as the alpha and omega of American film production and consumption, is not renowned for promoting cultural diversity, and one might reasonably conclude that the American Cinemathèque's victory in securing such palatial headquarters was at least in some respects a Pyrrhic one.

With the fanfare created by the announcement of the Cinema District, the El Capitán's grand reopening, and the promise of a restored Egyptian theater, the CRA's emphasis on laying claim to the movies as a way of reinvigorating commercial life appeared to be working. However, despite the movie theaters and the CRA's sponsorship of two film-related museums, even ardent supporters of the Hollywood Redevelopment Project could see that, as late as 1994 or 1995, the CRA had neither stimulated the commercial and cultural renaissance described in its charter nor attracted the kind of marquee investors it so desperately wanted.[17] The initial optimism was beginning to fade.

In 1995, however, David Malmouth, a former Disney executive who oversaw the renovation and relocation of Disney's New Amsterdam Theater in Times Square, pitched the CRA an idea on how to develop the corner of Hollywood Boulevard and Highland Avenue, the former site of the Hollywood Hotel. Malmouth, representing development firm TrizecHahn, proposed a massive urban entertainment center to be called, simply, Hollywood-Highland, the 'crown jewel' of the Hollywood Redevelopment Project, to which I alluded earlier. By virtually all accounts, the inception of the Hollywood-Highland project has finally stimulated interest from major commercial and entertainment-related investors within the designated Hollywood Redevelopment zone.[18]

Situated immediately next to and behind the Chinese Theater, the Hollywood-Highland project dwarfs virtually every other construction, renovation, or expansion project either planned or under way in the Hollywood Redevelopment zone. It is truly grandiose: spanning over eight acres, or nearly one and a half city blocks, the project will create over 650,000 square feet of commercial space that will include theme restaurants, studio showcase stores, retail shops, a 14-screen, 4,000-seat multiplex theater, a newly-remodeled 415-room hotel and a 3,300-seat live broadcast theater that will be home to the Academy Awards. The cost for the project is estimated at $385 million.

Hollywood-Highland offers a compelling example of how public administration, urban planning, and private investment have come together to forge an identity for Hollywood Boulevard. Although TrizecHahn's project will obviously provide business opportunities for a number of private entertainment-related interests, it nonetheless has the financial, legal, and political backing of the CRA, which has pledged $90 million (or 10 per cent of its total operating budget) to Hollywood-Highland. This money will finance the structure's underground parking lot and the Academy Theater, and has all but obliterated meaningful distinctions between 'community redevelopment' and 'commercial expansion.' In addition to its financial contribution, the CRA helped secure such a marquee investor for the project site through its partnership with the Metropolitan Transit Authority, whose $2-billion, seven-mile Red Line winds from the center of Downtown to Hollywood, and will eventually extend to Universal City and its own host of movie-themed attractions. Along this planned entertainment corridor, the CRA and MTA were together able to provide TrizecHahn with the added incentive of a dedicated subway station at Hollywood-Highland, despite the fact that a few blocks away at Hollywood and Vine, a $56-million station opened on June 12, 1999, boasting its own replica of the Yellow Brick Road from *The Wizard of Oz* as if to remind commuters and tourists alike they weren't in Kansas anymore.[19]

Like the Cinema District, the Hollywood museums, and even the Hollywood subway stations – all of which comply with the CRA's emphasis on marketing a fictionalized, or at the very least romanticized, Hollywood past – the Hollywood-Highland project is guided by a conceptually strategic pastiche which allows for the simulation of film industry history and urban history as commercial window-dressing. Conscious of how clear the past is to the CRA's grand illusion, Hollywood-Highland's historical sensibility and its willingness to play freely with that sensibility are made manifest in the fact that the project all but absorbs the Chinese Theater and features the first live-broadcast theater built specifically for the Academy Awards, thereby incorporating two of Hollywood's most globally recognizable icons under the roof of a single multi-use consumer space. Designed to collapse distinctions between the cinematic past of Hollywood and the hoped-for near-future of LA's consumer culture and tourist economy, Hollywood-Highland capitalizes on the signifying power of the former as a way of ensuring the latter. In addition to the Chinese and the new Academy Awards facility, one of the most prominently featured 'sets' in this distinctly postmodern space is a reproduction of the Babylon Court from D. W. Griffith's *Intolerance*, complete with Griffith's fabled white elephants. In its time, Griffith's set towered over the intersection of Sunset and Hollywood Boulevards for months after production was completed in 1916, at once a monument to the industry's prodigality and a metaphor for the city's collective investment in fusing architecture and cinema to create new forms of spectacle. In this sense, Hollywood-Highland's quotation of Griffith's set illustrates perfectly the complex spatial logic of cinematic, historical, and geographical recombination employed to conjure up 'the Hollywood that exists foremost in the expectations of the tourists who wander the boulevard in search of it.'[20]

Of course, even before Hollywood fell prey to urban neglect, tourists arrived on Hollywood Boulevard to the disappointing realisation that, to paraphrase Gertrude Stein's famous remark about Oakland, 'there was no there there.' As Carey McWilliams described Hollywood over fifty years ago, 'one of the most famous place-names in the world exists only as a state of mind, not as a geographical entity.'[21] Indeed, where were all those magical places from the opening of *Hollywood Hotel?* Tourists looking for stars had to settle for a star map or, after 1960, the Walk of Fame, while those in search of the studios were directed to Universal City, Burbank, Century City, or Culver City. Hollywood itself seems to have always been an insubstantial, ethereal set of signs more than an inhabitable *topos*.

But the CRA is working hard to forge a built environment out of this collective memory. With the help of hyperbolic projects like the Hollywood-Highland spectacle, the CRA's work in Hollywood might be described most simply as a recuperative effort to put a 'there' there. On a conceptual level this has meant working to erase the line between LA's material landscape and cinematic representations of it, a strategy that lays bare the historical importance of Hollywood film not only in articulating the city's cultural mythology, but also in shaping a material landscape in which that mythology can be inscribed, enacted, and consumed. On a practical level, the CRA's efforts to recreate an entertainment community out of a formerly dispersed geography has meant the aggressive recruitment of specific kinds of businesses – another reminder that this 'LA story' is subject to the CRA's 'final cut.' In the CRA's Hollywood business information packet, for instance, investors are reminded that 'there's no business like show business.' The brochure courts interested parties with the CRA's 'Entertainment Industry Attraction and Retention Program,' offering no-interest loans of up to $250,000 simply for relocating to Hollywood, with complete loan forgiveness if the business remains in Hollywood for a decade, or, as described in the dictum of the packet's enthusiastic boosterism: 'Stay here for 10 years and we'll make that loan disappear. Like Hollywood magic!'[22]

The more the Hollywood Redevelopment Project takes shape and continues to promote and recruit the entertainment industry as the *sine qua non* of the city, the more it is clear that projects like Hollywood-Highland will acquire spatial and representational hegemony in Los Angeles. Of course, it's easy to predict success for a project so thoroughly preconceived and so well-funded. As a chimerical shopping mall, theme park, movie theater, and general urban spectacle, it is likely to pique the curiosity of most LA locals as well as the millions of tourists who visit the region each year. Likely to become a fixture of the newly redeveloped Tinseltown, the Hollywood-Highland project epitomizes how a utopian consumer space can be forged out of an ebulliently eclectic architectural syntax. Celebrating the city, the film industry, and the consumption of both, the project's spatial logic makes concrete the triangular relationship between LA, Hollywood, and hegemonic consumerism.

The Hollywood-Highland project – and its unique ability to spatialize cultural history without historicizing cultural space – is at once exceptional and representative of the modes and sites of consumption being privileged within the Hollywood Redevelopment zone specifically, and in the emergent emphasis on themed urban environments more broadly. It is a space wherein the gaze of the moviegoer, the shopper, and the tourist become interchangeable, where the spectacular overwhelms the mundane and where Hollywood-the-place can be rendered in stucco façades of Hollywood-the-cultural-myth. Because it has been credited with drawing other investors and developers into the redevelopment area, the Hollywood-Highland project is an important point of consideration, for it speaks to the general strategies for renewal and revitalization employed by the CRA. Moreover, it invites us to consider whether or not these kinds of multimillion-dollar spatial fantasies can engender genuine urban reform and community redevelopment, as Los Angeles and the CRA overlook the city's history of deep racial and class divisions, re-creating LA in the image of *Oz* even as it future looks more and more like *Blade Runner*. The Yellow Brick Road at the Hollywood and Vine subway station reminds us of how clearly the CRA sees the Los Angeles of its dreams as being, while not exactly over the rainbow, at least on the other side of the screen.

NOTES

1. The Hollywood Redevelopment Plan was adopted on 7 May 1986. For more details of the proposed redevelopment initiatives, see 'Hollywood Redevelopment Plan: City Council Ordinance #161202 Project Guidelines.'
2. David Ferrell, 'Judge OKs Plan for Hollywood,' *Los Angeles Times*, 21 January 1989, p. 31; Evelyn DeWolfe, 'Developers Hope to Recapture Old Hollywood Glitter,' *Los Angeles Times*, 8 March 1987, p. 1.
3. David Thomson, 'Uneasy Street,' in David Reid (ed.), *Sex, Death and God in LA*, (Los Angeles: University of California Press, 1994), pp. 325, 327.
4. Jean Baudrillard, *America*, trans. Chris Turner (London: Verso, 1989), p. 56.
5. Mike Davis, *City of Quartz: Excavating the Future in Los Angeles* (New York: Vintage, 1992), p. 23.
6. Ibid., p. 18.
7. The CRA's function in LA is to 'eliminate slums and blight; revitalize older neighborhoods; build low- and moderate-income housing; encourage economic development; create new employment opportunities; support the best in urban

design, architecture and the arts; and ensure broad citizen participation in Agency endeavors.' Quoted from the Community Redevelopment Agency's website at http://www.cityofla.org/CRA/glauce.htm

8. For information regarding CRA specifications regarding minimum percentages of funds to be spent on housing, see 'Hollywood Redevelopment Plan: City Council Ordinance #161202,' p. 19. For details on the allotment of funds to individual residential, commercial, and civic projects during the five-year period 1995–9, see the CRA/LA, Hollywood Redevelopment Project, 'Hollywood 5 Year Implementation Plan: Health and Safety Code Section 334190' (4 May 1995), pp. 5–8.
9. The CRA/LA, Hollywood Redevelopment Project, 'Hollywood Five-Year Implementation Plan Progress Report', (28 January 1998), p. 1.
10. Duke Helfland, 'Hollywood: Is It Ready for Its Close-up?,' Los Angeles Times, 10 November 1996, p. A-32.
11. Dean Murphy, 'Hollywood Remake: New Cinema District Aimed at Restoring Film's Capital,' Los Angeles Times, 18 June 1991, p. B-1+.
12. Nicolai Ouroussoff, 'Could It Be Magic – Again?,' Los Angeles Times, 23 November 1997, p. F-6.
13. Sara Catania, ('Screen Test,') LA Weekly, 30 July–5 August 1999 (http://www.laweekly.com/ink/99/36/news-catania.shtml).
14. Carla Rivera, 'Bringing Back the Past,' Los Angeles Times, 10 April 1998, pp. B-1 +.
15. Catania, 'Screen Test.'
16. Robert Welkos, 'Ancient Egyptian's Reincarnation,' Los Angeles Times, 3 December 1998, p. F-6.
17. For more information on the CRA's involvement with Hollywood museum construction, see Hollywood Redevelopment Project, 'Hollywood Five-Year Implementation Plan Progress Report,' p. 4, and Hollywood Chamber of Commerce, 'Capital Investment in Hollywood' (March 1998), p. 2.
18. Since the LA City Council and the CRA approved construction of the Hollywood-Highland Project, an onslaught of projects has begun. For more information on specific project details, see Hollywood Chamber of Commerce, 'Capital Investment in Hollywood.'
19. Jeffrey Rabin, 'Hollywood Subway Line Opens Today,' Los Angeles Times, 12 June 1999, p. B-1, Hugo Martin, 'MTA Raises Curtain on Movie Glitz,' Los Angeles Times, 15 September 1998, pp. B-1+.
20. Greg Goldin, 'MALL-YWOOD,' LA Weekly, 18–24 December 1998, p. 30.
21. Carey McWilliams, Southern California: An Island on the Land (Salt Lake City: Gibbs Smith, 1995 (1946)), p. 330.
22. 'Hollywood Redevelopment Project,' Promotional Kit (Hollywood Chamber of Commerce, 1986), p. 4.

24

GLOBALISATION AND THE NEW MILLENNIUM

In the 1980s and 1990s, the overseas market counted for half of the majors' theatrical income and generated an even greater percentage of revenue through home video and television. The development and exploitation of world markets, specifically the rich and densely populated regions of Europe and Asia, led to strategic concerns with the global dimensions of film. This not only included questions about cinematic form, but also had significant implications for production, financing and labour practice.

In terms of the physical labour involved in the production of movies, Hollywood sought increasingly to exploit cheap labour markets during the 1990s. Similar to retail and manufacturing industries that source products using inexpensive factory labour, notably in Asia and South America, the film majors used 'runaway production' to keep down labour costs and to avoid troublesome domestic unions. Disney, for example, outsourced much of its animation work to Asia, where inkers and colourists were a lot cheaper to employ. At the same time, English-speaking countries such as Canada, Australia, New Zealand and the United Kingdom became emerging centres for runaway film production, a combination of tax incentives, currency imbalances and labour bargains meaning that studios could get more for their money using overseas production facilities.

While no big-budget movies were made overseas in 1990, twenty-four were made in 1998. Films such as *Titanic* (Mexico, 1997), *The Matrix* (Australia, 1999), *Mission: Impossible* (United Kingdom, 1996), *Mission: Impossible 2* (Australia, 2000), the *The Lord of the Rings* trilogy (New Zealand, 2001–3), and *The Bourne Identity* (Czech Republic, 2002) all drew upon offshore labour and studio facilities.

As a result, feature film production in Los Angeles almost halved between 1996 and 2000. Helping to facilitate this situation were national and regional film commissions, keen to attract investment by offering film companies highly competitive location opportunities. These would help producers find talent, locations and subsidies that would make offshore filming worthwhile. In this context, particular cities would often market themselves in terms of their specific ability to substitute for other cities and regions of the world. While Toronto often stood in for New York, the versatile sea and mountain scenery of Vancouver made it a key site of runaway film production. Meanwhile, Prague became popular for its European backdrops and atmosphere. In each case, the price of 'below-the-line' labour – a term for largely unsung screen workers and film crews – was far less expensive than in the United States.

An important dimension of globalisation in the film industry in the 1990s and 2000s was a higher degree of flexibility in Hollywood's (geographical) production of film and recruitment of labour. The sheer expense of film meant that studios and film companies looked increasingly towards offshore labour. At the same time, budgetary concerns led to collaborative methods of movie financing. For the majors, this functioned as a means of spreading risk, and involved production deals with other international media companies, typified by the agreement between Warner Bros. and the Australian company Village Roadshow to produce *The Matrix*. Such deals became known as 'equity co-productions' and significantly increased foreign financing in big-budget Hollywood films. Conversely, regionally specific films were often funded, wholly or in part, by Hollywood studios: the British comedy about Sheffield strippers, *The Full Monty* (1997), was owned by Fox. These arrangements served to complicate ideas about what exactly a 'British', 'French' or 'American' film might be. In industrial terms, the concept of national cinema became a lot more fluid as finance and labour moved across and between film industries.

This did not mean to say that national cinemas lost all sense of identity. While British talent, themes and backdrops formed the basis of popular genres including romantic comedy (*Love Actually* [2003]), social drama (*Billy Elliot* [2000]), and the crime picture (*Lock, Stock and Two Smoking Barrels* [1998]), the work of British *auteurs* such as Mike Leigh and Ken Loach, and emerging directors such as Shane Meadows and Lynne Ramsay, explored British life in more culturally specific ways. The austerity of Leigh's family portraits in *All or Nothing* (2002) and *Vera Drake* (2004), and Loach's concern with rail pri-vatisation in *The Navigators* (2001) was matched in this sense by Meadows' locational focus on the East Midlands (*Once Upon a Time in the Midlands* [2002]) and Ramsay's use of Scottish landscapes and characters in *Ratcatcher* (1999) and *Morvern Callar* (2002). Meanwhile, Michael Winterbottom portrayed very different concerns in *24 Hour Party People* (2002) and *9 Songs* (2004), one addressing the Manchester music scene of the 1980s and the other using rock and classical concerts in London to punctuate a series of erotic scenarios between two lovers.

If British cinema was defined by countervailing trends, shaped by the dynamics of the international and domestic film market and its appetite for both mass audience and niche movies, French national cinema was similar in kind. While art films such as *Baise-Moi* (2000) and Catherine Breillat's *A Ma Soeur!* (2001) dealt with the power dynamics of sexual encounter and rape, the emergence of Audrey Tautou as a French screen star in the early 2000s offered a cinematic counterpoint. In *Amélie* (2001) and *A Very Long Engagement* (2004), both directed by Jean-Pierre Jeunet, Tautou played a sexual innocent, a character whose child-like femininity formed the basis of fantastical and investigative journeys in the name of love. As interesting as the films themselves, and their articulation of French cinematic concerns, was the fierce legal battle that developed around their nationality, in particular *A Very Long Engagement*. Produced by Warner Bros., debate focused on whether the film could receive generous European film subsidies. This continued to expose the difficulties of how national film could or should be determined.

If these debates were often linked to a more general desire to resist Hollywood, one direct tactic of shoring up regional alliances came in the form of 'treaty co-productions'. These developed as a result of attempts by national governments to stimulate regional film production against the perceived onslaught of Hollywood. To receive funds, such films had to meet specific criteria about the use of regional industry and the promotion of cultural identity. In Europe, this was facilitated by the Council of Europe (and the body Eurimages discussed in Chapter 21) seeking to shore up a definable sense of European character via the medium of film. This gave rise to films such as Lars von Trier's *Breaking the Waves* (1996), about an unorthodox love affair in a traditional community, which was made by a Danish director in a Scottish setting, using a cast of British and Nordic actors. While fluid in its incorporation of 'European' elements, it was emblematic of attempts to use regional locations and labour, producing art films that could be sold on the festival circuit.

Sometimes, co-productions emerged between same-speaking countries. For example, the Argentine–Spanish production *Tango* (1998), by the Spanish director Carlos Saura, capitalised on a boost in Argentina's film economy in the mid-1990s after years of financial crisis. In Latin America, a fluctuating economic situation, brought about by the move from military dictatorship to plural democracy, meant that film industries in countries such as Brazil, Argentina and Mexico struggled to assert themselves or build regional alliances. However, the early 2000s saw a particular resurgence of Latin American cinema, notably that of Mexico. Alejandro González Iñárritu's *Amores Perros* (2000) and Alfonso Cuarón's *And Your Mother Too* (2002) marked a new cinematic moment that coincided with a change in Mexico's political order, emerging after the defeat in 2000 of the Institutional Revolutionary Party that had ruled Mexico for seventy-one years. Less inclined to reflect on political events, these focused on representations of youth. *And Your Mother Too*, for example, was a coming-of-age movie about a love triangle between two teenagers and an unhappily married Spaniard. Like *The Motorcycle Diaries* (2004), focusing on the young days of Che Guevara and also starring Gael Garcia Bernal, the film would translate the road movie to Latin American cultural and geographic landscapes.

Despite occasional success stories, and the growing importance of Spanish as a world language, Latin America did not generally press its influence within international markets. More successful on these terms, at least within the art house circuit, were European *auteurs* like Pedro Almodóvar. Continuing his concern with the mutability of gender and sexuality, *All About My Mother* (1999), *Talk to Her* (2002) and *Bad Education* (2004) would concentrate respectively on female friendships, family relations and male homosexuality. While developing a textured portrait of Spanish cultural life and history, *All About My Mother* also powerfully invoked classical Hollywood, in particular the Bette Davis melodrama *All About Eve* (1950). This was illustrative of the means by which European/art cinema rarely sat in opposition to Hollywood but often emerged in creative dialogue with its forms and conventions, even as it culturally or stylistically reworked them. The same was true, for example, of the cult French film *La Haine* (1995), a story of French inner city life that was powerfully indebted to American as well as French cinematic traditions, in particular the work of Martin Scorsese. At the same time, European films continued to be remade by Hollywood. While Alejandro Amenábar's Spanish film *Open your Eyes* (1997) was remade as *Vanilla Sky* (2001), starring Tom Cruise and Penelope Cruz, Amenábar would also direct the supernatural thriller *The Others* (2001), a film that while produced by Miramax, set in Jersey and influenced by Alfred Hitchcock, would use Spanish locations and crew.

The cross-pollination of film style and talent across national borders is nothing new within international film culture. However, such movement accelerated in the 1990s with the increased globalisation of markets. This influenced the personnel and production history of the largest Hollywood blockbusters. For example, while the reinvention of comic book heroes such as *Batman* (1989) and *X-Men* (2000) was increasingly entrusted to independent *auteurs* such as Tim Burton and Bryan Singer, films were also frequently directed in the 2000s by filmmakers who straddled different cultural, as well as cinematic, traditions. The émigré Taiwanese director Ang Lee used his exposure to American popular culture to reimagine *Hulk* (2003), and Guillermo del Toro moved from Mexican and Spanish art film to a career in Hollywood that would encompass comic book blockbusters such as *Hellboy* (2004).

As new markets opened and film audiences grew, Hollywood focused on the global potential of its products, and on styles and strategies that would widen the basis of a film's appeal. While international markets have always been important to the majors, films were increasingly made with a global audience in mind. In industrial terms, event movies such as the historical epics *Gladiator* (2000) and *Troy* (2004), and fantasy franchises like *Harry Potter* (2001–) and *The Lord of the Rings*, were specifically designed as global films. They relied on stories and effects that could translate well across regions and continents; they were released in quick succession in the main regional markets of North America, Europe and Asia; and they were made away from the film capital of Los Angeles. For instance, although it was produced by Universal and Dreamworks, *Gladiator* was not filmed in Hollywood. It was directed by the Englishman Ridley Scott, it had a multinational cast and it was filmed in locations ranging from Venice to Morocco. Similarly, while *Lord of the Rings* was directed by Peter Jackson and filmed in his native New Zealand, the *Harry Potter* franchise was shot principally in Britain and, by the third instalment, had been offered to the Mexican director Alfonso Cuarón. While few film industries could challenge the dominance of Hollywood in terms of the distribution power of the majors, individual films were becoming subject to greater intercultural influence.

This was also true of the Bollywood blockbuster, shaped by film traffic in and between British and Indian markets. India's huge domestic market, and rising international profile in Europe, Japan and North America, meant that theatrical film production continued to outpace that of Hollywood in domestic volume and penetration. While the Indian government lifted restrictions on film imports in 1994, Hollywood could only capture 10 per cent of the box office, its films priced out of the market by cheaper ticket admissions and the general popularity of indigenous Hindi, and other regional language, productions. These took the form of Hindi blockbusters such as *Dilwale Dulhania Le Jayenge* (1995). Maintaining key components of melodrama, romance, spectacle, exotic locations, comedy, and song and dance, the Hindi blockbuster was also increasingly framed for audiences within the Indian diaspora. In other words, they were made to resonate and appeal to audiences in the UK, Canada and the United States. It is in this respect that *Dilwale Dulhania Le Jayenge* begins with an Indian newsagent, resident in London, pining for his mythic home in the Punjab. This theme would be replayed in love stories such as *Kabhi Khushi Kabhie Gham* (2001), a popular 'Bollywood' blockbuster that also focused on characters displaced to the UK.

Partly as a result of a new volatility in the Indian film industry – caused by the impact of commercial television in the 1980s – new markets became attractive to Indian directors. While this was reflected in changes to the Hindi blockbuster, co-productions with European and North American firms led to a number of films targeted at major film festivals, including Mira Nair's *Salaam Bombay!* (1988) and Shekhar Kapur's *Bandit Queen* (1994). Nair would subsequently set and make a number of films in the United States, such as *Mississippi Masala* (1991), and later films including *Monsoon Wedding* (2001) would be set back in India. Addressing suburban British Asian communities in Britain, Gurinder Chadha used her experience of growing up in England, watching Indian cinema, as the basis for *Bhaji on the Beach* (1993). This drew upon Bollywood traditions of romance in telling a story of an Indian woman visiting the English seaside resort of Blackpool. Chadha would also focus on

554

the tensions of multicultural assimilation in the comedy drama about women's football, *Bend It Like Beckham* (2002).

These examples were representative of the diasporic cinema that became increasingly manifest in the 1990s and 2000s, reflecting in different ways on the postwar movement of peoples between countries and continents. Whether a result of decolonisation or other migrationary pressures, the twentieth century was defined by the dispersion and displacement of peoples, either seeking or forced to leave their homelands to find new lives in foreign lands. Diasporic cinema was not linked to any particular country or cinema, but represented a diverse thematic strand of filmmaking, concerned with the varied cultural experiences of second- and third-generation migrants.

This often reflected the movement of peoples towards the so-called developed world. While *Samia* (2000), by Moroccan director Philippe Faucon, examined the life of second-generation Arabs from North Africa living in Paris, the Turkish director Kutlug Ataman addressed the German Turk community in *Lola and Billy the Kid* (1999). Diasporic films could range significantly in style. For example, *East is East* (1999) was a mainstream comedy about a British-Asian family, focusing on the struggle between the rigid traditionalism of a Pakistani father, who runs a chip shop in the North of England, and his English wife and their very British children. This differed from the art house tendencies of Atom Egoyan. A Canadian director born in Egypt with Armenian heritage, Egoyan punctuated his work with video footage that, in films such as *Calendar* (1993), played experimentally with themes of identity and memory. All of these films addressed the experience of cultural displacement but used very different perspectives and formal effects.

Diasporic cinema examined the transnational flow of peoples, communities and cultures in explicit, thematic ways. Global processes were expressed at a more fundamental level, however, in forms of interchange taking place between particular film industries. If the production and consumption of film is linked inextricably to transnational movements of capital, technology and labour, some of the most interesting developments in the globalisation of film were levelled in and between the US and Asian film industries.

In East Asia during the 1990s and 2000s, film production in Hong Kong, Singapore, Taiwan and Indonesia fed upon the vast market for Chinese language film, encouraging regional investment and Asian co-productions that would also involve Japan and South Korea. These created a number of influential cinematic trends linked with the region, especially the development of animation and martial arts genres. Animation became especially associated with the Japanese film industry in the 1990s. While in economic terms the film industry was in a poor state, diminishing box office revenues leading to the bankruptcy of venerable film companies such as Nakkatsu, Japan continued to make its presence felt internationally. Not only did Japanese companies such as Sony and Matsushita own Hollywood studios, Japan successfully exported signature products such as *animé* film.

These were animated feature films that derived from Japanese comic books, or *manga*. Unlike the classic animation of Disney, *animé* used sharp angles, rapid editing and computer-generated imagery in often violent, yet touching, narratives that developed a cult following in both domestic and international markets. Hayao Miyazaki became closely associated with the success of *animé*, producing features such as *Princess Mononoke* (1997) and *Spirited Away* (2001). The latter concerned a little girl's adventures in a world of gods and monsters and became the highest grossing Japanese film of all time, and the first non-US film to earn more than $200 million outside the United States. While other developments in computer-generated animation, such as Richard Linklater's *Waking Life* (2001) and Sylvian Comet's *Belleville Rendez-Vous* (2003), moved animation away from the family entertainment vehicles of Disney and Pixar, Miyazaki became animation's most influential contemporary *auteur*.

In the global film market, Japanese cultural forms were often taken up or re-made by Hollywood. Japanese horror films such as *Ringu* (1998) were successfully remade by Hollywood: *The Ring* (2002) combined traditional Japanese ghost stories with the conventions of modern teen horror and *manga* was also embraced in particular forms of Western filmmaking. Notably, Quentin Tarantino interposed a *manga* sequence in *Kill Bill: Volume 1* (2003), a film with deliberate interests in Asian genre traditions, specifically samurai and kung fu cinema from Japan and Hong Kong. Like *The Matrix* before it, which drew upon Hong Kong action choreography and also *manga* in some of its spin-offs, *Kill Bill* was emblematic of the new cross-cultural popularity of martial arts.

The influence of Hong Kong cinema was especially significant in this context, exporting actors, directors and choreographers to Hollywood. This is examined by Leon Hunt's analysis of Jet Li in this chapter's reading. While the popularity of martial arts led to increased cultural traffic between American and Asian film industries, it also gave rise to major foreign-language blockbusters. *Crouching Tiger, Hidden Dragon* (2000), for example, was specifically designed to appeal to a wide audience. Internationally financed by companies in the United States, Europe, Taiwan and Hong Kong, *Crouching Tiger* was directed by Ang Lee, and made as an ode to his childhood memories of cinema in Taiwan. Using Mandarin dialogue, the film was made in the *wuxia* tradition, focusing on the tale of a noble swordsman. Lee combined elegant fight scenes with traditional *wuxia* concerns with martial arts chivalry, appealing to art house as well as youth audiences. While the film performed variably in the Asian market, it became a stellar success internationally, grossing over $200 million.

The success of *Crouching Tiger* was replicated in other Chinese language films, notably in Zhang Yimou's *Hero* (2002). While martial arts cinema was embraced by Hollywood in its pursuit of action spectacle and crossover stars, so Asian cinema also sought to emulate Hollywood production values in its creation of quality commercial cinema. Using internationally known stars, exquisite costumes and a generous number of special effects, the film was designed to cater to international tastes, synthesising art house and action-film conventions. As with other films of the period, *Hero* signified the growing difficulty of making clear distinctions between what a local Asian film and what a global Hollywood film might be in industrial or aesthetic terms. Indeed, adapting film to foreign markets had implications for Asian cinema as well as for Hollywood. This created a number of generically hybridised films that could play locally and globally. While *Hero* deliberately sought to compete in the global film market, other box office triumphs, such as the Hong Kong film *Shaolin Soccer* (2001), represented a martial arts–sports movie that successfully tapped local humour while appealing in style and theme to a wider market audience.

While often charged with cultural imperialism, Hollywood does not simply foist its wares on unsuspecting markets, or consume all oxygen for local film development. The late 1990s saw a particular resurgence of Asian film as it moved within, and against, the power of global Hollywood. Together with that of Japan, China and Hong Kong, the film industries of South Korea and Thailand saw local film perform particularly well in the early 2000s. The release of the terrorist thriller *Shiri* in 1999, for example, beat *Titanic* to become the highest grossing film in South Korean history, quickly surpassed by *Joint Security Area* (2000) and *Friend* (2001). Meanwhile, Thai cinema garnered roughly 30 per cent of the market in 2001, Thai film ranging from blockbusters such as *Suriyothai* (2002) to movies such as *Tears of the Black Tiger* (2000), offering a localised pastiche of the Hollywood western. As this last case may suggest, the success of local film at the domestic box office was often linked to the appropriation of stylistic elements from popular Hollywood films. While this at some level suggests the residual power of Hollywood, it also reveals the complex, and by no means unidirectional, flow of cross-cultural borrowing taking place between different film industries.

Entering the new millennium, Hollywood became increasingly sensitive to other regional industries and cinematic traditions, largely as a means of maximising its own aesthetic and industrial potential. Hollywood film began to incorporate a wider range of intercultural influences, intent on broadening its look, style and market appeal within global markets. Sometimes, this led directly to films that dwelt on specific cross-cultural experiences. Sofia Coppola's *Lost in Translation* (2003), for example, examined the jet lag and disorientation of a Hollywood actor (Bill Murray) and a young American wife (Scarlett Johansson) drawn together in their encounter with Tokyo, a place at once familiar when judged from within a luxury hotel but strange and disconcerting in the streets, bars and restaurants beyond.

If wider questions of 'translation' became key to Hollywood's success in local and global markets, these led to specific kinds of representational strategy in mainstream film. The attempt to bridge cultural and racial difference, for example, had a particular bearing on the kinds of star that would emerge in the early 2000s. Within action genres, the rise of Asian stars in Hollywood like Jackie Chan, Chow Yun-Fat and Jet Li paralleled the emergence of multiracial actors like Vin Diesel and The Rock. While linked to the performance of Hollywood film in 'non-white' export markets, the significance given to stars with indeterminate racial identities also responded to the ethnic diversity of youth-oriented popular culture in the United States. Films such as *The Fast and the Furious* (2001) and 'hip-hop kung fu' such as *Romeo Must Die* (2000) were more purposely 'multicultural' (or at least less white) in this context, especially in the figuration of the heroic protagonist.

Hollywood comedy was also drawn in different directions in its treatment of ethnicity and race. While romantic comedies such as *Maid in Manhattan* (2002) replayed the formula of *Pretty Woman* (1990), this time based around the Latino star image of Jennifer Lopez, black comedies such as *Barbershop* (2002) focused on a day in the life of an urban black community in Chicago, using an ailing black hairdressing salon to examine, in part, the legacies of civil rights. As with multiracial action cinema, however, these must be seen as developments within a system that still ultimately privileged whiteness as the industrial and ideological norm. Perhaps more significant than *The Fast and the Furious* or *Barbershop*, in this respect, were films that returned to established Hollywood stars, such as Tom Cruise in thrillers like *Minority Report* (2002); and that saw the emergence of powerful comedy coteries forming around the likes of Ben Stiller, Owen Wilson and Wes Anderson, whose work ranged from slapstick comedies such as *There's Something About Mary* (1998) and *Meet the Parents* (2000) to more idiosyncratic films like Anderson's *Rushmore* (1998), *The Royal Tenenbaums* (2001) and *The Life Aquatic with Steve Zissou* (2004).

In terms of Hollywood's more general output in global film markets during the early 2000s, the popularity of action and comedy genres was matched by a cycle of supernatural films especially associated with the Indian-born American director M. Night Shymalan. From *The Sixth Sense* (1999) and *Unbreakable* (2000) to *Signs* (2002) and *The Village* (2004), these films were all based on foreboding and revelation, their quality of surprise differing in part from an alternative cinematic impetus to rework, re-imagine or simply re-release classic genre films. For example, while Todd Haynes reworked Douglas Sirk's *All that Heaven Allows* (1955) in *Far From Heaven* (2002), inscribing a post-sixties sense of sexual and racial politics, Gus Van Sant restaged, shot for shot, Alfred Hitchcock's *Psycho* (1998). These art house adaptations met with other kinds of generic rekindling, especially found in the remake of 1970s classic horror, including *Dawn of the Dead* (2004) and *Assault on Precinct 13* (2005).

An alternative representational form that enjoyed a particular renaissance in the early 2000s was documentary. While films like *Spellbound* (2002) offered a cheerful portrait of youthful endeavour, following eight children competing in a national spelling competition, documentary subjects were more often polemically charged, or based on political and social revelation. In the latter case, Errol Morris' *Fog of War* (2003) detailed 'lessons' from the life of

one-time secretary of defence Robert S. McNamara, while the British documentary maker Nick Broomfield brought a more imposing interview-style to
his investigation of the shooting of hip-hop star Tupac Shakur in *Biggie and
Tupac* (2002). In more polemical terms, Morgan Spurlock's *Super Size Me*
(2004) built a case against the dietary inflictions of fast food in the United
States, and Michael Moore mounted a wider critique of American corporate
and political power. Specifically, in *Bowling for Columbine* (2002) Moore
addressed American gun culture and in *Fahrenheit 9/11* (2004) focused on the
mendacious administration of George W. Bush. Winning the Palme d'Or in
Cannes, and becoming an international blockbuster of its own kind, *Fahrenheit
9/11* demonstrated the political and financial currency of documentary film, as
well as the divisions of thinking about how best to examine, and understand,
the nature of American global power.

In cinematic terms, American global power is frequently examined through the
lens of political economy, a form of analysis that concentrates on the industrial
practices of Hollywood, especially as they relate both to policies of trade liberalisation that helped open up lucrative new markets in the 1990s, and to the
continuing means by which Hollywood has sought to establish itself as a
'universal' cinematic norm. Leon Hunt takes a different approach in his essay
'Transnational Dragons and "Asian Weapons": Kung Fu and the Hong Kong
Diaspora'. Concerned with questions about the cultural hegemony of
Hollywood, he examines the degree to which it is possible to imagine
Hollywood *yielding* to other cinemas rather than simply imposing itself
globally or appropriating talent and aesthetics from other regions. Hunt
focuses on the pivotal case of Hong Kong and examines how martial arts stars
and choreographers fared in Western cinematic vehicles in the late 1990s and
early 2000s. To this end, he explores the Hollywood career of Jet Li and the
choreographic work of Yuen Wo-ping, discussing what he calls the 'in-
betweenness' of Hong Kong–Hollywood action cinema.

In critical terms, Hunt is concerned with the complex forms of transnational
flow that shape, in this case, action film. Rather than simply combine elements
from figuratively 'Western' and 'Eastern' cinematic traditions, he suggests a
certain convergence of their aesthetics and technologies. This does not absent
questions of power. Indeed, Hunt draws a distinction between *The Matrix*, a
film that marginalises the Asian expertise that it so clearly draws upon, and
'transnational prestige martial arts cinema' (*Crouching Tiger* and *Hero*) that
does more than simply graft Asian action onto Hollywood forms. In broad
terms, Hunt considers the potential losses *and* opportunities for Asian
filmmaking as it has become aesthetically integrated with Hollywood.

Methodologically, Hunt's account is driven by concerns with cinematic
representation; he is concerned with the 'aesthetic space' of action film as it
emerges from, and in relation to, the 'Hong Kong diaspora'. He combines
textual analysis with specific consideration of the production history and

filmmaking processes that have used, and in some cases circumscribed, Asian creative talent. While the concentration on diasporic flow from Hong Kong delimits a wider industrial picture of the means by which Hollywood functions in relation to Asian markets – investing, for example, in local language film production and stimulating Asian film industries in both intentional and non-intentional ways – his analysis provides an acute picture of globalisation in its cultural, rather than specifically economic, dimension.

- What kind of evidence does Leon Hunt use to underpin his argument about diasporic Hong Kong action cinema?
- What assumptions can be made about the meaning of films (and stars) in different regional markets, and what research might you have to do to measure similarities or variations in cultural response?
- Can you think of any different instances or historical moments where genres or stars have moved beyond their regional confines, and influenced other cinemas? How might you examine this?

TRANSNATIONAL DRAGONS AND 'ASIAN WEAPONS': KUNG FU AND THE HONG KONG DIASPORA

Leon Hunt

'It's kind of a combination of East meets West', says stunt co-ordinator Gary Hymes of the action scenes in Jet Li's The One. This deceptively benign cliché has become a popular way of describing what David Bordwell calls the 'Hong-Kongification of American cinema' (2000a: 19).[1] 'The fastest hands in the East versus the biggest mouth in the West' was the tagline for Rush Hour (1998), marking a clear division of star labour – physical (Jackie Chan) and verbal (Chris Tucker) – which, in turn, reinforces some broader binary oppositions (nature/culture, body/intellect). But the meeting of 'East' and 'West' is not just a matter of combining stars from different industries, but of converging aesthetics and technologies. The Matrix arguably established a new template for the 'Asianisation' of Hollywood – Hong Kong choreography combined with what Hymes calls 'our technology' (for example, CGI).

Many longstanding fans have been disappointed by Jackie Chan and Jet Li's Hollywood fight scenes and found Yuen Wo-ping's Matrix choreography inferior to his earlier work – too short, too slow, lacking the intricate rhythms and dynamic power of their Hong Kong films. Already, the meeting of 'East' and 'West' does not look quite so neat. Then there are other issues inevitable in such a crossover – how have Chinese stars fared in a national cinema that has traditionally marginalised Asians? Is it possible to imagine an embryonic

Leon Hunt, *Kung Fu Cult Masters* (London: Wallflower Press, 2003).

Chinese-American action aesthetic, or has Hong Kong talent simply fallen to the insatiable appetite of the globalising entertainment industry?

What interests me particularly is the 'in-betweenness' of Hong Kong-Hollywood action, and the mutation of this indeterminate aesthetic space. In the 1970s, the 'kung fu craze' allowed a handful of Hong Kong stars to make international films, most notably Bruce Lee, the only one to truly 'crossover'. In several cases, these films used Hong Kong choreographers and even entire crews, but directors and writers were invariably Westerners. The post-1990s diaspora suggests not the trans-pacific traffic of the 1970s, but the de-territorialisation of global culture, the sense of 'Hong Kong cinema' put into some futuristic matter transporter, materialising here and there, often in fragments. The sense of atoms re-assembling, *Star Trek* fashion, is perhaps most frequently seen in the dialogue between different *action technologies*, the very different spectacular regimes embodied by CGI and wirework.

Hollywood has assimilated three kinds of 'Hong Kong action' – the high-octane gunplay of John Woo and Chow Yun-fat,[2] the stunt-filled action-comedy of Jackie Chan and Sammo Hung, and the 'wire fu' of Tsui Hark, Yuen Wo-ping and Jet Li. Obviously, the second and the third are of particular relevance here, but they also raise implications about the production methods of different national cinemas, the valuing of certain types of cinematic labour (cho-reography) and for culturally specific constructions of the 'real'.

In some ways, 'Hong Kongified' Hollywood can be seen to be positioned pre-cariously between 'Asiaphilia' and Asiaphobia. Both can be seen in the way *Enter the Dragon* both fetishises the 'Orient' and replays 'Yellow Peril' archetypes, but this ambivalence is even more blatant in *Lethal Weapon 4*, in which Jet Li made his US debut as a sadistic Triad. Hollywood's 'romance' with the 'Orient' has always been deeply contradictory, and is made no less so by the requirements of 'political correctness'. Gina Marchetti detects a kind of postmodern Orientalism in films like the Chinatown-set *Year of the Dragon* (1985), in which ' "yellow peril" clichés coexist with antiracist discourses . . . Chinatown functions as pure style with neon dragons, pop songs, lion dances, and displays of martial artistry' (1993: 203). Marchetti could easily be describing *Lethal Weapon 4* (1998), where 'colourful' Chinatown is also a front for money laundering and traffic in illegal immigrants. The film's 'good' Chinese seek assimilation in the great democratic 'melting pot', like the immigrant Hongs, who belong to a history of frail, passive Chinese in Hollywood cinema. Jet Li is offered to us simultaneously as dynamic spectacle – 'How the hell did he do that?' marvels Mel Gibson's Riggs after he dismantles a gun at lightning speed – and inscrutable Other, garrotting old men and kicking pregnant women. Such spectacle, as Marchetti argues, pulls in two directions:

It both attracts and repulses, encouraging viewer identification while keeping that involvement at a distance. Moments of spectacle that feature ethnic and racial differences can define and reinforce the boundaries

561

between ethnic and racial groups to keep the dominant culture's own power intact. However, these moments also often include violent eruptions that challenge the dominant culture's ability to define those differences and boundaries. Violence bursts forth against the racial and ethnic status quo, and the viewer may identify with this antiestablishment aspect of the spectacle as well as with its ostensible condemnation (207).

The climax of *Lethal Weapon 4* is a case in point, as Riggs and Murtaugh (Danny Glover) face off against Wah Sing Ku (Li). Our two aging heroes have good reason to hesitate before taking on the impossibly agile martial arts master, but ultimately must prove to themselves that they are not 'too old for this shit'. The fight can also be understood in the light of Riggs's status as Vietnam vet – he has faced the Asian Other before and acquired martial arts skills in the 'Encounter with Asia'. Li has performed some unconscionable acts in the film, speaks only one line of dialogue in English, and is ultimately exterminated as though he was not human. But there is another set of generic determinants that inform the scene – the spectacle (familiar from numerous kung fu films) of a five-foot-six Chinese man taking on two six-foot-plus American men. Earlier in the film, Riggs and Murtaugh throw their weight around in a Chinese restaurant, make references to Green cards and joke about 'flied lice' – change the dynamics a little and the scene could be lifted from *Way of the Dragon* or Li's *gwailophobic Born to Defence*. For the Jet Li/Hong Kong/kung fu fan, it is no great leap to see his character as an underdog antihero, his violence partially motivated by legitimate rage (even though he oppresses other Chinese) and a response to the heroes' casual racism. However, I think *Lethal Weapon 4* is smart (or cynical) enough to second-guess all of this, thus exemplifying the kind of postmodern racial politics that Marchetti is talking about. It both plays to a 'dominant' reading of the sadistic, mysterious 'Oriental' and allows some notional (if limited and peripheral) identification with him for the 'cult' audience that Li's casting was clearly meant to attract.[3] Just before his final fight, Li is 'humanised' by a moving scene with his dying brother, the character he has been trying to release from a Chinese prison throughout the film. The romancing of the Other (usually prior to its destruction or co-opting) can be seen as characteristic of what Christopher Sharrett calls the 'sacrificial excess' of late capitalism. Such texts are marked by 'a sacrificial violence that acknowledges the Other by its obliteration, a strategy that admits both the credulity and the scepticism of the spectator; the 'specialness' of the Other and our sympathies with it are acknowledged as its monstrous aspect is confirmed' (1996: 257). But, perhaps more significantly, this sacrifice also seems to be in the service of renewal of a cinema that (like its protagonists) fears that it may be 'too old for this shit'. Thus, Hollywood both incorporates and symbolically annihilates its 'younger', more dynamic, counterpart.

To some extent, Hollywood's 'Hong Kongification' can be seen as the latest manifestation of America's 'Encounter with Asia', a conquest rather than the benign meeting implied by 'East' meeting 'West', After all, one of the factors in the diasporic journey of Hong Kong film-makers was Hollywood's conquest of the South-East Asian market. And yet there are problems, too, with regarding certain cultural forms as off-limits, as the essential property of a particular group – Hong Kong cinema has, after all, had global aspirations for some time. Steve Fore suggests that Jackie Chan's later Hong Kong films were already starting to 'disembed' him from 'a core of cultural meanings and experiences characteristic of the Hong Kong ecumene' (2001: 117), his persona restructured for the global marketplace. This was evident in their (often exoticised) use of international locations and Chan's globetrotting persona – Fore likens these films to the James Bond series, even down to their ethnocentric representation of other cultures (116). Kwai-cheung Lo sees Hong Kong identity as being doubly negated in the transnational/Hollywood films made by Hong Kong film-makers. In the first instance, Hollywood negates Hong Kong diegetically, by characterising its Chinese leads as 'Mainland Chinese at the expense of Hong Kong's particularity' (Lo 2001: 466).[4] But Hong Kong's construction of a 'local' identity was already contingent on a 'certain negation of Chineseness' – thus, 'Hong Kong's transnational crossing to Hollywood initiates another negation that negates the very symbolic realm common to Chineseness' (467). Lo asks whether this 'negation of negation' can be seen as a 'strategic move for the becoming of a new postcolonial subject leading up to and after 1997' (478). Ding-Tzann Lii (1998) goes further by suggesting that Hong Kong cinema, at its peak, represented a form of 'marginal imperialism', which both reproduces the dynamics of traditional imperialism and poses a threat to it – the Jackie Chan/James Bond comparison is suggestive in the light of such a hypothesis. On the one hand, Hong Kong's Asian expansionism contributed to the underdevelopment of Taiwanese cinema, just as Hollywood did to Hong Kong itself after 1993. But Lii also argues that there are significant (cultural if not economic) differences between 'core' and 'marginal' imperialism – the latter represents a 'rupture' in global capitalism 'where the peripheral "Other" surfaces as a subject' (1998: 127) – in this case, Hong Kong's 'localised' media imperialism contributed to an 'Asianisation', blending into other Asian countries and 'creating a synthesis-form with a higher cognitive order' (128). One might expect the dynamics to be rather different, however, when core imperialism (in this case, Hollywood) absorbs its peripheral counterpart (Hong Kong). Lii distinguishes between *incorporation*, where the "Other" is transformed by imperialism, and *yielding*, a 'synthesis which transcends both the self and the Other' (134). Ackbar Abbas seemingly has something similar in mind for his hypothetical 'third space', where 'East and West are overcome and discredited as separate notions, and another space or a space of Otherness is introduced' (1996: 300). But is it possible to imagine Hollywood *yielding* to Hong Kong, rather than simply appropriating its talent and aesthetics? Steve Fore was (initially) optimistic, likening the exodus to Hollywood's European émigrés of the 1930s and 1940s – he described them as 'transnational design professionals' belonging to 'image-projecting and con-sciousness-transforming industries' (1997a: 133). Lii, like Fore, is hopeful that 'Hollywood movies will be changed dramatically' and that 'Jackie Chan . . . will definitely be of equal importance to Stallone and Schwarzenegger' (1998: 136). Instead, Chan found himself 'of equal importance' to Chris Tucker and Owen Wilson – in *Rush Hour 2* (2001), he had even slipped to second billing. It was not until *The One* that a former Hong Kong star, Jet Li, received sole top billing in a Hollywood film – he was, after all, playing both lead roles.

[. . .]

Kissed by the Dragon: Jet Li in Hollywood

Not unlike Jackie Chan, the repackaging of Jet Li for Western multiplexes was founded on a combination of carefully chosen English-language roles and dubbed versions of his more 'Westernised' Hong Kong films. His scene-stealing debut in *Lethal Weapon 4* was followed by a repackaged *Black Mask*, dubbed and restored with a hip-hop soundtrack. *Black Mask's* US soundtrack was a reminder of Hollywood's continuing belief in the symbiotic relationship between kung fu movies and urban black youth. *Romeo Must Die* (2000) was described in advance publicity as a 'hip-hop kung fu movie', and Li was cast opposite the late r'n'b Diva Aaliyah – he appeared in the promo video for her hit single 'Try Again'.[5] 'I know hip-hop', Li's Han Sing insists at one point, turning his baseball cap around and tugging his trousers down slightly, as the narrative works hard to ally him with Afro-American culture. The film deals with tensions between Afro-American and Chinese-American criminal empires operating on the Oakland waterfront. The conflict comes down to competing patriarchs. Isaak O'Day (Delroy Lindo), father of Aaliyah's Trish, is avuncular, a doting father who wants to go legit but is betrayed by his manipulative enforcer (Isaiah Washington), while Ch'u Sing (Henry O), betrays both of his sons, allowing Hong Kong cop Han to take the fall for him (we first meet Li in a Hong Kong prison) and having his younger son killed when he threatens to rock the boat. Han overthrows his Chinese father, while his 'forbidden' romance with Trish finds him a new father, namely Isaak. But *Romeo Must Die* does not work quite as neatly as this reading might suggest, largely because of its inability to integrate Li successfully into the film. Its nominal star is often a peripheral figure – we are 45 minutes in before his backstory is explained, and his 'romance' with Trish largely has to be taken on trust. While the narrative seeks to displace Han from his Chinese family, Li (the star) works best within the 'Chinese' scenes, delivering his lines in Mandarin and bringing his usual quiet intensity to the scenes with his father. At the opposite extreme, when Trish takes him to a club, cajoles him into dancing and then sings to him – a showcase for Aaliyah's talents, just as the fights are for Li's – his acute embarrassment and discomfort are all too evident. If the film cannot integrate Jet Li into his own film, it stumbles even more over its incorporation of 'Hong Kong action'.

Romeo Must Die is, visually, a post-*Matrix* film, but it does not have its predecessor's fantasy remit to explain why fighters float weightlessly in mid-air, the air around them looking like a computer simulation. While most of the film follows 'realistic' conventions, the CGI-enhanced wirework looks as though it has strayed in from a very different movie.

If Jackie Chan's unassuming persona once seemed at odds with Hollywood's conception of an action hero, Jet Li's chaste asceticism seems to have posed a similar conundrum; a number of Western critics have commented on his 'lack of chemistry' with female leads, as though sexual potency was the ultimate test of a leading man.[6] In the very different context of Hong Kong cinema, Li has worked perfectly well as a romantic lead of sorts, albeit a reserved one who needs women to take the lead. But Li's English-language films sometimes feel the need to 'explain' his sexual reticence. In *Kiss of the Dragon*, Bridget Fonda's hooker-with-a-heart comes right out with it and asks him if he is gay – quizzed about his 'type', he has earlier blurted out that 'I don't have (a) type'. *Lethal Weapon 4* envelopes the question in a racial jibe – 'Enter the Drag Queen', smirks Mel Gibson, trying to provoke Li into making a move. The scene recalls a similar moment from Bruce Lee's original, pre-*Big Boss*, Hollywood career, menacing James Garner's eponymous hero in *Marlowe*: 'Say, you're pretty light on your feet', offers Garner, 'Perhaps just a little bit gay?' In *The One*, Li's bad guy Yulaw arrives at a prison colony, prompting one inmate to comment on his 'pretty mouth'. 'I'm nobody's bitch!', he roars before beating them all senseless, *'you are mine!' Lethal Weapon 4* draws on a sado-polymorphous decadence familiar from the 'Yellow Peril' fantasy – he smiles sensuously as he garrottes one of his own gang. *Kiss of the Dragon* seems especially titillated by the enigma of Li's sexuality – making his first contact in Paris, he receives the terse instruction, 'Men's toilet – *now*!'

Romeo Must Die was perceived by many to have 'wasted' Li, and *Kiss of the Dragon* was made partly in response to fan's comments on the Jet Li website. As co-star Bridget Fonda says, 'he's doing something that's absolutely real . . . we're not talking special effects, we're not talking what the camera can make it look like', while Li promised 'no cable, no special effects, just hardcore fighting' (DVD commentary): The fights carry some kinetic force, even if they lack the grace of Li's best work. An early fight plays like a more brutal variation on Jackie Chan as Li makes use of steam irons, spin-dryers and a meticulously projected billiard ball. Later, he takes out twenty odd karate experts with fighting sticks, his arms a blur. *Kiss of the Dragon* has its shortcomings – it gets rather too much mileage out of having Fonda slapped around and humiliated by various brutal pimps. But one could never mistake it for anything other than a Jet Li vehicle, and its rapid production seemed to accomodate Hong Kong cinema's guerrilla filmmaking. The film grew out of what seems to have been a genuine collaboration across national cinemas – a Hong Kong star (Li co-produced and devised the original story) and choreographer (Corey Yuen), a French director (Chris Nahon) and a producer whose career blurs the line between 'French' and 'American' cinema (Luc Besson).

Kiss of the Dragon is described in its pressbook as a combination of Luc Besson's *Leon* (1994) and Li's *Fist of Legend*. The debt to *Leon* is a fairly obvious one – the metallic hues of Thierry Argogast's cinematography, a Mephistophelian cop villain (Tcheky Karyo replacing Gary Oldman), and an immigrant hero whose facility in combat is matched by his naïvety with women. Jean Reno's Leon must, of course, contend with underage Natalie Portman, but co-writer Robert Mark Kamen played to a blurring of Li's on and offscreen persona:

> Jet is the most straightforward and upstanding man I've ever met in my life, and we made Liu the same way. Luc and I asked ourselves what's the most uncomfortable position we could put the character in . . . And Luc said, 'Oh, it's very simple; she's a prostitute'. (*Kiss of the Dragon* Pressbook)

The connection to *Fist of Legend* is more tenuous, except as an assurance that *Kiss of the Dragon* would showcase a grittier Li than *Romeo Must Die* had done. Liu Juan, a Beijing special agent, is closer to the character Li played in *Bodyguard from Beijing*, a tough 'professional' whose defences the heroine must break down. Liu has 'no wife, no children. His only dedication is to his work.' In *Bodyguard from Beijing*, romantic and political union are conflated, but *Kiss of the Dragon* has rather less on its mind. Nevertheless, there is evidence of a yielding to both 'Hong Kong' and 'China'. If the 'Coming to America' narrative stresses the need for the Asian hero to accommodate to the West, *Kiss of the Dragon*'s postcard Paris (Eiffel Tower, Arc de Triomphe, Place de la Concorde) is a moral cesspool to be cleaned up by the upright Chinese cop. At one point, he flattens several policemen with the French Tricolour. Franco-Chinese relations are less than amicable – 'What is our miserable history compared to yours?' sneers Tcheky Karyo's psychotic Richard. Liu's expertise is defined by both 'History' and 'Technology' – deprived of his gun, he makes imaginative use of acupuncture needles sellotaped to his wrist. The titular, and fatal, 'kiss' is given to Richard by one of these needles, sending all of his blood on a one-way trip to his head, whereupon it exits via his nose, mouth, ears and eyes.

How to read this apparent European self-loathing, this yielding to the other? The film sends out conflicting messages about racial difference, messages coded through differently proportioned bodies. We are forever reminded of how everyone towers over Li, a device often used to stress his deceptive vulnerability in an unfamiliar locale. But as he assures Fonda's Jessica that she can trust him, a long shot seems designed to underline the fact that she, too, is significantly taller than her Chinese Knight. The shot looks like a visual joke, but at whose expense? Jet Li's? Our assumptions about bodies and their capacity for certain kinds of action? In one scene, Liu trounces the pimp who slaps Jessica once too often – 'I would really appreciate it if you don't do that again', he says slowly, but the warning falls on deaf ears. Just when the fight seems to be over, a huge figure fills the doorway – a large, black fighter removes his coat to reveal a mass of muscles. A slow tracking shot sutures us into Liu's reaction – *now* he is going to have his work cut out! But this film backs speed over size every time, and Liu cuts his gigantic opponent down to size. At least one commentator has seen this sequence as exhibiting an 'unchallenged, conventional' racism, making stereotypical and dehumanising use of the figure of the black behemoth (White 2001: 13). But how might one read this scene in relation to Li's later fight with the white, blonde-haired brothers, one of whose gigantic build suggests an equally stereotypical Aryan *übermensch*?

The One, like its scenery-chewing villain Yulaw (Jet Li), travels across parallel universes policed by 'Multiverse' agents. Yulaw is himself a former agent, corrupted by the discovery that the death of his parallel 'selves' empowers his remaining incarnations exponentially until there is 'only one'. One other 'self' remains – L.A. county sheriff Gabe (also Li), who finds himself Yulaw's target. The film was originally designed as a pretext for World Wrestling Entertainment star The Rock to lay the smackdown on himself, and the film was re-written to incorporate Li's 'spiritual' concerns when he took over as lead. *The One*'s most interesting concession to its star is the equipping of his two characters with different fighting styles. Yulaw, who adheres to the principle that 'the shortest distance between two points is a straight line', practices the straight-line attack of *xingyi*, an 'internal' style with a 'hard', forward rolling power; a *xingyi* boxer, so the saying goes, 'never backs up' (Allen 2001: 37). The gentler Gabe, yin to Yulaw's yang, practices the 'soft', circular *bagua*, which has its basis in Taoist circle-walking meditations derived from the *I Ching*. The specificity of the film's fighting styles, and particularly their use as shorthand characterisation, indicates *The One*'s debt to the Hong Kong martial arts tradition, which frequently makes economical, accessible and instructive use of characters with contrasting fighting styles. Granted, Li's *bagua* 'shapes' are the best thing about the film, even as the sub-*Matrix* effects seem annoyingly determined to upstage them. But the film does not feel the need to explain the protagonists' opposed styles – only martial arts fans and practitioners would be able to name them – so that, in effect, they function largely as both 'exotic' stylisation and a means of telling 'good' Jet Li from 'bad.' The film makes references to 'balance', but it seems to derive from conflicting discourses and origins. One version is implicitly indebted to Taoism and the interdependence of yin and yang – both Gabe and Yulaw need to survive at the end of the film to preserve this harmony. But the grey-suited Multiverse bureaucrats invoke a 'balance' that seems more suggestive of a moribund status quo in need of shaking up by the anarchic Yulaw, finally seen kicking ass on an intergalactic prison colony as the camera pulls back into an elaborate 'effects' shot. *The One* is interesting, but incoherent, partly because its primary agenda is to be as many things to as many people as possible. Of course, Hong Kong cinema can be overeager to please, too, and in any case, there is some yielding going on in *The One*. *Kung Fu Qigong* magazine used the film's release as a focus for a special *bagua/xingyi* issue which further served to orient a cult audience towards reading *The One* as a 'real' martial arts film (Burr 2001; Allen 2001). But, ultimately, *The One* and, conversely, the isolated success of *Kiss of the Dragon*, suggest that Li's Western vehicles need building from the ground up for his physical and acting talents to shine, and for his quietly heroic persona to make sense. Even more so than Chan, he seems especially vulnerable in his disembedding from Chinese generic traditions. Take away the *bagua* and the FX and *The One* starts to look worryingly like a Jean-Claude Van Damme vehicle, as several unsympathetic critics pointed out.

'All Under Heaven': Breaking Out of The (Hollywood) Matrix

The choreographer-as-star is the most recent development in Hong Kong's infiltration of Western cinema. Jackie Chan largely choreographs his own fight scenes, as Bruce Lee did, even though he has sometimes had to liaise with American stunt co-ordinators. Jet Li brought Corey Yuen with him to work on his first four English-language vehicles, and Yuen recently directed the Luc Besson-produced *The Transporter* (2002). Meanwhile, Sammo Hung choreographed Tsui Hark's Van Damme vehicles *Double Team* (1997) and *Knock Off* (1999), while Donnie Yen worked on *Highlander: Endgame* (2000) and *Blade 2* (2002) as well as appearing in *Shanghai Knights* (2003). However, it is Yuen Wo-ping who has enjoyed the highest profile, for his contribution to *The Matrix*, *Crouching Tiger, Hidden Dragon* and Quentin Tarantino's forthcoming *Kill Bill*.[7] Nevertheless, Yuen was conspicuously absent from *Crouching Tiger*'s Academy Award nominations – no such category presently exists (unlike special effects), another indicator of how different kinds of cinematic labour (and spectacle) are valued. Yuen has been in the forefront of every major development in martial arts-based Hong Kong action, from comedy to modern day action, and his career found a new lease of life in the 'new wave' martial arts films of the early 1990s. Ackbar Abbas has argued that the *Once Upon a Time in China* series was distinguished by 'its mastery of *special effects*' (1996: 298), but it would be misleading to suggest that performative skill completely disappeared because Hong Kong wirework has largely remained a pro-filmic spectacle. Neverthless, this points to the dialogue between different action technologies in recent Hollywood films. Hong Kong's representation of 'speed' – undercranked action – remains too low-tech for Hollywood, too reminiscent of silent cinema, however exciting it is when done well. Compare Donnie Yen's breakneck-speed 'invisible kicks' in *Iron Monkey* with *The Matrix*'s digital 'bullet-time' for two very different representations of martial arts velocity. But wirework and CGI could profitably converge – in Hong Kong, wires are 'lit out' (Orick and Mathies 1999: 58), but *Crouching Tiger* used 300 digital wire-removals as well as effects like sky replacement in scenes like Chow Yun-fat's bamboo-treetop duel with Zhang Ziyi (Lee and Schamus 2000: 122). *Hero*, choreographed by another wire-fu maestro Ching Siu-tung, uses similar technology when Jet Li fights Tony Leung on the surface of a lake or Zhang Ziyi takes to the treetops once more in her fight with Maggie Cheung's Flying Snow.

The Matrix seemed to create a new genre, 'Cyber-fu', in which kung fu skills are downloaded from a computer programme. In one emblematic scene, Trinity (Carrie Anne-Moss) floats into the air and holds the pose as the camera circles her, until this suspended moment is broken by a lethal kick. She dodges bullets by running up and around the walls of the room, but the final *pièce de résistance* is an over-the-shoulder kick to the face of a police officer who unwisely grabs her from behind. *The Matrix* did not only set a new standard for special effects; it also initiated a trend for 'authenticating' Hollywood stars when Yuen had the cast trained so that they could perform their own fight scenes.

'Our sense of reality is different from their sense of reality', explains Richard Donner on the DVD commentary for *Lethal Weapon 4*, explaining his modification of Hong Kong action. Hollywood, Bordwell suggests, is 'unusually fastidious about realism of detail, restraint of emotion, and plausibility of plot' (2000a: 19). Hong Kong cinema, too, has its own hierarchies of 'realism' – wirework is much less extravagant in modern-day films than period fantasies. In Hollywood, wirework initially came in through the fantasy door.[8] What *The Matrix* does is to download and authenticate Hong Kong 'reality', to reconstitute it as a virtual action space into which it can insert its protagonists. Morpheus (Lawrence Fishburne) explains to Neo that in the digital world, 'rules like gravity . . . are no different than the rules of the computer system. Some of them can be bent, others can be broken'. As some commentators have noted (King 2000: 191), *The Matrix* is only superficially dystopian and easily seduced by possibilities of the virtual action world. By the end of the film, Neo and Trinity do not just 'do' John Woo – with the sort of limitless ammo usually only enjoyed by Lara Croft – they *outdo* him as they scale walls, performing cartwheels as countless spent shells litter the floor. *Romeo Must Die*'s 'failure' to incorporate wirework seemed to lie precisely in its inability to negotiate a coherent 'reality' for its interfamilial/interracial crime drama and wired-up action – 'This isn't *The Matrix*, idiots!!!' commented one disgruntled viewer (Internet Movie Database 2000).

But there is another narrative embedded in *The Matrix*, where the 'utopia' of Hollywood showcasing Hong Kong talent gives way to a 'dystopia' of appropriation and marginalisation – there was some hope of Jet Li appearing in the sequels, but Joel Silver clearly felt the money could be better spent. In any case, the film's downloading of 'Hong Kong' can also be seen as a metaphor for the Wachowski's use of Yuen Wo-ping. In Hong Kong, fight choreographers are like Second Unit directors, sometimes more. Fight scenes are not storyboarded or scripted – action and camera angles are semi-improvised by the stunt director's team, pretty much 'edited' in camera with little coverage and no 'masters' (see Bordwell 2000: 210–47). Hollywood's authorial discourses, however, favour the deification of the director(s). According to Larry Wachowski:

> Wo(-ping) was the choreographer, but we were the ones who were in
> complete control at all times . . . He positioned the camera where he

thought it should be – Hong Kong choreographers always pick out the camera angles – and then Andy and I would look at them. Some of them we liked, some of them we didn't like – Many times Wo's shots just didn't meet our criteria, so we added moving camera shots, dollies, stuff like that around sections that we wanted. (Quoted in Persons 1999: 21)

Yuen had a slightly different interpretation:

In American movies, they're all storyboarded and they leave little room for inspiration on the set. It's good that everything's organised, but if I have any inspiration on the set, it's only good if the actors can follow. Jet Li and Jackie Chan can follow, but not these actors. (Quoted in Fischer 1999: 26)

The fight scenes were scripted and storyboarded by the Wachowskis, based on scenes from Yuen's Hong Kong films. They showed the storyboards to Yuen, who shot video footage using his stunt-team; the footage was shown to the Wachowskis, who approved and/or vetoed scenes. The cast were then 'taught' the moves from the videos so that they could perform them in the final film (Orick and Mathies 1999: 58–9). Spontaneity is not the only casualty in the martial arts scenes – postmodern appropriation can erase any sense of context or resonance. When Neo mimics Bruce Lee (cockily thumbing his nose) and Wong Fei-hung's signature stance (arm extended, palm turned upwards in 'invitation'), he points to the limits of 'de-territorialised' images and commodities. *The Matrix* does not need Jet Li precisely because 'goods mean more and people mean less' in certain transnational image-flows.

In some ways, *The Matrix* and its many imitators offer worst-case scenarios for the future of diasporic Hong Kong action – Asian expertise absorbed into a cinema that continues to marginalise Asian performers. In 1997, Steve Fore envisioned a 'best-case scenario' with 'directors, cinematographers, actors, and other personnel oscillating semi-permanently between hemispheres, working on a range of projects with different geolinguistic emphases' (1997a: 135).[9] Until recently, only Jackie Chan displayed anything like this kind of mobility – *Rush Hour* was followed by the more 'local' *Gorgeous/Bor Lei Jun* (1999), *Shanghai Noon* by *The Accidental Spy/Te Wu Mi Cheng* (2001), *Rush Hour 2* by *Highbinders* (2002). Jet Li, too, seems to be pursuing a degree of international mobility, not only with *Kiss of the Dragon* but Zhang Yimou's *Hero*, a Mandarin-language historical martial arts epic distributed and partly funded by Miramax.

It is difficult to predict the long-term influence and the significance of the crossover success of *Crouching Tiger*, but *Hero*, the most expensive Chinese film to date, suggests that it was not a one-off. There are some complex issues raised by what was seen as *Crouching Tiger's* comparative 'failure' in parts of Asia (Rose 2001), but in many ways, Ang Lee's film seemed to realise precisely the kind of cinema Fore might have envisioned – an émigré Taiwanese director, a script produced by an ongoing process of translation between Chinese and American writers, two stars and a choreographer from Hong Kong, one Taiwanese and one Mainland star. Most importantly, it suggested that Asian action had a broader range of options than simply being grafted onto variable Hollywood films until another 'fad' came along. Seemingly conceived as a pan-Asian blockbuster, *Crouching Tiger* played in the West as what *Sight and Sound's* cover copy dubbed 'Martial Arthouse' (December 2000), seemingly bestowing cultural capital on a lowbrow genre (at least for critics whose exposure to the genre was narrow), Ang Lee's film succeeded partly by appealing to audiences who would not normally watch kung fu films, thus the inherent appeal of Jane Austen seemingly let loose in *jianghu*. At its worst, the film's Western success could be construed as 'a visually and narratively exoticised representation of China's past that does not challenge white, Western stereotypes of the "Orient"' (Fore 1997b: 248).[10] Yet its breathtaking action scenes confirm that there was more going on than a particularly sophisticated manifestation of neo-Orientalism – cult Asian-American magazine *Giant Robot* dubbed it 'the best kung fu movie ever' (Ko 2001: 20–1). Yuen Wo-ping's choreography blends wirework, CGI and performative skill so artfully that Abbas' 'space of otherness' starts to materialise in bamboo forests, crowded taverns and across the rooftops of Qing-era Beijing – it is not just 'East' and 'West' which are overcome, but 'past' and 'future', technology and the performing body.

Taken together, *Crouching Tiger* and *Hero* augur well for a transnational (and 'Asianised') prestige martial arts cinema; sumptuous production values, state-of-the-art choreography, to-die-for Chinese casts and distinguished auteurs not usually associated with 'chop sockies'. In some ways, *Hero* seems packaged to replicate *Crouching Tiger's* Western success, with a virtually identical score by Tan Dun and similarly CGI-enhanced wirework, although Chris Doyle's photography (as several reviews have noted) also recalls *Ashes of Time* (as does the casting of Cheung and Leung). If its fights surpass its predecessor, some of this is attributable to its cast; many kung fu fans were eager to see Jet Li and Donnie Yen's first on-screen duel since *Once Upon a Time in China 2*. But there are important differences, too. Ang Lee's description of *Crouching Tiger* as '*Sense and Sensibility* with martial arts' underlines its cross-cultural conception, but *Hero* is more Sinicist in outlook. The film is set during the Warring States Era (403–221 BC), during which Qin Shihuang (Chen Daoming), King of Qin, sought to conquer and 'unify' China; the film has been widely read as a metaphor for the PRC's desire to unify China, Hong Kong and Taiwan. But the film's notion of 'All Under Heaven', like its tyrant King, is decidedly ambivalent. Qin Shihuang is both a Sinicist visionary (he built the Great Wall and founded China's first Dynasty) and a homogenising dictator who will erase local 'difference'; he tells would-be assassin Nameless (Jet Li) that he will standardise written Chinese. Nameless and Broken Sword (Tony Leung) spare the King and sacrifice themselves in anticipation of a unified

China, a 'message' that has not found favour with all of the film's reviewers. *Hero*, interestingly, has outperformed *Crouching Tiger* in South-East Asia, and was nominated for an Academy Award, but it remains to be seen whether it will repeat its predecessor's success in the West. Of course, global mass media, too, threatens to unite 'all under heaven' in the most homogenising way. *Crouching Tiger* and *Hero* find *wu xia* hero(in)es, as stealthy, resourceful and irresistible as Nameless, Broken Sword and Flying Snow, still storming the global 'palace'. The 'palace' seems unlikely to surrender, much less fall, to this invasion, but there is evidence that it is starting to *yield*.

NOTES

1. It is also, of course, a familiar cliché in the characterisation of Hong Kong. In the production featurette *Location: Hong Kong with Enter the Dragon* (1973), the 'jewel of South-East Asia' is described as 'a curious mixture of modern metropolis and ancient Chinese culture'.
2. Interestingly, Chow is the only Hong Kong star to crossover *without* martial arts skills, even though the later acquired some for *Crouching Tiger*. *Bullet Proof Monk* (2003) was quick to capitalise on them.
3. The 'flied lice' jokes suggest that this cult audience was probably not imagined as Chinese. 'I was condemned in Hong Kong and Shanghai' says director Richard Donner, 'but that was about it' (DVD Commentary). In fact, *Lethal Weapon 4* was heavily criticised by Chinese-Americans for its racist depictions.
4. By contrast, Hong Kong did exist in the realm of the real – the media coverage of the Handover.
5. His most recent Hollywood film, *Cradle 2 the Grave* [2003], teams him with hip-hop star DMX, who plays a cameo role in *Romeo Must Die*. Li's weakest film to date finds him even more peripheral than in *Romeo Must Die*.
6. For an interesting account of Asian-American perceptions of Li's sexuality, see Stringer 2003.
7. Tarantino's eclectic cast includes David Carradine, Lau Kar-fau and Sonny Chiba, while star Uma Thurman is clad in a variation on *Game of Death*'s famous jumpsuit. Lau's character in named 'Bai Mei', but whether this is more than fantasy name-dropping remains to be seen.
8. I am thinking especially of fantasy television shows like *Xena – Warrior Princess* (1995–2000) and *Buffy the Vampire Slayer* (1996–). In *Xena*, particularly, the campy tone seemed to license over-the-top wire-aided stunts.
9. A pan-Asian cinema that fits this description has existed for a while, but had not until recently extended beyond South-East Asia.
10. In British cinemas, at least, the wire-and-CGI-aided scenes of Bight seemed to inspire giggles as well as gasps, another way in which the film could be both enjoyed and marginalised. The 'exoticising' of *Crouching Tiger* can be partly attributed to what Fore calls 'semiotic repture' [1997a: 134]. One of the casualties of cultural translation. According to Ang Lee, 'the film is a kind of dream of China, a China that probably never existed, except in my boyhood fantasies in Taiwan' (Lee and Schamus 2000: 7).

WORKS CITED

Abbas, Ackbar (1996) 'Cultural Studies in a Postculture', in Carry Nelson and Dilip Parameshwar Gaonkar (eds) *Disciplinarity and Dissent in Cultural Studies*. London and New York: Routledge.

Allen, Frank (2001) 'The Line and the Circle: Comparing the Fighting Arts of Hsing-i vs. Bagua', *Kung Fu/Qigong*, December: 36–8.

Bordwell, David (2000) *Planet Hong Kong: Popular Cinema and the Art of Entertainment*. Cambridge, Massachusetts and London: Harvard University Press.

Burr, Martha (2000) 'Jet Li is Still the Hero', *Kung Fu Qigong*, 4: 30–7, 40–1, 121–2.

Burr, Martha (2001) 'The Big Jet Li Interview', *Kung Fu Qigong*, December: 16–29.

Fischer, Dennis (1999) 'Matrix Martial Arts', *Cinéfantastique*, 31, 5: 26.

Fore, Steve (1997a) 'Home, Migration, Identity: Hong Kong Workers Join the Chinese Diaspora', in Law Kar (ed.) *Fifty years of Electric Shadows*. Hong Kong: Hong Kong International Film Festival/Urban Council, 130–5.

Fore, Steve (1997b) 'Jackie Chan and the Cultural Dynamics of Global Entertainment', in Sheldon Hsiao-peng Lu (ed.) (1997) *Transnational Chinese Cinemas: Identity Nationhood, Gender*. Honolulu: University of Hawaii Press, 239–62.

Fore, Steve (2001) 'Life Imitates Entertainment: Home and Dislocation in the Films of Jackie Chan' in Esther Yau (ed.) *At Full Speed: Hong Kong Cinema in a Borderless World*. Minneapolis and London: University of Minnesota Press, 115–41.

Internet Movie Database (2000) 'User Comments: *Romeo Must Die*', http://us.imdb.com/commentsShow? 165929.

King, Geoff (2000) *Spectacular Narratives: Hollywood in the Age of the Blockbuster*. London and New York: I. B. Tauris.

Ko, Claudine (2001) '*Crouching Tiger*: Its the Best Kung Fu Movie Ever', *Giant Robot*, 20: 20–1.

Lee, Ang and Schamus, James (2000) *Crouching Tiger, Hidden Dragon: A Portrait of the Ang Lee Film*. London: Faber.

Lii, Ding-Tzann (1998) 'A Colonised Empire: Reflections on the Expansion of Hong Kong Films in Asian Countries' in Kuan-Hsing Chen (ed.) *Trajectories: Inter-Asia Cultural Studies*. London and New York: Routledge. 122–41.

Lo, Kwai-cheung (2001) 'Transnationalism of the Local in Hong Kong Cinema of the 1990s', in Esther Yau (ed.) (2001) *At Full Speed: Hong Kong Cinema in a Borderless World*. Minneapolis and London: University of Minnesota Press, 261–76.

Marchetti, Gina (1993) *Romance and the 'Yellow Peril'; Race, Sex and Discursive Strategies in Hollywood Fiction*. Berkeley, Los Angeles and London: University of California Press.

Orick, Josh and Eric Mathies (1999) 'Wired Style: Wire Work Special', *Giant Robot*, 16: 57–62.

Persons, Mitch (1999) 'Matrix: The Wachowski Brothers', *Cinéfantastique*, 31, 5: 20–1.

Pestilence Darryl (1998) 'Bruce Li: An Appreciation', *Asian Cult Cinema*, 18: 43–6.

Rose, Steve (2001) 'The Film is so slow – it's like grandma telling stories'. *The Guardian: G2*, February 13: 14–15.

Sharrett, Christopher (1996) 'The Horror Film in Neoconservative Culture', in Barry Keith Grant (ed.) *The Dread of Difference: Gender and the Horror Film*. Austin: University of Texas Press. 253–76.

Stringer, Julian (2003) 'Talking About Jet Li: Transnational Chinese Movie Stardom and Asian-American Internet Reception', in Gary Rawnsley and Ming-yeh Rawnsley (eds) *Political Communication in Greater China: The Construction and Reflection of Identity*. London and New York: Routledge-Curzon.

White, Armand (2001) 'Reality Bites', *Sight and Sound*, 11, 8: 12–13.

BIBLIOGRAPHY

Abel, Richard (1984), *French Cinema: The First Wave, 1915–1929*, Princeton: Princeton University Press.

Abel, Richard (1991), *The Ciné Goes to Town: French Cinema, 1896–1914*, Berkeley: University of California Press.

Abel, Richard (1999), *The Red Rooster Scare: Making Cinema American, 1900–1910*, Berkeley: University of California Press.

Abel, Richard (ed.) (1995), *Silent Film*, New Brunswick: Rutgers University Press.

Acland, Charles (2003), *Screen Traffic: Movies, Multiplexes and Global Culture*, Durham, NC: Duke University Press.

Adorno, Theodor and Max Horkheimer [1947] (1979), *Dialectic of Enlightenment*, London: Verso.

Aitken, Ian (1990), *Film and Reform: John Grierson and the Documentary Film Movement*, London: Routledge.

Aitken, Ian (ed.) (1998), *The Documentary Film Movement: An Anthology*, Edinburgh: Edinburgh University Press.

Allen, Robert (1990), 'From Exhibition to Reception: Reflections on the Audience in Film History', *Screen* 31 (4), pp. 347–56.

Allen, Robert, and Douglas Gomery (1985), *Film History: Theory and Practice*, Boston, MA: McGraw-Hill.

Allen, Robert, Melvyn Stokes, and Richard Maltby (eds) (2004), *Hollywood Abroad: Audiences and Cultural Exchange*, London: BFI.

Altman, Rick (2004), *Silent Film Sound*, New York: Columbia University Press.

Ambler, Charles (2001), 'Popular Films and Colonial Audiences: The Movies in Northern Rhodesia', *American Historical Review* (Feb.), pp. 81–105.

Anderson, Christopher (1994), *Hollywood TV: The Studio System in the Fifties*, Austin: University of Texas Press.

Armes, Roy (1978), *A Critical History of British Cinema*, Oxford: Oxford University Press.

Armes, Roy (1987), *Third World Film Making and the West*, Berkeley: University of California Press.

Ashby, Justine and Andrew Higson (2000), *British Cinema, Past and Present*, London: Routledge.

Austin, Bruce A. (1988), *Immediate Seating*, Belmont: Wadsworth Publishing Company.

Austin, Thomas (2002), *Hollywood, Hype and Audiences: Selling and Watching Popular Film in the 1990s*, Manchester: Manchester University Press.

Balio, Tino (1993), *Grand Design: Hollywood as a Modern Business Enterprise, 1930–1939*, New York: Charles Scribner's Sons.

Balio, Tino (ed.) (1985), *The American Film Industry*, Madison: University of Wisconsin Press.

Balio, Tino (ed.) (1990), *Hollywood in the Age of Television*, Boston: Unwin Hyman.

Bamford, Kenton (1999), *Distorted Images*, London: I. B. Tauris.

Barker, Martin (2003), *Knowing Audiences: Judge Dredd, Its Friends, Fans and Foes*, Luton: University of Luton.

Barker, Martin, Jane Arthurs and Ramaswami Harindranath (2001), *The Crash Controversy*, London: Wallflower Press.

Barnouw, Erik (1974), *Documentary: A History of Nonfiction Film*, New York: Oxford University Press.

Barr, Charles (ed.) (1987), *All Our Yesterdays: 90 Years of British Cinema*, London: BFI.

Barton, Ruth (2004), *Irish National Cinema*, London: Routledge.

Basinger, Jeanine (2000), *Silent Stars*, Middletown: Wesleyan University Press.

Bazin, André, (2004), *What is Cinema? Volume 1*, Berkeley: University of California Press.

Belton, John (1922), *Widescreen Cinema*, Cambridge, MA: Harvard University Press.

Beltrán, Mary (2005), 'The New Hollywood Racelessness: Only the Fast, Furious (and Multiracial) Will Survive', *Cinema Journal* 44 (2), pp. 50–67.

Berenstein, Rhona (1995), *Attack of the Leading Ladies*, New York: Columbia University Press.

Bernstein, Matthew (ed.) (1999), *Controlling Hollywood: Censorship and Regulation in the Studio Era*, New Brunswick: Rutgers University Press.

Berry, Chris (ed.) (1991), *Perspectives on Chinese Cinema*, London: BFI.

Biskind, Peter (1999), *Easy Riders, Raging Bulls: How the Sex-Drugs-and-Rock 'N' Roll Generation Saved Hollywood*, New York: Simon and Schuster.

Blake, Michael (1993), *Lon Chaney: The Man Behind the Thousand Faces*, Bloomington: Indiana University Press.

Bordwell, David (1993), *The Cinema of Eisenstein*, Cambridge, MA: Harvard University Press.

Bordwell, David (2000), *Planet Hong Kong: Popular Cinema and the Art of Entertainment*, Cambridge, MA: Harvard University Press.

Bordwell, David and Noel Carroll (eds) (1996), *Post-Theory: Reconstructing Film Studies*, Madison: University of Wisconsin Press.

Bordwell, David, Janet Staiger and Kristin Thompson (1985), *The Classical Hollywood Cinema: Film Style and Mode of Production to 1960*, London: Routledge.

Bowser, Eileen (1990), *The Transformation of Cinema, 1907–1915*, Berkeley: University of California Press.

Bowser Pearl, Jane Gaines and Charles Musser (eds) (2001), *Oscar Micheaux and his Circle: African-American Filmmaking and Race Cinema of the Silent Era*, Bloomington: Indiana University Press.

Brode, Douglas (2004), *From Walt to Woodstock: How Disney Made the Counter-Culture*, Denton: University of North Texas Press.

Brunsdon, Charlotte (1997), *Screen Tastes: From Soap Opera to Satellite Dishes*, London: Routledge.

Budd, Mike (ed.) (1990), *The Cabinet of Dr Caligari: Texts, Contexts*, New Brunswick: Rutgers University Press.

Burch, Noel (1990), *Life to these Shadows*, London: BFI.

Burton, Julianne (1986), *Cinema and Social Change in Latin America: Conversations with Filmmakers*, Austin: University of Texas Press.

Butler, Ivan (1971), *To Encourage the Art of the Film*: The Story of the British Film Institute, London: Robert Hale.

Butsch, Richard (2000), *The Making of American Audiences: From Stage to Television, 1750–1990*, Cambridge: Cambridge University Press.

Cadullo, Burt (ed.) (1997), *Bazin at Work: Major Essays and Reviews from the Forties and Fifties*, London: Routledge.

Chabria, S. (ed.) (1994), *Light of Asia: Silent Cinema in India, 1912–1934*, Bloomington: Indiana University Press.

Chanan, Michael (1980), *The Dream that Kicks: The Prehistory and Early Years of Cinema in Britain*, London: Routledge and Kegan Paul.

Chapman, James (2004), *Cinemas of the World*, London: Reaktion Books.

Charney, Leo and Vanessa R. Schwartz (eds) (1995), *Cinema and the Invention of Modern Life*, Berkeley: University of California Press.

Cherchi Usai, Paolo (1994), *Burning Passions: An Introduction to the Study of Silent Film*, London: BFI.

Cherchi Usai, Paolo (2001), *The Death of Cinema: History, Cultural Memory and the Digital Dark Age*, London: BFI.

Christie, Ian (1994), *The Last Machine: Early Cinema and the Birth of the Modern World*, London: BBC Educational Developments.

Clark, Paul (1987), *Chinese Cinema: Culture and Politics since 1949*, New York: Cambridge University Press.

Cohan, Steven (1997), *Masked Men: Masculinity and the Movies in the Fifties*, Bloomington: Indiana University Press.

Collins, Jim Hilary Radner and Ava Preacher Collins (eds) (1992), *Film Theory Goes to the Movies*, London: Routledge.

Collins, Jim (1995), *Architectures of Excess: Cultural Life in the Information Age*, New York: Routledge.

Cook, David (2000), *Lost Illusions: American Cinema in the Shadow of Watergate and Vietnam 1970–1979*, New York: Charles Scribner's Sons.

Cowie, Peter (2005), *Revolution!: The Explosion of World Cinema in the Sixties*, London: Faber and Faber.

Crafton, Donald (1993), *Before Mickey: The Animated Film, 1898–1928*, Chicago: University of Chicago Press.

Crafton, Donald (1997), *The Talkies: American Cinema's Transition to Sound, 1926–1931*, New York: Charles Scribner's Sons.

Darley, Andrew (2000), *Visual Digital Culture*, London: Routledge.

DeBauche, Leslie Midkiff (1997), *Reel Patriotism: The Movies and World War I*, Madison: University of Wisconsin Press.

DeCordova, Richard (1990), *Picture Personalities: The Emergence of the Star System in America*, Urbana: University of Illinois Press.

Desai, Jigna (2004), *Beyond Bollywood: The Cultural Politics of South Asian Diasporic Film*, London: Routledge.

Desser, David (1988), *Eros Plus Massacre: An Introduction to the Japanese New Wave Cinema*, Bloomington: Indiana University Press.

Desser, David and Garth Jowett (eds) (2000), *Hollywood Goes Shopping*, Minneapolis: Minnesota University Press.

Diawara, Manthia (1992), *African Cinema: Politics and Culture*, Bloomington: Indiana University Press.

Diawara, Manthia (1993), *Black American Cinema*, London: Routledge.

Dickinson, Margaret and Sarah Street (1985), *Cinema and State: The Film Industry and the Government, 1927–1984*, London: BFI.

Doane, Mary Ann (1987), *The Desire to Desire: The Woman's Films of the 1940s*, Bloomington: Indiana University Press.

Docherty, David, David Morrison and Michael Tracey (1988), *The Last Picture Show?: Britain's Changing Film Audience*, London: BFI.

Doherty, Thomas (1989), *Teenagers and Teenpics: The Juvenilization of American Movies in the 1950s*, Boston, MA: Unwin Hyman.

Donald, James (ed.) (1989), *Fantasy and the Cinema*, London: BFI.

Dyer, Richard (1987), *Heavenly Bodies: Film Stars and Society*, London: BFI.

Dyer, Richard (1998), *Stars*, London: BFI.

Eisenstein, Sergei (1947), *The Film Sense*, New York: Harcourt, Brace and World.

Eisenstein, Sergei (1949), *Film Form: Essays in Film Theory*, New York: Harcourt, Brace and World.

Eisner, Lotte (1969), *The Haunted Screen*, London: Thames and Hudson.

Elsaesser, Thomas (1989), *New German Cinema: A History*, London: Macmillan.

Elsaesser, Thomas (2000), *Weimar Cinema and After: Germany's Historical Imaginary*, London: Routledge.

Elsaesser, Thomas (ed.) (1990), *Early Cinema: Space, Frame, Narrative*, London: BFI.

Erb, Cynthia (1998), *Tracking King Kong: A Hollywood Icon in World Culture*, Detroit: Wayne State University Press.

Eyles, Allen (2005), *Odeon Cinemas 2: From J. Arthur Rank to the Multiplex*, London: BFI.

Eyles, Allen (2005), *Odeon Cinemas: Oscar Deutsch Entertains Our Nation*, London: BFI.

Fischer, Lucy and Marcia Landy (eds) (2004), *Stars: The Film Reader*, London: Routledge.

Fitzsimmons, Linda and Sarah Street (1998), *Moving Performance: British Stage and Screen, 1890s–1920s*, Trowbridge: Flicks Books.

Fowler, Catherine (ed.) (2002), *The European Cinema Reader*, London: Routledge.

Friedberg, Anne (1993), *Window Shopping: Cinema and the Postmodern*, Berkeley: University of California Press.

Fuller, Kathryn and Kathryn Fuller-Seeley (1996), *At the Picture Show: Small-Town Audiences and the Creation of Movie Fan Culture*, Washington, DC: Smithsonian Books.

Fullerton, John (1998), *Celebrating 1895: The Centenary of Cinema*, Bloomington: Indiana University Press.

Gaines, Jane and Charlotte Herzog (eds) (1990), *Fabrications: Costuming and the Female Body*, London: Routledge.

Ganti, Tejaswini (2004), *Bollywood*, London: Routledge.

Garnham, Nicholas (1990), *Capitalism and Communication: Global Culture and the Economics of Information*, London: Sage.

Geraghty, Christine (2000), *British Cinema in the Fifties: Gender, Genre, and the 'New Look'*, London: Routledge.

Gittings, Chris (2001), *Canadian National Cinema*, London: Routledge.

Gledhill, Christine (2004), *Reframing British Cinema, 1918–1928: Between Restraint and Passion*, London: BFI.

Gledhill, Christine (ed.) (1987), *Home is Where the Heart is: Studies in Melodrama and the Woman's Film*, London: BFI.

Gledhill, Christine and Linda Williams (eds) (2000), *Reinventing Film Studies*, London: Arnold.

Gomery, Douglas (1992), *Shared Pleasures: A History of Movie Presentation in the United States*, Madison: University of Wisconsin Press.

Gomery, Douglas (2004), *The Coming of Sound*, London: Routledge.

Gomery, Douglas (2005), *The Hollywood Studio System*, London: BFI.

Grainge, Paul (ed.) (2003), *Memory and Popular Film*, Manchester: Manchester University Press.

Gray, Ann (1992), *Video Playtime: The Gendering of a Leisure Technology*, London: Routledge.

Gray, Richard (1996), *Cinemas in Britain*, Lund Humphries Publishers.

Grierson, John (1966), *Grierson on Documentary*, London: Faber and Faber.

Grieveson, Lee (2004), *Policing Cinema: Movies and Censorship in Early-Twentieth Century America*, Berkeley: University of California Press.

Grieveson, Lee and Peter Krämer (eds) (2004), *The Silent Cinema Reader*, London: Routledge.

Guerrero, Ed (1993), *Framing Blackness: The African American Image in Film*, Philadelphia: Temple University Press.

Gunning, Tom (1990), 'The Cinema of Attractions: Early Film, its Spectator and the Avant-Garde', in Thomas Elsaesser (ed.), *Early Cinema: Space, Frame, Narrative*, London: BFI, pp. 56–62.

Hake, Sabine (2001), *German National Cinema*, London: Routledge.

Hall, Ben (1961), *Best Remaining Seats*, Bramhall House.

Handel, A. Leo (1976), *Hollywood Looks at its Audience: A Report of Film Audience Research*, London: Ayer Company Publishers.

Hansen, Miriam (1991), *Babel and Babylon: Spectatorship in American Silent Film*, Cambridge, MA: Harvard University Press.

Haralovich, Mary Beth (1982), 'Advertising Heterosexuality', *Screen* 23 (2), pp. 50–60.

Harding, Colin and Simon Popple (1996), *In the Kingdom of Shadows: A Companion to Early Cinema*, Madison: Fairleigh Dickinson University Press.

Hardt, Ursula (1993), *Erich Pommer: Film Producer for Germany*, Los Angeles: University of California Press.

Hark, Ina Rae (ed.) (2002), *Exhibition, The Film Reader*, London: Routledge.

Harper, Sue (1994), *Picturing the Past: The Rise and Fall of the British Costume Film*, London: BFI.

Harper, Sue and Vincent Porter (2003), *British Cinema of the 1950s: The Decline of Deference*, Oxford: Oxford University Press.

Harries, Dan (ed.) (2002), *The New Media Book*, London: BFI.

Harvey, Sylvia (1978), *May '68 and Film Culture*, London: BFI.

Haskell, Molly (1987), *From Reverence to Rape: Treatment of Women in the Movies*, Chicago: University of Chicago Press.

Hayward, Susan (1993), *French National Cinema*, London: Routledge.

Hayward, Susan and Ginette Vincendeau (eds) (1990), *French Film, Texts and Contexts*, London: Routledge.

Heffernan, Kevin (2002), 'Inner City Exhibition and the Genre Film: Distributing *Night of the Living Dead*', *Cinema Journal* 41 (3), pp. 59–77.

Heffernan, Kevin (2004), *Ghouls, Gimmicks, and Gold: Horror Films and the American Movie Business, 1953–1968*, Durham, NC: Duke University Press.

Heider, Karl (1991), *Indonesian Cinema: National Culture on Screen*, Honolulu: University of Hawai'i Press.

Herman, Edward and Robert W. McChesney (1998), *Global Media*, London: Cassell.

Hesmondhalgh, David (2002), *The Cultural Industries*, London: Sage.

Higashi, Sumiko (1994), *Cecil B. DeMille and American Culture: The Silent Era*, Berkeley: University of California Press.

Higson, Andrew (1989), 'The Concept of National Cinema', *Screen* 30 (4), pp. 36–46.

Higson, Andrew (1995), *Waving the Flag: Constructing a National Cinema in Britain*, Oxford: Clarendon Press.

Higson, Andrew (ed.) (2001), *Young and Innocent: British Silent Cinema*, Exeter: Exeter University Press.

Hill, John (1987), *Sex, Class and Realism: British Cinema 1956–1963*, London: BFI.

Hill, John and Pamela Church Gibson (eds) (1998), *The Oxford Guide to Film Studies*, Oxford: Oxford University Press.

Hillier, Jim (ed.) (1985), *Cahiers du Cinéma: The 1950s*, London: BFI.

Hillier, Jim (1994), *The New Hollywood*, London: Continuum.

Hilmes, Michèle (1990), *Hollywood and Broadcasting: From Radio to Cable*, Urbana: University of Illinois Press.

Houston, Penelope (1994), *Keepers of the Frame: The Film Archives*, London: BFI.

Hozic, Aida A. (2001), *Hollyworld: Space, Power, and Fantasy in the American Economy*, Ithaca: Cornell University Press.

Hunt, Leon (1998), *British Low Culture: From Safari Suits to Sexploitation*, London: Routledge.

Hunt, Leon (2003), *Kung-Fu Cult Masters*, London: Wallflower.

Issari, Mohammad Ali (1989), *Cinema in Iran, 1900–1979*, Metuchen: Scarecrow.

Jacobs, Lea (1991), *The Wages of Sin: Censorship and the Fallen Woman Film, 1928–1942*, Madison: University of Wisconsin Press.

Jacobs, Lea (1993), 'Belasco, DeMille and the Development of Lasky Lighting', *Film History 5* (4), pp. 405–18.

Jacobs, Lewis (1968), *The Rise of the American Film: A Critical History with an Essay: Experimental Cinema in America, 1921–1947*, New York: Teachers College Press.

James, David (1989), *Allegories of Cinema: American Film in the Sixties*, Princeton: Princeton University Press.

Jancovich, Mark and Lucy Faire with Sarah Stubbings (2003), *The Place of the Audience: Cultural Geographies of Film Consumption*, London: BFI.

Jancovich, Mark, Antonio Lazaro-Reboll, Andrew Willis, Julian Stringer (eds) (2004), *Defining Cult Movies*, Manchester: Manchester University Press.

Jarvie, Ian (1992), *Hollywood's Overseas Campaign: The North Atlantic Movie Trade, 1920–1950*, Cambridge: Cambridge University Press.

Jenkins, Harry (1992), *What Made Pistachio Nuts?*, New York: Columbia University Press.

Jenkins, Henry and Kristine Brunovska Karnick (1994), *Classical Hollywood Comedy*, London: Routledge.

Johnson, Randal and Robert Stam (eds) (1995), *Brazilian Cinema*, New York: Columbia University Press.

Jones, Janna (2003), *The Southern Movie Palace: Rise, Fall, and Resurrection*, Gainesville: University Press of Florida.

Jowett, Garth (1976), *Film: The Democratic Art*, New York: Little, Brown.

Kaes, Anton (1989), *From Hitler to Heimat: The Return of History as Film*, Cambridge, MA: Harvard University Press.

Kaplan, E. Ann (ed.) (1999), *Women in Film Noir*, London: BFI.

Kapsis, E. Robert (1992), *Hitchcock: The Making of a Reputation*, Chicago: University of Chicago Press.

Kaur, Raminder (2005), *Bollyworld: Popular Indian Cinema through a Transnational Lens*, London: Sage.

Keil, Charlie and Shelley Stamp (eds) (2005), *American Cinema's Transitional Era*, Berkeley: University of California Press.

Kernan, Lisa (2004), *Coming Attractions: Reading American Movie Trailers*, Austin: University of Texas Press.

Kerr, Paul (ed.) (1986), *The Hollywood Film Industry*, London: Routledge and Kegan Paul.

Kindem, Gorham A. (1979), 'Hollywood's Conversion to Color: The Technological, Economic and Aesthetic Factors', *Journal of the University Film Association*, 31 (2), pp. 29–36.

Kinder, Marsha (1993), *Blood Cinema: The Reconstruction of National Identity in Spain*, Berkeley: University of California Press.

King, John (1990), *Magical Reels: A History of Cinema in Latin American*, London: Verso.

Klein, Christina (2005), 'Martial Arts and the Globalization of US and Asian Film Industries', *Comparative American Studies* 2 (3), pp. 360–84.

Kleinhans, Chuck, (1998), 'Independent Features: Hopes and Dreams', in Jon Lewis (ed.), *The New American Cinema*, Durham, NC: Duke University Press, pp. 307–27.

Klinger, Barbara (1989), 'Digressions as the Cinema: Reception and Mass Culture', *Cinema Journal* 28 (4), pp. 3–19.

Klinger, Barbara (1994), *Melodrama and Meaning: History, Culture and the Films of Douglas Sirk*, Bloomington: Indiana University Press.

Klinger, Barbara (1997), 'Film History Terminable and Interminable: Recovering the Past in Reception Studies', *Screen* 38 (2), pp. 107–28.

Klinger, Barbara (1998), 'The New Media Aristocrats: Home Theater and the Domestic Film Experience', *Velvet Light Trap* 42, pp. 4–19.

Koppes, Clayton R. and Gregory D. Black (1987), *Hollywood Goes to War: How Politics, Profits and Propaganda Shaped World War II Movies*, New York: Macmillan.

Koppes, Clayton R. and Gregory D. Black (1977), 'What to Show the World: The Office of War Information and Hollywood, 1942–1945', *Journal of American History* 64, pp. 87–105.

Kozarski, Richard (1990), *An Evening's Entertainment: The Age of the Silent Feature Picture, 1915–28*, New York: Charles Scribner's Sons.

Kracauer, Siegfried (1947), *From Caligari to Hitler*, Princeton: Princeton University Press.

Krämer, Peter (1998), 'Post-Classical Hollywood', in John Hill and Pamela Church Gibson (eds), *The Oxford Guide to Film Studies*, Oxford: Oxford University Press, pp. 289–309.

Krämer, Peter (2001), ' "It's Aimed at Kids – the Kid in Everybody": George Lucas, Star Wars and Children's Entertainment', *Scope: an Online Journal of Film Studies*.

Kuhn, Annette (1988), *Cinema, Censorship and Sexuality, 1909–1925*, London: Routledge.

Kuhn, Annette (2002), *An Everyday Magic: Cinema and Cultural Memory*, London: I. B. Tauris.

Leff, Leonard J. and Jerold R. Simmons (1990), *The Dame in the Kimono: Hollywood Censorship and the Production Code from the 1920s to the 1960s*, New York: Grove, Weidenfeld.

Lent, John A. (1990), *The Asian Film History*, London: Christopher Helm.

Lewis, Jon (ed.) (1998), *The New American Cinema*, Durham, NC: Duke University Press.

Lewis, Jon (2000), *Hollywood v. Hardcore: How the Struggle for Censorship Created the Modern Film Industry*, New York: New York University Press.

Lewis, Jon (ed.) (2002), *The End of Cinema as We Know it: American Film in the 1990s*, London: Pluto Press.

Leyda, Jay (1983), *Kino: The History of Russian and Soviet Film*, Princeton: Princeton University Press.

Litman, Barry (1998), *The Motion Picture Mega-Industry*, Boston, MA: Allen and Bacon.

Lovell, Alan and Peter Krämer (eds) (1999), *Screen Acting*, London: Routledge.

Lovell, Alan and Gianluca Sergi (2005), *Making Films in Contemporary Hollywood*, Oxford: Arnold.

McGilligan, Patrick and Paul Buhle (1999), *Tender Comrades: A Backstory of the Hollywood Blacklist*, New York: St. Martin's Press.

MacDonald, Scott (1993), *Avant-Garde Film: Motion Studies*, Cambridge: Cambridge University Press.

Maland J. Charles (1989), *Charles Chaplin and American Culture: The Evolution of a Star Image*, Princeton: Princeton University Press.

Maltby, Richard (1993), 'The Production Code and the Hays Office', in Tino Balio (ed.), *Grand Design: Hollywood as a Modern Business Enterprise, 1930–39*, Berkeley: University of California Press, pp. 37–72.

Maltby, Richard (2003), *Hollywood Cinema*, 2nd edn, Oxford: Blackwell.

Martin, Michael (ed.) (1996), *Cinemas of the Black Diaspora*, Detroit: Wayne State University Press.

May, Elaine Tyler (1988), *Homeward Bound: American Families in the Cold War Era*, New York: Basic Books.

May, Lary (1983), *Screening Out the Past: The Birth of Mass Culture and the Motion Picture Industry*, Chicago: University of Chicago Press.

Mayne, Judith (1993), *Cinema and Spectatorship*, London: Routledge.

Medved, Michael (1992), *Hollywood vs America: Popular Culture and the War on Traditional Values*, New York: HarperCollins.

Michalek, Boles Law and Frank Turaj (1988), *The Modern Cinema of Poland*, Bloomington: Indiana University Press.

Miller, Toby, Nitin Govil, John McMurria and Richard Maxwell (2001), *Global Hollywood*, London: BFI.

Mishra, Vijay (2002), *Bollywood Cinema*, London: Routledge.

Moran, Albert (1996), *Film Policy*, London: Routledge.

Moseley, Rachel (2003), *Growing up with Audrey Hepburn: Text, Audience, Resonance*, Manchester: Manchester University Press.

Moseley, Rachel (2005), *Fashioning Film Stars: Dress, Culture, Identity*, London: BFI.

Munby, Jonathan (1999), *Public Enemies, Public Heroes: Screening the Gangster from Little Caeser to Touch of Evil*, Chicago: University of Chicago Press.

Murphy, Robert (1992), *Sixties British Cinema*, London: BFI.

Murphy, Robert (ed.) (2000), *British Cinema of the 90s*, London: BFI.

Murphy, Robert (2002), *The British Cinema Book*, London: BFI.

Musser, Charles (1990), *The Emergence of Cinema: The American Screen to 1907*, New York: Charles Scribner's Sons.

Musser, Charles (1991), *Before the Nickelodeon: Edwin S. Porter and the Edison Manufacturing Company*, Berkeley: University of California Press.

Musser, Charles, with Carole Nelson (1991), *High Class Moving Pictures: Lyman H. Howe and the Forgotten Era of Traveling Exhibition 1880–1920*, Princeton: Princeton University Press.

Nadeau, Maurice (1989), *The History of Surrealism*, Cambridge: Belknap Press.

Naremore, James (1998), *More than Night: Film Noir and its Contexts*, Berkeley: University of California Press.

Nasaw, David (1999), *Going Out: The Rise and Fall of Public Amusements*, Cambridge, MA: Harvard University Press.

Neale, Steve (1985), *Cinema and Technology: Image, Sound, Colour*, London: Macmillan.

Neale, Steve (2000), *Genre and Hollywood*, London: Routledge.

Neale, Steve (ed.) (2002), *Genre and Contemporary Hollywood*, London: BFI.

Neale, Steve and Murray Smith (eds) (1998), *Contemporary Hollywood Cinema*, London: Routledge.

Noble, Andrea (2005), *Mexican National Cinema*, London: Routledge.

Noriega, Chon A. and Steven Ricci (eds) (1994), *The Mexican Cinema Project*, Los Angeles: UCLA Film and Television Archive.

Nowell-Smith, Geoffrey (ed.) (1999), *The Oxford History of World Cinema*, Oxford: Oxford University Press.

Nowell-Smith, Geoffrey and Steven Ricci (eds) (1998), *Hollywood and Europe: Economics, Culture and National Identity 1945–95*, London: BFI.

O'Regan, Tom (1996), *Australian National Cinema*, London: Routledge.

Pearson, Roberta E. (1992), *Eloquent Gestures: The Transformation of Performance Style in the Griffith Biograph Films*, Berkeley: University of California Press.

Peiss, Kathy (1987), *Cheap Amusements: Working Women and Leisure in Turn-of-the-Century New York*, Philadelphia: Temple University Press.

Polan, Dana (1986), *Power and Paranoia: History, Narrative and American Cinema, 1940–1950*, New York: Columbia University Press.

Prince, Stephen (2000), *A New Pot of Gold: Hollywood under the Electronic Rainbow, 1980–1989*, Berkeley: University of California Press.

Rabinovitz, Lauren (1988), *For the Love of Pleasure: Women, Movies and Culture in Turn-of-the Century Chicago*, New Brunswick: Rutgers University Press.

Ramsaye, Terry (1986), *Million and One Nights: A History of the Motion Picture through 1925*, Carmichael: Touchstone Books.

Rees, A. L. (1999), *A History of Experimental Film and Video*, London: BFI.

Reeves, Nicholas (1986), *Official British Film Propaganda during the First World War*, London: Routledge.

Richards, Jeffrey (1989), *The Age of the Dream Palace: Cinema and Society in Britain, 1930–39*, London: Routledge.

Richards, Jeffrey and Dorothy Sheridan (1987), *Mass Observation at the Movies*, London: Routledge.

Roddick, Nick (1983), *New Deal in Entertainment: Warner Bros in the 1930s*, London: BFI.

Rosen, Marjorie (1975), *Popcorn Venus: Women, Movies and the American Dream*, Peter Owen.

Ross, Steven (ed.) (2002), *Movies and American Society*, Oxford: Blackwell.

Ryall, Tom (2001), *Britain and the American Cinema*, London: Sage.

Ryan, Michael and Douglas Kellner (1988), *Camera Politica: Politics and Ideology of Contemporary Hollywood Film*, Bloomington: Indiana University Press.

Salt, Barry (2003), *Film Style and Technology: History and Analysis*, London: Starword.

Schaefer, Eric (1999), *Bold! Daring! Shocking! True!: A History of Exploitation Films, 1919–1959*, Durham, NC: Duke University Press.

Schatz, Thomas (1988), *The Genius of the System: Hollywood Filmmaking in the Studio Era*, New York: Pantheon.

Schatz, Thomas (1992), 'The New Hollywood', in Jim Collins, Hilary Radner, Ava Preacher Collins (eds), *Film Theory Goes to the Movies*, London: Routledge, pp. 8–36.

Schatz, Thomas (1999), *Boom and Bust: American Cinema in the 1940s*, Berkeley: University of California Press.

Seldes, Gilbert (1950), *The Great Audience*, New York: Viking.

Sergi, Gianluca (1998), 'Tales of the Silent Blast: *Star Wars* and Sound', *Journal of Popular Film and Television* 26 (1) (spring), pp. 13–22.

Sergi, Gianluca (2004), *The Dolby Era: Film Sound in Contemporary Hollywood*, Manchester: Manchester University Press.

Shary, Timothy (2002), *Generation Multiplex*, Austin: University of Texas Press.

Shen, Vivian (2005), *The Origins of Leftwing Cinema in China, 1932–37*, London: Routledge.

Shiel, Mark and Tony Fitzmaurice (eds) (2001), *Cinema and the City: Film and Urban Societies in a Global Context*, Oxford: Blackwell.

Shohat, Ella and Robert Stam (1994), *Unthinking Eurocentrism*, London: Routledge.

Skinner, James M. (1993), *The Cross and the Cinema: The Legion of Decency and the National Catholic Office for Motion Pictures, 1933–1970*, Westport: Praeger.

Sklar, Robert (1976), *Movie-Made America*, New York: Vintage.

Sklar, Robert and Charles Musser (eds) (1990), *Resisting Images: Essays on Cinema and History*, Philadelphia: Temple University Press.

Slide, Anthony (1992), *Nitrate Won't Wait: A History of Film Preservation in the United States*, Jefferson: McFarland and Co.

Smith, Jeff (1998), *Sounds of Commerce: Marketing Popular Film Music*, New York: Columbia University Press.

Soila, Titti, Astrid Soderbergh Widding and Gunnar Iverson (1998), *Nordic National Cinema*, London: Routledge.

Sorlin, Pierre (1991), *European Cinemas, European Societies, 1939–1990*, London: Routledge.

Sorlin, Pierre (1996), *Italian National Cinema*, London: Routledge.

Stacey, Jackie (1994), *Star Gazing: Hollywood Cinema and Female Spectatorship*, London: Routledge.

Staiger, Janet (1986), 'Man Produced Photoplays: Economic and Signifying Practices in the First Years of Hollywood', in P. Kerr (ed.) *The Hollywood Film Industry*, London and New York: Routledge and Kegan Paul, pp. 97–119.

Staiger, Janet (1990), 'Announcing Wares, Winning Patrons, Voicing Ideals: Thinking about the History and Theory of Film Advertising', *Cinema Journal* 29 (3), pp. 3–31.

Staiger, Janet (1992), *Interpreting Audiences: Studies in the Historical Reception of American Cinema*, Princeton: Princeton University Press.

Staiger, Janet (2000), *Perverse Spectators: The Practices of Film Reception*, New York: New York University Press.

Stamp, Shelley (2000), *Movie-Struck Girls: Women and Motion-Picture Culture after the Nickelodeon*, Princeton: Princeton University Press.

Stanfield, Peter (2001), *Hollywood, Westerns and the 1930s: The Lost Trail*, Exeter: Exeter University Press.

Stokes, Melvyn and Richard Maltby (eds) (1999a), *American Movie Audiences: From the Turn of the Century to the Early Sound Era*, London: BFI.

Stokes, Melvyn and Richard Maltby (eds) (1999b), *Identifying Hollywood's Audiences: Cultural Identity and the Movies*, London: BFI.

Stokes, Melvyn and Richard Maltby (eds) (2001), *Hollywood Spectatorship: Changing Perceptions of Cinema Audiences*, London: BFI.

Street, Sarah (1997), *British National Cinema*, London: Routledge.

Stringer, Julian (ed.) (2003), *Movie Blockbusters*, London: Routledge.

Stringer, Julian and Chi-Yun Ching (eds) (2005), *New Korean Cinema*, Edinburgh: Edinburgh University Press.

Studlar, Gaylyn (1991), 'The Perils and Pleasures of Fan Magazines in the 1920s', *Wide Angle* 13 (1), pp. 6–33.

Tasker, Yvonne (1993), *Spectacular Bodies: Gender, Genre and the Action Cinema*, London: Routledge.

Taylor, Greg (1999), *Artists in the Audience: Cults, Camp, and American Film Criticism*, Princeton: Princeton University Press.

Taylor, Richard (ed.) (1999), *The Eisenstein Reader*, London: BFI.

Taylor, Richard and Ian Christie (eds) (1988), *The Film Factory: Russian and Soviet Cinema in Documents*, London: Routledge.

Taylor, Richard and Ian Christie (eds) (1991), *Inside the Film Factory: New Approaches to Russian and Soviet Film*, New York and London: Routledge.

Teo, Stephen (1996), *Hong Kong Cinema: The Extra Dimensions*, London: BFI.

Thompson, Kristin (1985), *Exporting Entertainment: America in the World Film Market, 1907–1934*, London: BFI.

Thompson, Kristin and David Bordwell (2003), *Film History: An Introduction*, 2nd edn, New York: McGraw-Hill.

Toulmin, Vanessa, Simon Popple and Patrick Russell (eds) (2005), *The Lost World of Mitchell and Kenyon: Edwardian Britain on Film*, London: BFI.

Triana-Toribio, Núria (2002), *Spanish National Cinema*, London: Routledge.

Truffaut, François (1986), *Hitchcock by Truffaut: The Definitive Study*, London: Paladin.

Tsvian, Yuri (2004), *Lines of Resistance: Dziga Vetov and the Twenties*, trans. Julian Graffy, Bloomington: Indiana University Press.

Tudor, Andrew (1989), *Monsters and Mad Scientists: A Cultural History of the Horror Movie*, Oxford: Blackwell.

Turan, Kenneth (2002), *Sundance to Sarajevo: Film Festivals and the World they Made*, Berkeley: University of California Press.

Ukadike, Nwachukwu Frank (1994), *Black African Cinema*, Berkeley: University of California Press.

Uricchio, William and Roberta E. Pearson (1993), *Reframing Culture: The Case of the Vitagraph Quality Films*, Princeton: Princeton University Press.

Valentine, Maggie (1994), *The Show Starts on the Sidewalk: An Architectural History of the Movie Theatre*, New Haven: Yale University Press.

Vasey, Ruth (1995), *Diplomatic Representations: The World According to Hollywood, 1919–1930*, Madison: University of Wisconsin Press.

Waller, Gregory (1995), *Main Street Amusements: Movies and Commercial Entertainment in a Southern City, 1896–1930*, Washington, DC: Smithsonian Institute.

Waller, Gregory (2001), *Movie Going in America*, Oxford: Blackwell.

Wasko, Janet (1994), *Hollywood in the Information Age: Beyond the Silver Screen*, Cambridge: Polity Press.

Wasko, Janet (2001), *Understanding Disney*, Cambridge, Polity Press.

Wasson, Haidee (2005), *Museum Movies: The Museum of Modern Art and the Birth of Art Cinema*, Berkeley: University of California Press.

Whitfield, Stephen J. (1996), *The Culture of the Cold War*, Baltimore: Johns Hopkins University Press.

Wilinsky, Barbara (2001), *Sure Seaters: The Emergence of Art House Cinema*, Minneapolis: University of Minnesota Press.

Williams, Alan (1992), *Republic of Images: A History of French Filmmaking*, Cambridge, MA: Harvard University Press.

Williams, Linda (1999), *Hard Core: Power, Pleasure and the 'Frenzy of the Visible'*, Berkeley: University of California Press.

Williams, Linda Ruth and Michael Hammond (eds) (2006), *Contemporary American Cinema*, Maidenhead: Open University Press.

Willis, Andrew (ed.) (2004), *Film Stars: Hollywood and Beyond*, Manchester: Manchester University Press.

Winston, Brian (1995), *Claiming the Real: the Griersonian Documentary and its Legitimations*, London: BFI.

Wolf, Michael J. (1999), *The Entertainment Economy*, London: Penguin.

Wyatt, Justin (1994), *High Concept: Movies and Marketing in Hollywood*, Austin: University of Texas Press.

Wyver, John (1989), *The Moving Image: An International History of Film Television and Video*, Oxford: Blackwell.

Youngblood, Denise (1999), *The Magic Mirror: Moviemaking in Russia, 1908–1918*, Madison: University of Wisconsin Press.

Zhang, Yingjin (2004), *Chinese National Cinema*, London: Routledge.

Journals that focus on questions of film history include (but are not limited to):
Cinema Journal
Film History
Film Quarterly
Historical Journal of Film, Radio and Television
Iris
Journal of Film and Video
Journal of Popular British Cinema
Journal of Popular Film and Television
Scope: An Online Journal of Film Studies
Screen
The Moving Image
The Velvet Light Trap
Wide Angle

COPYRIGHT ACKNOWLEDGEMENTS

Grateful acknowledgement is made to the following sources for permission to reproduce material in this book previously published elsewhere. Every effort has been made to trace copyright holders, but if any have been inadvertently overlooked the publisher will be pleased to make the necessary arrangement at the first opportunity.

Extracts from *American Movie Audiences* edited by Melvyn Stokes and Richard Maltby, British Film Institute, 1999. © 1999 by British Film Institute.

Extracts from *Cinema and the Invention of Modern Life* edited by Leo Charney and Vanessa R. Schwartz, University of California Press, 1995. © 1995 by The Regents of the University of California.

Extracts from *Shared Pleasures: A History of Movie Presentation in the United States* by Douglas Gomery, The University of Wisconsin Press, 1992. © 1992 by The University of Wisconsin Press. Reproduced with the permission of the publisher.

'Social Mobility and the Fantastic' by Thomas Elsaesser, © 2004 by Thomsas Elsaesser (updated version). Original version of this article first published in *Wide Angle*, Vol. 5 no. 2, 1982. © 1982 by the author.

Extracts from *The Place of the Audience* by Mark Jancovich and Lucy Faire with Sarah Stubbings, British Film Institute, 2003. © 2003 by British Film Institute.

INDEX